HALSBURY'S
Laws of England

FIFTH EDITION
2017

Volume 33

This is volume 33 of the Fifth Edition of Halsbury's Laws of England, containing the title DISCRIMINATION.

The title DISCRIMINATION replaces the title of the same name contained in volume 33(2013). Upon receipt of volume 33 (2017), volume 33 (2013) may be archived.

For a full list of volumes comprised in a current set of Halsbury's Laws of England please see overleaf.

Fifth Edition volumes:

1 (2017), 1A (2017), 2 (2017), 3 (2011), 4 (2011), 5 (2013), 6 (2011), 7 (2015), 8 (2015), 9 (2017), 10 (2017), 11 (2015), 12 (2015), 12A (2015), 13 (2017), 14 (2016), 15 (2016), 15A (2016), 16 (2017), 17 (2017), 18 (2009), 19 (2011), 20 (2014), 21 (2016), 22 (2012), 23 (2016), 24 (2010), 25 (2016), 26 (2016), 27 (2015), 28 (2015), 29 (2014), 30 (2012), 31 (2012), 32 (2012), 33 (2017), 34 (2011), 35 (2015), 36 (2015), 37 (2013), 38 (2013), 38A (2013), 39 (2014), 40 (2014), 41 (2014), 41A (2014), 42 (2011), 43 (2011), 44 (2011), 45 (2010), 46 (2010), 47 (2014), 47A (2014), 48 (2015), 49 (2015), 50 (2016), 50A (2016), 51 (2013), 52 (2014), 53 (2014), 54 (2017), 54A (2017), 55 (2012), 56 (2017), 57 (2012), 58 (2014), 58A (2014), 59 (2014), 59A (2014), 60 (2011), 61 (2010), 62 (2016), 63 (2016), 64 (2016), 65 (2015), 66 (2015), 67 (2016), 68 (2016), 69 (2009), 70 (2012), 71 (2013), 72 (2015), 73 (2015), 74 (2011), 75 (2013), 76 (2013), 77 (2016), 78 (2010), 79 (2014), 80 (2013), 81 (2010), 82 (2010), 83 (2010), 84 (2013), 84A (2013), 85 (2012), 86 (2017), 87 (2017), 88 (2012), 88A (2013), 89 (2011), 90 (2011), 91 (2012), 92 (2015), 93 (2017), 94 (2017), 95 (2017), 96 (2012), 97 (2015), 97A (2014), 98 (2013), 99 (2012), 100 (2009), 101 (2009), 102 (2016), 103 (2016), 104 (2014)

Consolidated Index and Tables:

2017 Consolidated Index (A–E), 2017 Consolidated Index (F–O), 2017 Consolidated Index (P–Z), 2018 Consolidated Table of Statutes, 2018 Consolidated Table of Statutory Instruments, 2018 Consolidated Table of Cases (A–G), 2018 Consolidated Table of Cases (H–Q), 2018 Consolidated Table of Cases (R–Z, ECJ Cases)

Updating and ancillary materials:

2017 annual Cumulative Supplement; monthly Noter-up; annual Abridgments 1974–2016

December 2017

DLA Piper UK LLP Leeds

HALSBURY'S
Laws of England

Volume 33

2017

Members of the LexisNexis Group worldwide

United Kingdom	RELX (UK) Ltd, trading as LexisNexis, 1–3 Strand, London WC2N 5JR and 9–10 St Andrew Square, Edinburgh EH2 2AF
Australia	Reed International Books Australia Pty Ltd trading as LexisNexis, Chatswood, New South Wales
Austria	LexisNexis Verlag ARD Orac GmbH & Co KG, Vienna
Benelux	LexisNexis Benelux, Amsterdam
Canada	LexisNexis Canada, Markham, Ontario
China	LexisNexis China, Beijing and Shanghai
France	LexisNexis SA, Paris
Germany	LexisNexis GmbH, Dusseldorf
Hong Kong	LexisNexis Hong Kong, Hong Kong
India	LexisNexis India, New Delhi
Italy	Giuffrè Editore, Milan
Japan	LexisNexis Japan, Tokyo
Malaysia	Malayan Law Journal Sdn Bhd, Kuala Lumpur
New Zealand	LexisNexis New Zealand Ltd, Wellington
Singapore	LexisNexis Singapore, Singapore
South Africa	LexisNexis, Durban
USA	LexisNexis, Dayton, Ohio

FIRST EDITION	*Published in 31 volumes between 1907 and 1917*
SECOND EDITION	*Published in 37 volumes between 1931 and 1942*
THIRD EDITION	*Published in 43 volumes between 1952 and 1964*
FOURTH EDITION	*Published in 56 volumes between 1973 and 1987, with reissues between 1988 and 2008*
FIFTH EDITION	*Published between 2008 and 2014, with reissues from 2014*

ISBN 978-1-4743-0944-8

ISBN for the set: 9781405734394
ISBN for this volume: 9781474309448

Typeset by LexisNexis
Printed and bound by CPI Group (UK) Ltd, Croydon, CR0 4YY

Visit LexisNexis at www.lexisnexis.co.uk

Editor of this Volume

FRANCES WARD, LLB,
of the Middle Temple, Barrister

Managing Editor

HELEN HALVEY, LLB

DISCRIMINATION

Consultant Editor

ROBIN ALLEN QC,
Head of Cloisters Chambers;
a Bencher of Middle Temple

The law stated in this volume is in general that in force on 1 November 2017, although subsequent changes have been included wherever possible.

Any future updating material will be found in the Noter-up and annual Cumulative Supplement to Halsbury's Laws of England.

TABLE OF CONTENTS

HOW TO USE HALSBURY'S LAWS OF ENGLAND

Volumes

Each text volume of Halsbury's Laws of England contains the law on the titles contained in it as at a date stated at the front of the volume (the operative date).

Information contained in Halsbury's Laws of England may be accessed in several ways.

First, by using the tables of contents.

Each volume contains both a general Table of Contents, and a specific Table of Contents for each title contained in it. From these tables you will be directed to the relevant part of the work.

Readers should note that the current arrangement of titles can be found in the Noter-up.

Secondly, by using tables of statutes, statutory instruments, cases or other materials.

If you know the name of the Act, statutory instrument or case with which your research is concerned, you should consult the Consolidated Tables of statutes, cases and so on (published as separate volumes) which will direct you to the relevant volume and paragraph.

(Each individual text volume also includes tables of those materials used as authority in that volume.)

Thirdly, by using the indexes.

If you are uncertain of the general subject area of your research, you should go to the Consolidated Index (published as separate volumes) for reference to the relevant volume(s) and paragraph(s).

(Each individual text volume also includes an index to the material contained therein.)

Updating publications

The text volumes of Halsbury's Laws should be used in conjunction with the annual Cumulative Supplement and the monthly Noter-up.

The annual Cumulative Supplement

The Supplement gives details of all changes between the operative date of the text volume and the operative date of the Supplement. It is arranged in the same volume, title and paragraph order as the text volumes. Developments affecting particular points of law are noted to the relevant paragraph(s) of the text volumes.

For narrative treatment of material noted in the Cumulative Supplement, go to the annual Abridgment volume for the relevant year.

Destination Tables

In certain titles in the annual *Cumulative Supplement*, reference is made to Destination Tables showing the destination of consolidated legislation. Those Destination Tables are to be found either at the end of the titles within the annual *Cumulative Supplement*, or in a separate *Destination Tables* booklet provided from time to time with the *Cumulative Supplement*.

The Noter-up

The Noter-up is issued monthly and notes changes since the publication of the annual Cumulative Supplement. Also arranged in the same volume, title and paragraph order as the text volumes, the Noter-up follows the style of the Cumulative Supplement.

For narrative treatment of material noted in the Noter-up, go to the annual Abridgment volume for the relevant year.

REFERENCES AND ABBREVIATIONS

ACT	Australian Capital Territory
A-G	Attorney General
Admin	Administrative Court
Admlty	Admiralty Court
Adv-Gen	Advocate General
affd	affirmed
affg	affirming
Alta	Alberta
App	Appendix
art	article
Aust	Australia
B	Baron
BC	British Columbia
C	Command Paper (of a series published before 1900)
c	chapter number of an Act
CA	Court of Appeal
CAC	Central Arbitration Committee
CA in Ch	Court of Appeal in Chancery
CB	Chief Baron
CCA	Court of Criminal Appeal
CCR	County Court Rules 1981 (as subsequently amended)
CCR	Court for Crown Cases Reserved
CJEU	Court of Justice of the European Union
C-MAC	Courts-Martial Appeal Court
CO	Crown Office
COD	Crown Office Digest
CPR	Civil Procedure Rules
Can	Canada
Cd	Command Paper (of the series published 1900–18)
Cf	compare
Ch	Chancery Division
ch	chapter
cl	clause
Cm	Command Paper (of the series published 1986 to date)
Cmd	Command Paper (of the series published 1919–56)
Cmnd	Command Paper (of the series published 1956–86)
Comm	Commercial Court

Comr	Commissioner
Court Forms (2nd Edn)	Atkin's Encyclopaedia of Court Forms in Civil Proceedings, 2nd Edn. See note 2 post.
CrimPR	Criminal Procedure Rules
DC.............................	Divisional Court
DPP............................	Director of Public Prosecutions
EAT............................	Employment Appeal Tribunal
EC	European Community
ECJ	Court of Justice of the European Community (before the Treaty of Lisbon (OJ C306, 17.12.2007, p 1) came into force on 1 December 2009); European Court of Justice (after the Treaty of Lisbon (OJ C306, 17.12.2007, p 1) came into force on 1 December 2009)
EComHR	European Commission of Human Rights
ECSC..........................	European Coal and Steel Community
ECtHR Rules of Court	Rules of Court of the European Court of Human Rights
EEC...........................	European Economic Community
EFTA	European Free Trade Association
EGC	European General Court
EWCA Civ	Official neutral citation for judgments of the Court of Appeal (Civil Division)
EWCA Crim	Official neutral citation for judgments of the Court of Appeal (Criminal Division)
EWHC	Official neutral citation for judgments of the High Court
Edn	Edition
Euratom......................	European Atomic Energy Community
EU	European Union
Ex Ch	Court of Exchequer Chamber
ex p...........................	ex parte
Fam...........................	Family Division
Fed............................	Federal
Forms & Precedents (5th Edn)	Encyclopaedia of Forms and Precedents other than Court Forms, 5th Edn. See note 2 post
GLC	Greater London Council
HC.............................	High Court
HC.............................	House of Commons
HK.............................	Hong Kong
HL.............................	House of Lords
HMRC........................	Her Majesty's Revenue and Customs
IAT	Immigration Appeal Tribunal
ILM...........................	International Legal Materials

INLR	Immigration and Nationality Law Reports
IRC	Inland Revenue Commissioners
Ind	India
Int Rels	International Relations
Ir	Ireland
J	Justice
JA	Judge of Appeal
Kan	Kansas
LA	Lord Advocate
LC	Lord Chancellor
LCC	London County Council
LCJ	Lord Chief Justice
LJ	Lord Justice of Appeal
LoN	League of Nations
MR	Master of the Rolls
Man	Manitoba
n	note
NB	New Brunswick
NI	Northern Ireland
NS	Nova Scotia
NSW	New South Wales
NY	New York
NZ	New Zealand
OHIM	Office for Harmonisation in the Internal Market
OJ	The Official Journal of the European Union published by the Publications Office of the European Union
Ont	Ontario
P	President
PC	Judicial Committee of the Privy Council
PEI	Prince Edward Island
Pat	Patents Court
q	question
QB	Queen's Bench Division
QBD	Queen's Bench Division of the High Court
Qld	Queensland
Que	Quebec
r	rule
RDC	Rural District Council
RPC	Restrictive Practices Court
RSC	Rules of the Supreme Court 1965 (as subsequently amended)
reg	regulation
Res	Resolution

revsd	reversed
Rly	Railway
s	section
SA	South Africa
S Aust	South Australia
SC	Supreme Court
SI	Statutory Instruments published by authority
SR & O	Statutory Rules and Orders published by authority
SR & O Rev 1904	Revised Edition comprising all Public and General Statutory Rules and Orders in force on 31 December 1903
SR & O Rev 1948	Revised Edition comprising all Public and General Statutory Rules and Orders and Statutory Instruments in force on 31 December 1948
SRNI	Statutory Rules of Northern Ireland
STI	Simon's Tax Intelligence (1973–1995); Simon's Weekly Tax Intelligence (1996-current)
Sask	Saskatchewan
Sch	Schedule
Sess	Session
Sing	Singapore
TCC	Technology and Construction Court
TS	Treaty Series
Tanz	Tanzania
Tas	Tasmania
UDC	Urban District Council
UKHL	Official neutral citation for judgments of the House of Lords
UKPC	Official neutral citation for judgments of the Privy Council
UN	United Nations
V-C	Vice-Chancellor
Vict	Victoria
W Aust	Western Australia
Zimb	Zimbabwe

NOTE 1. A general list of the abbreviations of law reports and other sources used in this work can be found at the beginning of the Consolidated Table of Cases.

NOTE 2. Where references are made to other publications, the volume number precedes and the page number follows the name of the publication; eg the reference '12 Forms & Precedents (5th Edn) 44' refers to volume 12 of the Encyclopaedia of Forms and Precedents, page 44.

NOTE 3. An English statute is cited by short title or, where there is no short title, by regnal year and chapter number together with the name by which it is commonly known or a description of its subject matter and date. In the case of a foreign statute, the mode of citation generally follows the style of citation in use in the country concerned with the addition, where necessary, of the name of the country in parentheses.

NOTE 4. A statutory instrument is cited by short title, if any, followed by the year and number, or, if unnumbered, the date.

TABLE OF STATUTES

TABLE OF STATUTORY INSTRUMENTS

TABLE OF EUROPEAN UNION LEGISLATION

Primary Legislation

Secondary Legislation

Directives

Regulations

TABLE OF TREATIES AND CONVENTIONS, ETC

TABLE OF CASES

Decisions of the European Court of Justice are listed below numerically. These decisions are also included in the preceding alphabetical list.

DISCRIMINATION

Volume 33

1. SOURCES OF DISCRIMINATION LAW

(1) DOMESTIC LEGISLATION

(i) Application of the Equality Act 2010

1. Discrimination law and the Equality Act 2010.

The Equality Act 2010 (which received Royal Assent on 8 April 2010, with most of its provisions coming into force in October 2010[1]), brought together and re-stated previous equality law and made various further changes; its aim being to harmonise the provisions and to give a single approach where appropriate[2]. The Equality Act 2010 repealed most of the existing legislation[3], but the Equality Act 2006 remains in force so far as it relates to the constitution and operation of the Equality and Human Rights Commission[4].

An extensive Explanatory Memorandum was published with the Bill and this was revised and republished as Explanatory Notes[5] at the time when the Equality Act 2010 received Royal Assent. The Explanatory Notes are often relied on when considering the extent to which, if at all, the Act has made a substantive change to the law.

Case law relating to the interpretation of previous statutory provisions continues to be relevant and to have authority or persuasive value under similar or corresponding provisions of the new legislation.

There are a number of other issues related to discrimination that are dealt with elsewhere in this work, particularly offences of incitement to racial or religious hatred or hatred on the grounds of sexual orientation[6], and the law relating to maternity and paternity rights[7].

1   See the Equality Act 2010 s 216 (amended by the Scotland Act 2016 s 38(1), (9)); the Equality Act 2010 (Commencement No 1) Order 2010, SI 2010/1736; the Equality Act 2010 (Commencement No 2) Order 2010, SI 2010/1966; the Equality Act 2010 (Commencement No 3) Order 2010, SI 2010/2191; the Equality Act 2010 (Commencement No 4, Savings, Consequential, Transitional, Transitory and Incidental Provisions and Revocation) Order 2010, SI 2010/2317 (amended by SI 2010/2337); the Equality Act 2010 (Commencement No 5) Order 2011, SI 2011/96; the Equality Act 2010 (Commencement No 6) Order 2011, SI 2011/1066; the Equality Act 2010 (Commencement No 7) Order 2011, SI 2011/1636; the Equality Act 2010 (Commencement No 8) Order 2011, SI 2011/2646; the Equality Act 2010 (Commencement No 9) Order 2012, SI 2012/1569; the Equality Act 2010 (Commencement No 10) Order 2012, SI 2012/2184; the Equality Act 2010 (Commencement No 11) Order 2016, SI 2016/839; the Equality Act 2010 (Commencement No 12) Order 2017, SI 2017/107. As from a day to be appointed, the Equality Act 2010 s 216 is further amended by the Wales Act 2017 s 45(1), (4)–(6). At the date at which this volume states the law no such day had been appointed.

2   See PARA 2. As to the territorial application of the Equality Act 2010 see PARA 5.

3   See the Equality Act 2010 s 211, Sch 27 (amended by SI 2010/2279; and SI 2011/1060).

4   As to the Equality and Human Rights Commission see PARA 28 et seq.

5   At the date at which this volume states the law, the Explanatory Notes can be found at http://www.legislation.gov.uk/ukpga/2010/15/notes/contents.

6   As to incitement to racial hatred see CRIMINAL LAW vol 26 (2016) PARAS 570–577. As to incitement to religious hatred see CRIMINAL LAW vol 26 (2016) PARAS 578–586. As to incitement to hatred on the grounds of sexual orientation see CRIMINAL LAW vol 26 (2016) PARAS 587–595. As to racially or religiously aggravated offences see CRIMINAL LAW vol 25 (2016) PARAS 182–184, 393; CRIMINAL LAW vol 26 (2016) PARA 556). As to racial or religious hatred as an aggravating factor in the commission of crimes see also SENTENCING vol 92 (2015) PARA 588.

7   As to maternity and paternity leave etc see EMPLOYMENT vol 40 (2014) PARA 354 et seq. As to maternity and paternity pay etc see EMPLOYMENT vol 40 (2014) PARA 401 et seq.

2. Purposes of the Equality Act 2010.

The Equality Act 2010 has two main purposes:

(1)   to harmonise discrimination law; and

(2)   to strengthen the law to support progress on equality[1].

The Act places a duty on certain public bodies to consider socio-economic disadvantage when making strategic decisions about how to exercise their functions[2]. It also extends the circumstances in which a person is protected against discrimination, harassment or victimisation because of a protected characteristic (namely: age, disability, gender reassignment, marriage and civil partnership, pregnancy and maternity, race, religion or belief, sex and sexual orientation)[3], and allows people to make a claim if they are directly discriminated against because of a combination of two relevant protected characteristics[4]. The Act requires reasonable adjustments to be made to various premises and services so as to avoid placing disabled persons at a disadvantage when accessing them[5], and requires taxis, other private hire vehicles, public service vehicles (such as buses) and rail vehicles to be accessible to disabled persons and to allow them to travel in reasonable comfort[6].

The Act creates a duty on listed public bodies when carrying out their functions and on other persons when carrying out public functions to have due regard to:

(a)   the need to eliminate conduct which the Act prohibits;

(b)   the need to advance equality of opportunity between persons who share a relevant protected characteristic and those who do not; and

(c)   the need to foster good relations between people who share a relevant protected characteristic and people who do not[7].

The Act allows an employer, service provider or other organisation to take positive action so as to enable existing or potential employees or customers to overcome or minimise a disadvantage arising from a protected characteristic[8], and it extends the permission for political parties to use women-only shortlists for election candidates to 2030[9].

The Equality Act 2010 is enforced through the civil courts (in relation to services and public functions, premises, education and associations) and employment tribunals (in relation to work and related areas, and equal pay)[10].

1   See the Explanatory Notes to the Equality Act 2010. The long title of the Equality Act 2010 reads as follows: An Act to make provision to require Ministers of the Crown and others when making strategic decisions about the exercise of their functions to have regard to the desirability of reducing socio-economic inequalities; to reform and harmonise equality law and restate the greater part of the enactments relating to discrimination and harassment related to certain personal characteristics; to enable certain employers to be required to publish information about the differences in pay between male and female employees; to prohibit victimisation in certain circumstances; to require the exercise of certain functions to be with regard to the need to eliminate discrimination and other prohibited conduct; to enable duties to be imposed in relation to the exercise of public procurement functions; to increase equality of opportunity; to amend the law relating to rights and responsibilities in family relationships; and for connected purposes. There is to be paid out of money provided by Parliament any increase attributable to the Equality Act 2010 in the expenses of a Minister of the Crown: s 215.

As to the power for a Minister of the Crown to harmonise certain provisions in the Act with changes required to comply with EU obligations see ss 203, 204; and PARA 18.

2   Equality Act 2010 Explanatory Notes para 12. As to the duty on certain public bodies to have due regard to socio-economic inequalities in making strategic decisions see the Equality Act 2010 Pt 1 (ss 1–3); and PARA 302.

3   The Equality Act 2010 makes it unlawful to discriminate against, harass or victimise a person:

(1)   when providing a service (which includes the provision of goods or facilities) or when exercising a public function (see Pt 3 (ss 28–31), Schs 2, 3; and PARAS 84–104);

(2)   when disposing of (eg by selling or letting) or managing premises (see Pt 4 (ss 32–38), Schs 4, 5; and PARAS 105–115);

(3)   at work or in employment services (see Pt 5 (ss 39–83), Schs 6, 7, 8; and PARAS 116–172);
(4)   when providing places or access to facilities and services at an educational establishment (see Pt 6 (ss 84–99), Schs 10, 11, 12, 13, 14; and PARAS 173–197);
(5)   when making decisions as to the membership of associations, or access to associations' benefits, facilities and services (see ss 100–103, Schs 15, 16; and PARA 198 et seq).

Terms in contracts, collective agreements or rules of undertakings are unenforceable or void if they result in unlawful discrimination, harassment or victimisation: see Pt 10 (ss 142–148); and PARAS 274–275. As to protected characteristics under the Equality Act 2010 see PARAS 45–63.

4   Equality Act 2010 Explanatory Notes para 12. The key concepts of protected characteristics, the definitions of direct discrimination, discrimination arising from disability, indirect discrimination, harassment and victimisation are dealt with in the Equality Act 2010 Pt 2 (ss 4–27), Sch 1: see PARAS 45–63, 67–83. Part 8 (ss 108–112) prohibits other forms of conduct, including discriminating against or harassing an ex-employee or ex-pupil, instructing a third party to discriminate against another, or helping someone to discriminate against another: see PARAS 70, 80, 82, 83, 120, 237, 351. Part 14 (ss 191–197), Schs 22, 23 establishes exceptions to the prohibitions in the earlier parts of the Act in relation to a range of conduct: see PARAS 104, 320–334.
5   See the Equality Act 2010 ss 20–22, 189, 190, Sch 21; and PARAS 76, 237–271.
6   See the Equality Act 2010 Pt 12 (ss 160–188); and PARAS 211–236.
7   Equality Act 2010 Explanatory Notes para 12. As to the public sector equality duty see the Equality Act 2010 Pt 11 Ch 1 (ss 149–157), Schs 18, 19; and PARAS 276–301.
8   As to positive action see the Equality Act 2010 Pt 11 Ch 2 (ss 158–159); and PARA 299.
9   Equality Act 2010 Explanatory Notes para 12. As to the special provisions for political parties see ss 104–106; and PARAS 209–210.
10   As to enforcement see the Equality Act 2010 Pt 9 (ss 113–141), Sch 17; and PARAS 351–365.

3.   Exceptions to the general application of the Equality Act 2010.

There are a number of exceptions to the general provisions of the Equality Act 2010 in the areas of:

(1)   national security[1];
(2)   acts carried out pursuant to statutory requirements[2];
(3)   acts carried out pursuant to pre-existing statutory provisions for the protection of women[3];
(4)   religion[4];
(5)   charities[5];
(6)   supported employment for the disabled[6];
(7)   nationality or residence[7];
(8)   sport[8]; and
(9)   the provision of communal accommodation[9].

There are also a number of exceptions which are specific to the 'arenas' of discrimination enumerated by the Equality Act 2010, namely services and public functions[10], premises[11], work[12], education[13] and associations[14].

1   See PARA 321.
2   See PARA 322.
3   See PARA 323.
4   See PARA 324.
5   See PARA 325.
6   See PARA 326.
7   See PARA 327.
8   See PARA 328.
9   See PARA 329.
10   See PARAS 91–104.
11   See PARAS 110–115.
12   See PARAS 156–172.
13   See PARAS 195–197.
14   See PARAS 204–208.

4. Subordinate legislation under the Equality Act 2010.

Until 2010, most functions under discrimination legislation were carried out by a succession of specified Secretaries of State[1]. Unless there is express provision to the contrary, the power to make orders or regulations under the Equality Act 2010 is exercisable by a Minister of the Crown[2]. Certain regulations under the Act, however, must be made by the Secretary of State[3], and the Equality Act 2010, like many modern statutes, refers simply to 'the Secretary of State' rather than specifying a particular governmental department[4].

Orders, regulations or rules under the Act must (with certain exceptions[5]) be made by statutory instrument[6]. The Act makes detailed provision concerning the procedures to be employed when orders or regulations are made by Ministers of the Crown and the Treasury[7]. Although the matter of equal opportunities is not devolved to Wales, the Act does give the Welsh Ministers powers to make subordinate legislation under the Act and to amend certain provisions of the Act in their application to Wales, where necessary[8]. The Act also specifies the procedure for making such legislation[9].

1 Equality functions which had been exercised by the Secretary of State for Trade and Industry were transferred to the Secretary of State for Communities and Local Government (see the Secretary of State for Communities and Local Government Order 2006, SI 2006/1926, art 7), and then to the Lord Privy Seal (see the Transfer of Functions (Equality) Order 2007, SI 2007/2914, art 3), before being transferred to 'the Secretary of State' (see the Transfer of Functions (Equality) Order 2010, SI 2010/1839, art 3). As to the usage of the term 'Secretary of State' see note 4.

2 Equality Act 2010 s 207(1). As to the making of subordinate legislation generally see further STATUTES AND LEGISLATIVE PROCESS vol 96 (2012) PARA 1030 et seq.

3 See eg the power to make taxi accessibility regulations (see the Equality Act 2010 s 160; and PARA 215), the power to make public service vehicle accessibility regulations (see s 174; and PARA 224), the power to make rail vehicle accessibility regulations (see s 182; and PARA 233).

4 In any enactment, 'Secretary of State' means one of Her Majesty's principal secretaries of state: see the Interpretation Act 1978 s 5, Sch 1; and STATUTES AND LEGISLATIVE PROCESS vol 96 (2012) PARA 1209. The office of Secretary of State is a unified office, and in law each Secretary of State is capable of performing the functions of all or any of them: see CONSTITUTIONAL AND ADMINISTRATIVE LAW vol 20 (2014) PARA 153.

5 Ie a transitional exemption order under the Equality Act 2010 Sch 11 Pt 1 (see PARA 176), a transitional exemption order under Sch 12 Pt 1 (see PARA 186), an order under Sch 14 para 1(3) that does not modify an enactment (see PARA 187): see s 207(3).

6 Equality Act 2010 s 207(2). Section 207(2) does not require an exemption order to be made by statutory instrument; but such an order is as capable of being amended or revoked as an order made by statutory instrument: s 183(7) (added by the Deregulation Act 2015 Sch 10 paras 28, 29(1), (3)). Orders or regulations under the Equality Act 2010 may make different provision for different purposes, and may include consequential, incidental, supplementary, transitional, transitory or saving provision: s 207(4). Nothing in s 163(4) (see PARA 218), s 174(4) (see PARA 224) or s 182(3) (see PARA 233) affects the generality of the power for orders and regulations to make different provision for different purposes: s 207(5). As from a day to be appointed, the list of provisions in s 207(5) also includes s 181A(5) (see PARA 230) and s 181B(6) (see PARA 231): see s 207(5) (prospectively amended by the Bus Services Act 2017 s 17(2)). At the date at which this volume states the law no such day had been appointed. The power to include consequential, incidental, supplementary, transitional, transitory or saving provision in its application to the Equality Act 2010 s 139A (see EMPLOYMENT vol 40 (2014) PARA 609), s 153 (see PARA 285), s 154(2) (see PARA 277), s 155(5) (see PARAS 277, 285, 289), s 197 (see PARA 96) or s 216 (see PARA 1) or Sch 11 para 7(1) (see PARA 173) or Sch 14 para 1(3) or Sch 14 para 2(3) (see PARA 187), includes power to amend an enactment (including, in the case of s 139A, s 197 or s 216, to amend the Equality Act 2010 itself): see s 207(6) (amended by the Enterprise and Regulatory Reform Act 2013 s 98(1), (3)). Provision is made in relation to commencement orders: see the Equality Act 2010 ss 207(7), 216.

A statutory instrument containing an Order in Council under s 82 (offshore work: see PARA 116) is subject to annulment in pursuance of a resolution of either House of Parliament: s 207(8).

7 Where the power to make an order or regulations under the Equality Act 2010 is exercisable by a Minister of the Crown or the Treasury, a statutory instrument containing (whether alone or with other provision) an order or regulations that amend the Equality Act 2010 or another Act of Parliament, or an Act of the Scottish Parliament or an Act or Measure of the National Assembly for Wales, is subject to the affirmative procedure: s 208(1), (2). However, a statutory instrument is not subject to the affirmative procedure merely because it contains: an order under s 59 (local authority functions: see PARA 132), an order under s 151 (power to amend list of public authorities for the purposes of the public sector equality duty: see PARA 277) (that provides for the omission of an entry where the authority concerned has ceased to exist or the variation of an entry where the authority concerned has changed its name), or an order under Sch 14 para 1(3) (educational charities and endowments: see PARA 177) (that modifies an enactment): see s 208(3). A statutory instrument containing any of the following orders or regulations is subject to the affirmative procedure (see s 208(4), (5) (amended by the Enterprise and Regulatory Reform Act 2013 s 98(1), (4); and the Deregulation Act 2015 Sch 10 paras 28, 30(c))):

(1) regulations under the Equality Act 2010 s 30 (services: ships and hovercraft: see PARA 89);

(2) regulations under s 78 (gender pay gap information: see PARA 149);

(3) regulations under s 81 (work: ships and hovercraft: see PARA 116);

(4) an order under s 105 (election candidates: expiry of provision: see PARA 209);

(5) regulations under s 106 (election candidates: diversity information: see PARA 210);

(6) regulations under s 139A (equal pay audits: see EMPLOYMENT vol 40 (2014) PARA 609);

(7) regulations under s 153 or s 154(2) (public sector equality duty: powers to impose specific duties: see PARAS 277, 285);

(8) an order under s 203 (EU obligations: harmonisation: see PARA 18);

(9) regulations under Sch 20 para 9(3) (repealed) (rail vehicle accessibility: determination of turnover for purposes of penalties: see PARA 233).

As from a day to be appointed, the list of provisions in heads (1) to (9) above also includes reference to regulations under s 181A or s 181B (information for bus passengers: see PARAS 230–231): see s 208(5)(fa) (prospectively added by the Bus Services Act 2017 s 17(3)). At the date at which this volume states the law no such day had been appointed.

A statutory instrument that is not subject to the affirmative procedure by virtue of the Equality Act 2010 s 208(2) or s 208(4) is subject to the negative procedure: s 208(6). But a statutory instrument is not subject to the negative procedure merely because it contains an order under s 216 (commencement) that does not amend an Act of Parliament, an Act of the Scottish Parliament or an Act or Measure of the National Assembly for Wales, and is not made in reliance on s 207(7): s 208(7) (amended by the Deregulation Act 2015 Sch 10 paras 28, 30(c)).

If a statutory instrument is subject to the affirmative procedure, the order or regulations contained in it must not be made unless a draft of the instrument is laid before and approved by a resolution of each House of Parliament: Equality Act 2010 s 208(8). If a statutory instrument is subject to the negative procedure, it is subject to annulment in pursuance of a resolution of either House of Parliament: s 208(9). If a draft of a statutory instrument containing an order or regulations under s 2, s 151, s 153, s 154(2) or s 155(5) would otherwise be treated for the purposes of the Standing Orders of either House of Parliament as a hybrid instrument, it is to proceed in that House as if it were not a hybrid instrument: s 208(10).

8 See PARA 5. As to the Welsh Ministers and the Welsh Government established under the Government of Wales Act 2006 see ss 45–52; and CONSTITUTIONAL AND ADMINISTRATIVE LAW vol 20 (2014) PARA 373 et seq.

9 Where the power to make an order or regulations under the Equality Act 2010 is exercisable by the Welsh Ministers, a statutory instrument containing (whether alone or with other provision) any of the following orders or regulations is subject to the affirmative procedure (s 209(1), (2), (3)):

(1) regulations under s 2 (socio-economic inequalities: see PARA 302);

(2) an order under s 151 (power to amend list of public authorities for the purposes of the public sector equality duty: see PARA 277);

(3) regulations under s 153 or s 154(2) (public sector equality duty: powers to impose specific duties: see PARAS 277, 285);

(4) regulations under s 155(5) (public sector equality duty: power to modify or remove specific duties: see PARAS 277, 285, 289) that amend an Act of Parliament or an Act or Measure of the National Assembly for Wales.

However, a statutory instrument is not subject to the affirmative procedure merely because it contains an order under s 151 that provides for the omission of an entry where the authority concerned has ceased to exist, or for the variation of an entry where the authority concerned has changed its name: s 209(4).

A statutory instrument that is not subject to the affirmative procedure by virtue of s 209(2) is subject to the negative procedure: s 209(5). If a statutory instrument is subject to the affirmative procedure, the order or regulations contained in it must not be made unless a draft of the instrument is laid before and approved by a resolution of the National Assembly for Wales: s 209(6). If a statutory instrument is subject to the negative procedure, it is subject to annulment in pursuance of a resolution of the National Assembly for Wales: s 209(7). As to the National Assembly for Wales see CONSTITUTIONAL AND ADMINISTRATIVE LAW vol 20 (2014) PARA 351 et seq.

Provision is also made in respect of the procedure to be used where the Scottish Ministers have power to make an order, regulations or rules under the Equality Act 2010: see s 210.

(ii) Jurisdiction

5. Territorial application of the Equality Act 2010.

The Equality Act 2010 forms part of the law of England and Wales[1]. In relation to the provisions of the Act concerning discrimination at work[2], the Act makes no specific provision for its territorial application but leaves it to tribunals to determine whether the law applies, depending for example on the connection between the employment relationship and Great Britain[3]. In the context of the Employment Rights Act 1996, it has been held that working for a British employer would not in itself be sufficient to found jurisdiction in a tribunal in Great Britain[4]. Whilst there is no explicit provision in the Equality Act 2010 itself regarding territorial application regarding Part 5 of the Act, it does, however, contain a power to specify the territorial application of that part in relation to ships and hovercraft[5] and offshore work[6].

In a limited number of specific cases, express provision is made for particular provisions of the Act to apply (or potentially apply) outside the United Kingdom[7].

Under the Welsh devolution settlement the subject matter of equal opportunities is not devolved to Wales[8]. However, the Equality Act 2010 does give the Welsh Ministers power to amend certain provisions of the Act in their application to Wales, where necessary[9].

1   Equality Act 2010 s 217(1). The Act, apart from s 190 (improvements to let dwelling houses: see PARA 272) and Pt 15 (ss 198–201) (family property) (not yet fully in force), forms part of the law of Scotland: s 217(2). The law of Scotland is not covered in this work. As to discrimination law in Scotland see *Stair Memorial Encyclopaedia* DISCRIMINATION (Reissue).

    Equal opportunities and discrimination are 'transferred matters' under the Northern Ireland Act 1998: see the Equality Act 2010 Explanatory Notes para 19. Therefore (with some exceptions), the Equality Act 2010 does not form part of the law of Northern Ireland, and the Disability Discrimination Act 1995 remains in force there despite its repeal in relation to England and Wales: see the Equality Act 2010 Explanatory Notes paras 19, 20. Each of the following form part of the law of Northern Ireland: s 82 (offshore work: see PARA 116), s 105(3), (4) (expiry of Sex Discrimination (Election Candidates) Act 2002) (see PARA 209), and the Equality Act 2010 s 199 (abolition of presumption of advancement) (not yet in force): see s 217(3). The law of Northern Ireland is not covered in this work. As to discrimination law in Northern Ireland see Valentine: All Laws of Northern Ireland. As to the repeal of the Disability Discrimination Act 1995 and the introduction of the Equality Act 2010 see PARA 1.

2   Ie the Equality Act 2010 Pt 5 (ss 39–83) (see PARAS 116–172).

3   See the Equality Act 2010 Explanatory Notes paras 14, 15.

4   See *Lawson v Serco Ltd* [2006] UKHL 3, [2006] 1 All ER 823, [2006] IRLR 289; *Duncombe v Secretary of State for Children, Schools and Families (No 2)* [2011] UKSC 36, [2011] ICR 1312; *Ravat v Halliburton Manufacturing & Services Ltd* [2012] UKSC 1, [2012] ICR 389; *Bates van Winkelhof v Clyde & Co LLP* [2012] EWCA Civ 1207, [2013] ICR 883; *Dhunna v CreditSights Ltd* [2014] EWCA Civ 1238, [2015] ICR 105; *Jeffery v the British Council* (2016)

UKEAT/0036/16/JOJ, [2016] IRLR 935; and EMPLOYMENT vol 39 (2014) PARA 166. See also *Nica v Xian Jiaotong Liverpool University* (2017) UKEAT/0041/17/JOJ, [2017] All ER (D) 139 (Aug). As to the law relating to employment rights see further EMPLOYMENT.

5   See the Equality Act 2010 s 81; the Equality Act 2010 (Work on Ships and Hovercraft) Regulations 2011, SI 2011/1771; and PARA **116**.

6   See the Equality Act 2010 s 82; the Equality Act 2010 (Offshore Work) Order 2010, SI 2010/1835; and PARA **116**.

7   See the Equality Act 2010 Explanatory Notes para 15. For examples see the Equality Act 2010 s 29(9) (see PARA **85**) which provides for the prohibitions in respect of the provision of services or the exercise of public functions to apply in relation to race and religion or belief to the granting of entry clearance, even where the act in question takes place outside the United Kingdom. See also s 30 (see PARA **89**) which contains power to specify the territorial application of the services provisions of Pt 3 in relation to ships and hovercraft.

8   See the Equality Act 2010 Explanatory Notes para 18. As to Welsh devolution see the Government of Wales Act 1998, the Government of Wales Act 2006; and CONSTITUTIONAL AND ADMINISTRATIVE LAW vol 20 (2014) PARA 75 et seq.

9   The Welsh Ministers have power to add any relevant Welsh body to the bodies subject to the duty to consider socio-economic inequalities: see the Equality Act 2010 s 2; and PARA **302**. The Welsh Ministers have power to impose specific duties on relevant Welsh bodies in relation to the public sector equality duty (see ss 153–155; and PARAS **277, 285**) and to amend Sch 19 Pt 2 which specifies relevant Welsh bodies subject to the general public sector equality duty (see ss 151, 152; and PARA **277**).

6. Jurisdiction to determine matters relating to contraventions of the Equality Act 2010.

Contraventions of the provisions in the Equality Act 2010 relating to services and public functions[1], premises[2], education[3] and associations[4] are in general within the jurisdiction of the County Court[5] (although there are exceptions for certain immigration cases[6] and cases involving disabled pupils[7]). Contraventions relating to work[8] are generally within the jurisdiction of employment tribunals[9]. Proceedings relating to a breach of an equality clause or rule[10] are also within the jurisdiction of employment tribunals[11], although such proceedings may also be brought before the County Court where allowed[12]. Proceedings in relation to qualifications bodies will normally be brought in the employment tribunal[13]. Proceedings relating to a contravention of the Equality Act 2010 must be brought accordingly[14], although this is subject to any express provision of the Act conferring jurisdiction on a court or tribunal[15]. It does not preclude the bringing of proceedings[16] before the Equality and Human Rights Commission[17] and does not prevent a claim for judicial review[18] or certain proceedings[19] relating to immigration[20].

Where conduct has given rise to two or more separate proceedings under the Equality Act 2010, one of which involves instructing, causing or inducing a contravention[21], the County Court may transfer proceedings to an employment tribunal and an employment tribunal may transfer proceedings to the County Court[22].

These provisions are not affected by the investigative powers of the Equality and Human Rights Commission[23] and do not apply to proceedings for a criminal offence under the Equality Act 2010[24] or to proceedings under the Act relating to a penalty under the provisions concerning accessibility of transport for disabled persons[25].

1   Ie the Equality Act 2010 Pt 3 (ss 28–31): see PARAS **84–104**.
2   Ie the Equality Act 2010 Pt 4 (ss 32–38): see PARAS **105–115**.
3   Ie the Equality Act 2010 Pt 6 (ss 84–99): see PARAS **173–197**.
4   Ie the Equality Act 2010 Pt 7 (ss 100–107): see PARAS **198–210**.
5   See the Equality Act 2010 Pt 9 Ch 2 (ss 114–119); and PARAS **351–355**.

6   See the Equality Act 2010 s 115; and PARA 352.
7   See the Equality Act 2010 s 116, Sch 17; and PARA 356.
8   Ie the Equality Act 2010 Pt 5 (ss 39–83): see PARAS 116–172.
9   See the Equality Act 2010 Pt 9 Ch 3 (ss 120–126); and PARAS 357–359.
10 As to the meanings of 'equality clause' and 'equality rule' see PARA 117 note 4.
11 See the Equality Act 2010 Pt 9 Ch 4 (ss 127–135); and PARAS 360–364.
12 The reference to a 'contravention' of the Equality Act 2010 includes a reference to a breach of an
    equality clause or rule (s 113(5)), although Pt 9 Ch 2 (see PARAS 351–355) and Pt 9 Ch 3 (see
    PARAS 357–359) do not apply to proceedings relating to an equality clause or rule except in so far
    as Pt 9 Ch 4 provides for that (s 113(6)). See *Abdulla v Birmingham City Council* [2012] UKSC
    47, [2013] 1 All ER 649, [2013] IRLR 38 (decided under the Equal Pay Act 1970 (repealed)).
13 See *Michalak v General Medical Council* [2017] UKSC 71. As to qualifications bodies see PARAS
    129, 192–193.
14 Ie in accordance with the Equality Act 2010 Pt 9 (ss 113–141) (see PARAS 351–355): s 113(1).
15 Equality Act 2010 s 113(4).
16 Ie under the Equality Act 2006 Pt 1 (ss 1–42) (see PARAS 28–44, 339–350).
17 Equality Act 2010 s 113(2). As to the inquisitional and investigatory powers of the Commission
    see PARAS 339–344 (inquiries), 345–350 (investigations).
18 Equality Act 2010 s 113(3)(a).
19 Ie proceedings under the Immigration Acts (see IMMIGRATION AND ASYLUM) or under the Special
    Immigration Appeals Commission Act 1997 (see IMMIGRATION AND ASYLUM vol 57 (2012)
    PARAS 430–456).
20 Equality Act 2010 s 113(3)(b), (c).
21 Ie at least one of the proceedings being for a contravention of the Equality Act 2010 s 111 (see
    PARA 82).
22 Equality Act 2010 s 140(1)–(3), (6)(a) (amended by Crime and Courts Act 2013 Sch 9 para 52).
    A court or employment tribunal is to be taken for the purposes of the Equality Act 2010 Pt 9 to
    have jurisdiction to determine a claim or complaint transferred to it under s 140: see s 140(4).
23 Nothing in the Equality Act 2006 affects the entitlement of a person to bring proceedings under
    the Equality Act 2010 in respect of a contravention mentioned in the Equality Act 2006 s 24A(1)
    (see PARA 345): s 24A(4) (s 24A added by the Equality Act 2010 Sch 26 para 68). As to the
    Equality and Human Rights Commission see PARAS 28–44.
24 Equality Act 2010 s 113(7)(a).
25 Equality Act 2010 s 113(7)(b). As to penalties under Pt 12 (ss 160–188) (disabled persons;
    transport) see PARAS 211–236.

(iii) Non-statutory Codes of Practice

7. Codes of practice issued by the Equality and Human Rights Commission.

In exercise of its power under the Equality Act 2006[1], the Equality and Human Rights Commission[2] has issued the following codes of practice: (1) the Equality Act 2010 Code of Practice on Services, Public Functions and Associations (referred to as 'the Services Code'); (2) the Equality Act 2010 Code of Practice on Employment (referred to as 'the Employment Code'); and (3) the Equality Act 2010 Code of Practice on Equal Pay (referred to as 'the Equal Pay Code')[3]. These codes supersede various codes of practice, issued under previous discrimination legislation by former commissions which have since been dissolved[4].

The codes are designed to ensure or facilitate compliance with provisions in the Equality Act 2010. The Services Code covers Part 3 of the Equality Act 2010, which makes it unlawful to discriminate against, harass or victimise a person when providing a service (which includes the provision of goods or facilities) or when exercising a public function[5]. The Services Code also covers Part 7 of the Act, which makes it unlawful for associations to discriminate against, harass or victimise members, associates or guests[6]. The Employment Code covers certain provisions in Part 5 of the Act (which make it unlawful to discriminate against, harass or victimise a person at work or in employment services, and restrict the circumstances in which potential employees can be asked questions about disability or health[7]) and Part 10 of the Act (which relates to unenforceable terms in contracts, etc)[8]. The Equal Pay Code covers provisions in Part 5 of the Act relating to equal pay between men and women, pregnancy and maternity pay, and provisions making it unlawful for an employment contract to prevent an employee disclosing his or her pay[9].

The codes also cover the key concepts on which the Equality Act 2010 is based, including the characteristics which are protected under the Act and the definitions of discrimination and other conduct which are prohibited[10]. All the codes cover relevant provisions in Part 9 of the Act dealing with enforcement of its provisions[11].

1   Ie under the Equality Act 2006 s 14 (see PARA 43).

2   As to the Commission see PARA 28 et seq.

3   See the Equality Act 2010 Codes of Practice (Services, Public Functions and Associations, Employment, and Equal Pay) Order 2011, SI 2011/857, which brought the Equality Act 2010 Code of Practice — Employment Statutory Code of Practice (2011), the Equality Act 2010 Code of Practice — Services, Public Functions and Associations Statutory Code of Practice (2011), and the Equality Act 2010 Code of Practice — Equal Pay Statutory Code of Practice (2011) into force on 6 April 2011.

4   As to the dissolution of the former commissions see the Equality Act 2006 s 36; and PARA 28. As to the revocation of former codes of practice see the Former Equality Commissions' Codes of Practice (Employment, Equal Pay, and Rights of Access for Disabled Persons) (Revocation) Order 2011, SI 2011/776.

5   As to the Equality Act 2010 Pt 3 (ss 28–31) see PARAS 84–104. See the Equality Act 2010 Code of Practice — Services, Public Functions and Associations Statutory Code of Practice (2011) Ch 1 (Introduction), Ch 2 (Who has rights under Part 3 (services and public functions) and Part 7 (associations) of the Act?), Ch 3 (Who has obligations under Part 3 (services and public functions) and Part 7 (associations) of the Act?), Ch 4 (Direct discrimination), Ch 5 (Indirect discrimination), Ch 6 (Discrimination arising from disability), Ch 7 (Disabled persons: reasonable adjustments), Ch 8 (Harassment), Ch 9 (Victimisation and other unlawful acts), Ch 10 (Positive action), Ch 11 (Services and public functions), Ch 13 (Exceptions), Ch 14 (Enforcement).

6   As to the Equality Act 2010 Pt 7 (ss 100–107) see PARAS 198–210. See the Equality Act 2010 Code of Practice — Services, Public Functions and Associations Statutory Code of Practice (2011) Ch 12 (Associations).

7   See the Equality Act 2010 Pt 5 Ch 1 (ss 39–60), Ch 4 (ss 81–83); and PARAS 116–172. See the Equality Act 2010 Code of Practice — Employment Statutory Code of Practice (2011) Ch 1 (Introduction), Ch 2 (Protected characteristics), Ch 3 (Direct discrimination), Ch 4 (Indirect discrimination), Ch 5 (Discrimination arising from disability), Ch 6 (Duty to make reasonable adjustments), Ch 7 (Harassment), Ch 8 (Pregnancy and maternity), Ch 9 (Victimisation and other unlawful acts), Ch 10 (Obligations and liabilities under the Act), Ch 11 (Discrimination in work relationships other than employment), Ch 12 (Positive action), Ch 13 (Occupational requirements and other exceptions related to work), Ch 14 (Pay and benefits), Ch 15 (Enforcement), Ch 16 (Avoiding discrimination in recruitment), Ch 17 (Avoiding discrimination during employment), Ch 18 (Equality policies and practice in the workplace), Ch 19 (Termination of employment).

8   As to the Equality Act 2010 Pt 10 (ss 142–148) see PARAS 274–275. See note 7.

9   See the Equality Act 2010 Code of Practice — Equal Pay Statutory Code of Practice (2011) Part 1 (Equal pay law), Part 2 (Good equal pay practice).

10 See PARAS 45–83.

11 As to enforcement see the Equality Act 2010 Pt 9 (ss 113–141); and PARAS 351–365.

(2) THE EUROPEAN CONVENTION ON HUMAN RIGHTS AND THE EUROPEAN SOCIAL CHARTER

8. The European Convention on Human Rights.

The European Convention on Human Rights[1] provides that the enjoyment of the rights and freedoms set forth in the Convention must be secured without discrimination on any ground such as sex, race, colour, language, religion, political or other opinion, national or social origin, association with a national minority, property, birth or other status[2]. Those grounds are referred to as 'the protected grounds'[3], although there are other characteristics and statuses, not explicitly referred to in the Convention, in relation to which the European Court of Human Rights has found a violation of the prohibition on discrimination[4]. This provision does not create a free standing right to equality but confers such right only in respect of the enjoyment of other rights guaranteed by the Convention[5]. Inequality of treatment will not necessarily violate the Convention if it can be reasonably and objectively justified[6].

Other rights protected under the Convention which may give rise to discrimination issues are:

(1) the right to a fair hearing[7];
(2) the right to respect for private and family life (including the right to marry)[8];
(3) freedom of thought, conscience and religion[9];
(4) freedom of expression[10];
(5) freedom of assembly and association[11];
(6) the protection of property[12]; and
(7) the right to education[13].

The prohibition on discrimination and the other rights referred to above are 'Convention rights' and it is therefore unlawful as a matter of English law for any public authority to act incompatibly with them[14]. Individuals may pursue and rely on Convention rights in domestic courts, which may provide a remedy for a breach of such rights[15].

1 Ie the Convention for the Protection of Human Rights and Fundamental Freedoms (Rome, 4 November 1950; TS 71 (1953); Cmd 8969): see generally RIGHTS AND FREEDOMS vol 88A (2013) PARA 88.

2 See the European Convention on Human Rights art 14; and RIGHTS AND FREEDOMS vol 88A (2013) PARA 506. See also *R (on the application of Mormoroc) v Secretary of State for Justice* [2017] EWCA Civ 989, [2017] All ER (D) 111 (July) (cited in PARA 67). As to the meaning of 'discrimination' in the context of the Convention see RIGHTS AND FREEDOMS vol 88A (2013) PARA 512.

3 As to where the European Court of Human Rights has found that there has been discrimination on each of the protected grounds see RIGHTS AND FREEDOMS vol 88A (2013) PARAS 514–518.

4 As to these see RIGHTS AND FREEDOMS vol 88A (2013) PARAS 519–528.

5 See RIGHTS AND FREEDOMS vol 88A (2013) PARA 509. This is known as the 'ambit' test: see further RIGHTS AND FREEDOMS vol 88A (2013) PARAS 510–511.

6 As to justified interferences with the prohibition on discrimination see RIGHTS AND FREEDOMS vol 88A (2013) PARAS 529–533.

7 See the European Convention on Human Rights art 6; and RIGHTS AND FREEDOMS vol 88A (2013) PARAS 243–300.

8 See the European Convention on Human Rights arts 8, 12; and RIGHTS AND FREEDOMS vol 88A (2013) PARAS 317–350 (right to respect for private life), 351–367 (right to family life and right to marry).

9 See the European Convention on Human Rights art 9; and RIGHTS AND FREEDOMS vol 88A (2013) PARAS 368–397.

10 See the European Convention on Human Rights art 10; and RIGHTS AND FREEDOMS vol 88A (2013)
    PARAS 398–435.
11 See the European Convention on Human Rights art 11; and RIGHTS AND FREEDOMS vol 88A (2013)
    PARAS 436–460 (assembly), 461–493 (association).
12 See the European Convention on Human Rights Protocol 1 art 1; and RIGHTS AND FREEDOMS vol
    88A (2013) PARAS 534–547.
13 See the European Convention on Human Rights Protocol 1 art 2; and RIGHTS AND FREEDOMS vol
    88A (2013) PARAS 548–571.
14 See the Human Rights Act 1998 ss 1(1)(a), (b) (3), 2, 6, Sch 1; and RIGHTS AND FREEDOMS vol 88A
    (2013) PARAS 14, 21, 23. Primary legislation and subordinate legislation, so far as it is possible,
    must be read and given effect to in a way which is compatible with the Convention rights,
    including the European Convention on Human Rights art 14: see the Human Rights Act 1998 s
    3; and RIGHTS AND FREEDOMS vol 88A (2013) PARA 16.
15 See the Human Rights Act 1998 ss 7, 8; and RIGHTS AND FREEDOMS vol 88A (2013) PARAS 27–29.

9.   The European Social Charter.

The European Social Charter was adopted by member states of the Council of
Europe[1] in 1961[2] and revised in 1999[3]. It is designed to guarantee social and
economic rights augmenting the human rights guaranteed by the European
Convention on Human Rights[4], and its preamble states that the enjoyment of
social rights should be secured without discrimination on grounds of race, colour,
sex, religion, political opinion, national extraction or social origin[5].

1   As to the Council of Europe see RIGHTS AND FREEDOMS vol 88A (2013) PARA 87.
2   See the European Social Charter (Turin, 18 October 1961; TS 38 (1965); Cmnd 2643). The United
    Kingdom ratified the Charter on 11 July 1962.
3   See the European Social Charter (Strasbourg, 3 May 1996; ETS 163). The United Kingdom has
    signed but not ratified the revised Charter.
4   Ie the Convention for the Protection of Human Rights and Fundamental Freedoms (Rome, 4
    November 1950; TS 71 (1953); Cmd 8969) (see RIGHTS AND FREEDOMS vol 88A (2013) PARA 88).
5   See the European Social Charter preamble.

(3) EUROPEAN UNION LAW

(i) The Treaties

10.   The Treaty on European Union and the Treaty on the Functioning of the
         European Union.

The Treaty on European Union[1] affirms that principles of equality and
non-discrimination are central to the aims and objectives of the EU, declaring that
the EU is founded on the values of respect for human dignity, freedom, democracy,
equality, the rule of law and respect for human rights, including the rights of
persons belonging to minorities, and that those values are common to the member
states in a society in which pluralism, non-discrimination, tolerance, justice,
solidarity and equality between women and men prevail[2]. The Treaty also declares
that the EU is to combat social exclusion and discrimination and to promote, inter
alia, equality between women and men[3].

The Treaty on the Functioning of the European Union[4] confers powers on the
EU Council to take action to combat discrimination[5], and these powers are the
source of the Equality Directives that now underpin much of United Kingdom law
in this area[6]. The Treaty also requires the EU to make the combating of
discrimination a central feature of its policy-making[7], and makes particular

provision in connection with the elimination of gender discrimination and the promotion of gender equality[8].

The EU Charter[9] is the principal mechanism through which the EU seeks to promote and protect its values within the EU, and has the same legal value as the Treaty on European Union and the Treaty on the Functioning of the European Union[10]. The Treaty on European Union also provides that the fundamental rights guaranteed by the European Convention on Human Rights[11] constitute general principles of EU law[12]. By these mechanisms the EU Charter is given the binding effect of a Treaty and pre-existing human rights protection within the EU and its member states continue to be part of EU law[13].

1 Ie the Treaty on European Union (Maastricht, 7 February 1992; Cm 1934) ('Treaty on European Union'). The Treaty has been amended and renumbered by the Treaty of Amsterdam Amending the Treaty on European Union, the Treaties Establishing the European Communities and Related Acts (Amsterdam, 2 October 1997, ECS 14 (1997); Cm 3780) and by the Treaty of Lisbon Amending the Treaty Establishing the European Union and the Treaty Establishing the European Community (Lisbon, 13 December 2007, ECS 13 (2007); Cm 7294) (the 'Lisbon Treaty').
2 See the Treaty on European Union art 2.
3 See the Treaty on European Union art 3.3.
4 Ie the Treaty on the Functioning of the European Union (Rome, 25 March 1957; TS 1 (1973); Cmnd 5179) ('TFEU'). The Treaty was formerly known as the Treaty Establishing the European Community (often abbreviated to 'EC Treaty'; and also known as the Treaty of Rome); it has been renamed and its provisions renumbered by the Lisbon Treaty (see note 1) which came into force on 1 December 2009. The Treaty on the Functioning of the European Union is also sometimes referred to as the 'EU Treaty'.
5 See the TFEU art 19.1 ('Without prejudice to the other provisions of the Treaties and within the limits of the powers conferred by them upon the Union, the Council, acting unanimously in accordance with a special legislative procedure and after obtaining the consent of the European Parliament, may take appropriate action to combat discrimination based on sex, racial or ethnic origin, religion or belief, disability, age or sexual orientation'). Article 19 forms part of Part II (arts 18–25), which is expressly concerned with non-discrimination and citizenship.
6 As to the Equality Directives see PARAS 12–18.
7 See the TFEU art 10 ('In defining and implementing its policies and activities, the Union shall aim to combat discrimination based on sex, racial or ethnic origin, religion or belief, disability, age or sexual orientation').
8 See the TFEU art 8 ('In all its activities, the Union shall aim to eliminate inequalities, and to promote equality, between men and women), and art 157 ('Each member state shall ensure that the principle of equal pay for male and female workers for equal work or work of equal value is applied . . .'). See *Brierley v Asda Stores Ltd* (2017) UKEAT/0011/17/DM, [2017] All ER (D) 141 (Aug), where the Employment Appeal Tribunal held, in declining to make a reference to the European Court of Justice, that although the point is not 'acte clair', the better view is that TFEU art 157 is directly effective in a claim founded on equal pay for work of equal value. As to equal pay under European law see PARAS 150–154. As to equality of terms see PARA 136 et seq.
9 Ie the Charter of Fundamental Rights of the European Union (OJ C364, 18.12.2000, p 1) (see PARA 11).
10 See the Treaty on the European Union art 6.1 ('The Union recognises the rights, freedoms and principles set out in the Charter of Fundamental Rights of the European Union . . . which shall have the same legal value as the Treaties. The provisions of the Charter shall not extend in any way the competences of the Union as defined in the Treaties . . .').
11 Ie the Convention for the Protection of Human Rights and Fundamental Freedoms (Rome, 4 November 1950; TS 71 (1953); Cmd 8969) (see PARA 8).
12 See the Treaty on the European Union arts 6.2, 6.3 ('The Union shall accede to the [European Convention on Human Rights]. Such accession shall not affect the Union's competences as defined in the Treaties. Fundamental rights, as guaranteed by the [European Convention on Human Rights] and as they result from the constitutional traditions common to the member states, shall constitute general principles of the Union's law').
13 See the text and notes 1–12; and Opinion 2/13, ECLI:EU:C:2014:2454, [2015] All ER (EC) 463.

11. EU Charter on Fundamental Rights.

The United Kingdom is a signatory to the EU Charter on Fundamental Rights[1] and must act consistently with it when implementing EU law or acting in the scope of the law of the Union[2]. The Charter declares that everyone is equal before the law[3], that discrimination based on any ground such as sex, race, colour, ethnic or social origin, genetic features, language, religion or belief, political or any other opinion, membership of a national minority, property, birth, disability, age or sexual orientation is prohibited[4], and that equality between men and women is to be ensured in all areas, including employment, work and pay[5]. Since these provisions duplicate to a degree the anti-discrimination provisions contained in the European Convention on Human Rights[6] the protection they offer to persons within the United Kingdom is consistent with that provided by the Convention: however, this does not preclude the grant of wider protection under EU law[7]. Thus, where there is a breach of the Charter, there may be an obligation to disapply domestic law; whereas where there is a breach of the Convention, the Human Rights Act 1998 would only require a declaration of incompatibility[8].

1 Ie the Charter of Fundamental Rights of the European Union (OJ C202, 7.6.2016, p 389) ('EU Charter of Fundamental Rights'). As to the Charter and its central position in EU law see further PARA 10; and RIGHTS AND FREEDOMS vol 88A (2013) PARA 97.
2 See the EU Charter of Fundamental Rights art 51. See *Benkharbouche v Secretary of State for Foreign and Commonwealth Affairs, Secretary of State for Foreign and Commonwealth Affairs and Libya v Janah Constitutional Law* [2017] UKSC 62.
3 See the EU Charter of Fundamental Rights art 20.
4 See the EU Charter of Fundamental Rights art 21.1.
5 See the EU Charter of Fundamental Rights art 23.
6 Ie the Convention for the Protection of Human Rights and Fundamental Freedoms (Rome, 4 November 1950; TS 71 (1953); Cmd 8969) art 14 (see PARA 8). As to the Convention generally see RIGHTS AND FREEDOMS vol 88A (2013) PARA 88.
7 See the EU Charter of Fundamental Rights art 52.3.
8 See *Benkharbouche v Secretary of State for Foreign and Commonwealth Affairs, Secretary of State for Foreign and Commonwealth Affairs and Libya v Janah Constitutional Law* [2017] UKSC 62; and RIGHTS AND FREEDOMS vol 88A (2013) PARA 18.

(ii) The Equality Directives

12. Equal treatment: men and women.

The Equal Treatment Directive[1] puts into effect in the member states the principle of equal treatment for men and women[2] as regards access to employment, including promotion, and to vocational training and as regards working conditions and, on certain conditions, social security[3]. Member states must take the necessary measures to ensure that:

(1)   any laws, regulations and administrative provisions contrary to the principle of equal treatment are abolished[4];

(2)   any provisions contrary to the principle of equal treatment which are included in contracts or collective agreements, internal rules of undertakings or in rules governing the independent occupations and professions and workers' and employers' organisations are or may be declared, null and void or may be amended[5]; and

(3)   occupational social security schemes containing such provisions may not be approved or extended by administrative measures[6].

Member states are required to:

(a)   ensure that judicial, administrative and conciliation procedures for the enforcement of obligations under the Equal Treatment Directive are available to all persons who consider themselves wronged by failure to apply the principle of equal treatment to them[7];

(b)   ensure that legal entities which have, in accordance with the criteria laid down by their national law, a legitimate interest in ensuring that the provisions of the Directive are complied with, may engage in any judicial and administrative procedures for the enforcement of obligations under the Directive[8];

(c)   introduce into their national legal systems necessary measures for compensation or reparation for loss or damage sustained as a result of discrimination[9]; and

(d)   introduce into their national legal systems such measures as are necessary to protect employees against dismissal or other adverse treatment by the employer as a reaction to a complaint aimed at enforcing compliance with the principle of equal treatment[10].

1   Ie Parliament and Council Directive (EC) 2006/54 (OJ L204, 26.7.2006, p 23) on the implementation of the principle of equal opportunities and equal treatment of men and women in matters of employment and occupation. This Directive repealed and consolidated Council Directive (EC) 75/117 (OJ L45, 19.2.75, p 19) on the approximation of the laws of the member states relating to the application of the principle of equal pay for men and women; Council Directive (EC) 76/207 (OJ L 39, 14.2.76, p 40) on the implementation of the principle of equal treatment for men and women as regards access to employment, vocational training and promotion, and working conditions (the former 'Equal Treatment Directive'); Council Directive (EC) 86/378 (OJ L225, 12.8.86, p 40) on the implementation of the principle of equal treatment for men and women in occupational social security schemes; Council Directive (EC) 97/80 (OJ L14, 20.1.98, p 6) on the burden of proof in cases of discrimination based on sex; and Council Directive (EC) 98/52 (OJ L205, 22.7.98, p 66) on the extension of EC Directive 97/80 on the burden of proof in cases of discrimination based on sex to the United Kingdom of Great Britain and Northern Ireland.

2   Parliament and Council Directive (EC) 2006/54 (OJ L204, 26.7.2006, p 23) also applies to transsexuals, and it is therefore contrary to the Directive to dismiss a person because he or she has undergone, or intends to undergo, gender reassignment: see Case C-13/94 *P v S* [1996] ICR 795, [1996] All ER (EC) 397, ECJ (decided under Council Directive (EC) 76/207 (OJ L39, 14.2.76, p 40) (see note 1)).

3   See Parliament and Council Directive (EC) 2006/54 (OJ L204, 26.7.2006, p 23) art 1. For the purposes of the Directive, discrimination includes: harassment and sexual harassment, as well as any less favourable treatment based on a person's rejection of or submission to such conduct; instruction to discriminate against persons on grounds of sex; and any less favourable treatment of a woman related to pregnancy or maternity leave: see art 2.2. In connection with the principle of equal treatment generally under Parliament and Council Directive (EC) 2006/54 (OJ L204, 26.7.2006, p 23) and under the former Equal Treatment Directive (see note 1) see the following cases: Case 222/84 *Johnston v Chief Constable of the Royal Ulster Constabulary* [1987] QB 129, [1986] 3 All ER 135, ECJ; Case 318/86 *EC Commission v France* [1988] ECR 3559, [1989] 3 CMLR 663, ECJ; Case C-394/96 *Brown v Rentokil Ltd* [1998] All ER (EC) 791, [1998] ECR I-4185, ECJ; Case C-273/97 *Sirdar v Army Board* [1999] All ER (EC) 928, [2000] ICR 130, ECJ; Case C-285/98 *Kreil v Bundesrepublik Deutschland* [2000] ECR I-69, [2002] 1 CMLR 1047, (2000) Times, 22 February, ECJ; Case C-407/98 *Abrahamsson v Fogelqvist* [2000] ECR I-5539, [2002] ICR 932, ECJ; Case E-1/02 *EFTA Surveillance Authority v Kingdom of Norway* [2003] 1 CMLR 725, [2003] IRLR 318, EFTA Ct; Case C-226/98 *Jørgensen v Foreningen AF Speciallaeger* [2000] ECR I-2447, [2000] IRLR 726, ECJ; Case C-476/99 *Lommers v Minister Van Landbouw, Natuurbeheer en Visserij* [2002] ECR I-2891, [2004] 2 CMLR 1141, ECJ; Case C-320/01 *Busch v Klinikum Neustadt GmbH & Co Betriebs-KG* [2003] All ER (EC) 985, [2003] IRLR 625, ECJ; Case C-5/12 *Montull v Instituto Nacional de la Seguridad Social* [2013] IRLR 976, ECJ; Case C-363/12 *Z v A Government Department* [2014] IRLR 563, ECJ; Case C-167/12 *CD v ST* ECLI:EU:C:2014:169, [2014] IRLR 551, ECJ.

4   See Parliament and Council Directive (EC) 2006/54 (OJ L204, 26.7.2006, p 23) art 23(a).

5   See Parliament and Council Directive (EC) 2006/54 (OJ L204, 26.7.2006, p 23) art 23(b).

6   See Parliament and Council Directive (EC) 2006/54 (OJ L204, 26.7.2006, p 23) art 23(c).

7 See Parliament and Council Directive (EC) 2006/54 (OJ L204, 26.7.2006, p 23) art 17.1. These provisions are without prejudice to national rules relating to time limits for bringing actions as regards the principle of equal treatment: art 17.3.

8 See Parliament and Council Directive (EC) 2006/54 (OJ L204, 26.7.2006, p 23) art 17.2.

9 See Parliament and Council Directive (EC) 2006/54 (OJ L204, 26.7.2006, p 23) art 18. Such compensation or reparation may not be restricted by the fixing of a prior upper limit, except in cases where the employer can prove that the only damage suffered by an applicant as a result of discrimination within the meaning of the Directive is the refusal to take his or her job application into consideration: art 18. It is contrary to art 18 to lay down an upper limit on the amount of compensation recoverable by a victim of discrimination in respect of the loss and damage sustained: see Case C-271/91 *Marshall v Southampton and South West Hampshire Area Health Authority (Teaching) (No 2)* [1994] QB 126, [1993] 4 All ER 586, ECJ; Case C-180/95 *Draehmpaehl v Urania Immobilienservice ohG* [1997] All ER (EC) 719, [1998] ICR 164, ECJ. It is also contrary to the provision for national legislation to require a finding of fault on the part of the employer before compensation can be awarded for discrimination: see Case C-180/95 *Draehmpaehl v Urania Immobilienservice ohG*. Note that the cases cited above were decided under Council Directive (EC) 76/207 (OJ L39, 14.2.76, p 40) (see note 1).

10 See Parliament and Council Directive (EC) 2006/54 (OJ L204, 26.7.2006, p 23) art 24.

13. Equal treatment: race and ethnic origin.

There is a European Directive prohibiting racial discrimination[1]. The purpose of this Directive is to lay down a framework for combating discrimination on the grounds of racial or ethnic origin, with a view to putting into effect in the member states the principle of equal treatment[2], which means that there must be no direct or indirect discrimination based on racial or ethnic origin[3]. The Directive applies to all persons, as regards both the public and private sectors, including public bodies, in relation to conditions for access to employment and occupation, access to vocational guidance and training, employment and working conditions, including dismissals and pay, membership of and involvement in an organisation of workers or employers, social protection including social security and healthcare, social advantages, education, and access to goods and services including housing[4]. There are exceptions relating to genuine occupational requirements[5] and the taking of positive action with a view to ensuring equality[6]. Member states must ensure that there are enforcement provisions similar to those that exist for the purposes of the Equal Treatment Directive[7].

1 Ie Council Directive (EC) 2000/43 (OJ L180, 10.07.2000, p 22) implementing the principle of equal treatment between persons irrespective of racial or ethnic origin.

2 See Council Directive (EC) 2000/43 (OJ L180, 10.07.2000, p 22) art 1.

3 See Council Directive (EC) 2000/43 (OJ L180, 10.07.2000, p 22) art 2.1. In connection with discrimination under these provisions see Case C-54/07 *Centrum voor Gelijkheid van Kansen en voor Racismebestrijding v Firma Feryn NV* [2008] All ER (EC) 1127, [2008] IRLR 732, ECJ.

4 See Council Directive (EC) 2000/43 (OJ L180, 10.07.2000, p 22) art 3.1.

5 See Council Directive (EC) 2000/43 (OJ L180, 10.07.2000, p 22) art 4.

6 See Council Directive (EC) 2000/43 (OJ L180, 10.07.2000, p 22) art 5.

7 See Council Directive (EC) 2000/43 (OJ L180, 10.07.2000, p 22) arts 7–9. As to the Equal Treatment Directive (ie Parliament and Council Directive (EC) 2006/54 (OJ L204, 26.7.2006, p 23) on the implementation of the principle of equal opportunities and equal treatment of men and women in matters of employment and occupation) see PARA 12. See also Case C-415/10 *Meister v Speech Design Carrier Systems GmbH* [2012] 2 CMLR 1119, [2012] ICR 1006, ECJ, [2014] All ER (EC) 231.

14. Religion or belief, disability, age or sexual orientation.

European Union legislation sets out a general framework[1] for combating discrimination on the grounds of religion or belief, disability[2], age or sexual orientation as regards employment and occupation, with a view to putting into effect in the member states the principle of equal treatment[3]. Member states must ensure that any laws, regulations and administrative provisions contrary to the principle of equal treatment are abolished, and any provisions contrary to the principle of equal treatment which are included in contracts or collective agreements, internal rules of undertakings or rules governing the independent occupations and professions and workers' and employers' organisations are, or may be, declared null and void or are amended[4].

The Directive applies to all persons, as regards both the public and private sectors, including public bodies, in relation to:

(1)   conditions for access to employment, to self-employment or to occupation;

(2)   access to vocational guidance and vocational training;

(3)   employment and working conditions, including dismissals and pay; and

(4)   membership of organisations of workers or employers[5].

Member states may impose occupational requirements for the application of these provisions[6], and may provide that differences of treatment on grounds of age do not constitute discrimination if they are objectively and reasonably justified by a legitimate aim[7].

In order to guarantee compliance with the principle of equal treatment in relation to persons with disabilities, reasonable accommodation must be provided[8]. Member states are not prevented from taking positive action for combating discrimination[9]. Member states must ensure that there are enforcement provisions similar to those that exist for the purposes of the Equal Treatment Directive[10], and are required to disseminate information about provisions adopted pursuant to these provisions[11], and to promote dialogue between the social partners with a view to fostering equal treatment[12].

1   Ie Council Directive (EC) 2000/78 (OJ L303, 2.12.2000, p 16) on establishing a general framework for equal treatment in employment and occupation. This Directive is without prejudice to measures laid down by national law which, in a democratic society, are necessary for public security, for the maintenance of public order and the prevention of criminal offences, for the protection of health and for the protection of the rights and freedoms of others: art 2.5.

2   Sickness does not amount to disability: Case C-13/05 *Navas v Eurest Colectividades SA* [2007] All ER (EC) 59, [2006] IRLR 706, ECJ. See also Case C-303/06 *Coleman v Attridge Law* [2008] All ER (EC) 1105, [2008] IRLR 722, ECJ (less favourable treatment or harassment as primary carer of disabled child contrary to prohibition of direct discrimination or harassment). A condition caused by illness may amount to a disability where that results in a condition which hinders the full and effective participation of the individual in professional life: see Cases C-335/11 and C-337/11 *HK Danmark (acting on behalf of Ring) v Dansk almennyttigt Boligselskab; HK Danmark (acting on behalf of Werge) v Dansk Arbejdsgiverforening (acting on behalf of Pro Displat A/S)* [2013] IRLR 571, [2013] EqLR 528, CJEU (Council Directive (EC) 2000/78 (OJ L303, 2.12.2000, p 16) must be interpreted consistently with the Convention on the Rights of Persons with Disabilities (New York, 13 December 2006; TS 10 (2010); Cm 7905) (see PARA 25)). See Case C-354/13 *Fag og Arbejde (FOA) v Kommunernes Landsforening (KL)* ECLI:EU:C:2014:2463, [2015] All ER (EC) 265, ECJ (obesity of worker may constitute disability).

3   See Council Directive (EC) 2000/78 (OJ L303, 2.12.2000, p 16) art 1. The 'principle of equal treatment' means that there must be no direct or indirect discrimination whatsoever on any of the grounds referred to in art 1: art 2.1. See Case C-229/08 *Wolf v Stadt Frankfurt am Main* [2010] All ER (EC) 939, [2010] IRLR 244, ECJ. Where national law allows same-sex civil partnerships but not same-sex marriages, a provision in a collective agreement giving additional benefits to married employees amounts to direct discrimination on the ground of sexual orientation: Case C-267/12 *Hay v Crédit Agricole Mutuel de Charente-Maritime et des Deux-Sèvres* [2014] 2 CMLR 961, [2013] All ER (D) 201 (Dec), ECJ. In Case C-157/15 *Achbita v G4S Secure Solutions* ECLI:EU:C:2017:203, [2017] IRLR 466, [2017] All ER (D) 108 (Mar), it was held that Council Directive (EC) 2000/78 (OJ L303, 2.12.2000, p 16) art 2(2)(a) had to be interpreted as meaning that the prohibition on wearing an Islamic headscarf which arose from an internal rule of a private undertaking prohibiting the visible wearing of any political, philosophical or religious sign in the workplace did not constitute direct discrimination based on religion or belief within the meaning of the Directive. By contrast, such an internal rule of a private undertaking could constitute indirect discrimination within the meaning of art 2(2)(b) if it was established that the apparently

neutral obligation it imposed resulted, in fact, in persons adhering to a particular religion or belief being put at a particular disadvantage, unless it was objectively justified by a legitimate aim, such as the pursuit by the employer, in its relations with its customers, of a policy of political, philosophical and religious neutrality, and the means of achieving that aim were appropriate and necessary, which it was for the referring court to ascertain.

4   See Council Directive (EC) 2000/78 (OJ L303, 2.12.2000, p 16) art 16.

5   See Council Directive (EC) 2000/78 (OJ L303, 2.12.2000, p 16) art 3.1. The Directive does not cover differences of treatment based on nationality or payments of any kind made by state schemes or similar, including state social security or social protection schemes (see art 3.2, 3.3), and does not extend to voluntary workers (see *X v Mid Sussex Citizens Advice Bureau* [2012] UKSC 59, [2013] 1 All ER 1038, [2013] IRLR 146).

6   See Council Directive (EC) 2000/78 (OJ L303, 2.12.2000, p 16) art 4. See Case C-416/13 *Perez v Ayuntamiento de Oviedo* [2015] IRLR 158, ECJ (maximum age limit for applicants to join police service was unlawful); Case C-188/15 *Bougnaoui v Micropole SA* ECLI:EU:C:2017:204, [2017] IRLR 447, [2017] All ER (D) 107 (Mar) (art 4(1) should be interpreted as meaning that the willingness of an employer to take account of the wishes of a customer no longer to have the services of that employer provided by a worker wearing an Islamic headscarf could not be considered a genuine and determining occupational requirement within the meaning of that provision).

7   See Council Directive (EC) 2000/78 (OJ L303, 2.12.2000, p 16) art 6. In connection with legislation governing age-dependent employee benefits see Case C-499/08 *Ingeniørforeningen i Danmark v Region Syddanmark* [2012] All ER (EC) 342, [2011] 1 CMLR 1140, ECJ; Case C-132/11 *Tyrolean Airways Tiroler Luftfahrt Gesellschaft mbH v Betriebsrat Bord der Tyrolean Airways Tiroler Luftfahrt Gesellschaft mbH* [2012] 3 CMLR 464, [2012] IRLR 781, ECJ; Cases C-250/09, C-268/09 *Georgiev v Tehnicheski universitet — Sofia, filial Plovdiv* [2012] All ER (EC) 840, [2011] 2 CMLR 179, ECJ. See Case C-416/13 *Perez v Ayuntamiento de Oviedo* [2015] IRLR 158, ECJ (cited in note 6); Case C-20/13 *Unland v Land Berlin* ECLI:EU:C:2015:561, [2015] All ER (D) 249 (Oct) (new national remuneration system founded on discrimination based on age lawful provided different treatment justified by aim of protecting acquired rights).

8   See Council Directive (EC) 2000/78 (OJ L303, 2.12.2000, p 16) art 5. 'Reasonable accommodation for disabled persons' means that employers must take appropriate measures, where needed in a particular case, to enable a person with a disability to have access to, participate in, or advance in employment, or to undergo training, unless such measures would impose a disproportionate burden on the employer: see art 5. A burden is not disproportionate when it is sufficiently remedied by measures existing within the framework of the disability policy of the member state concerned: see art 5. Article 5 does not require an employer to make reasonable adjustments for the benefit of an employee's disabled child: *Hainsworth v Ministry of Defence* [2014] EWCA Civ 763, [2014] IRLR 728.

9   See Council Directive (EC) 2000/78 (OJ L303, 2.12.2000, p 16) art 7. See Case C-406/15 *Milkova v Izpalnitelen direktor na Agentsiata za privatizatsia i sledprivatizatsionen control* [2017] All ER (D) 128 (Mar) (art 7(2) should be construed as allowing legislation of a member state, which conferred on employees with certain disabilities specific advance protection in the event of dismissal, without conferring such protection on civil servants with the same disabilities, unless it had been established that there had been an infringement of the principles of equal treatment, that being a matter for the referring court to determine). Member states may introduce or maintain provisions which are more favourable to the protection of the principle of equal treatment than those laid down in the Directive and may not reduce existing protection against discrimination: see art 8.

10 See Council Directive (EC) 2000/78 (OJ L303, 2.12.2000, p 16) arts 9–11. As to the Equal Treatment Directive (ie Parliament and Council Directive (EC) 2006/54 (OJ L204, 26.7.2006, p 23) on the implementation of the principle of equal opportunities and equal treatment of men and women in matters of employment and occupation) see PARA **12**.

11 See Council Directive (EC) 2000/78 (OJ L303, 2.12.2000, p 16) art 12.

12 See Council Directive (EC) 2000/78 (OJ L303, 2.12.2000, p 16) art 13. Member states are also required to encourage dialogue with appropriate non-governmental organisations which have a legitimate interest in contributing to the fight against discrimination with a view to promoting the principle of equal treatment: see art 14.

15.   Self-employment.

There is a European Directive[1] laying down a framework for putting into effect in the member states the principle of equal treatment between men and women engaged in an activity in a self-employed capacity, or contributing to the pursuit of such an activity[2]. The Directive covers self-employed workers, namely all persons pursuing a gainful activity for their own account, and their spouses and life partners (not including employees and business partners)[3]. The principle of equal treatment in this context means that there must be no discrimination whatsoever on grounds of sex in the public or private sectors, either directly or indirectly, for instance in relation to the establishment, equipment or extension of a business or the launching or extension of any other form of self-employed activity[4]. Member states must ensure that there are enforcement provisions similar to those that exist for the purposes of the Equal Treatment Directive[5].

1 Ie Parliament and Council Directive (EU) 2010/41 (OJ L180, 15.07.2010, p 1) on the application of the principle of equal treatment between men and women engaged in an activity in a self-employed capacity.
2 See Parliament and Council Directive (EU) 2010/41 (OJ L180, 15.07.2010, p 1) art 1. The Directive covers only those aspects of employment not covered by Parliament and Council Directive (EC) 2006/54 (OJ L204, 26.7.2006, p 23) on the implementation of the principle of equal opportunities and equal treatment of men and women in matters of employment and occupation (see PARA 12) and Council Directive (EEC) 79/7 (OJ L6, 10.1.79, p 24) on the progressive implementation of the principle of equal treatment for men and women in matters of social security (see PARA 16): Parliament and Council Directive (EU) 2010/41 (OJ L180, 15.07.2010, p 1) art 1.
3 See Parliament and Council Directive (EU) 2010/41 (OJ L180, 15.07.2010, p 1) art 2.
4 See Parliament and Council Directive (EU) 2010/41 (OJ L180, 15.07.2010, p 1) art 4.1. Harassment and sexual harassment are deemed to be discrimination on grounds of sex and therefore prohibited: art 4.2.
5 See Parliament and Council Directive (EU) 2010/41 (OJ L180, 15.07.2010, p 1) arts 9, 10. As to the Equal Treatment Directive (ie Parliament and Council Directive (EC) 2006/54 (OJ L204, 26.7.2006, p 23) on the implementation of the principle of equal opportunities and equal treatment of men and women in matters of employment and occupation) see PARA 12.

16. Social security.

The Social Security Directive[1] was passed to implement progressively, in the field of social security and other elements of social protection, the principle of equal treatment for men and women in matters of social security[2]. The Directive applies to the working population (including self-employed persons, workers and self-employed persons whose activity is interrupted by illness, accident or involuntary unemployment, and persons seeking employment) and to retired or invalided workers and self-employed persons[3]. The Directive applies to statutory schemes which provide protection against certain risks[4] and social assistance, in so far as it is intended to supplement or replace the statutory schemes[5].

The Directive states that the principle of equal treatment means that there must be no discrimination whatsoever on ground of sex either directly, or indirectly by reference in particular to marital or family status, in particular as concerns:

(1)   the scope of the schemes and the conditions of access to them;
(2)   the obligation to contribute and the calculation of contributions; and
(3)   the calculation of benefits including increases due in respect of a spouse and for dependants and the conditions governing the duration and retention of entitlement to benefits[6].

The principle of equal treatment is without prejudice to the provisions relating to the protection of women on the grounds of maternity[7].

The Directive requires member states to take the measures necessary to ensure that any laws, regulations and administrative provisions contrary to the principle of equal treatment are abolished[8] and to introduce into their national legal systems such measures as necessary to enable all persons who consider themselves wronged by failure to apply the principle of equal treatment to pursue their claims by judicial process, possibly after recourse to other competent authorities[9].

The Directive is without prejudice to the right of member states to exclude from its scope a number of matters connected with age-dependant pensions and benefits[10].

1 Ie Council Directive (EEC) 79/7 (OJ L6, 10.1.79, p 24) on the progressive implementation of the principle of equal treatment for men and women in matters of social security.

2 See Council Directive (EEC) 79/7 (OJ L6, 10.1.79, p 24) art 1.

3 See Council Directive (EEC) 79/7 (OJ L6, 10.1.79, p 24) art 2. 'Working population' does not apply to people who are not working or seeking work, or to persons whose occupation or efforts to find work were not interrupted by one of the risks referred to in art 3 (see the text and note 4); and 'activity' means an economic activity: Case C-77/95 *Züchner v Handelskrankenkasse (Ersatzkasse) Bremen* [1997] All ER (EC) 359, [1996] ECR I- 5689, ECJ. See also Case 150/85 *Drake v Chief Adjudication Officer* [1987] QB 166, [1986] 3 All ER 65, ECJ; Cases 48/88, 106–107/88 *Achterberg-Te Riele v Sociale Verzekeringsbank* [1989] ECR 1963, [1990] 3 CMLR 323, ECJ.

4 See Council Directive (EEC) 79/7 (OJ L6, 10.1.79, p 24) art 3.1(a). The risks referred to in the text are sickness, invalidity, old age, accidents at work and occupational diseases, and unemployment: see art 3.1(a). The Directive does not apply to the provisions concerning survivors' benefits nor to those concerning family benefits, except in the case of family benefits granted by way of increases of benefits due in respect of the risks referred to in art 3.1(a): art 3.2.

5 See Council Directive (EEC) 79/7 (OJ L6, 10.1.79, p 24) art 3.1(b). The operation of the Directive is not excluded where the benefit which forms part of a statutory scheme is not paid to the disabled person himself but to a third party: see Case 150/85 *Drake v Chief Adjudication Officer* [1987] QB 166, [1986] 3 All ER 65, ECJ. In order to fall within the scope of Council Directive (EEC) 79/7 (OJ L6, 10.1.79, p 24) a social security benefit must constitute the whole or part of a statutory scheme providing protection against one of the specified risks or a form of social assistance with the same objective: Cases C-63/91, 64/91 *Jackson v Chief Adjudication Officer* [1993] QB 367, [1993] 3 All ER 265, ECJ.

6 See Council Directive (EEC) 79/7 (OJ L6, 10.1.79, p 24) art 4.1. Article 4.1 precludes legislation refusing a pension to a person who has undergone male to female gender reassignment and is aged 60, on the ground that she has not attained the pensionable age for men of 65: see Case C-423/04 *Richards v Secretary of State for Work and Pensions* [2006] All ER (EC) 895, [2006] ICR 1181, ECJ; *Timbrell v Secretary of State for Work and Pensions* [2010] EWCA Civ 701, [2010] ICR 1369, [2011] 1 FLR 332. Council Directive (EEC) 79/7 art 4(1) precludes national legislation under which the different life expectancies of men and women are applied as an actuarial factor for the calculation of a statutory social benefit payable due to an accident at work when, by applying that factor, the lump sum compensation paid to a man is less than that which would have been paid to a woman of the same age and in a similar situation: Case C-318/13 *Re X* ECLI:EU:C:2014:2133, [2014] IRLR 975, ECJ.

7 See Council Directive (EEC) 79/7 (OJ L6, 10.1.79, p 24) art 4.2. See *Walter v Secretary of State for Social Security* [2001] EWCA Civ 1913, [2002] 1 CMLR 27, [2002] ICR 540.

8 See Council Directive (EEC) 79/7 (OJ L6, 10.1.79, p 24) art 5.

9 See Council Directive (EEC) 79/7 (OJ L6, 10.1.79, p 24) art 6.

10 See Council Directive (EEC) 79/7 (OJ L6, 10.1.79, p 24) art 7.1. In connection with these matters see Case C-9/91 *R v Secretary of State for Social Security, ex p Equal Opportunities Commission* [1992] 3 All ER 577, [1992] ICR 782, ECJ (determination of a statutory pensionable age that differs according to sex); *Thomas v Chief Adjudication Officer* [1991] 2 QB 164, [1991] 3 All ER 315, CA (the application of different age limits when determining applications for disability allowances was not a necessary consequence of fixing different pensionable ages for men and women); Case C-262/88 *Barber v Guardian Royal Exchange Assurance Group* [1991] 1 QB 344, [1990] 2 All ER 660, ECJ; Case C-382/98 *R v Secretary of State for Social Security, ex p Taylor* [2000] All ER(EC) 80, [1999] ECR I-8955, ECJ; *Trustee Solutions Ltd v Dubery* [2006] EWHC 1426 (Ch), [2007] 1 All ER 308, [2007] ICR 412; Case C-154/96 *Wolfs v Office National Des Pensions* [1998] ECR I-6173, [2000] 3 CMLR 1414, ECJ (member states may use different methods of calculating men's and women's retirement pensions when it maintains different pensionable ages according to sex); Case C-318/13 *Re X* ECLI:EU:C:2014:2133, [2014] IRLR 975, ECJ (cited in note 6).

    The question whether a requirement for a male to female transsexual to annul her marriage as a precondition of being recognised as a woman and being entitled to a state pension at the female pension age complies with Council Directive (EEC) 79/7 has been referred to the European Court of Justice: see *MB v Secretary of State for Work and Pensions* [2016] UKSC 53, [2016] All ER (D) 40 (Aug). At the date at which this volume states the law no ruling had been made by the European Court of Justice in this case.

17. Supply of goods and services.

There is a European Directive[1] the purpose of which is to lay down a framework for combating discrimination based on sex in access to and supply of goods and services, with a view to putting into effect in the member states the principle of equal treatment between men and women[2]. The Directive applies to all persons who provide goods and services to the public, although it does not prejudice the individual's freedom to choose a contractual partner and does not apply to the content of media and advertising, education or employment[3].

The principle of equal treatment in this context requires that there be no direct discrimination based on sex, including less favourable treatment of women for reasons of pregnancy and maternity, and no indirect discrimination based on sex, although these provisions are without prejudice to more favourable provisions concerning the protection of women as regards pregnancy and maternity[4]. The taking of positive action with a view to ensuring equality is not prohibited[5]. Member states must ensure that there are enforcement provisions similar to those that exist for the purposes of the Equal Treatment Directive[6].

1 Ie Council Directive (EC) 2004/113 (OJ L373, 21.12.2004, p 37) implementing the principle of equal treatment between men and women in the access to and supply of goods and services.
2 See Council Directive (EC) 2004/113 (OJ L373, 21.12.2004, p 37) art 1.
3 See Council Directive (EC) 2004/113 (OJ L373, 21.12.2004, p 37) art 3.
4 See Council Directive (EC) 2004/113 (OJ L373, 21.12.2004, p 37) art 4. Provision is made so that the use of gender as a factor in the calculation of premiums and benefits for the purposes of insurance and related financial services does not result in differences in individuals' premiums and benefits: see art 5.
5 See Council Directive (EC) 2004/113 (OJ L373, 21.12.2004, p 37) art 6.
6 See Council Directive (EC) 2004/113 (OJ L373, 21.12.2004, p 37) arts 8–10. As to the Equal Treatment Directive (ie Parliament and Council Directive (EC) 2006/54 (OJ L204, 26.7.2006, p 23) on the implementation of the principle of equal opportunities and equal treatment of men and women in matters of employment and occupation) see PARA 12.

18. Harmonisation of Equality Acts with EU obligations.

'Harmonising provision' is provision made in relation to relevant subject matter of the Equality Acts[1] which either:

(1) corresponds to provision made or to be made[2] in relation to so much of the subject matter of the Equality Acts as implements an EU obligation ('the implementing provision')[3]; or

(2) the Minister thinks is necessary or expedient in consequence of or related to provision so made[4] or the implementing provision[5].

If there is an EU obligation of the United Kingdom[6] which a Minister of the Crown thinks relates to the subject matter of the Equality Acts[7] and the Minister thinks that it is appropriate to make harmonising provision in the Equality Acts[8], the Minister may by order make the harmonising provision[9].

1 For these purposes 'the Equality Acts' are the Equality Act 2006 and the Equality Act 2010: s 203(5). 'Relevant subject matter' of the Equality Acts is so much of the subject matter of those Acts as does not implement an EU obligation: Equality Act 2010 s 203(8) (s 203(1)(a), (7), (8) amended by SI 2011/1043). The harmonisation provisions do not apply to the Equality Act 2010 s 203 or to Sch 24 or to the following provisions specified therein (see s 203(10), Sch 24):
  (1) Pt 1 (ss 1–3) (the public sector duty regarding socio-economic inequalities: see PARAS 302–304);
  (2) Pt 5 Ch 2 (ss 61–63) (occupational pensions: see PARAS 134–135);
  (3) s 78 (gender pay gap: see PARA 149);

(4)   s 106 (election candidates: diversity information: see PARA 210);

(5)   Pt 9 Chs 1–3, 5, except s 136 (ss 113–126, 137–141) (enforcement: see PARAS 6, 351 et seq);

(6)   ss 142, 146 (unenforceable terms, declaration in respect of void terms: see PARA 274);

(7)   Pt 11 Ch 1 (ss 149–157) (public sector equality duty: see PARAS 276–298);

(8)   Pt 12 (ss 160–188) (disabled persons: transport: see PARAS 215–236);

(9)   Pt 13 (ss 189–190) (disability: miscellaneous: see PARAS 237, 272);

(10)   s 197 (power to specify age exceptions: see PARA 96);

(11)   Pt 15 (ss 198–201) (family property: see PARA 5; and MATRIMONIAL AND CIVIL PARTNERSHIP LAW vol 72 (2015) PARAS 262, 285; TRUSTS AND POWERS vol 98 (2013) PARA 144);

(12)   Pt 16 (ss 202–218) (general and miscellaneous: see the text and notes 1–9; PARAS 1, 4, 5, 58, 74, 81; and CONSTITUTIONAL AND ADMINISTRATIVE LAW vol 20 (2014) PARA 196; MATRIMONIAL AND CIVIL PARTNERSHIP LAW vol 72 (2015) PARA 220;

(13)   Sch 1 (disability: supplementary provision: see PARAS 47–55);

(14)   Sch 3 (services and public functions: exceptions) Pt 3 (health and care) paras 13, 14 (see PARA 94), Sch 3 Pt 4 (immigration see PARA 96), Sch 3 Pt 5 (insurance see PARA 98), Sch 3 Pt 6 (marriage see PARA 99), Sch 3 Pt 7 (separate and single services see PARAS 100, 101) (except para 30), Sch 3 Pt 8 (television, radio and on-line broadcasting and distribution: see PARA 102), Sch 3 Pt 9 (transport: see PARA 103), Sch 3 Pt 10 (supplementary: see PARA 91);

(15)   Sch 4 (premises: reasonable adjustments: see PARAS 109, 241–244);

(16)   Sch 5 (premises: exceptions: see PARAS 113–114) (except para 1);

(17)   Sch 6 (office-holders: excluded offices: see PARA 128) (except so far as relating to colour or nationality or marriage and civil partnership);

(18)   Sch 8 (work: reasonable adjustments: see PARAS 155, 245–259);

(19)   Sch 9 (work: exceptions) Pt 1 (general: see PARAS 160–163) (except so far as relating to colour or nationality), Pt 2 (exceptions relating to age: see PARAS 164–169), Pt 3 (other exceptions: see PARAS 170–172) (except para 19 so far as relating to colour or nationality);

(20)   Sch 10 (education: accessibility for disabled pupils: see PARAS 178–181);

(21)   Sch 13 (education: reasonable adjustments: see PARAS 194, 260–264) (except paras 2, 5, 6, 9);

(22)   Sch 17 (education: disabled pupils: enforcement: see PARA 356);

(23)   Sch 18 (public sector equality duty: exceptions: see PARAS 279, 282–284);

(24)   Sch 19 (list of public authorities: see PARA 277);

(25)   Sch 20 (rail vehicle accessibility: compliance (repealed));

(26)   Sch 21 (reasonable adjustments: supplementary: see PARA 266 et seq);

(27)   Sch 22 (exceptions: statutory provisions) paras 2, 5 (see PARAS 159, 197);

(28)   Sch 23 (general exceptions: see PARAS 95, 97, 111, 112, 157, 196, 208, 327, 329) (except para 2); and

(29)   Sch 25 (information society services: see PARAS 335–338).

2   Ie in exercise of the power under the European Communities Act 1972 s 2(2) ('the implementing power'): Equality Act 2010 s 203(1)(b).

3   Equality Act 2010 s 203(6)(a), (7) (as amended: see note 1).

4   Ie in pursuance of the Equality Act 2010 s 203(6)(a) (see the text and notes 1–3).

5   Equality Act 2010 s 203(6)(b).

6   Ie an obligation which is to be implemented by the exercise of the implementing power: Equality Act 2010 s 203(1)(b).

7   Equality Act 2010 s 203(1)(a) (as amended: see note 1).

8   Equality Act 2010 s 203(1)(c).

9   Equality Act 2010 s 203(2). A harmonising provision may amend a provision of the Equality Acts: Equality Act 2010 s 203(9). If the Minister proposes to make an order under s 203, the Minister must consult persons and organisations the Minister thinks are likely to be affected by the harmonising provision: s 203(3). If, as a result of such consultation the Minister thinks it appropriate to change the whole or part of the proposal, the Minister must carry out such further consultation with respect to the changes as the Minister thinks appropriate: s 203(4).

If, after the conclusion of the consultation required under s 203 the Minister thinks it appropriate to proceed with the making of an order under s 203 he must lay before Parliament a draft of a statutory instrument containing the order together with an explanatory document (s 204(1)), which must introduce and give reasons for the harmonising provision (s 204(2)(a)), explain why the Minister thinks that the conditions in s 203(1) are satisfied (s 204(2)(b)), give details of the consultation carried out under s 203 (s 204(2)(c)), give details of the representations received as a result of the consultation (s 204(2)(d)) and give details of such changes as were made as a result of the representations (s 204(2)(e)). Where a person making representations in response to the consultation has requested the Minister not to disclose them, the Minister must not disclose them under s 204(2)(d) if, or to the extent that, to do so would (disregarding any connection with proceedings in Parliament) constitute an actionable breach of confidence: s 204(3). If information in representations made by a person in response to consultation under s 203 relates to another person, the Minister need not disclose the information under s 204(2)(d) if or to the extent that the Minister thinks that the disclosure of information could adversely affect the interests of that other person and the Minister has been unable to obtain the consent of that other person to the disclosure: s 204(4). The Minister may not act under s 204(1) before the end of the period of 12 weeks beginning with the day on which the consultation under s 203(3) begins: s 204(5).

A Minister of the Crown must report to Parliament on the exercise of the power under s 203(2) at the end of each period of 2 years succeeding the making of the first report under this provision: s 203(11)(b). The first report under this provision was required to be made at the end of the period of 2 years starting on 8 April 2010 (ie the day s 203 was brought into force by virtue of s 216(1)(b)): s 203(11)(a).

(4) UNITED NATIONS CHARTERS ETC

19. Charter of the United Nations.

The Charter of the United Nations[1] provides that the purposes of the United Nations include that of achieving international co-operation in solving international problems of an economic, social, cultural, or humanitarian character, and promoting and encouraging respect for human rights and for fundamental freedoms for all, without distinction as to race, sex, language, or religion[2]. Pursuant to this, all the principal instruments of the United Nations expressly prohibit discrimination within a general framework of rights[3], and there are also several free-standing multilateral human rights treaties promoting equality for specific groups[4].

1 Ie the Charter of the United Nations (San Francisco, 26 June 1945; TS 67 (1946); Cmd 7015). As to the United Nations see INTERNATIONAL RELATIONS LAW vol 61 (2010) PARA 519 et seq.
2 See the Charter of the United Nations art 1.3.
3 See eg the Universal Declaration of Human Rights (Paris, 10 December 1948; UN 2 (1949); Cmd 7662); the International Covenant on Civil and Political Rights (New York, 16 December 1966; TS 6 (1977); Cmnd 6702); and the International Covenant on Economic, Social and Cultural Rights (New York, 16 December 1966; TS 6 (1977); Cmnd 6702); and PARAS 20–22.
4 See eg the International Convention on the Elimination of All Forms of Racial Discrimination (New York, 7 March 1966; TS (1969) 77; Cmnd 4108), the International Convention on the Elimination of All Forms of Discrimination Against Women (New York, 18 December 1979; 1249 UNTS 13); the Convention on the Rights of Persons with Disabilities (New York, 13 December 2006; TS 10 (2010); Cm 7905); the Convention on the Protection of the Rights of All Migrant Workers and Members of Their Families (New York, 18 December 1990; UN General Assembly Resolution 158); and PARAS 23–26.

20. Universal Declaration of Human Rights.

The Universal Declaration of Human Rights[1] forms the basis of all human rights protection at the United Nations, although being declaratory in nature it places no direct legal obligations on states[2]. The Declaration commences with the statement that all human beings are born free and equal in dignity and rights, are endowed with reason and conscience and should act towards one another in a spirit of brotherhood[3], and declares that all persons are entitled to all the rights and freedoms set forth in the Declaration, without distinction of any kind, such as race, colour, sex, language, religion, political or other opinion, national or social origin, property, birth or other status[4]; that all are equal before the law and are entitled without any discrimination to equal protection of the law[5]; and that all are entitled to equal protection against any discrimination in violation of the Declaration and against any incitement to such discrimination[6].

1 Ie the Universal Declaration of Human Rights (Paris, 10 December 1948; UN 2 (1949); Cmd 7662). As to the declaration generally see RIGHTS AND FREEDOMS vol 88A (2013) PARA 100.
2 See the Universal Declaration of Human Rights preamble ('recognition of the inherent dignity and of the equal and inalienable rights of all members of the human family is the foundation of freedom, justice and peace in the world').
3 See the Universal Declaration of Human Rights art 1.
4 See the Universal Declaration of Human Rights art 2 (which goes on to provide that 'Furthermore, no distinction shall be made on the basis of the political, jurisdictional or international status of the country or territory to which a person belongs, whether it be independent, trust, non-self-governing or under any other limitation of sovereignty'). The Declaration also states that 'Everyone is entitled to a social and international order in which the rights and freedoms set forth in this Declaration can be fully realised' (art 28).
5 See the Universal Declaration of Human Rights art 7.
6 See the Universal Declaration of Human Rights art 7.

21. International Covenant on Civil and Political Rights.

Each state party to the International Covenant on Civil and Political Rights[1] undertakes to respect and to ensure to all individuals within its territory and subject to its jurisdiction the rights recognised in the Covenant without distinction of any kind, such as race, colour, sex, language, religion, political or other opinion, national or social origin, property, birth or other status[2]. It further provides that all persons are equal before the law and are entitled without any discrimination to the equal protection of the law, and that the law must prohibit any discrimination and guarantee to all persons equal and effective protection against discrimination on any ground such as race, colour, sex, language, religion, political or other opinion, national or social origin, property, birth or other status[3].

1 Ie the International Covenant on Civil and Political Rights (New York, 16 December 1966; TS 6 (1977); Cmnd 6702). The Covenant entered into force on 23 March 1976 and was ratified by the United Kingdom on 20 May 1976. As to the covenant generally see RIGHTS AND FREEDOMS vol 88A (2013) PARA 104.
2 See the International Covenant on Civil and Political Rights art 2.1.
3 See the International Covenant on Civil and Political Rights art 26.

22. International Covenant on Economic, Social and Cultural Rights.

Each state party to the International Covenant on Economic, Social and Cultural Rights[1] undertakes to guarantee that the rights enunciated in the Covenant will be exercised without discrimination of any kind as to race, colour, sex, language, religion, political or other opinion, national or social origin, property, birth or other status[2].

1 Ie the International Covenant on Economic, Social and Cultural Rights (New York, 16 December 1966; TS 6 (1977); Cmnd 6702). The Covenant entered into force on 3 January 1976, and was signed and ratified by the United Kingdom on 20 August 1976. As to the covenant generally see RIGHTS AND FREEDOMS vol 88A (2013) PARA 105.
2 See the International Covenant on Economic, Social and Cultural Rights art 2.2.

23. Convention on the Elimination of All Forms of Racial Discrimination.

The Convention on the Elimination of All Forms of Racial Discrimination[1] requires states parties to condemn racial discrimination[2], segregation and apartheid[3], to pursue policies aimed at eliminating racial discrimination[4], to take measures to combat prejudice and notions of racial superiority and the incitement of racial hatred[5], and to ensure equal treatment to persons of all races[6].

1 Ie the International Convention on the Elimination of All Forms of Racial Discrimination (New York, 7 March 1966; TS (1969) 77; Cmnd 4108). The Convention was adopted on 21 December 1965 and was ratified by the United Kingdom on 6 April 1969. See also RIGHTS AND FREEDOMS vol 88A (2013) PARA 108.

2 The Convention defines 'racial discrimination' as meaning any distinction, exclusion, restriction or preference based on race, colour, descent, or national or ethnic origin which has the purpose or effect of nullifying or impairing the recognition, enjoyment or exercise, on an equal footing, of human rights and fundamental freedoms in the political, economic, social, cultural or any other field of public life: see the International Convention for the Elimination of All Forms of Racial Discrimination art 1.1.

3 See the International Convention for the Elimination of All Forms of Racial Discrimination arts 2, 3.

4 See the International Convention for the Elimination of All Forms of Racial Discrimination art 4.

5 See the International Convention for the Elimination of All Forms of Racial Discrimination arts 4, 7.

6 See the International Convention for the Elimination of All Forms of Racial Discrimination arts 5, 6.

24. Convention on the Elimination of All Forms of Discrimination Against Women.

Parties to the Convention on the Elimination of All Forms of Discrimination against Women[1] condemn discrimination against women in all its forms and undertake to embody principles of equality in their constitutions and legislation[2], establish legal protection for women's rights[3], and take all appropriate measures to facilitate the advancement of women[4]. Particular provision is made for equal access to education, employment and healthcare[5], and in connection with marriage and family life[6]. Provision is made for the establishment of a Committee for monitoring compliance with the Convention[7]. An Optional Protocol to the Convention, providing for an individual complaints procedure and a procedure which allows the Committee to inquire into serious and systematic Convention violations, came into force in 2000[8].

1 Ie the International Convention on the Elimination of All Forms of Discrimination Against Women (New York, 18 December 1979; 1249 UNTS 13). The Convention was adopted by the General Assembly on 18 December 1979 and entered into force on 3 September 1981. The Convention defines 'discrimination against women' as any distinction, exclusion or restriction made on the basis of sex which has the effect or purpose of impairing or nullifying the recognition, enjoyment or exercise by women, irrespective of their marital status, on a basis of equality of men and women, of human rights and fundamental freedoms in the political, economic, social, cultural, civil or any other field: see the International Convention for the Elimination of All Forms of Discrimination Against Women art 1. The United Kingdom ratified the Convention on 7 May 1986. See also RIGHTS AND FREEDOMS vol 88A (2013) PARA 109.

2 See the International Convention for the Elimination of All Forms of Discrimination Against Women art 2(a), (b), (d)–(g).

3 See the International Convention for the Elimination of All Forms of Discrimination Against Women art 2(c).

4 See the International Convention for the Elimination of All Forms of Discrimination Against Women arts 3–9.

5 See the International Convention for the Elimination of All Forms of Discrimination Against Women arts 10–12; and see further as to the right to education RIGHTS AND FREEDOMS vol 88A (2013) PARA 550.

6 See the International Convention for the Elimination of All Forms of Discrimination Against Women art 16; and see further RIGHTS AND FREEDOMS vol 88A (2013) PARA 354.

7 See the International Convention for the Elimination of All Forms of Discrimination Against Women art 17.

8 The United Kingdom acceded to the Optional Protocol on 17 December 2004 and it entered into force on 17 March 2005.

25. Convention on the Rights of Persons with Disabilities.

The stated purposes of the Convention on the Rights of Persons with Disabilities[1] is to promote, protect and ensure the full and equal enjoyment of all human rights and fundamental freedoms by all persons with disabilities[2], and to promote respect for their inherent dignity, and its principles are to ensure respect for inherent dignity, individual autonomy and independence, non-discrimination[3], full and effective participation and inclusion in society, respect for difference and acceptance of persons with disabilities, equality of opportunity, accessibility, equality between men and women, respect for the evolving capacities of children with disabilities and respect for the right of children with disabilities to preserve their identities[4]. There is an Optional Protocol allowing for individual or group complaint[5].

1   Ie the Convention on the Rights of Persons with Disabilities (New York, 13 December 2006; TS 10 (2010); Cm 7905). The Convention entered into force on 3 May 2008 and was ratified by the United Kingdom on 8 June 2009. See also RIGHTS AND FREEDOMS vol 88A (2013) PARA 110.
2   The Convention defines 'persons with disabilities' as including those who have long-term physical, mental, intellectual or sensory impairments which in interaction with various barriers may hinder their full and effective participation in society on an equal basis with others: see the Convention on the Rights of Persons with Disabilities art 1.
3   The Convention defines 'discrimination on the basis of disability' as any distinction, exclusion or restriction on the basis of disability which has the purpose or effect of impairing or nullifying the recognition, enjoyment or exercise, on an equal basis with others, of all human rights and fundamental freedoms in the political, economic, social, cultural, civil or any other field: see the Convention on the Rights of Persons with Disabilities art 2.
4   See the Convention on the Rights of Persons with Disabilities arts 1, 3.
5   The United Kingdom ratified the Optional Protocol on 7 August 2009.

26. Convention on the Protection of the Rights of Migrant Workers.

The Convention on the Protection of the Rights of Migrant Workers[1] sets out a number of rights to which migrant workers[2] and their families are entitled[3], and parties to the Convention undertake to respect and to ensure those rights to all migrant workers and members of their families without distinction of any kind such as to sex, race, colour, language, religion or conviction, political or other opinion, national, ethnic or social origin, nationality, age, economic position, property, marital status, birth or other status[4].

1   Ie the Convention on the Protection of the Rights of All Migrant Workers and Members of Their Families (New York, 18 December 1990; UN General Assembly Resolution 158). The United Kingdom has not signed or ratified the Convention. See also RIGHTS AND FREEDOMS vol 88A (2013) PARA 111.
2   The Convention defines 'migrant worker' as a person who is to be engaged, is engaged or has been engaged in a remunerated activity in a state of which he or she is not a national: see the Convention on the Protection of the Rights of All Migrant Workers and Members of Their Families art 2.1.
3   See the Convention on the Protection of the Rights of All Migrant Workers and Members of Their Families arts 8–35: these are broadly the rights guaranteed in such instruments as the Universal Declaration of Human Rights (Paris, 10 December 1948; UN 2 (1949); Cmd 7662) (see PARA 20) and the Convention for the Protection of Human Rights and Fundamental Freedoms (Rome, 4 November 1950; TS 71 (1953); Cmd 8969) (see PARA 8), with additional rights that are specific to the status of migrant workers such as the right not to be arbitrarily expelled.
4   See the Convention on the Protection of the Rights of All Migrant Workers and Members of Their Families art 7.

27. Convention on the Rights of the Child.

The United Nations Convention on the Rights of the Child[1] sets out a number of rights which must be guaranteed to children, including the right to life[2] and rights relating to identity and dignity[3], family stability[4], education and development[5] and general welfare including protection from cruelty and exploitation[6], and requires parties to the Convention to respect and ensure those rights to each child within their jurisdiction without discrimination of any kind, irrespective of the child's or his or her parent's or legal guardian's race, colour, sex, language, religion, political or other opinion, national, ethnic or social origin, property, disability, birth or other status[7].

1 Ie the Convention on the Rights of the Child (New York, 20 November 1989; TS 44 (1992); Cm 1976). For Convention purposes a 'child' is human being below the age of 18 years unless under the law applicable to the child, majority is attained earlier: art 1. The Convention was adopted on 20 November 1989 and entered into force on 2 September 1990. The United Kingdom ratified the Convention on 15 January 1992. See also RIGHTS AND FREEDOMS vol 88A (2013) PARA 112.
2 See the Convention on the Rights of the Child art 6.
3 See the Convention on the Rights of the Child arts 7–8, 40.
4 See the Convention on the Rights of the Child arts 9–11, 16, 18.
5 See the Convention on the Rights of the Child arts 28–31.
6 See the Convention on the Rights of the Child arts 19–27, 32–39.
7 See the Convention on the Rights of the Child art 2.1.

2. THE EQUALITY AND HUMAN RIGHTS COMMISSION

(1) CONSTITUTIONAL AND ADMINISTRATIVE MATTERS

28. Establishment and constitution of the Commission.

The Equality Act 2006 established a Commission for Equality and Human Rights. From its inception this Commission has referred to itself as the Equality and Human Rights Commission[1].

The rules governing the constitution of the Equality and Human Rights Commission are set out in the Equality Act 2006[2]. The Secretary of State appoints the members of the Commission (known as 'Commissioners')[3], and the Commission appoints a chief executive with the consent of the Secretary of State[4].

1 Equality Act 2006 s 1. In the Equality Act 2006 and the Equality Act 2010, the Commission is referred to as the Commission for Equality and Human Rights. However, within months of the Equality Act 2006 coming into force, the Commission decided to call itself the Equality and Human Rights Commission, which name is used throughout this title. The Commission is a body corporate (see s 1) and operates as a non-departmental public body. The Commission is not regarded as the servant or agent of the Crown, and does not enjoy any status, immunity or privilege of the Crown: s 2, Sch 1 para 42 (amended by SI 2010/1839). Members of the Commission are disqualified from membership of the House of Commons: see the Equality Act 2006 Sch 1 para 44. The Commission replaced the Commission for Racial Equality, the Equal Opportunities Commission and the Disability Rights Commission, which were all dissolved on 1 October 2007: see the Equality Act 2006 ss 36–38 (s 38 amended by SI 2006/246); and the Equality Act 2006 (Dissolution of Commissions and Consequential and Transitional Provisions) Order 2007, SI 2007/2602 (amended by SI 2007/3555). The Commission is a relevant regulator for the purposes of the Small Business, Enterprise and Employment Act 2015 s 22 (and of ss 24A, 26): see the Business Impact Target (Relevant Regulators) Regulations 2017, SI 2017/344, reg 2 Schedule; and STATUTES AND LEGISLATIVE PROCESS vol 96 (2012) PARA 1047A. As to bodies corporate see COMPANIES vol 14 (2016) PARA 2; CORPORATIONS vol 24 (2010) PARA 301 et seq.
2 See the Equality Act 2006 Sch 1 paras 1, 2 (membership), Sch 1 para 3 (tenure of members), Sch 1 para 4 (appointment of chairman) (Sch 1 paras 1–4 amended by SI 2007/1388; and SI 2010/1839).
3 There must be not less than 10 or more than 15 individuals who are appointed as Commissioners: Equality Act 2006 Sch 1 para 1 (as amended: see note 2). Provision is made for the Commissioners' remuneration: see Sch 1 para 35 (Sch 1 paras 7, 35 amended by SI 2010/1839). Service as Commissioner is not employment in the civil service of the state: see the Equality Act 2006 Sch 1 para 42. As to the Secretary of State see PARA 4.
4 Equality Act 2006 Sch 1 para 7(1)(a), (2) (as amended: see note 3). It may also appoint other staff: see Sch 1 para 7(1)(b), (3) (as so amended). Provision is made for the remuneration of staff: see Sch 1 para 36. Service as an employee of the Commission is not employment in the civil service of the state: Sch 1 para 42.

29. Proceedings of the Commission and its committees.

The Equality and Human Rights Commission may regulate its own proceedings[1]. It has power to appoint Investigating Commissioners to carry out certain inquiries and investigations[2], and it may also establish advisory committees[3] and decision-making committees[4] in order to assist it in its functions[5].

1 See the Equality Act 2006 Sch 1 paras 5, 6, 10. Vacancies in offices or defects in appointment do not affect the validity of the Commission's proceedings: see Sch 1 para 33.
2 See the Equality Act 2006 Sch 1 para 9 (amended by SI 2010/1839). An Investigating Commissioner is not a Commissioner, but the Equality Act 2006 Sch 1 paras 3(1), (4), (5), 33 apply to him as if he were (and with the substitution of references to the Commission for references to the Secretary of State): see Sch 1 para 9(4) (as so amended). An Investigating Commissioner may (1) carry out an inquiry under s 16 (see PARA 35); (2) carry out an investigation under s 20 (see PARA 347); (3) give an unlawful act notice under s 21 (see PARA 347); and (4) enter into an agreement under s 23 (see PARA 350): see Sch 1 para 9(3). Service as an Investigating Commissioner is not employment in the civil service of the state: Sch 1 para 42(2). As to the Secretary of State see PARA 4.

3   See the Equality Act 2006 Sch 1 paras 11, 13, 14. Vacancies in offices or defects in appointment
     do not affect the validity of the proceedings of a committee: see Sch 1 para 34. Provision is made
     for the remuneration of committee members: see Sch 1 para 37 (amended by SI 2010/1839).
4   See the Equality Act 2006 Sch 1 para 12, 13, 14. The Commission may delegate a function to a
     decision-making committee: Sch 1 para 15. As to the Scotland decision-making committee see
     Sch 1 paras 16–23 (amended by SI 2014/406). As to the Wales decision-making committee see
     Sch 1 paras 24–31 (amended by SI 2014/406).
5   One of these decision-making committees, known as the 'Disability Committee', to which the
     Commission delegated certain of its statutory functions in relation to disability matters, was
     dissolved on 31 March 2017: see the Equality Act 2006 (Dissolution of the Disability Committee)
     Order 2014, SI 2014/406. As to the functions and duties of the Commission see PARA 31 et seq.

30.   The strategic plan, and other administrative and financial matters.

The Equality and Human Rights Commission is under a duty to prepare and
publish a plan showing:

(1)   activities or classes of activity to be undertaken by the Commission in
        pursuance of its functions under the Equality Act 2006;
(2)   an expected timetable for each activity or class; and
(3)   priorities for different activities or classes, or principles to be applied in
        determining priorities[1].

The Commission must regularly review the plan[2], and revise it if necessary[3].
Before preparing or reviewing a plan the Commission is under a duty to make
consultations, invite representations and take account of any representations so
made[4].

For each financial year the Commission must prepare a report on the
performance of its functions in that year[5]. This annual report must, in particular,
indicate in what manner and to what extent the Commission's performance of its
functions has accorded to its strategic plan[6].

The Secretary of State pays to the Commission such sums as appear to him
reasonably sufficient for the purpose of enabling the Commission to perform its
functions[7]. The Commission may also make a charge for certain services it
provides[8]. Provision is made for the keeping of accounts[9].

1   Equality Act 2006 s 4(1), (5). The Commission must send the plan and each revision to the
     Secretary of State, who must lay a copy before Parliament: s 4(4) (amended by SI 2010/1889). As
     to the Secretary of State see PARA 4.
2   Ie review it at least once during the period of three years beginning with its completion, at least
     once during each period of three years beginning with the completion of a review, and at such
     other times as the Commission thinks appropriate: see the Equality Act 2006 s 4(2).
3   Equality Act 2006 s 4(3).
4   Before preparing or reviewing a plan the Commission must (Equality Act 2006 s 5):
     (1)   consult such persons having knowledge or experience relevant to the Commission's
             functions as the Commission thinks appropriate;
     (2)   consult such other persons as the Commission thinks appropriate;
     (3)   issue a general invitation to make representations, in a manner likely in the
             Commission's opinion to bring the invitation to the attention of as large a class of
             persons who may wish to make representations as is reasonably practicable; and
     (4)   take account of any representations made.
5   As to the annual report see the Equality Act 2006 Sch 1 para 32.
6   Equality Act 2006 Sch 1 para 32(2). The reference in the text to the Commission's strategic plan
     is to the plan under s 4 (see the text and notes 1–3).
7   Equality Act 2006 Sch 1 para 38 (Sch 1 paras 38, 40 amended by SI 2010/1839).
8   Equality Act 2006 Sch 1 para 39 (amended by the Enterprise and Regulatory Reform Act 2013 s
     64(11)). The Commission may charge for services provided under the Equality Act 2006 s 13 (see
     PARA 40): see Sch 1 para 39.
9   See the Equality Act 2006 Sch 1 paras 40, 41 (Sch 1 para 40 as amended : see note 7).

(2) DUTIES AND POWERS OF THE COMMISSION

31. Commission's general duty.

The Equality and Human Rights Commission[1] must exercise its functions under the Equality Act 2006[2] with a view to encouraging and supporting the development of a society in which:

(1)   people's ability to achieve their potential is not limited by prejudice or discrimination[3];

(2)   there is respect for and protection of each individual's human rights[4];

(3)   there is respect for the dignity and worth of each individual[5];

(4)   each individual has an equal opportunity to participate in society[6]; and

(5)   there is mutual respect between groups[7] based on understanding and valuing of diversity and on shared respect for equality and human rights[8].

1   As to the establishment of the Equality and Human Rights Commission see PARA 28.
2   Ie under the Equality Act 2006 Pt 1 (ss 1–42).
3   Equality Act 2006 s 3(a). As to discrimination see PARA 67 et seq.
4   Equality Act 2006 s 3(b). As to the law relating to the protection of human rights see generally RIGHTS AND FREEDOMS.
5   Equality Act 2006 s 3(c).
6   Equality Act 2006 s 3(d).
7   For the purposes of Part 1, 'group' means a group or class of persons who share a common attribute in respect of age, disability, gender, gender reassignment within the meaning of the Equality Act 2010 s 7 (see PARA 56), race, religion or belief, or sexual orientation: Equality Act 2006 s 10(2)(a)–(g) (s 10(2)(d) substituted by the Equality Act 2010 s 211(1), Sch 26 paras 61, 63). A reference to a group includes a reference to a smaller group or smaller class, within a group, of persons who share a common attribute (in addition to the attribute by reference to which the group is defined) in respect of any of the matters specified in the Equality Act 2006 s 10(2)(a)–(g): s 10(3). 'Race' includes colour, nationality, ethnic origin and national origin: s 35. As to the meaning of 'religion or belief' see PARA 59; and as to the meaning of 'sexual orientation' see PARA 63 (both definitions applied by s 35 (amended by the Equality Act 2010 Sch 26 paras 61, 77 (amended by SI 2010/2279))).
8   Equality Act 2006 s 3(e).

32. Commission's duties in relation to equality and diversity.

The Equality and Human Rights Commission[1], by exercising the powers conferred by the Equality Act 2006[2], must:

(1)   promote understanding of the importance of equality and diversity[3];

(2)   encourage good practice in relation to equality and diversity[4];

(3)   promote equality of opportunity[5];

(4)   promote awareness and understanding of rights under the Equality Act 2010[6];

(5)   enforce the Equality Act 2010[7];

(6)   work towards the elimination of unlawful[8] discrimination[9]; and

(7)   work towards the elimination of unlawful harassment[10].

In promoting equality of opportunity between disabled persons and others, the Commission may, in particular, promote the favourable treatment of disabled persons[11].

In fulfilling a duty under the provisions described above the Commission must take account of any relevant human rights[12].

1   As to the establishment of the Equality and Human Rights Commission see PARA 28.
2   Ie the Equality Act 2006 Pt 1 (ss 1–42).
3   Equality Act 2006 s 8(1)(a). 'Diversity' means the fact that individuals are different; 'equality' means equality between individuals: s 8(2).

4   Equality Act 2006 s 8(1)(b).
5   Equality Act 2006 s 8(1)(c).
6   Equality Act 2006 s 8(1)(d) (s 8(1)(d), (e), (4) amended by the Equality Act 2010 Sch 26 para 62; and SI 2010/2279).
7   Equality Act 2006 s 8(1)(e) (as amended: see note 6).
8   In the Equality Act 2006 Pt 1 (except s 30(3) (see PARA 38)), 'unlawful' means contrary to a provision of the Equality Act 2010: Equality Act 2006 ss 8(2), 34(1). But action is not unlawful for the purposes of Pt 1 by reason only of the fact that it contravenes a duty under or by virtue of the Equality Act 2010 s 1 (public sector duty regarding socio-economic inequalities: see PARAS 302–304), s 149, s 153, s 154 (public sector equality duty: see PARAS 276–298), Pt 12 (disabled persons: transport: see PARA 215 et seq), or s 190 (disability: improvements to let dwelling houses: see PARA 272): Equality Act 2006 ss 8(2), 34(2) (amended by the Equality Act 2010 s 211(1), Sch 26 paras 61, 76).
9   Equality Act 2006 s 8(1)(f). See PARA 67 et seq.
10 Equality Act 2006 s 8(1)(g). See PARA 79.
11 Equality Act 2006 s 8(3). For these purposes, 'disabled person' means a person who (s 8(4) (as amended: see note 6)):
    (1)   is a disabled person within the meaning of the Equality Act 2010 (see PARA 47); or
    (2)   has been a disabled person within that meaning (whether or not at a time when that Act had effect).
12 Equality Act 2006 s 9(4) (amended by the Enterprise and Regulatory Reform Act 2013 s 64(3), (5)). As to the meaning of 'human rights' for this purpose see PARA 33 note 3.

33. Commission's duties in relation to human rights.

The Equality and Human Rights Commission[1], by exercising the powers conferred by the Equality Act 2006[2], must:
  (1)   promote understanding of the importance of human rights[3];
  (2)   encourage good practice in relation to human rights[4];
  (3)   promote awareness, understanding and protection of human rights[5]; and
  (4)   encourage public authorities to comply with their duty not to act in a way which is incompatible with a Convention right[6].

In determining what action to take exercising these duties, the Commission must have particular regard to the importance of exercising its statutory powers[7] in relation to the Convention rights[8].

In pursuance of these duties[9] the Commission may co-operate with persons interested in human rights within the United Kingdom or elsewhere[10].

1   As to the establishment of the Equality and Human Rights Commission see PARA 28.
2   Ie the Equality Act 2006 Pt 1 (ss 1–42).
3   Equality Act 2006 s 9(1)(a). In Pt 1, 'human rights' means the Convention rights within the meaning given by the Human Rights Act 1998 s 1 (see RIGHTS AND FREEDOMS vol 88A (2013) PARA 14), and other human rights: Equality Act 2006 s 9(2). A reference in Pt 1 (including in s 9) to human rights does not exclude any matter by reason only of its being a matter to which s 8 (equality and diversity: see PARA 32) relates: s 9(5) (amended by the Enterprise and Regulatory Reform Act 2013 s 64(3), (5)).
4   Equality Act 2006 s 9(1)(b).
5   Equality Act 2006 s 9(1)(c).
6   Equality Act 2006 s 9(1)(d). The text refers to the duty under the Human Rights Act 1998 s 6 (see RIGHTS AND FREEDOMS vol 88A (2013) PARA 23).
7   Ie the powers conferred by the Equality Act 2006 Pt 1.
8   Equality Act 2006 s 9(3). See RIGHTS AND FREEDOMS vol 88A (2013) PARA 14.
9   Ie its duties under the Equality Act 2006 s 9 (see the text and notes 1–8).
10 Equality Act 2006 s 18. This is expressed to be without prejudice to the generality of s 13 (see PARA 40). As to the meaning of 'United Kingdom' see PARA 85 note 1.

34. Commission's power to make grants.

In pursuance of any of its duties in relation to equality and diversity[1] and human rights[2], the Equality and Human Rights Commission[3] may make grants to another person[4]. Such a grant may be made subject to conditions (including conditions as to repayment)[5]. No other form of financial assistance may be given[6].

1 Ie under the Equality Act 2006 s 8 (see PARA 32).
2 Ie under the Equality Act 2006 s 9 (see PARAS 32, 33).
3 As to the establishment of the Equality and Human Rights Commission see PARA 28.
4 Equality Act 2006 s 17(1) (amended by the Enterprise and Regulatory Reform Act 2013 s 64(3), (9)).
5 Equality Act 2006 s 17(2).
6 A power under the Equality Act 2006 Pt 1 (ss 1–42) to co-operate with or assist a person may not be exercised by the provision of financial assistance otherwise than in accordance with s 17: s 17(3).

35. Commission's power to conduct inquiries and investigations.

The Equality and Human Rights Commission[1] may conduct an inquiry into a matter relating to any of its duties concerning equality and diversity[2] and human rights[3]. It also has power to investigate the commission of acts which are unlawful under the Equality Act 2010[4] and, where applicable, to issue 'unlawful act notices' and order the preparation of action plans for the purpose of addressing the unlawfulness[5]. Investigations may, but need not, arise from inquiries undertaken by the Commission[6]. The Commission may investigate whether a person has committed an unlawful act[7] and whether a person has complied with a requirement imposed by an unlawful act notice[8]. It may agree not to proceed with an investigation, or not to issue an unlawful act notice, in return for an undertaking not to commit an unlawful act or to refrain from other specified activities[9], and may also investigate failure to comply with such undertakings[10].

1 As to the establishment of the Equality and Human Rights Commission see PARA 28.
2 Ie under the Equality Act 2006 s 8 (see PARA 32).
3 Equality Act 2006 s 16(1) (amended by the Enterprise and Regulatory Reform Act 2013 s 64(3), (8)). The Commission's duties concerning human rights are those under the Equality Act 2006 s 9 (see PARAS 32, 33). As to the conduct of such inquiries see PARA 339 et seq.
4 As to the meaning of 'unlawful' see PARA 32 note 8. As to the Commission's investigatory powers see further PARA 339 et seq.
5 See the Equality Act 2006 ss 20–32; and PARAS 345–350. As to the unlawful acts to which the investigative provisions apply see PARA 345.
6 Ie an inquiry under the Equality Act 2006 s 16 (see the text and notes 1–3): see s 20(3); and PARA 347.
7 See the Equality Act 2006 s 20(1)(a); and PARA 347.
8 See the Equality Act 2006 s 20(1)(b); and PARA 347.
9 See the Equality Act 2010 s 23; and PARA 350.
10 See the Equality Act 2006 s 20(1)(c); and PARA 347.

36. Commission's power to conduct assessments.

The Equality and Human Rights Commission[1] may conduct an assessment as to the extent to which or the manner in which a person has complied with the public sector equality duty[2] and may issue notices requiring compliance with that duty[3]. As in the case of unlawful acts[4], the Commission may also agree not to proceed with an assessment in return for an undertaking not to commit or continue a breach[5].

1 As to the establishment of the Equality and Human Rights Commission see PARA 28.

2 See the Equality Act 2006 s 31(1). The text refers to a duty under or by virtue of the Equality Act 2010 s 149 (see PARAS **278–284**), s 153 (imposition of specific duties: see PARAS **285, 289**) or s 154 (see PARA **277**).
3 See the Equality Act 2006 ss 31, 32; and PARA **300**.
4 See PARA **35**.
5 See the Equality Act 2006 s 23(5); and PARA **301**.

37. Provision of legal assistance by the Commission.

The Equality and Human Rights Commission[1] may assist an individual who is or may become party to legal proceedings[2]:

(1)   if the proceedings relate or may relate (wholly or partly) to a provision of the Equality Act 2010[3] and the individual alleges that he has been the victim of behaviour contrary to a provision of that Act[4];

(2)   if the proceedings relate or may relate (wholly or partly) to a corresponding provision of European Union ('EU') law[5] and the individual alleges that he is disadvantaged by an enactment which is contrary to a provision of EU law or a failure by the United Kingdom to implement a right as required by EU law[6]; or

(3)   if and in so far as the proceedings concern or may concern the question of a landlord's reasonableness in relation to consent to the making of an improvement to a dwelling where the improvement would be likely to facilitate the enjoyment of the premises by the tenant or another lawful occupier having regard to a disability[7].

Where proceedings relate or may relate partly to a provision of the Equality Act 2010 and partly to other matters, assistance may in general be given only in respect of such aspects of the proceedings as relate to a provision of the Act[8].

Where the Commission has assisted an individual under these provisions in relation to proceedings and the individual becomes entitled to some or all of his costs in the proceedings (whether by virtue of an award or by virtue of an agreement)[9], the Commission's expenses in providing the assistance are charged on sums paid to the individual by way of costs and may be enforced as a debt due to the Commission[10].

1   As to the establishment of the Equality and Human Rights Commission see PARA **28**.
2   In giving assistance under these provisions the Commission may provide or arrange for the provision of legal advice, legal representation, facilities for the settlement of a dispute or any other form of assistance: Equality Act 2006 s 28(4). A legislative provision which requires insurance or an indemnity in respect of advice given in connection with a settlement agreement does not apply to advice provided by the Commission under s 28: s 28(11) (amended by the Enterprise and Regulatory Reform Act 2013 s 23(4)). As to settlement agreements see PARA **275**. These provisions are without prejudice to the effect of any restriction imposed, in respect of representation by virtue of an enactment or in accordance with the practice of a court: s 28(10).
3   Equality Act 2006 s 28(1)(a) (s 28(1)(a), (b), (5), (6)(a), (b), (7)(a), (b), (8), (9), (12) amended by the Equality Act 2010 Sch 26 para 72; and SI 2010/2279).
4   Equality Act 2006 s 28(1)(b) (as amended: see note 3). Assistance may not be given under s 28(1) in relation to alleged behaviour contrary to a provision of the Equality Act 2010 Pt 12 (ss 160–188) (disabled persons: transport: see PARAS **215–236**): Equality Act 2006 s 28(5) (as so amended).
5   Ie a provision of EU law which relates to discrimination on grounds of sex (including reassignment of gender), racial origin, ethnic origin, religion, belief, disability, age or sexual orientation, and confers rights on individuals: Equality Act 2006 s 28(12) (as amended (see note 3); s 28(12), (13) further amended by SI 2011/1043). As to European Union Law see PARA **10** et seq.
6   Equality Act 2006 s 28(12), (13) (as amended: see notes 3, 5). As to the meaning of 'United Kingdom' see PARA **85** note 1.
7   Equality Act 2006 s 28(2).
8   Where proceedings relate or may relate partly to a provision of the Equality Act 2010 and partly to other matters assistance may be given under the Equality Act 2006 s 28(1) (see the text and notes

1–4) in respect of any aspect of the proceedings while they relate to a provision of that Act (s 28(6)(a) (as amended: see note 3)), but if the proceedings cease to relate to a provision of the Act, assistance may not be continued under s 28(1) in respect of the proceedings (except in so far as it is permitted by virtue of s 28(7) or (8)) (s 28(6)(b) (as so amended)). Section 28(7) provides that the Lord Chancellor may by order disapply s 28(6)(b), and enable the Commission to give assistance under s 28(1), in respect of legal proceedings which when instituted, related (wholly or partly) to a provision of the Equality Act 2006 (s 28(7)(a) (as so amended)), have ceased to relate to the provision of the Act (s 28(7)(b) (as so amended)), and relate (wholly or partly) to any of the Convention rights within the meaning given by the Human Rights Act 1998 s 1 (Equality Act 2006 s 28(7)(c) (as so amended)). Section 28(8) (as so amended; amended by SI 2010/1839) provides that the Secretary of State may by order enable the Commission to give assistance under the Equality Act 2006 s 28 in respect of legal proceedings in the course of which an individual who is or has been a disabled person relies or proposes to rely on a matter relating to his disability (although such an order may not permit assistance in relation to alleged behaviour contrary to a provision of the Equality Act 2010 Pt 12). At the date at which this volume states the law no such order had been made. An order under the Equality Act 2006 s 28(7) or (8) may make provision generally or only in relation to proceedings of a specified kind or description (which in the case of an order under s 28(7) may, in particular, refer to specified provisions of the Equality Act 2010) or in relation to specified circumstances: Equality Act 2006 s 28(9) (as so amended). As to the Convention rights under the Human Rights Act 1998 s 1 see RIGHTS AND FREEDOMS vol 88A (2013) PARA 14. As to the Secretary of State see PARA 4.

9   Equality Act 2006 s 29(1). Costs may be awarded to an individual claimant in respect of expenses borne by a backing organisation: *Taiwo v Olaigbe* (2013) UKEAT/0254/12/KN, [2013] All ER (D) 294 (Mar); affirmed on other grounds [2014] EWCA Civ 279, [2014] 1 WLR 3636, [2014] IRLR 448.

10 Equality Act 2006 s 29(2). A requirement to pay money to the Commission under s 29(2) ranks after a requirement imposed by virtue of the Legal Aid, Sentencing and Punishment of Offenders Act 2012 s 25 (see LEGAL AID vol 65 (2015) PARA 150): Equality Act 2006 s 29(3) (amended by the Legal Aid, Sentencing and Punishment of Offenders Act 2012 Sch 5 para 67). For the purposes of the Equality Act 2006 s 29(2) the Commission's expenses must be calculated in accordance with such provision (if any) as the Secretary of State makes for the purpose by regulations; and regulations may, in particular, provide for the apportionment of expenditure incurred by the Commission partly for one purpose and partly for another or for general purposes: s 29(5) (amended by SI 2010/1839). At the date at which this volume states the law no such regulations had been made.

38. Institution of, and intervention in, legal proceedings by the Commission.

The Equality and Human Rights Commission[1] has capacity to institute or intervene in legal proceedings, whether for judicial review or otherwise, if it appears to the Commission that the proceedings are relevant to a matter in connection with which the Commission has a function[2]. This does not create a cause of action and is subject[3] to any limitation or restriction imposed by virtue of an enactment or in accordance with the practice of a court[4].

1   As to the establishment of the Equality and Human Rights Commission see PARA 28.
2   Equality Act 2006 s 30(1). The Commission may, in the course of legal proceedings for judicial review which it institutes (or in which it intervenes), rely on the Human Rights Act 1998 s 7(1)(b) (breach of Convention rights: see RIGHTS AND FREEDOMS vol 88A (2013) PARA 27); and for that purpose:
    (1)   the Commission need not be a victim or potential victim of the unlawful act to which the proceedings relate (Equality Act 2006 s 30(3)(a));
    (2)   the Commission may act only if there is or would be one or more victims of the unlawful act (s 30(3)(b));
    (3)   the Human Rights Act 1998 7(3) (see RIGHTS AND FREEDOMS vol 88A (2013) PARA 28) does not apply (Equality Act 2006 s 30(3)(c)); and
    (4)   no award of damages may be made to the Commission (whether or not the exception in the Human Rights Act 1998 s 8(3) (see RIGHTS AND FREEDOMS vol 88A (2013) PARA 29) applies) (Equality Act 2006 s 30(3)(d)).
    As to the meaning of 'victim' see the Human Rights Act 1998 s 7(7); and RIGHTS AND FREEDOMS vol 88A (2013) PARA 28 (definition applied by the Equality Act 2006 s 30(3)).
3   Ie except as provided by the Equality Act 2006 s 30(3) (see note 2).
4   Equality Act 2006 s 30(4).

39. Commission's duty of non-disclosure.

A person who is or was a Commissioner[1], an Investigating Commissioner[2], an employee of the Equality and Human Rights Commission[3] or a member of a committee established by the Commission[4] commits an offence if he discloses certain information without authorisation[5]. This duty of non-disclosure applies to information acquired by the Commission:

(1)   by way of representations made in relation to, or otherwise in the course of, an inquiry[6];

(2)   by way of representations made in relation to, or otherwise in the course of, an investigation[7];

(3)   by way of representations made in relation to, or otherwise in the course of, a public sector duty assessment[8];

(4)   by way of representations made in relation to, or otherwise in connection with, a public sector duty compliance notice[9]; or

(5)   from a person with whom the Commission enters into, or considers entering into, an agreement[10].

Disclosure is authorised, however, where it is made:

(a)   for the purpose of the exercise of certain specified functions of the Commission[11];

(b)   in a report of an inquiry, investigation or assessment published by the Commission[12];

(c)   in pursuance of an order of a court or tribunal[13];

(d)   with the consent of each person to whom the disclosed information relates[14];

(e)   in a manner that ensures that no person to whom the disclosed information relates can be identified[15];

(f)   for the purpose of civil or criminal proceedings to which the Commission is party[16]; or

(g)   if the information was acquired by the Commission more than 70 years before the date of the disclosure[17].

However, this does not authorise, nor may the Commission make, a disclosure of information provided by or relating to an intelligence service unless the service has authorised the disclosure[18].

1   As to the appointment and tenure of Commissioners see PARA 28.
2   As to Investigating Commissioners see PARA 29.
3   As to the establishment of the Equality and Human Rights Commission see PARA 28.
4   As to committees see PARA 29.
5   Equality Act 2006 s 6(1). A person guilty of an offence under s 6(1) is liable on summary conviction to a fine not exceeding level 5 on the standard scale: s 6(6). As to the powers of magistrates' courts to issue fines on summary conviction see SENTENCING vol 92 (2015) PARA 176.
6   Equality Act 2006 s 6(2)(a). The text refers to an inquiry under s 16 (see PARA 35).
7   Equality Act 2006 s 6(2)(b). The text refers to an investigation under s 20 (see PARA 347).
8   Equality Act 2006 s 6(2)(c). The text refers to an assessment under s 31 (see PARA 36).
9   Equality Act 2006 s 6(2)(d). The text refers to a notice under s 32 (see PARA 300).
10 Equality Act 2006 s 6(2)(e). The text refers to an agreement under s 23: see PARA 301.
11 Equality Act 2006 s 6(3)(a). The specified functions are those under s 16, s 20, s 21 (unlawful act notices: see PARAS 339, 347), s 24 (applications to court: see PARAS 346, 350), s 25 (now repealed), s 31, or s 32.
12 Equality Act 2006 s 6(3)(b).
13 Equality Act 2006 s 6(3)(c).
14 Equality Act 2006 s 6(3)(d).
15 Equality Act 2006 s 6(3)(e).
16 Equality Act 2006 s 6(3)(f).
17 Equality Act 2006 s 6(3)(g).

18 Equality Act 2006 s 6(4). 'Intelligence service' means the Security Service, the Secret Intelligence Service, and the Government Communications Headquarters: s 6(5). As to the Security Service, the Secret Intelligence Service and he Government Communications Headquarters see CONSTITUTIONAL AND ADMINISTRATIVE LAW vol 20 (2014) PARA 243 et seq.

(3) ADVICE, CONSULTATION AND GUIDANCE

40. Commission's power to publish information, advice etc.

In pursuance of its statutory duties in relation to equality and diversity[1] and human rights[2], the Equality and Human Rights Commission[3] may:

(1)   publish or otherwise disseminate ideas or information[4];

(2)   undertake research[5];

(3)   provide education or training[6];

(4)   give advice or guidance (whether about the effect or operation of an enactment or otherwise)[7];

(5)   arrange for a person to do anything within heads (1) to (4)[8];

(6)   act jointly with, co-operate with or assist a person doing anything within heads (1) to (4)[9].

1 Ie under the Equality Act 2006 s 8 (see PARA 32).
2 Ie under the Equality Act 2006 s 9 (see PARA 33).
3 As to the establishment of the Equality and Human Rights Commission see PARA 28.
4 Equality Act 2006 s 13(1)(a) (amended by the Enterprise and Regulatory Reform Act 2013 s 64(7)).
5 Equality Act 2006 s 13(1)(b).
6 Equality Act 2006 s 13(1)(c).
7 Equality Act 2006 s 13(1)(d). The reference to giving advice in s 13(1)(d) does not include a reference to preparing, or assisting in the preparation of, a document to be used for the purpose of legal proceedings: s 13(2).
8 Equality Act 2006 s 13(1)(e).
9 Equality Act 2006 s 13(1)(f).

41. Commission's duty to monitor the law.

The Equality and Human Rights Commission[1] has a duty to monitor the effectiveness of the equality and human rights enactments[2].

The Commission may:

(1)   advise central government[3] about the effectiveness of any of the equality and human rights enactments[4];

(2)   recommend to central government the amendment, repeal, consolidation (with or without amendments) or replication (with or without amendments) of any of the equality and human rights enactments[5];

(3)   advise central or devolved government[6] about the effect of an enactment (including an enactment in or under an Act of the Scottish Parliament)[7];

(4)   advise central or devolved government about the likely effect of a proposed change of law[8].

1 As to the establishment of the Equality and Human Rights Commission see PARA 28.
2 Equality Act 2006 s 11(1). A reference to the equality and human rights enactments is a reference to the Human Rights Act 1998, the Equality Act 2006 and the Equality Act 2010: Equality Act 2006 s 11(3)(c) (definition substituted by the Equality Act 2010 s 211(1), Sch 26 paras 61, 64; and amended by SI 2010/2279).
3 'Central government' means Her Majesty's Government: Equality Act 2006 s 11(3)(a).
4 Equality Act 2006 s 11(2)(a).
5 Equality Act 2006 s 11(2)(b).

6 'Devolved government' means the Scottish Ministers, the Welsh Ministers, the First Minister for Wales and the Counsel General to the Welsh Government: Equality Act 2006 s 11(3)(b) (definition amended by SI 2007/1388; and modified by the Wales Act 2014 s 4(4)(a)).
7 Equality Act 2006 s 11(2)(c).
8 Equality Act 2006 s 11(2)(d).

42. Commission's duty to monitor progress.

The Equality and Human Rights Commission[1] must from time to time identify:

(1) changes in society that have occurred or are expected to occur and are relevant to the Commission's duties in relation to equality and diversity and human rights[2];

(2) outcomes (that is the results at which to aim for the purpose of encouraging and supporting changes in society that are consistent with those duties)[3]; and

(3) indicators (that is the factors by reference to which progress towards those results may be measured)[4].

In identifying outcomes and indicators the Commission must:

(a) consult such persons having knowledge or experience relevant to the Commission's functions as the Commission thinks appropriate[5];

(b) consult such other persons as the Commission thinks appropriate[6];

(c) issue a general invitation to make representations, in a manner likely in the Commission's opinion to bring the invitation to the attention of as large a class of persons who may wish to make representations as is reasonably practicable[7]; and

(d) take account of any representations made[8].

From time to time the Commission must monitor progress towards each identified outcome by reference to any relevant identified indicator[9], and must publish a report on such progress[10] and send it to the Secretary of State[11].

1 As to the establishment of the Equality and Human Rights Commission see PARA 28.
2 Equality Act 2006 s 12(1)(a) (s 12(1)(a), (b) amended by the Enterprise and Regulatory Reform Act 2013 s 64(6)). As to the Commission's duties in relation to equality and diversity and human rights see PARAS 32, 33.
3 Equality Act 2006 s 12(1)(b) (as amended: see note 2).
4 Equality Act 2006 s 12(1)(c).
5 Equality Act 2006 s 12(2)(a).
6 Equality Act 2006 s 12(2)(b).
7 Equality Act 2006 s 12(2)(c).
8 Equality Act 2006 s 12(2)(d).
9 Equality Act 2006 s 12(3).
10 The Commission must publish a report on progress towards the identified outcomes by reference to the identified indicators:
   (1) within the period of three years beginning with the 1 October 2007 (Equality Act 2006 s 12(4)(a); Equality Act 2006 (Commencement No 3 and Savings) Order 2007, SI 2007/2603); and
   (2) within each period of five years beginning with the date on which a report is published (Equality Act 2006 s 12(4) (amended by the Enterprise and Regulatory Reform Act 2013 s 64(2))).
11 The Secretary of State then lays a copy before Parliament: Equality Act 2006 s 12(5) (amended by SI 2010/1839). As to the Secretary of State see PARA 4.

43. Commission's power to issue codes of practice.

The Equality and Human Rights Commission[1] may issue a code of practice[2] in connection with any matter addressed by the Equality Act 2010[3].

A code of practice must contain provision designed:

(1) to ensure or facilitate compliance with the Equality Act 2010 or an enactment made under that Act[4]; or

(2)   to promote equality of opportunity[5].

The Commission may also issue a code of practice giving practical guidance to landlords and tenants[6]. The Commission must comply with a direction of the Secretary of State to issue a code in connection with a specified matter if the matter is not a matter addressed by the Equality Act 2010, but the Secretary of State expects to add it by order[7].

Before issuing a code the Commission must publish proposals, and consult such persons as it thinks appropriate[8]. It must also submit a draft to the Secretary of State, who must either approve it and notify the Commission before laying it before Parliament, or otherwise give the Commission written reasons why he does not approve the draft[9]. If approved, the code comes into force in accordance with provision made by the Secretary of State by order[10].

The Commission may revise a code issued by it[11]. Codes may be revoked by order made by the Secretary of State, at the request of the Commission[12].

A failure to comply with a provision of a code does not of itself make a person liable to criminal or civil proceedings[13]. However, a code is admissible in evidence in criminal or civil proceedings, and must be taken into account by a court or tribunal in any case in which it appears to the court or tribunal to be relevant[14].

1   As to the establishment of the Equality and Human Rights Commission see PARA 28.
2   As to the codes of practice issued by the Commission see PARA 44.
3   Equality Act 2006 s 14(1) (s 14(1) substituted, s 14(2), (3), (5), (9) amended, by the Equality Act 2010 s 211(1), Sch 26 paras 61, 65(1)–(5); and SI 2010/2279).
4   Equality Act 2006 s 14(2)(a) (as amended: see note 3).
5   Equality Act 2006 s 14(2)(b).
6   Equality Act 2006 s 14(3) (as amended: see note 3). Such practical guidance is to be about:
     (1)   circumstances in which a tenant requires the consent of his landlord to make a relevant improvement (as to the meaning of which see the Equality Act 2010 s 190(7); and PARA 272) to a dwelling house (Equality Act 2006 s 14(3)(a) (as so amended));
     (2)   reasonableness in relation to that consent (s 14(3)(b)); and
     (3)   the application in relation to relevant improvements to dwelling houses of the Landlord and Tenant Act 1927 s 19(2) (consent to improvements: see LANDLORD AND TENANT vol 62 (2016) PARA 364, the Housing Act 1980 ss 81–85 (tenant's improvements: see LANDLORD AND TENANT vol 63 (2016) PARA 680), the Housing Act 1985 ss 97–99 (tenant's improvements: see LANDLORD AND TENANT vol 63 (2016) PARAS 1075–1076) and the Equality Act 2010 s 190 (see PARA 272) (Equality Act 2006 s 14(3)(c) (as so amended)).
     The Commission may also issue a code of practice giving practical guidance to landlords and tenants of houses in Scotland: see s 14(4).
7   Equality Act 2006 s 14(5) (as amended (see note 3); further amended by SI 2010/1839). The Secretary of State may by order amend the Equality Act 2006 s 14 so as to vary the range of matters that codes of practice under that provision may address: s 15(6) (ss 15(3), (6), 14(7)–(10) amended by SI 2010/1839). As to the Secretary of State see PARA 4.
8   Equality Act 2006 s 14(6).
9   Equality Act 2006 s 14(7) (as amended: see note 7).
10 See the Equality Act 2006 s 14(8)(b) (as amended: see note 7). Where a draft is laid before Parliament, if neither House passes a resolution disapproving the draft within 40 days the Commission may issue the code in the form of the draft, and it comes into force in accordance with provision made by the Secretary of State by order: s 14(8) (as so amended). The 40 day period specified in s 14(8) begins with the date on which the draft is laid before both Houses (or, if laid before each House on a different date, with the later date), and is taken not to include a period during which Parliament is prorogued or dissolved, or during which both Houses are adjourned for more than four days: s 15(2).
     If, or in so far as, a code relates to a duty imposed by or under the Equality Act 2010 s 149, s 153 or s 154 (public sector equality duty: see PARAS 277, 278) the Secretary of State must consult the Scottish Ministers and the Welsh Ministers before approving a draft or making a commencement order: Equality Act 2006 s 14(9) (as amended: see notes 3, 7). In relation to a code

of practice under s 14(4) (see note 6), the Secretary of State must consult the Scottish Ministers before approving a draft, or making an order: s 14(10) (as so amended).

11 See the Equality Act 2006 s 15(1).
12 Equality Act 2006 s 15(3) (as amended: see note 7).
13 Equality Act 2006 s 15(4).
14 Equality Act 2006 s 15(4)(a), (b). However, a code issued under s 14(4) (guidance to landlords and tenants in Scotland: see note 6) does not have to be taken into account: see s 15(4)(b), (5).

44. Current codes of practice.

The Equality and Human Rights Commission[1] has issued[2] a number of codes of practice which are intended to complement and facilitate the understanding of and compliance with the Equality Act 2010[3], namely:

(1) the Equality Act 2010 Code of Practice on Services, Public Functions and Associations (referred to as 'the Services Code')[4];

(2) the Equality Act 2010 Code of Practice on Employment (referred to as 'the Employment Code')[5]; and

(3) the Equality Act 2010 Code of Practice on Equal Pay (referred to as 'the Equal Pay Code')[6].

1 As to the establishment of the Equality and Human Rights Commission see PARA 28.
2 Ie under its power in the Equality Act 2006 ss 14, 15 (see PARA 43).
3 See PARA 2.
4 See the Equality Act 2010 Code of Practice — Services, Public Functions and Associations Statutory Code of Practice (2011); and PARA 7.
5 See the Equality Act 2010 Code of Practice — Employment Statutory Code of Practice (2011); and PARA 7.
6 See the Equality Act 2010 Code of Practice — Equal Pay Statutory Code of Practice (2011); and PARA 7.

3. PROTECTED CHARACTERISTICS

(1) PROTECTED CHARACTERISTICS UNDER THE EQUALITY ACT 2010

(i) The Protected Characteristics

45. Characteristics protected under the Equality Act 2010.
The following characteristics are 'protected characteristics'[1] under the Equality Act 2010: age[2]; disability[3]; gender reassignment[4]; marriage and civil partnership[5]; pregnancy and maternity[6]; race[7]; religion or belief[8]; sex[9]; and sexual orientation[10]. Although these same characteristics had enjoyed protection under previous discrimination legislation[11], the Equality Act 2010 consolidates the law and brings them together under a single statutory regime.

1 Equality Act 2010 s 4.
2 As to age see PARA 46.
3 As to disability see PARAS 47–55.
4 As to gender reassignment see PARAS 56, 61.
5 As to marriage and civil partnership see PARA 57.
6 As to pregnancy and maternity see PARAS 62, 73–74.
7 As to race see PARA 58.
8 As to religion or belief see PARA 59.
9 As to sex see PARA 60.
10 As to sexual orientation see PARA 63.
11 See PARA 1.

(ii) Age

46. Protected characteristic of age.
In relation to the protected characteristic[1] of age, a reference to a person who has a particular protected characteristic is a reference to a person of a particular age group[2]; and a reference to persons who share a protected characteristic is a reference to persons of the same age group[3].

1 As to protected characteristics generally see PARA 45.
2 Equality Act 2010 s 5(1)(a). A reference to an age group is a reference to a group of persons defined by reference to age, whether by reference to a particular age or to a range of ages: s 5(2).
3 Equality Act 2010 s 5(1)(b). See note 2.

(iii) Disability

A. STATUTORY DEFINITION OF DISABILITY

47. Protected characteristic of disability.
A person (P) has a disability if P has a physical or mental impairment, and the impairment has a substantial and long-term adverse effect on P's ability to carry out normal day-to-day activities[1]. A reference to a disabled person is a reference to a person who has a disability[2]. This definition may be modified in situations within the scope of European Union ('EU') law, in particular by the provisions of the equality directive on equal treatment in employment and occupation[3].

In relation to the protected characteristic of disability a reference to a person who has a particular protected characteristic is a reference to a person who has a particular disability; and a reference to persons who share a protected characteristic is a reference to persons who have the same disability[4].

The Equality Act 2010, apart from certain provisions[5], applies in relation to a person who has had a disability as it applies in relation to a person who has the disability[6]. Accordingly, with certain exceptions[7], a reference (however expressed) to a person who has a disability includes a reference to a person who has had the disability[8] and a reference (however expressed) to a person who does not have a disability includes a reference to a person who has not had the disability[9].

A question as to whether a person had a disability at a particular time ('the relevant time') is to be determined, for the purposes of these provisions[10], as if the provisions of, or made under, the Equality Act 2010 were in force when the act complained of was done had been in force at the relevant time[11].

1 Equality Act 2010 s 6(1). As to the meaning of 'impairment' see PARA 48; and as to substantial and long term effects see PARA 49 et seq. A Minister of the Crown may issue guidance about matters to be taken into account in deciding any question for these purposes: s 6(5). Such guidance may give examples of effects which it would, or would not, be reasonable, in relation to particular activities, to regard as substantial adverse effects; and substantial adverse effects which it would, or would not, be reasonable to regard as long term: s 6(6), Sch 1 paras 10, 11. In determining whether a person is a disabled person, an adjudicating body must take account of such guidance as it thinks is relevant: Sch 1 para 12(1). For these purposes an 'adjudicating body' is a court, a tribunal, or a person (other than a court or tribunal) who may decide a claim relating to a contravention of Pt 6 (ss 84–99) (education: see PARAS 173–197): Sch 1 para 12(2). Before issuing the guidance, the Minister must publish a draft of it, consider any representations made to him about the draft, and make such modifications as he thinks appropriate in the light of such representations: Sch 1 para 13. If the Minister decides to proceed with the proposed guidance, a draft of it must be laid before Parliament: Sch 1 para 14. A guidance comes into force on the day appointed by order by the Minister: Sch 1 para 15. The Minister may review the whole or part of a guidance and reissue it; or by order revoke the guidance: Sch 1 para 16(1). A reference to guidance includes a reference to a guidance which has been revised and reissued: Sch 1 para 16(2). As to guidance issued under these provisions see Equality Act 2010 — Guidance on matters to be taken into account in determining questions relating to the definition of disability (2011); and the Equality Act 2010 (Guidance on the Definition of Disability) Appointed Day Order 2011, SI 2011/1159.
2 Equality Act 2010 s 6(2).
3 Ie Council Directive (EC) 2000/78 (OJ L303, 2.12.2000, p 16) on establishing a general framework for equal treatment in employment and occupation (see PARA 14). In Advocate General Geelhoed's Opinion in Case C-13/05 *Chacon Navas v Eurest Colectividades SA* [2006] IRLR 706, ECJ, it was said at [65]–[66] '. . . a uniform Community interpretation of 'disability' is needed for substantive reasons, if only to ensure a minimum of the necessary uniformity in the personal and substantial scope of the prohibition of discrimination. The persons to be protected and the delineation of the functional limitations to be considered must not vary. Otherwise, the protection afforded by that prohibition of discrimination would vary within the Community'. None the less, in developing a uniform interpretation of the term 'disability', account should be taken of the aforementioned dynamic aspect of society's perception of the phenomenon of 'disability' as a functional limitation resulting from a mental or physical defect, the evolution of medical and biomedical understanding, and the major contextual differences in the assessment of a wide variety of disabilities'. Paragraph (e) in the preamble to the Convention on the Rights of Persons with Disabilities (New York, 13 December 2006; TS 10 (2010); Cm 7905) (see RIGHTS AND FREEDOMS vol 88A (2013) PARA 110), ratified by the European Union ('EU') on 23 December 2010 (see Council Decision (EC) 2010/48 (OJ L23, 27.1 2010, p 35) concerning the conclusion, by the European Community, of the United Nations Convention on the Rights of Persons with Disabilities, noted this dynamic nature of disability, stating: 'Recognising disability is an evolving concept and that disability results from the interaction between persons with impairments and attitudinal and environmental barriers that hinder their full and effective participation in society on an equal basis with others'. And this in turn has led the European Court of Justice to take a more adaptive approach to the concept in Case C-335/11 HK *Danmark (acting on behalf of Ring) v Dansk almennyttigt Boligselskab* ECLI:EU:C:2013:222, [2013] ICR 851, [2014] All ER (EC)

1161, ECJ; and Case C-354/13 *Fag og Arbejde (FOA) v Kommunernes Landsforening (KL)* ECLI:EU:C:2014:2463, [2015] All ER (EC) 265, [2015] ICR 322.
4 Equality Act 2010 s 6(3). As to protected characteristics generally see PARA 45.
5 Ie the Equality Act 2010 Pt 12 (ss 160–188) (disabled persons and transport: see PARA 215 et seq); and s 190 (improvements to let dwelling houses: see PARA 272).
6 Equality Act 2010 s 6(4).
7 See note 4.
8 Equality Act 2010 s 6(4)(a).
9 Equality Act 2010 s 6(4)(b).
10 Ie for the purposes of the Equality Act 2010 s 6 (see the text and notes 1–8).
11 Equality Act 2010 Sch 1 para 9(1). The relevant time may be a time before the coming into force of the provision of the Equality Act 2010 to which the question relates: Sch 1 para 9(2).

48. Physical or mental impairment.

'Physical or mental impairment' is not defined in the Equality Act 2010. The term should be given its ordinary meaning[1]. Regulations may make provision for a condition of a prescribed description to be, or not to be, an impairment[2]. Addiction to alcohol, nicotine or any other substance is to be treated as not amounting to an impairment for these purposes[3].

1 Equality Act 2010 — Guidance on matters to be taken into account in determining questions relating to the definition of disability (2011) para A3; and see *McNicol v Balfour Beatty Rail Maintenance Ltd* [2002] EWCA Civ 1074 at [17], [2002] ICR 1498, [2002] IRLR 711 (decided under the Disability Discrimination Act 1995 (now repealed)). An employer must form its own judgement, and not simply rely on advice given by occupational health advisers, as to whether an employee is disabled: *Gallop v Newport City Council* [2013] EWCA Civ 1583, [2014] IRLR 211. Although the Guidance provides a list of impairments from which disability may arise, that list is not exhaustive list of conditions that qualify as 'impairments': see Equality Act 2010 — Guidance on matters to be taken into account in determining questions relating to the definition of disability (2011) paras A4, A6. For these purposes 'impairment' includes sensory impairments such as those affecting sight or hearing: see para A5.
   An impairment may result from an illness or it may consist of an illness; and the presence of a physical cause is not necessary for there to be a physical impairment, as long as there are physical symptoms: see *McNicol v Balfour Beatty Rail Maintenance Ltd* at [17]; *College of Ripon and York St John v Hobbs* [2002] IRLR 185 at [32], [2001] All ER (D) 259 (Nov), EAT (decided under the Disability Discrimination Act 1995 (now repealed)). See also *J v DLA Piper UK LLP* (2010) UKEAT/0263/09/RN at [40], [2010] ICR 1052, [2010] IRLR 936 (decided under the Disability Discrimination Act 1995). Cf *Rugamer v Sony Music Entertainment UK Ltd, McNicol v Balfour Beatty Rail Maintenance Ltd* [2002] ICR 381, [2001] IRLR 644, EAT (decided under the Disability Discrimination Act 1995 (now repealed)).
2 Equality Act 2010 s 6(6), Sch 1 para 1. For the purposes of the Act, the following conditions are to be treated as not amounting to impairments: (1) a tendency to set fires; (2) a tendency to steal; (3) a tendency to physical or sexual abuse of other persons; (4) exhibitionism; and (5) voyeurism: Equality Act 2010 (Disability) Regulations 2010, SI 2010/2128, reg 4(1). For these purposes the condition known as seasonal allergic rhinitis (broadly, the condition commonly known as hay-fever) will be treated as not amounting to an impairment, however, this does not prevent that condition from being taken into account for the purposes of the Equality Act 2010 where it aggravates the effect of any other condition: Equality Act 2010 (Disability) Regulations 2010, SI 2010/2128, reg 4(2), (3).
   A claimant may have both a legitimate impairment and an excluded condition and in such circumstances, the critical question is one of causation, ie, the reason for the less favourable treatment of the claimant. If the reason was the legitimate impairment, then prima facie discrimination, subject to the defence of justification, is made out; if the reason was the excluded condition and not the legitimate impairment, then the claim fails by reason of the claimant's disability: *Edmund Nuttall Ltd v Butterfield* [2006] ICR 77 at [29], [2005] IRLR 751, EAT, describing as unhelpful the previous decision in *Murray v Newham Citizens Advice Bureau Ltd* [2003] ICR 643, [2003] IRLR 340, EAT, which held that the exclusion only applied where the condition in question was a 'freestanding' condition producing the tendency or conduct mentioned. See also *Governing Body of X Endowed Primary School v Special Educational Needs and Disability Tribunal* [2009] EWHC 1842 (Admin), [2009] IRLR 1007, [2010] ELR 1.
   An employee, who exhibits various symptoms with no identifiable cause, and which are further affected by his obesity, is disabled. The definition of 'disability' depends on whether there is

impairment; not on the cause of that impairment: see *Walker v SITA Information Networking Computing Ltd* (2013) UKEAT/0097/12/KN, [2013] All ER (D) 317 (May).

3   Equality Act 2010 (Disability) Regulations 2010, SI 2010/2128, reg 3(1). This does not apply to addiction which was originally the result of administration of medically prescribed drugs or other medical treatment: reg 3(2). For these purposes 'addiction' includes a dependency: reg 2. The exclusion in reg 3 may not apply if the claimant relies on some other condition as the disability, even if that condition was caused by alcohol addiction: *Power v Panasonic UK Ltd* [2003] IRLR 151, 72 BMLR 1, EAT (decided under the Disability Discrimination (Meaning of Disability) Regulations 1996, SI 1996/1455 (revoked)).

49.   Substantial and adverse effect.

A substantial adverse effect means more than minor or trivial effect[1]. When determining whether an impairment[2] has a substantial effect, the comparison is not with the population at large; rather, what is required is to compare the difference between the way in which the person carries out the activity in question and how he would carry it out if not impaired[3].

An impairment which consists of a severe disfigurement is to be treated as having a substantial adverse effect on the ability of the person concerned to carry out normal day-to-day activities[4]. Regulations may make provision for an effect of a prescribed description on the ability of a person to carry out normal day-to-day activities[5] to be treated as being, or as not being, a substantial adverse effect[6].

1   See the Equality Act 2010 s 212(1) ('substantial' means more than minor or trivial); and see *Goodwin v Patent Office* [1999] ICR 302, [1999] IRLR 4. See also the Equality Act 2010 Code of Practice — Employment Statutory Code of Practice (2010) Appendix 1 para 8.
      The definition of 'substantial' in the Equality Act 2010 s 212 does not create a spectrum running smoothly from those matters which are clearly of substantial effect to those matters which are clearly trivial, but provides for a bifurcation: unless a matter can be classified as within the heading 'trivial' or 'insubstantial' it must be treated as substantial; there is little room for any form of sliding scale between one and the other: *Aderemi v London and South Eastern Railway Ltd* (2012) UKEAT/0316/12/KN at [14], [2013] ICR 591, [2013] All ER (D) 201 (Feb).
2   As to physical and mental impairments see PARA 48.
3   See *Paterson v Metropolitan Police Comr* [2007] ICR 1522 at [27], [2007] IRLR 763. As to what to take into account when considering whether an impairment has substantial effect, including the time taken to carry out an activity, and the way in which an activity is carries out see Equality Act 2010 — Guidance on matters to be taken into account in determining questions relating to the definition of disability (2011) para B2 et seq. As to guidance on what should be taken into account in deciding whether a person's ability to carry out normal day-to-day activities might be restricted by the effects of the person's impairment see para D13 et seq. See also *Aderemi v London and South Eastern Railway Ltd* (2012) UKEAT/0316/12/KN, [2013] ICR 591, [2013] All ER (D) 201 (Feb); and note 1.
4   Equality Act 2010 Sch 1 para 3(1). Regulations may provide that in prescribed circumstances a severe disfigurement is not to be treated as having that effect: Sch 1 para 3(2). Regulations may, in particular, make provision in relation to deliberately acquired disfigurement: Sch 1 para 3(3). For these purposes, a severe disfigurement is not to be treated as having a substantial adverse effect on the ability of the person concerned to carry out normal day-to-day activities if it consists of:
      (1)   a tattoo (which has not been removed) (Equality Act 2010 (Disability) Regulations 2010, SI 2010/2128, reg 5(a)); or
      (2)   a piercing of the body for decorative or other non-medical purposes, including any object attached through the piercing for such purposes (reg 5(b)).
5   As to normal day-to-day activities see PARA 50.
6   Equality Act 2010 Sch 1 para 4. For the purposes of the Equality Act 2010, where a child under six years of age has an impairment which does not have a substantial and long-term adverse effect on the ability of that child to carry out normal day-to-day activities, the impairment is to be taken to have a substantial and long-term adverse effect on the ability of that child to carry out normal day-to-day activities where it would normally have that effect on the ability of a person aged six years or over to carry out normal day-to-day activities: Equality Act 2010 (Disability) Regulations 2010, SI 2010/2128, reg 6.

50. Normal day-to-day activities.

The Equality Act 2010 does not define 'normal day-to-day activities'[1]. Although 'normal day-to-day activities' is not intended to include activities which are normal only for a small group of people, a normal day-to-day activity is not necessarily one that is carried out by a majority of people[2]. A normal day-to-day activity may include an activity which is something only done at work[3].

1 See Equality Act 2010 — Guidance on matters to be taken into account in determining questions relating to the definition of disability (2011) paras D2–D3. Previously, the Disability Discrimination Act 1995 s 1(1), Sch 1 para 4(1) (now repealed) listed 'normal day-to-day' activities. This list has been omitted from the Equality Act 2010. See also Equality Act 2010 Code of Practice — Employment Statutory Code of Practice (2010) Appendix 1 para 14 et seq. As to an illustrative and non-exhaustive list of factors which may be regarded as having a substantial adverse effect on normal day-to-day activities see Equality Act 2010 — Guidance on matters to be taken into account in determining questions relating to the definition of disability (2011) Appendix. What is a day-to-day activity is best left unspecified: easily recognised, but defined with difficulty: see *Goodwin v Patent Office* [1999] ICR 302 at [36], [1999] IRLR 4, EAT.
2 See Equality Act 2010 — Guidance on matters to be taken into account in determining questions relating to the definition of disability (2011) paras D4–D5. See also *Ekpe v Metropolitan Police Comr* [2001] ICR 1084, [2001] IRLR 605, EAT.
3 See *Paterson v Metropolitan Police Comr* [2007] ICR 1522, [2007] IRLR 763, EAT. Cf Equality Act 2010 — Guidance on matters to be taken into account in determining questions relating to the definition of disability (2011) paras D8–D10.

51. Effect of medical treatment.

An impairment[1] is to be treated as having a substantial adverse effect[2] on the ability of the person concerned to carry out normal day-to-day activities[3] if measures[4] are being taken to treat or correct it, and but for that, it would be likely to have that effect[5].

1 As to physical and mental impairments see PARA **48**.
2 As to the meaning of 'substantial adverse effect' see PARA **49**.
3 As to 'normal day-to-day activities' see PARA **50**.
4 For these purposes, 'measures' includes, in particular, medical treatment and the use of a prosthesis or other aid: Equality Act 2010 Sch 1 para 5(2).
5 Equality Act 2010 Sch 1 para 5(1). These provisions do not apply in relation to the impairment of a person's sight, to the extent that the impairment is, in the person's case, correctable by spectacles or contact lenses or in such other ways as may be prescribed; or in relation to such other impairments as may be prescribed, in such circumstances as are prescribed: Sch 1 para 5(3). For these purposes, 'likely' should be interpreted as 'could well happen': see Equality Act 2010 — Guidance on matters to be taken into account in determining questions relating to the definition of disability (2011) para B12.

52. Progressive conditions.

If a person (P) has a progressive condition[1], as of result of which P has an impairment[2] which has, or had, an effect on his ability to carry out normal day-to-day activities[3], but the effect is not, or was not, a substantial adverse effect[4], P is taken to have an impairment which has a substantial adverse effect if the condition is likely to result in P having such an impairment[5].

1 Regulations may make provision for a condition of a prescribed description to be treated as being, or as not being, progressive: Equality Act 2010 Sch 1 para 8(3). At the date at which this volume states the law no such regulations had been made. As to examples of progressive conditions see Equality Act 2010 — Guidance on matters to be taken into account in determining questions relating to the definition of disability (2011) para B17.
    Cancer, HIV infection and multiple sclerosis are each a disability: Equality Act 2010 Sch 1 para 6(1). HIV infection is infection by a virus capable of causing the Acquired Immune Deficiency Syndrome: Sch 1 para 6(2).
2 As to physical and mental impairments see PARA **48**.
3 As to 'normal day-to-day activities' see PARA **50**.

4 Equality Act 2010 Sch 1 para 8(1). As to the meaning of 'substantial adverse effect' see PARA 49.
5 Equality Act 2010 Sch 1 para 8(2).

53. Meaning of 'long-term'.

The effect of an impairment[1] is long-term if it has lasted for at least 12 months, it is likely to last for at least 12 months, or it is likely[2] to last for the rest of the life of the person affected[3].

1 As to physical and mental impairments see PARA 48.
2 'Likely' means 'could well happen': see Equality Act 2010 — Guidance on matters to be taken into account in determining questions relating to the definition of disability (2011) para C3; and PARA 51 note 5. As to factors to take into account when assessing the likelihood of an effect lasting for 12 months see para C4.
3 Equality Act 2010 Sch 1 para 2(1). Regulations may prescribe circumstances in which, despite this provision, an effect is to be treated as being, or as not being, long-term: Sch 1 para 2(4). See the Equality Act 2010 (Disability) Regulations 2010, SI 2010/2128, reg 6; and PARA 49 note 6. The effect of an illness or condition likely to develop or which has developed from another illness or condition forms part of the assessment of whether the effect of the original impairment is likely to last or has lasted at least 12 months: *Patel v Oldham Metropolitan Borough Council* [2010] ICR 603, [2010] IRLR 280.

54. Recurring effects.

If an impairment[1] ceases to have a substantial adverse effect[2] on a person's ability to carry out normal day-to-day activities[3], it is to be treated as continuing to have that effect if that effect is likely to recur[4].

1 As to physical and mental impairments see PARA 48.
2 As to the meaning of 'substantial adverse effect' see PARA 49.
3 As to 'normal day-to-day activities' see PARA 50.
4 Equality Act 2010 Sch 1 para 2(2). For these purposes, the likelihood of an effect recurring is to be disregarded in such circumstances as may be prescribed: Sch 1 para 2(3). 'Likely' means that recurrence 'could well happen', rather than is more probable than not: *Boyle v SCA Packaging Ltd (Equality and Human Rights Commission intervening)* [2009] UKHL 37, [2009] ICR 1056, [2009] 4 All ER 1181; and *F v Cleveland Police Authority* (2012) UKEAT/0586/11/JOJ at [29], [2012] All ER (D) 52 (May). The likelihood of recurrence should be considered taking all the circumstances of the case into account, including what the person could be reasonably expected to do to prevent the recurrence: see Equality Act 2010 — Guidance on matters to be taken into account in determining questions relating to the definition of disability (2011) para C9. As to the questions that a tribunal should ask itself when considering the Equality Act 2010 Sch 1 para 2(2) see *Swift v Chief Constable of Wiltshire Constabulary* [2004] ICR 909 at [19] et seq, [2004] IRLR 540, EAT.

B. DEEMED DISABILITY

55. Persons of prescribed descriptions deemed to have disabilities.

Regulations may provide for persons of prescribed descriptions to be treated as having disabilities[1]. A person is deemed to have a disability, and hence to be a disabled person, for the purposes of the Equality Act 2010[2], where that person is certified as blind, severely sight impaired, sight impaired or partially sighted by a consultant ophthalmologist[3].

Regulations may also prescribe circumstances in which a person who has a disability is to be treated as no longer having the disability[4].

1 Equality Act 2010 Sch 1 para 7(1). These provisions do not affect the other provisions of Sch 1 (see PARA 47 et seq): Sch 1 para 7(3).
2 See PARA 47 et seq.
3 Equality Act 2010 (Disability) Regulations 2010, SI 2010/2128, reg 7. A 'consultant ophthalmologist' means a consultant or honorary consultant appointed in the medical speciality of ophthalmology, who is employed for the purposes of providing any service as part of the health

service continued under the National Health Service Act 2006 s 1(1), (2) (see HEALTH SERVICES vol 54 (2017) PARA 9), the National Health Service (Wales) Act 2006 s 1(1), (2) (see HEALTH SERVICES vol 54 (2017) PARA 97), the National Health Service (Scotland) Act 1978 s 1(1) or the Health and Social Care (Reform) Act (Northern Ireland) 2009 s 2(1)(a): Equality Act 2010 (Disability) Regulations 2010, SI 2010/2128, reg 2.

4   Equality Act 2010 Sch 1 para 7(2). See note 1.

(iv) Gender Reassignment

56. Protected characteristic of gender reassignment.

A person has the protected characteristic of gender reassignment if the person is proposing to undergo, is undergoing or has undergone a process (or part of a process) for the purpose of reassigning the person's sex by changing physiological or other attributes of sex[1].

In relation to the protected characteristic of gender reassignment a reference to a person who has a particular protected characteristic is a reference to a transsexual person[2]; and a reference to persons who share a protected characteristic is a reference to transsexual persons[3].

1   Equality Act 2010 s 7(1). See also PARA 61. As to protected characteristics generally see PARA 45.
2   A reference to a transsexual person is a reference to a person who has the protected characteristic of gender reassignment: Equality Act 2010 s 7(2).
3   Equality Act 2010 s 7(3).

(v) Marriage and Civil Partnership

57. Protected characteristic of marriage and civil partnership.

A person has the protected characteristic of marriage and civil partnership if the person is married or is a civil partner[1]. In relation to the protected characteristic of marriage and civil partnership a reference to a person who has a particular protected characteristic is a reference to a person who is married or is a civil partner[2]; and a reference to persons who share a protected characteristic is a reference to persons who are married or are civil partners[3].

1   Equality Act 2010 s 8(1). As to protected characteristics generally see PARA 45. As to marriage and civil partnership generally see MATRIMONIAL AND CIVIL PARTNERSHIP LAW vol 72 (2015) PARA 1 et seq.
2   Equality Act 2010 s 8(2)(a).
3   Equality Act 2010 s 8(2)(b).

(vi) Race

58. Protected characteristic of race.

Race includes colour, nationality, ethnic or national origins[1]. In relation to the protected characteristic of race a reference to a person who has a particular protected characteristic is a reference to a person of a particular racial group[2]; and a reference to persons who share a protected characteristic is a reference to persons of the same racial group[3].

The protected characteristic of race does not necessarily include caste, which is an autonomous concept. However, many of the facts relevant in considering caste in many of its forms might be capable of doing so since the term 'ethnic origins' has a wide and flexible ambit, including characteristics determined by 'descent'[4]. A Minister of the Crown must by order amend the Equality Act 2010[5] so as to provide for caste to be an aspect of race; and may by order amend the Act so as to provide for an exception to a provision of the Act to apply, or not to apply, to caste or to apply, or not to apply, to caste in specified circumstances[6].

If a charitable instrument[7] enables the provision of benefits to persons of a class defined by reference to colour, it has effect for all purposes as if it enabled the provision of such benefits to persons of the class which results if the reference to colour is ignored or, if the original class is defined by reference only to colour, to persons generally[8].

1   Equality Act 2010 s 9(1). As to protected characteristics generally see PARA 45. As to what constitutes an 'ethnic group' see *Mandla v Dowell Lee* [1983] 2 AC 548, [1983] 1 All ER 1062 (decided under the Race Relations Act 1976 (repealed)), where the House of Lords held that the two essential characteristics of such a group are:
    (1)   a long shared history, of which the group is conscious as distinguishing it from other groups, and the memory of which it keeps alive; and
    (2)   a cultural tradition of its own, including family and social occasions and manners, often, but not necessarily associated with religious observance.
    The non-essential relevant characteristics were identified as:
    (a)   a common geographical origin, or descent from a small number of common ancestors;
    (b)   a common language, not necessarily peculiar to the group;
    (c)   a common literature peculiar to the group;
    (d)   a common religion different from neighbouring groups or the general community; and
    (e)   being a minority, or an oppressed or dominant group within a larger community.
    The definition may include converts and exclude apostates. Gipsies are a racial group (*Commission for Racial Equality v Dutton* [1989] QB 783, [1989] 1 All ER 306, CA (decided under the Race Relations Act 1976 (repealed))); as are Roma (*European Roma Rights Centre v Immigration Officer at Prague Airport (United Nations High Commissioner for Refugees intervening)* [2004] UKHL 55, [2005] 2 AC 1, [2005] 1 All ER 527 (decided under the Race Relations Act 1976 (repealed))); and Jews (*Seide v Gillette Industries Ltd* [1980] IRLR 427, EAT (decided under the Race Relations Act 1976 (repealed))). English-speaking inhabitants of Wales do not constitute a racial group; the difference in language alone is not sufficient to distinguish them from the Welsh-speaking inhabitants: *Gwynedd County Council v Jones* [1986] ICR 833, EAT (decided under the Race Relations Act 1976 (repealed)). Muslims are not a racial group, but a group defined by religion: *Nyazi v Rymans Ltd* (10 May 1988, unreported) EAT/6/88 (Transcript) (decided under the Race Relations Act 1976 (repealed)). Rastafarians lack a sufficiently long shared history to be a racial group; and the Employment Appeal Tribunal also doubted whether they had a sufficient cultural tradition: *Crown Suppliers (Property Services Agency) v Dawkins* [1991] ICR 583, [1991] IRLR 327, EAT; affd [1993] ICR 517, sub nom *Dawkins v Department of the Environment* [1993] IRLR 284, CA (decided under the Race Relations Act 1976 (repealed)).

2   Equality Act 2010 s 9(2)(a). A 'racial group' is a group of persons defined by reference to race; and a reference to a person's racial group is a reference to a racial group into which the person falls: s 9(3). The fact that a racial group comprises two or more distinct racial groups does not prevent it from constituting a particular racial group: s 9(4).

3   Equality Act 2010 s 9(2)(b).

4   See *Chandhok v Tirkey* [2015] IRLR 195, EAT (person with protected characteristic of race entitled to try to prove alleged caste considerations came within heading 'ethnic or national origins').

5   Ie the Equality Act 2010 s 9 (see the text and notes 1–4).

6   Equality Act 2010 s 9(5) (amended by the Enterprise and Regulatory Reform Act 2013 s 97(1)–(4)). As to the carrying out of a review by a Minister of the Crown of the effect of the Equality Act 2010 s 9(5) (and orders made under it) and whether it remains appropriate see the Enterprise and Regulatory Reform Act 2013 s 97(5)–(10). Orders or regulations under the Equality Act 2010 may include consequential, incidental, supplementary, transitional, transitory or saving provision: s 207(4)(b) (see PARA 4). The power under s 207(4)(b), in its application to s 9(5), includes the power to amend the Equality Act 2010: s 9(6).

7   As to the meaning of 'charitable instrument' see PARA 325 note 5.

8   Equality Act 2010 s 193(4). As to exceptions relating to charities generally see PARA 325.

(vii) Religion and Belief

59. Protected characteristic of religion or belief.

Religion means any religion and a reference to religion includes a reference to a lack of religion[1]. Belief means any religious or philosophical belief and a reference to belief includes a reference to a lack of belief[2]. In relation to the protected characteristic of religion or belief a reference to a person who has a particular protected characteristic is a reference to a person of a particular religion or belief[3]; and a reference to persons who share a protected characteristic is a reference to persons who are of the same religion or belief[4].

1 Equality Act 2010 s 10(1). As to protected characteristics generally see PARA 45.
2 Equality Act 2010 s 10(2). It has been suggested that for a philosophical belief to be protected, it must be worthy of respect in a democratic society, not be incompatible with human dignity and not conflict with the fundamental rights of others: see *Nicholson v Grainger plc* [2010] 2 All ER 253, [2010] ICR 360, EAT (decided under the Equality (Religion or Belief) (Amendment) Regulations 2003, SI 2003/1660). See also *R (Williamson) v Secretary of State for Education and Employment* [2005] UKHL 15, [2005] 2 AC 246, [2005] 2 All ER 1; and *Campbell and Cosans v UK* [1982] ECHR 7511/76, (1982) 4 EHRR 293. Cf Application 47335/06 *Redfearn v United Kingdom* [2012] ECHR 47335/06, [2013] IRLR 51, ECtHR.
   The protection is broad and it is not necessary for a belief to be shared by others in order for it to be a religious belief, nor need a specific belief be a mandatory requirement of an established religion for it to qualify as a religious belief: *Eweida v British Airways plc* [2009] ICR 303, [2009] IRLR 78, EAT (decided under the Employment Equality (Religion or Belief) Regulations 2003, SI 2003/1660). The matters considered in *Eweida v British Airways plc* were subsequently brought before the European Court of Human Rights under the Convention for the Protection of Human Rights and Fundamental Freedoms (Rome, 4 November 1950; TS 71 (1953); Cmd 8969) (the European Convention on Human Rights) art 9 (freedom of religion and belief: see RIGHTS AND FREEDOMS vol 88A (2013) PARA 368): see *Eweida v United Kingdom* [2013] ECHR 48420/10, [2013] All ER (D) 69 (Jan), ECtHR (in which the applicants were employed by local authorities and were dismissed after refusing on religious grounds to officiate at civil partnership ceremonies and to counsel same sex couples, which violated the authorities' non-discrimination policies: the European Court of Human Rights found that the authorities' policies and actions in these matters pursued a legitimate aim and, in balancing the applicant's right to manifest their religious beliefs against the principles of non-discrimination, did not exceed the margin of appreciation). See also *Gareddu v London Underground Ltd* UKEAT/0086/16/DM, [2016] All ER (D) 140 (Dec) (employee had not been genuine in asserting that that he required a five-week period over the summer off work, in order to attend religious festivals with his family, as a manifestation of his religion or belief); *Trayhorn v Secretary of State for Justice* (2017) UKEAT/0304/16/RN, [2017] All ER (D) 97 (Sep).
   'Religion' includes the more commonly recognised religions in the United Kingdom such as the Baha'i faith, Buddhism, Christianity, Hinduism, Islam, Jainism, Judaism, Rastafarianism, Sikhism and Zoroastrianism; it is for the courts to determine what constitutes a religion: Equality Act 2010 Code of Practice — Employment Statutory Code of Practice (2010) para 2.53. Although a religion need not be mainstream or well known to gain protection, it must have a clear structure and belief system: para 2.54. The following beliefs have been recognised by the courts: a belief that an individual should not tell lies under any circumstances (see *Hawkins v Universal Utilities Ltd t/a Unicom* ET/2501234/2012, [2013] EqLR 651); a commitment to public service for the common good (see *Anderson v Chesterfield High School* [2014] EqLR 343)); and left-wing democratic social beliefs (see *Henderson v General Municipal and Boilermakers Union* [2015] IRLR 451, EAT).
3 Equality Act 2010 s 10(3)(a).
4 Equality Act 2010 s 10(3)(b).

(viii) Gender

A. SEX

60. Protected characteristic of sex.

In relation to the protected characteristic of sex, a reference to a person who has a particular protected characteristic is a reference to a man or to a woman[1]; and a reference to persons who share a protected characteristic is a reference to persons of the same sex[2].

1 Equality Act 2010 s 11(a). As to protected characteristics generally see PARA 45.
2 Equality Act 2010 s 11(b). For these purposes 'man' means a male of any age; and 'woman' means a female of any age: s 212(1).

B. GENDER REASSIGNMENT

61. Gender reassignment.

In the case of the protected characteristic of gender reassignment[1], specific provision is made in the following cases:

(1) where a transsexual person[2] who is absent from work because of gender reassignment is treated less favourably than would be the case if the absence was because of sickness or injury[3];

(2) where a person ('A') harasses another ('B') by engaging in unwanted conduct that is related to gender reassignment, where such conduct has the purpose or effect of violating B's dignity or creating an intimidating, hostile, degrading, humiliating or offensive environment for them, and because of B's rejection of or submission to the conduct, B is treated less favourably by A than would have been the case if B had not rejected or submitted to the conduct[4].

Provision is also made in the Equality Act 2010 for exceptions to apply to the prohibition on discrimination because of gender assignment[5] in certain specified cases in respect of marriage[6], separate and single services[7], sport[8], occupational requirements[9] and communal accommodation[10].

1 As to the protected characteristic of gender assignment see PARA 56.
2 As to the meaning of 'transsexual person' see PARA 56 note 2.
3 See the Equality Act 2010 s 16; and PARA 72.
4 See the Equality Act 2010 s 26; and PARA 79.
5 See the Equality Act 2010 s 13, 16, 19; and PARAS 67, 72, 75.
6 See PARA 99.
7 See PARA 100.
8 See PARA 104.
9 See PARAS 160, 161.
10 See PARA 329.

C. PREGNANCY AND MATERNITY

62. Pregnancy and maternity.

In the case of the protected characteristic of pregnancy and maternity[1], specific provision is made:

(1) in cases concerning discrimination at work[2], where:

(a) a person (A), in the protected period[3] in relation to a woman's pregnancy, treats that woman[4] unfavourably because of the pregnancy, or because of illness suffered by her as a result of it[5];

    (b)   A treats her unfavourably because she is on compulsory maternity leave[6];

    (c)   A treats her unfavourably because she is exercising or seeking to exercise, or has exercised or sought to exercise, the right to ordinary or additional maternity leave[7];

(2)   in non-work cases, where a person (A) treats a woman unfavourably because of a pregnancy of hers[8], or where, in the period of 26 weeks beginning with the day on which she gives birth, A treats her unfavourably because she has given birth[9].

Provision is also made in the Equality Act 2010 for pregnancy and maternity equality of terms[10] and for exceptions to apply to the prohibition on discrimination because of pregnancy and maternity[11] in certain specified cases concerning terms of employment whilst on maternity leave[12], the protection of women[13] and restriction on membership of associations on the grounds of health and safety[14].

1   As to pregnancy and maternity as a protected characteristic under the Equality Act 2010 see s 4; and PARA **45**.

2   As to discrimination at work see the Equality Act 2010 Pt 5 (ss 39-83); and PARAS **116**-172.

3   As to the meaning of 'protected period' see PARA **74** note 4.

4   As to the meaning of 'woman' see PARA **60** note 2.

5   See the Equality Act 2010 s 18(2); and PARA **74**.

6   See the Equality Act 2010 s 18(3); and PARA **74**.

7   See the Equality Act 2010 s 18(4); and PARA **74**.

8   See the Equality Act 2010 s 17(2); and PARA **73**.

9   See the Equality Act 2010 s 17(3); and PARA **73**.

10   See PARAS **145–147**.

11   See the Equality Act 2010 s 13, 17–19; and PARAS **67**, **73–75**.

12   See PARA **117** note 4.

13   See PARAS **158**, **197**, **323**.

14   See PARA **206**.

(ix) Sexual Orientation

63. Protected characteristic of sexual orientation.

Sexual orientation means a person's sexual orientation towards persons of the same sex, persons of the opposite sex, or persons of either sex[1]. In relation to the protected characteristic of sexual orientation a reference to a person who has a particular protected characteristic is a reference to a person who is of a particular sexual orientation[2]; a reference to persons who share a protected characteristic is a reference to persons who are of the same sexual orientation[3].

1   Equality Act 2010 s 12(1).

2   Equality Act 2010 s 12(2)(a). As to protected characteristics generally see PARA **45**.

3   Equality Act 2010 s 12(2)(b).

(2) PROTECTED CHARACTERISTICS UNDER OTHER LEGISLATION

(i) Part-time Status

64. Part-time work.
There is a Framework Agreement on Part-time Work implemented by European Union ('EU') legislation[1]. The purpose of the Framework Agreement is:

(1)   to provide for the removal of discrimination against part-time workers and to improve the quality of part-time work[2];

(2)   to facilitate the development of part-time work on a voluntary basis and to contribute to the flexible organisation of working time in a manner which takes into account the needs of employers and workers[3].

The Framework Agreement provides that, in respect of employment conditions, part-time workers must not be treated in a less favourable manner than comparable full-time workers solely because they work part-time, unless different treatment is justified on objective grounds, and where appropriate, the principle of *pro rata temporis* applies[4]. Obstacles which may limit opportunities for part-time work must be reviewed and, where appropriate, eliminated[5]. Employers should give consideration to requests by workers to increase or decrease their working hours, to measures to facilitate access to part-time work at all levels of the enterprise; and, where appropriate, to measures to facilitate access by part-time workers to vocational training[6].

Part-time workers regulations[7] have been made for the purpose of securing that persons in part-time employment are treated for such purposes and to such extent as the regulations may specify, no less favourably than persons in full-time employment[8]. The regulations provide that a part-time worker has the right not to be treated by his employer less favourably than the employer treats a comparable full-time worker as regards the terms of his contract; or by being subjected to any other detriment by any act, or deliberate failure to act, of his employer[9], but the right so conferred applies only if the treatment is on the ground that the worker is a part-time worker, and only if the treatment is not justified on objective grounds[10]. The part-time workers regulations make provision for the treatment of workers becoming part-time or returning part-time after an absence[11]; for an employee's dismissal for applying the regulations to be regarded as unfair[12]; for workers not to be subjected to detriment for applying the regulations[13]; and for complaints to an employment tribunal pursuant to the regulations[14].

1   See the Framework Agreement on Part-time Work concluded on 6 June 1997 between the general cross-industry organisations (the 'Framework Agreement') which is annexed to and implemented by Council Directive (EC) 97/81 (OJ L14, 20.1.98, p 9) concerning the Framework Agreement on part-time work (the 'Part-time Work Directive'): see art 1; and EMPLOYMENT vol 39 (2014) PARA 73. As to the effect of the Part-time Work Directive on an occupational pension based on length of service, in respect of periods of service which had been completed before the Directive had entered into force see *O'Brien v Ministry of Justice* [2017] UKSC 46, [2017] All ER (D) 74 (Jul).

2   See the Framework Agreement cl 1(a).

3   See the Framework Agreement cl 1(b).

4   See the Framework Agreement cl 4; and EMPLOYMENT vol 39 (2014) PARA 73.

5   See the Framework Agreement cl 5(1); and EMPLOYMENT vol 39 (2014) PARA 73. A worker's refusal to transfer from full-time to part-time work should not of itself constitute a valid reason for termination of employment: see the Framework Agreement cl 5(2); and EMPLOYMENT vol 39 (2014) PARA 73.

6   See the Framework Agreement cl 5(3); and EMPLOYMENT vol 39 (2014) PARA 73.

7 Ie the Part-time Workers (Prevention of Less Favourable Treatment) Regulations 2000, SI 2000/1551 (see EMPLOYMENT vol 39 (2014) PARA 75 et seq).
8 The Part-time Workers (Prevention of Less Favourable Treatment) Regulations 2000, SI 2000/1551, which came into force on 1 July 2000, are made under the Employment Act 1999 s 19(1) and implement the Part-time Work Directive: see EMPLOYMENT vol 39 (2014) PARAS 74–75.
9 See the Part-time Workers (Prevention of Less Favourable Treatment) Regulations 2000, SI 2000/1551, reg 5(1); and EMPLOYMENT vol 39 (2014) PARA 76.
10 See the Part-time Workers (Prevention of Less Favourable Treatment) Regulations 2000, SI 2000/1551, reg 5(2); and EMPLOYMENT vol 39 (2014) PARA 76.
11 See the Part-time Workers (Prevention of Less Favourable Treatment) Regulations 2000, SI 2000/1551, regs 3–4; and EMPLOYMENT vol 39 (2014) PARA 77.
12 See the Part-time Workers (Prevention of Less Favourable Treatment) Regulations 2000, SI 2000/1551, reg 7; and EMPLOYMENT vol 39 (2014) PARA 78.
13 See the Part-time Workers (Prevention of Less Favourable Treatment) Regulations 2000, SI 2000/1551, reg 7; and EMPLOYMENT vol 39 (2014) PARA 79.
14 See the Part-time Workers (Prevention of Less Favourable Treatment) Regulations 2000, SI 2000/1551, reg 8; and EMPLOYMENT vol 39 (2014) PARA 80. As to the liability of employers and principals under the regulations, special classes of person under the regulations, and codes of practice see EMPLOYMENT vol 39 (2014) PARAS 81–83.

(ii) Fixed-term Work

65. Fixed-term contracts.

There is a Framework Agreement on Fixed-term Work implemented by European Union ('EU') legislation[1]. The purpose of the Framework Agreement is:
(1)   to improve the quality of fixed-term work by ensuring the application of the principle of non-discrimination[2];
(2)   to establish a framework to prevent abuse arising from the use of successive fixed-term employment contracts or relationships[3].

The Framework Agreement provides that, in respect of employment conditions, fixed-term workers[4] must not be treated in a less favourable manner than comparable permanent workers[5] solely because they have a fixed-term contract or relationship, unless different treatment is justified on objective grounds, and where appropriate, the principle of *pro rata temporis* applies[6]. To prevent abuse arising from the use of successive fixed-term contracts or relationships, member states must, where there are no equivalent legal measures to prevent abuse, introduce one or more of the following measures:
(a)   objective reasons justifying the renewal of such contracts or relationships[7];
(b)   the maximum total duration of successive fixed-term employment contracts or relationships[8];
(c)   the number of renewals of such contracts or relationships[9].

Employers must inform fixed-term workers about vacancies and, as far as possible, are to facilitate access by fixed-term workers to appropriate training opportunities[10].

Fixed-term work regulations[11] have been made for the purpose of securing that employees in fixed-term employment are treated for such purposes and to such extent as the regulations may specify, no less favourably than employees in permanent employment and for the purpose of preventing abuse arising from the use of successive periods of fixed-term employment[12]. The regulations provide that a fixed-term employee has the right not to be treated by his employer less favourably than the employer treats a comparable permanent employee as regards the terms of his contract; or by being subjected to any other detriment by any act, or deliberate failure to act, of his employer[13], however the right so conferred applies only if the treatment is on the ground that the employee is a fixed-term employee, and the treatment is not justified on objective grounds[14]. The fixed-term work regulations make provision for the treatment of successive fixed-term contracts[15]; for an employee's dismissal for applying the regulations to be regarded as unfair[16]; for employees not to be subjected to detriment for applying the regulations[17]; and for complaints to an employment tribunal pursuant to the regulations[18].

1 See the Framework Agreement on Fixed-term Work concluded on 18 March 1999 between the general cross-industry organisations (the 'Framework Agreement') which is annexed to and put into effect by Council Directive (EC) 99/70 (OJ L175, 10.7.99, p 43) concerning the framework agreement on fixed-term work concluded by ETUC, UNICE and CEEP (the 'Fixed-term Work Directive'): see art 1; and EMPLOYMENT vol 39 (2014) PARA 84.
2 See the Framework Agreement cl 1(a); and EMPLOYMENT vol 39 (2014) PARA 84.
3 See the Framework Agreement cl 1(b); and EMPLOYMENT vol 39 (2014) PARA 84.
4 As to the meaning of 'fixed-term worker' see the Framework Agreement cl 3(1); and EMPLOYMENT vol 39 (2014) PARA 84.
5 As to the meaning of 'comparable permanent worker' see the Framework Agreement cl 3(2); and EMPLOYMENT vol 39 (2014) PARA 84.
6 See the Framework Agreement cl 4; and EMPLOYMENT vol 39 (2014) PARA 84.
7 See the Framework Agreement cl 5(1)(a); and EMPLOYMENT vol 39 (2014) PARA 84.
8 See the Framework Agreement cl 5(1)(b); and EMPLOYMENT vol 39 (2014) PARA 84.
9 See the Framework Agreement cl 5(1)(c); and EMPLOYMENT vol 39 (2014) PARA 84.
10 See the Framework Agreement cl 6; and EMPLOYMENT vol 39 (2014) PARA 84.
11 Ie the Fixed-term Employees (Prevention of Less Favourable Treatment) Regulations 2000, SI 2002/2034 (see EMPLOYMENT vol 39 (2014) PARA 86.
12 The Fixed-term Employees (Prevention of Less Favourable Treatment) Regulations 2002, SI 2002/2034, which came into force on 1 October 2002, are made under the Employment Act 2002 s 45(1) for the purposes of implementing the Framework Agreement which is annexed to and put into effect by the Fixed-term Work Directive (see note 1): see EMPLOYMENT vol 39 (2014) PARAS 85–86.
13 See the Fixed-term Employees (Prevention of Less Favourable Treatment) Regulations 2002, SI 2002/2034, reg 3(1); and EMPLOYMENT vol 39 (2014) PARA 87. As to comparable employees see reg 2; and EMPLOYMENT vol 39 (2014) PARA 86.
14 See the Fixed-term Employees (Prevention of Less Favourable Treatment) Regulations 2002, SI 2002/2034, regs 3(3), 4; and EMPLOYMENT vol 39 (2014) PARA 87. As to the right to receive a written statement of reasons for less favourable treatment see reg 5; and EMPLOYMENT vol 39 (2014) PARA 87.
15 See the Fixed-term Employees (Prevention of Less Favourable Treatment) Regulations 2002, SI 2002/2034, reg 8; and EMPLOYMENT vol 39 (2014) PARA 88.
16 See the Fixed-term Employees (Prevention of Less Favourable Treatment) Regulations 2002, SI 2002/2034, reg 6(1), (3); and EMPLOYMENT vol 39 (2014) PARA 89.
17 See the Fixed-term Employees (Prevention of Less Favourable Treatment) Regulations 2002, SI 2002/2034, reg 6(2), (3); and EMPLOYMENT vol 39 (2014) PARA 90.
18 See the Fixed-term Employees (Prevention of Less Favourable Treatment) Regulations 2002, SI 2002/2034, regs 7, 7A; and EMPLOYMENT vol 39 (2014) PARA 91. As to the liability of employers and principals under the regulations; and special and excluded classes of person under the regulations see EMPLOYMENT vol 39 (2014) PARAS 92–94.

(iii) European Convention on Human Rights

66. Protection from discrimination under the European Convention on Human Rights.
The European Convention on Human Rights[1] prohibits discrimination on the grounds of sex, race, colour, language, religion, political or other opinion, national or social origin, association with a national minority, property, birth or

other status (the 'protected grounds')[2]. It is unlawful for any public authority in England and Wales to act incompatibly with this prohibition or with any of the other rights protected under the Convention[3].

1 Ie the Convention for the Protection of Human Rights and Fundamental Freedoms (Rome, 4 November 1950; TS 71 (1953); Cmd 8969 (see PARA 8: and RIGHTS AND FREEDOMS vol 88A (2013) PARA 88).

2 See the European Convention on Human Rights art 14; and PARA 8. See *Steinfeld v Secretary of State for Education* [2017] EWCA Civ 81, [2017] All ER (D) 158 (Feb) (no remedy for heterosexual couples wishing to enter into civil partnership).

3 See PARA 8.

4. PROHIBITED CONDUCT

(1) DISCRIMINATION

(i) Direct and Indirect Discrimination

67. Direct discrimination under the Equality Act 2010.
A person (A) discriminates against another (B) if, because of a protected characteristic[1], A treats B less favourably[2] than A treats or would treat others[3].

If the protected characteristic is disability[4], and B is not a disabled person[5], A does not discriminate against B only because A treats or would treat disabled persons more favourably than A treats B[6]. If the protected characteristic is marriage and civil partnership[7], these provisions apply to a contravention of the provisions on work[8] only if the treatment is because it is B who is married or a civil partner[9]. If the protected characteristic is race[10], less favourable treatment includes segregating B from others[11]. If the protected characteristic is sex[12], less favourable treatment of a woman[13] includes less favourable treatment of her because she is breast-feeding[14]; and in a case where B is a man[15], no account is to be taken of special treatment afforded to a woman in connection with pregnancy or childbirth[16].

1   As to protected characteristics see PARA 45 et seq. As to combined discrimination: dual characteristics see PARA 68. Immigration status is not included in the list of protected characteristics in the Equality Act 2010 s 13 and discrimination on account of an employee's immigration status does not amount to discrimination on account of race: *Taiwo v Olaigbe; Onu v Akwiwu* [2016] UKSC 31, [2016] 1 WLR 2653, [2016] All ER (D) 134 (Jun). See also *R (on the application of Mormoroc) v Secretary of State for Justice* [2017] EWCA Civ 989, 2017 All ER (D) 111 (July): the presumption that a foreign prisoner who had been notified of his liability to deportation, but no decision to deport had been made, was unsuitable to be considered for early release on home detention curfew was not discriminatory under the Equality Act 2010 s 13, or art 14 of the European Convention on Human Rights, as it did not draw a distinction on the grounds of nationality, but on the basis of liability or eligibility to deportation. The characteristic needs to be a cause of the less favourable treatment, but does not need to be the only or even the main cause: Employment Statutory Code of Practice (2010) para 3.11. If the complainant received less favourable treatment because of a protected characteristic, direct discrimination is established; conscious motivation is not required: *Nagarajan v London Regional Transport* [2000] 1 AC 501, [1999] 4 All ER 65, HL (decided under the Race Relations Act 1976 (repealed)). See also *R (on the application of E) v Governing Body of JFS (Secretary of State for Children, School and Families, interested parties) (United Synagogue intervening)* [2009] UKSC 15, [2010] 2 AC 728, [2010] 1 All ER 319 (decided under the Race Relations Act 1976 (repealed)). Where there are mixed motives for less favourable treatment, and the unlawful motive or motives are a sufficient weight in the decision-making process to be treated as a cause of the treatment, there will be unlawful discrimination: *O'Donoghue v Redcar and Cleveland Borough Council* [2001] EWCA Civ 701, [2001] IRLR 615, [2001] All ER (D) 192 (May) (decided under the Sex Discrimination Act 1975 (repealed)). In a case where discrimination is not inherent in the impugned act, direct discrimination is made out where the motivation for that act, conscious or unconscious, was the claimant possessed the protected characteristic: *Geller v Yeshurun Hebrew Congregation* [2016] ICR 1028, [2016] All ER (D) 229 (Mar), EAT. See also *Reynolds v CLFIS (UK) Ltd* [2015] EWCA Civ 439, [2015] All ER (D) 20 (May); and *Tainted Dismissals*, Spencer Keen: 165 NLJ 7662, p 14. See *R (on the application of Coll) v Secretary of State for Justice (Howard League for Penal Reform intervening)* [2017] UKSC 40, [2017] 1 WLR 2093, [2017] All ER (D) 142 (May), where the court declared that the provision of approved premises for prisoners released on licence in England and Wales by the respondent Secretary of State constituted direct discrimination against woman which was unlawful unless justified and no justification had been shown by the Secretary of State.

2   See the text and notes 10–14. As to comparison of cases see PARA 77.
    Whether a person is afforded less favourable treatment than another is a matter to be determined objectively: *James v Eastleigh Borough Council* [1990] 2 AC 751, [1990] 2 All ER 607,

[1990] ICR 554, HL (decided under the Sex Discrimination Act 1975 (repealed)); applied in *Hall v Bull* [2012] EWCA Civ 83, [2012] 2 All ER 1017, [2012] 1 WLR 2514; affd [2013] UKSC 73, [2014] 1 All ER 919. See also *Black v Wilkinson*[2013] EWCA Civ 820, [2013] 4 All ER 1053; *Interim Executive Board of X School v Her Majesty's Chief Inspector of Education, Children's Services and Skills* [2016] EWHC 2813 (Admin), [2016] All ER (D) 105 (Nov). It is not enough to show simply that the complainant has been treated differently; there must be a quality in the treatment that enables the complainant reasonably to complain about it: *Khan v Chief Constable of West Yorkshire Police* [2001] UKHL 48 at [76], [2001] 4 All ER 834, sub nom *Chief Constable of West Yorkshire Police v Khan* [2001] ICR 1063 at [76] (decided under the Race Relations Act 1976 (repealed)). However, a complainant does not need to have suffered economic loss in order to demonstrate less favourable treatment: *Khan v Chief Constable of West Yorkshire Police* at [52]. The fact that a complainant considers that she or he is being less favourably treated does not of itself establish that there is less favourable treatment: *Burrett v West Birmingham Health Authority* [1994] IRLR 7, EAT (decided under the Sex Discrimination Act 1975 (repealed)). In *R (on the application of C) v Secretary of State for Work and Pensions* [2017] UKSC 72, [2017] All ER (D) 170 (Oct), it was held that the policy of the Department for Work and Pensions (DWP) of holding information on its centralised database about a customer, including name, former name and Gender Recognition Certificate, for the life of the individual concerned and for 50 years and a day thereafter, did not treat transgender customers less favourably than others on the database and was accordingly not discriminatory under the Equality Act 2010 s 13. See also the Employment Statutory Code of Practice (2010) para 3.4 et seq. As to hypothetical comparators generally see para 3.24 et seq.

3 Equality Act 2010 s 13(1). As to the irrelevance of an alleged discriminator's characteristics see PARA 78. Section 13 is subject to s 17(6) (see PARA 73) and s 18(7) (see PARA 74): s 13(8).

4 As to the protected characteristic of disability see PARAS 47–55.

5 As to the meaning of 'disabled person' see PARA 47.

6 Equality Act 2010 s 13(3).

7 As to the protected characteristic of marriage and civil partnership see PARA 57.

8 Ie the Equality Act 2010 Pt 5 (ss 39–83) (work: see PARAS 116–172).

9 Equality Act 2010 s 13(4).

10 As to the protected characteristic of race see PARA 58. See also *Taiwo v Olaigbe; Onu v Akwiwu* [2016] UKSC 31, [2016] 1 WLR 2653, [2016] All ER (D) 134 (Jun) (cited in note 1).

11 Equality Act 2010 s 13(5).

12 As to the protected characteristic of sex see PARA 60. See also *HM Chief Inspector of Education, Children's Services and Skills v Interim Executive Board of Al-Hijrah School (Secretary of State for Education intervening)* [2017] EWCA Civ 1426, [2017] All ER (D) 79 Oct (it was direct discrimination, contrary to the Equality Act 2010 ss 13, 85 (see PARA 173) for a mixed-sex school to have complete segregation of male and female pupils over a certain age for all lessons, breaks, school clubs and trips).

13 As to the meaning of 'woman' see PARA 60 note 2.

14 Equality Act 2010 s 13(6)(a). This does not apply for the purposes of Pt 5: s 13(7).

15 As to the meaning of 'man' see PARA 60 note 2.

16 Equality Act 2010 s 13(6)(b). 'Special treatment afforded to women in connection with pregnancy or childbirth' must be construed as referring only to treatment accorded to a woman so far as it constitutes a proportionate means of achieving the legitimate aim of compensating her for the disadvantages occasioned by her pregnancy or her maternity leave: see *Eversheds Legal Services Ltd v de Belin* (2011) UKEAT/0352/10/JOJ, UKEAT/0444/10/JOJ, [2011] ICR 1137, [2011] IRLR 448, EAT (the Equality Act 2010 s 13(6)(b) did not justify automatically giving the maximum score to an employee on maternity leave in a redundancy exercise, which resulted in the redundancy of a male employee who otherwise would have been retained). See Case C-7/12 *Riezniece v Zemkopibas minisrija* [2013] IRLR 828, ECJ (redundancy selection procedure unlawful where performance of woman returning from maternity leave based on assessment earlier than others in pool).

68.   Combined discrimination: dual characteristics.

As from a day to be appointed[1], the following provisions have effect.

A person (A) discriminates against another (B) if, because of a combination of two relevant protected characteristics, A treats B less favourably than A treats or would treat a person who does not share either of those characteristics[2]. The relevant protected characteristics are:

(1)   age[3];
(2)   disability[4];
(3)   gender reassignment[5];
(4)   race[6];
(5)   religion or belief[7];
(6)   sex[8];
(7)   sexual orientation[9].

For the purposes of establishing a contravention of these provisions[10], B need not show that A's treatment of B is direct discrimination because of each of the characteristics in the combination (taken separately)[11]. But B cannot establish such a contravention if, in reliance on another provision[12] or any other enactment, A shows that A's treatment of B is not direct discrimination because of either or both of the characteristics in the combination[13].

A Minister of the Crown may by order amend these provisions so as to:

(a)   make further provision about circumstances in which B can, or in which B cannot, establish[14] a contravention[15];

(b)   specify other circumstances in which the provisions[16] do not apply[17].

1   The provisions of the Equality Act 2010 s 14 come into force on a day to be appointed. At the date at which this volume states the law no such day had been appointed and the government has announced that it has decided not to bring forward this provision. There is existing case law on dual discrimination which has been applied in cases both before and after the inception of the Equality Act 2010. In *Bahl v the Law Society* [2004] EWCA Civ 1070, [2004] IRLR 799 the Court of Appeal explicitly ruled that each ground of alleged discrimination had to be separately considered, and a ruling made in respect of each, even if the claimant had experienced them as inextricably linked. Since then, cases have been allowed that depend on two factors to be used: see *Ministry of Defence v DeBique* [2010] IRLR 471, [2009] All ER (D) 258 (Nov). See also *Mandla v Dowell Lee* [1983] 2 AC 548, [1983] 1 All ER 1062 (where only a male Sikh would be disadvantaged); *Burton and Rhule v De Vere Hotels* [1997] ICR 1, [1996] IRLR 596 (two distinct and separate torts of sex discrimination and race discrimination); *Nwoke v Government Legal Service and Civil Service Comrs* [1996] 28 EOR 6, [1996] IT/43021/94.

2   Equality Act 2010 s 14(1) (not yet in force). The provisions of s 14(1) do not apply to a combination of characteristics that includes disability in circumstances where, if a claim of direct discrimination because of disability were to be brought, it would come within s 116 (special educational needs: see PARA 356): s 14(5) (not yet in force). As to the irrelevance of the alleged discriminator's characteristics see s 24(2); and PARA 78. The references to direct discrimination are to a contravention of the Act by virtue of s 13 (see PARA 67): s 14(7) (not yet in force).

3   As to the protected characteristic of age see PARA 46.

4   As to the protected characteristic of disability see PARAS 47–55.

5   As to the protected characteristic of gender reassignment see PARAS 56, 61.

6   As to the protected characteristic of race see PARA 58.

7   As to the protected characteristic of religion or belief see PARA 59.

8   As to the protected characteristic of sex see PARA 60.

9   Equality Act 2010 s 14(2) (not yet in force). As to the protected characteristic of sexual orientation see PARA 63.

10   Ie by virtue of the Equality Act 2010 s 14(1) (see the text and notes 1–2).

11   Equality Act 2010 s 14(3) (not yet in force).

12   Ie of the Equality Act 2010.

13   Equality Act 2010 s 14(4) (not yet in force).

14   See note 10.

15   See note 12.

16   Ie the Equality Act 2010 s 14(1) (see the text and notes 1–2).

17   Equality Act 2010 s 14(6) (not yet in force).

69. Direct discrimination justifiable in case of age.

If the protected characteristic is age[1], A does not discriminate against B[2] if A can show A's treatment of B to be a proportionate means of achieving a legitimate aim[3].

1   As to the protected characteristic of age see PARA 46. As to protected characteristics generally see PARA 45 et seq.
2   Ie under the Equality Act 2010 s 13(1) (see PARA 67).
3   Equality Act 2010 s 13(2). The questions of 'legitimate aim' and 'proportionate means' must be considered as separate issues, and not conflated: *MacCulloch v Imperial Chemical Industries plc* [2008] ICR 1334 at [26], [2008] IRLR 846 at [26], EAT (decided under the Employment Equality (Age) Regulations 2006, SI 2006/1031). The approach to justification of direct age discrimination is different from that of indirect discrimination: *Seldon v Clarkson Wright and Jakes* [2012] UKSC 16, [2012] 3 All ER 1301, [2012] ICR 716. As to indirect discrimination see PARA 75. Direct discrimination may only be justified if the relevant act seeks to achieve a legitimate aim of a public interest nature related to employment policy, the labour market and vocational training, in contrast with reasons individual to the situation to the particular employer, such as cost reduction; this is a narrower test than for justification of indirect discrimination: *Seldon v Clarkson Wright and Jakes* at [54]–[55], [73]. Cf Case no C-141/11 *Hornfeldt v Posten Meddelande AB* [2013] All ER (EC) 593, [2012] IRLR 785, ECJ. See *Seldon v Clarkson Wright & Jakes (No 2)* [2014] IRLR 748, EAT (aims of retention and workforce planning objectively justified particular retirement age of 65 for partners in firm of solicitors); *Lockwood v Department of Work and Pensions* [2013] EWCA Civ 1195, [2014] 1 All ER 250 (voluntary redundancy scheme, allowing higher payments to older employees on basis that they encountered greater difficulties in reacting to loss of employment, proportionate means of achieving legitimate aim).

70. Discrimination in relationships that have ended.

A person (A) must not discriminate against another (B) if the discrimination arises out of and is closely connected to a relationship which used to exist between them[1] and conduct of a description constituting the discrimination would, if it occurred during the relationship, contravene the equality provisions[2].

1   Equality Act 2010 s 108(1)(a). It does not matter whether the relationship ends before or after the commencement of s 108 (ie 1 October 2010, by virtue of the Equality Act 2010 (Commencement No 4, Savings, Consequential, Transitional, Transitory and Incidental Provisions and Revocation) Order 2010, SI 2010/2317): Equality Act 2010 s 108(3).
2   Equality Act 2010 s 108(1)(b). The equality provisions are the Equality Act 2010: as to direct discrimination under the Equality Act 2010 see PARA 67. Conduct is not a contravention of s 108 in so far as it also amounts to victimisation of B by A: s 108(7). As to post-termination of employment victimisation see *Jessemey v Rowstock Ltd* [2014] EWCA Civ 185, [2014] 3 All ER 409; *Taiwo v Olaigbe; Onu v Akwiwu* [2016] UKSC 31, [2016] 1 WLR 2653, [2016] All ER (D) 134 (Jun). As to victimisation see PARA 81.

71. Discrimination arising from disability.

A person (A) discriminates against a disabled person[1] (B) if A treats B unfavourably because of something arising in consequence of B's disability[2], and A cannot show that the treatment is a proportionate means of achieving a legitimate aim[3]. These provisions do not apply if A shows that A did not know, and could not reasonably have been expected to know, that B had the disability[4].

1   As to the meaning of 'disabled person' see PARA 47. As to direct discrimination see PARA 67.
2   As to the meaning of 'disability' see PARA 47. Unfavourable treatment need not be 'because' of a person's disability for there to be discrimination arising from disability: *Williams v Ystrad Mynach College* (Case 1600019/2011) [2012] EqLR 89 at [65]. Cf 'unfavourably' with 'less favourably' in the Equality Act 2010 s 13 (see PARA 67).
    There must be a connection between whatever led to the unfavourable treatment and the disability: Employment Statutory Code of Practice (2010) para 5.8.
    Liability for discrimination 'arising from disability' no longer depends on a requirement to use a non-disabled comparator: *Wickland (Holdings) Ltd v Telchadder* [2012] EWCA Civ 635 at [44], [2012] HLR 564, [2012] All ER (D) 51 (Jun) (revsd on other grounds [2014] UKSC 57, [2015] 1

P & CR 133, [2014] All ER (D) 51 (Nov)); *Burnip v Birmingham City Council; Trengove v Walsall Metropolitan Council; Gorry v Wiltshire Council* [2012] EWCA Civ 629 at [13], [2012] LGR 954. Cf *Lewisham London Borough Council v Malcolm* [2008] UKHL 43, [2008] 1 AC 1399, [2008] 4 All ER 525, in which the House of Lords held that the appropriate comparator in a case of disability-related discrimination under the Disability Discrimination Act 1995 s 3A(1) was a non-disabled person who was otherwise in the same circumstances as the disabled claimant. The narrow construction introduced by *Lewisham London Borough Council v Malcolm* was reversed by the introduction of the Equality Act 2010 s 15 (see the text and notes 3–4). See also *Khan v Chief Constable of West Yorkshire Police* [2001] UKHL 48, [2001] 4 All ER 834, sub nom *Chief Constable of West Yorkshire Police v Khan* [2001] ICR 1063 (see PARA 67 note 2); *IPC Media Ltd v Millar* [2013] IRLR 707, EAT; *Grosset v City of York Council* UKEAT/0015/16/BA, [2016] All ER (D) 186 (Nov); *Visram v ICTS (UK) Ltd* (2017) UKEAT/0344/15/LA, [2017] All ER (D) 229 (Jul) See also Employment Statutory Code of Practice (2010) para 5.6.

3   Equality Act 2010 s 15(1). This protection against discrimination arising from disability is in addition to s 13 (see PARA 67) and s 19 (see PARA 75).

Although the Equality Act 2010 does not define 'proportionate means of achieving a legitimate aim', the term is taken from European Union law: Employment Statutory Code of Practice (2010) paras 4.28, 4.31. The aim should be legal, should not be discriminatory in itself and must represent a real, objective consideration: para 4.28. The health, welfare and safety of individuals may qualify as legitimate aims, as may reasonable business needs and economic efficiency, however, an employer solely aiming to reduce costs cannot expect to satisfy the test: paras 4.28–4.29. Even if the aim is legitimate, the means of achieving it must also be proportionate: paras 4.30–4.31.

Less favourable treatment will be incapable of objective justification where there was an obviously less discriminatory means of achieving the same legitimate aim: see *Williams v Ystrad Mynach College* (Case 1600019/2011, 12 August 2011, unreported) at [85]–[86].

4   Equality Act 2010 s 15(2).

72. Absence from work due to gender reassignment.

A person (A) discriminates against a transsexual person[1] (B) if, in relation to an absence of B's that is because of gender reassignment[2], A treats B less favourably than A would treat B if B's absence was because of sickness or injury[3], or B's absence was for some other reason and it is not reasonable for B to be treated less favourably[4].

1   As to the meaning of 'transsexual person' see PARA 56 note 2.
2   As to the meaning of 'gender reassignment' see PARA 56. A person's absence is 'because of gender reassignment' if it is because the person is proposing to undergo, is undergoing or has undergone the process (or part of the process) mentioned in the Equality Act 2010 s 7(1) (see PARA 56): s 16(3).
3   Equality Act 2010 s 16(2)(a). These provisions have effect for the purposes of Pt 5 (ss 39–83) (work: see PARAS 116–172) to the protected characteristic of gender reassignment: s 16(1). As to protected characteristics generally see PARA 45 et seq; and as to the protected characteristic of gender reassignment see PARA 56. See also PARA 61.
4   Equality Act 2010 s 16(2)(b). See note 3.

73. Pregnancy and maternity discrimination; non-work cases.

A person (A) discriminates against a woman[1] if A treats her unfavourably because of a pregnancy of hers[2]. A discriminates against a woman if, in the period of 26 weeks beginning with the day on which she gives birth, A treats her unfavourably because she has given birth[3].

The provisions relating to direct discrimination[4], so far as relating to sex discrimination[5], do not apply[6] to anything done in relation to a woman in so far as it is because of a pregnancy of hers[7] or because she has given birth[8].

1   As to the meaning of 'woman' see PARA 60 note 2.
2   Equality Act 2010 s 17(2). These provisions have effect for the purposes of the application to the protected characteristic of pregnancy and maternity of Pt 3 (ss 28–31) (services and public functions: see PARAS 84–104); Pt 4 (ss 32–38) (premises: see PARAS 105–115); Pt 6 (ss 84–99)

(education: see PARAS **173–197**); and Pt 7 (ss 100–107) (associations: see PARAS **198–210**): Equality Act 2010 s 17(1). As to the protected characteristics generally see PARA **45** et seq.

3 Equality Act 2010 s 17(3). For these purposes, the day on which a woman gives birth is the day on which she gives birth to a living child; or she gives birth to a dead child (more than 24 weeks of the pregnancy having passed): s 17(5).

   The reference in s 17(3) to treating a woman unfavourably because she has given birth includes, in particular, a reference to treating her unfavourably because she is breast-feeding: s 17(4).

4 Ie the Equality Act 2010 s 13 (see PARA **67**).

5 For these purposes 'sex discrimination' is discrimination within the Equality Act 2010 s 13 (see PARA **67**) because of sex; and discrimination within s 19 (see PARA **75**) where the relevant protected characteristic is sex: s 25(8).

6 Equality Act 2010 s 17(6).

7 Ie under the Equality Act 2010 s 17(2) (see the text and note 2).

8 Ie under the Equality Act 2010 s 17(3) (see the text and note 3).

74. Pregnancy and maternity discrimination; work cases.

The following provisions have effect for the purposes of the application of the provisions of the Equality Act 2010 relating to work[1] to the protected characteristic of pregnancy and maternity[2]. A person (A) discriminates against a woman[3] if, in the protected period[4] in relation to a pregnancy of hers[5], A treats her unfavourably because of the pregnancy, or because of illness suffered by her as a result of it[6]. A discriminates against a woman if A treats her unfavourably because she is on compulsory maternity leave[7]. A discriminates against a woman if A treats her unfavourably because she is exercising or seeking to exercise, or has exercised or sought to exercise, the right to ordinary or additional maternity leave[8].

The direct discrimination provisions of the 2010 Act[9], so far as relating to sex discrimination[10], do not apply to treatment of a woman in so far as it is in the protected period in relation to her and it is because of the pregnancy[11], or because of illness suffered by her as a result of it[12]; or it is because she is on compulsory maternity[13] leave or is exercising or seeking to exercise, or has exercised or sought to exercise[14] the right to ordinary or additional maternity leave[15].

1 Ie the Equality Act 2010 Pt 5 (ss 39–83) (see PARAS **116–172**).

2 Equality Act 2010 s 18(1).

3 As to the meaning of 'woman' see PARA **60** note 2.

4 The 'protected period', in relation to a woman's pregnancy, begins when the pregnancy begins, and ends if she has the right to ordinary and additional maternity leave, at the end of the additional maternity leave period or (if earlier) when she returns to work after the pregnancy; or if she does not have that right, at the end of the period of two weeks beginning with the end of the pregnancy: Equality Act 2010 s 18(6). See *Lyons v DWP/Jobcentre Plus* Case No 2202190/11 (post-natal depression; held that there was no direct pregnancy/maternity discrimination under the Equality Act 2010 s 18 as the case did not fall within the scope of the beginning of pregnancy to the end of maternity leave). A reference to a woman on maternity leave is a reference to a woman on compulsory maternity leave, ordinary maternity leave, or additional maternity leave: s 213(1), (2). A reference to a woman on compulsory maternity leave is a reference to a woman absent from work because she satisfies the conditions prescribed for the purposes of the Employment Rights Act 1996 s 72(1) (see EMPLOYMENT vol 40 (2014) PARA 355): Equality Act 2010 s 213(3). A reference to a woman on ordinary maternity leave is a reference to a woman absent from work because she is exercising the right to ordinary maternity leave: s 213(4). A reference to the right to ordinary maternity leave is a reference to the right conferred by the Employment Rights Act 1996 s 71(1) (see EMPLOYMENT vol 40 (2014) PARA 355): Equality Act 2010 s 213(5). A reference to a woman on additional maternity leave is a reference to a woman absent from work because she is exercising the right to additional maternity leave: s 213(6). A reference to the right to additional maternity leave is a reference to the right conferred by the Employment Rights Act 1996 s 73(1) (see EMPLOYMENT vol 40 (2014) PARA 355): Equality Act 2010 s 213(7). 'Additional maternity leave period' has the meaning given in the Employment Rights Act 1996 s 73(2) (see EMPLOYMENT vol 40 (2014) PARA 355): Equality Act 2010 s 213(8).

5   There is no protection under the Equality Act 2010 for discrimination by association; ie where the complainant is treated unfavourably because of a partner's pregnancy, see *Kulikaoskas v MacDuff Shellfish* UKEATS/62/09, [2011] ICR 48, EAT (where, in a case decided under the Sex Discrimination Act 1975 (repealed), it was held that EU law did not allow for a claim of associative discrimination under the Act).

6   Equality Act 2010 s 18(2). For these purposes, if the treatment of a woman is in implementation of a decision taken in the protected period, the treatment is to be regarded as occurring in that period (even if the implementation is not until after the end of that period): s 18(5).

    As to examples of 'unfavourable treatment' see the Employment Statutory Code of Practice (2010) paras 8.21–8.23. Cf 'unfavourably' with 'less favourably' in the Equality Act 2010 s 13 (see PARA 67).

7   Equality Act 2010 s 18(3).

8   Equality Act 2010 s 18(4).

9   Ie the Equality Act 2010 s 13 (see PARA 67).

10 As to the meaning of 'sex discrimination' see PARA 73 note 5.

11 Ie under the Equality Act 2010 s 18(2)(a) (see the text and note 6).

12 Ie under the Equality Act 2010 s 18(2)(b) (see the text and note 6).

13 Ie under the Equality Act 2010 s 18(3) (see the text and note 7).

14 Ie under the Equality Act 2010 s 18(4) (see the text and note 8).

15 Equality Act 2010 s 18(7).

75.   Indirect discrimination under the Equality Act 2010.

A person (A) discriminates against another (B) if A applies to B a provision, criterion or practice[1] which is discriminatory in relation to a relevant protected characteristic of B's[2].

For these purposes, a provision, criterion or practice is discriminatory in relation to a relevant protected characteristic of B's if:

(1)   A applies, or would apply, it to persons with whom B does not share the characteristic[3];

(2)   it puts, or would put, persons with whom B shares the characteristic at a particular disadvantage when compared with persons with whom B does not share[4];

(3)   it puts, or would put, B at that disadvantage[5]; and

(4)   A cannot show it to be a proportionate means of achieving a legitimate aim[6].

It is not necessary for a claimant in an indirect discrimination claim to show more than the fact that a particular provision, criterion or practice disadvantages both them and the group sharing their protected characteristic. Whereas it had been held that it was also necessary to show why the disadvantage occurred and that it was somehow connected with the relevant protected characteristic, the Supreme Court has now definitively stated that the extra step of proving that the causation of the disadvantage derives from the protected characteristic is not required[7].

1   'Provision, criterion or practice' is not defined by the Equality Act 2010 but should be construed widely to include, for example, any formal or informal policies, rules, practices, arrangements, criteria, conditions, prerequisites, qualifications or provisions: see the Employment Statutory Code of Practice (2010) para 4.5. A 'practice' cannot be a one-off; it must have an element of repetition about it: see *Nottingham City Transport Ltd v Harvey* (2012) UKEAT/0032/12/JOJ, [2013] All ER (D) 267 (Feb). In *R (on the application of C) v Secretary of State for Work and Pensions* [2017] UKSC 72, [2017] All ER (D) 170 (Oct), it was held that the policy of the Department for Work and Pensions (DWP) of holding information on its centralised database about a customer, including name, former name and Gender Recognition Certificate, for the life of the individual concerned and for 50 years and a day thereafter, did not treat transgender customers less favourably than others on the database and was accordingly not discriminatory under the Equality Act 2010 s 13. See generally Employment Statutory Code of Practice (2010) para 4.5 et seq.

2   Equality Act 2010 s 19(1). The relevant protected characteristics are: age (see PARA 46), disability (see PARAS 47–55), gender reassignment (see PARA 56), marriage and civil partnership (see PARA

57), race (see PARA 58), religion or belief (see PARA 59), sex (see PARA 60) and sexual orientation (see PARA 63): Equality Act 19(3).

3   Equality Act 2010 s 19(2)(a).

4   Equality Act 2010 s 19(2)(b). As to comparison by reference to circumstances under s 19 see PARA 77; and Employment Statutory Code of Practice (2010) para 4.17 et seq.

5   Equality Act 2010 s 19(2)(c). The wording 'would put' allows challenges to provisions, criteria or practices which have not yet been applied but which would have a discriminatory effect if they were applied: Employment Statutory Code of Practice (2010) para 4.7.

The Equality Act 2010 does not define 'disadvantage'. It could include a denial of an opportunity or choice, deterrence, rejection or exclusion; the disadvantage does not have to be quantifiable: see the Employment Statutory Code of Practice (2010) para 4.9. As to examples of a disadvantage in this context see para 4.10 et seq. It is a typical feature of indirect discrimination that some members of the disadvantaged group will not in fact suffer the disadvantage: *Essop v Home Office (UK Border Agency), Naeem v Secretary of State for Justice* [2017] UKSC 27, [2017] 3 All ER 551, [2017] 1 WLR 1343.

6   Equality Act 2010 s 19(2)(d). This test of proportionality must be read in light of, and comply with, the jurisprudence of the Court of Justice of the European Union in relation to the former Equal Treatment Directive (see now Parliament and Council Directive (EC) 2006/54 (OJ L204, 26.7.2006, p 23) on the implementation of the principle of equal opportunities and equal treatment of men and women in matters of employment and occupation; and PARA 12): *Homer v Chief Constable of West Yorkshire Police* [2012] UKSC 15 at [22], [2012] 3 All ER 1287, [2012] ICR 704. As to the Equal Treatment Directive (ie Parliament and Council Directive (EC) 2006/54 (OJ L204, 26.7.2006, p 23) on the implementation of the principle of equal opportunities and equal treatment of men and women in matters of employment and occupation) see PARA 12. The test should be approached in two stages (see the Employment Statutory Code of Practice (2010) para 4.27. See also PARA 71 note 3):

(1)   is the aim of the provision, criterion or practice legal and non-discriminatory, and one that represents a real, objective consideration?; and

(2)   if the aim is legitimate, is the means of achieving it proportionate — ie, appropriate and necessary in all the circumstances?.

To be proportionate, a measure has to be both an appropriate means of achieving the legitimate aim and (reasonably) necessary in order to do so: *Homer v Chief Constable of West Yorkshire Police* at [22]. Applying this test entails a comparison of the impact of the provision, criterion or practice upon the affected group as against the importance of the aim to the employer; to some extent, the answer depends on whether there were non-discriminatory alternatives available: *Homer v Chief Constable of West Yorkshire Police* at [24]–[25]. See also *Harrod v Chief Constable of West Midlands Police* [2017] EWCA Civ 191, [2017] All ER (D) 13 (Apr) (an employer's decision about how to allocate his resources, and specifically his financial resources, should constitute a 'legitimate aim' even if it was shown that he could have afforded to make a different allocation with a lesser impact on the class of employee in question); *R (on the application of Unison) v Lord Chancellor* [2017] UKSC 51; [2017] All ER (D) 174 (Jul) (charging higher employment tribunal fees for claims which were brought by a higher proportion of women than men (type B claims) had not been shown to be a proportionate means of achieving the stated aims of the fees regime). See also *Trayhorn v Secretary of State for Justice* (2017) UKEAT/0304/16/RN, [2017] All ER (D) 97 (Sep) (employment tribunal did not err in holding that any restriction on claimant's religious belief was a proportionate means of achieving the legitimate aim of maintaining order and safety in a prison). In *R (on the application of C) v Secretary of State for Work and Pensions* [2017] UKSC 72, [2017] All ER (D) 170 (Oct), in a claim of indirect discrimination against persons who had undergone gender reassignment, it was held that a policy carried out by the Department for Work and Pensions setting out special procedures for dealing with the records of certain categories of customer which required extra protection (the SCR policy) was a proportionate means of achieving a legitimate aim for the purpose of the Equality Act 2010 s 19(2)(d).

7   See *Essop v Home Office (UK Border Agency), Naeem v Secretary of State for Justice* [2017] UKSC 27, [2017] 3 All ER 551, [2017] 1 WLR 1343.

(ii) Failure to Make Adjustments for Disabled Persons

76. Failure to make reasonable adjustments.

The duty imposed by the Equality Act 2010[1] to make reasonable adjustments for disabled persons[2] is comprised of three requirements[3]; and a failure to comply with those requirements is a failure to comply with the duty to make reasonable adjustments[4].

A person ('A') discriminates against a disabled person if A fails to comply with that duty in relation to that person[5].

1 Ie imposed by the Equality Act 2010 s 20 (see PARAS **237, 245**).
2 As to the duty to make reasonable adjustments for disabled persons see the Equality Act 2010 ss 20–22, Schs 2, 4, 8, 13, 15, 21; and PARA 237 et seq.
3 As to the three requirements see the Equality Act 2010 s 20; and PARAS **237, 245**.
4 See the Equality Act 2010 s 21(1): and PARA **238**.
5 See the Equality Act 2010 s 21(2): and PARA **238**. There is power to make regulations in relation to the duty to make reasonable adjustments: see s 22; and PARA **237**.

(iii) Comparison by Reference to Circumstance

77. Comparison.

In a comparison of cases for the purposes of the provisions on direct discrimination[1], combined discrimination[2] or indirect discrimination[3] there must be no material difference between the circumstances relating to each case[4]. The circumstances relating to a case include a person's abilities if:

(1)   on a comparison for the purposes of the direct discrimination provisions[5], the protected characteristic[6] is disability[7];

(2)   on a comparison for the purposes of the combined discrimination provisions[8], one of the protected characteristics in the combination is disability[9].

If the protected characteristic is sexual orientation[10], the fact that one person (whether or not the person referred to as B) is a civil partner while another is married to a person of the opposite sex is not a material difference between the circumstances relating to each case[11]. If the protected characteristic is sexual orientation, the fact that one person (whether or not the person referred to as B) is married to a person of the same sex while another is married to a person of the opposite sex is not a material difference between the circumstances relating to each case[12].

1 Ie the Equality Act 2010 s 13 (see PARA **67**).
2 Ie the Equality Act 2010 s 14 (see PARA **68**).
3 Ie the Equality Act 2010 s 19 (see PARA **75**).
4 Equality Act 2010 s 23(1).
5 See note 1.
6 As to protected characteristics under the Equality Act 2010 see PARAS **45–63**.
7 Equality Act 2010 s 23(2)(a). As to the protected characteristic of disability see PARAS **47–55**.
8 See note 2.
9 Equality Act 2010 s 23(2)(b).
10 As to the protected characteristic of sexual orientation see PARA **63**.
11 Equality Act 2010 s 23(3) (amended by the Marriage (Same Sex Couples) Act 2013 Sch 7 para 43(1), (2)). See *Bull v Hall* [2013] UKSC 73, [2014] 1 All ER 919, [2013] 1 WLR 3471.
12 Equality Act 2010 s 23(4) (added by the Marriage (Same Sex Couples) Act 2013 Sch 7 para 43(1), (3)). A hypothetical comparator may be used: *Shamoon v Chief Constable of the Royal Ulster Constabulary* [2003] UKHL 11, [2003] NI 174, [2003] 2 All ER 26 (decided under the Sex Discrimination (Northern Ireland) Order 1976, SI 1976/1042).

(iv) Irrelevance of Alleged Discriminator's Characteristics

78. Irrelevance of characteristics.

For the purpose of establishing a contravention of the Equality Act 2010 by virtue of the provisions on direct discrimination[1] it does not matter whether the person (A)[2] has the protected characteristic[3].

For the purpose of establishing a contravention of the Equality Act 2010 by virtue of the provisions on combined discrimination[4] it does not matter whether A has one of the protected characteristics in the combination[5]; or whether A has both[6].

1   Ie the Equality Act 2010 s 13(1) (see PARA 67).
2   Ie the person (A) who discriminates against another (B) (see PARA 67).
3   Equality Act 2010 s 24(1). As to protected characteristics under the Equality Act 2010 see PARAS 45–63.
4   Ie the Equality Act 2010 s 14(1) (see PARA 68).
5   Equality Act 2010 s 24(2)(a).
6   Equality Act 2010 s 24(2)(b).

(2) HARASSMENT

79. Harassment.

A person (A) harasses[1] another (B) if:
(1)   A engages in unwanted conduct[2] related to a relevant protected characteristic[3], and the conduct has the purpose or effect of[4]:
    (a)   violating B's dignity[5]; or
    (b)   creating an intimidating, hostile, degrading, humiliating or offensive environment for B[6]; or
(2)   A engages in unwanted conduct of a sexual nature[7]; and the conduct has the purpose or effect referred to in head (1)[8]; or
(3)   A or another person engages in unwanted conduct of a sexual nature or that is related to gender reassignment[9] or sex[10], that conduct has the purpose or effect referred to head (1)[11] and because of B's rejection of or submission to the conduct, A treats B less favourably than A would treat B if B had not rejected or submitted to the conduct[12].

1   As to general guidance on the meaning of 'harassment' and the way in which a case of harassment should be approached see *Dhaliwal v Richmond Pharmacology* [2009] ICR 724, [2009] IRLR 336, EAT (decided under the Race Relations Act 1976 (repealed)). In *Dhaliwal v Richmond Pharmacology* at [22], the EAT warned against encouraging 'a culture of hypersensitivity or the imposition of legal liability in respect of every unfortunate phrase'. See also *Heafield v Times Newspapers Ltd* (2013) UKEATPA/1305/12/BA, [2013] NLJR 235, [2013] All ER (D) 265 (Feb); *Lindsay v London School of Economics and Political Science* [2013] EWCA Civ 1650, [2014] IRLR 218.
2   The Equality Act 2010 does not define 'unwanted conduct'. It covers a wide range of behaviour, including spoken or written words or abuse, imagery, graffiti, physical gestures, facial expressions, mimicry, jokes, pranks, acts affecting a person's surroundings or other physical behaviour: Employment Statutory Code of Practice (2010) para 7.7. For these purposes 'unwanted' means essentially the same as 'unwelcome' or 'uninvited'; it does not mean that express objection must be made to the conduct before it is deemed be unwanted: para 7.8. See also *Reed and Bull Information Systems Ltd v Stedman* [1999] IRLR 299, EAT (decided under the Sex Discrimination Act 1975 (repealed)); *Insitu Cleaning Co Ltd v Heads* [1995] IRLR 4, EAT (decided under the Sex Discrimination Act 1975 (repealed)). If the 'unwanted conduct' is alleged to be inaction, it must be shown that the inaction had the effect of creating the proscribed environment: *Conteh v Parking Partners Ltd* (2011) UKEAT/0288/10, [2011] ICR 341, [2011] EqLR 332, [2011] All ER (D) 223 (Feb), EAT.

3 Equality Act 2010 s 26(1)(a). For these purposes the relevant protected characteristics are: age (see PARA 46), disability (see PARA 47 et seq), gender reassignment (see PARA 56), race (see PARA 58), religion or belief (see PARA 59), sex (see PARA 60) and sexual orientation (see PARA 63): Equality Act 2010 s 26(5). As to examples of conduct 'related to' a protected characteristic see the Employment Statutory Code of Practice (2010) para 7.9 et seq.

4 It is not necessary to establish both 'purpose' and 'effect'; if the purpose of subjecting the worker to the conduct is to create any of the circumstances in head (1) in the text, that will be sufficient to establish unlawful harassment: see Employment Statutory Code of Practice (2010) paras 7.16–7.17.

5 Equality Act 2010 s 26(1)(b)(i).

6 Equality Act 2010 s 26(1)(b)(ii). It may be that third party behaviour has created an intimidating, hostile, degrading, humiliating or offensive environment in part, but the actions of an employer, to whom those third parties are not responsible, has made it worse, in which case the environment might be said to have been created by the actions of both: *Conteh v Parking Partners Ltd* (2011) UKEAT/0288/10, [2011] ICR 341, [2011] EqLR 332, EAT.

7 Equality Act 2010 s 26(2)(a). See note 2. Conduct 'of a sexual nature' can cover verbal, non-verbal or physical conduct including unwelcome sexual advances, touching, forms of sexual assault, sexual jokes, displaying pornographic photographs or drawings or sending emails with material of a sexual nature: Employment Statutory Code of Practice (2010) para 7.13.

8 Equality Act 2010 s 26(2)(b). See the text and notes 5–6. In deciding whether conduct has the effect referred to head (1)(a), (b) in the text, each of the following must be taken into account (s 26(4)):
    (1)   the perception of B; and
    (2)   the other circumstances of the case; and
    (3)   whether it is reasonable for the conduct to have that effect.

9 As to the protected characteristic of gender reassignment see PARA 56. See also PARA 61.

10 Equality Act 2010 s 26(3)(a). As to the protected characteristic of sex see PARA 60.

11 Equality Act 2010 s 26(3)(b). See the text and notes 5–7, 9.

12 Equality Act 2010 s 26(3)(c).

80. Harassment in relationships that have ended.

A person (A) must not harass another (B) if the harassment arises out of and is closely connected to a relationship which used to exist between them[1] and conduct of a description constituting the harassment would, if it occurred during the relationship, contravene the equality provisions[2].

1 Equality Act 2010 s 108(2)(a). It does not matter whether the relationship ends before or after the commencement of s 108 (ie 1 October 2010, by virtue of the Equality Act 2010 (Commencement No 4, Savings, Consequential, Transitional, Transitory and Incidental Provisions and Revocation) Order 2010, SI 2010/2317): Equality Act 2010 s 108(3).

2 Equality Act 2010 s 108(1)(b). The equality provisions are the Equality Act 2010; as to harassment under the Equality Act 2010 see PARA 79. Conduct is not a contravention of s 108 in so far as it also amounts to victimisation of B by A: s 108(7). As to victimisation see PARA 81.

(3) VICTIMISATION

81. Victimisation.

A person (A) victimises another person (B) if A subjects B to a detriment[1] because B does a protected act, or A believes that B has done, or may do, a protected act[2].

Each of the following is a 'protected act'[3]: (1) bringing proceedings under the Equality Act 2010[4]; (2) giving evidence or information in connection with proceedings under the 2010 Act[5]; (3) doing any other thing for the purposes of or in connection with the 2010 Act[6]; (4) making an allegation, whether or not express, that A or another person has contravened the 2010 Act[7].

Giving false evidence or information, or making a false allegation, is not a protected act if the evidence or information is given, or the allegation is made, in bad faith[8].

1 A 'detriment' does not include conduct which amounts to harassment: Equality Act 2010 s 212(1). As to examples of detriment see the Employment Statutory Code of Practice (2010) para 9.8 et seq. Enduring physical or psychological injury may, depending on the circumstances, constitute 'detriment': see *Jiad v Byford* [2003] EWCA Civ 135 at [21], [2003] IRLR 232 (decided under the Race Relations Act 1976 (repealed)). An employer does not cause 'detriment' by the honest and reasonable conduct of its defence to the protected proceedings: see *Derbyshire v St Helens Metropolitan Borough Council* [2007] UKHL 16, [2007] 3 All ER 81, [2007] ICR 841 (decided under the Sex Discrimination Act 1975 (repealed)).
    As to the requirement on employers not to victimise a person or employee see the Equality Act 2010 s 39(3), (4); and PARA 117.
2 Equality Act 2010 s 27(1). Section 27 applies only where the person subjected to a detriment is an individual: s 27(4). Where s 27 is applied by s 85(4) or s 85(5) (victimisation of pupils by schools: see PARA 175) the references to 'B' in s 27(1) include a reference to a parent or sibling of the child in question: s 86(1), (2). In the context of s 86, 'child' means a person who has not attained the age of 18; and 'sibling' means a brother or sister, a half-brother or half-sister, or a stepbrother or stepsister: s 86(5).
    Victimisation does not require conscious motivation on the part of the perpetrator: see *Nagarajan v London Regional Transport* [2000] 1 AC 501, [1999] 4 All ER 65, HL (decided under the Race Relations Act 1976 (repealed)). A tribunal is permitted to deal with a claim of victimisation at the same time as one of discrimination, but it must ensure that it can justify its decisions on both issues: *Durrani v Ealing LBC* [2013] All ER (D) 218 (Sep), EAT.
3 Equality Act 2010 s 27(2). As to other 'protected acts' in the context of pay discussions see also s 77(4); and PARA 148.
4 Equality Act 2010 s 27(2)(a).
5 Equality Act 2010 s 27(2)(b).
6 Equality Act 2010 s 27(2)(c).
7 Equality Act 2010 s 27(2)(d). In general, a reference to a contravention of the Equality Act 2010 does not include a reference to a breach of an equality clause or rule, unless there is express provision to the contrary: see s 212(9). In s 27, the reference to contravening the Equality Act 2010 includes a reference to committing a breach of an equality clause or rule: s 27(5). A reference to a breach of an equality clause or rule is a reference to a breach of a term modified by, or included by virtue of, an equality clause or rule: s 212(8). As to the meanings of 'equality clause' and 'equality rule' see PARA 117 note 4. As to equality clauses or rules generally see PARA 136 et seq.
8 Equality Act 2010 s 27(3). Where s 27 is applied by s 85(4) or (5) (victimisation of pupils by schools: see PARA 175), giving false evidence or information, or making a false allegation, in good faith is not a protected act in a case where the evidence or information is given, or the allegation is made, by a parent or sibling of the child and the child has acted in bad faith (s 86(3)), and giving false evidence or information, or making a false allegation, in bad faith, is a protected act in a case where the evidence or information is given, or the allegation is made, by a parent or sibling of the child and the child has acted in good faith (s 86(4)).

(4) ANCILLARY AND THIRD PARTY CONDUCT

82. Instructing, causing or inducing contraventions.

A person (A) must not instruct another (B) to do in relation to a third person (C) anything which contravenes the provisions on services and public functions[1], premises[2], work[3], education[4] or associations[5], the provisions in connection with relationships that have ended[6], or the provision relating to aiding contraventions[7]. This is referred to as a 'basic contravention', and a person (A) also must not cause or induce[8] another (B) to do in relation to a third person (C) anything which is a basic contravention[9]. These provisions apply only if the relationship between A and B is such that A is in a position to commit a basic contravention in relation to B[10].

Proceedings for a contravention of these provisions may be brought by either B or C[11], or by the Equality and Human Rights Commission[12]. For the purpose of bringing proceedings it does not matter whether the basic contravention occurs or any other proceedings are, or may be, brought in relation to A's conduct[13].

1　Ie the Equality Act 2010 Pt 3 (ss 28–31) (see PARAS 84–104).
2　Ie the Equality Act 2010 Pt 4 (ss 32–38) (see PARAS 105–115).
3　Ie the Equality Act 2010 Pt 5 (ss 39–83): (see PARAS 116–172).
4　Ie the Equality Act 2006 Pt 6 (ss 84–99) (see PARAS 173–197).
5　Ie the Equality Act 2006 Pt 7 (ss 100–107) (see PARAS 198–210).
6　Ie the Equality Act 2006 s 108(1), (2) (see PARAS 70, 80).
7　Equality Act 2010 s 111(1). The provision relating to aiding contraventions is s 112(1) (see PARA 83).
8　Inducement may be direct or indirect: Equality Act 2010 s 111(4). A reference in s 111 to causing or inducing a person to do something includes a reference to attempting to cause or induce the person to do it: s 111(8).
9　Equality Act 2010 s 111(2), (3).
10　Equality Act 2010 s 111(7).
11　Ie proceedings may be brought by B, if B is subjected to a detriment as a result of A's conduct (Equality Act 2010 s 111(5)(a)) or by C, if C is subjected to a detriment as a result of A's conduct (s 111(5)(b)).
12　Equality Act 2010 s 111(5)(c). As to the Commission see PARAS 28–44.
13　Equality Act 2010 s 111(6).

83. Aiding contraventions of the Equality Act 2010.

A person (A) must not knowingly help another (B) to do anything which contravenes the provisions of the Equality Act 2010 on services and public functions[1], premises[2], work[3], education[4] or associations[5], the provisions in connection with relationships that have ended[6], or the provisions relating to instructing, causing or inducing contraventions[7]. This is referred to as a 'basic contravention'[8]. It is not a contravention of these provisions if A relies on a statement by B that the act for which the help is given does not contravene the equality provisions[9] and it is reasonable for A to do so[10].

1　Ie the Equality Act 2010 Pt 3 (ss 28–31) (see PARAS 84–104).
2　Ie the Equality Act 2010 Pt 4 (ss 32–38) (see PARAS 105–115).
3　Ie the Equality Act 2010 Pt 5 (ss 39–83) (see PARAS 116–172).
4　Ie the Equality Act 2006 Pt 6 (ss 84–99) (see PARAS 173–197).
5　Ie the Equality Act 2006 Pt 7 (ss 100–107) (see PARAS 198–210).
6　Ie the Equality Act 2006 s 108(1), (2) (see PARAS 70, 80).
7　Equality Act 2010 s 112(1). The provision relating to instructing, causing or inducing contraventions is s 111 (see PARA 82).
8　Equality Act 2010 s 112(1). The reference in s 112(1) to a basic contravention does not include a reference to disability discrimination in contravention of Pt 6 Ch 1 (ss 84–89) (schools: see PARAS 173–175): s 112(6).
9　Equality Act 2010 s 112(2)(a). The equality provisions are the provisions of the Equality Act 2010. B commits an offence if B knowingly or recklessly makes a statement mentioned in s 112(2)(a) which is false or misleading in a material respect: s 112(3). A person guilty of an offence under s 112(3) is liable on summary conviction to a fine not exceeding level 5 on the standard scale: s 112(4). As to the powers of magistrates' courts to issue fines on summary conviction see SENTENCING vol 92 (2015) PARA 176.
10　Equality Act 2010 s 112(2)(b).

5. SERVICES AND PUBLIC FUNCTIONS

(1) APPLICATION OF THE EQUALITY ACT 2010 TO SERVICES AND PUBLIC FUNCTIONS

84. Application of Part 3 of the Equality Act 2010.

Part 3 of the Equality Act 2010[1], which prohibits discrimination, harassment and victimisation by people who supply services (which includes goods and facilities) or perform public functions, does not apply to:

(1)   the protected characteristic of age[2], so far as relating to persons who have not attained the age of 18[3];

(2)   the protected characteristic of marriage and civil partnership[4];

(3)   discrimination[5], harassment[6] or victimisation[7] that is prohibited by the provisions in the Equality Act 2010[8] relating to premises[9], work[10] or education[11], or that would be so prohibited but for an express exception[12];

(4)   a breach of an equality clause or rule[13];

(5)   anything that would be a breach of an equality clause or rule but for[14] the defence of material factor[15] or an occupational pension scheme[16];

(6)   a breach of a non-discrimination rule[17].

1   Ie the Equality Act 2010 Pt 3 (ss 28–31) (see PARA 85 et seq).

2   As to the protected characteristic of age see PARA 46. As to protected characteristics generally see PARA 45 et seq.

3   Equality Act 2010 s 28(1)(a). Nothing in s 28 is to be regarded as an express exception: s 212(13).

4   Equality Act 2010 s 28(1)(b). See note 3. As to the protected characteristic of marriage and civil partnership see PARA 57.

5   As to direct discrimination see the Equality Act 2010 s 13; and PARA 67; and as to indirect discrimination see s 19; and PARA 75.

6   As to harassment see PARA 79.

7   As to victimisation see PARA 81.

8   Equality Act 2010 s 28(2)(a). See note 3.

9   Ie the Equality Act 2010 Pt 4 (ss 32–38): see PARAS 105–115.

10   Ie the Equality Act 2010 Pt 5 (ss 39–83): see PARAS 116–172.

11   Ie the Equality Act 2010 Pt 6 (ss 84–99) (see PARAS 173–197).

12   Equality Act 2010 s 28(2)(b). See note 3. The effect of this provision is that if an act of discrimination, harassment or victimisation is made unlawful by other Parts of the Equality Act 2010 covering premises, work or education, then those provisions, rather than the provisions covering services and public functions, apply. A reference (however expressed) to an act includes a reference to an omission; and a reference (however expressed) to an omission includes (unless there is express provision to the contrary) a reference to: a deliberate omission to do something, a refusal to do it, a failure to do it: s 212(2), (3).

13   Equality Act 2010 s 28(3)(a). See note 3. The effect of this is that if the act in question results in a breach of an equality clause in a person's terms of work or a non-discrimination rule in an occupational pension scheme, Pt 3 will not apply. As to the meanings of 'equality clause' and 'equality rule' see PARA 117 note 4. As to the meaning of 'breach of an equality clause or rule' see PARA 81 note 7. As to equality clauses or rules generally see PARA 136 et seq.

14   Equality Act 2010 s 28(3)(b). See note 3.

15   Ie under the Equality Act 2010 s 69 (see PARA 142)

16   Ie under the Equality Act 2010 Sch 7 Pt 2 (paras 3–6) (see PARAS 139–140).

17   Equality Act 2010 s 28(3)(c). See note 3. As to the meaning of 'non-discrimination rule' see PARA 134 notes 4–10.

(2) PROVISION OF SERVICES AND EXERCISE OF PUBLIC FUNCTIONS

85. Provision of services: discrimination.

A person (a 'service provider') concerned with the provision of a service[1] to the public or a section of the public[2], for payment or not, must not discriminate[3] against a person requiring the service[4] by not providing the person with the service[5]. A service-provider (A) must not, in providing the service, discriminate against a person (B) as to the terms on which A provides the service to B[6]; by terminating the provision of the service to B[7]; or by subjecting B to any other detriment[8].

1 Although the Equality Act 2010 does not define 'service', a wide range of services are covered. As to a non-exhaustive list of 'services' see the Equality Act 2010 Code of Practice — Services, Public Functions and Associations Statutory Code of Practice (2010) para 11.3. Services are covered regardless of whether they are provided by a private, voluntary or public body: para 11.5. A reference to the 'provision of a service' includes:
   (1)   a reference to the provision of goods or facilities (Equality Act 2010 s 31(1), (2));
   (2)   a reference to the provision of a service in the exercise of a public function (s 31(1), (3)).
A 'public function' is a function that is a function of a public nature for the purposes of the Human Rights Act 1998: Equality Act 2010 s 31(1), (4). As to a function of a public nature for the purposes of the Human Rights Act 1998 see RIGHTS AND FREEDOMS vol 88A (2013) PARA 26. Public functions are not only carried out by public authorities and may also be carried out by private or voluntary organisations (eg prisons): Equality Act 2010 Code of Practice — Services, Public Functions and Associations Statutory Code of Practice (2010) para 11.14. As to an illustrative list of actions covered by 'public function' see para 11.16.
   As to more specific examples of 'services, goods or facilities' see *Farah v Metropolitan Police Comr* [1998] QB 65, [1997] 1 All ER 289, CA (assistance by police officer) (decided under the Race Relations Act 1976 (repealed)); *Savjani v IRC* [1981] QB 458, [1981] 1 All ER 1121, CA (tax advice from a tax officer) (decided under the Race Relations Act 1976 (repealed)); *Tejani v Superintendent Registrar for the District of Peterborough* [1986] IRLR 502, CA (registration of births, deaths and marriages) (decided under the Race Relations Act 1976 (repealed)); *Jones v Royal Liver Friendly Society* (1982) Times, 2 December, CA (ability to stand for election to the governing body of a friendly society) (decided under the Sex Discrimination Act 1975 (repealed)); *R v North West Lancashire Health Authority, ex p A* (21 December 1998, unreported) (affd [2000] 1 WLR 977, (1999) Times, 24 August, [1999] All ER (D) 911, CA) (surgical treatment) (decided under the Sex Discrimination Act 1975 (repealed)); *Bain v Bowles* [1991] IRLR 356, CA (provision of advertising space) (decided under the Sex Discrimination Act 1975 (repealed)); *Conwell v Newham London Borough Council* [2000] 1 All ER 696, [2000] ICR 42, EAT (child in care) (decided under the Race Relations Act 1976 (repealed)); *Hall v Bull* [2012] EWCA Civ 83, [2012] 2 All ER 1017 (affd [2013] UKSC 73, [2014] 1 All ER 919) (hotel services); *Southern Pacific Mortgage Ltd v V* [2015] EW Misc B42 (CC) (provision of loans); and *Paulley v FirstGroup plc* [2017] UKSC 4, [2017] 2 All ER 1, [2017] 1 WLR 423 (bus services).
   Where an employee arranges for another person to provide a service only to the employer's employees, the employer is not to be regarded as the service-provider, but the employees are to be regarded as a section of the public: Equality Act 2010 s 31(1), (5).
   In the application of s 29, so far as relating to race or religion or belief, to the granting of entry clearance (within the meaning of the Immigration Act 1971: see IMMIGRATION AND ASYLUM vol 57 (2012) PARA 28), it does not matter whether an act is done within or outside the United Kingdom: Equality Act 2010 s 29(9). 'United Kingdom' means Great Britain and Northern Ireland: Interpretation Act 1978 s 5, Sch 1. 'Great Britain' means England, Scotland and Wales: Union with Scotland Act 1706 preamble art I; Interpretation Act 1978 s 22(1), Sch 2 para 5(a). Neither the Channel Islands nor the Isle of Man are within the United Kingdom. See further CONSTITUTIONAL AND ADMINISTRATIVE LAW vol 20 (2014) PARA 3. The Equality Act 2010 s 29(9) does not affect the application of any other provision of the Act to conduct outside England and Wales or Scotland: s 29(10). 'England' means, subject to any alteration of the boundaries of local government areas, the area consisting of the counties established by the Local Government Act 1972 s 1 (see LOCAL GOVERNMENT vol 69 (2009) PARAS 5, 24), and Greater London and the Isles of Scilly: Interpretation Act 1978 Sch 1. 'Wales' means the combined area of the counties which were created by the Local Government Act 1972 s 20 (as originally enacted) (see LOCAL GOVERNMENT vol 69 (2009) PARAS 5, 37), but subject to any alteration made under s 73 (consequential alteration

of boundary following alteration of watercourse) (see LOCAL GOVERNMENT vol 69 (2009) PARA 90): Interpretation Act 1978 Sch 1 (definition substituted by the Local Government (Wales) Act 1994 s 1(3), Sch 2 para 9). As to local government areas see LOCAL GOVERNMENT vol 69 (2009) PARA 22 et seq; and as to boundary changes see LOCAL GOVERNMENT vol 69 (2009) PARA 56 et seq. As to Greater London see LONDON GOVERNMENT vol 71 (2013) PARA 14.

    In relation to the provision of a service by either House of Parliament, the service-provider is the Corporate Officer of the House concerned; and if the service involves access to, or use of, a place in the Palace of Westminster which members of the public are allowed to enter, both Corporate Officers are jointly the service-provider: Equality Act 2010 s 31(1), (8).

2   Examples of cases in which goods, facilities or services were not held to be provided to the public or a section of it include: *Charter v Race Relations Board* [1973] AC 868, [1973] 1 All ER 512, HL (a Conservative club) (decided under the Race Relations Act 1968 (repealed)); *Dockers' Labour Club and Institute Ltd v Race Relations Board* [1976] AC 285, [1974] 3 All ER 592, HL (a working men's club, which belonged to a union of clubs) (decided under the Race Relations Act 1968 (repealed)).

    Examples of cases in which goods, facilities or services have been held to be provided to the public or a section of it include: *Gill v El Vino Co Ltd* [1983] QB 425, [1983] 1 All ER 398, CA (wine bars) (decided under the Sex Discrimination Act 1975 (repealed)); *Bateson v YMCA* [1980] NI 135 (snooker rooms) (decided under the Sex Discrimination (Northern Ireland) Order 1976, SI 1976/1042); *Alexander v Home Office* [1988] 2 All ER 118, [1988] 1 WLR 968, CA (prisons) (decided under the Race Relations Act 1976 (repealed)). See also *James v Eastleigh Borough Council* [1990] 2 AC 751, [1990] ICR 554, HL (unlawful for a section of the public to be defined in a way that incorporates discrimination) (decided under the Sex Discrimination Act 1975 (repealed)).

3   As to direct discrimination see PARA 67; and as to indirect discrimination see PARA 75.

4   A reference to a 'person requiring a service' includes a reference to a person who is seeking to obtain or use the service: Equality Act 2010 s 31(1), (6).

5   Equality Act 2010 s 29(1). A reference to a 'service-provider not providing a person with a service' includes a reference to the service-provider not providing the person with a service of the quality that the service-provider usually provides to the public (or the section of it which includes the person); or the service-provider not providing the person with the service in the manner in which, or on the terms on which, the service-provider usually provides the service to the public (or the section of it which includes the person): s 31(1), (7).

    As to exceptions to s 29 see PARAS **91–104**

6   Equality Act 2010 s 29(2)(a).

7   Equality Act 2010 s 29(2)(b).

8   Equality Act 2010 s 29(2)(c).

86. Provision of services: harassment.

A service-provider[1] must not, in relation to the provision of the service[2], harass[3] a person requiring the service[4], or a person to whom the service-provider provides the service[5].

1   As to service-providers see PARA 85.

2   As to the provision of a service see PARA 85 note 1.

3   As to harassment see the Equality Act 2010 s 26; and PARA 79. In the application of s 26 for the purposes of s 29(3) (see the text and notes 4–5) and s 29(6) (see PARA 88), neither religion or belief, nor sexual orientation is a relevant protected characteristic: s 29(8). As to the protected characteristic of religion or belief see PARA 59; and as to the protected characteristic of sexual orientation see PARA 63.

    Where the Equality Act 2010 disapplies a prohibition on harassment in relation to a specified protected characteristic, the disapplication does not prevent conduct relating to that characteristic from amounting to a detriment for the purposes of discrimination within s 13 because of that characteristic: s 212(5).

4   Equality Act 2010 s 29(3)(a). As to the meaning of 'person requiring the service' see PARA 85 note 4.

5   Equality Act 2010 s 29(3)(b).

87.   Provision of services: victimisation.

A service-provider[1] must not victimise[2] a person requiring the service[3] by not providing the person with the service[4]. A service-provider (A) must not, in providing the service, victimise a person (B) as to the terms on which A provides the service to B[5]; by terminating the provision of the service to B[6]; or by subjecting B to any other detriment[7].

1   As to service-providers see PARA 85.
2   As to victimisation see the Equality Act 2010 s 27; and PARA 81.
3   As to the meaning of 'person requiring the service' see PARA 85 note 4.
4   Equality Act 2010 s 29(4). As to the application of s 29 to the granting of entry clearance see PARA 85 note 1. As to the meaning of 'service-provider not providing a person with a service' see PARA 85 note 5.
5   Equality Act 2010 s 29(5)(a).
6   Equality Act 2010 s 29(5)(b).
7   Equality Act 2010 s 29(5)(c).

88.   Public function that is not provision of service.

A person must not, in the exercise of a public function[1] that is not the provision of a service[2] to the public or a section of the public[3], do anything that constitutes discrimination[4], harassment[5] or victimisation[6].

1   As to the meaning of 'public function' see PARA 85 note 1.
2   As to the meaning of 'provision of a service' see PARA 85 note 1.
3   As to examples of a 'section of the public' see PARA 85 note 2.
4   As to direct discrimination see PARA 67; and as to indirect discrimination see PARA 75.
5   As to harassment see the Equality Act 2010 s 26; and PARA 79. See also s 29(8); and PARA 86 note 3.
6   Equality Act 2010 s 29(6). A person does not contravene s 29(6), so far as relating to the protected characteristic of sex, if he does anything he must do pursuant to a requirement of an enactment: see Sch 22 para 1(1); and PARA 92. As to sex as a protected characteristic see PARA 60. As to victimisation see s 27; and PARA 81. As to the application of s 29 to the granting of entry clearance see PARA 85 note 1. This provision is broad and would cover refusing to allow someone to benefit from the exercise of a function or treating someone in a worse manner in the exercise of a function: see Equality Act 2010 Code of Practice — Services, Public Functions and Associations Statutory Code of Practice (2010) para 11.26.

89.   Ships and hovercraft.

Part 3 of the Equality Act 2010[1] applies only in such circumstances as are prescribed in relation to transporting people by ship or hovercraft[2]; or a service provided on a ship or hovercraft[3]. It does not matter whether the ship or hovercraft is within or outside the United Kingdom[4].

1   Ie the Equality Act 2010 ss 28–31 (see PARA 84 et seq).
2   Equality Act 2010 s 30(1)(a). 'Prescribed' means prescribed by regulations: s 212(1). At the date at which this volume states the law no such regulations had been made, but a number of enactments have been applied for these purposes as set out in the Equality Act 2010 (Commencement No 4, Savings, Consequential, Transitional, Transitory and Incidental Provisions and Revocation) Order 2010, SI 2010/2317, art 10, Schs 1, 2. For these purposes 'ship' has the same meaning as in the Merchant Shipping Act 1995 (see SHIPPING AND MARITIME LAW vol 93 (2017) PARA 229): Equality Act 2010 s 30(4). 'Hovercraft' has the same meaning as in the Hovercraft Act 1968 (see SHIPPING AND MARITIME LAW vol 93 (2017) PARA 381): Equality Act 2010 s 30(5).
    The Equality Act 2010 s 29(6) (exercise of a public function that is not the provision of a service: see PARA 88) applies in relation to the matters mentioned in s 30(1)(a), (b) (see note 3); but in so far as it relates to disability discrimination, s 29(6) applies to those matters only in such circumstances as are prescribed: s 30(2). At the date at which this volume states the law no such regulations had been prescribed. 'Disability discrimination' is discrimination within s 13 (see PARA 67) because of disability; discrimination within s 15 (see PARA 71); discrimination within s 19 (see

PARA 75) where the relevant protected characteristic is disability; discrimination within s 21 (see PARA 238): s 25(2). As to the meaning of 'disability' and as to the protected characteristic of disability see PARAS 47–55.

3   Equality Act 2010 s 30(1)(b). Nothing in s 30 affects the application of any other provision of the Equality Act 2010 to conduct outside England and Wales or Scotland: s 30(6). As to the meanings of 'England' and 'Wales' see PARA 85 note 1.

4   Equality Act 2010 s 30(3). As to the meaning of 'United Kingdom' see PARA 85 note 1.

(3) DUTY TO MAKE REASONABLE ADJUSTMENTS

90. Duty to make reasonable adjustments for disabled persons.

A duty to make reasonable adjustments for disabled persons[1] applies to a service-provider[2] and to a person who exercises a public function[3] that is not the provision of a service[4] to the public or a section of the public[5]. In this respect such persons are required to comply with first, second and third requirements set out in the Equality Act 2010[6], namely:

(1)   Where a provision, criterion or practice of the association's puts a disabled person at a substantial disadvantage in relation to a relevant matter in comparison with persons who are not disabled, the association is required to take such steps as it is reasonable to have to take to avoid the disadvantage[7].

(2)   Where a physical feature puts a disabled person at a substantial disadvantage in relation to a relevant matter in comparison with persons who are not disabled, the association is required to take such steps as it is reasonable to have to take to avoid the disadvantage[8].

(3)   Where a disabled person would, but for the provision of an auxiliary aid, be put at a substantial disadvantage in relation to a relevant matter in comparison with persons who are not disabled, the association is required to take such steps as it is reasonable to have to take to provide the auxiliary aid[9].

The full details of the steps which service-providers and persons who exercise public functions must take in order to make reasonable adjustments are set out elsewhere in this title[10].

1   As to the duty to make reasonable adjustments for disabled persons see further PARA 237 et seq.
2   Equality Act 2010 s 29(7)(a). As to service-providers see PARA 85. See also the Equality Act 2010 s 55(7); and PARA 155.
3   As to the meaning of 'public function' see PARA 85 note 1.
4   As to the meaning of 'provision of a service' see PARA 85 note 1.
5   Equality Act 2010 s 29(7)(b). As to examples of a 'section of the public' see PARA 85 note 2.
6   Equality Act 2010 s 31(9), Sch 2 para 1.
7   See the Equality Act 2010 s 20(3); and PARA 237.
8   See the Equality Act 2010 s 20(4); and PARA 237.
9   See the Equality Act 2010 s 20(5); and PARA 237.
10   See PARAS 239–240.

(4) EXCEPTIONS IN RELATION TO SERVICES AND PUBLIC FUNCTIONS

91. Constitutional matters.

The provisions in the Equality Act 2010 on the provision of services[1] do not apply to the following:

(1) the exercise of a function of Parliament[2] or a function exercisable in connection with proceedings in Parliament[3];

(2) preparing, making or considering an Act of Parliament[4], a Bill for an Act of Parliament[5], an Act of the National Assembly for Wales[6] or a Bill for an Act of the National Assembly for Wales[7];

(3) preparing, making, approving or considering a Measure of the National Assembly for Wales[8] or a proposed Measure of the National Assembly for Wales[9];

(4) preparing, making, confirming, approving or considering an instrument which is made under an enactment[10] by a Minister of the Crown[11]; the Welsh Ministers, the First Minister for Wales or the Counsel General to the Welsh Government[12];

(5) preparing, making, confirming, approving or considering an instrument[13] concerning the Church of England made by the General Synod[14];

(6) the preparation, making, consideration, approval or confirmation of an instrument made by Her Majesty in Council[15] or the Privy Council[16];

(7) anything done in connection with the imposition of a requirement or condition which comes within certain[17] statutory exceptions[18];

(8) a judicial function[19];

(9) anything done on behalf of, or on the instructions of, a person exercising a judicial function[20];

(10) a decision not to commence or continue criminal proceedings[21];

(11) anything done for the purpose of reaching, or in pursuance of, a decision not to commence or continue criminal proceedings[22];

(12) so far as relating to relevant discrimination[23], anything done for the purpose of ensuring the combat effectiveness of the armed forces[24];

(13) the Security Service[25], the Secret Intelligence Service[26], the Government Communications Headquarters[27], or a part of the armed forces which is, in accordance with a requirement of the Secretary of State, assisting the Government Communications Headquarters[28].

1 Ie the Equality Act 2010 s 29 (see PARA 84 et seq). As to exceptions from the Equality Act 2010 generally, and as to further exceptions in specific circumstances, see PARAS 320–338.
2 Equality Act 2010 s 31(1), (10), Sch 3 para 1(1)(a). Sch 3 para 1(1) does not permit anything to be done to or in relation to an individual unless it is done by or in pursuance of a resolution or other deliberation of either House or a Committee of either House: Sch 3 para 1(2).
   As to the power of a minister to amend these provisions see Sch 3 para 35.
3 Equality Act 2010 Sch 3 para 1(1)(b). See note 2.
4 Equality Act 2010 Sch 3 para 2(1)(a).
5 Equality Act 2010 Sch 3 para 2(1)(b).
6 Equality Act 2010 Sch 3 para 2(1)(e). As to the National Assembly for Wales and the Welsh Government generally see the Government of Wales Act 2006 Pts 1, 2 (ss 1–92); and CONSTITUTIONAL AND ADMINISTRATIVE LAW vol 20 (2014) PARAS 351 et seq, 373 et seq.
7 Equality Act 2010 Sch 3 para 2(1)(f). See note 6.
8 Equality Act 2010 Sch 3 para 2(2)(a). See note 6.
9 Equality Act 2010 Sch 3 para 2(2)(b). See note 6.

10 For these purposes 'enactment' means an enactment contained in an Act of Parliament; an Act or Measure of the National Assembly for Wales; or subordinate legislation: Equality Act 2010 s 212(1). 'Subordinate legislation' means subordinate legislation within the meaning of the Interpretation Act 1978 (see STATUTES AND LEGISLATIVE PROCESS vol 96 (2012) PARA 608) or an Act or Measure of the National Assembly for Wales: Equality Act 2010 s 212(1). See note 6.

11 Equality Act 2010 Sch 3 para 2(3)(a).

12 Equality Act 2010 Sch 3 para 2(3)(c) (modified by the Wales Act 2014 s 4(4)). See note 6.

13 Ie an instrument to which the Synodical Government Measure 1969 Sch 2 art 6(a) applies (see ECCLESIASTICAL LAW vol 34 (2011) PARA 110).

14 Equality Act 2010 Sch 3 para 2(4).

15 Equality Act 2010 Sch 3 para 2(5)(a).

16 Equality Act 2010 Sch 3 para 2(5)(b). As to the Privy Council see CONSTITUTIONAL AND ADMINISTRATIVE LAW vol 20 (2014) PARA 268.

17 Ie within the Equality Act 2010 Sch 22 (see PARAS 320, 322).

18 Equality Act 2010 Sch 3 para 2(6).

19 Equality Act 2010 Sch 3 para 3(1)(a). A reference in Sch 3 para 3(1) to a judicial function includes a reference to a judicial function conferred on a person other than a court or tribunal: Sch 3 para 3(2).

20 Equality Act 2010 Sch 3 para 3(1)(b). See note 19.

21 Equality Act 2010 Sch 3 para 3(1)(c). See note 19. As to decisions as to charge and prosecution see CRIMINAL PROCEDURE vol 27 (2015) PARA 43 et seq.

22 Equality Act 2010 Sch 3 para 3(1)(d). See notes 19, 21.

23 For these purposes 'relevant discrimination' is age discrimination, disability discrimination, gender reassignment discrimination, sex discrimination: Equality Act 2010 Sch 3 para 4(2). 'Age discrimination' is discrimination within s 13 (see PARA 67) because of age; or discrimination within s 19 (see PARA 75) where the relevant protected characteristic is age: s 25(1). As to the relevant protected characteristic of age see PARA 46. 'Gender reassignment discrimination' is discrimination within s 13 (see PARA 67) because of gender reassignment, discrimination within s 16 (see PARA 72) or discrimination within s 19 (see PARA 75) where the relevant protected characteristic is gender reassignment: s 25(3). As to the relevant protected characteristic of gender reassignment see PARAS 56, 61. As to the meaning of 'disability discrimination' see PARA 89 note 2.

24 Equality Act 2010 Sch 3 para 4(1). 'Armed forces' means any of the naval, military or air forces of the Crown: s 212(1).

25 Equality Act 2010 Sch 3 para 5(a). As to the Security Service see CONSTITUTIONAL AND ADMINISTRATIVE LAW vol 20 (2014) PARA 243.

26 Equality Act 2010 Sch 3 para 5(b). As to the Secret Intelligence Service see CONSTITUTIONAL AND ADMINISTRATIVE LAW vol 20 (2014) PARA 244.

27 Equality Act 2010 Sch 3 para 5(c). As to the Government Communications Headquarters see CONSTITUTIONAL AND ADMINISTRATIVE LAW vol 20 (2014) PARA 245.

28 Equality Act 2010 Sch 3 para 5(d). As to the Secretary of State see PARA 4.

92. Contraventions pursuant to other enactments.

A person does not contravene the provisions of the Equality Act 2010 on services[1], so far as relating to the protected characteristics of age[2], disability[3], religion or belief[4], sexual orientation[5] and (in the exercise of a public function that is not the provision of a service[6]) sex[7], if he does anything he must do pursuant to a requirement of an enactment[8]. A person also does not contravene those provisions so far as relating to the protected characteristics of disability, religion or belief or sexual orientation if he does anything he must do pursuant to a relevant requirement or condition imposed by virtue of an enactment[9].

1 Ie the Equality Act 2010 s Pt 3 (ss 28–31) (see PARA 84 et seq). As to exceptions from the Equality Act 2010 generally, and as to further exceptions in specific circumstances, see PARAS 320–338.

2 As to age as a protected characteristic see PARA 46.

3 As to disability as a protected characteristic see PARAS 47–55.

4 As to religion or belief as a protected characteristic see PARA 59.

5 As to sexual orientation as a protected characteristic see PARA 63.

6 Ie in the context of the Equality Act 2010 s 29(6) (see PARA 88).

7   As to sex as a protected characteristic see PARA 60.
8   Equality Act 2010 Sch 22 para 1(1). As to the meaning of 'enactment' see PARA 91 note 10. For the purposes of Sch 22 para 1, a reference to an 'enactment' includes a reference to a Measure of the General Synod of the Church of England and an enactment passed or made on or after 8 April 2010 (ie the date on which the Equality Act 2010 was passed (ie received the royal assent)): Sch 22 para 1(3). See ECCLESIASTICAL LAW vol 34 (2011) PARA 111.
9   Equality Act 2010 Sch 22 para 1(1). A reference in Sch 22 para 1 to a relevant requirement or condition is a requirement or condition imposed (whether before or after 8 April 201) by a Minister of the Crown, the National Assembly for Wales (constituted by the Government of Wales Act 1998), the Welsh Ministers, the First Minister for Wales or the Counsel General to the Welsh Government: see the Equality Act 2010 Sch 22 para 1(4) (modified by the Wales Act 2014 s 4(4)(a)).

93. Education.

The provisions of the Equality Act 2010 on the provision of services[1] do not apply to the following:
(1)   in its application to a local authority in England and Wales[2], so far as relating to age discrimination[3] or religious or belief-related discrimination[4]:
   (a)   the exercise of the authority's functions under the Education Act 1996[5] in respect of the provision of schools[6];
   (b)   the exercise of its functions under its general responsibility for education under the Education Act 1996[7] in so far as it relates to a function[8] in respect of the provision of schools[9];
(2)   in its application to a local authority in England and Wales, so far as relating to sex discrimination[10], the exercise of the authority's functions in relation to the establishment of a school[11];
(3)   so far as relating to age discrimination, anything done in connection with:
   (a)   the curriculum of a school[12];
   (b)   admission to a school[13];
   (c)   transport to or from a school[14];
   (d)   the establishment, alteration or closure of schools[15];
(4)   so far as relating to religious or belief-related discrimination, in relation to anything done in connection with:
   (a)   the curriculum of a school[16];
   (b)   admission to a school which has a religious ethos[17];
   (c)   acts of worship or other religious observance organised by or on behalf of a school (whether or not forming part of the curriculum)[18];
   (d)   the responsible body of a school which has a religious ethos[19];
   (e)   transport to or from a school[20];
   (f)   the establishment, alteration or closure of schools[21].

The provisions on the provision of services[22], so far as relating to disability discrimination[23], do not require a local authority in England or Wales exercising functions under the Education Acts[24] to remove or alter a physical feature[25].

1   Ie the Equality Act 2010 s 29 (see PARA 84 et seq). As to exceptions from the Equality Act 2010 generally, and as to further exceptions in specific circumstances, see PARAS 320–338.
2   As to the meanings of 'England' and 'Wales' see PARA 85 note 1. As to the meaning of 'local authority' see s 89(10); and PARA 173 note 1 (definition applied by the Equality Act 2010 Sch 3 para 12).
3   As to the meaning of 'age discrimination' see PARA 91 note 23.

4 'Religious or belief-related discrimination' is discrimination within the Equality Act 2010 s 13 (see PARA 67) because of religion or belief or discrimination within s 19 (see PARA 75) where the relevant protected characteristic is religion or belief: s 25(7). As to the relevant protected characteristic of religion or belief see PARA 59.

5 Ie under the Education Act 1996 s 14 (see EDUCATION vol 35 (2015) PARA 31).

6 Equality Act 2010 s 31(1), (10), Sch 3 para 6(a). As to the meaning of 'school' see s 89(5), (6); and PARA 173 note 1 (definition applied by the Equality Act 2010 Sch 3 para 12).

7 Ie under the Education Act 1996 s 13 (see EDUCATION vol 35 (2015) PARA 27).

8 Ie under the Education Act 1996 s 14 (see EDUCATION vol 35 (2015) PARA 31).

9 Equality Act 2010 Sch 3 para 6(b).

10 As to the meaning of 'sex discrimination' see PARA 73 note 5.

11 Equality Act 2010 Sch 3 para 8(1). Nothing in Sch 3 para 8(1) is to be taken as disapplying s 29 in relation to the exercise of the authority's functions under the Education Act 1996 s 14 (see EDUCATION vol 35 (2015) PARA 31): Equality Act 2010 Sch 3 para 8(2).

12 Equality Act 2010 Sch 3 para 9(a).

13 Equality Act 2010 Sch 3 para 9(b).

14 Equality Act 2010 Sch 3 para 9(c).

15 Equality Act 2010 Sch 3 para 9(d).

16 Equality Act 2010 Sch 3 para 11(a).

17 Equality Act 2010 Sch 3 para 11(b).

18 Equality Act 2010 Sch 3 para 11(c).

19 Equality Act 2010 Sch 3 para 11(d).

20 Equality Act 2010 Sch 3 para 11(e).

21 Equality Act 2010 Sch 3 para 11(f).

22 Ie the Equality Act 2010 s 29 (see PARA 84 et seq).

23 As to the meaning of 'disability discrimination' see PARA 89 note 2.

24 'The Education Acts' has the meaning given in the Education Act 1996 s 578 (see EDUCATION vol 35 (2015) PARA 1): Equality Act 2010 s 212(1).

25 Equality Act 2010 Sch 3 para 10(1).

94. Health and care.

A person operating a blood service[1] does not contravene the provisions of the Equality Act 2010 on the provision of services[2] only by refusing to accept a donation of an individual's blood if the refusal is because of an assessment of the risk to the public, or to the individual, based on clinical, epidemiological or other data obtained from a source on which it is reasonable to rely[3], and the refusal is reasonable[4].

A service-provider (A) who refuses to provide the service to a pregnant woman[5] does not discriminate against her[6] because she is pregnant if A reasonably believes that providing her with the service would, because she is pregnant, create a risk to her health or safety[7], A refuses to provide the service to persons with other physical conditions[8], and the reason for that refusal is that A reasonably believes that providing the service to such persons would create a risk to their health or safety[9]. A service-provider who provides, or offers to provide, the service to a pregnant woman on conditions does not discriminate against her[10] because she is pregnant if the conditions are intended to remove or reduce a risk to her health or safety[11], A reasonably believes that the provision of the service without the conditions would create a risk to her health or safety[12], A imposes conditions on the provision of the service to persons with other physical conditions[13], and the reason for the imposition of those conditions is that A reasonably believes that the provision of the service to such persons without those conditions would create a risk to their health or safety[14].

A person (A) does not contravene the provisions on the provision of services[15] only by participating in arrangements under which (whether or not for reward) A takes into A's home, and treats as members of A's family, persons requiring particular care and attention[16].

1 A 'blood service' is a service for the collection and distribution of human blood for the purposes of medical services: Equality Act 2010 s 31(1), (10), Sch 3 para 13(2). 'Blood' includes blood components: Sch 3 para 13(3).
2 Ie the Equality Act 2010 s 29 (see PARA 84 et seq). As to exceptions from the Equality Act 2010 generally, and as to further exceptions in specific circumstances, see PARAS 320–338.
3 Equality Act 2010 Sch 3 para 13(1)(a).
4 Equality Act 2010 Sch 3 para 13(1)(b).
5 As to the meaning of 'woman' see PARA 60 note 2.
6 Ie in contravention of the Equality Act 2010 s 29 (see PARA 84 et seq). As to direct discrimination see PARA 67; and as to indirect discrimination see PARA 75.
7 Equality Act 2010 Sch 3 para 14(1)(a).
8 Equality Act 2010 Sch 3 para 14(1)(b).
9 Equality Act 2010 Sch 3 para 14(1)(c).
10 Ie in contravention of the Equality Act 2010 s 29 (see PARA 84 et seq).
11 Equality Act 2010 Sch 3 para 14(2)(a).
12 Equality Act 2010 Sch 3 para 14(2)(b).
13 Equality Act 2010 Sch 3 para 14(2)(c).
14 Equality Act 2010 Sch 3 para 14(2)(d).
15 Ie under the Equality Act 2010 s 29 (see PARA 84 et seq).
16 Equality Act 2010 Sch 3 para 15.

95. Nationality or residence.

A person does not contravene the provisions of the Equality Act 2010 on services[1] by doing anything which discriminates against another because of the other's nationality[2], or which involves him discriminating against another person by applying to that other person a provision, criterion or practice which relates to that person's place of ordinary residence or the length of time that person has been present or resident in or outside the United Kingdom or an area within it[3], if the thing in question is done:

(1)   in pursuance of an enactment[4];
(2)   in pursuance of an instrument made by a member of the executive under an enactment[5];
(3)   to comply with a requirement imposed by a member of the executive by virtue of an enactment[6];
(4)   in pursuance of arrangements made by or with the approval of, or for the time being approved by, a Minister of the Crown[7];
(5)   to comply with a condition imposed by a Minister of the Crown[8].

1 Ie the Equality Act 2010 s Pt 3 (ss 28–31): see PARA 84 et seq. As to exceptions from the Equality Act 2010 generally, and as to further exceptions in specific circumstances, see PARAS 320–338.
2 Equality Act 2010 Sch 23 para 1(2).
3 Equality Act 2010 Sch 23 para 1(3).
4 Equality Act 2010 Sch 23 para 1(1)(a). As to the meaning of 'enactment' see PARA 91 note 10.
5 Equality Act 2010 Sch 23 para 1(1)(b).
6 Equality Act 2010 Sch 23 para 1(1)(c). This applies to a requirement imposed before or after 8 April 2010 (ie the date on which the Equality Act 2010 was passed (ie received the royal assent)): Sch 23 para 1(1)(c).
7 Equality Act 2010 Sch 23 para 1(1)(d). This applies to arrangements made before or after 8 April 2010: Sch 23 para 1(1)(d).
8 Equality Act 2010 Sch 23 para 1(1)(e). This applies to conditions imposed before or after 8 April 2010: Sch 23 para 1(1)(e).

96. Immigration.

The provisions of the Equality Act 2010 on the provision of services[1] do not apply to the following:

(1)   in relation to age discrimination[2], anything done by a relevant person[3] in the exercise of functions exercisable by virtue of a relevant enactment[4];

(2)   in relation to disability discrimination[5], a decision[6] (or anything done for the purposes of or in pursuance of such a decision[7]), whether or not taken in accordance with immigration rules[8], on the ground that doing so is necessary for the public good[9], to:

    (a)   to refuse entry clearance[10];

    (b)   to refuse[11], to cancel[12] or to vary[13] leave to enter or remain[14] in the United Kingdom[15];

    (c)   to refuse an application to vary leave to enter or remain in the United Kingdom[16];

(3)   in relation to disability discrimination, a decision taken, or guidance given, by the Secretary of State[17] in connection with a decision within head (2)[18]; or a decision taken in accordance with guidance given by the Secretary of State in connection with a decision within head (2)[19];

(4)   in relation to race discrimination[20], anything done by a relevant person[21] in the exercise of functions exercisable by virtue of a relevant enactment[22];

(5)   in relation to religion or belief-related discrimination[23], a decision (or anything done for the purposes of or in pursuance of such a decision[24]) taken in accordance with immigration rules[25]:

    (a)   to refuse entry clearance[26] or leave to enter the United Kingdom, or to cancel leave to enter or remain in the United Kingdom on the grounds that the exclusion of the person from the United Kingdom is conducive to the public good[27]; or

    (b)   to vary leave to enter or remain in the United Kingdom, or to refuse an application to vary leave to enter or remain in the United Kingdom, on the grounds that it is undesirable to permit the person to remain in the United Kingdom[28];

(6)   in relation to religion or belief-related discrimination, a decision (or anything done for the purposes of such a decision[29]) taken on certain grounds[30], whether or not taken in accordance with immigration rules, in connection with an application for entry clearance or for leave to enter or remain in the United Kingdom[31];

(7)   in relation to religion or belief-related discrimination, a decision taken, or guidance given, by the Secretary of State in connection with a decision within head (5)[32] or head (6)[33] or a decision taken in accordance with guidance given by the Secretary of State in connection with a decision within head (5) or head (6)[34].

1   Ie under the Equality Act 2010 s 29: see PARA **84** et seq. As to exceptions from the Equality Act 2010 generally, and as to further exceptions in specific circumstances, see PARAS **320–338**.

2   Equality Act 2010 s 31(10), Sch 3 para 15A(1) (Sch 3 para 15A added by SI 2012/2466). As to the meaning of 'age discrimination' see PARA **91** note 23

    The Equality Act 2010 (Age Exceptions) Order 2012, SI 2012/2466, was made under the Equality Act 2010 s 197, which provides that a Minister of the Crown may by order amend the Equality Act 2010 (apart from Pt 5 (ss 39–83) (work: see PARAS **116–172**) and Pt 6 Chapter 2 (ss 90–94) (further and higher education: see PARAS **182–191**)) to provide that any of the following does not contravene that Act so far as relating to age specified conduct (ie conduct of a specified description, conduct carried out in specified circumstances or conduct by or in relation to a person of a specified description); anything done for a specified purpose; or anything done in pursuance of arrangements of a specified description: s 197(1), (2), (9). Such an order may confer on a Minister of the Crown or the Treasury a power to issue guidance about the operation of the order (including, in particular, guidance about the steps that may be taken by persons wishing to rely on an exception provided for by the order) (s 197(3)(a)); require the Minister or the Treasury to carry out consultation before issuing guidance under a power so conferred (s 197(3)(b)); and make provision (including provision to impose a requirement) that refers to guidance issued under a power so conferred (s 197(3)(c)). Guidance given by a Minister of the Crown or the Treasury in anticipation of the making of an order under s 197 is, on the making of the order, to be treated as if it has been issued in accordance with the order: s 197(4). For the purposes of satisfying a requirement imposed by virtue of s 197(3)(b), the Minister or the Treasury may rely on consultation carried out before the making of the order that imposes the requirement (including consultation carried out before 19 June 2012 (the date in which s 197 came into force by virtue of the Equality Act 2010 (Commencement No 9) Order 2012, SI 2012/1569)) (Equality Act 2010 s 197(5)), and provision by virtue of s 197(3)(c) may, in particular, refer to provisions of the guidance that themselves refer to a document specified in the guidance (s 197(6)). Guidance issued (or treated as issued) under a power conferred by virtue of s 197(3)(a) comes into force on such day as the person who issues the guidance may by order appoint; and such an order may include the text of the guidance or of extracts from it: s 197(7). Section 197 is not affected by any provision of the Equality Act 2010 which makes special provision in relation to age: s 197(8).

3   A 'relevant person' is a Minister of the Crown acting personally, or a person acting in accordance with a relevant authorisation: Equality Act 2010 Sch 3 para 15A(3) (as added: see note 2). A 'relevant authorisation' is a requirement imposed or express authorisation given with respect to a particular case or class of case, by a Minister of the Crown acting personally; and with respect to a particular class of case, by a relevant enactment or by an instrument made under or by virtue of a relevant enactment: Sch 3 para 15A(4) (as so added). The 'relevant enactments' are the Immigration Acts, the Special Immigration Appeals Commission Act 1997 (see IMMIGRATION AND ASYLUM), a provision made under the European Communities Act 1972 s 2(2) (general implementation of treaties) which relates to immigration or asylum, and a provision of EU law which relates to immigration or asylum: Equality Act 2010 Sch 3 para 15A(5) (as so added). See generally IMMIGRATION AND ASYLUM. The reference to 'the Immigration Acts' does not include a reference to the Immigration Act 1971 ss 28A–28K (see IMMIGRATION AND ASYLUM vol 57 (2012) PARA 233 et seq) or the Asylum and Immigration (Treatment of Claimants, etc) Act 2004 s 14 (see IMMIGRATION AND ASYLUM vol 57 (2012) PARA 233): Equality Act 2010 Sch 3 para 15A(6) (as so added).

4   Equality Act 2010 Sch 3 para 15A(2) (as added: see note 2). As to the meaning of 'enactment' see PARA 91 note 10.

5   Equality Act 2010 Sch 3 para 16(1). As to the meaning of 'disability discrimination' see PARA 89 note 2.

6   Equality Act 2010 Sch 3 para 16(2)(a).

7   Equality Act 2010 Sch 3 para 16(2)(b).

8   As to the meaning of 'immigration rules' see the Immigration Act 1971 (IMMIGRATION AND ASYLUM vol 57 (2012) PARA 6) (applied by the Equality Act 2010 Sch 3 para 19).

9   Equality Act 2010 Sch 3 para 16(3).

10   Equality Act 2010 Sch 3 para 16(3)(a).

11   Equality Act 2010 Sch 3 para 16(3)(b).

12   Equality Act 2010 Sch 3 para 16(3)(c).

13   Equality Act 2010 Sch 3 para 16(3)(d).

14   As to the meaning of 'leave to enter or remain' see the Immigration Act 1971 (IMMIGRATION AND ASYLUM vol 57 (2012) PARA 15) (applied by the Equality Act 2010 Sch 3 para 19).

15   As to the meaning of 'the United Kingdom' see PARA 85 note 1.

16   Equality Act 2010 Sch 3 para 16(3)(e).

17   As to the Secretary of State see PARA 4.

18   Equality Act 2010 Sch 3 para 16(4)(a).

19   Equality Act 2010 Sch 3 para 16(4)(b).

20   Ie race discrimination so far as relating to nationality or ethnic or national origins: Equality Act 2010 Sch 3 para 17(1). 'Race discrimination' is discrimination within s 13 (see PARA 67) because of race, or discrimination within s 19 (see PARA 75) where the relevant protected characteristic is race: s 25(6). As to the relevant protected characteristic of race see PARA 58.

21   A 'relevant person' is a Minister of the Crown acting personally, or a person acting in accordance with a relevant authorisation: Equality Act 2010 Sch 3 para 17(3). A 'relevant authorisation' is a requirement imposed or express authorisation given with respect to a particular case or class of case, by a Minister of the Crown acting personally; or, with respect to a particular class of case, by a relevant enactment or by an instrument made under or by virtue of a relevant enactment:

Sch 3 para 17(4). The relevant enactments are the Immigration Acts, the Special Immigration Appeals Commission Act 1997 (see IMMIGRATION AND ASYLUM), a provision made under the European Communities Act 1972 s 2(2) (general implementation of treaties) which relates to immigration or asylum, and a provision of EU law which relates to immigration or asylum: Equality Act 2010 Sch 3 para 17(5) (amended by SI 2010/2279). The reference to 'the Immigration Acts' does not include a reference to the Immigration Act 1971 ss 28A–28K (see IMMIGRATION AND ASYLUM vol 57 (2012) PARA 233 et seq) or the Asylum and Immigration (Treatment of Claimants, etc) Act 2004 s 14 (see IMMIGRATION AND ASYLUM vol 57 (2012) PARA 233): Equality Act 2010 Sch 3 para 17(6).
22 Equality Act 2010 Sch 3 para 17(2).
23 Equality Act 2010 Sch 3 para 18(1). As to religious or belief-related discrimination see PARA 93 note 4.
24 Equality Act 2010 Sch 3 para 18(2).
25 Equality Act 2010 Sch 3 para 18(3).
26 As to the meaning of 'entry clearance' see the Immigration Act 1971 (IMMIGRATION AND ASYLUM vol 57 (2012) PARA 28) (applied by the Equality Act 2010 Sch 3 para 19).
27 Equality Act 2010 Sch 3 para 18(3)(a).
28 Equality Act 2010 Sch 3 para 18(3)(b).
29 Equality Act 2010 Sch 3 para 18(4).
30 The grounds referred to are (Equality Act 2010 Sch 3 para 18(6)):
    (1)   that a person holds an office or post in connection with a religion or belief or provides a service in connection with a religion or belief;
    (2)   that a religion or belief is not to be treated in the same way as certain other religions or beliefs; or
    (3)   the grounds that the exclusion from the United Kingdom of a person to whom head (1) applies is conducive to the public good.
31 Equality Act 2010 Sch 3 para 18(5).
32 Ie the Equality Act 2010 Sch 3 para 18(3) (see text and notes 25–28).
33 Ie the Equality Act 2010 Sch 3 para 18(5) (see text and notes 29–31).
34 Equality Act 2010 Sch 3 para 18(7).

97. Exceptions relating to religion or belief, and charity.

Religious organisations[1], other than organisations whose sole or main purpose is commercial[2], do not contravene the provisions of the Equality Act 2010 on services[3], so far as relating to religion or belief[4] or sexual orientation[5], only by restricting:

(1)   membership of the organisation[6];

(2)   participation in activities undertaken by the organisation or on its behalf or under its auspices[7];

(3)   the provision of goods, facilities or services in the course of activities undertaken by the organisation or on its behalf or under its auspices[8];

(4)   the use or disposal of premises owned or controlled by the organisation[9],

and a person does not contravene the provisions on services, so far as relating to religion or belief or sexual orientation, only by doing of those things on behalf of or under the auspices of the organisation[10].

A minister[11] does not contravene the provisions on services, so far as relating to religion or belief or sexual orientation[12], only by restricting:

(a)   participation in activities carried on in the performance of the minister's functions in connection with or in respect of the organisation[13]; or

(b)   the provision of goods, facilities or services in the course of activities carried on in the performance of the minister's functions in connection with or in respect of the organisation[14].

It is not a contravention of the provisions relating to services[15] for a person, in relation to an activity which is carried on for the purpose of promoting or supporting a charity, to restrict participation in the activity to persons of one sex[16].

1 Ie an organisation the purpose of which is:
   (1)   to practise a religion or belief (Equality Act 2010 Sch 23 para 2(1)(a));
   (2)   to advance a religion or belief (Sch 23 para 2(1)(b));
   (3)   to teach the practice or principles of a religion or belief (Sch 23 para 2(1)(c));
   (4)   to enable persons of a religion or belief to receive any benefit, or to engage in any activity, within the framework of that religion or belief (Sch 23 para 2(1)(d)); or
   (5)   to foster or maintain good relations between persons of different religions or beliefs (Sch 23 para 2(1)(e)).
2 Equality Act 2010 Sch 23 para 2(2).
3 Ie the Equality Act 2010 Pt 3 (ss 28–31) (see PARA 84 et seq). As to exceptions from the Equality Act 2010 generally, and as to further exceptions in specific circumstances, see PARAS 320–338.
4 As to religion or belief as a protected characteristic see PARA 59. The Equality Act 2010 Sch 23 para 2(3)–(5) (see the text and notes 6–14) permits a restriction relating to religion or belief only if it is imposed because of the purpose of the organisation or to avoid causing offence, on grounds of the religion or belief to which the organisation relates, to persons of that religion or belief: Sch 23 para 2(6).
5 As to sexual orientation as a protected characteristic see PARA 63. The Equality Act 2010 Sch 23 para 2(3)–(5) (see the text and notes 6–14) permit a restriction relating to sexual orientation only if it is imposed because it is necessary to comply with the doctrine of the organisation or to avoid conflict with the strongly held religious convictions of a significant number of the religion's followers (in the case of a religion) or the strongly held convictions relating to the belief of a significant number of the belief's followers (in the case of a belief): Sch 23 para 2(7), (9). In the application of these provisions in relation to sexual orientation, Sch 23 para 2(1)(e) (see note 1) must be ignored: Sch 23 para 2(11).
      Schedule 23 para 2 does not permit anything which is prohibited by s 29 (requirement that service providers must provide services to the public without discrimination: see PARA 84 et seq), so far as relating to sexual orientation, if it is done on behalf of a public authority and under the terms of a contract between the organisation and the public authority: Sch 23 para 2(10). As to the meaning of 'public authority' for these purposes see s 150(1); and PARA 277 (definition applied by Sch 23 para 2(13)(b)).
6 Equality Act 2010 Sch 23 para 2(3)(a).
7 Equality Act 2010 Sch 23 para 2(3)(b).
8 Equality Act 2010 Sch 23 para 2(3)(c).
9 Equality Act 2010 Sch 23 para 2(3)(d). As to the meaning of 'disposal' see PARA 106 note 1 (definition applied by Sch 23 para 2(13)(a)). In the application of these provisions in relation to sexual orientation, in Sch 23 para 2(3)(d) 'disposal' does not include disposal of an interest in premises by way of sale if the interest being disposed of is the entirety of the organisation's interest in the premises or the entirety of the interest in respect of which the organisation has power of disposal: Sch 23 para 2(12).
10 Equality Act 2010 Sch 23 para 2(4).
11 In the Equality Act 2010 Sch 23 para 2(5), the reference to a minister is a reference to a minister of religion, or other person, who performs functions in connection with a religion or belief to which the organisation relates and holds an office or appointment in, or is accredited, approved or recognised for the purposes of the organisation: Sch 23 para 2(8).
12 See notes 4, 5.
13 Equality Act 2010 Sch 23 para 2(5)(a).
14 Equality Act 2010 Sch 23 para 2(5)(b).
15 Ie the Equality Act 2010 s 29 (see PARA 84 et seq).
16 See the Equality Act 2010 s 193(7); and PARA 325.

98. Insurance etc.

The provisions of the Equality Act 2010 on the provision of services[1] do not apply to the following:

(1)   the provision of a relevant financial service[2] if the provision is in pursuance of arrangements made by an employer for the service-provider[3] to provide the service[4] to the employer's employees, and other persons, as a consequence of the employment[5];

(2)   so far as relating to age discrimination[6], doing anything in connection with the provision of a financial service[7];

(3)   so far as relating to disability discrimination[8], doing anything in connection with insurance business[9] if that thing is done by reference to information that is both relevant to the assessment of the risk to be insured and from a source on which it is reasonable to rely[10] and it is reasonable to do that thing[11];

(4)   so far as relating to relevant discrimination[12], doing anything in connection with insurance business[13] in relation to an existing insurance policy[14].

1   Ie under the Equality Act 2010 s 29 (see PARA 84 et seq). As to exceptions from the Equality Act 2010 generally, and as to further exceptions in specific circumstances, see PARAS 320–338.

2   'Relevant financial service' means insurance or a related financial service, or a service relating to membership of or benefits under a personal pension scheme (within the meaning given by the Pension Schemes Act 1993 s 1: see PERSONAL AND OCCUPATIONAL PENSIONS vol 80 (2013) PARA 208): Equality Act 2010 s 31(10), Sch 3 para 20(2).

3   As to the meaning of 'service-provider' see PARA 85.

4   As to the provision of a service see PARA 85 note 1.

5   Equality Act 2010 Sch 3 para 20(1). As to the meaning of 'employment' see PARA 116 (definition applied by s 212(1)).

6   As to the meaning of 'age discrimination' see PARA 91 note 23.

7   Equality Act 2010 Sch 3 para 20A(1) (Sch 3 para 20A added by SI 2012/2466). 'Financial service' includes a service of a banking, credit, insurance, personal pension, investment or payment nature: Equality Act 2010 Sch 3 para 20A(3) (as so added). The Equality Act 2010 (Age Exceptions) Order 2012, SI 2012/2466, was made under the Equality Act 2010 s 197: see PARA 96 note 2.

       Where a person (A) conducts an assessment of risk for the purposes of providing the financial service to another person (B), A may rely on Sch 3 para 20A(1) only if the assessment of risk, so far as it involves a consideration of B's age, is carried out by reference to information which is relevant to the assessment of risk and from a source on which it is reasonable to rely: Sch 3 para 20A(2) (as so added).

8   As to the meaning of 'disability discrimination' see PARA 89 note 2.

9   'Insurance business' means business which consists of effecting or carrying out contracts of insurance; and that definition is to be read with the Financial Services and Markets Act 2000 s 22, any relevant order under the 2000 Act, and Sch 2 to the 2000 Act (see FINANCIAL SERVICES REGULATION vol 50 (2016) PARAS 107–109): Equality Act 2010 Sch 3 para 21(2).

10 Equality Act 2010 Sch 3 para 21(1)(a).

11 Equality Act 2010 Sch 3 para 21(1)(b).

12 'Relevant discrimination' is age discrimination, disability discrimination, gender reassignment discrimination, pregnancy and maternity discrimination, race discrimination, religious or belief-related discrimination, sex discrimination or sexual orientation discrimination: Equality Act 2010 Sch 3 para 23(2). As to the meaning of 'age discrimination' see PARA 91 note 23; as the meaning of 'disability discrimination' see PARA 89 note 2; as to the meaning of 'gender reassignment discrimination' see PARA 91 note 23; as to the meaning of 'race discrimination' see PARA 96 note 20; as to the meaning of 'religious or belief-related discrimination' see PARA 93 note 4; and as to the meaning of 'sex discrimination' see PARA 73 note 5. 'Pregnancy and maternity discrimination' is discrimination within s 17 (see PARA 73) or s 18 (see PARA 74): s 25(5). 'Sexual orientation discrimination' is discrimination within s 13 (see PARA 67) because of sexual orientation, or discrimination within s 19 (see PARA 75) where the relevant protected characteristic is sexual orientation: s 25(9).

13 As to the meaning of 'insurance business' see note 9 (definition applied by the Equality Act 2010 Sch 3 para 23(6)).

14 Equality Act 2010 Sch 3 para 23(1). An 'existing insurance policy' is a policy of insurance entered into before 1 October 2010, or, so far as the provisions of Sch 3 Pt 5 apply to the protected

characteristic of age, 1 October 2012: see Sch 3 para 23(3); and the Equality Act 2010 (Commencement No 4, Savings, Consequential, Transitional, Transitory and Incidental Provisions and Revocation) Order 2010, SI 2010/2317, art 2; Equality Act 2010 (Commencement No 9) Order 2012, SI 2012/1569, art 3.

The Equality Act 2010 Sch 3 para 23(1) does not apply where an existing insurance policy was renewed, or the terms of such a policy were reviewed, on or after 1 October 2010, or, so far as the provisions of Sch 3 Pt 5 apply to the protected characteristic of age, 1 October 2012: see Sch 3 para 23(4); and the Equality Act 2010 (Commencement No 4, Savings, Consequential, Transitional, Transitory and Incidental Provisions and Revocation) Order 2010, SI 2010/2317, art 2; Equality Act 2010 (Commencement No 9) Order 2012, SI 2012/1569, art 3. A review of an existing insurance policy which was part of, or incidental to, a general reassessment by the service-provider of the pricing structure for a group of policies is not a review for these purposes: Equality Act 2010 Sch 3 para 23(5).

99. Marriage: gender reassignment and same sex couples.

So far as relating to gender reassignment discrimination[1], a person (A) does not contravene the provisions of the Equality Act 2010 on the provision of services[2]:

(1)   only because of anything done in reliance on the provisions in the Marriage Act 1949[3] relating to the solemnisation of marriages involving a person of acquired gender[4];

(2)   where A is a person whose consent to the solemnisation of the marriage of a person (B) is required under the provisions of the Marriage Act 1949[5], by refusing to consent if A reasonably believes that B's gender has become the acquired gender[6] under the Gender Recognition Act 2004[7];

(3)   by refusing to solemnise, in accordance with a form, rite or ceremony[8], the marriage of B if A reasonably believes that B's gender has become the acquired gender under the Gender Recognition Act 2004[9];

(4)   only because the person[10] does not:

    (a)   conduct a relevant marriage[11];

    (b)   is not present at, does not carry out, or does not otherwise participate in, a relevant marriage[12]; or

    (c)   does not consent to a relevant marriage being conducted[13],

for the reason that the marriage is the marriage of a same sex couple[14].

1   As to the meaning of 'gender reassignment discrimination' see PARA 91 note 23.
2   Ie under the Equality Act 2010 s 29 (see PARA 84 et seq). As to exceptions from the Equality Act 2010 generally, and as to further exceptions in specific circumstances, see PARAS 320–338.
3   Ie the Marriage Act 1949 s 5B (see MATRIMONIAL AND CIVIL PARTNERSHIP LAW vol 72 (2015) PARA 103).
4   Equality Act 2010 s 31(1), (10), Sch 3 para 24(1).
5   Ie under the Marriage Act 1949 s 44(1) (see MATRIMONIAL AND CIVIL PARTNERSHIP LAW vol 72 (2015) PARA 85 et seq).
6   As to the acquired gender under the Gender Recognition Act 2004 see REGISTRATION CONCERNING THE INDIVIDUAL vol 88 (2012) PARA 267.
7   Equality Act 2010 Sch 3 para 24(2).
8   The Equality Act 2010 Sch 3 para 24(4) applies to a person who may, in a case that comes within the Marriage Act 1949 (other than the case mentioned in the Equality Act 2010 Sch 3 para 24(1) (see the text and notes 3–4)), solemnise marriages according to a form, rite or ceremony of a body of persons who meet for religious worship: Sch 3 para 24(3).
9   Equality Act 2010 Sch 3 para 24(4).
10 'Person' includes a religious organisation but does not include a registrar, a superintendent registrar or the Registrar General: see the Marriage (Same Sex Couples) Act 2013 s 2(4) (definition applied by the Equality Act 2010 Sch 3 para 25A(2) (Sch 25A added by the Marriage (Same Sex Couples) Act 2013 s 2(6)).
11 Equality Act 2010 Sch 3 para 25A(1)(a) (as added: see note 10). 'Relevant marriage' means:
    (1)   a marriage of a same sex couple solemnized in accordance with the Marriage Act 1949 s 26A or s 26B (marriage in a place of worship or in another place according to religious rites or usages); Pt 5 (ss 68–71) (marriage in a naval, military or air force chapel); the

Marriage (Registrar General's Licence) Act 1970 s 1 (deathbed marriage), where the marriage is according to religious rites or usages; or an armed forces overseas marriage order, where the marriage is according to religious rites or usages, including any ceremony forming part of, or connected with, the solemnization of such a marriage; and

(2) a marriage ceremony read or celebrated in accordance with the Marriage Act 1949 s 46 in respect of a same sex couple (religious ceremony after registrar's marriage of same sex couple),

and a reference to conducting a relevant marriage is to be read accordingly: see the Marriage (Same Sex Couples) Act 2013 s 2(4) (definition applied by the Equality Act 2010 Sch 3 para 25A(2) (as so added)). As to formalities for marriage see MATRIMONIAL AND CIVIL PARTNERSHIP LAW vol 72 (2015) PARA 57 et seq.

12 Equality Act 2010 Sch 3 para 25A(1)(b) (as added: see note 10).
13 Equality Act 2010 Sch 3 para 25A(1)(c) (as added: see note 10).
14 Equality Act 2010 Sch 3 para 25A(1) (as added: see note 10). See MATRIMONIAL AND CIVIL PARTNERSHIP LAW vol 72 (2015) PARA 2.

100. Separate and single services.

A person (A) does not contravene the provisions of the Equality Act 2010 on the provision of services[1], so far as relating to sex discrimination[2], in the following circumstances:

(1) by providing[3] separate services for persons of each sex if a joint service for persons of both sexes would be less effective[4] and the limited provision is a proportionate means of achieving a legitimate aim[5];

(2) by providing[6] separate services differently for persons of each sex if a joint service for persons of both sexes would be less effective[7], the extent to which the service is required by one sex makes it not reasonably practicable to provide the service otherwise than as a separate service provided differently for each sex[8], and the limited provision is a proportionate means of achieving a legitimate aim[9];

(3) by providing[10] a service only to persons of one sex if any of certain conditions[11] is satisfied[12] and the limited provision is a proportionate means of achieving a legitimate aim[13];

(4) where A is a minister[14], by providing a service only to persons of one sex or separate services for persons of each sex, if the service is provided for the purposes of an organised religion[15], it is provided at a place which is (permanently or for the time being) occupied or used for those purposes[16], and the limited provision of the service is necessary in order to comply with the doctrines of the religion or is for the purpose of avoiding conflict with the strongly held religious convictions of a significant number of the religion's followers[17].

A person does not contravene the provisions on the provision of services, so far as relating to gender reassignment discrimination[18], only because of anything done in relation to certain matters[19] if the conduct in question is a proportionate means of achieving a legitimate aim[20].

If a service is generally provided only for persons who share a protected characteristic[21], a person (A) who normally provides the service for persons who share that characteristic does not contravene the provisions on the provision of services by insisting on providing the service in the way A normally provides it[22] or if A reasonably thinks it is impracticable to provide the service to persons who do not share that characteristic, by refusing to provide the service[23].

1 Ie under the Equality Act 2010 s 29 (see PARA 84 et seq). As to exceptions from the Equality Act 2010 generally, and as to further exceptions in specific circumstances, see PARAS 320–338.
2 As to the meaning of 'sex discrimination' see PARA 73 note 5.

3 Equality Act 2010 s 31(10), Sch 3 para 26(1). Schedule 3 para 26 applies to a person exercising a public function in relation to the provision of a service as it applies to the person providing the service: Sch 3 para 26(3). As to the meanings of 'public function' and 'provision of a service' see PARA 85 note 1.

4 Equality Act 2010 Sch 3 para 26(1)(a).

5 Equality Act 2010 Sch 3 para 26(1)(b).

6 Equality Act 2010 Sch 3 para 26(2). See note 3.

7 Equality Act 2010 Sch 3 para 26(2)(a).

8 Equality Act 2010 Sch 3 para 26(2)(b).

9 Equality Act 2010 Sch 3 para 26(2)(c).

10 Equality Act 2010 Sch 3 para 27(1). Schedule 3 para 27 applies to a person exercising a public function in relation to the provision of a service as it applies to the person providing the service: Sch 3 para 27(8). See note 3.

11 For these purposes, the conditions are that:
    (1) only persons of that sex have need of the service (Equality Act 2010 Sch 3 para 27(2));
    (2) the service is also provided jointly for persons of both sexes and the service would be insufficiently effective were it only to be provided jointly (Sch 3 para 27(3));
    (3) a joint service for persons of both sexes would be less effective and the extent to which the service is required by persons of each sex makes it not reasonably practicable to provide separate services (Sch 3 para 27(4));
    (4) the service is provided at a place which is, or is part of a hospital, or another establishment for persons requiring special care, supervision or attention (Sch 3 para 27(5));
    (5) the service is provided for, or is likely to be used by, two or more persons at the same time, and the circumstances are such that a person of one sex might reasonably object to the presence of a person of the opposite sex (Sch 3 para 27(6));
    (6) there is likely to be physical contact between a person (A) to whom the service is provided and another person (B), and B might reasonably object if A were not of the same sex as B (Sch 3 para 27(7)).
    See also note 10.

12 Equality Act 2010 Sch 3 para 27(1)(a).

13 Equality Act 2010 Sch 3 para 27(1)(b).

14 The reference to a 'minister' is a reference to a minister of religion, or other person, who performs functions in connection with the religion, and holds an office or appointment in, or is accredited, approved or recognised for purposes of, a relevant organisation in relation to the religion: Equality Act 2010 Sch 3 para 29(2). An organisation is a 'relevant organisation' in relation to a religion if its purpose is to practise the religion, to advance the religion, to teach the practice or principles of the religion, to enable persons of the religion to receive benefits, or to engage in activities, within the framework of that religion, or to foster or maintain good relations between persons of different religions: Sch 3 para 29(3). An organisation is not a 'relevant organisation' in relation to a religion if its sole of main purpose is commercial: Sch 3 para 29(4).

15 Equality Act 2010 Sch 3 para 29(1)(a).

16 Equality Act 2010 Sch 3 para 29(1)(b).

17 Equality Act 2010 Sch 3 para 29(1)(c).

18 As to the meaning of 'gender reassignment discrimination' see PARA 91 note 23.

19 The matters are the provision of separate services for persons of each sex, the provision of separate services differently for persons of each sex, and the provision of a service only to persons of one sex: Equality Act 2010 Sch 3 para 28(2).

20 Equality Act 2010 Sch 3 para 28(1).

21 As to protected characteristics generally see PARA 45.

22 Equality Act 2010 Sch 3 para 30(a).

23 Equality Act 2010 Sch 3 para 30(b).

101. Age exceptions.

So far as relating to age discrimination[1], a person (P) does not contravene the provisions of the Equality Act 2010 on the provision of services[2] by:

(1) giving a concession in respect of a service[3] to persons of a particular age group[4];

(2) providing a relevant holiday service[5] to persons of a particular age group[6];

(3)   where P provides a service[7] the provision of which is prohibited by or under an enactment[8] to persons under the age specified in or under the enactment ('the statutory age')[9] and displays on the premises on which the service is provided an age warning[10] in relation to the provision of the service[11], not providing a service to a person who appears to P, or an employee or agent of P's, to be under the age specified in the age warning in relation to the provision of the service[12] and on being required to do so by P or the employee or agent, fails to produce satisfactory identification[13].

So far as relating to age discrimination, a person (A) who is the owner[14] of a protected site[15] does not contravene the provisions on the provision of services by:

(a)   entering into a mobile home agreement[16] with a person (B) that entitles only persons who have attained a particular age to station and occupy a mobile home[17] on land forming part of the site[18];

(b)   refusing to permit assignment[19] by B of a mobile home agreement to any person other than a person who has attained a particular age[20];

(c)   imposing a requirement in park rules[21] that mobile homes stationed on land forming part of the site and occupied under mobile home agreements may be occupied only by persons who have attained a particular age[22];

(d)   imposing in or under a mobile home rental agreement[23] with a person (C) a requirement that the mobile home to which the agreement relates may be occupied only by persons who have attained a particular age[24]; or

(e)   refusing to permit assignment by C of a mobile home rental agreement to any person other than a person who has attained a particular age[25].

1   As to the meaning of 'age discrimination' see PARA **91** note 23.
2   Ie under the Equality Act 2010 s 29 (see PARA **84** et seq). As to exceptions from the Equality Act 2010 generally, and as to further exceptions in specific circumstances, see PARAS **320–338**.
3   The reference to a 'concession in respect of a service' is a reference to a benefit, right or privilege having the effect that the manner in which the service is provided is, or the terms on which it is provided are, more favourable than the manner in which, or the terms on which, it is usually provided to the public (or, where it is provided to a section of the public, that section): Equality Act 2010 s 31(1), (10), Sch 3 para 30A(2) (Sch 3 paras 30A–30D added by SI 2012/2466). As to examples of a 'section of the public' see PARA **85** note 2. The Equality Act 2010 (Age Exceptions) Order 2012, SI 2012/2466, was made under the Equality Act 2010 s 197: see PARA **96** note 2.
4   Equality Act 2010 Sch 3 para 30A(1) (as added: see note 3).
5   For these purposes, 'relevant holiday service' means (see the Equality Act 2010 Sch 3 para 30B(2) (as added: see note 3)) a service:
    (1)   which involves the provision of at least two of the following together for a single price;
          (a)   travel;
          (b)   accommodation;
          (c)   access to activities or services not ancillary to travel or accommodation which form a significant part of the service or its cost;
    (2)   the provision of which is for a period of more than 24 hours or includes the provision of overnight accommodation;
    (3)   which P provides only to persons of the age group in question; and
    (4)   an essential feature of which is the bringing together of persons of that age group with a view to facilitating their enjoyment of facilities or services designed with particular regard to persons of that age group.
    For the purposes of head (1)(a) above, 'travel' includes an option for an individual to make alternative travel arrangements to those included in the relevant holiday service as offered by P: Sch 3 para 30B(4) (as so added).
6   Equality Act 2010 Sch 3 para 30B(1) (as added: see note 3). P may not rely on Sch 3 para 30B(1) unless, before providing a person with a relevant holiday service, P provides the person with a

written statement that the service is provided only to persons of the age group in question: Sch 3 para 30B(3) (as so added).

7   As to the meaning of 'provision of a service' see PARA 85 note 1. For these purposes a reference to the 'provision of a service' includes a reference to provision of access to the service: Equality Act 2010 Sch 3 para 30C(4)(a) (as added: see note 3).

8   As to the meaning of 'enactment' see PARA 91 note 10.

9   Equality Act 2010 Sch 3 para 30C(1)(a) (as added: see note 3).

10   An 'age warning' in relation to the provision of a service is a statement to the effect that the service will not be provided to a person who appears to P, or an employee or agent of P's, to be under the age specified in the statement, and on being required to do so by P or the employee or agent, fails to produce satisfactory identification: Equality Act 2010 Sch 3 para 30C(2) (as added: see note 3). For these purposes 'satisfactory identification', in relation to a person, means a valid document which, in the case of licensed premises where an age condition applies, meets that condition, and in any other case includes a photograph of the person and establishes that the person has attained the statutory age in relation to the provision of a service: Sch 3 para 30C(4)(b) (as so added). 'Licensed premises' means premises in respect of which a relevant premises licence within the meaning of the Licensing Act 2003 s 19A (see LEISURE AND ENTERTAINMENT vol 67 (2016) PARA 74) has effect. 'Age condition' means a condition specified in an order under s 19A(1) (see LEISURE AND ENTERTAINMENT vol 67 (2016) PARA 74) requiring the age of certain persons to be verified in the manner specified in the condition before they are served alcohol in premises where the condition applies: Equality Act 2010 Sch 3 para 30C(4)(b) (as so added).

11   Equality Act 2010 Sch 3 para 30C(1)(b) (as added: see note 3).

12   Equality Act 2010 Sch 3 para 30C(3)(a) (as added: see note 3).

13   Equality Act 2010 Sch 3 para 30C(3)(b) (as added: see note 3).

14   As to the meaning of 'owner' see LANDLORD AND TENANT vol 64 (2016) PARAS 1762, 1763 (definition applied by the Equality Act 2010 Sch 3 para 30D(5) (as added (see note 3); definition amended by the Mobile Homes (Wales) Act 2013 Sch 4 para 11)).

15   As to the meaning of 'protected site' see LANDLORD AND TENANT vol 64 (2016) PARAS 1762, 1763 (definition applied by the Equality Act 2010 Sch 3 para 30D(5) (as added: see note 3); definition amended by the Mobile Homes (Wales) Act 2013 Sch 4 para 11)).

16   A 'mobile home agreement' means an agreement to which the Mobile Homes Act 1983 or the Mobile Homes (Wales) Act 1983 applies: Equality Act 2010 Sch 3 para 30D(5) (as added (see note 3); definition amended by the Mobile Homes (Wales) Act 2013 Sch 4 para 11)). See also LANDLORD AND TENANT vol 64 (2016) PARAS 1767, 1768 et seq.

17   As to the meaning of 'mobile home' see LANDLORD AND TENANT vol 64 (2016) PARAS 1761, 1762 (definition applied by the Equality Act 2010 Sch 3 para 30D(5) (as added (see note 3); definition amended by the Mobile Homes (Wales) Act 2013 Sch 4 para 11)).

18   Equality Act 2010 Sch 3 para 30D(1)(a) (as added: see note 3). A may not rely on Sch 3 para 30D(1) or (3) unless, before doing something mentioned in those provisions, A provides B or C, as the case may be, with a written statement to the effect that the mobile home in question may be occupied only by persons who have attained the age in question: Equality Act 2010 Sch 3 para 30D(4) (as so added).

19   As to assignment of contracts generally see CHOSES IN ACTION vol 13 (2017) PARAS 6, 13 et seq.

20   Equality Act 2010 Sch 3 para 30D(1)(b) (as added: see note 3). See also note 18.

21   For these purposes 'park rules' means rules applying to residents of mobile homes on the protected site and required to be observed by a term in the mobile home agreement or the mobile home rental agreement as the case may be: Equality Act 2010 Sch 3 para 30D(5) (as added: see note 3).

22   Equality Act 2010 Sch 3 para 30D(2) (as added: see note 3).

23   For these purposes 'mobile home rental agreement' means an agreement (other than an arrangement to occupy a mobile home for the purposes of a holiday) under which a person ('the occupier') is entitled to occupy a mobile home on the protected site as the occupier's residence whether for a specified period or for successive periods of a specified duration subject to payment of money and the performance of other obligations: Equality Act 2010 Sch 3 para 30D(5) (as added: see note 3).

24   Equality Act 2010 Sch 3 para 30D(3)(a) (as added: see note 3). See also note 18.

25   Equality Act 2010 Sch 3 para 30D(3)(b) (as added: see note 3). See also note 18. As to assignment of contracts generally see CHOSES IN ACTION vol 13 (2017) PARAS 6, 13 et seq.

102. Television, radio and online broadcasting and distribution.

The provisions of the Equality Act 2010 on the provision of services[1] do not apply[2] to the provision of a content service[3].

1   Ie under the Equality Act 2010 s 29 (see PARA 84 et seq). As to exceptions from the Equality Act 2010 generally, and as to further exceptions in specific circumstances, see PARAS 320–338.
2   Equality Act 2010 s 31(1), (10), Sch 3 para 31(1). This provision does not apply to the provision of an electronic communications network, electronic communications service or associated facility: Sch 3 para 31(2). As to the meanings of 'electronic communications network', 'electronic communications service' and 'associated facility' see TELECOMMUNICATIONS vol 97 (2015) PARA 53 (definitions applied by the Equality Act 2010 Sch 3 para 31(2)).
3   As to the meaning of 'content service' see TELECOMMUNICATIONS vol 97 (2015) PARA 53 (definition applied by the Equality Act 2010 Sch 3 para 31(1)).

103. Transport.

So far as relating to disability discrimination[1], the provisions of the Equality Act 2010 on the provision of services[2] do not apply to:

(1)   transporting people by air[3];

(2)   a service provided on a vehicle for transporting people by air[4];

(3)   anything governed by the provisions[5] concerning the rights of disabled persons and persons with reduced mobility when travelling by air[6];

(4)   transporting people by land, unless a listed[7] vehicle is concerned[8];

(5)   anything governed by the provisions[9] concerning the rights of passengers in bus and coach transport[10]; or

(6)   anything governed by the provisions[11] concerning the rights and obligations of rail passengers[12].

1   Equality Act 2010 s 31(10), Sch 3 para 32. As to the meaning of 'disability discrimination' see PARA 89 note 2.
2   Ie under the Equality Act 2010 s 29 (see PARA 84 et seq). As to exceptions from the Equality Act 2010 generally, and as to further exceptions in specific circumstances, see PARAS 320–338.
3   Equality Act 2010 Sch 3 para 33(1)(a).
4   Equality Act 2010 Sch 3 para 33(1)(b).
5   Ie Council Regulation (EC) 1107/2006 (OJ L204, 26.7.2006, p 1) concerning the rights of disabled persons with reduced mobility when travelling by air (implemented by the Civil Aviation (Access to Air Travel for Disabled Persons and Persons with Reduced Mobility) Regulations 2014, SI 2014/2833 (amended by SI 2016/729). See AVIATION vol 2 (2017) PARA 728. Cf *Stott v Thomas Cook Tour Operators Ltd* [2014] UKSC 15, [2014] AC 1347, [2014] 2 All ER 461.
6   Equality Act 2010 Sch 3 para 33(2).
7   Ie unless the vehicle concerned is:
     (1)   a hire-vehicle designed and constructed for the carriage of passengers and comprising no more than eight seats in addition to the driver's seat (Equality Act 2010 Sch 3 para 34(1)(a) (Sch 3 para 34 amended by SI 2010/2279));
     (2)   a hire-vehicle designed and constructed for the carriage of passengers, comprising more than eight seats in addition to the driver's seat and having a maximum mass not exceeding five tonnes (Equality Act 2010 Sch 3 para 34(1)(b) (as so amended));
     (3)   a hire-vehicle designed and constructed for the carriage of goods and having a maximum mass not exceeding 3.5 tonnes (Equality Act 2010 Sch 3 para 34(1)(c) (as so amended));
     (4)   a vehicle licensed under the Local Government (Miscellaneous Provisions) Act 1976 s 48 (see ROAD TRAFFIC vol 90 (2011) PARA 1194) or the Private Hire Vehicles (London) Act 1998 s 7 (see LONDON GOVERNMENT vol 71 (2013) PARA 234) (or under a provision of a local Act corresponding to either of those provisions) (Equality Act 2010 Sch 3 para 34(1)(d) (as so amended));
     (5)   a public service vehicle (within the meaning given by the Public Passenger Vehicles Act 1981 s 1: see ROAD TRAFFIC vol 90 (2011) PARA 896) (Equality Act 2010 Sch 3 para 34(1)(f) (as so amended));
     (6)   a vehicle built or adapted to carry passengers on a railway or tramway (within the meaning, in each case, of the Transport and Works Act 1992: see RAILWAYS AND TRAMWAYS vol 86 (2017) PARA 310) (Equality Act 2010 Sch 3 para 34(1)(g) (as so amended));

(7)   a taxi (Equality Act 2010 Sch 3 para 34(1)(h) (as so amended));
(8)   a vehicle deployed to transport the driver and passengers of a vehicle that has broken
        down or is involved in an accident (Equality Act 2010 Sch 3 para 34(1)(i) (as so
        amended)); or
(9)   a vehicle deployed on a system using a mode of guided transport (within the meaning of
        the Transport and Works Act 1992: see RAILWAYS AND TRAMWAYS vol 86 (2017)
        PARA 310) (Equality Act 2010 Sch 3 para 34(1)(j) (as so amended)).

8   Equality Act 2010 Sch 3 para 34(1) (as amended: see note 7).
9   Ie European Parliament and Council Regulation (EU) 181/2011 (OJ L55, 28.2.2011, p 1)
    concerning the rights of passengers in bus and coach transport (see CONSUMER PROTECTION vol 21
    (2016) PARA 590).
10 Equality Act 2010 Sch 3 para 34(1A) (Sch 3 para 34 as amended (see note 7); Sch 3 para 34(1A)
    added by SI 2013/1865).
11 Ie European Parliament and Council Regulation (EC) 1371/2007 (OJ L315, 3.12.2007, p 14) on
    rail passengers' rights and obligations (see CARRIAGE AND CARRIERS vol 7 (2015) PARAS 688–690).
12 Equality Act 2010 Sch 3 para 34A (added by SI 2010/2279).

104. Transsexual persons and sport.

A person does not contravene the provisions of the Equality Act 2010 on
services[1], so far as relating to gender reassignment[2], only by doing anything in
relation to the participation of a transsexual person as a competitor in a
gender-affected activity[3] if it is necessary to do so to secure in relation to the
activity fair competition[4] or the safety of competitors[5].

1   Ie the Equality Act 2010 s 29 (see PARA 84 et seq). As to exceptions from the Equality Act 2010
    generally, and as to further exceptions in specific circumstances, see PARAS 320–338.
2   As to gender reassignment as a protected characteristic see PARAS 56, 61.
3   As to the meaning of 'gender-affected activity' see PARA 328.
4   Equality Act 2010 s 195(2)(a).
5   Equality Act 2010 s 195(2)(b).

6. PREMISES

(1) APPLICATION OF THE EQUALITY ACT 2010 TO PREMISES

105. Application of Part 4 of the Equality Act 2010.

Part 4 of the Equality Act 2010[1], which prohibits discrimination, harassment and victimisation in relation to the disposal, management and occupation of premises, does not apply to:

(1)　the protected characteristics of age[2] or marriage and civil partnership[3];

(2)　discrimination[4], harassment[5] or victimisation[6] that is prohibited by the provisions applying to work[7] or education[8] or that would be so prohibited but for an express exception[9];

(3)　the provision of accommodation if the provision is generally for the purpose of short stays by individuals who live elsewhere[10]; or is for the purpose only of exercising a public function[11] or providing a service[12] to the public or a section of the public[13];

(4)　a breach of an equality clause or rule[14];

(5)　anything that would be a breach of an equality clause or rule but for[15] the defence of material factor[16] or an exception in relation to occupational pension schemes[17];

(6)　a breach of a non-discrimination rule[18].

1　Ie the Equality Act 2010 Pt 4 (ss 32–38) (see PARA 106 et seq).
2　As to the protected characteristic of age see PARA 46.
3　Equality Act 2010 s 32(1). Nothing in s 32 is to be regarded as an express exception: s 212(13). 'Marriage and civil partnership discrimination' is:
　(1)　discrimination within s 13 (direct discrimination: see PARA 67) because of marriage and civil partnership (s 25(4)(a));
　(2)　discrimination within s 19 (indirect discrimination: see PARA 75) where the relevant protected characteristic is marriage and civil partnership (s 25(4)(b)).
　As to the protected characteristic of marriage and civil partnership see PARA 57.
4　As to direct discrimination see PARA 67 et seq; and as to indirect discrimination see PARA 75.
5　As to harassment see PARA 79.
6　As to victimisation see PARA 81.
7　Ie the Equality Act 2010 Pt 5 (ss 39–83) (see PARAS 116–172).
8　Ie the Equality Act 2010 Pt 6 (ss 84–99) (see PARAS 173–197).
9　Equality Act 2010 s 32(2). See note 3. The effect of this is that, if an act of discrimination, harassment or victimisation is made unlawful by other Parts of the Act covering work or education, then those provisions, rather than the provisions covering premises, apply.
10　Equality Act 2010 s 32(3)(a). See note 3.
11　As to the meaning of 'public function' see PARA 85 note 1 (definition applied by Equality Act 2010 s 32(4)).
12　As to the meaning of 'provision of a service' see PARA 85 note 1 (definition applied by Equality Act 2010 s 32(4)).
13　Equality Act 2010 s 32(3)(b). See note 3.
14　Equality Act 2010 s 32(5)(a). See note 3. As to the meanings of 'equality clause' and 'equality rule' see PARA 117 note 4. As to the meaning of 'breach of an equality clause of rule' see PARA 81 note 7. As to equality clauses or rules generally see PARA 136 et seq.
15　Equality Act 2010 s 32(5)(b). See note 3.
16　Ie under the Equality Act 2010 s 69 (see PARA 142).
17　Ie under the Equality Act 2010 Sch 7 Pt 2 (paras 3–6) (see PARA 140).
18　Equality Act 2010 s 32(5)(c). See note 3. As to the meaning of 'non-discrimination rule' see PARA 134.

(2) DISPOSAL AND MANAGEMENT OF PREMISES

106. Disposals etc.

A person (A) who has the right to dispose of premises[1] must not[2] discriminate[3] or victimise[4] against another (B):

(1)   as to the terms on which A offers to dispose of the premises to B[5];

(2)   by not disposing of the premises to B[6];

(3)   in A's treatment of B with respect to things done in relation to persons seeking premises[7].

Where an interest in a commonhold unit[8] cannot be disposed of[9] unless a particular person is a party to the disposal, that person must not discriminate against or victimise a person by not being a party to the disposal[10].

A person who has the right to dispose of premises must not, in connection with anything done in relation to their occupation[11] or disposal, harass[12] a person who occupies them[13] or a person who applies for them[14].

1   For these purposes, a reference to 'disposing of premises' includes, in the case of premises subject to a tenancy, a reference to assigning the premises, sub-letting them, or parting with possession of them: Equality Act 2010 s 38(1), (3). A reference to 'disposing of premises' also includes a reference to granting a right to occupy them: s 38(1), (4). A reference to 'premises' is a reference to the whole or part of the premises: s 38(1), (2). A reference to a 'tenancy' is to a tenancy created (whether before or after the passing of the 2010 Act) by a lease or sub-lease, by an agreement for a lease or sub-lease, by a tenancy agreement, or in pursuance of an enactment, and a reference to a tenant is to be construed accordingly: s 38(1), (6). As to the creation of a tenancy see LANDLORD AND TENANT vol 62 (2016) PARA 1.

2   As to exceptions to these provisions see PARAS 110–115.

3   As to direct discrimination see PARA 67; and as to indirect discrimination see PARA 75.

4   As to victimisation see PARA 81.

5   Equality Act 2010 s 33(1)(a), (4)(a).

6   Equality Act 2010 s 33(1)(b), (4)(b).

7   Equality Act 2010 s 33(1)(c), (4)(c).

8   As to the meaning of 'commonhold unit' see REAL PROPERTY AND REGISTRATION vol 87 (2017) PARA 1131 (definition applied by the Equality Act 2010 s 38(1), (7)).

9   A reference to 'disposing of an interest in a commonhold unit' includes a reference to creating an interest in a commonhold unit: Equality Act 2010 s 38(1), (5).

10 Equality Act 2010 s 33(2), (5).

11 A reference to 'occupation', in relation to premises, is a reference to lawful occupation: Equality Act 2010 s 212(6).

12 As to harassment see PARA 79.

13 Equality Act 2010 s 33(3)(a). In the application of s 26 (harassment: see PARA 79) for these purposes, neither religion or belief (see PARA 59), nor sexual orientation (see PARA 63) is a relevant protected characteristic: s 33(6). However, conduct relating to those characteristics may amount to a detriment for the purposes of discrimination within s 13: see PARA 86 note 3.

14 Equality Act 2010 s 33(3)(b). See note 13.

107. Permission for disposal.

A person whose permission is required for the disposal of premises[1] must not[2]:

(1)   discriminate[3] against another by not giving permission for the disposal of the premises to the other[4];

(2)   in relation to an application for permission to dispose of the premises, harass[5] a person who applies for permission to dispose of the premises[6]; or to whom the disposal would be made if permission were given[7];

(3)   victimise[8] another by not giving permission for the disposal of the premises to the other[9].

These provisions do not apply to anything done in the exercise of a judicial function[10].

1 As to the meaning of 'disposal of premises' see PARA 106 note 1.
2 As to exceptions to these provisions see PARAS 110–115.
3 As to direct discrimination see PARA 67; and as to indirect discrimination see PARA 75.
4 Equality Act 2010 s 34(1).
5 As to harassment see PARA 79.
6 Equality Act 2010 s 34(2)(a). In the application of s 26 (harassment: see PARA 79) for these purposes, neither religion or belief (see PARA 59), nor sexual orientation (see PARA 63) is a relevant protected characteristic: s 34(4). However, conduct relating to those characteristics may amount to a detriment for the purposes of discrimination within s 13: see s 212(5); and PARA 86 note 3.
7 Equality Act 2010 s 34(2)(b). See note 6.
8 As to victimisation see PARA 81.
9 Equality Act 2010 s 34(3).
10 Equality Act 2010 s 34(5).

108. Management.

A person (A) who manages premises[1] must not[2]:
(1)   discriminate[3] against or vicitimise[4] a person (B) who occupies the premises[5]:
    (a)   in the way in which A allows B, or by not allowing B, to make use of a benefit or facility[6];
    (b)   by evicting B (or taking steps for the purpose of securing B's eviction)[7];
    (c)   by subjecting B to any other detriment[8];
(2)   harass[9] a person who occupies them[10] or who applies for them[11].

1 As to the meaning of 'premises' see PARA 106 note 1.
2 As to exceptions to these provisions see PARAS 110–115.
3 As to direct discrimination see PARA 67; and as to indirect discrimination see PARA 75.
4 As to victimisation see PARA 81.
5 Equality Act 2010 s 35(1), (3).
6 Equality Act 2010 s 35(1)(a), (3)(a).
7 Equality Act 2010 s 35(1)(b), (3)(b).
8 Equality Act 2010 s 35(1)(c), (3)(c).
9 As to harassment see PARA 79.
10 Equality Act 2010 s 35(2)(a). In the application of s 26 (harassment: see PARA 79) for these purposes, neither religion or belief (see PARA 59), nor sexual orientation (see PARA 63) is a relevant protected characteristic: s 35(4). However, conduct relating to those characteristics may amount to a detriment for the purposes of discrimination within s 13: see s 212(5); and PARA 86 note 3.
11 Equality Act 2010 s 35(2)(b). See note 10.

(3) DUTY TO MAKE REASONABLE ADJUSTMENTS

109. Duty to make reasonable adjustments for disabled persons.

A duty to make reasonable adjustments for disabled persons[1] applies to:
(1)   a controller of let premises[2];
(2)   a controller of premises to let[3]; and
(3)   a commonhold association[4].
As from a day to be appointed, this duty also applies to a responsible person in relation to common parts[5].

Where such a duty is imposed by Part 4 of the Equality Act 2010[6] such persons must comply with the requirements as set out in the Equality Act 2010[7]. The full details of the steps which such persons must take in order to make reasonable adjustments to premises are set out elsewhere in this title[8].

1   As to the general duty to make reasonable adjustments for disabled persons see PARA 237.
2   Equality Act 2010 s 36(1)(a). A 'controller of let premises' is a person by whom premises are let; or a person who manages them: Equality Act 2010 s 36(2). As to the meaning of 'premises' see PARA 106 note 1. A reference to 'letting' includes a reference to sub-letting; and for the purposes of heads (1)–(2) in the text, a reference to 'let premises' includes premises subject to a right to occupy: s 36(7).
    For the purposes of s 36 and Sch 4, regulations may make provision as to:
    (1)   circumstances in which premises are to be treated as let, or as not let, to a person (Sch 4 para 9(1), (2)(a));
    (2)   circumstances in which premises are to be treated as being, or as not being, to let (Sch 4 para 9(1), (2)(b));
    (3)   who is to be treated as being, or as not being, a person entitled to occupy premises otherwise than as tenant or unit-holder (Sch 4 para 9(1), (2)(c));
    (4)   who is to be treated as being, or as not being, a person by whom premises are let (Sch 4 para 9(1), (2)(d));
    (5)   who is to be treated as having, or as not having, premises to let (Sch 4 para 9(1), (2)(e));
    (6)   who is to be treated as being, or as not being, a manager of premises (Sch 4 para 9(1), (2)(f)).
    Provision made by virtue of Sch 4 para 9 may amend Sch 4: Sch 4 para 9(3). At the date at which this volume states the law no such regulations have been made.
3   Equality Act 2010 s 36(1)(b). A 'controller of premises to let' is a person who has premises to let; or a person who manages them: Equality Act 2010 s 36(3).
4   Equality Act 2010 s 36(1)(c). The reference to 'commonhold association' is a reference to the association in its capacity as the person who manages a commonhold unit: s 36(4). As to the meanings of 'commonhold association' and 'commonhold unit' see REAL PROPERTY AND REGISTRATION vol 87 (2017) PARAS 1107, 1131 (definitions applied by the Equality Act 2010 s 38(1), (7)).
    Section 36 does not apply to premises of such description as may be prescribed by regulations: s 36(8). At the date at which this volume states the law no such regulations had been made.
5   Equality Act 2010 s 36(1)(d) (not yet in force). At the date at which this volume states the law no day had been appointed for s 36(1)(d), (5), (6) to be brought into force. 'A responsible person in relation to common parts' is:
    (1)   where the premises to which the common parts relate are let, and are not part of commonhold land, a person by whom the premises are let (s 36(5)(a) (not yet in force));
    (2)   where the premises to which the common parts relate are part of commonhold land, the commonhold association (s 36(5)(b) (not yet in force)).
    'Common parts' are:
    (a)   in relation to let premises (which are not part of commonhold land), the structure and exterior of, and any common facilities within or used in connection with, the building or part of a building which includes the premises (s 36(6)(b) (not yet in force));
    (b)   in relation to commonhold land, every part of the commonhold which is not for the time being a commonhold unit in accordance with the commonhold community statement (s 36(6)(b) (not yet in force)).
    As to the meanings of 'commonhold land' and 'commonhold community statement' see REAL PROPERTY AND REGISTRATION vol 87 (2017) PARAS 1104, 1112 (definitions applied by s 38(1), (7)).
6   See the Equality Act 2010 s 38(8), Sch 4 para 1.
7   See the Equality Act 2010 Sch 4 para 1.
8   See the Equality Act 2010 Sch 4 paras 1–9; and PARAS 241–244.

(4) EXCEPTIONS IN RELATION TO PREMISES

110.   Contraventions pursuant to other enactments.
A person does not contravene the provisions of the Equality Act 2010 on premises[1], so far as relating to the protected characteristics of age[2], disability[3], religion or belief[4], or sexual orientation[5], if he does anything he must do pursuant to a requirement of an enactment[6]. A person also does not contravene those provisions so far as relating to the protected characteristics of disability, religion

or belief or sexual orientation if he does anything he must do pursuant to a relevant requirement or condition imposed by virtue of an enactment[7].

1   Ie the Equality Act 2010 s Pt 4 (ss 32–38) (see PARA 105 et seq). As to exceptions from the Equality Act 2010 generally, and as to further exceptions in specific circumstances, see PARAS 320–338.
2   As to age as a protected characteristic see PARA 46.
3   As to disability as a protected characteristic see PARAS 47–55.
4   As to religion or belief as a protected characteristic see PARA 59.
5   As to sexual orientation as a protected characteristic see PARA 63.
6   Equality Act 2010 Sch 22 para 1(1). As to the meaning of 'enactment' see PARA 92 note 8.
7   Equality Act 2010 Sch 22 para 1(1). As to the meaning of 'a relevant requirement or condition' see PARA 92 note 9.

111. Nationality or residence.

A person does not contravene the provisions of the Equality Act 2010 on premises[1] by doing anything which discriminates against another because of the other's nationality[2], or which involves him discriminating against another person by applying to that other person a provision, criterion or practice which relates to that person's place of ordinary residence or the length of time that person has been present or resident in or outside the United Kingdom or an area within it[3], if the thing in question is done:

(1)   in pursuance of an enactment[4];
(2)   in pursuance of an instrument made by a member of the executive under an enactment[5];
(3)   to comply with a requirement imposed by a member of the executive by virtue of an enactment[6];
(4)   in pursuance of arrangements made by or with the approval of, or for the time being approved by, a Minister of the Crown[7];
(5)   to comply with a condition imposed by a Minister of the Crown[8].

1   Ie the Equality Act 2010 s Pt 4 (ss 32–38) (see PARA 105 et seq). As to exceptions from the Equality Act 2010 generally, and as to further exceptions in specific circumstances, see PARAS 320–338.
2   Equality Act 2010 Sch 23 para 1(2).
3   Equality Act 2010 Sch 23 para 1(3).
4   Equality Act 2010 Sch 23 para 1(1)(a).
5   Equality Act 2010 Sch 23 para 1(1)(b).
6   Equality Act 2010 Sch 23 para 1(1)(c). This applies to a requirement imposed before or after 8 April 2010 (ie the date on which the Equality Act 2010 was passed (ie received the royal assent)): Sch 23 para 1(1)(c).
7   Equality Act 2010 Sch 23 para 1(1)(d). This applies to arrangements made before or after 8 April 2010: Sch 23 para 1(1)(d).
8   Equality Act 2010 Sch 23 para 1(1)(e). This applies to conditions imposed before or after 8 April 2010: Sch 23 para 1(1)(e).

112. Religion or belief.

Religious organisations[1], other than organisations whose sole or main purpose is commercial[2], do not contravene the provisions of the Equality Act 2010 on premises[3], so far as relating to religion or belief[4] or sexual orientation[5], only by restricting:

(1)   membership of the organisation[6];
(2)   participation in activities undertaken by the organisation or on its behalf or under its auspices[7];
(3)   the provision of goods, facilities or services in the course of activities undertaken by the organisation or on its behalf or under its auspices[8];
(4)   the use or disposal of premises owned or controlled by the organisation[9],

and a person does not contravene the provisions on premises, so far as relating to religion or belief or sexual orientation, only by doing of those things on behalf of or under the auspices of the organisation[10].

A minister[11] does not contravene the provisions on premises, so far as relating to religion or belief or sexual orientation[12], only by restricting:

(a)   participation in activities carried on in the performance of the minister's functions in connection with or in respect of the organisation[13]; or

(b)   the provision of goods, facilities or services in the course of activities carried on in the performance of the minister's functions in connection with or in respect of the organisation[14].

1 As to the meaning of 'religious organisation' for these purposes see PARA 97 note 1.
2 Equality Act 2010 Sch 23 para 2(2).
3 Ie the Equality Act 2010 s Pt 4 (ss 32–38) (see PARA 105 et seq). As to exceptions from the Equality Act 2010 generally, and as to further exceptions in specific circumstances, see PARAS 320–338.
4 As to religion or belief as a protected characteristic see PARA 59; and as to restrictions on the permitted discrimination see the Equality Act 2010 Sch 23 para 2(6); and PARA 97 note 4.
5 As to sexual orientation as a protected characteristic see PARA 63; and as to restrictions on the permitted discrimination see the Equality Act 2010 Sch 23 para 2(7), (9)–(11); and PARA 97 note 5.
6 Equality Act 2010 Sch 23 para 2(3)(a).
7 Equality Act 2010 Sch 23 para 2(3)(b).
8 Equality Act 2010 Sch 23 para 2(3)(c).
9 Equality Act 2010 Sch 23 para 2(3)(d). As to the meaning of 'disposal' for these purposes see the Equality Act 2010 Sch 23 para 2(12), (13)(a); and PARA 97 note 9.
10 Equality Act 2010 Sch 23 para 2(4).
11 As to the meaning of 'minister' for these purposes see the Equality Act 2010 Sch 23 para 2(8); and PARA 97 note 11.
12 See notes 4, 5.
13 Equality Act 2010 Sch 23 para 2(5)(a).
14 Equality Act 2010 Sch 23 para 2(5)(b).

113. Owner-occupier.

Where there is a private disposal of premises[1] by an owner occupier[2]:

(1)   the prohibition against discrimination by a person who has the right to dispose of premises[3] applies only in so far as it relates to race[4];

(2)   the prohibition against discrimination by a person whose permission is required for the disposal of premises[5] does not apply in so far as it relates to religion or belief[6] or sexual orientation[7].

A duty to make reasonable adjustments[8] does not apply:

(a)   in the case of a controller of let premises[9], if the premises are, or have been, the only main home of a person by whom they are let[10]; and, since entering into the letting, neither that person nor any other by whom they are let has used a manager[11] for managing the premises[12];

(b)   in the case of a controller of premises to let[13], if the premises are, or have been, the only or main home of a person who has them to let[14]; and neither that person nor any other who has the premises to let uses the services of an estate agent[15] for letting the premises[16].

1 A disposal is a private disposal only if the owner-occupier does not use the services of an estate agent for the purpose of disposing of the premises; or publish (or cause to be published) an advertisement in connection with their disposal: Equality Act 2010 s 38(9), Sch 5 para 1(2). For these purposes, 'estate agent' means a person who, by way of profession or trade, provides services for the purpose of finding premises for persons seeking them; or assisting in the disposal of premises; and 'owner-occupier' means a person who owns an estate or interest in premises; and occupies the whole of them: Sch 5 para 1(5). As to the meanings of 'disposal of premises' and 'premises' see PARA 106 note 1. As to the meaning of 'trade' see PARA 239 note 8.

2   Equality Act 2010 Sch 5 para 1(1).
3   Ie under the Equality Act 2010 s 33(1) (see PARA 106). As to exceptions from the Equality Act
    2010 generally, and as to further exceptions in specific circumstances, see PARAS 320–338.
4   Equality Act 2010 Sch 5 para 1(3). As to the protected characteristic of race see PARA 58.
5   Ie under the Equality Act 2010 s 34(1) (see PARA 107).
6   As to the protected characteristic of religion or belief see PARA 59.
7   Equality Act 2010 Sch 5 para 1(4). As to the protected characteristic of sexual orientation see
    PARA 63.
8   As to the duty to make reasonable adjustments see PARAS 109, 241–244.
9   Ie under the Equality Act 2010 s 36(1)(a) (see PARA 109).
10 Equality Act 2010 Sch 5 para 2(1)(a).
11 A manager is a person who, by profession or trade, manages let premises: Equality Act 2010 Sch 5
    para 2(2).
12 Equality Act 2010 Sch 5 para 2(1)(b).
13 Ie under the Equality Act 2010 s 36(1)(b) (see PARA 109).
14 Equality Act 2010 Sch 5 para 2(3)(a).
15 As to the meaning of 'estate agent' see note 1 (definition applied by the Equality Act 2010 Sch 5
    para 2(4)).
16 Equality Act 2010 Sch 5 para 2(3)(b).

114.   Small premises.

The following provisions apply to anything done by a person in relation to the
disposal[1], occupation[2] or management of part of small premises[3] if:

(1)   the person or a relative[4] of that person resides, and intends to continue
        to reside, in another part of the premises[5]; and

(2)   the premises include parts (other than storage areas and means of
        access) shared with residents of the premises who are not members of
        the same household as the resident mentioned in head (1)[6].

The provisions relating to prohibition against discrimination by:

(a)   a person who has the right to dispose of premises[7];

(b)   a person whose permission is required for the disposal of premises[8]; and

(c)   a person who manages premises[9],

apply only in so far as they relate to race[10].

A duty to make reasonable adjustments[11] does not apply[12] if:

(i)   the premises in question are small premises[13];

(ii)   the relevant person[14] or a relative[15] of that person resides, and intends to
        continue to reside, in another part of the premises[16]; and

(iii)   the premises include parts (other than storage areas and means of
        access) shared with residents of the premises who are not members of
        the same household as the resident mentioned in head (ii)[17].

1   As to the meaning of 'disposal of premises' see PARA 106 note 1. As to exceptions from the
    Equality Act 2010 generally, and as to further exceptions in specific circumstances, see PARAS
    320–338.
2   As to the meaning of 'occupation' see PARA 106 note 11.
3   Equality Act 2010 s 38(9), Sch 5 para 3(1). A Minister of the Crown may by order amend Sch 5
    paras 3, 4 (see the text and notes 4–17): Sch 5 para 5. At the date at which this volume states the
    law no such order had been made. As to the meaning of 'premises' see PARA 106 note 1. Premises
    are small if:
        (1)   the only other persons occupying the accommodation occupied by the resident
                mentioned in head (1) in the text are members of the same household (Sch 5 para
                3(3)(a));
        (2)   the premises also include accommodation for at least one other household (Sch 5 para
                3(3)(b));
        (3)   the accommodation for each of those other households is let, or available for letting, on
                a separate tenancy or similar agreement (Sch 5 para 3(3)(c)); and

(4)   the premises are not normally sufficient to accommodate more than two other households (Sch 5 para 3(3)(d)).

Premises are also small if they are not normally sufficient to provide residential accommodation for more than six persons (in addition to the resident mentioned in head (1) in the text and members of the same household): Sch 5 para 3(4).

4   For these purposes, 'relative' means:
   (1)   spouse or civil partner (Sch 5 para 3(5)(a));
   (2)   unmarried partner (Sch 5 para 3(5)(b));
   (3)   parent or grandparent (Sch 5 para 3(5)(c));
   (4)   child or grandchild (whether or not legitimate) (Sch 5 para 3(5)(d));
   (5)   the spouse, civil partner or unmarried partner of a child or grandchild (Sch 5 para 3(5)(e));
   (6)   brother or sister (whether of full blood or half-blood) (Sch 5 para 3(5)(f)); or
   (7)   a relative within heads (3)–(6) whose relationship arises as a result of marriage or civil partnership (Sch 5 para 3(5)(g)).

For these purposes, a reference to an unmarried partner is a reference to the other member of a couple consisting of a man and a woman who are not married to each other but are living together as husband and wife; or two people of the same sex who are not civil partners of each other but are living together as if they were: Sch 5 para 3(6). 'Parent', in relation to England and Wales, has the same meaning as in the Education Act 1996 (see EDUCATION vol 35 (2015) PARA 7): Equality Act 2010 s 212(1). Spouse includes a person who is married to a person of the same sex: see the Marriage (Same Sex Couples) Act 2013 Sch 3 paras 1(1)(c), 2, 3.

5   Equality Act 2010 Sch 5 para 3(1)(a).
6   Equality Act 2010 Sch 5 para 3(1)(b).
7   Ie under the Equality Act 2010 s 33(1) (see PARA 106).
8   Ie under the Equality Act 2010 s 34(1) (see PARA 107).
9   Ie under the Equality Act 2010 s 35(1) (see PARA 108).
10   Equality Act 2010 Sch 5 para 3(2). As to the protected characteristic of race see PARA 58.
11   Ie under the Equality Act 2010 s 36(1) (see PARA 109).
12   Equality Act 2010 Sch 5 para 4(1). See note 3.
13   Equality Act 2010 Sch 5 para 4(1)(a). As to the meaning of 'small premises' see note 3 (definition applied by Sch 5 para 4(3)).
14   The relevant person is the person who, for the purposes of the Equality Act 2010 s 36(1) (see PARA 109) is the controller of the premises; or the responsible person in relation to the common parts to which the premises relate: Sch 5 para 4(2). As to the meanings of 'controller of let premises' and 'controller of premises to let' see PARA 109 notes 2–3. As to the meaning of 'responsible person in relation to common parts' see PARA 109 note 5.
15   As to the meaning of 'relative' see note 4 (definition applied by Sch 5 para 4(3)).
16   Equality Act 2010 Sch 5 para 4(1)(b).
17   Equality Act 2010 Sch 5 para 4(1)(c).

115.   Exceptions relating to transsexual persons and sport.

A person does not contravene the provisions of the Equality Act 2010 on the disposal and management of premises[1], so far as relating to gender reassignment[2], only by doing anything in relation to the participation of a transsexual person as a competitor in a gender-affected activity[3] if it is necessary to do so to secure in relation to the activity fair competition[4] or the safety of competitors[5].

1   Ie the Equality Act 2010 ss 33, 34, or 35 (see PARAS 106–108). As to exceptions from the Equality Act 2010 generally, and as to further exceptions in specific circumstances, see PARAS 320–338.
2   As to gender reassignment as a protected characteristic see PARAS 56, 61.
3   As to the meaning of 'gender-affected activity' see PARA 328.
4   Equality Act 2010 s 195(2)(a).
5   Equality Act 2010 s 195(2)(b).

7. WORK

(1) EMPLOYMENT

(i) Employees

116. 'Employee' and 'employment'.

For the purposes of the provisions of the Equality Act 2010 concerning discrimination at work[1] 'employment' means:

(1)   employment under a contract of employment[2], a contract of apprenticeship[3] or a contract personally to do work[4];

(2)   Crown employment[5];

(3)   employment as a relevant member of the House of Commons staff[6]; and

(4)   employment as a relevant member of the House of Lords staff[7].

and references to an 'employer' or an 'employee', or to 'employing' or 'being employed', are construed accordingly[8].

Those provisions apply to service in the armed forces as they apply to employment by a private person[9]; apply in relation to work on ships[10], work on hovercraft[11] and seafarers[12] in certain circumstances[13]; and extend subject to modifications, to offshore work[14].

1   Ie the Equality Act 2010 Pt 5 (ss 39–83) (see PARA 117 et seq).

2   As to contracts of employment see EMPLOYMENT vol 39 (2014) PARA 2.

3   As to contracts of apprenticeship see EMPLOYMENT vol 39 (2014) PARA 112.

4   Equality Act 2010 s 83(1), (2)(a). There is no employment relationship for these purposes where the dominant purpose of the contract is not to carry out work personally: see *Patterson v Legal Services Commission* [2003] EWCA Civ 1558, [2004] ICR 312, [2004] IRLR 153 (decided under the Race Relations Act 1976). See also *Halawi v WDFG UK Ltd (t/a World Duty Free)* [2014] EWCA Civ 1387, [2015] IRLR 50 (no requirement to perform work personally); *Capita Translation and Interpreting Ltd v Siacuinas* UKEAT/0181/16/RN, EAT.

5   Equality Act 2010 s 83(2)(b). 'Crown employment' means employment under or for the purposes of a government department or any officer or body exercising on behalf of the Crown functions conferred by a statutory provision: Employment Rights Act 1996 s 191(3) (applied by the Equality Act 2010 s 83(1), (9)); and see EMPLOYMENT vol 39 (2014) PARA 163.

6   Equality Act 2010 s 83(2)(c). 'Relevant member of the House of Commons staff' means any person who was appointed by the House of Commons Commission or is employed in the refreshment department; or who is a member of the Speaker's personal staff: see the Employment Rights Act 1996 s 195(5); and EMPLOYMENT vol 39 (2014) PARA 165 (definition applied by the Equality Act 2010 s 83(1), (5)). Such a member of staff is an employee of the person who is the employer of that member under the Employment Rights Act 1996 s 195(6) (see EMPLOYMENT vol 39 (2014) PARA 165) or, if s 195(7) applies in the case of that member (see EMPLOYMENT vol 39 (2014) PARA 165), the person who is the employer of that member under s 195(7): Equality Act 2010 s 83(5)(a), (b).

7   Equality Act 2010 s 83(2)(d). 'Relevant member of the House of Lords staff' means any person who is employed under a contract of employment with the Corporate Officer of the House of Lords: see the Employment Rights Act 1996 s 194(6); and EMPLOYMENT vol 39 (2014) PARA 164 (definition applied by the Equality Act 2010 s 83(1), (6)).

8   A reference to an employer or an employee, or to employing or being employed, is (subject to the Equality Act 2010 s 212(11): see PARA 134 note 4) to be read with s 83(2), (3); and a reference to an employer also includes a reference to a person who has no employees but is seeking to employ one or more other persons: see s 83(4).

9   Equality Act 2010 s 83(3). For this purpose references to terms of employment, or to a contract of employment, are to be read as including references to terms of service; and references to associated employers are to be ignored: s 83(3).

10   As to the meaning of 'ship' see the Merchant Shipping Act 1995 s 313(1); and SHIPPING AND MARITIME LAW vol 93 (2017) PARA 229 (definition applied by the Equality Act 2010 s 81(3)).

11 As to the meaning of 'hovercraft' see the Hovercraft Act 1968 s 4(1); and SHIPPING AND MARITIME LAW vol 93 (2017) PARA 381 (definition applied by the Equality Act 2010 s 81(4)).

12 'Seafarer' means a person employed or engaged in any capacity on board a ship or hovercraft: Equality Act 2010 s 81(5).

13 Ie in the circumstances prescribed by the Equality Act 2010 (Work on Ships and Hovercraft) Regulations 2011, SI 2011/1771: Equality Act 2010 s 81(1). For these purposes it does not matter whether employment arises or work is carried out within or outside the United Kingdom: s 81(2). Nothing in s 81 affects the application of any other provision of the Equality Act 2010 to conduct outside England and Wales or Scotland: s 81(6). As to the meanings of 'United Kingdom', 'England', 'Wales' and 'Scotland' see PARA 85 note 1.

14 See the Equality Act 2010 (Offshore Work) Order 2010, SI 2010/1835 (made under the Equality Act 2010 s 82).

117. Employees and applicants: discrimination and victimisation.

An employer (A), must not discriminate against[1] or victimise[2] a person (B):

(1)   in the arrangements A makes for deciding to whom to offer employment[3];

(2)   as to the terms on which A offers B employment[4];

(3)   by not offering B employment[5].

A must not discriminate against or victimise an employee of A's (B):

(a)   as to B's terms of employment[6];

(b)   in the way A affords B access, or by not affording B access, to opportunities for promotion, transfer or training or for receiving any other benefit, facility or service[7];

(c)   by dismissing B[8];

(d)   by subjecting B to any other detriment[9].

1   As to direct discrimination see PARA 67; and as to indirect discrimination see PARA 75.

2   As to victimisation see PARA 81.

3   Equality Act 2010 s 39(1)(a), (3)(a). 'Arrangements' extend beyond setting up, to the manner of operation and may cover the interview process: see *Nagarajan v London Regional Transport* [2000] 1 AC 501, [1999] 4 All ER 65, HL (decided under the Race Relations Act 1976); *Mallon v Corus Constructions and Industrial* (2003) 147 Sol Jo LB 1150, [2003] All ER (D) 191 (Sep), EAT (decided under the Disability Discrimination Act 1995). See also the Equality Act 2010 Code of Practice — Employment Statutory Code of Practice (2010) para 10.8. As to a partial exception to the Equality Act 2010 s 39(1)(a) in connection with occupational requirements (including religious requirements) see Sch 9 paras 1–3; and PARAS 160–161; as to an exception relating to employment in the armed forces see Sch 9 para 4(1), (2); and PARA 163.

4   Equality Act 2010 s 39(1)(b), (3)(b). Section 39(1)(b), so far as relating to sex (see PARA 60) or pregnancy and maternity (see PARAS 62, 73–74), does not apply to a term that relates to pay:

(1)   unless, were B to accept the offer, an equality clause or rule would have effect in relation to the term (s 39(6)(a)); or

(2)   if head (1) does not apply, except in so far as making an offer on terms including that term amounts to a contravention of s 39(1)(b) by virtue of s 13 (see PARA 67), s 14 or s 18 (see PARA 74) (s 39(6)(b)).

'Equality clause' means a sex equality clause or maternity equality clause: s 212(1). As to the meaning of 'sex equality clause' see s 66; and PARA 139 (definition applied by s 212(1)). As to the meaning of 'maternity equality clause' see s 73; and PARA 147 (definition applied by s 212(1)). 'Equality rule' means a sex equality rule or maternity equality rule: s 212(1). As to the meaning of 'sex equality rule' see s 67; and PARA 140 (definition applied by s 212(1)). As to the meaning of 'maternity equality rule' see s 75; and PARA 146 (definition applied by s 212(1)). As to examples of terms on which an employer might offer employment see the Equality Act 2010 Code of Practice — Employment Statutory Code of Practice (2010) para 10.9.

A person does not contravene the Equality Act 2010 s 39(1)(b) or (2), so far as relating to pregnancy and maternity, by depriving a woman who is on maternity leave of any benefit from the terms of her employment relating to pay: s 83(11), Sch 9 para 17(1). For this purpose the reference to 'benefit from the terms of a woman's employment relating to pay' does not include a reference to:

(a)   maternity-related pay (ie pay to which a woman is entitled as a result of being pregnant or in respect of times when she is on maternity leave) (including maternity-related pay that is increase-related) (Sch 9 para 17(2)(a), (6));

(b)   pay (including increase-related pay) in respect of times when she is not on maternity leave (Sch 9 para 17(2)(b)); or

(c)   pay by way of bonus in respect of times when she is on compulsory maternity leave (Sch 9 para 17(2)(c)).

For these purposes:

(i)   a reference to terms of a woman's employment is a reference to terms of her employment that are not in her contract of employment, her contract of apprenticeship or her contract to do work personally (Sch 9 para 17(4));

(ii)   'pay' means benefits that consist of the payment of money to an employee by way of wages or salary and that are not benefits whose provision is regulated by the contract referred to above (Sch 9 para 17(5)); and

(iii)   pay is increase-related in so far as it is to be calculated by reference to increases in pay that the woman would have received had she not been on maternity leave (Sch 9 para 17(3)).

As to pregnancy and maternity as a protected characteristic see PARAS 62, 73–74.

5   Equality Act 2010 s 39(1)(c), (3)(c). For a partial exception to these provisions in connection with occupational requirements (including religious requirements) see Sch 9 paras 1–3; and PARAS 160–161; for an exception relating to employment in the armed forces see Sch 9 para 4(1), (2); and PARA 163.

6   Equality Act 2010 s 39(2)(a), (4)(a). See also the Equality Act 2010 Code of Practice — Employment Statutory Code of Practice (2010) para 10.12. Discrimination on account of an employee's immigration status does not amount to discrimination on account of race: see *Taiwo v Olaigbe; Onu v Akwiwu* [2016] UKSC 31, [2016] 1 WLR 2653, [2016] All ER (D) 134 (Jun). The Equality Act 2010 s 39(2) (so far as relating to employment) has no effect in relation to a term of a woman's work that is modified by a maternity equality clause or rule or in relation to a term of a woman's work that relates to pay but in relation to which a maternity equality clause or rule has no effect: see s 76(1), (1A), (3); and PARA 147. The inclusion in the woman's terms of a term that requires modification by virtue of s 73(2) or (3) (see PARA 147) is not pregnancy and maternity discrimination for these purposes: s 76(2). As to an exception relating to maternity pay see note 4; as to an exception relating to the provision of public services see Sch 9 para 19; and PARA 171.

7   Equality Act 2010 s 39(2)(b), (4)(b). See note 6. A reference, however expressed, to providing or affording access to a benefit, facility or service (other than in the context of the provision of an information society service within the meaning of Sch 25: see PARAS 335–338), includes a reference to facilitating access to the benefit, facility or service: s 212(4), Sch 25 para 7(8). This can include a refusal to investigate complaints of unfair treatment, as long as the refusal is on a prohibited ground: see *Eke v Customs and Excise Comrs* [1981] IRLR 334, EAT (decided under the Race Relations Act 1976). See *R (on the application of Hottak) v Secretary of State for Foreign and Commonwealth Affairs* [2016] EWCA Civ 438, [2016] 1 WLR 3791, [2016] All ER (D) 67 (May) (unsuccessful discrimination claim by Afghan interpreters employed by British armed forces in Afghanistan that their benefits scheme was less generous than scheme for Iraqi locally employed staff). For a partial exception to these provisions in connection with occupational requirements (including religious requirements) see the Equality Act 2010 Sch 9 paras 1–3; and PARAS 160–161; for an exception relating to employment in the armed forces see Sch 9 para 4(1), (2); and PARA 163; for applicable modifications in relation to these exceptions see Sch 9 para 6(5). There are also exceptions to this provision in connection with the provision of childcare: see Sch 9 para 15(2)(a); and PARA 168.

8   Equality Act 2010 s 39(2)(c), (4)(c). See note 6. In s 39(2)(c), (4)(c), the reference to dismissing B includes a reference to the termination of B's employment:

(1)   by the expiry of a period (including a period expiring by reference to an event or circumstance) (s 39(7)(b));

(2)   by an act of B's (including giving notice) in circumstances such that B is entitled, because of A's conduct, to terminate the employment without notice (s 39(7)(b)).

Head (1) does not apply if, immediately after the termination, the employment is renewed on the same terms: s 39(8). In the case of a person in Crown employment, or in employment as a relevant member of the House of Commons staff, a reference to the person's dismissal is a reference to the termination of the person's employment: s 83(1), (7). As to the meaning of 'Crown employment' see PARA 116 note 5. As to a partial exception to these provisions in connection with occupational requirements (including religious requirements) see Sch 9 paras 1–3; and PARAS 160–161; as to applicable modifications in relation to this exceptions see Sch 9 para 6(6).

9 Equality Act 2010 s 39(2)(d), (4)(d). See note 6. As to the meaning of 'detriment' see PARA 81 note 1. Post-termination of employment victimisation is prohibited by the Equality Act 2010: *Jessemey v Rowstock Ltd* [2014] EWCA Civ 185, [2014] 3 All ER 409.

118. Employees and applicants: harassment.

An employer (A) must not, in relation to employment[1] by A, harass[2] a person (B):

(1)   who is an employee of A's[3]; or

(2)   who has applied to A for employment[4].

1 As to the meanings of 'employment', 'employee' and 'employer' see PARA 116
2 As to harassment see PARA 79.
3 Equality Act 2010 s 40(1)(a).
4 Equality Act 2010 s 40(1)(b).

119. Contract workers.

A principal[1] must not discriminate[2] against or victimise[3] a contract worker[4]:

(1)   as to the terms on which the principal allows the worker to do the work[5];

(2)   by not allowing the worker to do, or to continue to do, the work[6];

(3)   in the way the principal affords the worker access, or by not affording the worker access, to opportunities for receiving a benefit, facility or service[7];

(4)   by subjecting the worker to any other detriment[8].

A principal must not, in relation to contract work, harass[9] a contract worker[10].

1 A 'principal' is a person who makes work available for an individual who is:
    (1)   employed by another person (Equality Act 2010 s 41(5)(a)); and
    (2)   supplied by that other person in furtherance of a contract to which the principal is a party (whether or not that other person is a party to it) (s 41(5)(b)).
2 As to direct discrimination see PARA 67; and as to indirect discrimination see PARA 75.
3 As to victimisation see PARA 81.
4 A 'contract worker' is an individual supplied to a principal in furtherance of a contract such as is mentioned in note 1 head (2): Equality Act 2010 s 41(7). 'Contract work' is work such as is mentioned in s 41(5) (see note 1): s 41(6).
5 Equality Act 2010 s 41(1)(a), (3)(a). As to an exception relating to the provision of public services see Sch 9 para 19; and PARA 171.
6 Equality Act 2010 s 41(1)(b), (3)(b). As to a partial exception to these provisions in connection with occupational requirements (including religious requirements) see Sch 9 paras 1–3; and PARAS 160–161; for modifications in connection with this exception see Sch 9 para 6(7). See also note 5.
7 Equality Act 2010 s 41(1)(c), (3)(c). As to the meaning of 'benefit, facility or service' see PARA 117 note 7. There are exceptions to this provision in connection with the provision of childcare: see Sch 9 para 15; and PARA 168. See also note 5.
8 Equality Act 2010 s 41(1)(d), (3)(d). As to the meaning of 'detriment' see PARA 81 note 1. See also note 5.
9 As to harassment see PARA 79
10 Equality Act 2010 s 41(2).

120. Vicarious liability.

Anything done[1] by a person (A) in the course of A's employment[2] must be treated as also done by the employer[3]; and anything done by an agent for a principal, with the authority of the principal, must be treated as also done by the principal[4]. It does not matter whether the thing is done with the employer's or principal's knowledge or approval[5]. In proceedings against A's employer (B) in respect of anything alleged to have been done by A in the course of A's employment it is a defence for B to show that B took all reasonable steps to prevent A from doing that thing or from doing anything of that description[6].

If a person who is an employee or agent[7] does something which by virtue of these provisions[8] is treated as having been done by his employer or principal[9], and the doing of that thing by the person amounts to a contravention of the Equality Act 2010[10] by the employer or principal[11], that is a contravention[12]. It does not matter whether, in any proceedings, the employer is found[13] not to have contravened the Act[14]. However, it is not a contravention of the Act if:

(1)   the person relies on a statement by the employer or principal that doing that thing is not a contravention thereof[15] and it is reasonable for the person to do so[16];

(2)   a specified person[17] does not conduct a relevant marriage[18], is not present at, does not carry out, or does not otherwise participate in, a relevant marriage, or does not consent to a relevant marriage being conducted, for the reason that the marriage is the marriage of a same sex couple[19].

1   These provisions do not apply to offences under the Equality Act 2010 (other than offences under Pt 12 (ss 160–188) (disabled persons: transport: see PARAS **215–236**)): s 109(5).

2   The common law rules on 'in the course of employment' are not to be applied in relation to vicarious liability (see *Jones v Tower Boot Co Ltd* [1997] 2 All ER 406, [1997] IRLR 168, CA (decided under the Sex Discrimination Act 1975 and the Race Relations Act 1976 (both repealed))), and the phrase may therefore cover apparently social activities if in fact work-related (see *Chief Constable of Lincolnshire Police v Stubbs* [1999] IRLR 81, EAT (decided under the Sex Discrimination Act 1975 (repealed))).

3   Equality Act 2010 s 109(1). As to the meanings of 'employment', 'employee' and 'employer' see PARA **116** Thus both employer and employee are liable where these provisions apply: see eg *Read v Tiverton District Council* [1977] IRLR 202, IT (decided under the Sex Discrimination Act 1975 (repealed)).

4   Equality Act 2010 s 109(2). As to the meaning of 'principal' see PARA **119** note 1. In contrast to the position in relation to ordinary vicarious liability (ie that the common law tests are not to be applied), vicarious liability in the context of agency is to be construed in the light of common law rules of agency: see eg *Yearwood v Metropolitan Police Comr* [2004] ICR 1660, [2004] All ER (D) 457 (May), EAT (decided under the Sex Discrimination Act 1975 and the Race Relations Act 1976 (both repealed)). See also *Ministry of Defence v Kemeh* [2014] EWCA Civ 91, [2014] IRLR 377(decided under the Race Relations Act 1976 (repealed)).

5   Equality Act 2010 s 109(3).

6   Equality Act 2010 s 109(4). In connection with this defence see eg *Palmer v Southend-on-Sea Borough Council* [1984] IRLR 119, [1984] ICR 372, CA (decided under the Employment Protection (Consolidation) Act 1978 s 67 (repealed)); *Balgobin and Francis v London Borough of Tower Hamlets* [1987] IRLR 401, [1987] ICR 829 (decided under the Sex Discrimination Act 1975 (repealed)).

7   Equality Act 2010 s 110(1)(a).

8   Ie by virtue of the Equality Act 2010 s 109(1) or s 109(2) (see the text and notes 1–4).

9   Equality Act 2010 s 110(1)(b).

10   As to the Equality Act 2010 see PARAS **1–4**.

11   Equality Act 2010 s 110(1)(c). The reference in s 110(1)(c) to a contravention of the Equality Act 2010 does not include a reference to disability discrimination in contravention of Pt 6 Ch 1 (ss 84–89) (schools: see PARAS **173–175**): s 110(7).

12   Ie a contravention of the Equality Act 2010 s 110 (see the text and notes 7–11, 13–19).

13   Ie by virtue of the Equality Act 2010 s 109(4) (see the text and note 6).

14   Equality Act 2010 s 110(2).

15   Equality Act 2010 s 110(3)(a). A person commits an offence if he knowingly or recklessly makes a statement mentioned in s 110(3)(a) which is false or misleading in a material respect: s 110(4). A person guilty of an offence under s 110(4) is liable on summary conviction to a fine not exceeding level 5 on the standard scale: s 110(5). As to the powers of magistrates' courts to issue fines on summary conviction see SENTENCING vol 92 (2015) PARA 176.

16   Equality Act 2010 s 110(3)(b).

17 Ie a 'person' within the meaning of the Marriage (Same Sex Couples) Act 2013 s 2 (see MATRIMONIAL AND CIVIL PARTNERSHIP LAW vol 72 (2015) PARA 1): Equality Act 2010 s 110(5B) (s 110(5A), (5B) added by the Marriage (Same Sex Couples) Act 2013 s 2(5)).

18 As to the meaning of 'relevant marriage' see the Marriage (Same Sex Couples) Act 2013 s 2(4); and MATRIMONIAL AND CIVIL PARTNERSHIP LAW vol 72 (2015) PARA 1 (definition applied by the Equality Act 2010 s 110(5B) (as added: see note 17)).

19 Equality Act 2010 s 110(5A) (as added: see note 17). See MATRIMONIAL AND CIVIL PARTNERSHIP LAW vol 72 (2015) PARA 1.

(ii) Police Officers

121. Identity of employer.

For the purposes of Part 5 of the Equality Act 2010[1], holding the office of constable is to be treated as employment[2]:

(1)　by the chief officer[3], in respect of any act done by the chief officer in relation to a constable or appointment to the office of constable[4];

(2)　by the responsible authority[5], in respect of any act done by the authority in relation to a constable or appointment to the office of constable[6].

For these purposes, holding an appointment as a police cadet[7] is to be treated as employment:

(a)　by the chief officer, in respect of any act done by the chief officer in relation to a police cadet or appointment as one[8];

(b)　by the responsible authority, in respect of any act done by the authority in relation to a police cadet or appointment as one[9].

1 Ie the Equality Act 2010 ss 39–83 (see PARA 116 et seq).

2 As to the meaning of 'employment' see PARA 116.

3 'Chief officer' means:
   (1)　in relation to an appointment under a relevant Act, the chief officer of police for the police force to which the appointment relates (Equality Act 2010 s 43(1), (2)(a));
   (2)　in relation to any other appointment, the person under whose direction and control the body of constables or other persons to which the appointment relates is (s 43(1), (2)(b));
   (3)　in relation to a constable or other person under the direction and control of a chief officer of police, that chief officer of police (s 43(1), (2)(c));
   (4)　in relation to any other constable or any other person, the person under whose direction and control the constable or other person is (s 43(1), (2)(d)).

   For these purposes, the 'relevant Acts' are the Metropolitan Police Act 1839 (see LONDON GOVERNMENT vol 71 (2013) PARAS 310–313; POLICE AND INVESTIGATORY POWERS vol 84 (2013) PARA 127), the City of London Police Act 1839 (see LONDON GOVERNMENT vol 71 (2013) PARAS 310–313; POLICE AND INVESTIGATORY POWERS vol 84 (2013) PARAS 122, 129), and the Police Reform and Social Responsibility Act 2011 (see POLICE AND INVESTIGATORY POWERS): Equality Act 2010 s 43(1), (8) (amended by the Police Reform and Social Responsibility Act 2011 Sch 16 paras 380, 382(b)).

4 Equality Act 2010 s 42(1)(a). Section 42(1) does not apply to service with the Civil Nuclear Constabulary: see s 42(3). As to the Civil Nuclear Constabulary see ENERGY AND CLIMATE CHANGE vol 44 (2011) PARA 924 et seq. Section 42(1) does not apply to a constable at NCA: see s 42(4) (s 42(4), (5) amended by the Crime and Courts Act 2013 Sch 8 para 181). 'NCA' means the National Crime Agency; and a reference to a constable at NCA is a reference to a constable seconded to it to serve as an NCA officer: Equality Act 2010 s 43(1), (5) (s 42(5) substituted by the Crime and Courts Act 2013 Sch 8 para 182). A constable at NCA is to be treated as employed by it, in respect of any act done by it in relation to the constable: Equality Act 2010 s 42(5) (as so amended). As to NCA see POLICE AND INVESTIGATORY POWERS vol 84 (2013) PARA 379. See *P v Metropolitan Police Commissioner* [2017] UKSC 65, [2017] All ER (D) 133 (Oct), where it was held that the Equality Act 2010 s 42(1) was to be interpreted as applying to the exercise of disciplinary functions by misconduct panels in relation to police constables.

5 'Responsible authority' means (see the Equality Act 2010 s 43(1), (3) (amended by the Police Reform and Social Responsibility Act 2011 Sch 16 paras 380, 382(a))):
   (1)　in relation to an appointment under a relevant Act, the local policing body or police authority that maintains the police force to which the appointment relates;

(2)   in relation to any other appointment, the person by whom a person would (if appointed) be paid;

(3)   in relation to a constable or other person under the direction and control of a chief officer of police, the local policing body or police authority that maintains the police force for which that chief officer is the chief officer of police;

(4)   in relation to any other constable or any other person, the person by whom the constable or other person is paid.

6   Equality Act 2010 s 42(1)(b).
7   For these purposes, 'police cadet' means a person appointed to undergo training with a view to becoming a constable: Equality Act 2010 s 43(1), (4).
8   Equality Act 2010 s 42(2)(a).
9   Equality Act 2010 s 42(2)(b).

(iii) Partners

122.   Duty on partnerships not to discriminate etc.

A firm[1] or proposed firm[2] must not discriminate[3] against or victimise[4] a person:

(1)   in the arrangements it makes for deciding to whom to offer a position as a partner[5];

(2)   as to the terms on which it offers the person a position as a partner[6];

(3)   by not offering the person a position as a partner[7].

A firm (A) must not discriminate against or victimise a partner:

(a)   as to the terms on which B is a partner[8];

(b)   in the way A affords B access, or by not affording B access, to opportunities for promotion, transfer or training or for receiving any other benefit, facility or service[9];

(c)   by expelling B[10];

(d)   by subjecting B to any other detriment[11].

A firm must not, in relation to a position as a partner, harass[12], a partner[13]; or a person who has applied for the position[14]. A proposed firm must not, in relation to a position as a partner, harass a person who has applied for the position[15].

1   For these purposes persons who have entered into partnership with one another are called collectively a 'firm': Partnership Act 1890 s 4(1) (applied by the Equality Act 2010 s 46(1), (2)). 'Partnership' is the relation which subsists between persons carrying on a business in common with a view of profit: Partnership Act 1890 s 1(1) (applied by the Equality Act 2010 s 46(1), (2)). See PARTNERSHIP vol 79 (2014) PARA 1
2   'Proposed firm' means persons proposing to form themselves into a partnership: Equality Act 2010 s 46(1), (3).
3   As to direct discrimination see PARA 67; and as indirect discrimination see PARA 75.
4   As to victimisation see PARA 81.
5   Equality Act 2010 s 44(1)(a), (5)(a). In the application of s 44 to a limited partnership within the meaning of the Limited Partnership Act 1907 (see PARTNERSHIP vol 79 (2014) PARA 218), 'partner' means a general partner within the meaning of the 1907 Act: Equality Act 2010 s 44(8); and see PARTNERSHIP vol 79 (2014) PARA 218. As to the meaning of 'arrangements' see PARA 117 note 3. As to a partial exception to these provisions in connection with occupational requirements (including religious requirements) see Sch 9 paras 1–3; and PARAS 160–161.
6   Equality Act 2010 s 44(1)(b), (5)(b).
7   Equality Act 2010 s 44(1)(c), (5)(c). As to a partial exception to these provisions in connection with occupational requirements (including religious requirements) see Sch 9 paras 1–3; and PARAS 160–161.
8   Equality Act 2010 s 44(2)(a), (6)(a). As to an exception relating to the provision of public services see Sch 9 para 19; and PARA 171.
9   Equality Act 2010 s 44(2)(b), (6)(b). As to the meaning of 'benefit, facility or service' see PARA 117 note 7. As to a partial exception to these provisions in connection with occupational requirements (including religious requirements) see Sch 9 paras 1–3; and PARAS 160–161; for applicable

modifications in relation to these exceptions see Sch 9 para 6(5). There are also exceptions to this provision in connection with the provision of childcare: see Sch 9 para 15; and PARA **168**. See also note 8.

10 Equality Act 2010 s 44(2)(c), (6)(c). A reference to expelling a partner of a firm or a member of an LLP includes a reference to the termination of the person's position as such:

    (1)   by the expiry of a period (including a period expiring by reference to an event or circumstance) (s 46(1), (6)(a));

    (2)   by an act of the person (including giving notice) in circumstances such that the person is entitled, because of the conduct of other partners or members, to terminate the position without notice (s 46(1), (6)(b));

    (3)   (in the case of a partner of a firm) as a result of the dissolution of the partnership (s 46(1), (6)(c)).

Heads (1) and (3) do not apply if, immediately after the termination, the position is renewed on the same terms: s 46(1), (7). As to the meaning of 'LLP' see PARA **123** note 1. As to a partial exception to these provisions in connection with occupational requirements (including religious requirements) see Sch 9 paras 1–3; and PARAS **160–161**; as to applicable modifications in relation to this exception see Sch 9 para 6(6). See also note 8.

11 Equality Act 2010 s 44(2)(d), (6)(d). As to the meaning of 'detriment' see PARA **81** note 1. See also note 8.

12 As to harassment see PARA **79**.

13 Equality Act 2010 s 44(3)(a).

14 Equality Act 2010 s 44(3)(b).

15 Equality Act 2010 s 44(4).

123. Duty on limited liability partnerships not to discriminate etc.

An LLP[1] or proposed LLP[2] must not discriminate[3] against or victimise[4] a person:

    (1)   in the arrangements it makes for deciding to whom to offer a position as a member[5];

    (2)   as to the terms on which it offers the person a position as a member[6];

    (3)   by not offering the person a position as a member[7].

An LLP (A) must not discriminate against or victimise a member (B):

    (a)   as to the terms on which B is a member[8];

    (b)   in the way A affords B access, or by not affording B access, to opportunities for promotion, transfer or training or for receiving any other benefit, facility or service[9];

    (c)   by expelling B[10];

    (d)   by subjecting B to any other detriment[11].

An LLP must not, in relation to a position as a member, harass[12] a member[13] or a person who has applied for the position[14]. A proposed LLP must not, in relation to a position as a member, harass a person who has applied for the position[15].

1 For these purposes, 'LLP' means a limited liability partnership within the meaning of the Limited Liability Partnerships Act 2000 (see PARTNERSHIP vol 79 (2014) PARA 233): Equality Act 2010 s 46(1), (4).

2 'Proposed LLP' means persons proposing to incorporate an LLP with themselves as members: Equality Act 2010 s 46(1), (5).

3 As to direct discrimination see PARA **67**; and as indirect discrimination see PARA **75**.

4 As to victimisation see PARA **81**.

5 Equality Act 2010 s 45(1)(a), (5)(a). As to the meaning of 'arrangements' see PARA **117** note 3. As to a partial exception to these provisions in connection with occupational requirements (including religious requirements) see Sch 9 paras 1–3; and PARAS **160–161**.

6 Equality Act 2010 s 45(1)(b), (5)(b).

7 Equality Act 2010 s 45(1)(c), (5)(c). As to a partial exception to these provisions in connection with occupational requirements (including religious requirements) see Sch 9 paras 1–3; and PARAS **160–161**.

8 Equality Act 2010 s 45(2)(a), (6)(a). As to an exception relating to the provision of public services see Sch 9 para 19; and PARA **171**.

9 Equality Act 2010 s 45(2)(b), (6)(b). As to the meaning of 'benefit, facility or service' see PARA 117 note 7. For a partial exception to these provisions in connection with occupational requirements (including religious requirements) see Sch 9 paras 1–3; and PARAS 160–161; for applicable modifications in relation to these exceptions see Sch 9 para 6(5). There are also exceptions to this provision in connection with the provision of childcare: see Sch 9 para 15; and PARA 168. See also note 8.

10 Equality Act 2010 s 45(2)(c), (6)(c). For a partial exception to these provisions in connection with occupational requirements (including religious requirements) see Sch 9 paras 1–3; and PARAS 160–161; for applicable modifications in relation to this exception see Sch 9 para 6(6). See also note 8.

11 Equality Act 2010 s 45(2)(d), (6)(d). As to the meaning of 'detriment' see PARA 81 note 1. See also note 8.

12 As to harassment see PARA 79.

13 Equality Act 2010 s 45(3)(a).

14 Equality Act 2010 s 45(3)(b).

15 Equality Act 2010 s 45(4).

(iv) The Bar

124. Duty on barristers not to discriminate etc.

A barrister[1] (A) must not discriminate against[2] or victimise[3] a person (B):

(1) in the arrangements A makes for deciding to whom to offer a pupillage or tenancy[4]; or

(2) as to the terms on which A offers B a pupillage or tenancy[5];

(3) by not offering B a pupillage or tenancy[6].

A must not discriminate against or victimise B who is a pupil or tenant:

(a) as to the terms on which B is a pupil or tenant[7];

(b) in the way A affords B access, or by not affording B access, to opportunities for training or gaining experience or for receiving any other benefit, facility or service[8];

(c) by terminating the pupillage[9];

(d) by subjecting B to pressure to leave chambers[10];

(e) by subjecting B to any other detriment[11].

A barrister must not, in relation to a pupillage or tenancy, harass[12] the pupil or tenant[13] or a person who has applied for the pupillage or tenancy[14].

A person must not, in relation to instructing a barrister discriminate against a barrister by subjecting the barrister to a detriment[15]; harass the barrister[16]; or victimise the barrister[17].

1 As to the meaning of 'barrister' see LEGAL PROFESSIONS vol 66 (2015) PARA 805. The provisions of the Equality Act 2010 s 47 (see the text and notes 2–17), apart from s 47(6) (see the text and notes 15–17) apply in relation to a barrister's clerk as they apply in relation to a barrister; and for that purpose the reference to a barrister's clerk includes a reference to a person who carries out the functions of a barrister's clerk: s 47(8). As to a barrister's clerk see LEGAL PROFESSIONS vol 66 (2015) PARA 836.

2 As to direct discrimination see PARA 67; and as indirect discrimination see PARA 75.

3 As to victimisation see PARA 81.

4 Equality Act 2010 s 47(1)(a), (4)(a). As to pupillage see LEGAL PROFESSIONS vol 66 (2015) PARA 835 et seq. As to the meaning of 'arrangements' see PARA 117 note 3.

5 Equality Act 2010 s 47(1)(b), (4)(b). A reference to a tenant includes a reference to a barrister who is permitted to work in chambers (including as a squatter or door tenant); and a reference to a tenancy is to be construed accordingly: s 47(9).

6 Equality Act 2010 s 47(1)(c), (4)(c).

7 Equality Act 2010 s 47(2)(a), (5)(a).

8 Equality Act 2010 s 47(2)(b), (5)(b). As to the meaning of 'benefit, facility or service' see PARA 117 note 7. There are exceptions to this provision in connection with the provision of childcare: see Sch 9 para 15; and PARA 168.

9 Equality Act 2010 s 47(2)(c), (5)(c).

10 Equality Act 2010 s 47(2)(c), (5)(d).

11 Equality Act 2010 s 47(2)(c), (5)(e). As to the meaning of 'detriment' see PARA 81 note 1.

12 As to harassment see PARA 79.

13 Equality Act 2010 s 47(3)(a).

14 Equality Act 2010 s 47(3)(b).

15 Equality Act 2010 s 47(6)(a).

16 Equality Act 2010 s 47(6)(b).

17 Equality Act 2010 s 47(6)(c).

(v) Office-holders

125. Personal offices: duty not to discriminate etc.

The following provisions apply in relation to personal offices[1]. A person (A) who has the power to make an appointment to a personal office must not discriminate against[2] or victimise[3] a person (B):

(1)   in the arrangements A makes for deciding to whom to offer the appointment[4];

(2)   as to the terms on which A offers B the appointment[5];

(3)   by not offering B the appointment[6].

A person (A) who is a relevant person[7] in relation to a personal office must not discriminate against or victimise a person (B) appointed to the office:

(a)   as to the terms of B's appointment[8];

(b)   in the way A affords B access, or by not affording B access, to opportunities for promotion, transfer or training or for receiving any other benefit, facility or service[9];

(c)   by terminating B's appointment[10];

(d)   by subjecting B to any other detriment[11].

A person who has the power to make an appointment to a personal office must not, in relation to the office, harass[12] a person seeking, or being considered for, the appointment[13].

A relevant person in relation to a personal office must not, in relation to that office, harass a person appointed to it[14].

1 Equality Act 2010 s 49(1). A 'personal office' is an office or post:

    (1)   to which a person is appointed to discharge a function personally under the direction of another person (ss 49(2)(a), 52(2)); and

    (2)   in respect of which an appointed person is entitled to remuneration (ss 49(2)(b), 52(2)).

For the purposes of head (1) above, a person is to be regarded as discharging functions personally under the direction of another person if that other person is entitled to direct the person as to when and where to discharge the functions: s 49(10). For the purposes of head (2) above, a person is not to be regarded as entitled to remuneration merely because the person is entitled to payments:

    (a)   in respect of expenses incurred by the person in discharging the functions of the office or post (s 49(11)(a)); or

    (b)   by way of compensation for the loss of income or benefits the person would or might have received had the person not been discharging the functions of the office or post (s 49(11)(b)).

2 As to direct discrimination see PARA 67; and as to indirect discrimination see PARA 75.

3 As to victimisation see PARA 81.

4 Equality Act 2010 s 49(3)(a), (5)(a). As to the meaning of 'arrangements' see PARA 117 note 3. As to a partial exception to these provisions in connection with occupational requirements (including religious requirements) see Sch 9 paras 1–3; and PARAS 160–161.

5 Equality Act 2010 s 49(3)(b), (5)(b). Section 49(3)(b), so far as relating to sex or pregnancy and maternity, does not apply to a term that relates to pay:

    (1)   unless, were B to accept the offer, an equality clause or rule would have effect in relation to the term (s 49(12)(a)); or

    (2)   if head (1) does not apply, except in so far as making an offer on terms including that term amounts to a contravention of s 49(3)(b) by virtue of s 13 (see PARA 67), s 14 or s 18 (see PARA 74): (s 49(12)(b)).

As to the meaning of 'equality clause' and 'equality rule' see PARA 117 note 4. As to the protected characteristic of sex see PARA 60; and as to pregnancy and maternity discrimination see PARA 73–74.

6 Equality Act 2010 s 49(3)(c), (5)(c). For a partial exception to these provisions in connection with occupational requirements (including religious requirements) see Sch 9 paras 1–3; and PARAS 160–161.

7 For the purposes of ss 49–51 (see PARA 126 et seq) 'relevant person', in relation to an office, means the person who, in relation to a term of appointment, has the power to set the term; the person who, in relation to access to an opportunity, has the power to afford access to the opportunity (or, if there is no such person, the person who has the power to make the appointment); the person who, in relation to terminating an appointment, has the power to terminate the appointment; the person who, in relation to subjecting an appointee to any other detriment, the person who has the power in relation to the matter to which the conduct in question relates (or, if there is no such person, the person who has the power to make the appointment); and the person who, in relation to harassing an appointee, has the power in relation to the matter to which the conduct in question relates: see the Equality Act 2010 s 52(1), (6). But a reference to a relevant person does not in any case include the House of Commons, the House of Lords, the National Assembly for Wales or the Scottish Parliament: see s 52(1), (6).

8 Equality Act 2010 s 49(6)(a), (8)(a). Section 49(6) (so far as relating to appointment to a personal office) has no effect in relation to a term of a woman's work that is modified by a maternity equality clause or rule or in relation to a term of a woman's work that relates to pay but in relation to which a maternity equality clause or rule has no effect: see s 76(1), (1A), (3); and PARA 147. The inclusion in the woman's terms of a term that requires modification by virtue of the Equality Act 2010 s 73(2) or (3) (see PARA 147) is not pregnancy and maternity discrimination for these purposes: s 76(2). For an exception relating to the provision of public services see Sch 9 para 19; and PARA 171.

9 Equality Act 2010 s 49(6)(b), (8)(b). See note 8. As to the meaning of 'benefit, facility or service' see PARA 117 note 7. As to a partial exception to these provisions in connection with occupational requirements (including religious requirements) see Sch 9 paras 1–3; and PARAS 160–161; as to applicable modifications in relation to this exception see Sch 9 para 6(5). There are also exceptions to this provision in connection with the provision of childcare: see Sch 9 para 15; and PARA 168.

10 Equality Act 2010 s 49(6)(c), (8)(c). See note 8. A reference to terminating a person's appointment includes a reference to termination of the appointment:

    (1)   by the expiry of a period (including a period expiring by reference to an event or circumstance) (s 52(1), (7)(a));

    (2)   by an act of the person (including giving notice) in circumstances such that the person is entitled, because of the relevant person's conduct, to terminate the appointment without notice (s 52(1), (7)(b)).

Head (1) above does not apply if, immediately after the termination, the appointment is renewed on the same terms: s 52(1), (8). As to a partial exception to these provisions in connection with occupational requirements (including religious requirements) see Sch 9 paras 1–3; and PARAS 160–161; for applicable modifications in relation to this exception see Sch 9 para 6(6).

11 Equality Act 2010 49(6)(d), (8)(d). See note 8. As to the meaning of 'detriment' see PARA 81 note 1.

12 As to harassment see PARA 79.

13 Equality Act 2010 s 49(4).

14 Equality Act 2010 s 49(7).

126. Public offices: duty not to discriminate etc.

The following provisions[1] apply in relation to public offices[2].

Where a person (A), has the power to make an appointment to certain public offices[3], A must not:

    (1)   discriminate[4] against or victimise[5] a person (B):

(a)   in the arrangements A makes for deciding to whom to offer the appointment[6];

(b)   as to the terms on which A offers B the appointment[7];

(c)   by not offering B the appointment[8];

(2)   in relation to the office, harass[9] a person seeking, or being considered for, the appointment[10].

A person (A) who is a relevant person[11] in relation to certain public offices[12] must not discriminate against or victimise a person (B) appointed to the office:

(i)   as to B's terms of appointment[13];

(ii)   in the way A affords B access, or by not affording B access, to opportunities for promotion, transfer or training or for receiving any other benefit, facility or service[14];

(iii) by terminating the appointment[15];

(iv)   by subjecting B to any other detriment[16].

A person (A) who is a relevant person in relation to certain public offices[17] must not discriminate against or victimise a person (B) appointed to the office:

(A)   as to B's terms of appointment[18];

(B)   in the way A affords B access, or by not affording B access, to opportunities for promotion, transfer or training or for receiving any other benefit, facility or service[19];

(C)   by subjecting B to any other detriment (other than by terminating the appointment)[20].

A relevant person in relation to a public office must not, in relation to that office, harass[21] a person appointed to it[22].

1   Ie the Equality Act 2010 ss 50, 51 (see the text and notes 2–22; and PARA 127).
2   Equality Act 2010 s 50(1). A 'public office' is:
    (1)   an office or post, appointment to which is made by a member of the executive (s 50(2)(a));
    (2)   an office or post, appointment to which is made on the recommendation of, or subject to the approval of, a member of the executive (s 50(2)(b));
    (3)   an office or post, appointment to which is made on the recommendation of, or subject to the approval of, the House of Commons, the House of Lords, the National Assembly for Wales or the Scottish Parliament (s 50(2)(c));
    (4)   an office or post, appointment to which is made by the Lord Chief Justice or the Senior President of Tribunals (s 50(2)(d) (added by the Crime and Courts Act 2013 Sch 13 para 50(1), (2))).
    An office or post which is both a personal office (see PARA 125) and a public office is to be treated as being a public office only: Equality Act 2010 s 52(1), (4). The following are members of the executive:
    (a)   a Minister of the Crown (s 212(7)(a));
    (b)   a government department (s 212(7)(b));
    (c)   the Welsh Ministers, the First Minister for Wales or the Counsel General to the Welsh Government (s 212(7)(c) (modified by the Wales Act 2014 s 4(4)(a))).
3   Ie within the Equality Act 2010 s 50(2)(a), (b) or s 50(2)(d) (see note 2). Appointment to an office or post does not include election to it: s 52(1), (5).
4   As to direct discrimination see PARA 67; and as to indirect discrimination see PARA 75.
5   As to victimisation see PARA 81.
6   Equality Act 2010 s 50(3)(a), (5)(a) (s 50(3)–(6), (9) amended by the Crime and Courts Act 2013 Sch 13 para 50(1), (3)). As to the meaning of 'arrangements' see PARA 117 note 3. For a partial exception to these provisions in connection with occupational requirements (including religious requirements) see the Equality Act 2010 Sch 9 paras 1–3; and PARAS 160–161.
7   Equality Act 2010 s 50(3)(b), (5)(b). Section 50(3)(b), so far as relating to sex or pregnancy and maternity, does not apply to a term that relates to pay:
    (1)   unless, were B to accept the offer, an equality clause or rule would have effect in relation to the term (s 50(12)(a)); or

(2)   if head (1) does not apply, except in so far as making an offer on terms including that
term amounts to a contravention of s 50(3)(b) by virtue of s 13 (see PARA 67), s 14 or
s 18 (see PARA 74) (s 50(12)(b)).

As to the meaning of 'equality clause' and 'equality rule' see PARA 117 note 4. As to the protected
characteristic of sex see PARA 60; and as to pregnancy and maternity discrimination see PARAS
73–74.

8   Equality Act 2010 s 50(3)(c), (5)(c). For a partial exception to these provisions in connection with
occupational requirements (including religious requirements) see Sch 9 paras 1–3; and PARAS
160–161.
9   As to harassment see PARA 79.
10   Equality Act 2010 s 50(4) (as amended: see note 6).
11   As to the meaning of 'relevant person' see PARA 125 note 7.
12   Ie within the Equality Act 2010 s 50(2)(a), (b) or s 50(2)(d) (see note 2).
13   Equality Act 2010 s 50(6)(a), (9)(a) (as amended: see note 6). Section 50(6) (so far as relating to
appointment to a public office) has no effect in relation to a term of a woman's work that is
modified by a maternity equality clause or rule or in relation to a term of a woman's work that
relates to pay but in relation to which a maternity equality clause or rule has no effect: see s 76(1),
(1A), (3); and PARA 147. The inclusion in the woman's terms of a term that requires modification
by virtue of s 73(2) or (3) (see PARA 147) is not pregnancy and maternity discrimination for these
purposes: s 76(2). For an exception relating to the provision of public services see Sch 9 para 19;
and PARA 171.
14   Equality Act 2010 s 50(6)(b), (9)(b). See note 13. As to the meaning of 'benefit, facility or service'
see PARA 117 note 7. As to a partial exception to these provisions in connection with occupational
requirements (including religious requirements) see Sch 9 paras 1–3; and PARAS 160–161; for
applicable modifications in relation to this exception see Sch 9 para 6(5). There are also exceptions
to this provision in connection with the provision of childcare: see Sch 9 para 15; and PARA 168.
15   Equality Act 2010 s 50(6)(c), (9)(c). See note 13. As to the meaning of 'terminating a person's
appointment' see PARA 125 note 10. For a partial exception to these provisions in connection with
occupational requirements (including religious requirements) see Sch 9 paras 1–3; and PARAS
160–161; for applicable modifications in relation to this exception see Sch 9 para 6(6).
16   Equality Act 2010 s 50(6)(d), (9)(d). See note 13. As to the meaning of 'detriment' see PARA 81
note 1.
17   Ie within the Equality Act 2010 s 50(2)(c) (see note 2).
18   Equality Act 2010 s 50(7)(a), (10)(a). As to an exception relating to the provision of public services
see Sch 9 para 19; and PARA 171.
19   Equality Act 2010 s 50(7)(b), (10)(b). See note 18.
20   Equality Act 2010 s 50(7)(c), (10)(c). See note 18.
21   As to harassment see PARA 79.
22   Equality Act 2010 s 50(8).

127. Public offices: recommendations for appointments etc.

A person (A) who has the power to make a recommendation for or give
approval to an appointment to a certain public office[1] must not:

(1)   discriminate against[2] or victimise[3] a person (B):

   (a)   in the arrangements A makes for deciding who to recommend for
appointment or to whose appointment to give approval[4];
   (b)   by not recommending B for appointment to the office[5];
   (c)   by making a negative recommendation of B for appointment to
the office[6];
   (d)   by not giving approval to the appointment of B to the office[7].

(2)   in relation to the office, harass[8] a person seeking or being considered for
the recommendation or approval[9].

1   Ie a public office within the Equality Act 2010 s 50(2)(a), (b) or s 50(2)(d) (see PARA 126 note 2)
(definition applied by s 52(1), (3)). A reference in s 51 to a person who has the power to make a
recommendation for or give approval to an appointment to a public office within s 50(2)(a) or s
50(2)(d) (see PARA 126 note 2) is a reference only to a relevant body which has that power; and
for that purpose 'relevant body' means a body established by or in pursuance of an enactment; or

by a member of the executive: s 51(5) (s 51(1), (2), (3), (5) amended by the Crime and Courts Act 2013 Sch 13 para 51). As to appointment to an office see PARA 126 note 3. As to the meaning of 'enactment' see PARA 91 note 10.

2   As to direct discrimination see PARA 67; and as to indirect discrimination see PARA 75.
3   As to victimisation see PARA 81.
4   Equality Act 2010 s 51(1)(a), (3)(a) (as amended: see note 1). As to the meaning of 'arrangements' see PARA 117 note 3. For a partial exception to these provisions in connection with occupational requirements (including religious requirements) see Sch 9 paras 1–3; and PARAS 160–161.
5   Equality Act 2010 s 51(1)(b), (3)(b).
6   Equality Act 2010 s 51(1)(c), (3)(c).
7   Equality Act 2010 s 51(1)(d), (3)(d).
8   As to harassment see PARA 79.
9   Equality Act 2010 s 51(2) (as amended: see note 1).

128. Excluded offices.

An office or post is not a personal or public office[1]:

(1)   in so far as certain provisions[2] apply in relation to the office or post[3]; or would apply in relation to the office or post but for the operation of some other provision of the Equality Act 2010[4];

(2)   if it is a political office[5];

(3)   if it is life peerage[6], or any other dignity or honour conferred by the Crown[7];

(4)   if it is the office of diocesan or suffragan bishop[8].

1   A reference to a personal or public office, or to an appointment to a personal or public office, is to be construed in accordance with the Equality Act 2010 s 52 (see PARAS 125–127): s 83(1), (8). As to the meaning of 'personal office' see PARA 125 note 1; and as to the meaning of public office see PARA 126 note 2.
2   Ie one or more of the provisions mentioned in the Equality Act 2010 s 52(1), (9), Sch 6 para 1(2)(a)–(2)(g), namely, s 39 (employment: see PARA 117); s 41 (contract work: see PARA 119); s 44 (partnerships: see PARA 122); s 45 (LLPs: see PARA 123); s 47 (barristers: see PARA 124); and s 55 (employment services: see PARA 130) so far as applying to the provision of work experience within s 56(2)(a) (see PARA 130) or arrangements within section 56(2)(c) (see PARA 130) for such provision.
3   Equality Act 2010 Sch 6 para 1(1)(a).
4   Equality Act 2010 Sch 6 para 1(1)(b).
5   Equality Act 2010 Sch 6 para 2(1). A political post is one of the following offices or posts: see Sch 6 para 2(2). In the Houses of Parliament, a political post is an office of the House of Commons held by a member of that House; an office of the House of Lords held by a member of that House; a ministerial office within the meaning of the House of Commons Disqualification Act 1975 s 2 (see PARLIAMENT vol 78 (2010) PARA 909); the office of Leader of the Opposition within the meaning of the Ministerial and Other Salaries Act 1975 (see CONSTITUTIONAL AND ADMINISTRATIVE LAW vol 20 (2014) PARA 118); the office of the Chief Opposition Whip, or of an Assistant Opposition Whip, within the meaning of the 1975 Act (see CONSTITUTIONAL AND ADMINISTRATIVE LAW vol 20 (2014) PARA 118: see the Equality Act 2010 Sch 6 para 2(2). In the National Assembly for Wales; a political post is an office of the National Assembly for Wales held by a member of the Assembly; the office of a member of the Welsh Government: see Sch 6 para 2(2) (modified by the Wales Act 2014). In local government in England (outside London), a political post is an office of a county council, district council or parish council in England held by a member of the council; an office of the Council of the Isles of Scilly held by a member of the Council: see the Equality Act 2010 Sch 6 para 2(2); and LOCAL GOVERNMENT vol 69 (2009) PARA 24 et seq. In local government in London, a political post is an office of the Greater London Authority held by the Mayor of London or a member of the London Assembly; an office of a London borough council held by a member of the council; an office of the Common Council of the City of London held by a member of the Council: see Sch 6 para 2(2); and LONDON GOVERNMENT vol 71 (2013) PARA 1 et seq. In local government in Wales, a political post is an office of a county council, county borough council or community council in Wales held by a member of the council: see Sch 6 para 2(2); and LOCAL GOVERNMENT vol 69 (2009) PARA 37 et seq. In political parties, a political post is an office of a registered political party: see Sch 6 para 2(2). The reference to a registered political party is a reference to a party

registered in the Great Britain register under the Political Parties, Elections and Referendums Act 2000 Pt 2 (ss 22–40) (see CONSTITUTIONAL AND ADMINISTRATIVE LAW vol 20 (2014) PARA 103 et seq): Equality Act 2010 Sch 6 para 2(3).

6 Ie within the meaning of the Life Peerages Act 1958 (see CONSTITUTIONAL AND ADMINISTRATIVE LAW vol 20 (2014) PARA 569; PARLIAMENT vol 78 (2010) PARA 843; PEERAGES AND DIGNITIES vol 79 (2014) PARA 807).
7 Equality Act 2010 Sch 6 para 3.
8 Equality Act 2010 Sch 6 para 4 (added by the Bishops and Priests (Consecration and Ordination of Women) Measure 2014 s 2).

(vi) Qualifications Bodies

129. Duty on qualifications bodies not to discriminate etc.
A qualifications body[1] (A) must not discriminate against[2] or victimise[3] a person (B):

(1) in the arrangements A makes for deciding upon whom to confer a relevant qualification[4];

(2) as to the terms on which it is prepared to confer a relevant qualification on B[5];

(3) by not conferring a relevant qualification on B[6].

A qualifications body (A) must not discriminate against or victimise a person (B) upon whom A has conferred a relevant qualification:

(a) by withdrawing the qualification from B[7];

(b) by varying the terms on which B holds the qualification[8];

(c) by subjecting B to any other detriment[9].

A qualifications body must not, in relation to conferment by it of a relevant qualification, harass[10] a person who holds the qualification[11]; or a person who applies for it[12].

The application by a qualifications body of a competence standard[13] to a disabled person[14] is not disability discrimination[15] unless it is indirect discrimination[16].

1 For these purposes, a 'qualifications body' is an authority or body which can confer a relevant qualification: Equality Act 2010 s 54(1), (2). A 'relevant qualification' is an authorisation, qualification, recognition, registration, enrolment, approval or certification which is needed for, or facilitates engagement in, a particular trade or profession: s 54(1), (3). An authority or body is not a 'qualifications body' in so far as:
   (1) it can confer a qualification to which s 96 (see PARAS 192–193) applies (s 54(1), (4)(a));
   (2) it is the responsible body of a school to which s 85 (see PARAS 173–175) applies (s 54(1), (4)(b));
   (3) it is the governing body of an institution to which s 91 (see PARAS 182–185) applies (s 54(1), (4)(c));
   (4) it exercises functions under the Education Acts (Equality Act 2010 s 54(1), (4)(d)).
   Political parties are not 'qualifications bodies' for these purposes: see *Watt (formerly Carter) v Ahsan* [2007] UKHL 51, [2008] 1 AC 696, [2008] 1 All ER 869 (decided under the Race Relations Act 1976 (repealed)). As to the meaning of 'the Education Acts' see PARA 93 note 24. As to the meanings of 'trade' and 'profession' see PARA 239 note 8.
2 As to direct discrimination see PARA 67; and as to indirect discrimination see PARA 75. As to a partial exception to these provisions in connection with religious requirements see the Equality Act 2010 Sch 9 para 2; and PARA 161; for applicable modifications in relation to this exception see Sch 9 para 6(6). These provisions cover cases where a qualification *in fact* facilities a person's employment, whether or not it is intended by the authority or body granting it: see eg *British Judo Association v Petty* [1981] IRLR 484, [1981] ICR 660, EAT (decided under the Sex Discrimination Act 1975 (repealed)).
3 As to victimisation see PARA 81.
4 Equality Act 2010 s 53(1)(a), (4)(a). As to the meaning of 'arrangements' see PARA 117 note 3. A reference to 'conferring a relevant qualification' includes a reference to renewing or extending the

conferment of a relevant qualification: s 54(1), (5). These provisions are concerned with qualifications and not with the appointment of a particular person to a particular post: see eg *Malik v Post Office Counters Ltd* [1993] ICR 93, EAT. Appointments that are not covered by these provisions include the appointment of a justice of the peace (see *Arthur v A-G* [1999] ICR 631, EAT) and the selection of a candidate for election by a political party (see *Watt v Ahsan* [2007] UKHL 51, [2008] 1 All ER 869, [2008] IRLR 243 (decided under the Race Relations Act 1976 (repealed)). These provisions will also cover the granting of a legal aid franchise: see *Patterson v Legal Services Commission* [2003] EWCA Civ 1558, [2003] IRLR 742, CA (decided under the Race Relations Act 1976 (repealed)).

5 Equality Act 2010 s 53(1)(b), (4)(b). In this regard see eg *Bohon-Mitchell v Common Professional Examination Board and the Council of Legal Education* [1978] IRLR 525, IT (extra requirements imposed on overseas non-law graduates in order to complete the academic stage of training for the Bar held to be unlawful discrimination) (decided under the Race Relations Act 1976 (repealed)).
6 Equality Act 2010 s 53(1)(c), (4)(c).
7 Equality Act 2010 s 53(2)(a), (5)(a).
8 Equality Act 2010 s 53(2)(b), (5)(b).
9 Equality Act 2010 s 53(2)(c), (5)(c). As to the meaning of 'detriment' see PARA 81 note 1.
10 As to harassment see PARA 79.
11 Equality Act 2010 s 53(3)(a).
12 Equality Act 2010 s 53(3)(b).
13 For these purposes a 'competence standard' is an academic, medical or other standard applied for the purpose of determining whether or not a person has a particular level of competence or ability: Equality Act 2010 s 54(1), (6).
14 As to the meaning of 'disabled person' see PARA 47.
15 As to the meaning of 'disability discrimination' see PARA 89 note 2.
16 See the Equality Act 2010 s 53(7). As to indirect discrimination see s 19; and PARA 75.

(vii) Employment Service-providers

130. Duty on employment service-providers not to discriminate etc.

A person (an 'employment service-provider') concerned with the provision of an employment service[1] must not discriminate against[2] or victimise[3] a person:

(1)   in the arrangements the service-provider makes for selecting persons to whom to provide, or to whom to offer to provide, the service[4];

(2)   as to the terms on which the service-provider offers to provide the service to the person[5];

(3)   by not offering to provide the service to the person[6].

An employment service-provider (A) must not, in relation to the provision of an employment service, discriminate against or victimise a person (B):

(a)   as to the terms on which A provides the service to B[7];

(b)   by not providing the service to B[8];

(c)   by terminating the provision of the service to B[9];

(d)   by subjecting B to any other detriment[10].

A person or organisation does not contravene[11] these provisions[12] if he shows that:

(i)   his treatment of another person relates only to work the offer of which could be legitimately refused[13] to that other person[14] or only to training for such work[15]; or

(ii)   he acted in reliance on a statement made to him by a person with the power to offer the work in question to the effect that[16] his action would be lawful[17] and it was reasonable for him to rely on the statement[18].

An employment service-provider must not, in relation to the provision of an employment service, harass[19] a person who asks the service-provider to provide the service[20]; or a person for whom the service-provider provides the service[21].

1 For these purposes, the provision of an employment service includes (see the Equality Act 2010 s 56(1), (2)(a)–(h)):

(1)   the provision of vocational training;
(2)   the provision of vocational guidance;
(3)   making arrangements for the provision of vocational training or vocational guidance;
(4)   the provision of a service for finding employment for persons;
(5)   the provision of a service for supplying employers with persons to do work;
(6)   the provision of a service in pursuance of arrangements made under the Employment and Training Act 1973 s 2 (see EMPLOYMENT vol 40 (2014) PARA 634);
(7)   the provision of a service in pursuance of arrangements made or a direction given under the Employment and Training Act 1973 s 10 (see EMPLOYMENT vol 40 (2014) PARA 640);
(8)   an assessment related to the conferment of a relevant qualification within the meaning of the Equality Act 2010 s 53 (see PARA 129) (except in so far as the assessment is by the qualifications body which confers the qualification).

See *Rice v Fon-A-Car* [1980] ICR 133, EAT (decided under the Sex Discrimination Act 1975); *Commission for Racial Equality v Imperial Society of Teachers of Dancing* [1983] ICR 473, [1983] IRLR 315, EAT (decided under the Race Relations Act 1976 (repealed)).

For these purposes, 'vocational training' means training for employment; or work experience (including work experience the duration of which is not agreed until after it begins): Equality Act 2010 s 56(1), (6). A reference to 'training' includes a reference to facilities for training: s 56(1), (8).

Section 56 does not apply in relation to training or guidance:

(a)   so far as it is training or guidance in relation to which another provision of Pt 5 (ss 39–83: see PARA 116 et seq) applies (s 56(1), (3));
(b)   for pupils of a school to which s 85 (see PARAS 173–175) applies in so far as it is training or guidance to which the responsible body of the school has power to afford access (whether as the responsible body of that school or as the responsible body of any other school at which the training or guidance is provided) ((s 56(1), (4));
(c)   for students of an institution to which s 91 (see PARAS 182–185) applies in so far as it is training or guidance to which the governing body of the institution has power to afford access (s 56(1), (5)).

See *Blackwood v Birmingham & Solihull Mental Health NHS Foundation Trust* [2016] EWCA Civ 607, [2016] All ER (D) 168 (Jun) (Equality Act 2010 s 56(5) did not prevent employment tribunal determining complaint under Pt 5 of the Act about withdrawal of training or guidance to which institution had power to afford access where complaint alleged discrimination by the provider rather than the institution).

2   As to direct discrimination see PARA 67; and as to indirect discrimination see PARA 75. So far as relating to disability, these provisions do not apply to work experience in the armed forces: see Sch 9 para 4(3); and PARA 163.
3   As to victimisation see PARA 81.
4   Equality Act 2010 s 55(1)(a), (4)(a). As to the meaning of 'arrangements' see PARA 117 note 3.
5   Equality Act 2010 s 55(1)(b), (4)(b).
6   Equality Act 2010 s 55(1)(c), (4)(c).
7   Equality Act 2010 s 55(2)(a), (5)(a).
8   Equality Act 2010 s 55(2)(b), (5)(b).
9   Equality Act 2010 s 55(2)(c), (5)(c).
10   Equality Act 2010 s 55(2)(d), (5)(d). As to the meaning of 'detriment' see PARA 81 note 1.
11   Ie by virtue of the Equality Act 2010 s 13 (see PARA 67).
12   Ie the Equality Act 2010 s 55(1), (2) (see the text and notes 1–10). As to modifications in connection with this exception see Sch 9 para 6(6).
13   Ie in reliance on the Equality Act 2010 Sch 9 paras 1–4 (see PARAS 160–163). 'Work' means employment (see PARA 116), contract work (see PARA 119 note 4), a position as a partner or as a member of an LLP (see PARA 123), or an appointment to a personal or public office (see PARAS 125–128): Sch 9 para 6(3).
14   Equality Act 2010 Sch 9 paras 5(1).
15   Equality Act 2010 Sch 9 paras 5(2), 6(2).
16   Ie by virtue of the Equality Act 2010 Sch 9 para 5(1) or (2) (see the text and notes 11–15).
17   Equality Act 2010 Sch 9 para 5(3)(a). A person commits an offence by knowingly or recklessly making a statement such as is mentioned in Sch 9 para 5(3)(a) which in a material respect is false or misleading: Sch 9 para 5(4). A person guilty of such an offence is liable on summary conviction to a fine not exceeding level 5 on the standard scale: Sch 9 para 5(5). As to the powers of magistrates' courts to issue fines on summary conviction see SENTENCING vol 92 (2015) PARA 176.
18   Equality Act 2010 Sch 9 para 5(3)(b).
19   As to harassment see PARA 79.

20 Equality Act 2010 s 55(3)(a).
21 Equality Act 2010 s 55(3)(b).

(viii) Trade Organisations

131. Duty on trade organisations not to discriminate etc.

A trade organisation[1] (A) must not discriminate against[2] or victimise[3] a person (B):

(1)   in the arrangements A makes for deciding to whom to offer membership of the organisation[4];

(2)   as to the terms on which it is prepared to admit B as a member[5];

(3)   by not accepting B's application for membership[6].

A trade organisation (A) must not discriminate against or victimise a member (B):

(a)   in the way it affords B access, or by not affording B access, to opportunities for receiving a benefit, facility or service[7];

(b)   by depriving B of membership[8];

(c)   by varying the terms on which B is a member[9];

(d)   by subjecting B to any other detriment[10].

A trade organisation must not, in relation to membership of it, harass[11] a member[12]; or an applicant for membership[13].

1   A 'trade organisation' is:
    (1)   an organisation of workers (Equality Act 2010 s 57(7)(a));
    (2)   an organisation of employers (s 57(7)(b)); or
    (3)   any other organisation whose members carry on a particular trade or profession for the purposes of which the organisation exists: (s 57(7)(c)).
    As to the meaning of 'trade' see PARA 239 note 8. As to what constitutes a particular trade or profession see *Sadek v Medical Protection Society* [2004] EWCA Civ 865, [2004] 4 All ER 118, sub nom *Medical Protection Society v Sadek* [2004] ICR 1263. It does not include a professional body which entirely regulatory in function: see *General Medical Council v Cox* (2002) 70 BMLR 31, [2002] All ER (D) 383 (Mar), EAT.
2   As to direct discrimination see PARA 67; and as to indirect discrimination see PARA 75.
3   As to victimisation see PARA 81.
4   Equality Act 2010 s 57(1)(a), (4)(a). As to the meaning of 'arrangements' see PARA 117 note 3.
5   Equality Act 2010 s 57(1)(b), (4)(b).
6   Equality Act 2010 s 57(1)(c), (4)(c). An 'application for membership' does not include an application for pupillage: *Horton v Higham* [2004] EWCA Civ 941, [2004] 3 All ER 852, sub nom *Higham v Meurig Lestyn Horton* [2005] ICR 292. As to barristers see PARA 124
7   Equality Act 2010 s 57(2)(a), (5)(a). As to the meaning of 'benefit, facility or service' see PARA 117 note 7. There are exceptions to this provision in connection with the provision of childcare: see Sch 9 para 15; and PARA 168.
8   Equality Act 2010 s 57(2)(b), (5)(b).
9   Equality Act 2010 s 57(2)(c), (5)(c).
10 Equality Act 2010 s 57(2)(d), (5)(d). As to the meaning of 'detriment' see PARA 81 note 1.
11 As to harassment see PARA 79.
12 Equality Act 2010 s 57(3)(a).
13 Equality Act 2010 s 57(3)(b).

(ix) Local Authority Members

132. Duty on local authorities not to discriminate etc against members carrying out official business.

A local authority[1] must not:

(1)   discriminate against[2] or victimise[3] a member of the authority in relation to the member's carrying out of official business[4]:

    (a)   in the way the authority affords the member access, or by not affording the member access, to opportunities for training or for receiving any other facility[5];

    (b)   by subjecting the member to any other detriment[6];

(2)   in relation to a member's carrying out of official business, harass[7] the member[8].

1 For these purposes, 'local authority' means (see the Equality Act 2010 s 59(1), (2)):
    (1)   a county council in England;
    (2)   a district council in England;
    (3)   the Greater London Authority;
    (4)   a London borough council;
    (5)   the Common Council of the City of London;
    (6)   the Council of the Isles of Scilly;
    (7)   a parish council in England;
    (8)   a county council in Wales;
    (9)   a community council in Wales;
    (10)   a county borough council in Wales.
  See LOCAL GOVERNMENT vol 69 (2009) PARAS 24 et seq, 37 et seq; LONDON GOVERNMENT vol 71 (2013) PARA 1 et seq. As to the amendment of this list see s 59(1), (3).
2 As to direct discrimination see PARA 67; and as indirect discrimination see PARA 75.
3 As to victimisation see PARA 81.
4 A reference to the carrying-out of official business by a person who is a member of a local authority is a reference to the doing of anything by the person:
    (1)   as a member of the authority (Equality Act 2010 s 59(1), (4)(a));
    (2)   as a member of a body to which the person is appointed by, or appointed following nomination by, the authority or a group of bodies including the authority (s 59(1), (4)(b)); or
    (3)   as a member of any other public body (s 59(1), (4)(c)).
  'Member', in relation to the Greater London Authority, means the Mayor of London; or a member of the London Assembly: s 59(1), (5). See LONDON GOVERNMENT vol 71 (2013) PARA 67 et seq.
5 Equality Act 2010 s 58(1)(a), (3)(a). There are exceptions to this provision in connection with the provision of childcare: see Sch 9 para 15; and PARA 168.
6 Equality Act 2010 s 58(1)(b), (3)(b). A member of a local authority is not subjected to a detriment for the purposes of s 58(1)(b), (3)(b) only because the member is:
    (1)   not appointed or elected to an office of the authority (s 58(4)(a));
    (2)   not appointed or elected to, or to an office of, a committee or sub-committee of the authority (s 58(4)(b)); or
    (3)   not appointed or nominated in exercise of an appointment power of the authority (s 58(4)(c)).
  In head (3), an appointment power of a local authority is a power of the authority, or of a group of bodies including the authority, to make:
    (a)   appointments to a body (s 58(5)(a));
    (b)   nominations for appointment to a body (s 58(5)(b)).
  As to the meaning of 'detriment' generally see PARA 81 note 1.
7 As to harassment see PARA 79.
8 Equality Act 2010 s 58(2).

(x) Recruitment

133. Inquiries about disability and health.

A person (A) to whom an application for work[1] is made must not ask about the health of the applicant (B)[2] before offering work to B[3]; or where A is not in a position to offer work to B, before including B in a pool of applicants from whom A intends (when in a position to do so) to select a person to whom to offer work[4].

A does not contravene a relevant disability provision[5] merely by asking about B's health; but A's conduct in reliance on information given in response may be a contravention of a relevant disability provision[6].

These provisions[7] do not apply to a question that A asks in so far as asking the question is necessary for the purpose of:

(1) establishing whether B will be able to comply with a requirement to undergo an assessment or establishing whether a duty to make reasonable adjustments[8] is or will be imposed on A in relation to B in connection with a requirement to undergo an assessment[9];

(2) establishing whether B will be able to carry out a function that is intrinsic to the work concerned[10];

(3) monitoring diversity in the range of persons applying to A for work[11];

(4) taking action to which the provisions on positive action[12] would apply if references in those provisions to persons who share (or do not share) a protected characteristic[13] were references to disabled persons[14] (or persons who are not disabled) and the reference to the characteristic were a reference to disability[15]; or

(5) if A applies in relation to the work a requirement to have a particular disability, establishing whether B has that disability[16].

These provisions do not apply to anything done for the purpose of vetting applicants for work for reasons of national security[17].

1 'Work' means employment, contract work, a position as a partner, a position as a member of an LLP, a pupillage or tenancy, an appointment to a personal or public office, or the provision of an employment service; and the references in the Equality Act 2010 s 60(1) to offering a person work are, in relation to contract work, to be read as references to allowing a person to do the work: s 60(9).

2 For these purposes, whether or not a person has a disability is to be regarded as an aspect of that person's health: Equality Act 2010 s 60(13). As to the meaning of 'disability' see PARA 47.

3 Equality Act 2010 s 60(1)(a). See also the Equality Act 2010 Code of Practice — Employment Statutory Code of Practice (2010) para 10.25 et seq. A reference to 'offering work' is a reference to making a conditional or unconditional offer of work (and, in relation to contract work, is a reference to allowing a person to do the work subject to fulfilment of one or more conditions): s 60(10).

A contravention of s 60(1) (or a contravention of s 111 (see PARA 82) or s 112 (see PARA 83) that relates to a contravention of s 60(1)) is enforceable as an unlawful act under the Equality Act 2006 Pt 1 (ss 1–42) (and, by virtue of the Equality Act 2010 s 120(8), is enforceable only by the Commission under the Equality Act 2006 Pt 1): see the Equality Act 2010 s 60(2); and PARA 351 et seq. As to the Commission see PARA 28 et seq.

If B brings proceedings before an employment tribunal on a complaint that A's conduct in reliance on information given in response to a question about B's health is a contravention of a relevant disability provision (see note 5), in the application of s 136 (burden of proof: see PARA 365) to the proceedings, the particulars of the complaint are to be treated for the purposes of s 136(2) as facts from which the tribunal could decide that A contravened the provision: s 60(4), (5).

4 Equality Act 2010 s 60(1)(b). See note 3.

5 The following, so far as relating to discrimination within the Equality Act 2010 s 13 (see PARA 67) because of disability, are 'relevant disability provisions' (s 60(11)):

(1) s 39(1)(a) or s 39(1)(c) (see PARA 117);
(2) s 41(1)(b) (see PARA 119);
(3) s 44(1)(a) or s 44(1)(c) (see PARA 122);
(4) s 45(1)(a) or s 45(1)(c) (see PARA 123);
(5) s 47(1)(a) or s 47(1)(c) (see PARA 124);
(6) s 49(3)(a) or s 49(3)(c) (see PARA 125);
(7) s 50(3)(a) or s 50(3)(c) (see PARA 126);
(8) s 51(1) (see PARA 127);
(9) s 55(1)(a) or s 55 (1)(c) (see PARA 130).

6 Equality Act 2010 s 60(3).

7 Ie the Equality Act 2010 s 60.

8 As to the duty to make reasonable adjustments under the Equality Act 2010 Pt 5 see PARA 155. As to the general duty to make reasonable adjustments see PARA 237.

9 Equality Act 2010 s 60(6)(a). An 'assessment' is an interview or other process designed to give an indication of a person's suitability for the work concerned: s 60(12).
10 Equality Act 2010 s 60(6)(b). Where A reasonably believes that a duty to make reasonable adjustments would be imposed on A in relation to B in connection with the work, the reference to a function that is intrinsic to the work is to be read as a reference to a function that would be intrinsic to the work once A complied with the duty: s 60(7).
11 Equality Act 2010 s 60(6)(c).
12 Ie the Equality Act 2010 s 158 (see PARA 299).
13 As to protected characteristics see PARA 45 et seq.
14 As to the meaning of 'disabled person' see PARA 47.
15 Equality Act 2010 s 60(6)(d).
16 Equality Act 2010 s 60(6)(e). Section 60(6)(e) applies only if A shows that, having regard to the nature or context of the work:
    (1)   the requirement is an occupational requirement (s 60(8)(a)); and
    (2)   the application of the requirement is a proportionate means of achieving a legitimate aim (s 60(8)(b)).
17 Equality Act 2010 s 60(14).

(2) OCCUPATIONAL PENSION SCHEMES

134. Non-discrimination rule.

An occupational pension scheme[1] must be taken to include a non-discrimination rule[2] and the provisions of such a scheme have effect subject to the non-discrimination rule[3]. A non-discrimination rule is a provision by virtue of which a responsible person[4] (A):

(1)   must not discriminate[5] against another person (B) in carrying out any of A's functions in relation to the scheme[6];
(2)   must not, in relation to the scheme, harass[7] B[8];
(3)   must not, in relation to the scheme, victimise[9] B[10].

A breach of a non-discrimination rule is a contravention of Part 5 of the Equality Act 2010[11] for the purposes of enforcement[12].

1 As to the meaning of 'occupational pension scheme' see the Pension Schemes Act 1993 s 1 (definition applied by the Equality Act 2010 s 212(1)); PERSONAL AND OCCUPATIONAL PENSIONS vol 80 (2013) PARA 208.
2 Equality Act 2010 s 61(1). A non-discrimination rule does not apply in relation to a person who is a pension credit member of a scheme: s 61(5). However, ss 61, 120 (see PARA 357), s 126 (see PARA 359) and Sch 8 para 19 (and other such provisions of Sch 8 as apply for the purposes of Sch 8 para 19), in their application to communications, apply in relation to a disabled person who is a pension credit member as they apply in relation to a disabled person who is a deferred member or pensioner member of the scheme: s 63(1). 'Communications' include the provision of information and the operation of a dispute resolution procedure: s 63(2).
3 Equality Act 2010 61(3). A non-discrimination rule does not have effect in relation to an occupational pension scheme in so far as an equality rule has effect in relation to it (or would have effect in relation to it but for Sch 7 Pt 2 (paras 3–6) (exceptions): s 61(10).
4 The following are 'responsible persons':
    (1)   the trustees or managers of the scheme (Equality Act 2010 s 61(4)(a));
    (2)   an employer whose employees are, or may be, members of the scheme (s 61(4)(b));
    (3)   a person exercising an appointing function in relation to an office the holder of which is, or may be, a member of the scheme (s 61(4)(c)).
An 'appointing function' is any of the following:
    (a)   the function of appointing a person (s 61(6)(a));
    (b)   the function of terminating a person's appointment (s 61(6)(b));
    (c)   the function of recommending a person for appointment (s 61(6)(c));
    (d)   the function of approving an appointment (s 61(6)(d)).
'Member' in relation to an occupational pension scheme, means an active member, a deferred member or a pensioner member, within the meaning, in each case, of the Pensions Act 1995 s 124(1) (see PERSONAL AND OCCUPATIONAL PENSIONS vol 80 (2013) PARA 491): Equality Act 2010 s

212(10). 'Employer', 'deferred member', 'pension credit member', 'pensionable service', 'pensioner member' and 'trustees or managers' each have, in relation to an occupational pension scheme, the meaning given by the Pensions Act 1995 s 124 (see PERSONAL AND OCCUPATIONAL PENSIONS vol 80 (2013) PARA 250, 491, 303): Equality Act 2010 s 212(11). A reference to the accrual of rights under an occupational pension scheme is to be construed in accordance with the Pensions Act 1995 s 124 (see PERSONAL AND OCCUPATIONAL PENSIONS vol 80 (2013) PARA 250): Equality Act 2010 s 212(12).

5   As to direct discrimination see PARA 67; and as to indirect discrimination see PARA 75.
6   Equality Act 2010 s 61(2)(a).
7   As to harassment see PARA 79.
8   Equality Act 2010 s 61(2)(b).
9   As to victimisation see PARA 81.
10 Equality Act 2010 s 61(2)(c).
11 Ie the Equality Act 2010 ss 39–83 (see PARA 116 et seq).
12 Equality Act 2010 s 61(7). As to enforcement under Pt 9 (ss 113–141) see PARA 351 et seq. It is not a breach of a non-discrimination rule for the employer or the trustees or managers of a scheme to maintain or use in relation to the scheme rules, practices, actions or decisions relating to age which are of a description specified by order by a Minister of the Crown: s 61(8). As to the Equality Act (Age Exceptions for Pension Schemes) Order 2010, SI 2010/2133, see PARA 169 An order authorising the use of rules, practices, actions or decisions which are not in use before the order comes into force must not be made unless the minister consults such persons as the minister thinks appropriate: Equality Act 2010 s 61(9).

135. Non-discrimination alterations.

If the trustees or managers[1] of an occupational pension scheme[2] do not have power to make non-discrimination alterations to the scheme[3]; or if the trustees or managers of an occupational pension scheme have power to make non-discrimination alterations to the scheme but the procedure for doing so is liable to be unduly complex or protracted[4]; or involves obtaining consents which cannot be obtained or which can be obtained only with undue delay or difficulty[5], the trustees or managers may by resolution make non-discrimination alterations to the scheme[6].

1   As to the meaning of 'trustees or managers' see PARA 134 note 4.
2   As to the meaning of 'occupational pension scheme' see PARA 134 note 1.
3   Equality Act 2010 s 62(1). 'Non-discrimination alterations' to an occupational pension scheme are such alterations to the scheme as may be required for the provisions of the scheme to have the effect that they have in consequence of s 61(3) (see PARA 134): s 62(5). As to the meaning of the 'non-discrimination rule' see PARA 134.
4   Equality Act 2010 s 62(2)(a).
5   Equality Act 2010 s 62(2)(b).
6   Equality Act 2010 s 62(3). Non-discrimination alterations may have effect in relation to a period before the date on which they are made: s 62(4).

(3) EQUALITY OF TERMS

(i) Sex Equality

136. Relevant types of work.

The provisions relating to the equality of terms[1] apply where:
(1)   a person (A) is employed on work that is equal to the work that a comparator of the opposite sex (B) does[2];
(2)   a person (A) holding a personal or public office[3] does work that is equal to the work that a comparator of the opposite sex (B) does[4].

1   Ie the Equality Act 2010 ss 66–70 (see PARAS 139–143).

2   Equality Act 2010 s 64(1)(a). As to comparators see PARA **138**. The references in s 64(1) to the
    work that B does are not restricted to work done contemporaneously with the work done by A:
    s 64(2).
3   As to the meaning of 'personal or public office' see PARAS **125–126** (definition applied by the
    Equality Act 2010 s 83(8)). Section 42 (identity of employer: see PARA **121**) does not apply to Pt
    5 Ch 3 (ss 64–80) (see PARA **137** et seq); accordingly, for the purposes of Pt 5 Ch 3 only, holding
    the office of constable is to be treated as holding a personal office: s 79(8).
4   Equality Act 2010 s 64(1)(b). See note 2.

137. Equal work.

For the purposes of the provisions on equality of terms[1] A's work is equal to
that of B if it is like B's work[2]; rated as equivalent to B's work[3]; or of equal value
to B's work[4].

A's work is like B's work if A's work and B's work are the same or broadly
similar[5]; and such differences as there are between their work are not of practical
importance in relation to the terms of their work[6].

A's work is rated as equivalent to B's work if a job evaluation study[7] gives an
equal value to A's job and B's job in terms of the demands made on a worker[8]; or
would give an equal value to A's job and B's job in those terms were the evaluation
not made on a sex-specific system[9].

A's work is of equal value to B's work if it is neither like B's work nor rated as
equivalent to B's work[10]; but nevertheless equal to B's work in terms of the
demands made on A by reference to factors such as effort, skill and
decision-making[11].

1   Ie for the purpose of the Equality Act 2010 Pt 5 Ch 3 (ss 64–80) (see PARA **138** et seq).
2   Equality Act 2010 s 65(1)(a). See text and notes 5–6.
3   Equality Act 2010 s 65(1)(b). See text and notes 7–9.
4   Equality Act 2010 s 65(1)(c). See text and notes 10–11.
5   Equality Act 2010 s 65(2)(a). On a comparison of one person's work with another's for the
    purposes of determining whether A's work is like B's work, it is necessary to have regard to the
    frequency with which differences between their work occur in practice; and the nature and extent
    of the differences: s 65(3). The emphasis is on what is actually done rather than what may be
    required under the contract of employment: see *Redland Roof Tiles Ltd v Harper* [1977] ICR 349,
    EAT; *Capper Pass Ltd v Lawton* [1977] QB 852, [1977] ICR 83, EAT; *Shields v E Coombes
    (Holdings) Ltd* [1978] ICR 1159, sub nom *E Coombes (Holdings) Ltd v Shields* [1978] IRLR 263,
    CA. As to examples of 'like work' see *Capper Pass Ltd v Allan* [1980] ICR 194, [1980] IRLR 236,
    EAT; *Eaton Ltd v Nuttall* [1977] 3 All ER 1131, [1977] ICR 272, EAT; cf *Morgan v
    Middlesborough Borough Council* [2005] EWCA Civ 1432, [2005] All ER (D) 256 (Jul). All the
    decisions referred to above were decided under the Equal Pay Act 1970 (repealed). See also the
    Equality Act 2010 Code of Practice — Equal Pay Statutory Code of Practice (2010) para 36.
6   Equality Act 2010 s 65(2)(b). See note 5.
7   A 'job evaluation study' is a study undertaken with a view to evaluating, in terms of the demands
    made on a person by reference to factors such as effort, skill and decision-making, the jobs to be
    done:
    (1)   by some or all of the workers in an undertaking or group of undertakings (Equality Act
          2010 s 80(1), (5)(a)); or
    (2)   in the case of the armed forces, by some or all of the members of the armed forces
          (Equality Act 2010 s 80(1), (5)(b)).
    In the case of Crown employment, the reference in head (1) above to an 'undertaking' is to be
    construed in accordance with the Employment Rights Act 1996 s 191(4) (see EMPLOYMENT vol 39
    (2014) PARA 163): Equality Act 2010 s 80(1), (6). To be valid, a job evaluation study must (see the
    Equality Act 2010 Code of Practice — Equal Pay Statutory Code of Practice (2010) para 41):
    (a)   encompass both the woman's job and her comparator's;
    (b)   be thorough in its analysis and capable of impartial application (*Eaton Ltd v Nuttall*
          [1977] 3 All ER 1131, [1977] ICR 272, EAT (decided under the Equal Pay Act 1970
          (repealed)));

(c)   take into account factors connected only with the requirements of the job rather than the person doing the job (so for example how well someone is doing the job is not relevant); and

(d)   be analytical in assessing the component parts of particular jobs, rather than their overall content on a 'whole job' basis (*Bromley v H & J Quick Ltd* [1988] ICR 623, [1988] IRLR 249, CA (decided under the Equal Pay Act 1970 (repealed))).

Job evaluation studies must be non-discriminatory and not influenced by gender stereotyping or assumptions about women's and men's work: see the Equality Act 2010 Code of Practice — Equal Pay Statutory Code of Practice (2010) para 43.

8   Equality Act 2010 s 65(4)(a).
9   Equality Act 2010 s 65(4)(b). A system is sex-specific if, for the purposes of one or more of the demands made on a worker, it sets values for men different from those it sets for women: s 65(5).
10   Equality Act 2010 s 65(6)(a).
11   Equality Act 2010 s 65(6)(b).

138. Comparators.

For the purposes of the provisions on equality of terms[1], if A is employed, B is a comparator if:

(1)   B is employed by A's employer or by an associate of A's employer[2], and A and B work at the same establishment[3]; or

(2)   B is employed by A's employer or an associate of A's employer[4], B works at an establishment other than the one at which A works[5], and common terms apply at the establishments (either generally or as between A and B)[6].

If A holds a personal or public office[7], B is a comparator if B holds a personal or public office and the person responsible for paying A is also responsible for paying B[8].

If A is a relevant member of the House of Commons staff[9], B is a comparator if B is employed by the person who is[10] A's employer[11] or[12] B is employed by the person who is[13] A's employer[14], and if A is a relevant member of the House of Lords staff[15], B is a comparator if B is also a relevant member of the House of Lords staff[16].

1   Ie for the purpose of the Equality Act 2010 Pt 5 Ch 3 (ss 64–80) (see PARA 139 et seq).
2   Equality Act 2010 s 79(1), (2), (3)(a). For these purposes employers are 'associated' if one is a company of which the other (directly or indirectly) has control or both are companies of which a third person (directly or indirectly) has control: s 79(9). As to associated employers see EMPLOYMENT vol 39 (2014) PARA 3. The ordinary meaning of the word 'associated' is to be used: see *Glasgow City Council v Unison Claimants* [2014] CSIH 27 at 40–46, [2014] IRLR 532 at 541–543, Court of Session, per Lord Brodie, citing Lord Hoffman in *O'Neill v Phillips* [1999] 1 WLR 1092. Thus a local authority may be associated with a limited liability partnership.
3   Equality Act 2010 s 79(3)(b). If work is not done at an establishment, it is to be treated as done at the establishment with which it has the closest connection: s 80(3). There is no definition of an 'establishment'; the problem may arise whether a particular place of work is itself an establishment or merely part of one overall establishment: *Rice v Scottish Legal Life Assurance Society* [1976] IRLR 330, IT. See also *City of Edinburgh Council v Wilkinson* [2012] IRLR 202, [2012] EqLR 54 ('establishment' does not mean 'employer'). In connection with the meaning of 'establishment' see also the Trade Union and Labour Relations (Consolidation) Act 1992 s 188(1); and EMPLOYMENT vol 41A (2014) PARA 1185.
4   Equality Act 2010 s 79(4)(a).
5   Equality Act 2010 s 79(4)(b).
6   Equality Act 2010 s 79(4)(c). As to the function of the 'same employment' test see *North v Dumfries and Galloway Council* [2013] UKSC 45, [2013] 4 All ER 413 (decided under the Equal Pay Act 1970 (repealed)). In connection with predecessor and successor employees as comparators see *McArthys Ltd v Smith (No 2)* [1981] QB 180, [1981] 1 All ER 111, [1980] IRLR 209, CA (decided under the Equal Pay Act 1970 (repealed)). See note 3. Where there was a 'single source' of pay and conditions for both the employee and comparator, a comparison between them was permitted independently of whether unequal treatment arose from legislation or collective

agreements, and whether or not the employment was in the same establishment or service: see *Brierley v Asda Stores Ltd* (2017) UKEAT/0011/17/DM, [2017] All ER (D) 141 (Aug).

7   As to the meaning of 'personal office' see PARA **125** note 1; as to the meaning of 'public office' see PARA **126** note 2.
8   Equality Act 2010 s 79(5).
9   As to the meaning of 'relevant member of the House of Commons staff' see PARA **116** note 6.
10 Ie under the Employment Rights Act 1996 s 195(6) (see EMPLOYMENT vol 39 (2014) PARA 165).
11 Equality Act 2010 s 79(6)(a).
12 Ie if the Employment Rights Act 1996 s 195(7) (see EMPLOYMENT vol 39 (2014) PARA 165) applies in A's case.
13 Ie under the Employment Rights Act 1996 s 195(7) (see EMPLOYMENT vol 39 (2014) PARA 165).
14 Equality Act 2010 s 79(6)(b).
15 As to the meaning of 'relevant member of the House of Lords staff' see PARA **116** note 7.
16 Equality Act 2010 s 79(7).

139.   Sex equality clause.

If the terms of A's work do not (by whatever means) include a sex equality clause[1], they are to be treated as including one[2]. A sex equality clause is a provision that has the following effect:

(1)   if a term of A's is less favourable to A than a corresponding term of B's is to B, A's term is modified so as not to be less favourable[3];

(2)   if A does not have a term which corresponds to a term of B's that benefits B, A's terms are modified so as to include such a term[4].

A sex equality clause does not have effect in relation to terms of work affected by compliance with laws regulating the employment of women or the appointment of women to personal or public offices[5] or to terms of work affording special treatment to women in connection with pregnancy or childbirth[6].

1   See notes 3–4.
2   Equality Act 2010 s 66(1).
3   Equality Act 2010 s 66(2)(a). Section 66(2)(a) applies to a term of A's relating to membership of or rights under an occupational pension scheme only in so far as a sex equality rule would have effect in relation to the term: s 66(3). As to the meaning of 'occupational pension scheme' see PARA **134** note 1.
       In the case of work within s 65(1)(b) (see PARA **137**), a reference in s 66(2) to a term includes a reference to such terms (if any) as have not been determined by the rating of the work (as well as those that have): s 66(4).
4   Equality Act 2010 s 66(2)(b).
5   Equality Act 2010 Sch 7 para 1. As to the meaning of 'personal office' see PARA **125** note 1; as to the meaning of 'public office' see PARA **126** note 2.
6   Equality Act 2010 Sch 7 para 2.

140.   Sex equality rule.

If an occupational pension scheme[1] does not include a sex equality rule[2], it is to be treated as including one[3]. A sex equality rule is a provision that has the following effect:

(1)   if a relevant term[4] is less favourable to A than it is to B, the term is modified so as not to be less favourable[5];

(2)   if a term confers a relevant discretion[6] capable of being exercised in a way that would be less favourable to A than to B, the term is modified so as to prevent the exercise of the discretion in that way[7].

If the effect of a relevant matter[8] on a person (A) differs according to the effect it has on a person of the same sex as A, according to whether A is married, in a civil partnership, or for some other reason due to A's family status, a comparison for the purposes of these provisions of the effect of that matter on persons of the opposite sex must be with a person of the opposite sex to A who is in the same position as A and in particular[9]:

(a)   where A is married to someone of the opposite sex, A is to be compared to a person of the opposite sex to A ('B') where B is married to someone of the opposite sex to B[10];

(b)   where A is married to someone of the same sex as A or is in a civil partnership, A is to be compared to B where B is married to someone of the same sex as B or is in a civil partnership[11].

A sex equality rule does not have effect in relation to a difference as between men and women in the effect of a relevant matter if the difference is permitted in specified circumstances[12] relating to the calculation of state retirement pensions[13] or is attributable to certain actuarial matters[14].

1   As to the meaning of 'occupational pension scheme' see PARA 134 note 1.
2   See notes 4–7.
3   Equality Act 2010 s 67(1). These provisions, so far as relating to the terms on which persons become members of an occupational pension scheme, do not have effect in relation to pensionable service before 8 April 1976; and, so far as relating to the terms on which members of an occupational pension scheme are treated, does not have effect in relation to pensionable service before 17 May 1990: s 67(9), (10). As to the meaning of 'pensionable service' see PARA 134 note 4.
4   A term is relevant if it is a term on which persons become members of the scheme; or a term on which members of the scheme are treated: Equality Act 2010 s 67(3). The reference to a term on which members of a scheme are treated includes a reference to the term as it has effect for the benefit of dependants of members: see s 67(5).
5   Equality Act 2010 s 67(2)(a).
6   A discretion is relevant if its exercise in relation to the scheme is capable of affecting the way in which persons become members of the scheme; or the way in which members of the scheme are treated: Equality Act 2010 s 67(4). The reference to the way in which members of a scheme are treated includes a reference to the way in which they are treated as the scheme has effect for the benefit of dependants of members: s 67(6).
7   Equality Act 2010 s 67(2)(b).
8   A 'relevant matter' is (see the Equality Act 2010 s 67(8), Sch 7 para 3(2)):
        (1)   a relevant term (see note 4);
        (2)   a term conferring a relevant discretion (see note 6);
        (3)   the exercise of a relevant discretion in relation to an occupational pension scheme.
9   Equality Act 2010 s 67(7) (substituted by SI 2014/560).
10 Equality Act 2010 s 67(7)(b) (as substituted: see note 9).
11 Equality Act 2010 s 67(7)(b) (as substituted: see note 9).
12 Equality Act 2010 Sch 7 para 3(1). The reference in the text to specified circumstances is to the circumstances in which the difference is permitted by Sch 7 Pt 2 (paras 3–6). Regulations may amend the Equality Act 2010 Sch 7 Pt 2 so as to add, vary or omit provision about cases where a difference as between men and women in the effect of a relevant matter is permitted: Sch 7 para 6(1). The regulations may make provision about pensionable service before the date on which they come into force (but not about pensionable service before 17 May 1990): Sch 7 para 6(2). At the date at which this volume states the law no such regulations had been made.
13 Where a man and a woman are eligible, in prescribed circumstances, to receive different amounts by way of pension, the difference is permitted if, in prescribed circumstances, it is attributable only to differences between men and women in the benefits to which, in prescribed circumstances, the man and woman are or would be entitled under the Social Security Contributions and Benefits Act 1992 ss 43–55 (state retirement pensions: see WELFARE BENEFITS AND STATE PENSIONS vol 104 (2014) PARA 487 et seq) or Pensions Act 2014 ss 2–12 (state pension: see WELFARE BENEFITS AND STATE PENSIONS vol 104 (2014) PARA 523A): see the Equality Act 2010 Sch 7 para 4 (amended by SI 2016/224). As to the circumstances which have been prescribed for these purposes see the Equality Act 2010 (Sex Equality Rule) (Exceptions) Regulations 2010, SI 2010/2132, regs 2, 3 (reg 2 amended by SI 2015/1985).
14 A difference as between men and women is permitted if it consists of applying to the calculation of the employer's contributions to an occupational pension scheme actuarial factors which differ for men and women and are of such description as may be prescribed: Equality Act 2010 Sch 7

para 5(1). A difference as between men and women is also permitted if it consists of applying to the determination of benefits of such description as may be prescribed actuarial factors which differ for men and women: Sch 7 para 5(2). As to the circumstances which have been prescribed for these purposes see the Equality Act 2010 (Sex Equality Rule) (Exceptions) Regulations 2010, SI 2010/2132, reg 4 (amended: by SI 2014/1711).

141. Sex equality rule: consequential alteration of schemes.

If the trustees or managers[1] of an occupational pension scheme[2] do not have power to make sex equality alterations[3] to the scheme[4]; and if the trustees or managers of an occupational pension scheme have power to make sex equality alterations to the scheme but the procedure for doing so is liable to be unduly complex or protracted[5]; or involves obtaining consents which cannot be obtained or which can be obtained only with undue delay or difficulty[6] the trustees or managers may by resolution make sex equality alterations to the scheme[7].

1   As to the meaning of 'trustees or managers' see PARA 134 note 4.
2   As to the meaning of 'occupational pension scheme' see PARA 134 note 1.
3   'Sex equality alterations' to an occupational pension scheme are such alterations to the scheme as may be required to secure conformity with a sex equality rule: Equality Act 2010 s 68(5).
4   Equality Act 2010 s 68(1).
5   Equality Act 2010 s 68(2)(a).
6   Equality Act 2010 s 68(2)(b).
7   Equality Act 2010 s 68(3). Sex equality alterations may have effect in relation to a period before the date on which they are made: s 68(4).

142. Defence of material factor.

The sex equality clause[1] in A's terms has no effect in relation to a difference between A's terms and B's terms if the responsible person[2] shows that the difference is because of a material factor[3], reliance on which:

(1)   does not involve treating A less favourably because of A's sex than the responsible person treats B[4]; and

(2)   if the factor is within certain provisions[5], is a proportionate means of achieving a legitimate aim[6].

A sex equality rule[7] has no effect in relation to a difference between A and B in the effect of a relevant matter[8] if the trustees or managers[9] of the scheme in question show that the difference is because of a material factor which is not the difference of sex[10].

1   As to a sex equality clause see PARA 139
2   A person (P) is the responsible person in relation to another person if:
    (1)   P is the other's employer (Equality Act 2010 s 80(4)(a));
    (2)   P is responsible for paying remuneration in respect of a personal or public office that the other holds (s 80(4)(b)).
    As to the meaning of 'employer' see PARA 134 note 4.
3   For these purposes, a factor is not material unless it is a material difference between A's case and B's: Equality Act 2010 s 69(6).
    The employer must identify the factor and prove the following (see *Glasgow City Council v Marshall* [2000] 1 All ER 641 at 647, [2000] IRLR 272 at 274, HL (decided under the Equal Pay Act 1970 (repealed)); and the Equality Act 2010 Code of Practice — Equal Pay Statutory Code of Practice (2010) para 76):
    (1)   it is the real reason for the difference in pay and not a sham or pretence;
    (2)   it is causative of the difference in pay between the woman and her comparator;
    (3)   it is material: that is, significant and relevant; and
    (4)   it does not involve direct or indirect sex discrimination.
    In determining the reason for a pay disparity, a tribunal must look at the underlying reasons and not content itself with examining the immediate reason: *Bainbridge v Redcar and Cleveland Borough Council; Surtees v Middlesborough Borough Council* [2008] EWCA Civ 885 at [103], [2009] ICR 133, [2008] IRLR 776 (decided under the Equal Pay Act 1970 (repealed)). There is no need for a tribunal, as a matter of law, always to adopt a formulaic approach, in considering

whether there is sex-related pay discrimination; what matters is whether, in any particular case, a tribunal is satisfied on the evidence before them and the facts found that the pay difference is caused by a factor or factors which are related to the difference in sex between the applicant and her comparator: *Armstrong v Ministry of Defence* [2004] IRLR 672 at [42] (decided under the Equal Pay Act 1970); approved in *British Airways plc v Grundy (No 2)* [2007] EWCA Civ 1020 at [28], [2008] IRLR 74 per Sedley LJ.

Whether an explanation for a variation is limited by time may be relevant: see *Benveniste v University of Southampton* [1989] ICR 617, [1989] IRLR 122, CA (decided under the Equal Pay Act 1970 (repealed)) (explanation for variation financial constraints; when such constraints ended, explanation no longer valid); *Secretary of State for Justice (sued as national offenders management service) v Bowling* (2011) UKEAT/0297/11/SM, [2012] IRLR 382, EAT (decided under the Equal Pay Act 1970 (repealed)) (continuing effect).

As to examples of possible material factors see the Equality Act 2010 Code of Practice — Equal Pay Statutory Code of Practice (2010) para 77; and *Navy, Army and Air Force Institutes v Varley* [1977] 1 All ER 840, [1977] 1 WLR 149, [1977] ICR 11, EAT (decided under the Equal Pay Act 1970 (repealed)); *Shields v E Coomes (Holdings) Ltd* [1979] 1 All ER 456, [1978] 1 WLR 1408, [1978] ICR 1159, CA (decided under the Equal Pay Act 1970 (repealed)); *Jenkins v Kingsgate (Clothing Productions) Ltd (No 2)* [1981] ICR 715, [1981] IRLR 388, EAT (decided under the Equal Pay Act 1970 (repealed)). Where the material factor accounts for only part of the variation in pay, the woman is entitled to a pay increase to the extent that the defence is made out: Case C-127/92 *Enderby v Frenchay Health Authority* [1994] ICR 112, [1993] IRLR 591, ECJ. See also *Ratcliffe v North Yorkshire County Council* [1995] 3 All ER 597, [1995] IRLR 439, HL (decided under the Equal Pay Act 1970 (repealed)). See also *Wallace v Calmac Ferries Ltd* [2013] All ER (D) 242 (Dec), EAT; and *Webster v A-G of Trinidad and Tobago* [2015] UKPC 10, [2015] All ER (D) 110 (Mar).

4 Equality Act 2010 s 69(1)(a).
5 Ie within the Equality Act 2010 s 69(2). A factor is within s 69(2) if A shows that, as a result of the factor, A and persons of the same sex doing work equal to A's are put at a particular disadvantage when compared with persons of the opposite sex doing work equal to A's: s 69(2). As to equal work see PARA 137. As to indirect discrimination see PARA 75.
6 Equality Act 2010 s 69(1)(b). For these purposes, the long-term objective of reducing inequality between men's and women's terms of work is always to be regarded as a legitimate aim: s 69(3). The Equality Act 2010 does not include a list of aims that are accepted to be legitimate, and whether or not an employer's pay practice pursues a legitimate aim will depend on the facts and circumstances of the particular case: see the Equality Act 2010 Code of Practice — Equal Pay Statutory Code of Practice (2010) para 88. As to examples of proportionate means see the Equality Act 2010 Code of Practice — Equal Pay Statutory Code of Practice (2010) para 89.
7 As to a sex equality rule see PARA 140.
8 As to the meaning of 'relevant matter' see PARA 140 note 8 (definition applied by the Equality Act 2010 s 69(5)).
9 As to the meaning of 'trustees or managers' see PARA 134 note 4.
10 Equality Act 2010 s 69(4).

143. Exclusion of sex discrimination provisions.

The relevant sex discrimination provision[1] has no effect in relation to a term of A's that:

(1) is modified by, or included by virtue of, a sex equality clause[2] or rule[3]; or

(2) would be so modified or included but for the provisions on the defence of material factor[4] and exceptions in relation to occupational pension schemes[5].

Neither the inclusion in A's terms of a term that is less favourable[6], nor the failure to include in A's terms a corresponding term[7], is sex discrimination for the purposes of the relevant sex discrimination provision[8].

1 The relevant sex discrimination provision is, in relation to employment, the Equality Act 2010 s 39(2) (see PARA 117): see s 70(3). As to the meaning of 'employment' see PARA 117 note 3. The relevant sex discrimination is, in relation to appointment to a personal office, s 49(6) (see PARA 125): see s 70(3). As to the meaning of 'personal office' see PARA 125 note 1; and see also PARA 137 note 5. The relevant sex discrimination is, in relation to appointment to a public office, s 50(6)

(see PARA **126**): see s 70(3). As to the meaning of 'public office' see PARA **126** note 2. As to the meaning of 'sex discrimination' see PARA **73** note 5.

2   As to a sex equality clause see PARA **139**
3   Equality Act 2010 s 70(1)(a). As to a sex equality rule see PARA **140**
4   See the Equality Act 2010 s 70(1)(b). As to the defence of material factor see PARA **142**.
5   See the Equality Act 2010 s 70(1)(b).
6   Ie as referred to in the Equality Act 2010 s 66(2)(a) (see PARA **139**).
7   Ie as referred to in the Equality Act 2010 s 66(2)(b) (see PARA **139**).
8   Equality Act 2010 s 70(2). See note 1.

144. Sex discrimination in relation to contractual pay.

In relation to a term of a person's work that relates to pay[1], but in relation to which a sex equality clause[2] or rule[3] has no effect[4], the relevant sex discrimination provision[5] has no effect in relation to the term except in so far as treatment of the person amounts to a contravention of the provision by virtue of the provisions[6] on direct discrimination[7].

1   Equality Act 2010 s 71(1)(a). The terms of a person's work are:
    (1)   if the person is employed, the terms of the person's employment that are in the person's contract of employment, contract of apprenticeship or contract to do work personally (s 80(1), (2)(a));
    (2)   if the person holds a personal or public office, the terms of the person's appointment to the office (s 80(1), (2)(b)).
As to the meaning of 'personal or public office' see PARA **128** note 1; and see also PARA **137** note 5. As to the meaning of 'employment' see PARA **116**.
2   As to a sex equality clause see PARA **139**.
3   As to a sex equality rule see PARA **140**.
4   Equality Act 2010 s 71(1)(b).
5   As to the meaning of the 'relevant sex discrimination provision' see PARA **143** note 1 (definition applied by the Equality Act 2010 s 71(2)).
6   Ie the Equality Act 2010 ss 13, 14 (see PARA
7   Equality Act 2010 s 71(2).

(ii) Pregnancy and Maternity Equality

145. Modification of terms of maternity pay ('maternity equality clause').

If a term of a woman's work provides for maternity-related pay[1] to be calculated by reference to her pay at a particular time[2], and:
    (1)   after the time by reference to which the pay is calculated but before the end of the protected period[3] her pay increases[4] or would have increased had she not been on maternity leave[5];
    (2)   the maternity-related pay is not what her pay would have been had she not been on maternity leave[6] or the difference between the amount of statutory maternity pay to which she is entitled and what her pay would have been had she not been on maternity leave[7]; and
    (3)   the terms of her work do not provide for the maternity-related pay to be subject to a pay increase[8] or an increase that would have occurred[9] had she not been on maternity leave[10],

that term is modified to provide for the maternity-related pay to be subject to the applicable pay increase[11] or the increase that would have occurred[12] had she not been on maternity leave[13].

If a term of a woman's work provides for:
    (a)   pay (including pay by way of bonus) in respect of times before the woman is on maternity leave[14];

(b)   pay by way of bonus in respect of times when she is on compulsory maternity leave[15]; or

(c)   pay by way of bonus in respect of times after the end of the protected period[16],

but does not provide for her to be given the pay in circumstances in which she would have been given it had she not been on maternity leave[17], that term is modified so as to provide for her to be given it in circumstances in which it would normally be given[18].

If a term of a woman's work provides for pay after the end of the protected period[19] but does not provide for it to be subject to an increase to which it would have been subject had she not been on maternity leave, that term is modified so as to provide for it to be subject to the increase[20].

A maternity equality clause does not have effect in relation to terms of work affected by compliance with laws regulating the employment of women or the appointment of women to personal or public offices[21].

1   'Maternity-related pay' is pay (other than statutory maternity pay) to which a woman is entitled as a result of being pregnant or in respect of times when she is on maternity leave: Equality Act 2010 s 74(9). As to statutory maternity pay EMPLOYMENT vol 40 (2014) PARA 401 et seq. As to the terms of a person's work see PARA 144 note 1.
2   Equality Act 2010 s 74(1).
3   Equality Act 2010 s 74(2). A reference to the protected period is to be construed in accordance with s 18 (see PARA 74): s 74(10).
4   Equality Act 2010 s 74(2)(a).
5   Equality Act 2010 s 74(2)(b).
6   Equality Act 2010 s 74(3)(a).
7   Equality Act 2010 s 74(3)(b).
8   Ie an increase as mentioned in the Equality Act 2010 s 74(2)(a) (see the text and note 4).
9   Ie as mentioned in the Equality Act 2010 s 74(2)(b) (see the text and note 5).
10 Equality Act 2010 s 74(4).
11 Equality Act 2010 s 74(5)(a). The applicable pay increase is any increase mentioned in s 74(2)(a) (see the text and note 4).
12 Ie as mentioned in the Equality Act 2010 s 74(2)(b) (see the text and note 5):
13 Equality Act 2010 s 74(5)(b). As to the incorporation of these provisions in terms of employment see PARA 147.
14 Equality Act 2010 s 74(6)(a), (7)(a).
15 Equality Act 2010 s 74(7)(b).
16 Equality Act 2010 s 74(7)(c).
17 Equality Act 2010 s 74(6)(b).
18 Equality Act 2010 s 74(6). As to the incorporation of these provisions in terms of employment see PARA 147.
19 As to the protected period see note 3.
20 Equality Act 2010 s 74(8). As to the incorporation of these provisions in terms of employment see PARA 147.
21 Equality Act 2010 Sch 7 para 1. As to the meaning of 'personal office' see PARA 125 note 1; as to the meaning of 'public office' see PARA 126 note 2; and see also PARA 137 note 5.

146. Modification of occupational pension provisions ('maternity equality rule').

If:

(1)   a term relating to membership of an occupational pension scheme[1];

(2)   a term relating to the accrual of rights under the scheme[2]; or

(3)   a term providing for the determination of the amount of a benefit payable under the scheme[3],

does not treat time when a woman is on maternity leave[4] as it treats time when she is not, the term is modified so as to treat time when she is on maternity leave as time when she is not[5].

If a term of an occupational pension scheme confers a discretion the exercise of which is capable of affecting:

(a)   membership of the scheme[6];

(b)   the accrual of rights under the scheme[7]; or

(c)   the determination of the amount of a benefit payable under the scheme[8],

and that discretion is capable of being exercised so that time when a woman is on maternity leave is treated differently from time when she is not, the term is modified so as not to allow the discretion to be exercised in that way[9].

These provisions do not require a woman's contributions to the scheme in respect of time when she is on maternity leave to be determined otherwise than by reference to the amount she is paid in respect of that time[10].

1   Equality Act 2010 s 75(5)(a). As to the meaning of 'occupational pension scheme' see PARA **134** note 1.

2   Equality Act 2010 s 75(5)(b).

3   Equality Act 2010 s 75(5)(c).

4   For these purposes a reference to being on maternity leave includes a reference to having been on maternity leave: Equality Act 2010 s 75(10)(a). These provisions (ie s 75), so far as relating to time when a woman is on ordinary maternity leave but is not being paid by her employer, apply only in a case where the expected week of childbirth began on or after 6 April 2003 (s 75(8)); and so far as relating to time when a woman is on additional maternity leave but is not being paid by her employer, these provisions do not apply to the accrual of rights under the scheme in any case and apply for other purposes only in a case where the expected week of childbirth began on or after 5 October 2008 (s 75(9)). A reference to being 'paid' by an employer includes a reference to receiving statutory maternity pay from the employer: s 75(10)(b). As to statutory maternity pay see EMPLOYMENT vol 40 (2014) PARA 401 et seq.

5   Equality Act 2010 s 75(3).

6   Equality Act 2010 s 75(6)(a).

7   Equality Act 2010 s 75(6)(b).

8   Equality Act 2010 s 75(6)(c).

9   Equality Act 2010 s 75(4).

10 Equality Act 2010 s 75(7).

147.   Implied incorporation of maternity equality clause and maternity equality rule.

A provision that, in relation to the terms of a woman's work, has the effect of modifying those terms in accordance with the requirements for equality in maternity pay[1] is referred to as a 'maternity equality clause'[2], and a provision that has the effect of modifying terms of an occupational pension scheme in accordance with the requirements for equality in pension entitlements[3] is referred to as a 'maternity equality rule'[4]. If a woman is employed[5] or holds a personal or public office[6] but the terms of her work do not (by whatever means) include a maternity equality clause, or an occupational pension scheme[7] does not include a maternity equality rule, those terms or that scheme are to be treated as including such a clause or rule[8].

1   Ie a provision that, in relation to the terms of the woman's work, has the effect referred to in the Equality Act 2010 s 74(1), (6), (8) (see PARA **145**). As to the terms of a person's work see PARA **144** note 1.

2   Equality Act 2010 s 73(2).

3   Ie a provision that has the effect set out in the Equality Act 2010 s 75(3), (4) (see PARA **146**).

4   Equality Act 2010 s 75(2).

5   As to the meaning of 'employed' see PARA **116**.

6   As to the meaning of 'personal office' see PARA **125** note 1; as to the meaning of 'public office' see PARA **126** note 2; and see also PARA **137** note 5.

7   As to the meaning of 'occupational pension scheme' see PARA **134** note 1.

8   Equality Act 2010 ss 72, 73(1), 75(1). In the case of a term relating to membership of or rights under an occupational pension scheme, a maternity equality clause has only such effect as a

maternity equality rule would have: s 73(3). Section 39(2) (so far as relating to employment) (see PARA 117), s 49(6) (so far as relating to appointment to a personal office) (see PARA 125) and s 50(6) (so far as relating to appointment to a public office) (see PARA 126) have no effect in relation to a term of a woman's work that is modified by a maternity equality clause or rule or in relation to a term of a woman's work that relates to pay but in relation to which a maternity equality clause or rule has no effect: s 76(1), (1A), (3) (s 76(1A) added by SI 2010/2622).

(iii) Pay Disclosures

148. Discussions about pay.
A disclosure is a 'relevant pay disclosure' if made for the purpose of enabling the person who makes it, or the person to whom it is made, to find out whether or to what extent there is, in relation to the work in question, a connection between pay and having (or not having) a particular protected characteristic[1], and a term of a person's work is unenforceable against him if:

(1)   it purports to prevent or restrict him from disclosing or seeking to disclose information about the terms of his work in so far as he makes or seeks to make a relevant pay disclosure[2]; or

(2)   it purports to prevent or restrict him from seeking disclosure of information from a colleague[3] about the terms of the colleague's work in so far as he seeks a relevant pay disclosure from the colleague[4].

Seeking a disclosure that would be a relevant pay disclosure, making or seeking to make a relevant pay disclosure, and receiving information disclosed in a relevant pay disclosure, are 'protected acts' for the purposes of the general provisions on workplace victimisation[5].

1   Equality Act 2010 s 77(3). As to the protected characteristics see PARA 45 et seq.
2   Equality Act 2010 s 77(1). As to the terms of a person's work see PARA 144 note 1.
3   'Colleague' includes a former colleague in relation to the work in question: Equality Act 2010 s 77(2).
4   Equality Act 2010 s 77(2).
5   Equality Act 2010 s 77(4). For this purpose the general provisions on workplace victimisation are the Equality Act 2010 s 27 (see PARA 81) in relation to employment (so far as it applies to s 39(3) or s 39(4): see PARA 117), in relation to appointment to a personal office (so far as it applies to s 49(5) or s 49(8): see PARA 125), and in relation to appointment to a public office (so far as it applies to s 50(5) or s 50(9): see PARA 126): s 77(5). As to the meaning of 'personal office' see PARA 125 note 1; as to the meaning of 'public office' see PARA 126 note 2; and see also PARA 137 note 5.

149. Gender pay gap information.
Regulations may require employers to publish information relating to the pay of employees[1] for the purpose of showing whether, by reference to factors of such description as is prescribed, there are differences in the pay of male and female employees[2]. The regulations may prescribe:

(1)   descriptions of employer[3];
(2)   descriptions of employee[4];
(3)   how to calculate the number of employees that an employer has[5];
(4)   descriptions of information[6];
(5)   the time at which information is to be published[7];
(6)   the form and manner in which it is to be published[8].

In exercise of these powers regulations have been made which provide as follows[9]. A relevant employer must publish the following information[10]:

(a)   the difference between the mean hourly rate of pay of male full-pay relevant employees[11] and that of female full-pay relevant employees; and the difference between the median hourly rate of pay of male full-pay relevant employees and that of female full-pay relevant employees[12];

(b)   the difference between the mean bonus pay paid to male relevant employees and that paid to female relevant employees; and the difference between the median bonus pay paid to male relevant employees and that paid to female relevant employees[13];

(c)   the proportions of male and female relevant employees who were paid bonus pay[14]; and

(d)   the proportions of male and female full-pay relevant employees in the lower, lower middle, upper middle and upper quartile pay bands[15].

Regulations may also make provision in connection with the punishment for failure to comply with the regulations[16].

1   As to the meanings of 'employment', 'employee' and 'employer' see PARA **116**
2   Equality Act 2010 s 78(1). These requirements do not apply to an employer who has fewer than 250 employees, a person specified in Sch 19 (see PARA **277**), or a government department or part of the armed forces not specified in Sch 19: s 78(2).
3   Equality Act 2010 s 78(3)(a).
4   Equality Act 2010 s 78(3)(b).
5   Equality Act 2010 s 78(3)(c).
6   Equality Act 2010 s 78(3)(d).
7   Equality Act 2010 s 78(3)(e). Regulations under s 78(3)(e) may not require an employer, after the first publication of information, to publish information more frequently than at intervals of 12 months: s 78(4).
8   Equality Act 2010 s 78(3)(f).
9   See the Equality Act 2010 (Gender Pay Gap Information) Regulations 2017, SI 2017/172; and notes 10–16. As to the review of these regulations to be carried out by the Secretary of State see reg 16. As to the Secretary of State see PARA **4**.
10 The information is to be published for 2017 and each subsequent year and must be accompanied by a signed statement: see the Equality Act 2010 (Gender Pay Gap Information) Regulations 2017, SI 2017/172, regs 2(1), 14. The information and statement must be published on the employer's website for at least three years (see reg 15(1)); and the information and details of the person who signed the statement must be published on a website designated by the Secretary of State for that purpose (see reg 15(2)). The information required must be published within the period of 12 months beginning with the snapshot date (5 April) in the year to which the information required relates: see regs 1(2), 2(2). As to data not required to be included see reg 2(3). 'Relevant employer' means an employer who has 250 or more employees on the snapshot date but does not include a person specified in the Equality Act 2010 Sch 19 (see PARA **277**) or a government department or part of the armed forces not specified in that Schedule: see the Equality Act 2010 (Gender Pay Gap Information) Regulations 2017, SI 2017/172, reg 1(2), (6).
11 'Full-pay relevant employee' means a relevant employee who is not, during the relevant pay period (ie the pay period within which the snapshot date falls), being paid at a reduced rate or nil as a result of the employee being on leave; and 'relevant employee' means a person who is employed by the relevant employer on the snapshot date but does not include a partner in a firm: see the Equality Act 2010 (Gender Pay Gap Information) Regulations 2017, SI 2017/172, regs 1(2), (4), (5), 5(2). 'Pay period' in relation to a relevant employee means the period in respect of which the relevant employer pays the employee basic pay, whether weekly, fortnightly, monthly or any other period, or if the relevant employer does not pay the employee basic pay, the period in respect of which the employer most frequently pays the employee one of the elements of ordinary pay mentioned in reg 3(1)(b)–(e): reg 5(1). 'Ordinary pay' is defined in reg 3.
12 See the Equality Act 2010 (Gender Pay Gap Information) Regulations 2017, SI 2017/172, reg 2(1)(a), (1)(b). As to determination of the difference between the mean hourly rate of pay of male full-pay relevant employees and that of female full-pay relevant employees see regs 6–8. As to determination of the difference between the median hourly rate of pay of male full-pay relevant employees and that of female full-pay relevant employees see regs 6–7, 9.
13 See the Equality Act 2010 (Gender Pay Gap Information) Regulations 2017, SI 2017/172, reg 2(1)(c), (1)(d). As to determination of the difference between the mean bonus pay of male full-pay relevant employees and that of female full-pay relevant employees see reg 10. As to determination

of the difference between the median bonus pay of male full-pay relevant employees and that of female full-pay relevant employees see reg 11. 'Bonus pay' is defined in reg 4.

14 See the Equality Act 2010 (Gender Pay Gap Information) Regulations 2017, SI 2017/172, reg 2(1)(e). As to determination of the proportions of male and female relevant employees who were paid bonus pay see reg 12.

15 See the Equality Act 2010 (Gender Pay Gap Information) Regulations 2017, SI 2017/172, reg 2(1)(f). As to determination of the proportions of male and female full-pay relevant employees in the lower, lower middle, upper middle and upper quartile pay bands see reg 13.

16 See the Equality Act 2010 s 78(5). The regulations may provide for failure to comply to be an offence punishable on summary conviction by a fine not exceeding level 5 on the standard scale or to be enforced, otherwise than as an offence, by such means as are prescribed: s 78(5). As to the powers of magistrates' courts to issue fines on summary conviction see SENTENCING vol 92 (2015) PARA 176. The reference to a failure to comply with the regulations includes a reference to a failure by a person acting on behalf of an employer: s 78(6). At the date at which this volume states the law no such regulations had been made. In the event of persistent failure, the Equality Act 2006 would permit the Equality and Human Rights Commission to consider using its powers: see PARAS 35–36, 339 et seq.

(iv) Equal Pay under European Law

150. The principle of equal pay.

The Treaty on the Functioning of the European Union requires that men and women should receive equal pay for equal work and work of equal value[1]. This requirement is supplemented by elements of the Equal Treatment Directive[2]. The principle of equal pay forms part of the foundations of the EU[3].

The principle of equal pay applies to each element of remuneration[4]. Once discrimination in pay is established, the only proper way of complying with the equal pay requirement is to grant the disadvantaged person the benefits paid to the advantaged class[5]. These provisions are of direct effect and may be relied upon in national courts[6]: however, they do not provide a free-standing right of action in the employment tribunal[7].

1 See the Treaty on the Functioning of the European Union (Rome, 25 March 1957; TS 1 (1973); Cmnd 5179) art 157.1. The Treaty was formerly known as the Treaty Establishing the European Community; it has been renamed and its provisions renumbered: see PARA 10. As to reasonable time limits for bringing a claim under these provisions see *Rankin v British Coal Corpn* [1995] ICR 774, [1993] IRLR 69, EAT. As to the Treaty in the context of discrimination law see PARA 10.

2 Ie Parliament and Council Directive (EC) 2006/54 (OJ L204, 26.7.2006, p 23) on the implementation of the principle of equal opportunities and equal treatment of men and women in matters of employment and occupation: see PARA 12.

3 Case 43/74 *Defrenne v Sabena (No 2)* [1981] 1 All ER 122, [1976] ICR 547, ECJ; Case C-262/88 *Barber v Guardian Royal Exchange Assurance Group* [1991] 1 QB 344, [1990] ICR 616, ECJ.

4 Case C-262/88 *Barber v Guardian Royal Exchange Assurance Group* [1991] 1 QB 344, [1990] ICR 616, ECJ. See Case C-381/99 *Brunnhofer v Bank der Österreichischen Postsparkasse AG* [2001] All ER (EC) 693, [2001] ECR I-4961, ECJ. As to overtime payments for full-time and part-time workers see Case C-285/02 *Elsner-Lakeberg v Land Nordrhein-Westfalen* [2004] ECR I-5861, [2005] IRLR 209, ECJ.

5 Case C-408/92 *Smith v Avdel Systems Ltd* [1995] All ER (EC) 132, [1995] ICR 596, ECJ.

6 See Case C-170/84 *Bilka-Kaufhaus GmbH v Weber Von Hartz* [1987] ICR 110, [1986] IRLR 317, ECJ. See also PARA 153. As to the meaning of 'direct effect' see Case 26/62 *NV Algemene Transport en Expeditie Onderneming van Gend & Loos v Nederlandse Administratie der Belastingen* [1963] ECR 1, [1963] CMLR 105, ECJ. See also *Brierley v Asda Stores Ltd* (2017) UKEAT/0011/17/DM, [2017] All ER (D) 141 (Aug).

7 *Biggs v Somerset County Council* [1996] 2 All ER 734, [1995] ICR 811, EAT. Reliance must be placed on the statutory authority, modified, if necessary, by striking out any provisions incompatible with the Treaty on the Functioning of the European Union art 157.

151. The meaning of 'pay' in European law.

'Pay' is defined as the ordinary basic or minimum wage or salary and any other consideration, whether in cash or in kind, which the worker receives directly or indirectly, in respect of his employment, from his employer[1]. The European Court of Justice has adopted an extremely broad definition of 'pay'[2]. The term 'pay' includes salary, overtime rates where men and women work the same hours[3], automatic pay increases[4], bonus payments that amount to retroactive pay for work carried out during the course of the year[5], allowances for periods carrying out duties away from work[6], sick pay (provided it is paid by the employer rather than a social security body)[7] and certain non-monetary benefits[8].

Maternity pay constitutes pay for these purposes[9]. However, where maternity pay is lower than normal contractual remuneration[10] or sick pay[11] there is no breach of the principle of equal pay. This is because discrimination involves the application of different rules to comparable situations or the application of the same rule to different situations. The position of a woman absent on maternity leave is unique and is not comparable to that of a man at work or a man who is absent due to ill-health[12]. However, where a woman is absent from work for a pregnancy-related illness prior to the period of maternity leave there will be a breach of the principle of equal pay if she is not paid at the same rate as a man absent through ill-health[13]. Once she returns to work, a woman is entitled to the benefit of any pay rise that was implemented while she was absent on maternity leave[14].

Various payments made on or after the termination of employment constitute pay. These include notice monies[15], statutory and contractual redundancy payments[16], and unfair dismissal compensation[17].

1 See the Treaty on the Functioning of the European Union (Rome, 25 March 1957; TS 1 (1973); Cmnd 5179) art 157.2. The Treaty was formerly known as the Treaty Establishing the European Community; it has been renamed and its provisions renumbered: see PARA 10. As to the Treaty in the context of discrimination law see PARA 10.

2 See Case C-167/97 *R v Secretary of State for Employment, ex p Seymour-Smith* [1999] 2 AC 554, [1999] ICR 447, ECJ. See also Case C-381/99 *Brunnhofer v Bank der Österreichischen Postsparkasse AG* [2001] All ER (EC) 693, [2001] ECR I-4961, ECJ.

3 Where men and women work the same hours they are entitled to the same overtime rate; however, the principle of equal pay does not require that women who work part-time are paid overtime rates for work beyond their normal hours: Case C-399/92 *Stadt Lengerich v Helmig* [1996] ICR 35, [1995] IRLR 216, ECJ. See also Case C-236/98 *Jämställdhetsombudsmannen v Örebro Läns Landsting* [2000] ECR I-2189, [2000] 2 CMLR 708, [2001] ICR 249, ECJ.

4 Case C-184/89 *Nimz v Freie und Hansestadt Hamburg* [1991] ECR I-297, [1991] IRLR 222, ECJ; Case C-243/95 *Hill and Stapleton v Inland Revenue Comrs and Department of Finance* [1998] All ER (EC) 722, [1998] IRLR 466, ECJ; cf Case C-1/95 *Gerster v Freistaat Bayern* [1998] ICR 327, [1997] IRLR 699, ECJ.

5 Case C-333/97 *Lewen v Denda* [2000] All ER (EC) 261, [2000] IRLR 67, ECJ; Case C-281/97 *Krüger v Kreiskrankenhaus Ebersberg* [1999] ECR I-5127, [1999] IRLR 808, ECJ.

6 Case C-360/90 *Arbeiterwohlfahrt der Stadt Berlin eV v Bötel* [1992] ECR I-3589, [1992] IRLR 423, ECJ; Case C-457/93 *Kuratorium für Dialyse Und Nierentransplantation eV v Lewark* [1996] ECR I-243, [1996] IRLR 637, ECJ. Cf *Manor Bakeries Ltd v Nazir* [1996] IRLR 604, EAT.

7 Case 171/88 *Rinner-Kühn v FWW Spezial-Gebäudereinigung GmbH & Co KG* [1989] ECR 2743, [1989] IRLR 493, ECJ.

8 Case 12/81 *Garland v British Rail Engineering Ltd* [1982] ECR 359, [1982] IRLR 111, ECJ.

9 Case C-342/93 *Gillespie v Northern Health and Social Services Board* [1996] ICR 498, [1996] IRLR 214, ECJ. As to maternity rights see EMPLOYMENT vol 40 (2014) PARA 354 et seq.

10 Case C-342/93 *Gillespie v Northern Health and Social Services Board* [1996] ICR 498, [1996] IRLR 214, ECJ.

11 *Todd v Eastern Health and Social Services Board, Gillespie v Northern Health and Social Services Board (No 2)* [1997] IRLR 410, NI CA.

12 *Gillespie v Northern Health and Social Services Board (No 2)* [1997] IRLR 410, NI CA. See also
    Case C-411/96 *Boyle v Equal Opportunities Commission* [1998] All ER (EC) 879, [1998] IRLR
    717, ECJ; Case C-218/98 *Abdoulaye v Régie Nationale des Usines Renault SA* (1999) ECR I-5723,
    [1999] IRLR 811, ECJ; Case C-249/97 *Gruber v Silhouette International Schmeid GmbH & Co
    KG* [1999] ECR I-5295, [1999] All ER (D) 1013, ECJ.
        Employers can continue to pay higher wages in recognition of experience and length of service
    even if it is detrimental to women who have maternity leave but have no automatic right to the
    same pay as male colleagues who are doing the same job but have not had time off: see Case
    C-17/05 *Cadman v Health and Safety Executive* [2007] All ER (EC) 1, [2006] ICR 1623, ECJ.
13 Case C-66/96 *Pedersen* [1999] All ER (EC) 138, [1999] IRLR 55, ECJ.
14 Case C-342/93 *Gillespie v Northern Health and Social Services Board* [1996] ICR 498, [1996]
    IRLR 214, ECJ.
15 See *Secretary of State for Employment v Clark* [1997] 1 CMLR 613, sub nom *Clark v Secretary
    of State for Employment* [1997] ICR 64, CA.
16 Case C-262/88 *Barber v Guardian Royal Exchange Assurance Group* [1991] 1 QB 344, [1990]
    ICR 616, ECJ. See also *Hammersmith and Queen Charlotte's Special Hospital Authority v Cato*
    [1988] 1 CMLR 3, [1988] ICR 132, EAT.
17 Case C-167/97 *R v Secretary of State for Employment, ex p Seymour-Smith* [1999] 2 AC 554,
    [1999] ICR 447, ECJ. See also *Mediguard Services Ltd v Thame* [1994] ICR 751, [1994] IRLR
    504, EAT; followed in *Methilhill Bowling Club v Hunter* [1995] ICR 793, [1995] IRLR 232, EAT.

152. Equal pay and pensions.

The equal pay provisions of the Treaty on the Functioning of the European
Union[1] do not apply to social security pension schemes[2]. However, benefits paid
under the majority of EU occupational pension schemes are pay for those
purposes[3]. United Kingdom occupational pension schemes are covered by the
principle of equal pay, which will also apply to the majority of public sector
pension schemes[4]. The principle of equal pay extends to the right to join a pension
scheme[5] and to the payment of benefits under the scheme[6]. Men and women are
entitled to receive the same benefits at the same age[7]. Payments made to the
dependants of pension scheme members also constitute pay[8].

Compulsory employees' contributions constitute pay, and men and women are
entitled to equal gross pay before the deduction of such contributions[9]. However,
in a final salary pension scheme it is lawful for employers' contributions to vary
between men and women to take account of actuarial factors[10]. Where an element
of a pension derives from additional voluntary contributions, it does not amount
to pay for these purposes, as the pension scheme does no more than provide the
members with the arrangements for management of their contributions[11].

These provisions may be relied upon to mount a claim against the trustees of
an occupational pension fund, who may be required to exercise their powers
under the scheme in accordance with the principle of equal pay and, if necessary,
apply to the court for a variation of the trust deed[12].

1 Ie the Treaty on the Functioning of the European Union (Rome, 25 March 1957; TS 1 (1973);
   Cmnd 5179) art 157 (see PARAS 150–151).
2 Case 80/70 *Defrenne v Belgium* [1971] ECR 445, [1974] 1 CMLR 494, ECJ (the European Court
   of Justice drew a distinction between state benefits, determined by considerations of social policy,
   and schemes that provide benefits determined by the employment relationship).
3 Case 170/84 *Bilka-Kaufhaus GmbH v Weber Von Hartz* [1987] ICR 110, [1986] IRLR 317, ECJ
   (the European Court of Justice held that it was contrary to the Treaty on the Functioning of the
   European Union art 157 to exclude part-time employees from the benefits of an occupational
   pension scheme, where the exclusion affects a far greater number of women than men, unless the
   exclusion is based on objectively justified factors unrelated to any discrimination on grounds of
   sex); followed in Case C-50/96 *Deutsche Telekom v Schröder* [2000] ECR I743, [2002] 2 CMLR
   583, ECJ.
4 See Case C-262/88 *Barber v Guardian Royal Exchange Assurance Group* [1991] 1 QB 344, [1990]
   ICR 616, ECJ; Case C-200/91 *Coloroll Pension Trustees Ltd v Russell* [1995] All ER (EC) 23,
   [1995] ICR 179, ECJ; Case C-7/93 *Bestuur Van het Algemeen Burgerlijk Pensioenfonds v Beune*

[1995] All ER (EC) 97, [1995] IRLR 103, ECJ. See, however, indications to the contrary in Case 192/85 *Newstead v Department of Transport* [1988] 1 All ER 129, [1988] 1 WLR 612, ECJ; *Griffin v London Pension Fund Authority* [1993] ICR 564, [1993] IRLR 248, EAT.

5   Case C-170/84 *Bilka-Kauhaus GmbH v Weber Von Hartz* [1987] ICR 110, [1986] IRLR 317, ECJ (which strictly speaking did not concern the right to join a pension scheme but has been repeatedly quoted as authority for the proposition in subsequent cases); Case C-57/93 *Vroege v NCIV Instituut Voor Volkshuisvesting BV* [1995] All ER (EC) 193, [1995] ICR 635, ECJ; Case C-128/93 *Fisscher v Voorhuis Hengelo BV* [1995] All ER (EC) 193, [1995] ICR 635, ECJ; Case C-246/96 *Magorrian v Eastern Health and Social Services Board* [1998] All ER (EC) 38, [1998] ICR 979, ECJ.

6   Case C-262/88 *Barber v Guardian Royal Exchange Assurance Group* [1991] 1 QB 344, [1990] ICR 616, ECJ.

7   Case C-262/88 *Barber v Guardian Royal Exchange Assurance Group* [1991] 1 QB 344, [1990] ICR 616, ECJ. See also Case C-110/91 *Moroni v Collo GmbH* [1995] ICR 137, [1994] IRLR 130, ECJ; Case C-408/92 *Smith v Avdel Systems Ltd* [1995] All ER (EC) 132, [1995] ICR 596, ECJ; Case C-28/93 *Van den Akker v Stichting Shell Pensioenfonds* [1995] All ER (EC) 156, [1995] ICR 596, ECJ; cf Case C-132/92 *Birds Eye Walls Ltd v Roberts* [1993] ECR I-5579, sub nom C-132/92 *Roberts v Birds Eye Walls Ltd* [1994] ICR 338, ECJ.

8   Case C-109/91 *Ten Oever v Stichting Bedrijfspensioenfonds Voor Het Glazenwassers-en Schoonmaakbedrijf* [1995] ICR 74, [1993] IRLR 601, ECJ. See also Case C-117/01 *KB v National Health Service Pensions Agency* [2004] All ER (EC) 1089, [2004] ICR 781, ECJ.

9   Case 69/80 *Worringham v Lloyd's Bank Ltd* [1981] ICR 558, [1981] IRLR 178, ECJ; Case 192/85 *Newstead v Department of Transport* [1988] 1 All ER 129, [1988] 1 WLR 612, ECJ.

10 Case C-152/91 *Neath v Hugh Steeper Ltd* [1995] ICR 158, [1994] IRLR 91, ECJ; Case C-200/91 *Coloroll Pension Trustees Ltd v Russell* [1995] All ER (EC) 23, [1995] ICR 179, [1994] IRLR 586, ECJ.

11 Case C-200/91 *Coloroll Pension Trustees Ltd v Russell* [1995] All ER (EC) 23, [1995] ICR 179, [1994] IRLR 586, ECJ.

12 Case C-200/91 *Coloroll Pension Trustees Ltd v Russell* [1995] All ER (EC) 23, [1995] ICR 179, [1994] IRLR 586, ECJ.

153.   Establishing a breach of the principle of equal pay.

The principle of equal pay[1] has been described as a particular expression of the general principle of non-discrimination under EU law[2]. Although in the majority of the cases before the European Court of Justice there has been no suggestion that the applicant and her comparator were not engaged in equal work or work of equal value, the principle of equal pay cannot apply if this is not the case[3]. The situation of a woman and her comparator must be properly comparable[4].

Where a provision affects a considerably greater number[5] of women than men, it is contrary to the equal pay provisions[6] unless it is established that the exclusion is based on objectively justified factors unrelated to any discrimination on grounds of sex. The objective must correspond to a real need on the part of the undertaking, and the means chosen must be appropriate with a view to achieving the objective in question and be necessary to that end[7].

Although it is for the national court to determine whether a provision is objectively justified, the European Court of Justice has been prepared to give some guidance[8]. Where a pay structure disproportionately affects a group of employees that is predominantly made up of women it is for the employer to establish that the structure is objectively justified[9], particularly if the pay structure is lacking in transparency[10]. Mere generalisations about particular categories of workers do not provide objective justification[11].

The European Court of Justice has adopted a less restrictive approach where discrimination is alleged to result from the application of a legislative provision, on the grounds that social policy is a matter for the member states who are entitled to introduce legislative provisions provided they reasonably consider that the legislation in question is necessary in order to achieve a social policy aim unrelated to any discrimination on grounds of sex[12].

1   See PARAS 150–152.
2   Case C-342/93 *Gillespie v Northern Health and Social Services Board* [1996] All ER (EC) 284, [1996] ICR 498, ECJ. See also Case C-381/99 *Brunnhofer v Bank der Österreichischen Postsparkasse AG* [2001] All ER (EC) 693, [2001] ECR I-4961, ECJ (difference in pay received from commencement of employment cannot be justified by factors which can only be assessed after commencement of employment); applied in *Sharp v Caledonia Group Services Ltd* [2006] ICR 218, [2006] IRLR 4, EAT.
3   See Case C-309/97 *Angestelltenbetriebsrat der Wiener Gebietskrankenkasse v Wiener Gebietskrankenkasse* [1999] ECR I-2865, [1999] IRLR 804, ECJ.
4   For example, in the context of maternity pay see Case C-342/93 *Gillespie v Northern Health and Social Services Board* [1996] All ER (EC) 284, [1996] ICR 498, ECJ; Case C-411/96 *Boyle v Equal Opportunities Commission* [1998] All ER (EC) 879, [1998] IRLR 717, ECJ; Case C-218/98 *Abdoulaye v Régie Nationale des Usines Renault SA* [1999] ECR I-5723, [1999] IRLR 811; Case C-249/97 *Gruber v Silhouette International Schmied GmbH & Co KG* [1999] ECR I-5295, [1999] All ER (D) 1013, ECJ. See also *Barry v Midland Bank plc* [1999] 3 All ER 974, [1999] ICR 859, HL; *Brierley v Asda Stores Ltd* (2017) UKEAT/0011/17/DM, [2017] All ER (D) 141 (Aug).
5   The general approach was set out in Case 170/84 *Bilka-Kaufhaus GmbH v Weber Von Hartz* [1987] ICR 110, [1986] IRLR 317, ECJ. The European Court of Justice referred to exclusion of part-time workers from the pension scheme in question as affecting a 'far greater proportion' of women than men, and has settled on the test of whether the provision affects a considerably greater number of women than men: see eg Case C-167/97 *R v Secretary of State for Employment, ex p Seymour-Smith* [1999] 2 AC 554, [1999] ICR 447, ECJ. See also Case C-300 *Voss v Land Berlin* [2007] ECR I-10573, [2008] 1 CMLR 1313, ECJ (overtime remuneration at lower rate than normal hours for both full-time and part-time employees could have disproportionate effect on part-time employees). It is for the national court to assess the validity of the statistical material: Case C-127/92 *Enderby v Frenchay Health Authority* [1994] ICR 112, [1993] IRLR 591, ECJ. See also *R v Secretary of State for Employment, ex p Seymour-Smith* [2000] ICR 244, [2000] IRLR 263, HL.
6   Ie the Treaty on the Functioning of the European Union (Rome, 25 March 1957; TS 1 (1973); Cmnd 5179) art 157 (see PARAS 150–152).
7   Case 170/84 *Bilka-Kaufhaus GmbH v Weber Von Hartz* [1987] ICR 110, [1986] IRLR 317, ECJ.
8   For a consideration of specific factors see Case 170/84 *Bilka-Kaufhaus GmbH v Weber Von Hartz* [1987] ICR 110, [1986] IRLR 317, ECJ. See, however, Case 171/88 *Rinner-Kühn v FWW Spezial-Gebäudereinigung GmbH & Co KG* [1989] ECR 2743, [1989] IRLR 493, ECJ; Case 109/88 *Handels-og Kontorfunktionaerernes Forbund i Danmark v Dansk Arbejdsgiverforening* [1991] ICR 74, [1989] IRLR 532, ECJ; Case C-184/89 *Nimz v Freie und Hansestadt Hamburg* [1991] ECR I–297, [1991] IRLR 222, ECJ; Case C-127/92 *Enderby v Frenchay Health Authority* [1994] ICR 112, [1993] IRLR 591, ECJ; Case C-243/95 *Hill and Stapleton v Inland Revenue Comrs* [1998] All ER (EC) 722, [1998] IRLR 466, ECJ; Case C-167/97 *R v Secretary of State for Employment, ex p Seymour-Smith* [1999] 2 AC 554, [1999] ICR 447, ECJ. As a general rule, recourse to the criterion of length of service was appropriate to attain the legitimate objective of rewarding experience acquired which enabled a worker better to perform his duties; the employer did not have to justify recourse to this criterion unless the worker provided evidence capable of raising serious doubts: see Case C-17/05 *Cadman v Health and Safety Executive* [2006] All ER (EC) 1, [2006] ICR 1623, ECJ; *Wilson v Health and Safety Executive* [2009] EWCA Civ 1074, [2010] 1 CMLR 772, [2010] IRLR 59.
    As to the question of what the employer has to justify see also Case C-381/99 *Brunnhofer v Bank der Österreichischen Postsparkasse AG* [2001] All ER (EC) 693, [2001] ECR I-4961, ECJ; *Sharp v Caledonia Group Services Ltd* [2006] ICR 218, [2006] IRLR 4, EAT. One reading of Case C-381/99 *Brunnhofer v Bank der Österreichischen Postsparkasse AG* is that any proved inequality of treatment needs to be justified while generally the approach in the United Kingdom cases (at least until *Sharp v Caledonia Group Services Ltd*) has been that there has to be a sexually discriminatory practice (producing the unequal pay) before there is a burden on the employer to show objective justification; if not it is enough just to show a non-generic reason (eg different history of collective bargaining) without having to justify it: see *Tyldesley v TML Plastics Ltd* [1996] ICR 356, [1996] IRLR 395, EAT. See *Villalba v Merill Lynch & Co Inc* [2007] ICR 469, [2006] IRLR 437, EAT (where the Employment Appeal Tribunal took the line that objective justification is only necessary once a prima facie case of indirect sex discrimination has been made out); and see *Parliamentary Comr for Administration v Fernandez* [2004] 2 CMLR 59, [2004] ICR 123, EAT. See also *Best v Tyne and Wear Passenger and Transport Executive (t/a Nexus)* [2007]

ICR 523, [2006] All ER (D) 362 (Dec), EAT, where *Villalba v Merill Lynch & Co Inc* was applied; Case C-427/11 *Kenny v Ministry for Justice, Equality and Law Reform* [2013] IRLR 463, ECJ.

9　Case C-127/92 *Enderby v Frenchay Health Authority* [1994] ICR 112, [1993] IRLR 591, ECJ. Where one group of employees is disadvantaged in comparison to another group which is predominantly male, the employer is required objectively to justify the difference irrespective of whether the disadvantaged group contains a significant number of men: *Home Office v Bailey* [2005] EWCA Civ 327, [2005] ICR 1057, [2005] IRLR 369.

10　Case 109/88 *Handels-og Kontorfunktionaerernes Forbund i Danmark v Dansk Arbejdsgiverforening (acting for Danfoss)* [1991] ICR 74, [1989] IRLR 532.

11　Case 171/88 *Rinner-Kühn v FWW Spezial-Gebäudereinigung GmbH & Co KG* [1989] ECR 2743, [1989] IRLR 493, ECJ.

12　Case C-317/93 *Nolte v Landesversicherungsanstalt Hannover* [1996] All ER (EC) 212, [1996] IRLR 225, ECJ. See also Case C-167/97 *R v Secretary of State for Employment, ex p Seymour-Smith* [1999] 2 AC 554, [1999] ICR 447, ECJ. Cf Case C-281/99 *Kruger v Kreiskrankenhaus Ebersberg* [1999] ECR I-5127, [1999] IRLR 808, ECJ.

154. Equal Pay Audits.

Regulations under the Equality Act 2010[1] may make provision requiring an employment tribunal[2] to order the respondent to carry out an equal pay audit[3] in any case where the tribunal finds that there has been an equal pay breach[4].

An equal pay breach is:

(1)　a breach of an equality clause[5], or

(2)　a contravention in relation to pay of specified provisions of the Equality Act 2010[6], so far as relating to sex discrimination[7].

In exercise of this power, regulations[8] have been made which make provision as to the circumstances in which the tribunal must order an equal pay audit to be carried out and the circumstances in which an audit must not be ordered[9]. There are exemptions which apply to micro-businesses and new businesses[10]. Provision is also made as to the contents of tribunal orders and audits[11]; as to determining compliance with orders to carry out or publish audits[12]; and as to penalties for non-compliance[13].

1　Ie the Equality Act 2010 s 139A (see the text and notes 2–5; and EMPLOYMENT vol 40 (2014) PARA 609).

2　As to employment tribunals see EMPLOYMENT vol 41A (2014) PARA 1399 et seq.

3　An equal pay audit is an audit designed to identify action to be taken to avoid equal pay breaches occurring or continuing: see the Equality Act 2010 s 139A(3) (s 139A added by the Enterprise and Regulatory Reform Act 2013 s 98(1), (2)).

4　See the Equality Act 2010 s 139A(1); and EMPLOYMENT vol 40 (2014) PARA 609.

5　See the Equality Act 2010 s 139A(2)(a) (as added: see note 3). As to equality clauses see PARA 139.

6　Ie the provisions of the Equality Act 2010 ss 39(2) (see PARA 117), 49(6) (see PARA 125) or s 50(6) (see PARA 126).

7　See the Equality Act 2010 s 139A(1)(b) (as added: see note 3).

8　Ie the Equality Act 2010 (Equal Pay Audits) Regulations 2014, SI 2014/2559 (see the text and notes 9–13; and EMPLOYMENT vol 40 (2014) PARA 609).

9　See the Equality Act 2010 (Equal Pay Audits) Regulations 2014, SI 2014/2559, regs 2–3; and EMPLOYMENT vol 40 (2014) PARA 609.

10　See the Equality Act 2010 (Equal Pay Audits) Regulations 2014, SI 2014/2559, reg 4, Schedule; and EMPLOYMENT vol 40 (2014) PARA 609.

11　See the Equality Act 2010 (Equal Pay Audits) Regulations 2014, SI 2014/2559, regs 5, 6; and EMPLOYMENT vol 40 (2014) PARA 609.

12　Se the Equality Act 2010 (Equal Pay Audits) Regulations 2014, SI 2014/2559, regs 7–10; and EMPLOYMENT vol 40 (2014) PARA 609.

13　See the Equality Act 2010 (Equal Pay Audits) Regulations 2014, SI 2014/2559, reg 11; and EMPLOYMENT vol 40 (2014) PARA 609.

(4) DUTY TO MAKE REASONABLE ADJUSTMENTS

155. Duty to make reasonable adjustments for disabled persons.

A duty to make reasonable adjustments for disabled persons[1] applies to an employer[2], a principal (as well as to the employer of a contract worker)[3], a firm or proposed firm[4], a limited liability partnership or proposed limited liability partnership[5], a barrister[6], a person who has the power to make an appointment to a personal or public office and a relevant person in relation to a personal or public office[7], a person who has the power to make a recommendation for or give approval to an appointment to a public office[8], a qualifications body[9], an employment service-provider[10], a trade organisation[11], a local authority[12], and a responsible person in relation to an occupational pension scheme[13]. In this respect they are required to comply with the first, second and third requirements set out in the Equality Act 2010[14], namely:

(1)   where a provision, criterion or practice of the employer's puts a disabled person at a substantial disadvantage in relation to a relevant matter in comparison with persons who are not disabled, the employer is required to take such steps as it is reasonable to have to take to avoid the disadvantage[15];

(2)   where a physical feature puts a disabled person at a substantial disadvantage in relation to a relevant matter in comparison with persons who are not disabled, the employer is required to take such steps as it is reasonable to have to take to avoid the disadvantage[16];

(3)   where a disabled person would, but for the provision of an auxiliary aid, be put at a substantial disadvantage in relation to a relevant matter in comparison with persons who are not disabled, the employer is required to take such steps as it is reasonable to have to take to provide the auxiliary aid[17].

The full details of the steps which employers must take in order to make reasonable adjustments are set out elsewhere in this title[18].

1 As to the duty to make reasonable adjustments for disabled persons see further PARA 237 et seq.
2 Equality Act 2010 s 39(5). As to the meaning of 'employer' see PARA 116.
3 Equality Act 2010 s 41(4). As to the meaning of 'principal' see PARA 119 note 1; as to the meanings of 'contract worker' and 'contract work' see PARA 119 note 4.
4 Equality Act 2010 s 44(7). As to the meaning of 'firm' see PARA 122 note 1; as to the meaning of 'proposed firm' see PARA 122 note 2.
5 Equality Act 2010 s 45(7). As to the meaning of 'limited liability partnership' see PARA 123 note 1.
6 Equality Act 2010 s 47(7). As to the meaning of 'barrister' see PARA 124 note 1.
7 Equality Act 2010 ss 49(9), 50(11) (amended by the Crime and Courts Act 2013 Sch 13 para 50). As to the meaning of 'personal or public office' see PARAS 125–126.
8 Equality Act 2010 s 51(4) (amended by the Crime and Courts Act 2013 Sch 13 para 51).
9 Equality Act 2010 s 53(6). As to the meaning of 'qualifications body' see PARA 129 note 1.
10 Equality Act 2010 s 55(6). As to the meaning of 'employment service-provider' see PARA 130. A duty to make reasonable adjustments applies to an employment service-provider, except in relation to the provision of a vocational service: s 55(6). A reference to the 'provision of a vocational service' is a reference to the provision of an employment service within s 56(2)(a)–(d) (see PARA 130) (or an employment service within s 56(2)(f), (g) (see PARA 130) in so far as it is also an employment service s 56(2)(a)–(d)); and for that purpose:
    (1)   the references to an employment service within s 56(2)(a) do not include a reference to vocational training within the meaning given by s 56(6)(b) (s 56(1), (7)(b)); and
    (2)   the references to an employment service within s 56(2)(d) (also include a reference to a service for assisting persons to retain employment (s 56(1), (7)(a)).

A service-provider's duty to make reasonable adjustments under s 29(7)(a) (see PARA **239**) applies to a person concerned with the provision of a vocational service; but a failure to comply with that duty in relation to the provision of a vocational service is a contravention of Pt 5 (ss 39–83: see PARA **116** et seq) for the purposes of enforcement: see s 55(7). As to enforcement under Pt 9 (ss 113–141) see PARA **351** et seq.

11 Equality Act 2010 s 57(6). As to the meaning of 'trade organisation' see PARA **131** note 1.
12 Equality Act 2010 s 58(6). As to the meaning of 'local authority' see PARA **132** note 1.
13 Equality Act 2010 s 61(11). As to the meaning of 'responsible person' see PARA **134** note 4; as to the meaning of 'occupational pension scheme' see PARA **134** note 1.
14 Equality Act 2010 s 83(10), Sch 8 paras 1, 2(1).
15 See the Equality Act 2010 s 20(3); and PARA **237**.
16 See the Equality Act 2010 s 20(4); and PARA **237**.
17 See the Equality Act 2010 s 20(5); and PARA **237**.
18 See PARAS **245–259**.

(5) EXCEPTIONS IN RELATION TO WORK

(i) Statutory Provisions

156. Contraventions pursuant to enactments.

A person does not contravene the provisions of the Equality Act 2010 on work[1], so far as relating to the protected characteristics of age[2], disability[3], or religion or belief[4], if he does anything he must do pursuant to a requirement of an enactment[5]. A person also does not contravene those provisions so far as relating to the protected characteristics of disability or religion or belief if he does anything he must do pursuant to a relevant requirement or condition imposed by virtue of an enactment[6].

1 Ie the Equality Act 2010 s Pt 5 (ss 39–83): see PARA **116** et seq. As to exceptions from the Equality Act 2010 generally, and as to further exceptions in specific circumstances, see PARAS **320–338**.
2 As to age as a protected characteristic see PARA **46**.
3 As to disability as a protected characteristic see PARAS **47–55**.
4 As to religion or belief as a protected characteristic see PARA **59**.
5 Equality Act 2010 Sch 22 para 1(1). As to the meaning of 'enactment' see PARA **92** note 8.
6 Equality Act 2010 Sch 22 para 1(1). As to the meaning of 'a relevant requirement or condition' see PARA **92** note 9.

157. Nationality or residence.

A person does not contravene the provisions of the Equality Act 2010 on work[1] by doing anything which discriminates against another because of the other's nationality[2], or which involves him discriminating against another person by applying to that other person a provision, criterion or practice which relates to that person's place of ordinary residence or the length of time that person has been present or resident in or outside the United Kingdom or an area within it[3], if the thing in question is done:

(1)   in pursuance of an enactment[4];
(2)   in pursuance of an instrument made by a member of the executive under an enactment[5];
(3)   to comply with a requirement imposed by a member of the executive by virtue of an enactment[6];
(4)   in pursuance of arrangements made by or with the approval of, or for the time being approved by, a Minister of the Crown[7];

(5)   to comply with a condition imposed by a Minister of the Crown[8].

1   Ie the Equality Act 2010 s Pt 5 (ss 39–83) (see PARA 116 et seq). As to exceptions from the Equality Act 2010 generally, and as to further exceptions in specific circumstances, see PARAS 320–338.
2   Equality Act 2010 Sch 23 para 1(2).
3   Equality Act 2010 Sch 23 para 1(3).
4   Equality Act 2010 Sch 23 para 1(1)(a). As to the meaning of 'enactment' see PARA 91 note 10.
5   Equality Act 2010 Sch 23 para 1(1)(b).
6   Equality Act 2010 Sch 23 para 1(1)(c). This applies to a requirement imposed before or after 8 April 2010 (ie the date on which the Equality Act 2010 was passed (ie received the royal assent)): Sch 23 para 1(1)(c).
7   Equality Act 2010 Sch 23 para 1(1)(d). This applies to arrangements made before or after 8 April 2010: Sch 23 para 1(1)(d).
8   Equality Act 2010 Sch 23 para 1(1)(e). This applies to conditions imposed before or after 8 April 2010: Sch 23 para 1(1)(e).

158. Contraventions connected to the protection of women.
A person (P) does not contravene the provisions of the Equality Act 2010 on work[1], so far as relating to the protected characteristics of pregnancy and maternity[2], and sex[3], only by doing in relation to a woman (W) anything P is required to do to comply with:
(1)   a pre-1975 Act enactment[4] concerning the protection of women[5];
(2)   a specified statutory provision concerning health and safety at work[6], if it is done for the purpose of the protection of W (or a description of women which includes W)[7]; or
(3)   a requirement of a statutory provision[8] concerned with protection of women at work[9].

1   Ie the Equality Act 2010 s Pt 5 (ss 39–83) (see PARA 116 et seq). As to exceptions from the Equality Act 2010 generally, and as to further exceptions in specific circumstances, see PARAS 320–338.
2   As to pregnancy and maternity as a protected characteristic see PARAS 62, 73–74.
3   As to sex as a protected characteristic see PARA 60.
4   A 'pre-1975 Act enactment' is an enactment contained in an Act passed before 12 November 1975 (ie the date on which the Sex Discrimination Act 1975 (repealed) received the royal assent) and an instrument approved or made by or under such an Act (including one approved or made after 12 November 1975): see the Equality Act 2010 Sch 22 para 2(5). If an Act repeals and re-enacts (with or without modification) a pre-1975 enactment then the provision re-enacted must be treated as being in a pre-1975 enactment: Sch 22 para 2(6). References to the 'protection of women' are references to protecting women in relation to pregnancy or maternity or any other circumstances giving rise to risks specifically affecting women: Sch 22 para 2(2). It does not matter whether the protection is restricted to women: Sch 22 para 2(3). As to the meaning of 'enactment' see PARA 91 note 10.
5   Equality Act 2010 Sch 22 para 2(1)(a), (4)(a), (8).
6   Ie a 'relevant statutory provision' within the meaning of the Health and Safety at Work etc Act 1974 Pt 1 (ss 1–54) (see s 53; and HEALTH AND SAFETY AT WORK vol 52 (2014) PARA 302).
7   Equality Act 2010 Sch 22 para 2(1)(b).
8   Ie a provision specified in the Employment Act 1989 Sch 1 (repealed). For these purposes a reference to a provision in the Employment Act 1989 Sch 1 includes a reference to a provision for the time being having effect in place of it: Equality Act 2010 Sch 22 para 2(7).
9   Equality Act 2010 Sch 22 para 2(1)(c).

159. Crown employment and public office.
A person does not contravene the Equality Act 2010[1] by making or continuing in force rules restricting to persons of particular birth, nationality, descent or residence employment in the service of the Crown, employment by a prescribed public body[2], or holding a public office[3]. A person also does not contravene the

Act by publishing, displaying or implementing such rules[4] or by publishing the gist of such rules[5].

1 As to the Equality Act 2010 see PARAS 1–4. As to exceptions from the Equality Act 2010 generally, and as to further exceptions in specific circumstances, see PARAS 320–338.
2 For this purpose 'public body' means a body (whether corporate or unincorporated) exercising public functions (within the meaning given by the Equality Act 2010 s 31(4) (see PARA 300)): Sch 22 para 5(4). As to the prescribed public bodies see the Race Relations (Prescribed Public Bodies) (No 2) Regulations 1994, SI 1994/1986 (amended by SI 2017/80) (made under the Race Relations Act 1976 s 75(5)(a) (repealed); continued in force by the Equality Act 2010 (Commencement No 4, Savings, Consequential, Transitional, Transitory and Incidental Provisions and Revocation) Order 2010, SI 2010/2317, art 21(1), Sch 7).
3 Equality Act 2010 Sch 22 para 5(1)(a), (2). The reference in the text to 'holding a public office' is a reference to holding a public office within the meaning of s 50 (see PARA 126).
4 Equality Act 2010 Sch 22 para 5(1)(b).
5 Equality Act 2010 Sch 22 para 5(1)(c).

(ii) Occupational Requirements

160. Occupational requirements generally.
Certain of the provisions in the Equality Act 2010 relating to work[1] are not contravened[2] where a person or organisation applies in relation to work[3] a requirement to have a particular protected characteristic[4], if the person or organisation shows that, having regard to the nature or context of the work:

(1) it is an occupational requirement[5];
(2) the application of the requirement is a proportionate means of achieving a legitimate aim[6]; and
(3) the person to whom the requirement is applied does not meet it or (other than in the case of a requirement to be of a particular sex) the former person or organisation has reasonable grounds for not being satisfied that the person meets it[7].

1 Ie certain provisions of the Equality Act 2010 s Pt 5 (ss 39–83) (see PARA 116 et seq). Those provisions are s 39(1)(a), (c), (2)(b), (c) (duty of employers: see PARA 117), s 41(1)(b) (contract workers: see PARA 119), s 44(1)(a), (c), (2)(b), (c) (partnerships: see PARA 122), s 45(1)(a), (c), (2)(b), (c) (limited liability partnerships: see PARA 123), s 49(3)(a), (c), (6)(b), (c) (appointments to personal offices: see PARA 125), s 50(3)(a), (c), (6)(b), (c) (appointments to public offices: see PARA 126), and s 51(1) (recommendations for appointments: see PARA 127): Sch 9 para 1(2). As to exceptions from the Equality Act 2010 generally, and as to further exceptions in specific circumstances, see PARAS 320–338.
2 Ie by virtue of the Equality Act 2010 s 13 (direct discrimination: see PARAS 67, 69): Sch 9 para 6(1), (2).
3 Ie employment (see PARA 116), contract work (see PARA 119 note 4), a position as a partner or as a member of an LLP (see PARA 123), or an appointment to a personal or public office (see PARAS 125–128): Equality Act 2010 Sch 9 para 6(3).
4 As to the protected characteristics generally see PARA 45 et seq. References to a requirement to have a protected characteristic are to be read:
    (1) in the case of gender reassignment, as references to a requirement not to be a transsexual person (and s 7(3) (see PARA 56) is accordingly to be ignored) (Sch 9 para 1(3)(a)); and
    (2) in the case of marriage and civil partnership, as references to a requirement not to be married or a civil partner (and s 8(2) (see PARA 57) is accordingly to be ignored) (Sch 9 para 1(3)(a)).
    As to gender reassignment as a protected characteristic see PARA 56. As to marriage and civil partnership as a protected characteristic see PARA 57.
5 Equality Act 2010 Sch 9 paras 1(1)(a), 6(4).
6 Equality Act 2010 Sch 9 para 1(1)(b).
7 Equality Act 2010 Sch 9 para 1(1)(c), (4).

161. Exceptions relating to religion or belief.

Certain of the provisions in the Equality Act 2010 relating to work[1] are not contravened[2] where a person or organisation applies in relation to employment[3]:

(1)   a requirement to be of a particular sex[4];

(2)   a requirement not to be a transsexual person[5];

(3)   a requirement not to be married or a civil partner[6];

(4)   a requirement not to be married to a person of the same sex[7];

(5)   a requirement not to be married to, or the civil partner of, a person who has a living former spouse or civil partner[8];

(6)   a requirement relating to circumstances in which a marriage or civil partnership came to an end[9]; or

(7)   a requirement related to sexual orientation[10],

if the person or organisation shows that the employment is for the purposes of an organised religion[11], the application of the requirement engages the compliance or non-conflict principle[12], and the person to whom the requirement is applied does not meet it or (other than in the case of a requirement to be of a particular sex) has reasonable grounds for not being satisfied that the person meets it[13].

A person or organisation with an ethos based on religion or belief does not contravene certain of the provisions relating to work[14] by applying in relation to work[15] a requirement to be of a particular religion or belief if he shows that, having regard to that ethos and to the nature or context of the work it is an occupational requirement[16], the application of the requirement is a proportionate means of achieving a legitimate aim[17], and the person to whom the requirement is required does not meet it (or the person has reasonable grounds for not being satisfied that the person meets it)[18].

A person or organisation also does not contravene elements of the prohibition on discrimination by qualifications bodies[19] by applying in relation to a relevant qualification[20] one of the requirements listed above if he shows that:

(a)   the qualification is for the purposes of employment for the purposes of an organised religion[21]; and

(b)   the application of the requirement engages the compliance or non-conflict principle[22].

1   Ie certain provisions of the Equality Act 2010 s Pt 5 (ss 39–83): see PARA 116 et seq. Those provisions are s 39(1)(a), (c), (2)(b), (c) (duty of employers: see PARA 117), s 49(3)(a), (c), (6)(b), (c) (appointments to personal offices: see PARA 125), s 50(3)(a), (c), (6)(b), (c) (appointments to public offices: see PARA 126), and s 51(1) (recommendations for appointments: see PARA 127): Sch 9 para 2(2). As to exceptions from the Equality Act 2010 generally, and as to further exceptions in specific circumstances, see PARAS 320–338.

2   Ie by virtue of the Equality Act 2010 s 13 (direct discrimination: see PARAS 67, 69): Equality Act 2010 Sch 9 para 6(1), (2).

3   A reference in these provisions to 'employment' includes a reference to an appointment to a personal or public office: Equality Act 2010 Sch 9 para 2(7).

4   Equality Act 2010 Sch 9 paras 2(4)(a), 6(4).

5   Equality Act 2010 Sch 9 para 2(4)(b).

6   Equality Act 2010 Sch 9 para 2(4)(c).

7   Equality Act 2010 Sch 9 para 2(4)(ca) (added by the Marriage (Same Sex Couples) Act 2013 Sch 7 para 45). See *Reverend Canon Pemberton v Right Reverend Inwood, former acting Bishop of Southwell and Nottinghamshire* (2017) UKEAT/0072/16/BA, [2017] ICR 929, [2017] IRLR 2011.

8   Equality Act 2010 Sch 9 para 2(4)(d).

9   Equality Act 2010 Sch 9 para 2(4)(e).

10 Equality Act 2010 Sch 9 para 2(4)(f).

11 Equality Act 2010 Sch 9 para 2(1)(a).

12 Equality Act 2010 Sch 9 para 2(1)(b). The application of a requirement engages the compliance principle if the requirement is applied so as to comply with the doctrines of the religion: Sch 9 para

2(5). The application of a requirement engages the non-conflict principle if, because of the nature or context of the employment, the requirement is applied so as to avoid conflicting with the strongly held religious convictions of a significant number of the religion's followers: Sch 9 para 2(6).

13 Equality Act 2010 Sch 9 para 2(1)(c), (8).

14 Ie the Equality Act 2010 s 39(1)(a), (c), (2)(b), (c) (duty of employers: see PARA 117), s 41(1)(b) (contract workers: see PARA 119), s 44(1)(a), (c), (2)(b), (c) (partnerships: see PARA 122), s 45(1)(a), (c), (2)(b), (c) (limited liability partnerships: see PARA 123), s 49(3)(a), (c), (6)(b), (c) (appointments to personal offices: see PARA 125), s 50(3)(a), (c), (6)(b), (c) (appointments to public offices: see PARA 126), and s 51(1) (recommendations for appointments: see PARA 127): Sch 9 paras 1(2), 3.

15 Ie employment (see PARA 116), contract work (see PARA 119 note 4), a position as a partner or as a member of an LLP (see PARA 123), or an appointment to a personal or public office (see PARAS 125–128): Equality Act 2010 Sch 9 para 6(3).

16 Equality Act 2010 Sch 9 para 3(a).

17 Equality Act 2010 Sch 9 para 3(b).

18 Equality Act 2010 Sch 9 para 3(c). See *Jivraj v Hashwani* [2011] UKSC 40, [2012] 1 All ER 629, [2011] 1 WLR 1872.

19 Ie the Equality Act 2010 s 53(1) or s 53(2)(a) or s 53(2)(b) (see PARA 129).

20 As to the meaning of 'relevant qualification' see PARA 129 note 1.

21 Equality Act 2010 Sch 9 para 2(3)(a).

22 Equality Act 2010 Sch 9 para 2(3)(b).

162. Educational appointments and religious belief.

If, in connection with the employment of a person as the head teacher or principal of an educational establishment[1], the head, a fellow or other member of the academic staff of a college, or institution in the nature of a college, in a university[2], or a professorship of a university which is a canon professorship or one to which a canonry is annexed[3], a person does anything it is necessary to do to comply with:

(1)   a requirement of an instrument relating to the establishment that the head teacher or principal must be a member of a particular religious order[4];

(2)   a requirement of an instrument relating to the college or institution that the holder of the position must be a woman[5]; or

(3)   an Act or instrument in accordance with which the professorship is a canon professorship or one to which a canonry is annexed[6],

he does not contravene the provisions of the Equality Act 2010 on work[7] only by doing that act[8]. A person also does not contravene the Equality Act 2010[9] only by doing anything which is permitted for the purpose of:

(a)   statutory provisions[10] enabling the dismissal of teachers from schools of a religious character because of failure to give religious education efficiently[11];

(b)   statutory provisions[12] enabling religious considerations to be taken into account in making certain appointments at schools of a religious character[13];

(c)   statutory provisions[14] enabling independent schools of a religious character to give preferential treatment to applicants for teaching posts who observe certain religious practices[15]; and

(d)   statutory provisions[16] enabling academies with religious character to employ teachers who observe certain religious practices[17].

1 Equality Act 2010 Sch 22 para 3(2)(a). For these purposes an 'educational establishment' is: a school within the meaning of the Education Act 1996 (see s 4; and EDUCATION vol 35 (2015) PARA 91); a college, or institution in the nature of a college, in a university; an institution designated by order made, or having effect as if made, under the Education Reform Act 1988 s 129

(see EDUCATION vol 35 (2015) PARA 671); or an institution designated by order under the Further and Higher Education Act 1992 s 28 (see EDUCATION vol 35 (2015) PARA 572): Equality Act 2010 Sch 22 para 3(6)(a)–(c), (f).

2 Equality Act 2010 Sch 22 para 3(2)(b).
3 Equality Act 2010 Sch 22 para 3(2)(c).
4 Equality Act 2010 Sch 22 para 3(3)(a).
5 Equality Act 2010 Sch 22 para 3(3)(b). Schedule 22 para 3(3)(b) does not apply to an instrument taking effect on or after 16 January 1990 (the day on which the Employment Act 1989 s 5(3) (repealed) came into force): Equality Act 2010 Sch 22 para 3(4).
6 Equality Act 2010 Sch 22 para 3(3)(c).
7 Ie the Equality Act 2010 s Pt 5 (ss 39–83) (see PARA 116 et seq). As to exceptions from the Equality Act 2010 generally, and as to further exceptions in specific circumstances, see PARAS 320–338.
8 Equality Act 2010 Sch 22 para 3(1). A Minister of the Crown may by order provide that anything in Sch 22 para 3(1)–(3) (see the text and notes 1–7) does not have effect in relation to a specified educational establishment or university or a specified description of educational establishments: Sch 22 para 3(5). At the date at which this volume states the law no such orders had been made. These provisions do not affect Sch 9 para 2 (occupational requirements relating to religious employment: see PARA 161): Sch 22 para 3(7).
9 As to the Equality Act 2010 see PARAS 1–4.
10 Ie the School Standards and Framework Act 1998 58(6) or (7) (see EDUCATION vol 35 (2015) PARA 302).
11 Equality Act 2010 Sch 22 para 4(a).
12 Ie the School Standards and Framework Act 1998 s 60(4), (5) (see EDUCATION vol 35 (2015) PARA 304).
13 Equality Act 2010 Sch 22 para 4(b).
14 Ie the School Standards and Framework Act 1998 s 124A (see EDUCATION vol 35 (2015) PARA 378).
15 Equality Act 2010 Sch 22 para 4(c).
16 Ie the School Standards and Framework Act 1998 s 124AA(5)–(7) (see EDUCATION vol 35 (2015) PARA 379).
17 Equality Act 2010 Sch 22 para 4(d) (added by the Education Act 2011 s 62(1), (4)(c)).

163. Exceptions relating to the armed forces.

The provisions of the Equality Act 2010 relating to work[1], so far as relating to age[2] or disability[3], do not apply to service in the armed forces; and the provisions relating to employment service-providers[4], so far as relating to disability, do not apply to work experience in the armed forces[5]. Certain of the provisions relating to an employer's duty not to discriminate[6] are not contravened[7] where, in relation to service in the armed forces, a requirement to be a man[8] or a requirement not to be a transsexual person[9] is applied and it can be shown that the application is a proportionate means of ensuring the combat effectiveness of the armed forces[10].

1 Ie the Equality Act 2010 s Pt 5 (ss 39–83) (see PARA 116 et seq). As to exceptions from the Equality Act 2010 generally, and as to further exceptions in specific circumstances, see PARAS 320–338.
2 As to age as a protected characteristic see PARA 46.
3 As to disability as a protected characteristic see PARAS 47–55.
4 Ie the Equality Act 2010 s 55 (see PARA 130).
5 Equality Act 2010 Sch 9 para 4(3).
6 Ie the Equality Act 2010 s 39(1)(a), (c), (2)(b) (see PARA 117).
7 Ie contravened by virtue of the Equality Act 2010 s 13 (direct discrimination: see PARAS 67, 69): Sch 9 para 6(1), (2).
8 Equality Act 2010 Sch 9 para 4(1), (2)(a).
9 Equality Act 2010 Sch 9 para 4(2)(b).
10 Equality Act 2010 Sch 9 para 4(1).

(iii) Exceptions relating to Age

164. Benefits based on length of service.

It is not an age contravention[1] for a person (A) to put a person (B) at a disadvantage when compared with another (C), in relation to the provision of a benefit, facility or service[2] in so far as the disadvantage is because B has a shorter period of service than C[3]. If B's period of service exceeds five years, A may rely on this exception only if A reasonably believes that doing so fulfils a business need[4].

A person's period of service is whichever of the following A chooses:

(1)   the period for which the person has been working for A at or above a level (assessed by reference to the demands made on the person) that A reasonably regards as appropriate for these purposes[5]; or

(2)   the period for which the person has been working for A at any level[6].

1   For these purposes a reference to an age contravention is a reference to a contravention of the Equality Act 2010 s Pt 5 (ss 39–83) (see PARA **116** et seq), so far as relating to age: Sch 9 para 7. As to exceptions from the Equality Act 2010 generally, and as to further exceptions in specific circumstances, see PARAS **320–338**.
2   For these purposes the reference to a benefit, facility or service does not include a reference to a benefit, facility or service which may be provided only by virtue of a person's ceasing to work: Equality Act 2010 Sch 9 para 10(7).
3   Equality Act 2010 Sch 9 para 10(1).
4   Equality Act 2010 Sch 9 para 10(2).
5   Equality Act 2010 Sch 9 para 10(3)(a). The period for which a person has been working for A must be based on the number of weeks during the whole or part of which the person has worked for A (Sch 9 para 10(4)); however for that purpose A may, so far as is reasonable, discount periods of absence (Sch 9 para 10(5)(a)) and periods that A reasonably regards as related to periods of absence (Sch 9 para 10(5)(b)).
6   Equality Act 2010 Sch 9 para 10(3)(b). For the purposes of Sch 9 para 10(3)(b), a person is to be treated as having worked for A during any period in which the person worked for a person other than A if that period counts as a period of employment with A as a result of the Employment Rights Act 1996 s 218 (see EMPLOYMENT vol 39 (2014) PARA 135) (Sch 9 para 10(6)(a)) or, if Sch 9 para 10(6)(a) does not apply, that period is treated as a period of employment by an enactment pursuant to which the person's employment was transferred to A (Sch 9 para 10(6)(b)). As to the meaning of 'enactment' see PARAS **91** note 10, **92** note 8.

165. National minimum wage.

It is not an age contravention[1] for a person to pay a young worker[2] (A) at a lower rate than that at which the person pays an older worker[3] (B) if:

(1)   the hourly rate for the national minimum wage for a person of A's age is lower than that for a person of B's age[4]; and

(2)   the rate at which A is paid is below the single hourly rate[5].

It is not an age contravention for a person to pay an apprentice[6] who does not qualify for the national minimum wage at a lower rate than the person pays an apprentice who does[7].

1   As to the meaning of 'age contravention' see PARA **164** note 1. As to exceptions from the Equality Act 2010 generally, and as to further exceptions in specific circumstances, see PARAS **320–338**.
2   A young worker is a person who qualifies for the national minimum wage at a lower rate than the single hourly rate: Equality Act 2010 Sch 9 para 11(2). As to entitlement to the national minimum wage see EMPLOYMENT vol 39 (2014) PARA 169 et seq.
3   An older worker is a person who qualifies for the national minimum wage at a higher rate than that at which the young worker qualifies for it: Equality Act 2010 Sch 9 para 11(2).
4   Equality Act 2010 Sch 9 para 11(1)(a).
5   Equality Act 2010 Sch 9 para 11(1)(b). The single hourly rate is the rate prescribed under the National Minimum Wage Act 1998 s 1(3) (see EMPLOYMENT vol 39 (2014) PARA 199): Equality Act 2010 Sch 9 para 11(3).

6   An apprentice is a person who is employed under a contract of apprenticeship or as a result of provision made by virtue of the National Minimum Wage Act 1998 s 3(2)(a) (persons not qualifying: see EMPLOYMENT vol 39 (2014) PARA 186), is treated as employed under a contract of apprenticeship: Equality Act 2010 Sch 9 para 12(2). As to contracts of apprenticeship see EMPLOYMENT vol 39 (2014) PARA 112.
7   Equality Act 2010 Sch 9 para 12(1).

166. Redundancy.

It is not an age contravention[1] for a person to give a qualifying employee[2] an enhanced redundancy payment[3] of an amount less than that of an enhanced redundancy payment which the person gives to another qualifying employee, if each amount is calculated on the same basis[4].

1   As to the meaning of 'age contravention' see PARA 164 note 1. As to exceptions from the Equality Act 2010 generally, and as to further exceptions in specific circumstances, see PARAS 320–338.
2   A person is a qualifying employee if he:
     (1)   is entitled to a redundancy payment as a result of the Employment Rights Act 1996 s 135 (see EMPLOYMENT vol 41 (2014) PARA 836) (Equality Act 2010 Sch 9 para 13(3)(a));
     (2)   agrees to the termination of the employment in circumstances where the person would, if dismissed, have been so entitled (Sch 9 para 13(3)(b));
     (3)   would have been so entitled but for the Employment Rights Act 1996 s 155 (requirement for two years' continuous employment: see EMPLOYMENT vol 41 (2014) PARA 855) (Equality Act 2010 Sch 9 para 13(3)(c)); or
     (4)   agrees to the termination of the employment in circumstances where the person would, if dismissed, have been so entitled but for the Employment Rights Act 1996 s 155 (Equality Act 2010 Sch 9 para 13(3)(d)).
3   An enhanced redundancy payment is a payment the amount of which is calculated in accordance with the Employment Rights Act 1996 s 162(1)–(3) (see EMPLOYMENT vol 41 (2014) PARA 881): Equality Act 2010 Sch 9 para 13(4). A person making a calculation for these purposes:
     (1)   may treat a week's pay (references to which are to be read with the Employment Rights Act 1996 Pt 14 Ch 2 (ss 220–229) (see EMPLOYMENT vol 39 (2014) PARAS 143–148)) as not being subject to a maximum amount (Equality Act 2010 Sch 9 para 13(5)(a), (7));
     (2)   may treat a week's pay (references to which are to be read with the Employment Rights Act 1996 Pt 14 Ch 2 (see EMPLOYMENT vol 39 (2014) PARAS 143–148)) as being subject to a maximum amount above that for the time being specified in s 227(1) (see EMPLOYMENT vol 39 (2014) PARA 147) (Equality Act 2010 Sch 9 para 13(5)(b), (7)); and
     (3)   may multiply the appropriate amount (as defined in the Employment Rights Act 1996 s 162: see EMPLOYMENT vol 41 (2014) PARA 881) for each year of employment by a figure of more than one (Equality Act 2010 Sch 9 para 13(5)(c), (7)).
     Having made a calculation for the purposes of Sch 9 para 13(4) (whether or not in reliance on Sch 9 para 13(5)), a person may multiply the amount calculated by a figure of more than one: Sch 9 para 13(6). For these purposes the reference to 'the relevant date' in the Employment Rights Act 1996 s 162(1)(a) is, in the case of a person who is a qualifying employee by virtue of the Equality Act 2010 Sch 9 para 13(3)(b) or Sch 9 para 13(3)(d) (see note 2 head (4)), to be read as reference to the date of the termination of the employment: Sch 9 para 13(8).
4   Equality Act 2010 Sch 9 para 13(1). It is also not an age contravention to give enhanced redundancy payments only to those who are qualifying employees by virtue of Sch 9 para 13(3)(a) or Sch 9 para 13(3)(b) (see note 2 head (2)): Sch 9 para 13(2).

167. Insurance.

It is not an age contravention[1] for an employer[2] to make arrangements for, or afford access to, the provision of insurance or a related financial service[3] to or in respect of an employee for a period ending when the employee attains whichever is the greater of the age of 65, and the state pensionable age[4]. It is also not an age contravention for an employer to make arrangements for, or afford access to, the provision of insurance or a related financial service to or in respect of only such employees as have not attained whichever is the greater of the age of 65, and the state pensionable age[5].

1 As to the meaning of 'age contravention' see PARA 164 note 1. As to exceptions from the Equality Act 2010 generally, and as to further exceptions in specific circumstances, see PARAS 320–338.
2 As to the meaning of 'employer' see PARA 116
3 These provisions apply only where the insurance or related financial service is, or is to be, provided to the employer's employees or a class of those employees in pursuance of an arrangement between the employer and another person, or, where the employer's business includes the provision of insurance or financial services of the description in question, by the employer: Equality Act 2010 Sch 9 para 14(3) (Sch 9 para 14 substituted by SI 2011/1069).
4 Equality Act 2010 Sch 9 para 14(1) (as substituted: see note 3). The state pensionable age is the pensionable age determined in accordance with the rules in the Pensions Act 1995 Sch 4 para 1 (see WELFARE BENEFITS AND STATE PENSIONS vol 104 (2014) PARA 488): Equality Act 2010 Sch 9 para 14(4) (as so substituted).
5 Equality Act 2010 Sch 9 para 14(2) (as substituted: see note 3).

168. Childcare.

Certain of the provisions of the Equality Act 2010 relating to work[1] are not contravened, so far as relating to age[2], only by providing, or making arrangements for or facilitating the provision of, care[3] for children[4] of a particular age group[5]. Facilitating the provision of care for a child includes:

(1)   paying for some or all of the cost of the provision[6];
(2)   helping a parent of the child to find a suitable person to provide care for the child[7];
(3)   enabling a parent of the child to spend more time providing care for the child or otherwise assisting the parent with respect to the care that the parent provides for the child[8].

1 Ie certain provisions of the Equality Act 2010 s Pt 5 (ss 39–83) (see PARA 116 et seq). Those provisions are s 39(2)(b) (duty of employers: see PARA 117), s 41(1)(c) (contract workers: see PARA 119), s 44(2)(b) (partnerships: see PARA 122), s 45(2)(b) (limited liability partnerships: see PARA 123), s 47(2)(b) (barristers: see PARA 124), s 49(6)(b) (appointments to personal offices: see PARA 125), s 50(6)(b) (appointments to public offices: see PARA 126), s 57(2)(a) (trade organisations: see PARA 131), and s 58(3)(a) (official business of local authority members: see PARA 132): Sch 9 para 15(2). As to exceptions from the Equality Act 2010 generally, and as to further exceptions in specific circumstances, see PARAS 320–338.
2 As to age as a protected characteristic see PARA 46.
3 A reference to care includes a reference to supervision: Equality Act 2010 Sch 9 para 15(5).
4 A child is a person who has not attained the age of 17: Equality Act 2010 Sch 9 para 15(4).
5 Equality Act 2010 Sch 9 para 15(1).
6 Equality Act 2010 Sch 9 para 15(3)(a).
7 Equality Act 2010 Sch 9 para 15(3)(b).
8 Equality Act 2010 Sch 9 para 15(3)(c).

169. Contributions to personal pension schemes.

It is not an age contravention[1] for an employer[2] to maintain or use, with respect to contributions to personal pension schemes[3], practices, actions or decisions relating to age which are of a description specified by order[4].

1 As to the meaning of 'age contravention' see PARA 164 note 1. As to exceptions from the Equality Act 2010 generally, and as to further exceptions in specific circumstances, see PARAS 320–338.
2 As to the meaning of 'employer' in relation to a personal pension scheme see the Pensions Act 2004 s 318(1); and PERSONAL AND OCCUPATIONAL PENSIONS vol 80 (2013) PARA 503 (definition applied by the Equality Act 2010 Sch 9 para 16(3)).
3 As to the meaning of 'personal pension scheme' see the Pension Schemes Act 1993 s 1; and PERSONAL AND OCCUPATIONAL PENSIONS vol 80 (2013) PARA 780 (definition applied by the Equality Act 2010 Sch 9 para 16(3)).

4 For the applicable order see the Equality Act (Age Exceptions for Pension Schemes) Order 2010, SI 2010/2133 (amended by SI 2010/2285) (made under the Equality Act 2010 Sch 9 para 16(1)). An order authorising the use of practices, actions or decisions which are not in use before the order comes into force must not be made unless the Minister consults such persons as the Minister thinks appropriate: Sch 9 para 16(2).

(iv) Exceptions relating to Benefits, Public Services and Insurance Contracts

170. Marital status, sexual orientation and maternity pay.

A person does not contravene the provisions of the Equality Act 2010 on work[1], so far as relating to sexual orientation[2], by doing anything which prevents or restricts a person who is not married to a person of the opposite sex[3] from having access to a benefit, facility or service:

(1)   the right to which accrued before 5 December 2005[4]; or

(2)   which is payable in respect of periods of service before that date[5].

A person also does not contravene the provisions on work, so far as relating to sexual orientation, by providing married persons and civil partners (to the exclusion of all other persons) with access to a benefit, facility or service[6].

There are also exceptions from certain of the provisions on employer discrimination relating to payments to women on maternity leave[7].

1 Ie the Equality Act 2010 Pt 5 (ss 39–83) (see PARA 116 et seq). As to exceptions from the Equality Act 2010 generally, and as to further exceptions in specific circumstances, see PARAS 320–338.
2 As to sexual orientation as a protected characteristic see PARA 63.
3 Ie within the Equality Act 2010 Sch 9 para 18(1A). A person is within Sch 9 para 18(1A) if the person is a man who is married to a woman, or a woman who is married to a man, or married to a person of the same sex in a relevant gender change case: Sch 9 para 18(1A) (Sch 9 para 18(1) amended, Sch 9 para 18(1A), (1B) added, by the Marriage (Same Sex Couples) Act 2013 Sch 4 para 17). For these purposes, the reference to a relevant gender change case is a reference to a case where the married couple were of the opposite sex at the time of their marriage, and a full gender recognition certificate has been issued to one of the couple under the Gender Recognition Act 2004 (see REGISTRATION CONCERNING THE INDIVIDUAL vol 88 (2012) PARA 267 et seq): Equality Act 2010 Sch 9 para 18(1B) (as so added).
4 Equality Act 2010 Sch 9 para 18(1)(a) (as amended: see note 3). 5 December 2005 is the day on which the Civil Partnership Act 2004 s 1 was brought into force by the Civil Partnership Act 2004 (Commencement No 2) Order 2005, SI 2005/3175. It has been held that the Equality Act 2010 Sch 9 para 18 is incompatible with Council Directive (EC) 2000/78 (see PARA 14) and must be disapplied: see *Walker v Innospec* [2017] UKSC 47, [2017] IRLR 928, [2017] All ER (D) 77 (Jul).
5 Equality Act 2010 Sch 9 para 18(1)(b).
6 Equality Act 2010 Sch 9 para 18(2).
7 See the Equality Act 2010 Sch 9 para 17; and PARA 117 note 4.

171. Provision of services to the public.

Certain of the provisions of the Equality Act 2010 relating to work[1] are not contravened in relation to the provision of a benefit, facility or service to B if A is concerned with the provision (for payment or not) of a benefit, facility or service of the same description to the public[2]. These exceptions do not apply if:

(1)   the provision by A to the public differs in a material respect from the provision by A to comparable persons[3];

(2)   the provision to B is regulated by B's terms[4]; or

(3)   the benefit, facility or service relates to training[5].

1 Ie certain provisions of the Equality Act 2010 s Pt 5 (ss 39–83) (see PARA 116 et seq). Those provisions are s 39(2), (4) (duty of employers: see PARA 117), s 41(1), (3) (contract workers: see PARA 119), s 44(2), (6) (partnerships: see PARA 122), s 45(2), (6) (limited liability partnerships: see PARA 123), s 49(6), (8) (appointments to personal offices: see PARA 125), and s 50(6), (7), (9), (10)

(appointments to public offices: see PARA **126**): Sch 9 para 19(2). As to exceptions from the Equality Act 2010 generally, and as to further exceptions in specific circumstances, see PARAS **320–338**.

2 Equality Act 2010 Sch 9 para 19(1). A reference to 'the public' includes a reference to a section of the public which includes B: Sch 9 para 19(6).

3 Equality Act 2010 Sch 9 para 19(3)(a). 'Comparable persons' means:
    (1)   in relation to s 39(2) or s 39(4), the other employees (Sch 9 para 19(4)(a));
    (2)   in relation to s 41(1) or s 41(3), the other contract workers supplied to the principal (Sch 9 para 19(4)(b));
    (3)   in relation to s 44(2) or s 44(6), the other partners of the firm (Sch 9 para 19(4)(c));
    (4)   in relation to s 45(2) or s 45(6), the other members of the LLP (Sch 9 para 19(4)(d));
    (5)   in relation to s 49(6) or s 49(8) or s 50(6), (7), (9) or s 50(10), persons holding offices or posts not materially different from that held by B (Sch 9 para 19(4)(e)).

4 Equality Act 2010 Sch 9 para 19(3)(b). 'B's terms' means:
    (1)   the terms of B's employment (Sch 9 para 19(5)(a));
    (2)   the terms on which the principal allows B to do the contract work (Sch 9 para 19(5)(b));
    (3)   the terms on which B has the position as a partner or member (Sch 9 para 19(5)(c)); or
    (4)   the terms of B's appointment to the office (Sch 9 para 19(5)(d)).

5 Equality Act 2010 Sch 9 para 19(3)(c).

172. Insurance contracts.

It is not a contravention of the provisions of the Equality Act 2010 on work[1], so far as relating to relevant discrimination[2], to do anything in relation to an annuity, life insurance policy, accident insurance policy or similar matter involving the assessment of risk if:

    (1)   that thing is done by reference to actuarial or other data from a source on which it is reasonable to rely[3]; and

    (2)   it is reasonable to do it[4].

1 Ie the Equality Act 2010 Pt 5 (ss 39–83) (see PARA **116** et seq). As to exceptions from the Equality Act 2010 generally, and as to further exceptions in specific circumstances, see PARAS **320–338**.

2 'Relevant discrimination' is gender reassignment discrimination (see PARA **56**), marriage and civil partnership discrimination (see PARA **57**), pregnancy and maternity discrimination (see PARAS **73–74**) and sex discrimination (see PARA **60**): Equality Act 2010 Sch 9 para 20(2).

3 Equality Act 2010 Sch 9 para 20(1)(a).

4 Equality Act 2010 Sch 9 para 20(1)(b).

8. EDUCATION

(1) SCHOOLS

(i) Admission and Treatment

173. Admission.

The responsible body of a school[1] must not discriminate[2] against a person:

(1)   in the arrangements it makes for deciding who is offered admission as a pupil[3];

(2)   as to the terms on which it offers to admit the person as a pupil[4];

(3)   by not admitting the person as a pupil[5].

So far as relating to sex as a protected characteristic[6], these provisions[7] do not apply in relation to a single-sex school[8] or in relation to admission as a boarder to certain mixed schools[9]. These provisions also do not apply to certain schools of a religious character insofar as relating to religion or belief as a protected characteristic[10], and a person does not contravene these provisions, so far as relating to disability[11], only by applying a permitted form of selection[12].

1   In relation to England and Wales, the Equality Act 2010 s 85 (see the text and notes 2–5; and PARAS 174–175) applies to a school maintained by a local authority (s 85(7)(a)), an independent educational institution (other than a special school) (s 85(7)(b)), an alternative provision academy that is not an independent educational institution (s 85(7)(ba) (added by SI 2012/976)) and a special school (not maintained by a local authority) (Equality Act 2010 s 85(7)(c)). As to the meaning of 'school' see the Education Act 1996 s 4; and EDUCATION vol 35 (2015) PARA 91 (definition applied by the Equality Act 2010 s 89(5)(a)). A reference to a 'school' includes a reference to an independent educational institution in England; and a reference to an independent educational institution in England is to be construed in accordance with the Education and Skills Act 2008 Pt 4 Ch 1 (ss 92–141) (see EDUCATION vol 35 (2015) PARA 382 et seq): Equality Act 2010 s 89(6). A reference in these provisions to an 'independent educational institution' is a reference to an independent educational institution in England or an independent school in Wales: s 89(7). As to the meaning of 'independent school' in relation to Wales see the Education Act 1996 s 463; and EDUCATION vol 35 (2015) PARA 369 (definition applied by the Equality Act 2010 s 89(8)(a)). 'Local authority' means an English or Welsh local authority within the meaning of the Education and Inspections Act 2006 s 162 (see EDUCATION vol 35 (2015) PARA 26) (Equality Act 2010 s 89(10)); as to the meaning of 'special school' see the Education Act 1996 s 337; and EDUCATION vol 36 (2015) PARA 1041 (definition applied by the Equality Act 2010 s 89(9)). As to the meanings of 'England' and 'Wales' see PARA 85 note 1. Nothing in Pt 6 Ch 1 (ss 84–89) applies to anything done in connection with the content of the curriculum: s 89(2).

     The responsible body of a school to which these provisions apply is the local authority or governing body (if the school is within s 85(7)(a)) or the proprietor (if it is within s 85(7)(b), (ba) or (c)): s 85(9)(a), (b) (s 85(9)(b) amended by SI 2012/976). As to the meaning of 'proprietor' see the Education Act 1996 s 579(1); and EDUCATION vol 35 (2015) PARA 51 (definition applied by the Equality Act 2010 s 89(4)(a)).

     The Education Act 1996 ss 496, 497 (powers to give directions where responsible body of school in default of obligations, etc: see EDUCATION vol 35 (2015) PARAS 64, 65) apply to the performance of a duty under the Equality Act 2010 s 85: s 87(1). However, save in the case of a school in Wales (see s 87(A1) (added by the Schools Standards and Organisation (Wales) Act 2013 Sch 5 para 11(1), (2)), neither of the Education Act 1996 ss 496, 497 applies to the performance of a duty under the Equality Act 2010 s 85 by the proprietor of an independent educational institution (other than a special school) or an alternative provision academy that is not an independent educational institution: s 87(2) (amended by SI 2010/2279; SI 2012/976). As to the provisions which apply in the case of a school in Wales to the performance of a duty under the Equality Act 2010 s 85 see s 87(3), (4) (added by the Schools Standards and Organisation (Wales) Act 2013 Sch 5 para 11(1), (3)).

2   The Equality Act 2010 Pt 6 Ch 1 (ss 84–89) (see the text and notes 3–12; and PARAS 174–197) does not apply to the protected characteristics of age (see PARA 46), and marriage and civil

partnership (see PARA 57): s 84. Nothing in s 84 is to be regarded as an express exception: Equality Act 2010 s 212(13).

3 Equality Act 2010 s 85(1)(a). As to the meaning of 'pupil' see the Education Act 1996 s 3(1); and EDUCATION vol 35 (2015) PARA 20 (definition applied by the Equality Act 2010 s 89(3)(a)). See *R (on the application of E) v Governing Body of JFS* [2009] UKSC 15, [2010] 2 AC 728, [2010] 1 All ER 319 (in which the Supreme Court held that a school for Orthodox Jews which tested applicants for matrilineal descent was acting on the basis of ethnic origin and that their admission requirement therefore constituted direct racial discrimination contrary to the Race Relations Act 1976 s 1 (repealed); the school argued that because the matrilineal test was based on religious law the discrimination it had applied was religious and not racial and that what subjectively motivated the policy was compliance with religious law, not the ethnicity of the applicants to the school, but the court held that since there is no defence of justification to the prohibition of direct racial discrimination the motive of the discriminator is irrelevant (see *James v Eastleigh Borough Council* [1990] 2 AC 751, [1990] 2 All ER 607). See further RIGHTS AND FREEDOMS vol 88A (2013) PARA 378 (religious education in the context of the Convention for the Protection of Human Rights and Fundamental Freedoms (Rome, 4 November 1950; TS 71 (1953); Cmd 8969) (the European Convention on Human Rights art 9 (freedom of thought, conscience and religion)); and RIGHTS AND FREEDOMS vol 88A (2013) PARA 571 (prohibition of discrimination in education pursuant to in the context of Protocol 1 art 2 (the right to education)).

4 Equality Act 2010 s 85(1)(b). See *HM Chief Inspector of Education, Children's Services and Skills v Interim Executive Board of Al-Hijrah School (Secretary of State for Education intervening)* [2017] EWCA Civ 1426, [2017] All ER (D) 79 (Oct) (where a mixed-sex school had complete segregation of male and female pupils over a certain age, the restriction on the freedom of a girl pupil to mix or socialise with boy pupils and on a boy pupil to mix or socialise with girl pupils was detrimental to their education and discriminatory for the purposes of the Equality Act 2010 s 13 (see PARA 67) and s 85). See *G (by his litigation friend) v Head Teacher and Governors of St Gregory's Catholic Science College* [2011] EWHC 1452 (Admin), [2011] NLJR 884, [2011] All ER (D) 113 (Jun) (decided under the Race Relations Act 1976 (repealed)) (in which a school's decision that a male pupil of Afro-Caribbean descent could not wear his hair in cornrows was held to amount to potential indirect race discrimination but not sex discrimination).

5 Equality Act 2010 s 85(1)(c).

6 As to sex as a protected characteristic see PARA 60.

7 Ie the Equality Act 2010 s 85(1) (see the text and notes 1–5).

8 Equality Act 2010 s 89(12), Sch 11 para 1(1). A 'single-sex school' is a school which admits pupils of one sex only or (on the basis of the assumption that pupils of the opposite sex are to be disregarded if their admission to the school is exceptional or their numbers are comparatively small and their admission is confined to particular courses or classes), would be taken to admit pupils of one sex only: Sch 11 para 1(2), (3).

9 Equality Act 2010 Sch 11 para 2(1). The schools to which this exception applies are schools (other than single-sex schools) which have some pupils as boarders and others as non-boarders and which admit as boarders pupils of one sex only or (on the basis of the assumption that pupils of the opposite sex admitted as boarders are to be disregarded if their numbers are small compared to the numbers of other pupils admitted as boarders) would be taken to admit as boarders pupils of one sex only: Sch 11 para 2(3), (4).

10 Equality Act 2010 Sch 11 para 5 (amended by SI 2012/976). As to religion or belief as a protected characteristic see PARA 59. Section 85(1) (see the text and notes 1–5), so far as relating to religion or belief, do not apply in relation to:

   (1)   a school designated under the School Standards and Framework Act 1998 s 69(3) (foundation or voluntary school with religious character: see EDUCATION vol 36 (2015) PARA 914) (Equality Act 2010 Sch 11 para 5(a)); or

   (2)   a school (other than an alternative provision academy) listed in the register of independent schools for England or for Wales (see EDUCATION vol 35 (2015) PARA 417 et seq), if the school's entry in the register records that the school has a religious ethos (Sch 11 para 5(b) (as so amended)).

   A Minister of the Crown may by order amend the Equality Act 2010 Sch 11 paras 5, 6 (see above; and PARA 174) so as to add, vary or omit an exception to s 85 and so as to make provision about the construction or application of s 19(2)(d) (see PARA 75) in relation to s 85: Sch 11 para 7(1). This power is exercisable only in relation to religious or belief-related discrimination: Sch 11 para 7(2). Before making an order under Sch 11 para 7 the Minister must consult the Welsh Ministers, the Scottish Ministers, and such other persons as the Minister thinks appropriate: Sch 11 para 7(3). At the date at which this volume states the law no such orders had been made.

11 As to disability as a protected characteristic see PARAS 47–55.

12 Equality Act 2010 Sch 11 para 8(1). In relation to England and Wales, a 'permitted form of selection' is:

(1)   in the case of a maintained school (as defined in the School Standards and Framework Act 1998 s 22: see EDUCATION vol 35 (2015) PARA 99) which is not designated as a grammar school under s 104 (see EDUCATION vol 35 (2015) PARA 263), a form of selection mentioned in s 99(2) or (4) (see EDUCATION vol 35 (2015) PARA 258) (Equality Act 2010 Sch 11 para 8(2)(a), (4));

(2)   in the case of a maintained school which is so designated, its selective admission arrangements (within the meaning of the School Standards and Framework Act 1998 s 104) (Equality Act 2010 Sch 11 para 8(2)(b)); and

(3)   in the case of an independent educational institution, arrangements which provide for some or all of its pupils to be selected by reference to general or special ability or aptitude, with a view to admitting only pupils of high ability or aptitude (Equality Act 2010 Sch 11 para 8(2)(c)).

174. Discrimination against pupils in provision of education or services.

The responsible body of a school[1] must not discriminate[2] against a pupil[3]:

(1)   in the way it provides education for the pupil[4];
(2)   in the way it affords the pupil access to a benefit, facility or service[5];
(3)   by not providing education for the pupil[6];
(4)   by not affording the pupil access to a benefit, facility or service[7];
(5)   by excluding the pupil from the school[8];
(6)   by subjecting the pupil to any other detriment[9].

1   As to the schools to which these provisions apply, and as to the 'responsible bodies' of such schools, see PARA 173 note 1.
2   See PARA 173 note 2.
3   As to the meaning of 'pupil' see PARA 173 note 3.
4   Equality Act 2010 s 85(2)(a). In the case of a school which is a single-sex school by virtue of the assumption that pupils of the opposite sex are to be disregarded if their numbers are comparatively small and their admission is confined to particular courses or classes (ie by virtue of Sch 11 para 1(3)(b): see PARA 173 note 8), s 85(2)(a)–(d) (see the text and notes 5–7), so far as relating to sex as a protected characteristic (see PARA 60), does not prohibit confining pupils of the same sex to particular courses or classes: Sch 11 para 1(4). So far as relating to sex as a protected characteristic, s 85(2)(a)–(d) also do not apply in relation to boarding facilities at schools (other than single-sex schools) which have some pupils as boarders and others as non-boarders and which admit as boarders pupils of one sex only or (on the basis of the assumption that pupils of the opposite sex admitted as boarders are to be disregarded if their numbers are small compared to the numbers of other pupils admitted as boarders) would be taken to admit as boarders pupils of one sex only: Sch 11 para 2(2)–(4).
    So far as relating to religion or belief as a protected characteristic, s 85(2)(a)–(d) do not apply in relation to a school designated under the School Standards and Framework Act 1998 s 69(3) (foundation or voluntary school with religious character: see EDUCATION vol 36 (2015) PARA 914) (Equality Act 2010 Sch 11 para 5(a)) or a school (other than an alternative provision academy) listed in the register of independent schools for England or for Wales (see EDUCATION vol 35 (2015) PARA 417 et seq), if the school's entry in the register records that the school has a religious ethos (Sch 11 para 5(b) (amended by SI 2012/976)), and do not apply in relation to anything done in connection with acts of worship or other religious observance organised by or on behalf of a school (whether or not forming part of the curriculum) (Equality Act 2010 Sch 11 para 6). As to the meanings of 'England' and 'Wales' see PARA 85 note 1.
5   Equality Act 2010 s 85(2)(b). See note 4. As to providing or affording access to a benefit, facility or service see PARA 117 note 7.
6   Equality Act 2010 s 85(2)(c). See note 4.
7   Equality Act 2010 s 85(2)(d). See note 4.
8   Equality Act 2010 s 85(2)(e).
9   Equality Act 2010 s 85(2)(f). As to the meaning of 'detriment' see PARA 81 note 1. See *G (by his litigation friend) v Head Teacher and Governors of St Gregory's Catholic Science College* [2011] EWHC 1452 (Admin), [2011] NLJR 884, [2011] All ER (D) 113 (Jun) (decided under the Race Relations Act 1976 (repealed)) (in which a school's decision that a male pupil of Afro-Caribbean descent could not wear his hair in cornrows was held to amount to potential indirect race

discrimination but not sex discrimination); HM *Chief Inspector of Education, Children's Services and Skills v Interim Executive Board of Al-Hijrah School (Secretary of State for Education intervening)* [2017] EWCA Civ 1426, [2017] All ER (D) 79 (Oct) (segregation of male and female pupils in school with Islamic ethos held to be discriminatory).

175. Harassment and victimisation of pupils.

The responsible body of a school[1] must not:

(1) harass[2] a pupil[3] or a person who has applied for admission as a pupil[4];

(2) victimise[5] a person in the arrangements it makes for deciding who is offered admission as a pupil[6], as to the terms on which it offers to admit the person as a pupil[7], or by not admitting the person as a pupil[8]; or

(3) victimise a pupil:

    (a) in the way it provides education for the pupil[9];

    (b) in the way it affords the pupil access to a benefit, facility or service[10];

    (c) by not providing education for the pupil[11];

    (d) by not affording the pupil access to a benefit, facility or service[12];

    (e) by excluding the pupil from the school[13];

    (f) by subjecting the pupil to any other detriment[14].

1 As to the schools to which these provisions apply, and as to the 'responsible bodies' of such schools, see PARA 173 note 1.

2 As to the meaning of 'harassment' see the Equality Act 2010 s 26; and PARA 79. In the application of s 26 for this purpose neither gender reassignment (see PARAS 56, 61), religion or belief (see PARA 59), or sexual orientation (see PARA 63), is a relevant protected characteristic: s 85(10). See also PARA 173 note 2.

3 Equality Act 2010 s 85(3)(a). As to the meaning of 'pupil' see PARA 173 note 3.

4 Equality Act 2010 s 85(3)(b).

5 As to the meaning of 'victimisation' see the Equality Act 2010 ss 27, 86; and PARA 81.

6 Equality Act 2010 s 85(4)(a).

7 Equality Act 2010 s 85(4)(b).

8 Equality Act 2010 s 85(4)(c).

9 Equality Act 2010 s 85(5)(a).

10 Equality Act 2010 s 85(5)(b). As to providing or affording access to a benefit, facility or service see PARA 117 note 7.

11 Equality Act 2010 s 85(5)(c).

12 Equality Act 2010 s 85(5)(d).

13 Equality Act 2010 s 85(5)(e).

14 Equality Act 2010 s 85(5)(f). As to the meaning of 'detriment' see PARA 81 note 1.

176. Transitional exemptions for single-sex schools turning co-educational.

If the responsible body of a single-sex school[1] or a mixed boarding school[2] decides to alter its admissions arrangements so that the school will cease to be such a school, the body may apply for a transitional exemption order in relation to the school[3], the effect of which is to authorise:

(1) sex discrimination by the responsible body in the arrangements it makes for deciding who is offered admission as a pupil[4]; and

(2) the responsible body, in the circumstances specified in the order, not to admit a person as a pupil because of the person's sex[5].

A responsible body will not contravene the Equality Act 2010, so far as relating to sex discrimination[6], if, in accordance with a transitional exemption order or pending the determination of an application for a transitional exemption order in relation to the school, it does not admit a person as a pupil because of the person's sex[7].

1   As to the schools to which these provisions apply, and as to the 'responsible bodies' of such schools, see PARA 173 note 1. As to the meaning of 'single-sex school' in this context see PARA 173 note 8.
2   Ie a school to which the exemption set out in the Equality Act 2010 Sch 11 para 2 (see PARA 173 note 9).
3   Equality Act 2010 Sch 11 para 3(1), (2).
4   Equality Act 2010 Sch 11 para 3(3)(a). Such authorisations apply only during the period specified in the order as the transitional period: Sch 11 para 3(3).
        In the case of a maintained school within the meaning given by the Education and Inspections Act 2006 s 32 (see EDUCATION vol 35 (2015) PARA 132), a transitional exemption order may be made in accordance with such provision as is made in regulations under s 21 (orders made by local authority or adjudicator in relation to schools in England: see EDUCATION vol 35 (2015) PARA 133): Equality Act 2010 Sch 11 para 4(1). In the case of a school in Wales maintained by a local authority, a transitional exemption order may be made in accordance with the School Standards and Organisation (Wales) Act 2013 s 82 or Sch 3 Pt 3 (orders made by Welsh Ministers: see EDUCATION vol 35 (2015) PARA 10): Equality Act 2010 Sch 11 para 4(2) (amended by the School Standards and Organisation (Wales) Act 2013 Sch 5 para 28). In the case of a school in England or Wales not coming within any of the above provisions the responsible body may submit to the Equality and Human Rights Commission an application for the making of a transitional exemption order and the Commission may make the order: Sch 11 para 4(6). Such an application must specify the period proposed by the responsible body as the transitional period to be specified in the order, the stages within that period by which the body proposes to move to the position where s 85(1)(a), (c) (see PARA 173), so far as relating to sex, is complied with, and any other matters relevant to the terms and operation of the order applied for (Sch 11 para 4(7)), and the Commission must not make an order on such an application unless satisfied that the terms of the application are reasonable, having regard to the nature of the school's premises, the accommodation, equipment and facilities available, and the responsible body's financial resources (Sch 11 para 4(8)). As to the Commission see PARAS 28–44. As to the meanings of 'England' and 'Wales' see PARA 85 note 1.
5   Equality Act 2010 Sch 11 para 3(3)(b). See note 4.
6   See PARA 60.
7   Equality Act 2010 Sch 11 para 3(5).

177. Modification of discriminatory trust deeds.

If:

(1)   a trust deed or other instrument concerning property applicable for or in connection with the provision of education in a school in England and Wales[1] in any way restricts the benefits available under the instrument to persons of one sex[2];

(2)   a Minister of the Crown is satisfied that the removal or modification of the restriction would be conducive to the advancement of education without sex discrimination[3],

the Minister may, on application[4] by order make such modifications of the instrument as appear to the Minister expedient for removing or modifying the restriction[5]. Before making the order, the Minister must take account of representations[6].

1   Ie property applicable for or in connection with the provision of education in an establishment to which the Equality Act 2010 s 85 (see PARAS 173–175).
2   Equality Act 2010 s 99, Sch 14 para 1(1).
3   Equality Act 2010 Sch 14 para 1(2). As to sex as a protected characteristic see PARA 60.
4   Ie on the application of the trustees or the responsible body (within the meaning of the Equality Act 2010 s 85: see PARA 173): Sch 14 para 1(2). The Minister must require the applicant to publish a notice containing particulars of the proposed order and stating that representations may be made to the Minister within a period specified in the notice (which must be not less than one month beginning with the day after the date of the notice): Sch 14 para 1(6), (7). The applicant must

publish the notice in the manner specified by the Minister (Sch 14 para 1(8)), and the cost of publication may be paid out of the property of the trust (Sch 14 para 1(9)).

5   Equality Act 2010 Sch 14 para 1(3). If the trust was created by a gift or bequest, an order must not be made until the end of the period of 25 years after the date when the gift or bequest took effect, unless the donor or the personal representatives of the donor or testator consent in writing to making the application for the order: Sch 14 para 1(4), (5).

6   Equality Act 2010 Sch 14 para 1(10). The reference in the text to representations is to those made in accordance with the notice referred to in the Equality Act 2010 Sch 14 para 1(6) (see note 4).

(ii) Accessibility

178. Accessibility strategies and accessibility plans.
An 'accessibility strategy' is a strategy for, over a prescribed period:

(1)   increasing the extent to which disabled pupils[1] can participate in the schools' curriculums[2];

(2)   improving the physical environment of the schools for the purpose of increasing the extent to which disabled pupils are able to take advantage of education and benefits, facilities or services provided or offered by the schools[3]; and

(3)   improving the delivery to disabled pupils of information which is readily accessible to pupils who are not disabled[4].

An 'accessibility plan' is a plan for, over a prescribed period:

(a)   increasing the extent to which disabled pupils can participate in the school's curriculum[5];

(b)   improving the physical environment of the school for the purpose of increasing the extent to which disabled pupils are able to take advantage of education and benefits, facilities or services provided or offered by the school[6]; and

(c)   improving the delivery to disabled pupils of information which is readily accessible to pupils who are not disabled[7].

1   'Disabled pupil' includes a disabled person who may be admitted to the school as a pupil: Equality Act 2010 Sch 10 para 6(1), (4). As to the meaning of 'pupil' see PARA 173 note 3.

2   Equality Act 2010 Sch 10 para 1(2)(a). As to the schools to which these provisions apply see PARA 173 note 1.

3   Equality Act 2010 Sch 10 para 1(2)(b). As to providing or affording access to a benefit, facility or service see PARA 117 note 7. Regulations may prescribe services which are, or are not, to be regarded as being education or a benefit, facility or service for these purposes: Sch 10 para 6(1), (2). The power to make regulations is exercisable by a Minister of the Crown (in relation to England) or the Welsh Ministers (in relation to Wales): Sch 10 para 6(1), (3). As to the meanings of 'England' and 'Wales' see PARA 85 note 1. At the date at which this volume states the law no such regulations had been made.

4   Equality Act 2010 Sch 10 para 1(2)(c). The delivery in Sch 10 para 1(2)(c) must be within a reasonable time and in ways which are determined after taking account of the pupils' disabilities and any preferences expressed by them or their parents: Sch 10 para 1(3).

5   Equality Act 2010 Sch 10 para 3(2)(a).

6   Equality Act 2010 Sch 10 para 3(2)(b).

7   Equality Act 2010 Sch 10 para 3(2)(c). The delivery in Sch 10 para 3(2)(c) must be within a reasonable time and in ways which are determined after taking account of the pupils' disabilities and any preferences expressed by them or their parents: Sch 10 para 3(3).

179. Preparation and implementation of strategies and plans.
A local authority in England and Wales[1] must, in relation to schools for which it is the responsible body[2], prepare and implement an accessibility strategy[3] and further such strategies at such times as may be prescribed[4]; and the responsible body of a school in England and Wales must prepare and implement an

accessibility plan[5] and further such plans at such times as may be prescribed[6]. Plans and strategies must be in writing[7], copies must be made available to supervisory bodies[8], and the local authority or, as the case may be, responsible body must keep its accessibility strategy or plan under review during the period to which it relates and, if necessary, revise it[9]. Provision is also made in connection with the inspection of strategies[10] and plans[11].

1   As to the meaning of 'local authority' for these purposes see PARA 173 note 1. As to the meanings of 'England' and 'Wales' see PARA 85 note 1.
2   As to the schools to which these provisions apply see PARA 173 note 1. For the purposes of the Equality Act 2010 Sch 10 'responsible body' means:
    (1)   in relation to a maintained school or a maintained nursery school, the local authority or governing body (Sch 10 para 6(5)(a));
    (2)   in relation to a pupil referral unit, the local authority (Sch 10 para 6(5)(b));
    (3)   in relation to an independent educational institution or an alternative provision academy that is not an independent educational institution, the proprietor (Sch 10 para 6(5)(c) (amended by SI 2012/976)); and
    (4)   in relation to a special school not maintained by a local authority, the proprietor (Equality Act 2010 Sch 10 para 6(5)(d)).
    As to the meanings of 'maintained school' and 'maintained nursery school' for these purposes see the School Standards and Framework Act 1998 ss 20, 22; and EDUCATION vol 35 (2015) PARA 99) (definitions applied by the Equality Act 2010 Sch 10 para 6(7)). 'Governing body', in relation to a maintained school, means the body corporate (constituted in accordance with regulations under the Education Act 2002 s 19: see EDUCATION vol 35 (2015) PARA 195) which the school has as a result of s 19: Equality Act 2010 Sch 10 para 6(6). As to the meaning of 'independent educational institution' see PARA 173 note 1. As to pupil referral units see EDUCATION vol 35 (2015) PARAS 427–434. As to academies see EDUCATION vol 35 (2015) PARAS 345–367. As to special schools see EDUCATION vol 36 (2015) PARA 1041 et seq.
3   Equality Act 2010 Sch 10 para 1(1)(a), (6). As to the meaning of 'accessibility strategy' see PARA 178.
4   Equality Act 2010 Sch 10 para 1(1)(b).
5   Equality Act 2010 Sch 10 para 3(1)(a), (6). As to the meaning of 'accessibility plan' see PARA 178.
6   Equality Act 2010 Sch 10 para 3(1)(b).
7   Equality Act 2010 Sch 10 paras 1(4), 3(4).
8   A local authority in England or Wales must, if asked by a Minister of the Crown or, as the case may be, the Welsh Ministers give the Minister or Ministers a copy of its accessibility strategy: Equality Act 2010 Sch 10 para 2(6), (7). The proprietor of an independent educational institution (other than an academy) must, if asked, make a copy of the school's accessibility plan available for inspection at such reasonable times as the proprietor decides (Sch 10 para 4(2)); the proprietor of an independent educational institution in England (other than an academy) must, if asked by a Minister of the Crown, give the Minister a copy of the school's accessibility plan (Sch 10 para 4(3)); and the proprietor of an independent school in Wales (other than an academy) must, if asked by the Welsh Ministers, give them a copy of the school's accessibility plan (Sch 10 para 4(4)). As to the Welsh Ministers see PARA 4.
9   Equality Act 2010 Sch 10 paras 1(5), 3(5).
10 A local authority must, if asked, make a copy of its accessibility strategy available for inspection at such reasonable times as it decides: Equality Act 2010 Sch 10 para 2(5).
11 An inspection under the Education Act 2005 Pt 1 (ss 5–63) (see EDUCATION vol 36 (2015) PARA 1162 et seq) or the Education and Skills Act 2008 Pt 4 Ch 1 (ss 92–141) (regulation and inspection of independent education provision in England: see EDUCATION vol 35 (2015) PARA 382 et seq) may extend to the performance by the responsible body of its functions in relation to the preparation, publication, review, revision and implementation of its accessibility plan: Equality Act 2010 Sch 10 para 3(7), (8).

180. Matters to which regard must be had in preparation and implementation of strategies and plans.

In preparing an accessibility strategy[1] or accessibility plan[2] a local authority[3] or, as the case may be, the responsible body[4] must have regard to the need to allocate adequate resources for implementing the strategy or plan[5]. In preparing an accessibility strategy a local authority must also have regard to guidance[6] as to compliance with the requirement to keep the strategy under review[7] and as to the content of an accessibility strategy[8], the form in which it is to be produced[9] and persons to be consulted in its preparation[10].

1   As to the meaning of 'accessibility strategy' see PARA 178.
2   As to the meaning of 'accessibility plan' see PARA 178.
3   As to the meaning of 'local authority' for these purposes see PARA 173 note 1.
4   As to the meaning of 'responsible body' for these purposes see PARA 179 note 2.
5   Equality Act 2010 Sch 10 paras 2(1)(a), 4(1).
6   Guidance may be issued by a Minister of the Crown (for England) and by the Welsh Ministers (for Wales): Equality Act 2010 Sch 10 para 2(4). As to the meanings of 'England' and 'Wales' see PARA 85 note 1. As to the Welsh Ministers see PARA 4.
7   Ie guidance as to compliance with the Equality Act 2010 Sch 10 para 1(5) (see PARA 179): Sch 10 para 2(2).
8   Equality Act 2010 Sch 10 para 2(1)(b), (3)(a).
9   Equality Act 2010 Sch 10 para 2(3)(b).
10 Equality Act 2010 Sch 10 para 2(3)(c).

181. Default powers.

If:

(1)   the appropriate authority[1] is satisfied (whether or not on a complaint) that a responsible body has acted or is proposing to act unreasonably in the discharge of a duty relating to the preparation and implementation of accessibility strategies and plans[2] or has failed to discharge such a duty[3];

(2)   the appropriate authority is satisfied (whether or not on a complaint) that a responsible body of a specified school[4] has acted or is proposing to act unreasonably in the discharge of a duty the body has in relation to the provision to the authority of copies of the body's accessibility plan[5] or the inspection of that plan[6] or has failed to discharge the duty[7]; or

(3)   a Tribunal has made an order relating to the contravention of the education provisions on disability grounds[8] and the appropriate authority is satisfied (whether or not on a complaint) that the responsible body concerned has acted or is proposing to act unreasonably in complying with the order or has failed to comply with the order[9],

the appropriate authority may give a responsible body such directions as the authority thinks expedient as to the discharge by the body of the duty or compliance by the body with the order[10]. The power to give directions is restricted in connection with certain matters previously complained about[11]. A direction may be varied or revoked by the appropriate authority[12] and may be enforced[13] by a mandatory order[14].

1   For this purpose 'the appropriate authority is' the Secretary of State (in relation to the responsible body of a school in England) and the Welsh Ministers (in relation to the responsible body of a school in Wales): Equality Act 2010 Sch 10 para 5(10). As to the meaning of 'responsible body' for these purposes see PARA 179 note 2. As to the meanings of 'accessibility strategy' and 'accessibility plan' see PARA 178. As to the meanings of 'England' and 'Wales' see PARA 85 note 1. As to the Secretary of State and the Welsh Ministers see PARA 4.
2   Ie a duty under the Equality Act 2010 Sch 10 (see PARAS 178–180).
3   Equality Act 2010 Sch 10 para 5(1).
4   Ie specified in the Equality Act 2010 Sch 10 para 5(3). The schools are: those approved under the Education Act 1996 s 342 (non-maintained special schools: see EDUCATION vol 36 (2015) PARAS 1042–1043), academies, academy schools and alternative provision academies: Equality Act 2010 Sch 10 para 5(3) (amended by the Education Act 2011 Sch 13 para 20).

5 As to the provision of copies of accessibility plans see PARA 179 note 8.
6 As to the inspection of accessibility plans see PARA 179 note 11.
7 Equality Act 2010 Sch 10 para 5(2).
8 Ie an order under the Equality Act 2010 Sch 17 para 5 (see PARA 356).
9 Equality Act 2010 Sch 10 para 5(4).
10 Equality Act 2010 Sch 10 para 5(5). A direction may be given in relation to Sch 10 para 5(1) or (2) even if the performance of the duty is contingent on the opinion of the responsible body: Sch 10 para 5(6).
11 A direction may not in general be given to the responsible body of a school in England in respect of a matter that has been complained about to a Local Commissioner in accordance with the Apprenticeships, Skills, Children and Learning Act 2009 Pt 10 Ch 2 (ss 206–224) (parental complaints against governing bodies etc (repealed)), or that the appropriate authority thinks could have been so complained about (Equality Act 2010 Sch 10 para 5(7)), although this restriction on the giving of directions in those circumstances will not apply if the Local Commissioner has made a recommendation to the responsible body under the Apprenticeships, Skills, Children and Learning Act 2009 s 211(4) (statement following investigation (repealed)) in respect of the matter and the responsible body has not complied with the recommendation (Equality Act 2010 Sch 10 para 5(8)).
12 Equality Act 2010 Sch 10 para 5(9)(a).
13 Ie on the application of the appropriate authority: Equality Act 2010 Sch 10 para 5(9)(b).
14 Equality Act 2010 Sch 10 para 5(9)(b). As to enforcement by mandatory order see the Senior Courts Act 1981 s 31; and JUDICIAL REVIEW vol 61 (2010) PARA 602.

(2) FURTHER AND HIGHER EDUCATION

(i) Admission and Treatment

182. Admission.
The responsible body of an applicable further and higher education institution[1] must not discriminate[2] against a person:
   (1)   in the arrangements it makes for deciding who is offered admission as a student[3];
   (2)   as to the terms on which it offers to admit the person as a student[4];
   (3)   by not admitting the person as a student[5].
So far as relating to sex as a protected characteristic[6], these provisions[7] do not apply in relation to a single-sex institution[8] and so far as relating to sexual orientation[9], to the provision of services for married couples and civil partners[10]. These provisions also do not apply to certain institutions with a religious ethos insofar as relating to religion or belief as a protected characteristic[11], or in certain contexts to the provision of training[12].

1 In relation to England and Wales, the Equality Act 2010 s 91 (see the text and notes 2–5; and PARAS 183–185) applies to a university, any other institution within the higher education sector, an institution within the further education sector, and a 16 to 19 academy: Equality Act 2010 s 91(10) (s 91(10) amended, s 91(12)(aa) added, by the Education Act 2011 Sch 13 para 20). A reference to a 'university' includes a reference to a university college and a college, school or hall of a university (Equality Act 2010 s 94(1), (4)); as to the meaning of 'university' generally see the EDUCATION vol 35 (2015) PARA 621. A reference to an institution within the further or higher education sector is to be construed in accordance with the Further and Higher Education Act 1992 s 91 (see EDUCATION vol 35 (2015) PARAS 555, 619) (Equality Act 2010 s 94(1), (5)); 'further education' in relation to England and Wales has the meaning given in the Education Act 1996 s 2 (see EDUCATION vol 35 (2015) PARA 23) (Equality Act 2010 s 94(1), (6)(a)); and 'higher education' in relation to England and Wales, means education provided by means of a course of a description mentioned in the Education Reform Act 1988 Sch 6 (see EDUCATION vol 35 (2015) PARA 24) (Equality Act 2010 s 94(1), (7)(a)).
   The responsible body of an institution to which these provisions apply is:

(1)   in the case of a university or an institution within the higher or further education sector, the governing body (s 91(12)(a)); and

(2)   in the case of a 16 to 19 academy, the proprietor (within the meaning of the Education Act 1996 s 579(1) (see EDUCATION vol 35 (2015) PARA 51)) (Equality Act 2010 s 91(12)(aa) (as so added)).

As to the meanings of 'England' and 'Wales' see PARA 85 note 1. Nothing in Pt 6 Ch 2 (ss 90–94) applies to anything done in connection with the content of the curriculum: s 94(1), (2).

2   The Equality Act 2010 Pt 6 Ch 2 (ss 90–94) (see the text and notes 3–5; and PARAS 183–191) does not apply to the protected characteristic of marriage and civil partnership (see PARA 57): s 90. Nothing in s 90 is to be regarded as an express exception: s 212(13).

3   Equality Act 2010 s 91(1)(a). A reference to a student, in relation to an institution, is a reference to a person for whom education is provided by the institution: s 94(1), (3).

4   Equality Act 2010 s 91(1)(b).

5   Equality Act 2010 s 91(1)(c).

6   As to sex as a protected characteristic see PARA 60.

7   Ie the Equality Act 2010 s 91(1) (see the text and notes 1–5).

8   Equality Act 2010 Sch 12 para 1(1). A 'single-sex institution' is an institution to which s 91 applies (see note 1) which admits students of one sex only or (on the basis of the assumption that students of the opposite sex are to be disregarded if their admission to the institution is exceptional or their numbers are comparatively small and their admission is confined to particular courses or classes), would be taken to admit students of one sex only: Sch 12 para 1(2), (3).

9   As to sexual orientation as a protected characteristic see PARA 63.

10   A person does not contravene the Equality Act 2010 s 91, so far as relating to sexual orientation, by providing married persons and civil partners (to the exclusion of all other persons) with access to a benefit, facility or service: Sch 12 para 6.

11   See the Equality Act 2010 Sch 12 para 5. As to religion or belief as a protected characteristic see PARA 59. A Minister of the Crown may by order designate an institution for these purposes if satisfied that the institution has a religious ethos (Sch 12 para 5(2)), and the responsible body of an institution which is so designated does not contravene s 91(1), so far as relating to religion or belief, if, in the admission of students to a course at the institution it gives preference to persons of a particular religion or belief, it does so to preserve the institution's religious ethos, and the course is not a course of vocational training (Sch 12 para 5(1)). As to the institutions designated for this purpose see the Equality Act 2010 (Designation of Institutions with a Religious Ethos) (England and Wales) Order 2010, SI 2010/1915.

12   A person (P) does not contravene the Equality Act 2010 s 91(1) if P shows that P's treatment of another person relates only to training that would help fit that other person for work the offer of which the other person could be refused in reliance on Sch 9 Pt 1 (see PARA 117 et seq): Sch 12 para 4.

183.   Discrimination against students in provision of education or services.

The responsible body of an applicable further and higher education institution[1] must not discriminate[2] against a student[3]:

(1)   in the way it provides education for the student[4];

(2)   in the way it affords the student access to a benefit, facility or service[5];

(3)   by not providing education for the student[6];

(4)   by not affording the student access to a benefit, facility or service[7];

(5)   by excluding the student[8];

(6)   by subjecting the student to any other detriment[9].

1   As to the institutions to which these provisions apply, and as to the 'responsible bodies' of such institutions, see PARA 182 note 1.

2   See PARA 182 note 2. A person does not contravene the Equality Act 2010 s 91, so far as relating to sexual orientation as a protected characteristic (see PARA 63), by providing married persons and civil partners (to the exclusion of all other persons) with access to a benefit, facility or service: Sch 12 para 6.

3   As to the meaning of 'student' see PARA 182 note 3.

4   Equality Act 2010 s 91(2)(a). In the case of an institution which is a single-sex institution by virtue of the assumption that students of the opposite sex are to be disregarded if their numbers are comparatively small and their admission is confined to particular courses or classes (ie by virtue of Sch 12 para 1(3)(b): see PARA 182 note 8), s 91(2)(a)–(d) (see the text and notes 5–7), so far as

relating to sex as a protected characteristic (see PARA 60), does not prohibit confining students of the same sex to particular courses or classes: Sch 12 para 1(4).

A person (P) does not contravene s 91(2) if P shows that P's treatment of another person relates only to training that would help fit that other person for work the offer of which the other person could be refused in reliance on Sch 9 Pt 1 (see PARA 117 et seq): Sch 12 para 4.

5 Equality Act 2010 s 91(2)(b). See note 4 A person does not contravene s 91(2)(b) or s 91(2)(d), so far as relating to age as a protected characteristic (see PARA 46), only by providing, or making arrangements for or facilitating the provision of, care for children (ie persons who have not attained the age of 17) of a particular age group: Sch 12 para 7(1), (3). Facilitating the provision of care for a child includes paying for some or all of the cost of the provision, helping a parent of the child to find a suitable person to provide care for the child, and enabling a parent of the child to spend more time providing care for the child or otherwise assisting the parent with respect to the care that the parent provides for the child: Sch 12 para 7(2). A reference to 'care' includes a reference to supervision: Sch 12 para 7(4). As to providing or affording access to a benefit, facility or service see PARA 117 note 7.
6 Equality Act 2010 s 91(2)(c). See note 4.
7 Equality Act 2010 s 91(2)(d). See notes 4, 5.
8 Equality Act 2010 s 91(2)(e). See note 4.
9 Equality Act 2010 s 91(2)(f). See note 4. As to the meaning of 'detriment' see PARA 81 note 1.

184. Discrimination against disabled persons.

The responsible body of an applicable further and higher education institution[1] must not discriminate[2] against a disabled person[3]:

(1) in the arrangements it makes for deciding upon whom to confer a qualification[4];

(2) as to the terms on which it is prepared to confer a qualification on the person[5];

(3) by not conferring a qualification on the person[6];

(4) by withdrawing a qualification from the person or varying the terms on which the person holds it[7].

1 As to the institutions to which these provisions apply, and as to the 'responsible bodies' of such institutions, see PARA 182 note 1.
2 See PARA 182 note 2. A person does not contravene the Equality Act 2010 s 91, so far as relating to sexual orientation as a protected characteristic (see PARA 63), by providing married persons and civil partners (to the exclusion of all other persons) with access to a benefit, facility or service: Sch 12 para 6.
3 These provisions apply only to disability discrimination: Equality Act 2010 s 91(4). As to disability as a protected characteristic see PARAS 47–55.
4 Equality Act 2010 s 91(3)(a). A reference to conferring a qualification includes a reference to renewing or extending the conferment of a qualification and to authenticating a qualification conferred by another person: s 94(11A) (added by SI 2010/2279).
5 Equality Act 2010 s 91(3)(b).
6 Equality Act 2010 s 91(3)(c).
7 Equality Act 2010 s 91(3)(d).

185. Harassment and victimisation of students.

The responsible body of an applicable further and higher education institution[1] must not:

(1) harass[2] a student[3], a person who has applied for admission as a student[4] or a disabled person who holds or has applied for a qualification conferred by the institution[5];

(2) victimise[6] a person in the arrangements it makes for deciding who is offered admission as a student[7], as to the terms on which it offers to admit the person as a student[8], or by not admitting the person as a student[9];

(3) victimise a student:

(a) in the way it provides education for the student[10];
(b) in the way it affords the student access to a benefit, facility or service[11];
(c) by not providing education for the student[12];
(d) by not affording the student access to a benefit, facility or service[13];
(e) by excluding the student[14]; or
(f) by subjecting the student to any other detriment[15], or

(4) victimise a disabled person:
(a) in the arrangements it makes for deciding upon whom to confer a qualification[16];
(b) as to the terms on which it is prepared to confer a qualification on the person[17];
(c) by not conferring a qualification on the person[18]; or
(d) by withdrawing a qualification from the person or varying the terms on which the person holds it[19].

1   As to the institutions to which these provisions apply, and as to the 'responsible bodies' of such institutions, see PARA 182 note 1.
2   As to the meaning of 'harassment' see the Equality Act 2010 s 26; and PARA 79.
3   Equality Act 2010 s 91(5)(a). As to the meaning of 'student' see PARA 182 note 3.
4   Equality Act 2010 s 91(5)(b).
5   Equality Act 2010 s 91(5)(c). As to references to conferring a qualification see PARA 184 note 4.
6   As to the meaning of 'victimisation' see the Equality Act 2010 s 27; and PARA 81.
7   Equality Act 2010 s 91(6)(a).
8   Equality Act 2010 s 91(6)(b).
9   Equality Act 2010 s 91(6)(c).
10 Equality Act 2010 s 91(7)(a).
11 Equality Act 2010 s 91(7)(b). As to providing or affording access to a benefit, facility or service see PARA 117 note 7.
12 Equality Act 2010 s 91(7)(c).
13 Equality Act 2010 s 91(7)(d).
14 Equality Act 2010 s 91(7)(e).
15 Equality Act 2010 s 91(7)(f). As to the meaning of 'detriment' see PARA 81 note 1.
16 Equality Act 2010 s 91(8)(a).
17 Equality Act 2010 s 91(8)(b).
18 Equality Act 2010 s 91(8)(c).
19 Equality Act 2010 s 91(8)(d).

186. Transitional exemptions for single-sex institutions turning co-educational.

If the responsible body of a single-sex institution[1] decides to alter its admissions arrangements so that the institution will cease to be a single-sex institution, the body may apply for a transitional exemption order in relation to the institution[2], the effect of which is to authorise:

(1) sex discrimination by the responsible body in the arrangements it makes for deciding who is offered admission as a student[3]; and
(2) the responsible body, in the circumstances specified in the order, not to admit a person as a student because of the person's sex[4].

A responsible body will not contravene the Equality Act 2010, so far as relating to sex discrimination[5], if in accordance with a transitional exemption order or pending the determination of an application for a transitional exemption order in relation to the institution, it does not admit a person as a student because of the person's sex[6] or it discriminates in the arrangements it makes for deciding who is offered admission as a student[7].

1 As to the institutions to which these provisions apply, and as to the 'responsible bodies' of such institutions, see PARA 182 note 1.
2 Equality Act 2010 Sch 12 para 2(1).
3 Equality Act 2010 Sch 12 para 2(2)(a).
4 Equality Act 2010 Sch 12 para 2(2)(b). Such authorisations apply only during the period specified in the order as the transitional period: Sch 12 para 2(2).
  The responsible body of a single-sex institution may submit to the Equality and Human Rights Commission an application for the making of a transitional exemption order and the Commission may make the order: Sch 12 para 3(1). As to the Commission see PARAS 28–44. Such an application must specify the period proposed by the responsible body as the transitional period to be specified in the order, the stages, within that period, by which the body proposes to move to the position where s 91(1)(a)–(c) (see PARA 182), so far as relating to sex, is complied with, and any other matters relevant to the terms and operation of the order applied for: Sch 12 para 3(2). The Commission must not make an order on an application under Sch 12 para 3(1) unless satisfied that the terms of the application are reasonable, having regard to the nature of the institution's premises, the accommodation, equipment and facilities available and the responsible body's financial resources: Sch 12 para 3(3).
5 See PARA 60.
6 Equality Act 2010 Sch 12 para 2(4).
7 Equality Act 2010 Sch 12 para 2(5).

187. Modification of discriminatory trust deeds.

If:

(1)   a trust deed or other instrument concerning property applicable for or in connection with the provision of education in a further or higher education establishment in England and Wales[1] in any way restricts the benefits available under the instrument to persons of one sex[2];

(2)   a Minister of the Crown is satisfied that the removal or modification of the restriction would be conducive to the advancement of education without sex discrimination[3],

the Minister may, on application[4] by order make such modifications of the instrument as appear to the Minister expedient for removing or modifying the restriction[5]. Before making the order, the Minister must take account of representations[6].

1 Ie property applicable for or in connection with the provision of education in an establishment to which the Equality Act 2010 s 91 (see PARAS 182–185) applies: Sch 14 para 1(1)(a).
2 Equality Act 2010 Sch 14 para 1(1)(b).
3 Equality Act 2010 Sch 14 para 1(2). As to sex as a protected characteristic see PARA 60.
4 Ie on the application of the trustees or the responsible body (within the meaning of the Equality Act 2010 s 91: see PARA 182 note 1). The Minister must require the applicant to publish a notice containing particulars of the proposed order and stating that representations may be made to the Minister within a period specified in the notice (which must be not less than one month beginning with the day after the date of the notice): Sch 14 para 1(6), (7). The applicant must publish the notice in the manner specified by the Minister (Sch 14 para 1(8)), and the cost of publication may be paid out of the property of the trust (Sch 14 para 1(9)).
5 Equality Act 2010 Sch 14 para 1(3). If the trust was created by a gift or bequest, an order must not be made until the end of the period of 25 years after the date when the gift or bequest took effect, unless the donor or the personal representatives of the donor or testator consent in writing to making the application for the order: Sch 14 para 1(4), (5).
6 Equality Act 2010 Sch 14 para 1(10). The reference in the text to representations is to those made in accordance with the notice referred to in the Equality Act 2010 Sch 14 para 1(6) (see note 4).

(ii) Courses

188. Discrimination in enrolment.

The responsible body in relation to an applicable course of further or higher education[1] must not discriminate[2] against a person:

(1)   in the arrangements it makes for deciding who is enrolled[3] on the course[4];

(2)   as to the terms on which it offers to enrol the person on the course[5];

(3)   by not accepting the person's application for enrolment[6],

and the responsible body in relation to such a course must not discriminate against a person who is enrolled on the course in the services[7] it provides or offers to provide[8].

1   The Equality Act 2010 s 92 (see the text and notes 2–8; and PARA 189) applies to a course of further or higher education secured by a responsible body in England or Wales and a course of education provided by the governing body of a maintained school under the School Standards and Framework Act 1998 s 80 (see EDUCATION vol 35 (2015) PARA 588): Equality Act 2010 s 92(7)(a), (b). 'Course', in relation to further education, includes each component part of a course if there is no requirement imposed on persons registered for a component part of the course to register for another component part of the course; and 'maintained school' has the meaning given in the School Standards and Framework Act 1998 s 20(7) (see EDUCATION vol 35 (2015) PARA 99): Equality Act 2010 s 92(9). As to the meanings of 'further education' and 'higher education' see PARA 182 note 1. As to the meanings of 'England' and 'Wales' see PARA 85 note 1.

A 'responsible body' in relation to a course to which these provisions apply is a local authority in England or Wales (for the purposes of a course of further or higher education secured by a responsible body in England or Wales) or the governing body of a maintained school (for the purposes of a course of education provided by the governing body of a maintained school under the School Standards and Framework Act 1998 s 80): Equality Act 2010 s 92(8)(a), (b). For these purposes 'local authority' means an English local authority within the meaning of the Education and Inspections Act 2006 s 162 (in relation to England) and a Welsh local authority within the meaning of s 162 (in relation to Wales): Equality Act 2010 s 94(10). As to the Education and Inspections Act 2006 s 162 see EDUCATION vol 35 (2015) PARA 26

2   See PARA 182 note 2.

3   For these purposes 'enrolment' includes registration for a component part of a course: Equality Act 2010 s 92(9).

4   Equality Act 2010 s 92(1)(a).

5   Equality Act 2010 s 92(1)(b).

6   Equality Act 2010 s 92(1)(c).

7   For these purposes 'services' means services of any description which are provided wholly or mainly for persons enrolled on a course to which the Equality Act 2010 s 92 applies: Equality Act 2010 s 92(9).

8   Equality Act 2010 s 92(2).

189. Harassment and victimisation.

The responsible body in relation to an applicable course of further or higher education[1] must not harass[2] a person who seeks enrolment[3] on the course[4], is enrolled on the course[5], or is a user of services[6] provided by the body in relation to the course[7]. A responsible body also must not victimise[8] a person in the arrangements it makes for deciding who is enrolled on the course[9], as to the terms on which it offers to enrol the person on the course[10], or by not accepting the person's application for enrolment[11], and must not victimise a person who is enrolled on the course in the services it provides or offers to provide[12].

1   As to the courses to which these provisions apply, and as to the 'responsible bodies' in connection with such courses, see PARA 188 note 1.

2   As to the meaning of 'harassment' see the Equality Act 2010 s 26; and PARA 79.

3   As to the meaning of 'enrolment' see PARA 188 note 3.

4   Equality Act 2010 s 92(3)(a).

5   Equality Act 2010 s 92(3)(b).

6   As to the meaning of 'services' see PARA **188** note 7.
7   Equality Act 2010 s 92(3)(c).
8   As to the meaning of 'victimisation' see the Equality Act 2010 s 27; and PARA **81**.
9   Equality Act 2010 s 92(4)(a).
10 Equality Act 2010 s 92(4)(b).
11 Equality Act 2010 s 92(4)(c).
12 Equality Act 2010 s 92(5).

(iii) Recreational and Training Facilities

190. Discrimination in provision of facilities.
The body responsible for the provision of recreational and training facilities[1] must not discriminate[2] against a person:

(1)   in the arrangements it makes for deciding who is provided with the facilities[3];

(2)   as to the terms on which it offers to provide the facilities to the person[4]; or

(3)   by not accepting the person's application for provision of the facilities[5],

and must not discriminate against a person who is provided with the facilities in the services it provides or offers to provide[6].

1   The Equality Act 2010 s 93 (see the text and notes 2–6; and PARA **191**) applies to facilities secured by a local authority in England under the Education Act 1996 s 507A (see EDUCATION vol 35 (2015) PARA 503) or s 507B (see EDUCATION vol 35 (2015) PARA 504) and facilities secured by a local authority in Wales under s 508 (see EDUCATION vol 35 (2015) PARA 505): Equality Act 2010 s 93(7)(a), (b). A 'responsible body' for these purposes is a local authority in England (in connection with facilities secured by a local authority in England under the Education Act 1996 s 507A or s 507B) and a local authority in Wales (in connection with facilities secured by a local authority in Wales under s 508): Equality Act 2010 s 93(8)(a), (b). As to the meaning of 'local authority' see PARA **188** note 1.
2   See PARA **182** note 2. The Equality Act 2010 s 93 does not apply to the protected characteristic of age (see PARA **46**), so far as relating to persons who have not attained the age of 18: s 93(9).
3   Equality Act 2010 s 93(1)(a).
4   Equality Act 2010 s 93(1)(b).
5   Equality Act 2010 s 93(1)(c).
6   Equality Act 2010 s 93(2).

191. Harassment and victimisation.
The body responsible for the provision of recreational and training facilities[1] must not harass[2] a person who seeks to have the facilities provided[3], is provided with the facilities[4] or is a user of services provided by the body in relation to the facilities[5]. The responsible body also must not victimise[6] a person in the arrangements it makes for deciding who is provided with the facilities[7], as to the terms on which it offers to provide the facilities to the person[8] or by not accepting the person's application for provision of the facilities[9], and must not victimise a person who is provided with the facilities in the services it provides or offers to provide[10].

1   As to the recreational and training facilities to which these provisions apply, and as to the 'responsible bodies' in connection with such facilities, see PARA **190** note 1.
2   As to the meaning of 'harassment' see the Equality Act 2010 s 26; and PARA **79**.
3   Equality Act 2010 s 93(3)(a).
4   Equality Act 2010 s 93(3)(b).
5   Equality Act 2010 s 93(3)(c).
6   As to the meaning of 'victimisation' see the Equality Act 2010 s 27; and PARA **81**.
7   Equality Act 2010 s 93(4)(a).
8   Equality Act 2010 s 93(4)(b).

9   Equality Act 2010 s 93(4)(c).
10 Equality Act 2010 s 93(5).

(3) QUALIFICATIONS BODIES

192. Discrimination in conferment of qualifications.

A qualifications body[1] (A) must not discriminate[2] against a person (B):
(1)   in the arrangements A makes for deciding upon whom to confer a relevant qualification[3];
(2)   as to the terms on which it is prepared to confer a relevant qualification on B[4]; or
(3)   by not conferring a relevant qualification on B[5].

A qualifications body (A) must not discriminate against a person (B) upon whom A has conferred a relevant qualification:
(a)   by withdrawing the qualification from B[6];
(b)   by varying the terms on which B holds the qualification[7]; or
(c)   by subjecting B to any other detriment[8].

1   For these purposes a 'qualifications body' is an authority or body which can confer a relevant qualification (Equality Act 2010 s 97(1), (2)); an authority or body is not a qualifications body in so far as it is the responsible body of a school to which s 85 applies (see PARA 173 note 1), it is the governing body of an institution to which 91 applies (see PARA 182 note 1), or it exercises functions under the Education Acts (Equality Act 2010 s 97(1), (4)(a)–(c)); a qualifications body does not include an authority or body of such description, or in such circumstances, as may be prescribed (s 97(1), (5)). At the date at which this volume states the law no matters had been prescribed for these purposes. As to the meaning of 'the Education Acts' see PARA 93 note 24.
    A 'relevant qualification' is an authorisation, qualification, approval or certification of such description as may be prescribed by a Minister of the Crown (in relation to conferments in England) or the Welsh Ministers (in relation to conferments in Wales): s 97(1), (3)(a), (b). As to the meanings of 'England' and 'Wales' see PARA 85 note 1. For these purposes, a relevant qualification is conferred in a part of Great Britain if there are, or may reasonably be expected to be, persons seeking to obtain the relevant qualification who are or will be assessed for those purposes wholly or mainly in that part: ss 96(11), 97(7), (8). As to the relevant qualifications prescribed for these purposes see the Equality Act 2010 (General Qualifications Bodies) (Appropriate Regulator and Relevant Qualifications) Regulations 2010, SI 2010/2245, reg 4, Sch 1 (amended by SI 2017/705). A reference to conferring a relevant qualification includes a reference to renewing or extending the conferment of a relevant qualification and to authenticating a relevant qualification conferred by another person: s 97(6). As to reasonable adjustments to be made by qualifications bodies see also PARA 264.
2   The Equality Act 2010 Pt 6 Ch 3 (ss 95–97) (see the text and notes 3–8; and PARA 193) does not apply to the protected characteristic of marriage and civil partnership (see PARA 57): Equality Act 2010 s 95. Nothing in s 95 is to be regarded as an express exception: s 212(13). See *Michalak v General Medical Council* [2017] UKSC 71.
3   Equality Act 2010 s 96(1)(a). A reference to a student, in relation to an institution, is a reference to a person for whom education is provided by the institution: s 94(1), (3).
4   Equality Act 2010 s 96(1)(b).
5   Equality Act 2010 s 96(1)(c).
6   Equality Act 2010 s 96(2)(a).
7   Equality Act 2010 s 96(2)(b).
8   Equality Act 2010 s 96(2)(c). As to the meaning of 'detriment' see PARA 81 note 1.

193. Harassment and victimisation.

A qualifications body[1] must not, in relation to conferment by it of a relevant qualification[2], harass[3] a person who holds the qualification[4] or a person who applies for it[5]. A qualifications body (A) must not victimise[6] a person (B) in the arrangements A makes for deciding upon whom to confer a relevant qualification[7], as to the terms on which it is prepared to confer a relevant qualification on B[8], or by not conferring a relevant qualification on B[9], and must not victimise a person (B) upon whom it has conferred a relevant qualification by withdrawing the qualification from B[10], by varying the terms on which B holds the qualification[11] or by subjecting B to any other detriment[12].

1 As to the meaning of 'qualifications body' see PARA 192 note 1.
2 As to the meaning of 'relevant qualification', and as to the conferment of qualifications, see PARA 192 note 1.
3 As to the meaning of 'harassment' see the Equality Act 2010 s 26; and PARA 79.
4 Equality Act 2010 s 96(3)(a).
5 Equality Act 2010 s 96(3)(b).
6 As to the meaning of 'victimisation' see the Equality Act 2010 s 27; and PARA 81.
7 Equality Act 2010 s 96(4)(a).
8 Equality Act 2010 s 96(4)(b).
9 Equality Act 2010 s 96(4)(c).
10 Equality Act 2010 s 96(5)(a).
11 Equality Act 2010 s 96(5)(b).
12 Equality Act 2010 s 96(5)(c).

(4) DUTY TO MAKE REASONABLE ADJUSTMENTS

194. Duty to make reasonable adjustments.
   The responsible body of a school[1], the responsible body of an applicable further and higher education institution[2], the responsible body in relation to an applicable course of further or higher education[3], a body responsible for the provision of recreational and training facilities[4], and a qualifications body[5], are under a duty to make reasonable adjustments for disabled persons[6]. In this respect they are required to comply with first, second and third requirements (or, in the case of the responsible body of a school, the first and third requirements) set out in the Equality Act 2010[7], namely:
   (1)   Where a provision, criterion or practice of the applicable body puts a disabled person at a substantial disadvantage in relation to a relevant matter in comparison with persons who are not disabled, the body is required to take such steps as it is reasonable to have to take to avoid the disadvantage[8].
   (2)   Where a physical feature of premises occupied by the applicable body puts a disabled person at a substantial disadvantage in relation to a relevant matter in comparison with persons who are not disabled, the body is required to take such steps as it is reasonable to have to take to avoid the disadvantage[9].
   (3)   Where a disabled person would, but for the provision of an auxiliary aid, be put at a substantial disadvantage in relation to a relevant matter in comparison with persons who are not disabled, the applicable body is required to take such steps as it is reasonable to have to take to provide the auxiliary aid[10].
The full details of the steps which the applicable bodies must take in order to make reasonable adjustments are set out elsewhere in this title[11].

1 As to the schools to which these provisions apply, and as to the 'responsible bodies' of such schools, see PARA 173 note 1.
2 As to the institutions to which these provisions apply, and as to the 'responsible bodies' of such institutions, see PARA 182 note 1.

3   As to the courses to which these provisions apply, and as to the 'responsible bodies' in connection
     with such courses, see PARA **188** note 1.
4   As to the recreational and training facilities to which these provisions apply, and as to the
     'responsible bodies' in connection with such facilities, see PARA **190** note 1.
5   As to the meaning of 'qualifications body' see PARA **192** note 1.
6   Equality Act 2010 ss 85(6), 91(9), 92(6), 93(6), 96(6). As to the meaning of 'disabled person' see
     PARA **47**. As to the duty to make reasonable adjustments generally, and in connection with failure
     to comply with the duty to make adjustments, see PARAS **76**, 237–238.
7   See the Equality Act 2010 Sch 13 paras 1, 2(1), (2), 3(1), (2), 5(1), (2), 6(1), (2), 9(1), (2); and
     PARAS **260–264**. If the responsible body is the governing body of a maintained school (within the
     meaning given by s 92: see PARA **188** note 1), it is not required to comply with the second
     requirement: Sch 13 para 5(2).
8   See the Equality Act 2010 s 20(3); and PARA **237**.
9   See the Equality Act 2010 s 20(4); and PARA **237**.
10   See the Equality Act 2010 s 20(5); and PARA **237**.
11   See PARAS **260–264**.

(5) EXCEPTIONS IN RELATION TO EDUCATION

195. Contraventions pursuant to other enactments.

A person does not contravene the provisions of the Equality Act 2010 on
education (other than so far as relating to vocational training)[1], so far as relating
to the protected characteristic of age[2], disability[3], religion or belief[4], sex[5], or
sexual orientation[6], if he does anything he must do pursuant to a requirement of
an enactment[7]. A person also does not contravene those provisions (other than
those relating to vocational training) so far as relating to the protected
characteristics of disability, religion or belief or sexual orientation if he does
anything he must do pursuant to a relevant requirement or condition imposed by
virtue of an enactment[8].

1   Ie the Equality Act 2010 s Pt 6 (ss 84–99) (see PARA **173** et seq). As to exceptions from the Equality
     Act 2010 generally, and as to further exceptions in specific circumstances, see PARAS **320–338**.
2   As to age as a protected characteristic see PARA **46**.
3   As to disability as a protected characteristic see PARAS **47–55**.
4   As to religion or belief as a protected characteristic see PARA **59**.
5   As to sex as a protected characteristic see PARA **60**.
6   As to sexual orientation as a protected characteristic see PARA **63**.
7   Equality Act 2010 Sch 22 para 1(1), (2). As to the meaning of 'enactment' see PARA **92** note 8.
8   Equality Act 2010 Sch 22 para 1(1), (2). As to the meaning of 'a relevant requirement or condition'
     see PARA **92** note 9.

196. Exceptions relating to nationality or residence.

A person does not contravene the provisions of the Equality Act 2010 on
education[1] by doing anything which discriminates against another because of the
other's nationality[2], or which involves him discriminating against another person
by applying to that other person a provision, criterion or practice which relates to
that person's place of ordinary residence or the length of time that person has been
present or resident in or outside the United Kingdom or an area within it[3], if the
thing in question is done:
(1)   in pursuance of an enactment[4];
(2)   in pursuance of an instrument made by a member of the executive under
       an enactment[5];
(3)   to comply with a requirement imposed by a member of the executive by
       virtue of an enactment[6];

(4)   in pursuance of arrangements made by or with the approval of, or for the time being approved by, a Minister of the Crown[7];

(5)   to comply with a condition imposed by a Minister of the Crown[8].

1   Ie the Equality Act 2010 s Pt 6 (ss 84–99) (see PARA 173 et seq). As to exceptions from the Equality Act 2010 generally, and as to further exceptions in specific circumstances, see PARAS 320–338.
2   Equality Act 2010 Sch 23 para 1(2).
3   Equality Act 2010 Sch 23 para 1(3). As to the meaning of 'United Kingdom' see PARA 85 note 1.
4   Equality Act 2010 Sch 23 para 1(1)(a). As to the meaning of 'enactment' see PARA 91 note 10.
5   Equality Act 2010 Sch 23 para 1(1)(b).
6   Equality Act 2010 Sch 23 para 1(1)(c). This applies to a requirement imposed before or after 8 April 2010 (ie the date on which the Equality Act 2010 was passed (ie received the royal assent)): Sch 23 para 1(1)(c).
7   Equality Act 2010 Sch 23 para 1(1)(d). This applies to arrangements made before or after 8 April 2010: Sch 23 para 1(1)(d).
8   Equality Act 2010 Sch 23 para 1(1)(e). This applies to conditions imposed before or after 8 April 2010: Sch 23 para 1(1)(e).

197. Contraventions connected to the protection of women.

A person (P) does not contravene the provisions of the Equality Act 2010 on education[1], so far as relating to vocational training, so far as relating to the protected characteristics of pregnancy and maternity[2], and sex[3], only by doing in relation to a woman (W) anything P is required to do to comply with:

(1)   a pre-1975 Act enactment[4] concerning the protection of women[5];

(2)   a specified statutory provision concerning health and safety at work[6], if it is done for the purpose of the protection of W (or a description of women which includes W)[7]; or

(3)   a requirement of a statutory provision[8] concerned with protection of women at work[9].

1   Ie the Equality Act 2010 s Pt 6 (ss 84–99) (see PARA 173 et seq). As to exceptions from the Equality Act 2010 generally, and as to further exceptions in specific circumstances, see PARAS 320–338.
2   As to pregnancy and maternity as a protected characteristic see PARAS 62, 73–74.
3   As to sex as a protected characteristic see PARA 60.
4   As to the meaning of 'pre-1975 Act enactment' see PARA 158 note 4.
5   Equality Act 2010 Sch 22 para 2(1)(a), (4)(b), (8). As to references to the 'protection of women' see PARA 158 note 4.
6   Ie a 'relevant statutory provision' within the meaning of the Health and Safety at Work etc Act 1974 Pt 1 (ss 1–54) (see HEALTH AND SAFETY AT WORK vol 52 (2014) PARA 302).
7   Equality Act 2010 Sch 22 para 2(1)(b).
8   Ie a provision specified in the Employment Act 1989 Sch 1 (repealed). For these purposes a reference to a provision in the Employment Act 1989 Sch 1 includes a reference to a provision for the time being having effect in place of it: Equality Act 2010 Sch 22 para 2(7).
9   Equality Act 2010 Sch 22 para 2(1)(c).

9. ASSOCIATIONS

(1) APPLICATION OF THE EQUALITY ACT 2010 TO ASSOCIATIONS

198. Application of Part 7 of the Equality Act 2010 to associations.

Part 7 of the Equality Act 2010 prohibits discrimination, harassment and victimisation by associations[1]. However, it does not apply to the protected characteristic of marriage and civil partnership[2]. If an act of discrimination, harassment or victimisation is made unlawful by the Equality Act 2010 Part 3 (services and public functions)[3], Part 4 (premises)[4], Part 5 (work)[5] or Part 6 (education)[6], then those provisions, rather than the provisions of Part 7, apply[7]. The provisions of Part 7 do not apply to discrimination, harassment or victimisation that would be so prohibited but for an express exception[8].

For these purposes, an 'association' is an association of persons which has at least 25 members, and admission to membership of which is regulated by the association's rules and involves a process of selection[9]. It does not matter whether an association is incorporated, or whether its activities are carried on for profit[10].

1   See the Equality Act 2010 Pt 7 (ss 100–107); and PARA 199 et seq. As to discrimination see PARAS 67–78; as to harassment see PARAS 79–80; and as to victimisation see PARA 81.
2   Equality Act 2010 s 100(1). Nothing in s 100 is to be regarded as an express exception: s 212(13). As to the protected characteristics of marriage and civil partnership see PARA 57.
3   Ie the Equality Act 2010 Pt 3 (ss 28–31) (see PARAS 84–104).
4   Ie the Equality Act 2010 Pt 4 (ss 32–38) (see PARAS 105–115).
5   Ie the Equality Act 2010 Pt 5 (ss 39–83) (see PARAS 116–172).
6   Ie the Equality Act 2010 Pt 6 (ss 84–99) (see PARAS 173–197).
7   See the Equality Act 2010 s 100(2)(a). See note 2. See also the Equality Act 2010 Code of Practice — Services, Public Functions and Associations Statutory Code of Practice (2011) para 12.10.
8   Equality Act 2010 s 100(2)(b). See note 2. As to express exceptions see PARAS 204–208.
9   Equality Act 2010 s 107(1), (2). A Minister of the Crown may by order amend s 107(2) so as to substitute a different number for that for the time being specified there: s 107(3). Note that the Equality Act 2010 Pt 5, rather than Pt 7, applies to associations which are trade organisations, such as a business or professional organisation or a trade union: see the Equality Act 2010 Code of Practice — Services, Public Functions and Associations Statutory Code of Practice (2011) para 12.2. Organisations which do not have rules regulating admission or any selection process for membership (eg campaigning organisations, football team supporters' clubs, informal book groups etc) are not associations for this purpose: see the Equality Act 2010 Code of Practice — Services, Public Functions and Associations Statutory Code of Practice (2011) paras 12.7, 12.8.
10   Equality Act 2010 s 107(1), (4). An organisation that merely requires members of the public to pay a fee to join it without any form of selection (eg a nightclub or a gym), is not an association under the Equality Act 2010, even if it describes itself as a 'club' or refers to customers as 'members': see the Equality Act 2010 Code of Practice — Services, Public Functions and Associations Statutory Code of Practice (2011) para 12.6. Such bodies are involved in the provision of services to the public or a section of the public and their duties are covered by the Equality Act 2010 Pt 3 (ss 28–31); see also the Equality Act 2010 Code of Practice — Services, Public Functions and Associations Statutory Code of Practice (2011) Ch 11.

(2) PROHIBITED CONDUCT

199. Discrimination in relation to membership.

An association[1] (A) must not discriminate against a person (B):
(1)   in the arrangements A makes for deciding who to admit to membership[2];

(2)   as to the terms on which A is prepared to admit B to membership[3];
(3)   by not accepting B's application for membership[4].

An association (A) must not discriminate against a member (B):

(a)   in the way A affords B access, or by not affording B access, to a benefit, facility or service[5];
(b)   by depriving B of membership[6];
(c)   by varying B's terms of membership[7];
(d)   by subjecting B to any other detriment[8].

Associates[9] are also protected from discrimination. An association (A) must not discriminate against an associate (B):

(i)   in the way A affords B access, or by not affording B access, to a benefit, facility or service[10];
(ii)   by depriving B of B's rights as an associate[11];
(iii) by varying B's rights as an associate[12];
(iv)   by subjecting B to any other detriment[13].

1 As to the meaning of 'association' see PARA 198.
2 Equality Act 2010 s 101(1)(a). As to the statutory exceptions to s 101(1) see PARA 204 et seq. As to discrimination see PARAS 67–78. 'Membership' is membership of any description; and a reference to a member is to be construed accordingly: s 107(5); and see the Equality Act 2010 Code of Practice — Services, Public Functions and Associations Statutory Code of Practice (2011) para 12.12. 'Arrangements' can include how or to whom opportunities for membership are, or are not, publicised, forms of communication, application procedures, application forms, time of day, location and conduct of any selection process: see the Equality Act 2010 Code of Practice — Services, Public Functions and Associations Statutory Code of Practice (2011) para 12.23. For further guidance as to what is unlawful in relation to members see the Equality Act 2010 Code of Practice — Services, Public Functions and Associations Statutory Code of Practice (2011) para 12.25–12.32.
3 Equality Act 2010 s 101(1)(b). 'Terms for admission' can include level of joining fee, conditions and initiation procedures: see the Equality Act 2010 Code of Practice — Services, Public Functions and Associations Statutory Code of Practice (2011) para 12.24. 'Terms of membership' can include fees or charges, voting rights, right to stand for office or to represent the association externally, conditions for use of facilities or participation in events: see the Equality Act 2010 Code of Practice — Services, Public Functions and Associations Statutory Code of Practice (2011) para 12.28.
4 Equality Act 2010 s 101(1)(c).
5 Equality Act 2010 s 101(2)(a). As to the statutory exceptions to s 101(2) see PARAS 205–206. 'Benefit, facility or service' describes the wide range of material and non-material advantages enjoyed by members of an association and can include invitation or admission to meetings or events, use of equipment or facilities, discount schemes, bar or restaurant services, receipt of journals or newsletters: see the Equality Act 2010 Code of Practice — Services, Public Functions and Associations Statutory Code of Practice (2011) para 12.27.
6 Equality Act 2010 s 101(2)(b).
7 Equality Act 2010 s 101(2)(c).
8 Equality Act 2010 s 101(2)(d). Even if an association considers that they are acting in the best interests of a person they may be subjecting that person to a detriment: see the Equality Act 2010 Code of Practice — Services, Public Functions and Associations Statutory Code of Practice (2011) para 12.30.
9 A person is an 'associate', in relation to an association, if the person is not a member of the association, but in accordance with the association's rules, has some or all of the rights as a member as a result of being a member of another association: Equality Act 2010 s 107(6). A number of separate trades clubs are affiliated to a single parent body which organises a reciprocal associates scheme amongst its affiliates. Therefore, a member of a trades club in one location would also be an associate of other trades clubs that are affiliated to the parent body and are part of the scheme: see the Equality Act 2010 Code of Practice — Services, Public Functions and Associations Statutory Code of Practice (2011) para 12.13. As to further guidance in relation to associates see the Equality Act 2010 Code of Practice — Services, Public Functions and Associations Statutory Code of Practice (2011) paras 12.33–12.35.
10 Equality Act 2010 s 101(3)(a). As to the statutory exceptions to s 101(3) see PARAS 204–206.

11 Equality Act 2010 s 101(3)(b).
12 Equality Act 2010 s 101(3)(c).
13 Equality Act 2010 s 101(3)(d).

200. Harassment and victimisation in relation to membership.
Harassment and victimisation of members and associates are prohibited[1]. An association[2] must not harass a member, a person seeking to become a member, or an associate[3]. An association (A) must not victimise a person (B):

(1) in the arrangements A makes for deciding who to admit to membership[4];

(2) as to the terms on which A is prepared to admit B to membership[5];

(3) by not accepting B's application for membership[6].

An association (A) must not victimise a member (B):

(a) in the way A affords B access, or by not affording B access, to a benefit, facility or service[7];

(b) by depriving B of membership[8];

(c) by varying B's terms of membership[9];

(d) by subjecting B to any other detriment[10].

Similarly, an association (A) must not victimise an associate (B):

(i) in the way A affords B access, or by not affording B access, to a benefit, facility or service[11];

(ii) by depriving B of B's rights as an associate[12];

(iii) by varying B's rights as an associate[13];

(iv) by subjecting B to any other detriment[14].

1 As to harassment see PARAS 79–80; and as to victimisation see PARA 81.
2 As to the meaning of 'association' see PARA 198.
3 Equality Act 2010 s 101(4). As to the meaning of 'associate' see PARA 199 note 9. In the application of s 26 (harassment: see PARA 79) for the purposes of section 101(4), neither religion or belief, nor sexual orientation is a relevant protected characteristic: s 103(2). For further guidance as to what is unlawful see the Equality Act 2010 Code of Practice — Services, Public Functions and Associations Statutory Code of Practice (2011) paras 12.25–12.32 (members), and paras 12.33–12.35 (associates).
4 Equality Act 2010 s 101(5)(a). As to the meaning of 'membership' see PARA 199 note 2.
5 Equality Act 2010 s 101(5)(b).
6 Equality Act 2010 s 101(5)(c).
7 Equality Act 2010 s 101(6)(a).
8 Equality Act 2010 s 101(6)(b).
9 Equality Act 2010 s 101(6)(c).
10 Equality Act 2010 s 101(6)(d).
11 Equality Act 2010 s 101(7)(a).
12 Equality Act 2010 s 101(7)(b).
13 Equality Act 2010 s 101(7)(c).
14 Equality Act 2010 s 101(7)(d).

201. Discrimination in relation to guests.
An association[1] (A) must not discriminate[2] against a person (B):

(1) in the arrangements A makes for deciding who to invite, or who to permit to be invited, as a guest[3];

(2) as to the terms on which A is prepared to invite B, or to permit B to be invited, as a guest[4];

(3) by not inviting B, or not permitting B to be invited, as a guest[5].

An association (A) must not discriminate against a guest (B) invited by A or with A's permission (whether express or implied):

(a) in the way A affords B access, or by not affording B access, to a benefit, facility or service[6];

(b)   by subjecting B to any other detriment[7].

1 As to the meaning of 'association' see PARA 198.
2 As to discrimination see PARAS 67–78.
3 Equality Act 2010 s 102(1)(a). As to the statutory exceptions to s 102(1) see PARAS 204–205. A
   guest could be any person who is not a member but who is invited by the association or by a
   member of the association to enjoy or participate in some benefit, facility or service of the
   association: see the Equality Act 2010 Code of Practice — Services, Public Functions and
   Associations Statutory Code of Practice (2011) para 12.14. For further guidance as to what is
   unlawful in relation to guests see the Equality Act 2010 Code of Practice — Services, Public
   Functions and Associations Statutory Code of Practice (2011) paras 12.36–12.42.
4 Equality Act 2010 s 102(1)(b).
5 Equality Act 2010 s 102(1)(c).
6 Equality Act 2010 s 102(2)(a). As to the statutory exceptions to s 102(2) see PARAS 205–206.
7 Equality Act 2010 s 102(2)(b).

202.   Harassment and victimisation in relation to guests.
An association[1] must not harass[2] a guest or a person seeking to be a guest[3].
An association (A) must not victimise[4] a person (B):
(1)   in the arrangements A makes for deciding who to invite, or who to
        permit to be invited, as a guest[5];
(2)   as to the terms on which A is prepared to invite B, or to permit B to be
        invited, as a guest[6];
(3)   by not inviting B, or not permitting B to be invited, as a guest[7].
An association (A) must not victimise a guest (B) invited by A or with A's
permission (whether express or implied):
(a)   in the way A affords B access, or by not affording B access, to a benefit,
        facility or service[8];
(b)   by subjecting B to any other detriment[9].

1 As to the meaning of 'association' see PARA 198.
2 As to harassment see PARAS 79–80.
3 Equality Act 2010 s 102(3). In the application of s 26 (harassment: see PARA 79) for the purposes
   of section 102(3), neither religion or belief, nor sexual orientation is a relevant protected
   characteristic: s 103(2). As to who may be considered a guest see PARA 201 note 3. For further
   guidance as to what is unlawful in relation to guests see the Equality Act 2010 Code of Practice
   — Services, Public Functions and Associations Statutory Code of Practice (2011) paras
   12.36–12.42.
4 As to victimisation see PARA 81.
5 Equality Act 2010 s 102(4)(a).
6 Equality Act 2010 s 102(4)(b).
7 Equality Act 2010 s 102(4)(c).
8 Equality Act 2010 s 102(5)(a).
9 Equality Act 2010 s 102(5)(b).

(3) DUTY TO MAKE REASONABLE ADJUSTMENTS

203.   Duty to make reasonable adjustments for disabled persons.
Associations are under a duty to make reasonable adjustments for disabled
persons[1]. In this respect they are required to comply with first, second and third
requirements set out in the Equality Act 2010[2], namely:
(1)   Where a provision, criterion or practice of the association's puts a
        disabled person at a substantial disadvantage in relation to a relevant
        matter in comparison with persons who are not disabled, the
        association is required to take such steps as it is reasonable to have to
        take to avoid the disadvantage[3].

(2) Where a physical feature puts a disabled person at a substantial disadvantage in relation to a relevant matter in comparison with persons who are not disabled, the association is required to take such steps as it is reasonable to have to take to avoid the disadvantage[4].

(3) Where a disabled person would, but for the provision of an auxiliary aid, be put at a substantial disadvantage in relation to a relevant matter in comparison with persons who are not disabled, the association is required to take such steps as it is reasonable to have to take to provide the auxiliary aid[5].

The full details of the steps which associations must take in order to make reasonable adjustments are set out elsewhere in this title[6].

1 Equality Act 2010 s 103(1); and see the Equality Act 2010 Code of Practice — Services, Public Functions and Associations Statutory Code of Practice (2011) paras 12.43–12.45. As to the meaning of 'association' see PARA 198. As to reasonable adjustments for disabled persons see further PARA 237 et seq.
2 Equality Act 2010 s 107(8), Sch 15 para 1.
3 See the Equality Act 2010 s 20(3); and PARA 237.
4 See the Equality Act 2010 s 20(4); and PARA 237.
5 See the Equality Act 2010 s 20(5); and PARA 237.
6 See PARA 265.

(4) EXCEPTIONS IN RELATION TO ASSOCIATIONS

204. Restriction of membership to persons who share a protected characteristic.
The Equality Act 2010 specifies the following exceptions in the context of associations in relation to protected characteristics[1].

An association does not discriminate[2] by restricting membership[3] to persons who share a protected characteristic[4]. An association that restricts membership to persons who share a protected characteristic does not discriminate[5] by restricting the access by associates to a benefit, facility or service to such persons as share the characteristic[6]. An association that restricts membership to persons who share a protected characteristic does not discriminate[7] by inviting as guests, or by permitting to be invited as guests, only such persons as share the characteristic[8].

These exceptions, however, so far as relating to race, do not apply in relation to colour[9]. Nor do these exceptions apply to an association that is a registered political party[10].

1 As to the meaning of 'protected characteristic' see PARA 45. As to exceptions from the Equality Act 2010 generally, and as to further exceptions in specific circumstances, see PARAS 320–338.
2 Ie the association does not breach the Equality Act 2010 s 101(1) (see PARA 199). As to the meaning of 'association' see PARA 198.
3 As to the meaning of 'membership' see PARA 199 note 2. As to discrimination see PARAS 67–78.
4 Equality Act 2010 s 107(9), Sch 16 para 1(1).
5 Ie the association does not breach the Equality Act 2010 s 101(3) (see PARA 199).
6 Equality Act 2010 Sch 16 para 1(2).
7 Ie the association does not breach the Equality Act 2010 s 102(1) (see PARA 201).
8 Equality Act 2010 Sch 16 para 1(3).
9 Equality Act 2010 Sch 16 para 1(4).
10 Equality Act 2010 Sch 16 para 1(5). As to the special provisions for political parties see PARAS 209–210. As to further guidance on exceptions see the Equality Act 2010 Code of Practice — Services, Public Functions and Associations Statutory Code of Practice (2011) paras 12.46–12.51.

205. Membership concessions for persons of a particular age group.

The Equality Act 2010 specifies the following exceptions in relation to age-related concessions[1].

An association[2] does not discriminate[3], so far as relating to age discrimination, by giving a concession on admission to membership for:

(1)   persons of a particular age group[4]; or

(2)   persons who have been members of the association for more than a number of years specified by the association for this purpose[5].

An association does not discriminate[6], so far as relating to age discrimination, by giving a concession on access to a benefit, facility or service for:

(a)   members of a particular age group[7]; or

(b)   persons who have been members of the association for more than a number of years specified by the association for this purpose[8].

An association does not discriminate[9], so far as relating to age discrimination, by giving a concession on invitations of persons of a particular age group as guests[10].

An association does not discriminate[11], so far as relating to age discrimination, by giving a concession on access to a benefit, facility or service for guests of a particular age group[12].

1 Affording only persons of a particular age group access to a benefit, facility or service for a limited time is to be regarded as a concession: Equality Act 2010 Sch 16 para 1A(5) (Sch 16 para 1A added by SI 2012/2466). The reference to a concession in respect of something done by an association is a reference to a benefit, right or privilege having the effect that the manner in which, or the terms on which, it does it are more favourable than the manner in which, or the terms on which, it usually does the thing: Equality Act 2010 Sch 16 para 1A(6) (as so added). The Equality Act 2010 (Age Exceptions) Order 2012, SI 2012/2466, was made under the Equality Act 2010 s 197: see PARA 96 note 2. As to exceptions from the Equality Act 2010 generally, and as to further exceptions in specific circumstances, see PARAS 320–338.

2 As to the meaning of 'association' see PARA 198.

3 Ie an association does not contravene the Equality Act 2010 s 101(1) or s 101(2) (see PARA 199).

4 Equality Act 2010 Sch 16 para 1A(1)(a) (as added: see note 1). As to age discrimination see PARA 46.

5 Equality Act 2010 Sch 16 para 1A(1)(b) (as added: see note 1).

6 Ie an association does not contravene the Equality Act 2010 s 101(2) or s 101(3) (see PARA 199).

7 Equality Act 2010 Sch 16 para 1A(2)(a) (as added: see note 1).

8 Equality Act 2010 Sch 16 para 1A(2)(b) (as added: see note 1).

9 Ie an association does not contravene the Equality Act 2010 s 102(1) (see PARA 201).

10 Equality Act 2010 Sch 16 para 1A(3) (as added: see note 1).

11 Ie an association does not contravene the Equality Act 2010 s 102(2) (see PARA 201).

12 Equality Act 2010 Sch 16 para 1A(4) (as added: see note 1).

206. Membership restrictions to pregnant women on grounds of health and safety.

The Equality Act 2010 specifies the following exceptions in relation to pregnant women on the grounds of health and safety.

An association (A) must not discriminate against a person (B) as to the terms on which A is prepared to admit B to membership[1]. However, an association does not discriminate against a pregnant woman in contravention of this provision because she is pregnant if:

(1)   the terms on which A is prepared to admit her to membership include a term intended to remove or reduce a risk to her health or safety[2];

(2)   A reasonably believes that admitting her to membership on terms which do not include that term would create a risk to her health or safety[3];

(3)   the terms on which A is prepared to admit persons with other physical
         conditions to membership include a term intended to remove or reduce
         a risk to their health or safety[4]; and
(4)   A reasonably believes that admitting them to membership on terms
         which do not include that term would create a risk to their health or
         safety[5].

An association must not discriminate against a person (B) as to the terms on which
it is prepared to invite B, or to permit B to be invited, as a guest[6]. However, the
same exception applies, and therefore an association does not discriminate against
a pregnant woman in contravention of this provision because she is pregnant if the
conditions in heads (1) to (4) are met[7].

An association (A) must not discriminate against a member, associate or guest
in the way it affords them access, or by not affording them access, to a benefit,
facility or service[8]. However, an association does not discriminate against a
pregnant woman in contravention of these provisions because she is pregnant if:

(a)   the way in which A affords her access to a benefit, facility or service is
         intended to remove or reduce a risk to her health or safety[9];
(b)   A reasonably believes that affording her access to the benefit, facility or
         service otherwise than in that way would create a risk to her health or
         safety[10];
(c)   A affords persons with other physical conditions access to the benefit,
         facility or service in a way that is intended to remove or reduce a risk to
         their health or safety[11]; and
(d)   A reasonably believes that affording them access to the benefit, facility
         or service otherwise than in that way would create a risk to their health
         or safety[12].

An association (A) which does not afford a pregnant woman access to a benefit,
facility or service does not discriminate against her[13] because she is pregnant if:

(i)   A reasonably believes that affording her access to the benefit, facility or
         service would, because she is pregnant, create a risk to her health or
         safety[14];
(ii)   A does not afford persons with other physical conditions access to the
         benefit, facility or service[15]; and
(iii)   the reason for not doing so is that A reasonably believes that affording
         them access to the benefit, facility or service would create a risk to their
         health or safety[16].

An association must not discriminate against a member by varying his or her
terms of membership[17], and similarly must not discriminate against an associate
by varying his or her rights as an associate[18]. However, an association (A) does not
discriminate against a pregnant woman under these provisions because she is
pregnant if:

(A)   the variation of A's terms of membership, or rights as an associate, is
         intended to remove or reduce a risk to her health or safety[19];
(B)   A reasonably believes that not making the variation to A's terms or
         rights would create a risk to her health or safety[20];
(C)   A varies the terms of membership, or rights as an associate, of persons
         with other physical conditions[21];
(D)   the variation of their terms or rights is intended to remove or reduce a
         risk to their health or safety[22]; and

(E)   A reasonably believes that not making the variation to their terms or rights would create a risk to their health or safety[23].

1 See the Equality Act 2010 s 101(1)(b); and PARA 199. As to the meaning of 'association' see PARA 198. As to discrimination see PARAS 67–78. As to exceptions from the Equality Act 2010 generally, and as to further exceptions in specific circumstances, see PARAS 320–338.
2 Equality Act 2010 Sch 16 para 2(1)(a).
3 Equality Act 2010 Sch 16 para 2(1)(b).
4 Equality Act 2010 Sch 16 para 2(1)(c).
5 Equality Act 2010 Sch 16 para 2(1)(d).
6 See the Equality Act 2010 s 102(1)(b); and PARA 201.
7 Equality Act 2010 Sch 16 para 2(2).
8 See the Equality Act 2010 s 101(2)(a), (3)(a) (see PARA 199), s 102(2)(a) (see PARA 201).
9 Equality Act 2010 Sch 16 para 2(3)(a).
10 Equality Act 2010 Sch 16 para 2(3)(b).
11 Equality Act 2010 Sch 16 para 2(3)(c).
12 Equality Act 2010 Sch 16 para 2(3)(d).
13 Ie in contravention of the Equality Act 2010 s 101(2)(a), s 101(3)(a) or s 102(2)(a) (see PARAS 199, 201).
14 Equality Act 2010 Sch 16 para 2(4)(a).
15 Equality Act 2010 Sch 16 para 2(4)(b).
16 Equality Act 2010 Sch 16 para 2(4)(c).
17 See the Equality Act 2010 s 101(2)(c); and PARA 199.
18 See the Equality Act 2010 s 101(3)(c); and PARA 199.
19 Equality Act 2010 Sch 16 para 2(5)(a).
20 Equality Act 2010 Sch 16 para 2(5)(b).
21 Equality Act 2010 Sch 16 para 2(5)(c).
22 Equality Act 2010 Sch 16 para 2(5)(d).
23 Equality Act 2010 Sch 16 para 2(5)(e).

207.   Contraventions pursuant to enactments.

A person does not contravene the provisions of the Equality Act 2010 concerning associations[1], so far as relating to the protected characteristics of age[2], disability[3], religion or belief[4], sex[5], or sexual orientation[6], if he does anything he must do pursuant to a requirement of an enactment[7]. A person also does not contravene those provisions so far as relating to the protected characteristics of disability, religion or belief, or sexual orientation, if he does anything he must do pursuant to a relevant requirement or condition imposed by virtue of an enactment[8].

1 Ie the Equality Act 2010 s Pt 7 (ss 100–107) (see PARA 198 et seq). As to exceptions from the Equality Act 2010 generally, and as to further exceptions in specific circumstances, see PARAS 320–338.
2 As to age as a protected characteristic see PARA 46.
3 As to disability as a protected characteristic see PARAS 47–55.
4 As to religion or belief as a protected characteristic see PARA 59.
5 As to sex as a protected characteristic see PARA 60.
6 As to sexual orientation as a protected characteristic see PARA 63.
7 Equality Act 2010 Sch 22 para 1(1). As to the meaning of 'enactment' see PARA 92 note 8.
8 Equality Act 2010 Sch 22 para 1(1). As to the meaning of 'a relevant requirement or condition' see PARA 92 note 9.

208.   Exceptions relating to religion or belief.

Religious organisations[1], other than organisations whose sole or main purpose is commercial[2], do not contravene the provisions of the Equality Act 2010 concerning associations[3], so far as relating to religion or belief[4] or sexual orientation[5], only by restricting:

(1)   membership of the organisation[6];

(2)   participation in activities undertaken by the organisation or on its behalf or under its auspices[7];

(3)   the provision of goods, facilities or services in the course of activities undertaken by the organisation or on its behalf or under its auspices[8];

(4)   the use or disposal of premises owned or controlled by the organisation[9],

and a person does not contravene the provisions on associations, so far as relating to religion or belief or sexual orientation, only by doing any of those things on behalf of or under the auspices of the organisation[10].

A minister[11] does not contravene the provisions on associations, so far as relating to religion or belief or sexual orientation[12], only by restricting:

(a)   participation in activities carried on in the performance of the minister's functions in connection with or in respect of the organisation[13]; or

(b)   the provision of goods, facilities or services in the course of activities carried on in the performance of the minister's functions in connection with or in respect of the organisation[14].

1   As to the meaning of 'religious organisation' for these purposes see PARA 97 note 1.
2   See the Equality Act 2010 Sch 23 para 2(1), (2).
3   Ie the Equality Act 2010 s Pt 7 (ss 100–107) (see PARA 198 et seq). As to exceptions from the Equality Act 2010 generally, and as to further exceptions in specific circumstances, see PARAS 320–338.
4   As to religion or belief as a protected characteristic see PARA 59; and as to restrictions on the permitted discrimination see the Equality Act 2010 Sch 23 para 2(6); and PARA 97 note 4.
5   As to sexual orientation as a protected characteristic see PARA 63; and as to restrictions on the permitted discrimination see the Equality Act 2010 Sch 23 para 2(7), (9)–(11); and PARA 97 note 5.
6   Equality Act 2010 Sch 23 para 2(3)(a).
7   Equality Act 2010 Sch 23 para 2(3)(b).
8   Equality Act 2010 Sch 23 para 2(3)(c).
9   Equality Act 2010 Sch 23 para 2(3)(d). As to the meaning of 'disposal' for these purposes see the Equality Act 2010 Sch 23 para 2(12), (13)(a); and PARA 97 note 9.
10 Equality Act 2010 Sch 23 para 2(4).
11 As to the meaning of 'minister' for these purposes see the Equality Act 2010 Sch 23 para 2(8); and PARA 97 note 11.
12 See notes 4, 5.
13 Equality Act 2010 Sch 23 para 2(5)(a).
14 Equality Act 2010 Sch 23 para 2(5)(b).

(5) SPECIAL PROVISION FOR POLITICAL PARTIES

209.   Selection of candidates for registered political parties.
The Equality Act 2010 makes the following provision regarding the selection of candidates for associations which are registered political parties[1].

A person does not contravene Part 7 of the Act[2] only by acting in accordance with selection arrangements[3]. Selection arrangements are arrangements:

(1)   which the party makes for regulating the selection of its candidates in a relevant election[4];

(2)   the purpose of which is to reduce inequality in the party's representation in the body concerned[5]; and

(3)   which are a proportionate means of achieving that purpose[6].

The reference to inequality in a party's representation in a body is a reference to inequality between:

(a)   the number of the party's candidates elected to be members of the body who share a protected characteristic[7]; and

(b)   the number of the party's candidates so elected who do not share that characteristic[8].

Selection arrangements do not include short-listing only such persons as have a particular protected characteristic[9]. Where there is inequality in a party's representation, the Act permits a political party to adopt selection arrangements that would reserve a fixed number of places on their candidate shortlists for persons who share protected characteristics that are under-represented in the party's elected candidates on the relevant body[10]. However, for all protected characteristics other than sex, regardless of the scale of inequality of representation, such selection arrangements cannot require that all persons short-listed must have that characteristic[11]. Political parties are, however, permitted to select only women for their shortlist of candidates for election to a body in order to reduce inequality between women and men in that party's representation in the elected body concerned[12].

1   See the Equality Act 2010 s 104(1). As to the meaning of 'association' see PARA 198. A reference to a registered political party is a reference to a party registered in the Great Britain register under the Political Parties, Elections and Referendums Act 2000 Pt 2 (ss 22–40): Equality Act 2010 s 107(7). As to further guidance in relation to the selection of candidates for political parties see the Equality Act 2010 Code of Practice — Services, Public Functions and Associations Statutory Code of Practice (2011) paras 12.54–12.62.

2   Ie the Equality Act 2010 Pt 7 (ss 100–107) (see PARA 198 et seq).

3   Equality Act 2010 s 104(2).

4   Equality Act 2010 s 104(3)(a). The following elections are relevant elections: parliamentary elections; elections to the European Parliament; elections to the Scottish Parliament; elections to the National Assembly for Wales; local government elections within the meaning of the Representation of the People Act 1983 s 191, s 203 or s 204 (excluding elections for the Mayor of London): Equality Act 2010 s 104(8). See generally ELECTIONS AND REFERENDUMS.

5   Equality Act 2010 s 104(3)(b).

6   Equality Act 2010 s 104(3)(c). This is subject to the Equality Act 2010 s 104(7): see note 9. However, this is a time-limited provision. The words 'subject to subsection (7)' in s 104(3)(c) are repealed at the end of 2030, unless at any time before the end of 2030, a Minister of the Crown by order provides that a later time should be substituted for the time being specified: see s 105(1), (2). A party's selection arrangements can include their procedures for encouraging prospective candidates to come forward, for identifying suitable candidates and in determining how a final shortlist will be chosen: see the Equality Act 2010 Code of Practice — Services, Public Functions and Associations Statutory Code of Practice (2011) para 12.58. If a party achieves equality in respect of a particular protected characteristic in its representation on an elected body they will not be able to continue to reserve shortlist places for people who share that protected characteristic or take any other measures under the provisions described above as it would no longer be a proportionate act: see the Equality Act 2010 Code of Practice — Services, Public Functions and Associations Statutory Code of Practice (2011) para 12.62.

7   Equality Act 2010 s 104(4)(a). For the purposes of s 104(4), persons share the protected characteristic of disability if they are disabled persons (and s 6(3)(b) (see PARA 47) is accordingly to be ignored): s 104(5). As to the meaning of 'protected characteristics' see PARA 45. It is unlikely to be proportionate for a political party to adopt selection arrangements that focus exclusively on improving the representation of one particular group sharing a protected characteristic which would reduce further the selection prospects for people in other under-represented groups: see the Equality Act 2010 Code of Practice — Services, Public Functions and Associations Statutory Code of Practice (2011) para 12.59.

8   Equality Act 2010 s 104(4)(b). See note 7.

9   Equality Act 2010 s 104(6). But s 104(6) does not apply to the protected characteristic of sex: s 104(7). Section 104(3)(c) (see head (3) in the text) does not apply to short-listing in reliance on s 104(7): s 104(7).

10 See the Equality Act 2010 Code of Practice — Services, Public Functions and Associations Statutory Code of Practice (2011) para 12.60.

11 See the Equality Act 2010 Code of Practice — Services, Public Functions and Associations
   Statutory Code of Practice (2011) para 12.60.
12 See the Equality Act 2010 Code of Practice — Services, Public Functions and Associations
   Statutory Code of Practice (2011) para 12.63.

210. Duty to provide information about diversity in range of candidates etc.

As from a day to be appointed, the following provisions apply[1]. They relate
exclusively to associations which are registered as political parties[2].

If the party had candidates at a relevant election[3], the party must, in accordance
with regulations, publish information relating to protected characteristics of
persons who come within a description prescribed in the regulations[4]. This does
not apply to the protected characteristics of marriage and civil partnership, or
pregnancy and maternity[5]. One or more of the following descriptions may be
prescribed by the regulations:

(1)   successful applicants for nomination as a candidate at the relevant
      election;
(2)   unsuccessful applicants for nomination as a candidate at that election;
(3)   candidates elected at that election;
(4)   candidates who are not elected at that election[6].

The regulations may:

(a)   provide that the information to be published must relate to all protected
      characteristics or only to such as are prescribed[7];
(b)   provide that the information to be published must include a statement,
      in respect of each protected characteristic to which the information
      relates, of the proportion that the number of persons who provided the
      information to the party bears to the number of persons who were asked
      to provide it[8];
(c)   prescribe descriptions of information[9];
(d)   prescribe descriptions of political party to which the duty is to apply[10];
(e)   prescribe the time at which information is to be published[11];
(f)   prescribe the form and manner in which information is to be
      published[12];
(g)   prescribe the period for which information is to be published[13];
(h)   provide that the duty to publish information[14] applies only to such
      relevant elections as are prescribed[15];
(i)   provide that a by-election or other election to fill a vacancy is not to be
      treated as a relevant election or is to be so treated only to a prescribed
      extent[16];
(j)   provide for the duty to publish information[17] to apply in the case of
      additional descriptions of election[18].

However, nothing in provisions described above authorises a political party to
require a person to provide information to it[19].

1 At the date at which this volume states the law, no day had been appointed for the Equality Act
   2010 s 106 to be brought into force.
2 Equality Act 2010 s 106(1) (not yet in force). As to the meaning of 'registered political party' see
   PARA 209 note 1.
3 The following elections are relevant elections: parliamentary elections; elections to the European
   Parliament; elections to the Scottish Parliament; elections to the National Assembly for Wales:
   Equality Act 2010 s 106(5) (not yet in force). See generally ELECTIONS AND REFERENDUMS.
4 Equality Act 2010 s 106(2). The duty imposed by s 106(2) applies only in so far as it is possible
   to publish information in a manner that ensures that no person to whom the information relates
   can be identified from that information: s 106(4) (not yet in force). At the date at which this volume
   states the law, no such regulations had been made.

5 Equality Act 2010 s 106(6) (not yet in force). As to the protected characteristics of marriage and civil partnership see PARA 57.
6 Equality Act 2010 s 106(3) (not yet in force).
7 Equality Act 2010 s 106(7)(a) (not yet in force). However, this is expressed to be subject to s 106(6), which states that s 106 does not apply to the protected characteristics of marriage and civil partnership, or pregnancy and maternity.
8 Equality Act 2010 s 106(7)(b) (not yet in force).
9 Equality Act 2010 s 106(8)(a) (not yet in force).
10 Equality Act 2010 s 106(8)(b) (not yet in force). Provision by virtue of s 106(8)(b) may, in particular, provide that the duty to publish information imposed by s 106(2) (see the text to note 4) does not apply to a party which had candidates in fewer constituencies in the election concerned than a prescribed number: s 106(9) (not yet in force).
11 Equality Act 2010 s 106(8)(c) (not yet in force).
12 Equality Act 2010 s 106(8)(d) (not yet in force).
13 Equality Act 2010 s 106(8)(e) (not yet in force).
14 Ie the duty imposed by the Equality Act 2010 s 106(2) (see the text to note 4).
15 Equality Act 2010 s 106(10)(a) (not yet in force).
16 Equality Act 2010 s 106(10)(b) (not yet in force).
17 See note 14.
18 See the Equality Act 2010 s 106(10)(c) (not yet in force).
19 Equality Act 2010 s 106(11) (not yet in force).

10. ACCESSIBILITY ISSUES FOR DISABLED PERSONS

(1) STATUTORY MEASURES FOR ENSURING ACCESS FOR DISABLED PERSONS

211. Measures under the Equality Act 2010 to ensure disabled persons have access to public transport.

The Equality Act 2010 contains provisions aimed at ensuring that disabled persons have access to various forms of public transport[1]. These include, for example, provisions to enable disabled people to access taxis safely, even when seated in a wheelchair, and to be carried in safety and reasonable comfort[2], and provisions enabling technical standards to be specified for buses, coaches[3], trains, trams and other guided transport systems[4] so that they provide greater accessibility to disabled passengers including wheelchair users.

1   See the Equality Act 2010 Pt 12 (ss 160–188); and PARAS 215–235.
2   As to taxi accessibility see PARAS 215–223.
3   As to public service vehicle accessibility see PARAS 224–229.
4   As to rail vehicle accessibility see PARAS 233–234.

212. Measures under the Transport Act 2000 to ensure rail replacement services are suitable for disabled persons.

Where railway services have been temporarily interrupted or discontinued and substitute road services are provided for the carriage of passengers, there is a duty on the provider of such services to ensure that, so far as is reasonably practicable, the substitute road services allow disabled passengers to undertake their journeys safely and in reasonable comfort[1].

1   See the Transport Act 2000 s 248; and PARA 236.

213. Measures under the Equality Act 2010 to ensure disabled persons have access to services and premises.

The duty to make reasonable adjustments for the purposes of Equality Act 2010[1] requires service providers to take positive steps to ensure that disabled people can access services[2]. This goes beyond simply avoiding discrimination: it requires service providers to anticipate the needs of potential disabled customers for reasonable adjustments. The purpose of the duty to make reasonable adjustments is to provide access to a service as close as it is reasonably possible to get to the standard normally offered to the public at large (and their equivalents in relation to associations or the exercise of public functions)[3].

The duty comprises three requirements which apply where a disabled person is placed at a substantial disadvantage in comparison with non-disabled people. The first requirement covers changing the way things are done (such as changing a practice)[4], the second requirement covers making changes to the built environment (such as providing access to a building)[5], and the third requirement covers providing auxiliary aids and services (such as providing special computer software or providing a different service)[6].

The duty is anticipatory as it requires consideration of, and action in relation to, barriers that impede people with one or more kinds of disability prior to an individual disabled person seeking to use the service, avail themselves of a function or participate in the activities of an association[7]. Service providers should therefore not wait until a disabled person wants to use a service that they provide before they give consideration to their duty to make reasonable adjustments. They should anticipate the requirements of disabled people and the adjustments that may have to be made for them. Failure to anticipate the need for an adjustment may create additional expense, or render it too late to comply with the duty to make the adjustment. Furthermore, it may not in itself provide a defence to a claim of a failure to make a reasonable adjustment[8].

The duty is owed to disabled people at large, and applies regardless of whether the service provider knows that a particular person is disabled or whether it currently has disabled customers or members[9].

1 As to the duty to make reasonable adjustments see the Equality Act 2010 s 20; and PARA 237.
2 As to the specific duties in relation to services and public functions see the Equality Act 2010 Sch 2; and PARAS 239–240. As to the specific duties in relation to let premises see Sch 4; and PARAS 241–244. As to the specific duties in relation to work see Sch 8; and PARAS 245–259. As to the specific duties in relation to education see Sch 13; and PARAS 260–264. As to the specific duties in relation to associations see Sch 15; and PARA 265. For further guidance and examples see the Equality Act 2010 Code of Practice — Services, Public Functions and Associations Statutory Code of Practice (2011) Ch 7.
3 Equality Act 2010 Code of Practice — Services, Public Functions and Associations Statutory Code of Practice (2011) paras 7.3, 7.4.
4 As to the first requirement see the Equality Act 2010 s 20(3); and PARA 237.
5 As to the second requirement see the Equality Act 2010 s 20(4); and PARA 237.
6 As to the third requirement see the Equality Act 2010 s 20(5); and PARA 237.
7 Equality Act 2010 Code of Practice — Services, Public Functions and Associations Statutory Code of Practice (2011) para 7.20. See *Finnigan v Chief Constable of Northumbria Police* [2013] EWCA Civ 1191 at [31], (2013) 134 BMLR 1, [2014] 1 WLR 445 per Lord Dyson MR, citing Sedley LJ in *Roads v Central Trains Ltd* [2004] EWCA CIV 1541, (in the context of a case about the provision of services by a train operator) '[service providers] cannot be expected to anticipate the needs of every individual who may use their service , but what they are required to think about and provide for are features which may impede people with particular kinds of disability'.
8 Equality Act 2010 Code of Practice — Services, Public Functions and Associations Statutory Code of Practice (2011) para 7.21.
9 Equality Act 2010 Code of Practice — Services, Public Functions and Associations Statutory Code of Practice (2011) para 7.22.

214. Measures under the Chronically Sick and Disabled Persons Act 1970 to ensure access for disabled persons.

Providers of office premises, shop premises, railway premises, factories, educational institutions and premises to which the public are to be admitted are required, in the means of access to and within the premises, and in the parking facilities and sanitary conveniences to be available, to make such provision as it is practicable and reasonable to make (including, where applicable, provision for the display of notices and signs) for the needs of disabled visitors and users[1]. Housing authorities are required to take account of the needs of disabled persons in decisions concerning the provision of housing stock[2], and local authorities that undertake the provision of public sanitary conveniences are required to make such provision as is practicable and reasonable (including provision for the display of notices and signs) for the needs of disabled persons[3].

The Secretary of State and the Welsh Ministers[4] are required to lay before Parliament and the National Assembly for Wales a report on their proposals for ensuring or facilitating the improvement of means of access for disabled persons to buildings and premises[5], to public sanitary conveniences[6] and to sanitary conveniences provided in other specified places to which the public has access[7].

1 See the Chronically Sick and Disabled Persons Act 1970 ss 4(1), (2), 6–8, 8A(1), (2); BUILDING vol 6 (2011) PARA 103A; EDUCATION vol 36 (2015) PARA 1348; ENVIRONMENTAL QUALITY AND PUBLIC HEALTH vol 46 (2010) PARA 993; HEALTH AND SAFETY AT WORK vol 52 (2014) PARA 422.
2 See the Chronically Sick and Disabled Persons Act 1970 s 3; and HOUSING vol 56 (2017) PARA 401.

3   See the Chronically Sick and Disabled Persons Act 1970 ss 5(1), (2), (3), 7; and ENVIRONMENTAL
    QUALITY AND PUBLIC HEALTH vol 46 (2010) PARA 993.
4   As to the Secretary of State and the Welsh Ministers see PARA 4.
5   Chronically Sick and Disabled Persons Act 1970 s 8B(1)(a) (s 8B added by the Disabled Persons
    Act 1981 s 7). The buildings and premises referred to in the text those as are mentioned in the
    Chronically Sick and Disabled Persons Act 1970 ss 4, 8, 8A (see the text and note 1).
6   Chronically Sick and Disabled Persons Act 1970 s 8B(1)(b) (as added: see note 5).
7   Chronically Sick and Disabled Persons Act 1970 s 8B(1)(c) (as added: see note 5). The places
    specified are those normally used or proposed to be normally used for the holding of any
    entertainment, exhibition or sporting event to which members of the public are admitted either as
    spectators or otherwise, places normally used or proposed to be normally used for the sale of food
    or drink to members of the public for consumption at the place, and places used on some occasion
    or occasions or proposed to be used on some occasion or occasions for any of those purposes: s
    8B(2)(a), (b) (as so added).

(2) FORMS OF TRANSPORT: ACCESSIBILITY FOR DISABLED PERSONS

(i) Taxis and Private Hire Vehicles

215. Taxi accessibility regulations.

As from a day to be appointed the following provisions have effect[1].

The Secretary of State[2] may make regulations (known as 'taxi accessibility regulations') for securing that it is possible for disabled persons:

(1)   to get into and out of taxis in safety;
(2)   to do so while in wheelchairs;
(3)   to travel in taxis in safety and reasonable comfort;
(4)   to do so while in wheelchairs[3].

The regulations may, in particular, require a regulated taxi[4] to conform with provision as to:

(a)   the size of a door opening for the use of passengers;
(b)   the floor area of the passenger compartment;
(c)   the amount of headroom in the passenger compartment;
(d)   the fitting of restraining devices designed to ensure the stability of a wheelchair while the taxi is moving[5].

The regulations may require the driver of a regulated taxi which is plying for hire, or which has been hired, to comply with provisions as to the carrying of ramps or other devices designed to facilitate the loading and unloading of wheelchairs[6]. They may also require the driver of a regulated taxi in which a disabled person is being carried while in a wheelchair to comply with provisions as to the position in which the wheelchair is to be secured[7].

The driver of a regulated taxi which is plying for hire or has been hired commits an offence by failing to comply with a requirement of the regulations, or if the taxi fails to conform with any provision of the regulations with which it is required to conform[8].

1   At the date at which this volume states the law no day had been appointed for the Equality Act
    2010 s 160 to be brought into force.
2   As to the Secretary of State see PARA 4.
3   Equality Act 2010 s 160(1)(a)–(d) (not yet in force). At the date at which this volume states the law
    no such regulations had been made. 'Taxi' means a vehicle which is licensed under the Town Police
    Clauses Act 1847 s 37 (see ROAD TRAFFIC vol 90 (2011) PARA 1181) or the Metropolitan Public
    Carriage Act 1869 s 6 (see LONDON GOVERNMENT vol 71 (2013) PARA 233); and in the Equality Act

2010 ss 162, 165–167, also includes a taxi licensed under the Civic Government (Scotland) Act 1982 s 10, but does not include a vehicle drawn by a horse or other animal: Equality Act 2010 s 173(1).

4   'Regulated taxi' means a taxi to which taxi accessibility regulations are expressed to apply: Equality Act 2010 s 160(6) (not yet in force).
5   Equality Act 2010 s 160(2)(a)–(d) (not yet in force).
6   Equality Act 2010 s 160(3)(a) (not yet in force).
7   Equality Act 2010 s 160(3)(b) (not yet in force).
8   Equality Act 2010 s 160(4) (not yet in force). A person guilty of such an offence is liable on summary conviction to a fine not exceeding level 3 on the standard scale: s 160(5) (not yet in force). As to the powers of magistrates' courts to issue fines on summary conviction see SENTENCING vol 92 (2015) PARA 176.

216.   Exception in relation to the power to control numbers of licensed taxis.

Licensing authorities are permitted to control the number of taxis operating in their areas by refusing licences, if satisfied that there is no unmet demand for taxis in the area[1]. However, as from a day to be appointed, a licensing authority in England or Wales cannot refuse to license a wheelchair-accessible vehicle on the grounds of controlling taxi numbers, if the proportion of wheelchair-accessible vehicles operating in the area is smaller than the proportion prescribed in regulations by the Secretary of State[2].

1   See the Transport Act 1985 s 16; and ROAD TRAFFIC vol 90 (2011) PARA 1182. As to the meaning of 'taxi' see PARA 215 note 3.
2   If:
    (1)   an application for a licence in respect of a vehicle is made under the Town Police Clauses Act 1847 s 37 (see ROAD TRAFFIC vol 90 (2011) PARA 1181);
    (2)   it is possible for a disabled person:
          (a)   to get into and out of the vehicle in safety;
          (b)   to travel in the vehicle in safety and reasonable comfort; and
          (c)   to do the things mentioned in heads (a) and (b) while in a wheelchair of a size prescribed by the Secretary of State; and
    (3)   the proportion of taxis licensed in respect of the area to which the licence would (if granted) apply that conform to the requirement in head (2) is less than the proportion that is prescribed by the Secretary of State,
    then the Transport Act 1985 s 16 (which modifies the provisions of the Town Police Clauses Act 1847 about hackney carriages to allow a licence to ply for hire to be refused in order to limit the number of licensed carriages: see ROAD TRAFFIC vol 90 (2011) PARA 1182) does not apply in relation to the vehicle; and those provisions of the Town Police Clauses Act 1847 are to have effect subject to the Equality Act 2010 s 161: see s 161(1), (2) (in force only so far as it confers power to make regulations: see the Equality Act 2010 (Commencement No 4, Savings, Consequential, Transitional, Transitory and Incidental Provisions and Revocation) Order 2010, SI 2010/2317). At the date at which this volume states the law no such regulations had been made and no day had been appointed for the Equality Act 2010 s 161 to be brought into force for remaining purposes.

217.   Designated transport facilities.

Franchise agreements exist between operators of transport facilities[1] and operators of private hire cars, in order to provide services to members of the public so that they can travel from, for example, the mainline station to their destination. As from a day to be appointed, provisions will be brought into force requiring vehicles used under franchise agreements to ensure accessibility for disabled people as follows[2].

The Secretary of State[3] may by regulations provide for the application of any taxi provision[4] (with or without modification) to vehicles used for the provision of services under a franchise agreement, or drivers of such vehicles[5]. A franchise agreement is a contract entered into by the operator[6] of a designated[7] transport facility for the provision, by the other party to the contract, of hire car[8] services for members of the public using any part of the facility, and which involve vehicles entering any part of the facility[9].

1 'Transport facility' means premises which form part of a port, airport, railway station or bus station: Equality Act 2010 s 162(3) (not yet in force).
2 At the date at which this volume states the law no day had been appointed for the Equality Act 2010 s 162 to be brought into force.
3 See the Equality Act 2010 s 162(3), (4) (not yet in force). As to the Secretary of State see PARA 4.
4 In relation to England and Wales, 'taxi provision' means a provision of the Equality Act 2010 Pt 12 Ch 1 (ss 160–173) which applies in relation to taxis or drivers of taxis: see s 162(3) (not yet in force).
5 Equality Act 2010 s 162(1) (not yet in force).
6 'Operator', in relation to a transport facility, means a person who is concerned with the management or operation of the facility: Equality Act 2010 s 162(3) (not yet in force).
7 Ie designated by order made by the Secretary of State: see the Equality Act 2010 s 162(3) (not yet in force).
8 'Hire car' has such meaning as is prescribed by the Secretary of State: Equality Act 2010 s 162(3) (not yet in force).
9 Equality Act 2010 s 162(2) (not yet in force).

218. Taxi licence conditional on compliance with taxi accessibility regulations.

As from a day to be appointed the following provisions have effect[1].

A licence for a taxi[2] to ply for hire must not be granted unless the vehicle conforms with the provisions of taxi accessibility regulations[3] with which a vehicle is required to conform if it is licensed[4]. However, this does not apply if a licence is in force in relation to the vehicle at any time during the period of 28 days immediately before the day on which the licence is granted[5]. This is so that existing vehicles can continue to be used even if they do not meet the accessibility requirements, but provision is made so that this exception may be removed at some point[6].

1 At the date at which this volume states the law no day had been appointed for the Equality Act 2010 s 163 to be brought into force.
2 As to the meaning of 'taxi' see PARA 215 note 3.
3 As to the meaning of 'taxi accessibility regulations' see PARA 215.
4 Equality Act 2010 s 163(1) (not yet in force). A relevant licensing authority may apply for an order exempting it from the requirements of s 163: see PARA 219.
5 Equality Act 2010 s 163(2) (not yet in force).
6 The Secretary of State may by order provide for the Equality Act 2010 s 163(2) to cease to have effect on a specified date (s 163(3) (not yet in force)), and this power may be exercised differently for different areas or localities (s 163(4) (not yet in force)).

219. Exemption from taxi accessibility regulations.

As from a day to be appointed the following provisions have effect[1].

The Secretary of State may by regulations[2] provide for a relevant licensing authority[3] to apply for an exemption order exempting the authority from having to comply with the provision[4] which states that a licence for a taxi to ply for hire must not be granted unless the vehicle conforms with the provisions of taxi accessibility regulations with which a vehicle is required to conform if it is licensed[5].

Such regulations may, in particular, make provision requiring an authority proposing to apply for an exemption order:

(1)   to carry out such consultation as is specified;
(2)   to publish its proposals in the specified manner;
(3)   before applying for the order, to consider representations made about the proposal;

(4)   to make the application in the specified form[6].

An authority may apply for an exemption order only if it is satisfied:

(a)   that, having regard to the circumstances in its area, it is inappropriate for the relevant provision to apply[7]; and

(b)   that the application of that provision would result in an unacceptable reduction in the number of taxis in its area[8].

After consulting the Disabled Persons Transport Advisory Committee and such other persons as the Secretary of State thinks appropriate, the Secretary of State may:

(i)   make an exemption order in the terms of the application for the order;

(ii)   make an exemption order in such other terms as the Secretary of State thinks appropriate; or

(iii) refuse to make an exemption order[9].

The Secretary of State may by regulations make provision requiring a taxi plying for hire in an area in respect of which an exemption order is in force to conform with provisions of the regulations as to the fitting and use of swivel seats[10].

1   At the date at which this volume states the law no day had been appointed for the Equality Act 2010 s 164 to be brought into force.
2   At the date at which this volume states the law no such regulations had been made. As to the Secretary of State see PARA 4.
3   'Relevant licensing authority' means an authority responsible for licensing taxis in any area of England and Wales other than the area to which the Metropolitan Public Carriage Act 1869 (see LONDON GOVERNMENT vol 71 (2013) PARA 233) applies: Equality Act 2010 s 164(7) (not yet in force).
4   Ie the Equality Act 2010 s 163: see PARA 218.
5   Equality Act 2010 s 164(1) (not yet in force).
6   Equality Act 2010 s 164(2) (not yet in force). In s 164(2), 'specified' means specified in the regulations: s 164(2) (not yet in force).
7   Equality Act 2010 s 164(3)(a) (not yet in force). The relevant provision is the Equality Act 2010 s 163 (which states that a licence for a taxi to ply for hire must not be granted unless the vehicle conforms with the provisions of taxi accessibility regulations with which a vehicle is required to conform if it is licensed) (see PARA 218).
8   Equality Act 2010 s 164(3)(b) (not yet in force).
9   Equality Act 2010 s 164(4) (not yet in force).
10 Equality Act 2010 s 164(5) (not yet in force). 'Swivel seats' has such meaning as is specified in regulations under s 164(5): s 164(7) (not yet in force). Such regulations may make provision corresponding to s 163 (see PARA 218): s 164(6) (not yet in force).

220. Passengers in wheelchairs.

The Equality Act 2010[1] imposes duties on:

(1)   the driver of a designated taxi[2] which has been hired:

(a)   by or for a disabled person who is in a wheelchair[3]; or

(b)   by another person who wishes to be accompanied by a disabled person who is in a wheelchair[4];

(2)   the driver of a designated private hire vehicle[5], where a disabled person who is in a wheelchair, or another person who wishes to be accompanied by a disabled person who is in a wheelchair, has indicated to the driver that the person wishes to travel in the vehicle[6].

The duties are:

(i)   to carry the passenger[7] while in the wheelchair[8];

(ii)   not to make any additional charge for doing so[9];

(iii) if the passenger chooses to sit in a passenger seat, to carry the wheelchair[10];

(iv)   to take such steps as are necessary to ensure that the passenger is carried in safety and reasonable comfort[11];

(v)   to give the passenger such mobility assistance as is reasonably required[12].

However, the driver is not required, unless the vehicle is of a prescribed description[13], to carry more than one person in a wheelchair, or more than one wheelchair, on any one journey[14]. Nor is he required to carry a person in circumstances in which it would otherwise be lawful for the driver to refuse to carry the person[15].

A driver of a designated taxi or designated private hire vehicle commits an offence by failing to comply with a duty imposed on the driver by the provisions described above[16]. However, it is a defence for a person charged with the offence to show that at the time of the alleged offence the vehicle conformed to the accessibility requirements which applied to it, but it would not have been possible for the wheelchair to be carried safely in the vehicle[17].

A driver may apply for an exemption certificate which exempts him from the obligations imposed under these provisions[18]. A licensing authority[19] must issue a person with a certificate exempting the person from the duties imposed by the Equality Act 2010 in relation to carrying disabled persons in taxis and private hire vehicles[20] if satisfied that it is appropriate to do so on medical grounds; or on the ground that the person's physical condition makes it impossible or unreasonably difficult for the person to comply with those duties[21].

The driver of a designated taxi[22] or a designated private hire vehicle is exempt from those duties if an exemption certificate issued to the driver is in force[23], and the prescribed notice of the exemption is exhibited on the vehicle in the prescribed manner[24].

It is an offence to use an exemption certificate or a notice of exemption with intent to deceive[25].

1   Ie the Equality Act 2010 s 165 (see the text and notes 2–17).

2   For these purposes a taxi or private hire vehicle is 'designated' if it appears on a list maintained under the Equality Act 2010 s 167: s 165(3)(a). As to the meaning of 'taxi' see PARA 215 note 3. For the purposes of s 165, a licensing authority may maintain a list of vehicles which are either taxis or private hire vehicles, and which conform to such accessibility requirements as the licensing authority thinks fit: s 167(1), (2). A licensing authority may, if it thinks fit, decide that a vehicle may be included on the list only if it is being used, or is to be used, by the holder of a special licence under that licence: s 167(3). An appeal may be made against a decision to include a vehicle on a maintained list: see PARA 223. As to special licences see the Transport Act 1985 s 12 (use of taxis or hire cars in providing local services: see ROAD TRAFFIC vol 90 (2011) PARA 1218): Equality Act 2010 s 167(4). For the purposes of ss 166, 167, 'licensing authority', in relation to any area, means the authority responsible for licensing taxis or, as the case may be, private hire vehicles in that area: s 166(6). 'Accessibility requirements' are requirements for securing that it is possible for disabled persons in wheelchairs to get into and out of vehicles in safety; and to travel in vehicles in safety and reasonable comfort, either staying in their wheelchairs or not (depending on which they prefer): s 167(5). The Secretary of State may issue guidance to licensing authorities as to the accessibility requirements which they should apply for these purposes, and as to any other aspect of their functions under or by virtue of s 167: s 167(6). A licensing authority which maintains such a list must have regard to any such guidance: s 167(7). As to the Secretary of State see PARA 4.

3   Equality Act 2010 s 165(1)(a).

4   Equality Act 2010 s 165(1)(b).

5   For these purposes, 'private hire vehicle' means:

    (1)   a vehicle licensed under the Local Government (Miscellaneous Provisions) Act 1976 s 48 (Equality Act 2010 s 165(10)(a));

    (2)   a vehicle licensed under the Private Hire Vehicles (London) Act 1998 s 7 (Equality Act 2010 s 165(10)(b));

    (3)   a vehicle licensed under an equivalent provision of a local enactment (s 165(10)(c));

   (4) a private hire car licensed under the Civic Government (Scotland) Act 1982 s 10 (Equality Act 2010 s 165(10)(d)).

6 Equality Act 2010 s 165(2).
7 'The passenger' means the disabled person concerned: Equality Act 2010 s 165(3)(b).
8 Equality Act 2010 s 165(4)(a).
9 Equality Act 2010 s 165(4)(b).
10 Equality Act 2010 s 165(4)(c).
11 Equality Act 2010 s 165(4)(d).
12 Equality Act 2010 s 165(4)(e). Mobility assistance is assistance:
   (1) to enable the passenger to get into or out of the vehicle (s 165(5)(a));
   (2) if the passenger wishes to remain in the wheelchair, to enable the passenger to get into and out of the vehicle while in the wheelchair (s 165(5)(b));
   (3) to load the passenger's luggage into or out of the vehicle (s 165(5)(c));
   (4) if the passenger does not wish to remain in the wheelchair, to load the wheelchair into or out of the vehicle (s 165(5)(d)).
13 Ie prescribed by the Secretary of State. At the date at which this volume states the law no descriptions of vehicles had been prescribed for this purpose.
14 Equality Act 2010 s 165(6)(a).
15 Equality Act 2010 s 165(6)(b).
16 Equality Act 2010 s 165(7). A person guilty of such an offence is liable on summary conviction to a fine not exceeding level 3 on the standard scale: s 165(8). As to the powers of magistrates' courts to issue fines on summary conviction see SENTENCING vol 92 (2015) PARA 176.
17 Equality Act 2010 s 165(9).
18 See the Equality Act 2010 s 166; and the text and notes 19–24.
19 See note 2.
20 Ie the duties imposed by the Equality Act 2010 s 165 (see the text and notes 1–17).
21 Equality Act 2010 s 166(1). An appeal may be made against a refusal to issue an exemption certificate see PARA 223.
22 For these purposes, a taxi or private hire vehicle is 'designated' if it appears on a list maintained under the Equality Act 2010 s 167 (see note 2): s 166(5).
23 An exemption certificate is valid for such period as is specified in the certificate: Equality Act 2010 s 166(2).
24 Equality Act 2010 s 166(3), (4). The notice of exemption has been prescribed by the Equality Act 2010 (Taxis and Private hire Vehicles) (Passengers in Wheelchairs-Notices of Exemption) Regulations 2017, SI 2017/342, reg 1, Sch 1 (in relation to England), Sch 2 (in relation to Wales).
25 See PARA 235.

221. Assistance dogs in taxis.

The driver of a taxi[1] which has been hired:

 (1) by or for a disabled person who is accompanied by an assistance dog; or

 (2) by another person who wishes to be accompanied by a disabled person with an assistance dog[2],

must carry the disabled person's dog and allow it to remain with that person, and must not make any additional charge for doing so[3]. The driver of a taxi commits an offence by failing to comply with a duty imposed by these provisions[4].

However, a driver may apply for an exemption certificate which exempts him from these obligations. A licensing authority[5] must issue a person with a certificate exempting the person from these duties if satisfied that it is appropriate to do so on medical grounds[6]. In deciding whether to issue an exemption certificate the authority must have regard, in particular, to the physical characteristics of the taxi which the person drives or those of any kind of taxi in relation to which the person requires the certificate[7]. The driver of a taxi is exempt from those duties if an exemption certificate issued to the driver is in force[8] with respect to the taxi, and the prescribed notice of the exemption is exhibited on the taxi in the prescribed manner[9].

It is an offence to use an exemption certificate or a notice of exemption with intent to deceive[10].

1   As to the meaning of 'taxi' see PARA 215 note 3.
2   Equality Act 2010 s 168(1). 'Assistance dog' means:
    (1)   a dog which has been trained to guide a blind person;
    (2)   a dog which has been trained to assist a deaf person;
    (3)   a dog which has been trained by a prescribed charity to assist a disabled person who has a disability that consists of epilepsy or otherwise affects the person's mobility, manual dexterity, physical co-ordination or ability to lift, carry or otherwise move everyday objects;
    (4)   a dog of a prescribed category which has been trained to assist a disabled person who has a disability (other than one falling within head (3)) of a prescribed kind: s 173(1), (2).
   The prescribed charities for the purposes of the definition of 'assistance dog' in respect of taxis are set out in the Disability Discrimination Act 1995 (Taxis) (Carrying of Guide Dogs etc) (England and Wales) Regulations 2000, SI 2000/2990, reg 3 (substituted by SI 2010/2317). See also note 9.
3   Equality Act 2010 s 168(2).
4   Equality Act 2010 s 168(3). A person guilty of such an offence is liable on summary conviction to a fine not exceeding level 3 on the standard scale: s 168(4). As to the powers of magistrates' courts to issue fines on summary conviction see SENTENCING vol 92 (2015) PARA 176.
5   For these purposes, 'licensing authority' means:
    (1)   in relation to the area to which the Metropolitan Public Carriage Act 1869 applies, Transport for London (see LONDON GOVERNMENT vol 71 (2013) PARA 163 et seq);
    (2)   in relation to any other area in England and Wales, the authority responsible for licensing taxis in that area: Equality Act 2010 s 169(5).
6   Equality Act 2010 s 169(1). An appeal may be made against a refusal to issue an exemption certificate see PARA 223.
7   Equality Act 2010 s 169(2).
8   An exemption certificate is valid in respect of a specified taxi or a specified kind of taxi; for such period as is specified in the certificate: Equality Act 2010 s 169(3).
9   Equality Act 2010 s 169(4). As to exemption notices see the Disability Discrimination Act 1995 (Taxis) (Carrying of Guide Dogs etc) (England and Wales) Regulations 2000, SI 2000/2990, reg 2, Schs 1, 2 (amended by SI 2006/1616; SI 2010/2317). These regulations were made under the Disability Discrimination Act 1995, but now have effect as if made under the Equality Act 2010 s 169(4) following the repeal of the enabling provision: see the Equality Act 2010 (Commencement No 4, Savings, Consequential, Transitional, Transitory and Incidental Provisions and Revocation) Order 2010, SI 2010/2317, arts 21(1), 24, Sch 7, Sch 8 para 2.
10   See PARA 235.

222. Assistance dogs in private hire vehicles.

The operator[1] of a private hire vehicle[2] commits an offence by failing or refusing to accept a booking for the vehicle:

(1)   if the booking is requested by or on behalf of a disabled person or a person who wishes to be accompanied by a disabled person; and

(2)   the reason for the failure or refusal is that the disabled person will be accompanied by an assistance dog[3].

The operator commits an offence by making an additional charge for carrying an assistance dog which is accompanying a disabled person[4].

The driver[5] of a private hire vehicle commits an offence by failing or refusing to carry out a booking accepted by the operator:

(a)   if the booking is made by or on behalf of a disabled person or a person who wishes to be accompanied by a disabled person, and

(b)   the reason for the failure or refusal is that the disabled person is accompanied by an assistance dog[6].

A person guilty of an offence under these provisions is liable on summary conviction to a fine[7].

However, a driver may apply for an exemption certificate which exempts him from the offence[8]. A licensing authority must issue a driver with a certificate exempting the driver from the offence if satisfied that it is appropriate to do so on medical grounds[9]. In deciding whether to issue an exemption certificate the authority must have regard, in particular, to the physical characteristics of the private hire vehicle which the person drives or those of any kind of private hire vehicle in relation to which the person requires the certificate[10].

A driver does not commit an offence[11] if an exemption certificate issued to the driver is in force with respect to the private hire vehicle[12], and the prescribed notice of the exemption is exhibited on the vehicle in the prescribed manner[13].

It is an offence to use an exemption certificate or a notice of exemption with intent to deceive[14].

1 'Operator' means a person who holds a licence under the Private Hire Vehicles (London) Act 1998 s 3, the Local Government (Miscellaneous Provisions) Act 1976 s 55 or an equivalent provision of a local enactment: Equality Act 2010 s 170(5).
2 'Private hire vehicle' means a vehicle licensed under the Private Hire Vehicles (London) Act 1998 s 6, the Local Government (Miscellaneous Provisions) Act 1976 s 48 or an equivalent provision of a local enactment: Equality Act 2010 s 170(5). 'Licensing authority', in relation to any area in England and Wales, means the authority responsible for licensing private hire vehicles in that area: s 170(5).
3 Equality Act 2010 s 170(1). As to the meaning of 'assistance dog' see PARA 221 note 2. The prescribed charities for the purposes of the definition of 'assistance dog' in respect of private hire vehicles are set out in the Disability Discrimination Act 1995 (Private Hire Vehicles) (Carriage of Guide Dogs etc) (England and Wales) Regulations 2003, SI 2003/3122, reg 3 (substituted by SI 2010/2317). See also note 13.
4 Equality Act 2010 s 170(2).
5 'Driver' means a person who holds a licence under the Private Hire Vehicles (London) Act 1998 s 13 (see LONDON GOVERNMENT vol 71 (2013) PARA 234), the Local Government (Miscellaneous Provisions) Act 1976 s 51 (see ROAD TRAFFIC vol 90 (2011) PARA 1195), or an equivalent provision of a local enactment: Equality Act 2010 s 170(5).
6 Equality Act 2010 s 170(3).
7 Equality Act 2010 s 170(4). The fine referred to in the text is one not exceeding level 3 on the standard scale (see SENTENCING vol 92 (2015) PARA 176).
8 Ie an offence under the Equality Act 2010 s 170(3) (see the text to note 6).
9 Equality Act 2010 s 171(1), (5). An appeal may be made against a refusal to issue an exemption certificate see PARA 223.
10 Equality Act 2010 s 171(2), (5).
11 See note 8.
12 Equality Act 2010 s 171(4)(a), (5). An exemption certificate is valid in respect of a specified private hire vehicle or a specified kind of private hire vehicle for such period as is specified in the certificate: Equality Act 2010 s 171(3), (5).
13 Equality Act 2010 s 171(4)(b). As to notices of exemption see the Disability Discrimination Act 1995 (Private Hire Vehicles) (Carriage of Guide Dogs etc) (England and Wales) Regulations 2003, SI 2003/3122, reg 2 (amended by SI 2006/1617; SI 2010/2317). These regulations were made under the Disability Discrimination Act 1995, but now have effect as if made under the Equality Act 2010 s 171(4) following the repeal of the enabling provision: see the Equality Act 2010 (Commencement No 4, Savings, Consequential, Transitional, Transitory and Incidental Provisions and Revocation) Order 2010, SI 2010/2317, art 21(1), Sch 7.
14 See PARA 235.

223. Appeal against refusal to issue an exemption certificate or against decision to designate a vehicle.

A person who is aggrieved by the refusal of a licensing authority in England and Wales to issue an exemption certificate[1] may appeal to a magistrates' court before the end of the period of 28 days beginning with the date of the refusal[2]. On appeal, the magistrates' court may direct the licensing authority to issue the exemption certificate to have effect for such period as is specified in the direction[3].

A person who is aggrieved by the decision of a licensing authority to include a vehicle on a maintained list[4] may appeal to a magistrates' court before the end of the period of 28 days beginning with the date of the inclusion[5].

1   Ie under the Equality Act 2010 s 166 (see PARA 220), s 169 (see PARA 221) or s 171 (see PARA 222).
2   Equality Act 2010 s 172(1). As regards appeals against licensing authorities' decisions in Scotland see s 172(2).
3   Equality Act 2010 s 172(3).
4   Ie a list maintained under the Equality Act 2010 s 167 (see PARA 220 note 2).
5   Equality Act 2010 s 172(4).

(ii) Public Service Vehicles

224. PSV accessibility regulations.
The Secretary of State[1] may make regulations (known as 'PSV accessibility regulations') for securing that it is possible for disabled persons[2]:

(1)   to get on to and off regulated public service vehicles[3] in safety and without unreasonable difficulty (and, in the case of disabled persons in wheelchairs, to do so while remaining in their wheelchairs)[4]; and
(2)   to travel in such vehicles in safety and reasonable comfort[5].

The regulations may, in particular, make provision as to the construction, use and maintenance of regulated public service vehicles, including provision as to:

(a)   the fitting of equipment to vehicles;
(b)   equipment to be carried by vehicles;
(c)   the design of equipment to be fitted to, or carried by, vehicles;
(d)   the fitting and use of restraining devices designed to ensure the stability of wheelchairs while vehicles are moving;
(e)   the position in which wheelchairs are to be secured while vehicles are moving[6].

The regulations may make different provision as respects different classes or descriptions of vehicle and as respects the same class or description of vehicle in different circumstances[7].

A person commits an offence by:

(i)   contravening a provision of PSV accessibility regulations;
(ii)   using on a road a regulated public service vehicle which does not conform with a provision of the regulations with which it is required to conform;
(iii)   causing or permitting such a regulated public service vehicle to be used on a road[8].

If such an offence is committed by a body corporate and is committed with the consent or connivance of, or is attributable to neglect on the part of, a responsible person, the responsible person as well as the body corporate is guilty of the offence[9].

1   As to the Secretary of State see PARA 4.
2   As to the relationship between the PSV accessibility regulations and the duty to make reasonable adjustments see *First Group plc v Paulley* [2017] UKSC 4, [2017] 2 All ER 1, [2017] 1 WLR 423.
3   In the Equality Act 2010 s 174, 'public service vehicle' means a vehicle which is adapted to carry more than eight passengers; and is a public service vehicle for the purposes of the Public Passenger Vehicles Act 1981 (see ROAD TRAFFIC vol 90 (2011) PARA 896): Equality Act 2010 ss 174(3), 181. In Pt 12 Ch 2 (ss 174–181) 'regulated public service vehicle' means a public service vehicle to which PSV accessibility regulations are expressed to apply: s 174(3).
4   Equality Act 2010 ss 174(1)(a), 181.

5 Equality Act 2010 ss 174(1)(b), 181. The Secretary of State must not make regulations under s 174, s 176 or s 177 without consulting the Disabled Persons Transport Advisory Committee, and such other representative organisations as the Secretary of State thinks fit: s 174(5). The Public Service Vehicles Accessibility Regulations 2000, SI 2000/1970, which were made under the Disability Discrimination Act 1995, now have effect as if made under the Equality Act 2010 s 174(1), (2), (4) following the repeal of the enabling provision: see the Equality Act 2010 (Commencement No 4, Savings, Consequential, Transitional, Transitory and Incidental Provisions and Revocation) Order 2010, SI 2010/2317, arts 21(1), 24, Sch 7, Sch 8 para 1. As to the Disabled Persons Transport Advisory Committee see ROAD TRAFFIC vol 89 (2011) PARA 61.
6 Equality Act 2010 s 174(2). See note 5.
7 Equality Act 2010 s 174(4). See note 5.
8 Equality Act 2010 s 175(1). A person guilty of an offence under s 175 is liable on summary conviction to a fine not exceeding level 4 on the standard scale: s 175(2). As to the powers of magistrates' courts to issue fines on summary conviction see SENTENCING vol 92 (2015) PARA 176.
9 Equality Act 2010 s 175(3). A responsible person, in relation to a body corporate, is:
   (1)   a director, manager, secretary or similar officer (s 175(4)(a));
   (2)   a person purporting to act in the capacity of a person mentioned in head (1) (s 175(4)(b));
   (3)   in the case of a body corporate whose affairs are managed by its members, a member (s 175(4)(c)).
   If, in Scotland, an offence committed by a partnership or an unincorporated association is committed with the consent or connivance of, or is attributable to neglect on the part of, a partner or person concerned in the management of the association, the partner or person as well as the partnership or association is guilty of the offence: s 175(5).

225. Requirement for a public service vehicle accessibility certificate.

A regulated public service vehicle[1] must not be used on a road unless either a vehicle examiner has issued an accessibility certificate confirming that such provisions of PSV accessibility regulations[2] as are prescribed are satisfied in respect of the vehicle[3], or an approval certificate has been issued in respect of the vehicle[4].

Regulations may make provision:

(1)   with respect to applications for, and the issue of, accessibility certificates[5];

(2)   providing for the examination of vehicles in respect of which applications have been made[6];

(3)   with respect to the issue of copies of accessibility certificates which have been lost or destroyed[7].

The operator of a regulated public service vehicle commits an offence if the vehicle is used in contravention of the provisions described above[8]. It is also an offence to use an accessibility certificate with intent to deceive[9].

1 As to the meaning of 'regulated public service vehicle' see PARA 224 note 3.
2 As to the meaning of 'PSV accessibility regulations' see PARA 224.
3 Equality Act 2010 ss 176(1)(a), 181.
4 See the Equality Act 2010 ss 176(1)(b), 181. As to approval certificates see s 177; and PARA 226. As to fees payable see PARA 229.
5 Equality Act 2010 s 176(2)(a).
6 Equality Act 2010 s 176(2)(b).
7 Equality Act 2010 s 176(2)(c). This power to make regulations is exercisable by the Secretary of State: s 176(5). As to the Secretary of State see PARA 4. The Public Service Vehicles Accessibility Regulations 2000, SI 2000/1970, which were made under the Disability Discrimination Act 1995, now have effect as if made under the Equality Act 2010 s 176(2) following the repeal of the enabling provision: see the Equality Act 2010 (Commencement No 4, Savings, Consequential, Transitional, Transitory and Incidental Provisions and Revocation) Order 2010, SI 2010/2317, art 21(1), Sch 7. As to the provision that has been made in respect of accessibility certificates see the Public Service Vehicles Accessibility Regulations 2000, SI 2000/1970, regs 6–8, Sch 4.
8 Equality Act 2010 s 176(3). For the purposes of s 176, 'operator' has the same meaning as in the Public Passenger Vehicles Act 1981 (see ROAD TRAFFIC vol 90 (2011) PARA 896): Equality Act 2010

s 176(6). A person guilty of such an offence is liable on summary conviction to a fine not exceeding level 4 on the standard scale: s 176(4). As to the powers of magistrates' courts to issue fines on summary conviction see SENTENCING vol 92 (2015) PARA 176.
9   See PARA 235.

226. Requirement for public service vehicle approval certificate.
A regulated public service vehicle[1] must not be used on a road unless either a vehicle examiner has issued an accessibility certificate confirming that such provisions of PSV accessibility regulations[2] as are prescribed are satisfied in respect of the vehicle[3], or an approval certificate has been issued in respect of the vehicle[4].

The Secretary of State[5] may approve a vehicle for these purposes[6] if satisfied that prescribed provisions of PSV accessibility regulations[7] are satisfied in respect of the vehicle[8]. A vehicle which is so approved is referred to as a 'type vehicle'[9]. If a declaration in the prescribed form is made by an authorised person that a particular vehicle conforms in design, construction and equipment with a type vehicle[10], then a vehicle examiner may issue an approval certificate to confirm that it conforms to the type vehicle[11].

Regulations may make provision:
(1)   with respect to applications for, and grants of, approval;
(2)   with respect to applications for, and the issue of, approval certificates;
(3)   providing for the examination of vehicles in respect of which applications have been made;
(4)   with respect to the issue of copies of approval certificates in place of certificates which have been lost or destroyed[12].

The Secretary of State may at any time withdraw approval of a type vehicle[13]. If an approval is withdrawn no further approval certificates are to be issued by reference to the type vehicle[14], but an approval certificate issued by reference to the type vehicle before the withdrawal continues[15] to have effect[16].

It is an offence to use an approval certificate with intent to deceive[17].

1   As to the meaning of 'regulated public service vehicle' see PARA 224 note 3.
2   As to the meaning of 'PSV accessibility regulations' see PARA 224.
3   Equality Act 2010 s 176(1)(a). As to accessibility certificates see the Equality Act 2010 s 176; and PARA 225.
4   Equality Act 2010 s 176(1)(b).
5   Ie for the purposes of the Equality Act 2010 s 177 (see the text and notes 6–16).
6   As to the Secretary of State see PARA 4.
7   Ie such provisions of PSV accessibility regulations as are prescribed for the purposes of the Equality Act 2010 s 176 (see PARA 225).
8   Equality Act 2010 s 177(1). As to fees payable see PARA 229.
9   Equality Act 2010 s 177(2).
10 Equality Act 2010 s 177(3). 'Authorised person' means a person authorised by the Secretary of State for the purposes of s 177(3): s 177(9).
11 See the Equality Act 2010 s 177(4). As to fees payable see PARA 229.
12 Equality Act 2010 s 177(5). The power to make regulations under s 177 is exercisable by the Secretary of State: s 177(8). The Public Service Vehicles Accessibility Regulations 2000, SI 2000/1970, which were made under the Disability Discrimination Act 1995, now have effect as if made under the Equality Act 2010 s 177(3), (4), (5) following the repeal of the enabling provision: see the Equality Act 2010 (Commencement No 4, Savings, Consequential, Transitional, Transitory and Incidental Provisions and Revocation) Order 2010, SI 2010/2317, art 21(1), Sch 7. As to the provision that has been made in respect of accessibility certificates see the Public Service Vehicles Accessibility Regulations 2000, SI 2000/1970, regs 9–18, Schs 5, 6.
13 Equality Act 2010 s 177(6).
14 Equality Act 2010 s 177(7)(a).
15 Ie for the purposes of the Equality Act 2010 s 176 (see PARA 225).

16 Equality Act 2010 s 177(7)(b).
17 See PARA 235.

227. Special authorisations regarding public service vehicles.

The Secretary of State[1] may by order authorise the use on roads of:

(1) a regulated public service vehicle of a class or description specified by the order; or

(2) a regulated public service vehicle which is so specified[2].

Where such an order is made, nothing in the provisions of the Equality Act 2010 concerning public vehicle accessibility[3] prevents the use of a vehicle in accordance with the order[4].

The Secretary of State may also by order make provision for securing that provisions of PSV accessibility regulations apply to regulated public service vehicles of a specified description subject to any specified modifications or exceptions[5].

1 As to the Secretary of State see PARA 4.
2 Equality Act 2010 s 178(1). Section 207(2) (see PARA 4) does not require an order under s 178 that applies only to a specified vehicle, or to vehicles of a specified person, to be made by statutory instrument; but such an order is as capable of being amended or revoked as an order made by statutory instrument: s 178(5). Such an order may make the authorisation subject to such restrictions and conditions as are specified by or under the order: s 178(4). At the date at which this volume states the law no such order had been made.
3 Ie the Equality Act 2010 ss 174–177 (see PARAS 224–226).
4 Equality Act 2010 s 178(2).
5 Equality Act 2010 s 178(3). Such an order may make provision subject to such restrictions and conditions as are specified by or under the order: s 178(4).

228. Reviews and appeals.

If the Secretary of State refuses an application for the approval of a vehicle[1] and, before the end of the prescribed period, the applicant asks the Secretary of State to review the decision, and pays any required fee[2], then the Secretary of State must review the decision, and in doing so, must consider any representations made in writing by the applicant before the end of the prescribed period[3].

A person applying for an accessibility certificate or an approval certificate may appeal to the Secretary of State against the refusal of a vehicle examiner to issue the certificate[4].

An appeal must be made within the prescribed time and in the prescribed manner[5], and regulations may make provision as to the procedure to be followed in connection with appeals[6].

On the determination of an appeal, the Secretary of State may confirm, vary or reverse the decision appealed against[7]. He may also give directions to the vehicle examiner for giving effect to the Secretary of State's decision[8].

1 Ie under the Equality Act 2010 s 177(1): see PARA 226. As to the Secretary of State see PARA 4.
2 Equality Act 2010 s 179(1). The reference to a fee is to one fixed under s 180: see PARA 229.
3 Equality Act 2010 s 179(2). See note 6.
4 Equality Act 2010 s 179(3).
5 Equality Act 2010 s 179(4). See note 6.
6 Equality Act 2010 s 179(5). A power to make regulations under s 179 is exercisable by the Secretary of State: s 179(7). The Public Service Vehicles Accessibility Regulations 2000, SI 2000/1970, which were made under the Disability Discrimination Act 1995, now have effect as if made under the Equality Act 2010 s 179(1), (2) following the repeal of the enabling provision: see the Equality Act 2010 (Commencement No 4, Savings, Consequential, Transitional, Transitory and Incidental Provisions and Revocation) Order 2010, SI 2010/2317, art 21(1), Sch 7. As to the provision that has been made in respect of reviews and appeals see the Public Service Vehicles Accessibility Regulations 2000, SI 2000/1970, reg 19.

7 Equality Act 2010 s 179(6)(a).
8 Equality Act 2010 s 179(6)(b).

229. Fees.

The Secretary of State[1] may charge such fees[2], payable at such times, as are prescribed in respect of:
(1) applications for, and grants of, approval[3];
(2) applications for, and the issue of, accessibility certificates and approval certificates[4];
(3) copies of such certificates[5];
(4) reviews and appeals[6].

This power to make regulations is exercisable by the Secretary of State[7], who must, before making them, consult such representative organisations as he thinks fit[8].

The regulations may make provision for the repayment of fees, in whole or in part, in such circumstances as are prescribed[9].

1 As to the Secretary of State see PARA 4.
2 Fees received by the Secretary of State must be paid into the Consolidated Fund: Equality Act 2010 s 180(2). As to the Consolidated Fund see CONSTITUTIONAL AND ADMINISTRATIVE LAW vol 20 (2014) PARA 480.
3 Equality Act 2010 s 180(1)(a). As to grants of approval under s 177(1) see PARA 226.
4 Equality Act 2010 s 180(1)(b). As to accessibility certificates see PARA 225. As to approval certificates see PARA 226.
5 Equality Act 2010 s 180(1)(c).
6 Equality Act 2010 s 180(1)(d). As to reviews and appeals under s 179 see PARA 228.
7 Equality Act 2010 s 180(3). The Public Service Vehicles Accessibility Regulations 2000, SI 2000/1970, which were made under the Disability Discrimination Act 1995, now have effect as if made under the Equality Act 2010 s 180(1) following the repeal of the enabling provision: see the Equality Act 2010 (Commencement No 4, Savings, Consequential, Transitional, Transitory and Incidental Provisions and Revocation) Order 2010, SI 2010/2317, art 21(1), Sch 7. As to the provision that has been made in respect of fees see the Public Service Vehicles Accessibility Regulations 2000, SI 2000/1970, regs 7, 12, 17, 18 (all amended by SI 2009/876).
8 Equality Act 2010 s 180(5).
9 Equality Act 2010 s 180(4). See note 7.

230. Bus passenger information regulations.

As from a day to be appointed the following provisions have effect[1].

The Secretary of State[2] may, for the purpose of facilitating travel by disabled persons, make regulations requiring operators[3] of local services[4] to make available information about a local service to persons travelling on the service[5]. The regulations may make provision about the descriptions of information that are to be made available; and how information is to be made available[6]. The regulations may, in particular:
(1) require an operator of a local service to make available information of a prescribed description about:
(a) the name or other designation of the local service;
(b) the direction of travel;
(c) stopping places[7];
(d) diversions;
(e) connecting local services[8];
(2) specify:
(a) when information of a prescribed description is to be made available[9];

    (b)   how information of a prescribed description is to be made available, including requiring information to be both announced and displayed[10];

    (c)   standards for the provision of information, including standards based on an announcement being audible or a display being visible to a person of a prescribed description in a prescribed location[11];

    (d)   forms of communication that are not to be regarded as satisfying a requirement to make information available[12].

Regulations under these provisions may make different provision as respects different descriptions of vehicle and as respects the same description of vehicle in different circumstances[13].

1   At the date at which this volume states the law no day had been appointed for the Equality Act 2010 ss 181A, 181D to be brought into force.

2   As to the Secretary of State see PARA 4.

3   For these purposes, references to the operator of a passenger transport service of any description are to be construed in accordance with the Transport Act 1985 s 137(7) (see ROAD TRAFFIC vol 90 (2011) PARA 896): Equality Act 2010 s 181D(3) (ss 181A, 181D added by the Bus Services Act 2017 s 17(1)) (not yet in force).

4   'Local service' has the same meaning as in the Transport Act 1985 (see ROAD TRAFFIC vol 90 (2011) PARA 937): Equality Act 2010 s 181D(1) (as added: see note 3) (not yet in force).

5   Equality Act 2010 s 181A(1) (as added: see note 3) (not yet in force). Before making regulations under s 181A, the Secretary of State must consult the Welsh Ministers and the Scottish Ministers: s 181A(6) (as so added) (not yet in force). At the date at which this volume states the law no such regulations had been made. As to the Welsh Ministers see PARA 4. As to the Scottish Ministers see CONSTITUTIONAL AND ADMINISTRATIVE LAW vol 20 (2014) PARA 67.

6   Equality Act 2010 s 181A(2) (as added: see note 3) (not yet in force).

7   'Stopping place' has the same meaning as in the Transport Act 1985 (see ROAD TRAFFIC vol 90 (2011) PARA 938): Equality Act 2010 s 181D(1) (as added: see note 3) (not yet in force).

8   Equality Act 2010 s 181A(3) (as added: see note 3) (not yet in force). For these purposes, a local service ('service A') is a connecting local service in relation to another local service ('service B') if service A has a stopping place at, or in the vicinity of, a stopping place of service B: s 181D(2) (as so added) (not yet in force).

9   Equality Act 2010 s 181A(4)(a) (as added: see note 3) (not yet in force).

10 Equality Act 2010 s 181A(4)(b) (as added: see note 3) (not yet in force).

11 Equality Act 2010 s 181A(4)(c) (as added: see note 3) (not yet in force).

12 Equality Act 2010 s 181A(4)(d) (as added: see note 3) (not yet in force).

13 Equality Act 2010 s 181A(5) (as added: see note 3) (not yet in force).

231. Exemption from bus passenger information regulations.

As from a day to be appointed the following provisions have effect[1].

The Secretary of State[2] may by regulations make provision for securing that the provisions of bus passenger information regulations[3] do not apply or apply subject to such modifications or exceptions as the regulations may specify to:

    (1)   public service vehicles[4] of a prescribed description;

    (2)   operators[5] of a prescribed description;

    (3)   local services[6] of a prescribed description[7].

Such regulations may make different provision for different areas[8] and regulations under head (2) may, in particular, make provision by reference to an operator's size[9].

Regulations may also make provision for securing that the provisions of regulations on information for bus passengers do not apply or apply subject to such modifications or exceptions as the regulations may specify to:

    (a)   a prescribed public service vehicle;

    (b)   public service vehicles of a prescribed operator;

(c)   a prescribed local service[10].

Regulations under heads (1) to (3) or heads (a) to (c) may:

(i)   make the provision subject to such restrictions and conditions as are specified in the regulations[11];

(ii)   specify the period for which provisions of those regulations are to have effect[12].

1   At the date at which this volume states the law no day had been appointed for the Equality Act 2010 ss 181B, 181D to be brought into force.

2   As to the Secretary of State see PARA **4**.

3   Ie under the Equality Act 2010 s 181A (see PARA **230**).

4   'Public service vehicle' means a vehicle that is a public service vehicle for the purposes of the Public Passenger Vehicles Act 1981 (see ROAD TRAFFIC vol 90 (2011) PARA 896): Equality Act 2010 s 181D(1) (s 181D added by the Bus Services Act 2017 s 17(1)) (not yet in force).

5   As to the meaning of 'operator' see PARA **230** note 3.

6   As to the meaning of 'local service' see PARA **230** note 4.

7   Equality Act 2010 s 181B(1) (s 181B added by the Bus Services Act 2017 s 17(1)) (not yet in force). Before making regulations under the Equality Act 2010 s 181B, the Secretary of State must consult the Welsh Ministers and the Scottish Ministers: s 181B(8) (as so added) (not yet in force). At the date at which this volume states the law no such regulations had been made. The provisions of s 207(2) (see PARA **4**) do not require regulations under s 181B that apply only to a prescribed public service vehicle, public service vehicles of a prescribed operator, or a prescribed local service, to be made by statutory instrument; but such regulations are as capable of being amended or revoked as regulations made by statutory instrument: s 181B(7) (as so added) (not yet in force). As to the Welsh Ministers see PARA **4**. As to the Scottish Ministers see CONSTITUTIONAL AND ADMINISTRATIVE LAW vol 20 (2014) PARA 67.

8   Equality Act 2010 s 181B(6) (as added: see note 7) (not yet in force).

9   Equality Act 2010 s 181B(2) (as added: see note 7) (not yet in force).

10 Equality Act 2010 s 181B(3) (as added: see note 7) (not yet in force).

11 Equality Act 2010 s 181B(4) (as added: see note 7) (not yet in force).

12 Equality Act 2010 s 181B(5) (as added: see note 7) (not yet in force).

232.   Guidance on duties imposed by bus passenger information regulations.

As from a day to be appointed the following provisions have effect[1].

The Secretary of State[2] must issue guidance about the duties imposed on operators of local services[3] by bus passenger information regulations[4].

The Secretary of State must review the guidance so issued, at intervals not exceeding five years; and may revise it[5].

Before issuing the guidance or revising it in a way which would, in the opinion of the Secretary of State, result in a substantial change to it, the Secretary of State must consult:

(1)   the Welsh Ministers[6];

(2)   the Scottish Ministers[7];

(3)   the Passengers' Council[8];

(4)   such organisations representing disabled persons as the Secretary of State thinks fit[9];

(5)   such organisations representing operators of local services as the Secretary of State thinks fit[10]; and

(6)   such other persons as the Secretary of State thinks fit[11].

The Secretary of State must arrange for any guidance issued or revised under these provisions to be published in a way the Secretary of State considers appropriate[12].

1   At the date at which this volume states the law no day had been appointed for the Equality Act 2010 s 181C to be brought into force.

2   As to the Secretary of State see PARA **4**.

3   As to the meaning of 'operator' see PARA **230** note 3; and as to the meaning of 'local service' see PARA **230** note 4.

4 Equality Act 2010 s 181C(1) (s 181C added by the Bus Services Act 2017 s 17(1)) (not yet in force). The reference in the text to bus passenger information regulations is to those under the Equality Act 2010 s 181A (see PARA 230).
5 Equality Act 2010 s 181C(2) (as added: see note 4) (not yet in force).
6 Equality Act 2010 s 181C(3)(a) (as added: see note 4) (not yet in force). As to the Welsh Ministers see PARA 4.
7 Equality Act 2010 s 181C(3)(b) (as added: see note 4) (not yet in force). As to the Scottish Ministers see CONSTITUTIONAL AND ADMINISTRATIVE LAW vol 20 (2014) PARA 67.
8 Equality Act 2010 s 181C(3)(c) (as added: see note 4) (not yet in force). As to the Passengers' Council (renamed Transport Focus) see RAILWAYS AND TRAMWAYS vol 86 (2017) PARAS 5, 50.
9 Equality Act 2010 s 181C(3)(d) (as added: see note 4) (not yet in force). Such organisations as the Secretary of State must consult include the Disabled Persons Transport Advisory Committee (see ROAD TRAFFIC vol 89 (2011) PARA 61) and the committee established under the Transport (Scotland) Act 2001 s 72: see Equality Act 2010 s 181C(3)(d) (as so added) (not yet in force).
10 Equality Act 2010 s 181C(3)(e) (as added: see note 4) (not yet in force).
11 Equality Act 2010 s 181C(3)(f) (as added: see note 4) (not yet in force).
12 Equality Act 2010 s 181C(4) (as added: see note 4) (not yet in force).

(iii) Rail Vehicles

233. Rail vehicle accessibility regulations.
The Secretary of State[1] may make regulations (known as 'rail vehicle accessibility regulations') for securing that it is possible for disabled persons:
(1) to get on to and off regulated rail vehicles[2] in safety and without unreasonable difficulty;
(2) to do so while in wheelchairs;
(3) to travel in such vehicles in safety and reasonable comfort;
(4) to do so while in wheelchairs[3].

The regulations may, in particular, make provision as to the construction, use and maintenance of regulated rail vehicles including provision as to:
(a) the fitting of equipment to vehicles;
(b) equipment to be carried by vehicles;
(c) the design of equipment to be fitted to, or carried by, vehicles;
(d) the use of equipment fitted to, or carried by, vehicles;
(e) the toilet facilities to be provided in vehicles;
(f) the location and floor area of the wheelchair accommodation to be provided in vehicles;
(g) assistance to be given to disabled persons[4].

The regulations may contain different provision as respects different classes or descriptions of rail vehicle, as respects the same class or description of rail vehicle in different circumstances, and as respects different networks[5].

The Secretary of State must exercise the power to make rail vehicle accessibility regulations so as to secure that on and after 1 January 2020 every rail vehicle is a regulated rail vehicle[6].

1 As to the Secretary of State see PARA 4.
2 'Regulated rail vehicle' means a rail vehicle to which provisions of rail vehicle accessibility regulations are expressed to apply: Equality Act 2010 ss 182(4), 187(1). 'Rail vehicle' means a vehicle constructed or adapted to carry passengers on a railway, tramway or prescribed system other than a vehicle used in the provision of a service for the carriage of passengers on the trans-European rail system located in Great Britain: ss 182(4), 187(1) (definition amended by SI 2011/3066). As to the meaning of 'trans-European rail system' see the Railways (Interoperability) Regulations 2011, SI 2011/3066, reg 2(1): Equality Act 2010 s 182(5) (definition added by SI 2011/3066). A vehicle is used 'for carriage' if it is used for the carriage of passengers: Equality Act 2010 s 187(2). 'Prescribed system' means a system using a mode of guided transport ('guided transport' having the same meaning as in the Transport and Works Act 1992: see RAILWAYS

AND TRAMWAYS vol 86 (2017) PARA 310) that is specified in rail vehicle accessibility regulations: Equality Act 2010 s 182(5). 'Railway' and 'tramway' have the same meaning as in the Transport and Works Act 1992 (see RAILWAYS AND TRAMWAYS vol 86 (2017) PARA 310): Equality Act 2010 s 182(5). See further the Railways (Interoperability) Regulations 2011, SI 2011/3066; and RAILWAYS AND TRAMWAYS vol 86 (2017) PARA 211 et seq. As to the meaning of 'Great Britain' see PARA 85 note 1.

3   Equality Act 2010 ss 182(1), 187(1). Before making such regulations the Secretary of State must consult the Disabled Persons Transport Advisory Committee, and such other representative organisations as the Secretary of State thinks fit: s 182(8). As to the Disabled Persons Transport Advisory Committee see ROAD TRAFFIC vol 89 (2011) PARA 61.

    The Rail Vehicle Accessibility (Non-Interoperable Rail System) Regulations 2010, SI 2010/432, which were made under the Disability Discrimination Act 1995, now have effect as if made under the Equality Act 2010 s 182 following the repeal of the enabling provision: see the Equality Act 2010 (Commencement No 4, Savings, Consequential, Transitional, Transitory and Incidental Provisions and Revocation) Order 2010, SI 2010/2317, art 21(1), Sch 7. The Rail Vehicle Accessibility (Non-Interoperable Rail System) Regulations 2010, SI 2010/432, set accessibility standards (ie standards designed to improve accessibility for disabled persons) which operators of applicable rail vehicles must comply with if such vehicles are to be used for the carriage of passengers: see regs 3–5, Schs 1–4 (reg 3 amended by SI 2015/1682). See also RAILWAYS AND TRAMWAYS vol 86 (2017) PARA 40.

4   Equality Act 2010 s 182(2).
5   Equality Act 2010 s 182(3). 'Network' means any permanent way or other means of guiding or supporting rail vehicles, or any section of it: s 182(4).
6   Equality Act 2010 s 182(6). However, s 182(6) does not affect s 182(3) (see the text and note 5), s 183(1) (see PARA **234**) or s 207(4)(a): see s 182(7).

234. Exemptions from rail vehicle accessibility regulations.

The Secretary of State[1] may make an exemption order[2] which:

(1)   authorises the use for carriage[3] of a regulated rail vehicle[4] even though the vehicle does not conform with the provisions of rail vehicle accessibility regulations[5] with which it is required to conform[6];

(2)   authorises a regulated rail vehicle to be used for carriage otherwise than in conformity with the provisions of rail vehicle accessibility regulations with which use of the vehicle is required to conform[7].

The Secretary of State may make an exemption order in the terms of the application for the order, or make an exemption order in such other terms as he thinks appropriate, or he may refuse to make an exemption order[8]. He may make an exemption order subject to such conditions and restrictions as are specified in the order[9].

After the end of each calendar year the Secretary of State must prepare and lay before Parliament a report on the exercise in that year of the power to make exemption orders[10].

1   As to the Secretary of State see PARA 4.
2   Numerous exemption orders which were made by the Secretary of State in respect of particular railways under the Disability Discrimination Act 1995 s 47 now have effect as if made under the Equality Act 2010 s 183 following the repeal of the enabling provision. See the Rail Vehicle Accessibility (East Hayling Light Railway Vehicles) Exemption Order 2002, SI 2002/285; the Rail Vehicle Accessibility (Cairngorm Funicular Railway) Exemption Order 2002, SI 2002/657 (amended by SI 2011/2705); the Rail Vehicle Accessibility (Middleton Railway Drewry Car) Exemption Order 2002, SI 2002/1188 (amended by SI 2011/2705); the Rail Vehicle Accessibility (Isle of Wight Railway LCDR No 2515 Vehicle) Exemption Order 2002, SI 2002/1694. These orders were made under the Disability Discrimination Act 1995 s 47 (repealed) but continue in force by virtue of the Equality Act 2010 (Commencement No 4, Savings, Consequential, Transitional, Transitory and Incidental Provisions and Revocation) Order 2010, SI 2010/2317, art 21(1), Sch 7.

    The Secretary of State has exercised the power in the Equality Act 2010 s 183 to make new exemption orders: see the Rail Vehicle Accessibility (Non-Interoperable Rail System) (London Underground Metropolitan Line S8 Vehicles) Exemption Order 2011, SI 2011/70; the Rail Vehicle

Accessibility (Middleton Railway Drewry Car) and (Cairngorm Funicular Railway) Exemption Order 2011, SI 2011/2705; the Rail Vehicle Accessibility (Non-Interoperable Rail System) (London Underground Circle, District and Hammersmith & City Lines S7 Vehicles) Exemption Order 2012, SI 2012/105 (partially expired in December 2017); and the Rail Vehicle Accessibility (B2007 Vehicles) Exemption Order 2015, SI 2015/1631.

3   As to the meaning of 'for carriage' in this context see PARA 233 note 2.
4   As to the meaning of 'regulated rail vehicle' see PARA 233 note 2.
5   As to the meaning of 'rail vehicle accessibility regulations' see PARA 233.
6   Equality Act 2010 s 183(1)(a). The authority under s 183(1)(a) or s 183(1)(b) may be for:
    (1)   a regulated rail vehicle that is specified or of a specified description (s 183(2)(a));
    (2)   use in specified circumstances of a regulated rail vehicle (s 183(2)(b)); or
    (3)   use in specified circumstances of a regulated rail vehicle that is specified or of a specified description (s 183(2)(c)).
    'Specified' means as specified in an exemption order: s 183(6).
7   Equality Act 2010 s 183(1)(b). See note 6.
8   Equality Act 2010 s 183(4). Before making an order, the Secretary of State must consult the Disabled Persons Transport Advisory Committee and such other persons as he thinks appropriate: s 183(4). The provisions of s 207(2) (orders, regulations to be made by statutory instrument: see PARA 4) do not require an exemption order to be made by statutory instrument; but such an order is as capable of being amended or revoked as an order made by statutory instrument: s 183(7) (added by the Deregulation Act 2015 Sch 10 paras 28, 29(1), (3)). The Rail Vehicle Accessibility (Applications for Exemption Orders) Regulations 2010, SI 2010/427, which were made under the Disability Discrimination Act 1995, have effect as if made under the Equality Act 2010 s 183(3)(repealed) following the repeal of the enabling provision (see the Equality Act 2010 (Commencement No 4, Savings, Consequential, Transitional, Transitory and Incidental Provisions and Revocation) Order 2010, SI 2010/2317, art 21(1), Sch 7). As to the Disabled Persons Transport Advisory Committee see ROAD TRAFFIC vol 89 (2011) PARA 61.
9   Equality Act 2010 s 183(5).
10 See the Equality Act 2010 s 185 (amended by the Deregulation Act 2015 Sch 10 paras 28, 30).

(iv) Using Documents with Intent to Deceive

235. Offence of using documents with intent to deceive.

Exemption certificates[1], accessibility certificates[2], approval certificates[3] and certain notices[4] issued under the Equality Act 2010 (together referred to as 'relevant documents') must not be used with intent to deceive[5].

A person commits an offence if, with intent to deceive, he:

(1)   forges, alters or uses a relevant document;
(2)   lends a relevant document to another person;
(3)   allows a relevant document to be used by another person;
(4)   makes or has possession of a document which closely resembles a relevant document[6].

Knowingly making a false statement for the purpose of obtaining an accessibility certificate or an approval certificate is also an offence[7].

1   Ie an exemption certificate issued under the Equality Act 2010 s 166 (see PARA 220), s 169 (see PARA 221) or s 171 (see PARA 222).
2   Ie an accessibility certificate issued under the Equality Act 2010 s 176 (see PARA 225).
3   Ie an approval certificate issued under the Equality Act 2010 s 177 (see PARA 226).
4   Ie a notice of a kind mentioned in the Equality Act 2010 s 166(3)(b) (see PARA 220), s 169(4)(b) (see PARA 221) or s 171(4)(b) (see PARA 222).
5   See the Equality Act 2010 s 188(1).
6   Equality Act 2010 s 188(2). A person guilty of such an offence is liable on summary conviction, to a fine not exceeding the statutory maximum; and liable on conviction on indictment, to imprisonment for a term not exceeding 2 years or to a fine or to both: s 188(3). As to the powers of magistrates' courts to issue fines on summary conviction see SENTENCING vol 92 (2015) PARA 176.

7   Equality Act 2010 s 188(4). A person guilty of such an offence is liable on summary conviction to
    a fine not exceeding level 4 on the standard scale: s 188(5). As to the powers of magistrates' courts
    to issue fines on summary conviction see SENTENCING vol 92 (2015) PARA 176.

(v) Suitability of Rail Replacement Road Services

236. Substituted services to be suitable for disabled passengers.
Where a person who provides services for the carriage of passengers by
railway[1] provides or secures the provision of substitute road services[2], or the
provision of such services is secured by the Secretary of State or the National
Assembly for Wales[3], then provision is made by the Transport Act 2000 to ensure
that such substitute road services are suitable for disabled passengers[4].

In providing or securing the provision of the services, the person providing
them, the Secretary of State or the National Assembly for Wales must ensure, so
far as is reasonably practicable, that the substitute road services allow disabled
passengers to undertake their journeys safely and in reasonable comfort[5]. In the
event of any failure by a person to comply with this duty[6], he is liable to pay
damages in respect of any expenditure reasonably incurred, or other loss
sustained, by a disabled passenger in consequence of the failure[7].

However, the Secretary of State may by order grant exemption from the duty[8]
to any class or description of persons who provide services for the carriage of
passengers by railway, or to any particular person who provides such services, in
respect of all substitute road services or any class or description of such services[9].

1   As to railways see generally RAILWAYS AND TRAMWAYS vol 86 (2017) PARA 1 et seq.
2   'Substitute road services' means services for the carriage of passengers by road which are provided
    where railway services have been temporarily interrupted or discontinued: Transport Act 2000 s
    248(7).
3   As to the Secretary of State and the National Assembly for Wales see PARA 4.
4   Transport Act 2000 s 248(1) (amended by the Railways Act 2005 s 59(1), Sch 12 para 17(1), (4)).
    For these purposes, a passenger is disabled if he has a disability, or has suffered an injury, which
    seriously impairs his ability to walk: Transport Act 2000 s 248(8).
5   Transport Act 2000 s 248(2) (amended by the Railways Act 2005 Sch 12 para 17(1), (5)).
6   Ie the duty under the Transport Act 2000 s 248(2) (see the text and note 5).
7   Transport Act 2000 s 248(3) (amended by the Railways Act 2005 s 59(6), Sch 12 para 17(1), (6),
    Sch 13 Pt 1).
8   See note 6.
9   Transport Act 2000 s 248(4). Before making such an order the Secretary of State must consult the
    Disabled Persons Transport Advisory Committee, and such other representative organisations as
    he thinks fit: s 248(5). As to the Disabled Persons Transport Advisory Committee see ROAD TRAFFIC
    vol 89 (2011) PARA 61.
        In exercise of this power, the Secretary of State has made the Railways (Substitute Road
    Services) (Exemptions) Order 2006, SI 2006/1935, which grants exemption to certain operators
    from the Transport Act 2000 s 248(2) in respect of all substitute road services other than those
    provided in relation to the railway passenger services specified in the Schedule.

(3) DUTY TO MAKE REASONABLE ADJUSTMENTS FOR DISABLED PERSONS

(i) The General Duty to Make Reasonable Adjustments

237. Duty to make adjustments in relation to disabled persons.

Where the Equality Act 2010 imposes a duty to make reasonable adjustments on a person, the provisions on adjustments[1] apply, and for those purposes, a person on whom the duty is imposed is referred to as 'A'[2].

The duty comprises the following three requirements[3]:

(1)   the first requirement is a requirement, where a provision, criterion or practice[4] of A's puts a disabled person[5] at a substantial disadvantage[6] in relation to a relevant matter[7] in comparison with persons who are not disabled, to take such steps as it is reasonable to have to take to avoid the disadvantage[8];

(2)   the second requirement is a requirement, where a physical feature[9] puts a disabled person at a substantial disadvantage in relation to a relevant matter in comparison with persons who are not disabled, to take such steps as it is reasonable to have to take to avoid the disadvantage[10];

(3)   the third requirement is a requirement, where a disabled person would, but for the provision of an auxiliary aid[11], be put at a substantial disadvantage in relation to a relevant matter in comparison with persons who are not disabled, to take such steps as it is reasonable to have to take to provide the auxiliary aid[12].

A person (A) who is subject to a duty to make reasonable adjustments is not (subject to express provision to the contrary) entitled to require a disabled person, in relation to whom A is required to comply with the duty, to pay to any extent A's costs of complying with the duty[13]. A duty to make reasonable adjustments may continue to apply where a relationship has ended[14].

1   Ie the Equality Act 2010 ss 20–22 and the applicable Schedule. The applicable Schedules are as follows (see s 20(13), Table):
    (1)   in relation to the Pt 3 (services and public functions: see PARAS 84–104), see Sch 2;
    (2)   in relation to Pt 4 (premises: see PARAS 105–115), see Sch 4;
    (3)   in relation to Pt 5 (work: see PARAS 116–172), see Sch 8;
    (4)   in relation to Pt 6 (education: see PARAS 173–197), see Sch 13;
    (5)   in relation to Pt 7 (associations: see PARAS 198–210), see Sch 15; and
    (6)   in relation to each of the Parts in heads (1)–(5), see Sch 21.
    As to further guidance and examples see the Equality Act 2010 Code of Practice — Services, Public Functions and Associations Statutory Code of Practice (2011) Ch 7.
2   Equality Act 2010 s 20(1). If an employer proposes an adjustment which is incompatible with the terms of the contract of employment, the employee is entitled to decline it; the adjustment will not be effective without agreement, that is to say without a variation of the contract: *G4S Cash Solutions (UK) Ltd v Powell* [2016] IRLR 820, EAT. The limits of the duty to make reasonable adjustments for disabled employees are explored in Time to Adjust, Spencer Keen: 167 NLJ 7728, p 10.
3   Equality Act 2010 s 20(2). A reference in s 21 (see PARA 238) or s 22 (see note 8) or an applicable Schedule (see note 1) to the first, second or third requirement is to be construed in accordance with s 20: s 20(8). Regulations may prescribe descriptions of persons to whom the first, second or third requirement does not apply: s 22(1)(b). At the date at which this volume states the law no such regulations had been made. Provision made by virtue of s 22 may amend an applicable Schedule: s 22(3).
    A failure to make a reasonable adjustment cannot be justified: see the Equality Act 2010 — Employment Statutory Code of Practice (2010) para 6.30; and see the Equality Act 2010 Code of

Practice — Services, Public Functions and Associations Statutory Code of Practice (2011) para 7.14.

4   'Provision, criterion or practice' is not defined by the Equality Act 2010 but should be construed widely: see the Equality Act 2010 Code of Practice — Employment Statutory Code of Practice (2010) para 6.10 (see PARA 75 note 1); and the Equality Act 2010 Code of Practice — Services, Public Functions and Associations Statutory Code of Practice (2011) para 7.43. Regulations may make provision as to what is, or what is not, a provision, criterion or practice: Equality Act 2010 s 22(2)(b). At the date at which this volume states the law no such regulations had been made.

5   As to the meaning of 'disabled person' see PARA 47.

6   As to the meaning of 'substantial' see PARA 49 note 1. Whether such a disadvantage exists in a particular case is a question of fact, and is assessed on an objective basis: Equality Act 2010 Code of Practice — Employment Statutory Code of Practice (2010) para 6.15. See also *Rowan v Environment Agency* [2008] ICR 218, [2008] IRLR 20, EAT (decided under the Disability Discrimination Act 1995 (repealed)) (an employment tribunal considering a claim that an employer has discriminated against an employee by failing to comply with the duty to make reasonable adjustments must identify:

(1)   the provision, criterion or practice applied by or on behalf of an employer; or
(2)   the physical feature of premises occupied by the employer;
(3)   the identity of non-disabled comparators (where appropriate); and
(4)   the nature and extent of the substantial disadvantage suffered by the claimant).

There is no requirement to identify a comparator or comparator group whose circumstances are the same or nearly the same as the disabled person's: Equality Act 2010 Code of Practice — Employment Statutory Code of Practice (2010) para 6.16. The more general comparative exercise required in a reasonable adjustments claim, involving a class or group of non-disabled comparators, differs from that which is understood and applied in the individual, like-for-like comparison required in cases of direct discrimination: *Walters v Fareham College Corpn* [2009] IRLR 991, [2009] All ER (D) 102 (Aug), EAT. See also *MM v Secretary of State for Work and Pensions* [2013] EWCA Civ 1565, [2014] 2 All ER 289 (mental health patients placed at substantial disadvantage when required to undergo work capability assessment for determination of eligibility for employment and support allowance). As to direct discrimination see PARA 67.

7   What constitutes a 'relevant matter' depends on the applicable Schedule. See note 1.

8   Equality Act 2010 s 20(3). Where the first or third requirement relates to the provision of information, the steps which it is reasonable for A to have to take include steps for ensuring that in the circumstances concerned the information is provided in an accessible format: s 20(6).

The Equality Act 2010 does not specify any particular factors that should be taken into account when determining whether a step is reasonable; what is a reasonable step for an employer to take will depend on all the circumstances of each individual case: Equality Act 2010 Code of Practice — Employment Statutory Code of Practice (2010) para 6.23. As to examples of reasonable steps and as to some of the factors which might be taken into account when determining whether a step is reasonable see Equality Act 2010 Code of Practice — Employment Statutory Code of Practice (2010) para 6.24 et seq. There is no reason why the duty of reasonable adjustment should be read as excluding any requirement on an employer to protect an employee's pay in conjunction with other measures to counter the employee's disadvantage through disability; the question will always be whether it is reasonable for the employer to have to take that step: *G4S Cash Solutions (UK) Ltd v Powell* [2016] IRLR 820, EAT.

Regulations may prescribe matters to be taken into account in deciding whether it is reasonable for A to take a step for the purposes of a prescribed provision of an applicable Schedule: Equality Act 2010 s 22(1)(a). Regulations may also make provision as to circumstances in which it is, or in which it is not, reasonable for a person of a prescribed description to have to take steps of a prescribed description: s 22(2)(a). See the Equality Act 2010 (Disability) Regulations 2010, SI 2010/2128, regs 9–14, Schedule.

The fact that the claimant's disability was caused by an employer's failings can be relevant to the assessment of reasonableness: *HM Prison Service v Johnson* [2007] IRLR 951, EAT (decided under the Disability Discrimination Act 1995 (repealed)). There is nothing to suggest that the duty only arises where an employer knows or ought to know that particular steps are available to him: see *Price-Job v Camden London Borough Council* (2007) 152 Sol Jo (no 2) 31, [2007] All ER (D) 259 (Dec), EAT (decided under the Disability Discrimination Act 1995 (repealed)). There is no reason why the duty of reasonable adjustment should be read as excluding any requirement on an employer to protect an employee's pay in conjunction with other measures to counter the employee's disadvantage through disability; the question will always be whether it is reasonable for the employer to have to take that step: *G4S Cash Solutions (UK) Ltd v Powell* [2016] IRLR 820, EAT. See note 2.

9 A reference in the Equality Act 2010 s 20, s 21 (see PARA 238) or s 22 or an applicable Schedule (see note 1), apart from Sch 4 paras 2–4 (see PARAS 241–244) to a 'physical feature' is a reference to a feature arising from the design or construction of a building; a feature of an approach to, exit from or access to a building; a fixture or fitting, or furniture, furnishings, materials, equipment or other chattels, in or on premises; or any other physical element or quality: s 20(10). As to examples of 'physical features' see the Equality Act 2010 Code of Practice — Employment Statutory Code of Practice (2010) para 6.12. Regulations may make provision as to things which are, or which are not, to be treated as physical features, and things which are, or which are not, to be treated as alterations of physical features: Equality Act 2010 s 22(2)(c), (d). At the date at which this volume states the law no such regulations had been made.

10 Equality Act 2010 s 20(4). In relation to the second requirement, a reference in s 20 or an applicable Schedule to avoiding a substantial disadvantage includes a reference to removing the physical feature in question, altering it, or providing a reasonable means of avoiding it: s 20(9).

11 A reference in the Equality Act 2010 ss 20, 21, 22 or an applicable Schedule to an 'auxiliary aid' includes a reference to an auxiliary service: s 20(11). An auxiliary aid is something which provides support or assistance to a disabled person and can include provision of a specialist piece of equipment: Equality Act 2010 Code of Practice — Employment Statutory Code of Practice (2010) para 6.13. Regulations may make provision as to things which are, or which are not, to be treated as auxiliary aids: Equality Act 2010 s 22(2)(e). See the Equality Act 2010 (Disability) Regulations 2010, SI 2010/2128, reg 8.

12 Equality Act 2010 s 20(5). See note 8; and as to 'disabled persons' in this context see note 5.

13 Equality Act 2010 s 20(7).

14 See the Equality Act 2010 s 108(4) (amended by SI 2010/2279), which provides that a duty to make reasonable adjustments applies to A (in the context of discrimination in a relationship that has ended: see the Equality Act 2010 s 108(1); and PARA 70) if B (in that context) is placed at a substantial disadvantage as mentioned in s 20 (see the text and notes 1–13). For the purposes of s 108(4), ss 20–22 (see the text and notes 1–13; and PARA 238) and the applicable Schedules are to be construed as if the relationship had not ended: s 108(5).

238. Failure to comply with duty to make reasonable adjustments.

A failure to comply with the first, second or third requirement[1] is a failure to comply with a duty to make reasonable adjustments[2]. A person ('A') discriminates[3] against a disabled person[4] if A fails to comply with that duty in relation to that person[5].

1 As to the first, second and third requirements see PARA 237.
2 Equality Act 2010 s 21(1). As to the duty to make reasonable adjustments see PARA 237.
3 As to direct discrimination see PARA 67; and as to indirect discrimination see PARA 75
4 As to the meaning of 'disabled person' see PARA 47.
5 Equality Act 2010 s 21(2). A provision of an applicable Schedule which imposes a duty to comply with the first, second or third requirement applies only for the purpose of establishing whether A has contravened the Equality Act 2010 by virtue of s 21(2); a failure to comply is, accordingly, not actionable by virtue of another provision of the Equality Act 2010 or otherwise: s 21(3). As to the meaning of 'an applicable Schedule' see PARA 237 note 1.

(ii) Reasonable Adjustments to be made in the Provision of Services and the Exercise of Public Functions

239. Reasonable adjustments to be made by service-providers etc.

A duty to make reasonable adjustments[1] applies to a service-provider[2] and a person who exercises a public function[3] that is not the provision of a service[4] to the public or a section of the public[5]. Where a duty to make reasonable adjustments is imposed on a person (A)[6] by the Equality Act 2010 Pt 3[7], A must comply with the first, second and third requirements as follows[8].

The first requirement is a requirement, where a provision, criterion or practice[9] of A's puts disabled persons generally at a substantial disadvantage[10] in relation to the provision of the service, or the exercise of the function, by A[11] in comparison with persons who are not disabled, to take such steps as it is reasonable to have to take to avoid the disadvantage[12].

The second requirement is a requirement, where a physical feature[13] puts disabled persons generally at a substantial disadvantage in relation to the provision of the service, or the exercise of the function, by A in comparison with persons who are not disabled, to take such steps as it is reasonable to have to take to avoid the disadvantage or to adopt a reasonable alternative method of providing the service or exercising the function[14].

The third requirement is a requirement, where disabled persons generally would, but for the provision of an auxiliary aid[15], be put at a substantial disadvantage in relation to the provision of the service, or the exercise of the function, by A in comparison with persons who are not disabled, to take such steps as it is reasonable to have to take to provide the auxiliary aid[16].

1   As to the duty to make reasonable adjustments see PARA 237.
2   Equality Act 2010 s 29(7)(a). As to service-providers see PARA 85.
3   As to the meaning of 'public function' see PARA 279 note 1.
4   As to the meaning of 'provision of a service' see PARA 85 note 1.
5   Equality Act 2010 s 29(7)(b). As to examples of a 'section of the public' see PARA 85 note 2.
6   Equality Act 2010 s 31(9), Sch 2 para 1.
7   Ie the Equality Act 2010 Pt 3 (ss 28–31): see PARAS 84–104.
8   Equality Act 2010 Sch 2 para 2(1). As to the first, second and third requirements see PARA 237. If A is a service-provider, nothing in Sch 2 para 2 requires A to take a step which would fundamentally alter the nature of the service, or the nature of A's trade or profession: Sch 2 para 2(7). 'Profession' includes a vocation or occupation; and 'trade' includes any business: s 212(1). If A exercises a public function, nothing in Sch 2 para 2 requires A to take a step which A has no power to take: Sch 2 para 2(8).
9   As to the meaning of 'provision, criterion or practice' see PARA 237 note 4.
10 Being placed at a substantial disadvantage in relation to the exercise of a function means:
    (1)   if a benefit is or may be conferred in the exercise of the function, being placed at a substantial disadvantage in relation to the conferment of the benefit (Equality Act 2010 Sch 2 para 2(5)(a)); or
    (2)   if a person is or may be subjected to a detriment in the exercise of the function, suffering an unreasonably adverse experience when being subjected to the detriment (Sch 2 para 2(5)(b)).
11 These are referred to as 'relevant matters': see the Equality Act 2010 Sch 2 para 2(4).
12 Equality Act 2010 s 20(3), Sch 2 para 2(2).
13 In relation to the second requirement, a physical feature includes a physical feature brought by or on behalf of A, in the course of providing the service or exercising the function, on to premises other than those that A occupies (as well as including a physical feature in or on premises that A occupies): Equality Act 2010 Sch 2 para 2(6).
14 See the Equality Act 2010 s 20(4), Sch 2 para 2(2), (3). See *Allen v Royal Bank of Scotland Group plc* [2009] EWCA Civ 1213, 112 BMLR 30, [2010] 1 EGLR 13 (decided under the Disability Discrimination Act 1995 (repealed)). It is not reasonable for a provider of services or a public authority carrying out its functions to have to remove or alter a physical feature where the feature concerned was provided in or in connection with a building for the purpose of assisting people to have access to the building or to use facilities provided in the building; and satisfies the relevant design standard: Equality Act 2010 (Disability) Regulations 2010, SI 2010/2128, reg 9(1), (2). Whether a physical feature satisfies the relevant design standard is determined in accordance with the Equality Act 2010 (Disability) Regulations 2010, SI 2010/2128, Schedule: see reg 9(3).
15 As to the meaning of 'auxiliary aid' see PARA 237 note 11.
16 Equality Act 2010 s 20(5), Sch 2 para 2(2).

240.   Reasonable adjustments in relation to transport.

Where a person ('A') is concerned with the provision of a service[1] which involves transporting people by land, air or water[2] it is never reasonable for A, in fulfilling his duty to make reasonable adjustments for the benefit of disabled persons, to have to take a step which would:

(1)   involve the alteration or removal of a physical feature of a vehicle used in providing the service[3];

(2)   affect whether vehicles are provided[4];

(3)   affect what vehicles are provided[5];

(4)   affect what happens in the vehicle while someone is travelling in it[6].

1   As to the meaning of 'provision of a service' see PARA 85 note 1.

2   Equality Act 2010 s 31(9), Sch 2 para 3(1). Schedule 2 applies where a duty to make reasonable adjustments is imposed on A by Pt 3 (ss 28–31) (see PARAS 84–104): Sch 2 para 1. As to the duty to make reasonable adjustments see PARA 237

3   Equality Act 2010 Sch 2 para 3(2)(a). A may not, for the purpose of complying with the first, second or third requirement rely on Sch 2 para 3(2) if A provides the service by way of a hire-vehicle built to carry no more than eight passengers: Sch 2 para 3(5). As to the first, second and third requirements see PARAS 237, 239.

    For the purposes of Sch 2 para 3(5) in its application to the second requirement (see PARAS 237, 239), a part of a vehicle is to be regarded as a physical feature if it requires alteration in order to facilitate the provision of:

    (1)   hand controls to enable a disabled person to operate braking and accelerator systems in the vehicle (Sch 2 para 3(6)(a)); or

    (2)   facilities for the stowage of a wheelchair (Sch 2 para 3(6)(b)).

    For the purposes of head (1) above, fixed seating and in-built electrical systems are not physical features; and for the purposes of head (2) above, fixed seating is not a physical feature: Sch 2 para 3(7). As to the meaning of 'physical feature' see PARAS 237 note 9, 239 note 13.

    Regulations may amend Sch 2 para 3 so as to provide for Sch 2 para 3(2) not to apply, or to apply only so far as is prescribed, in relation to vehicles of a prescribed description: Sch 2 para 3(10). At the date at which this volume states the law no such regulations had been made.

4   Equality Act 2010 Sch 2 para 3(2)(b). See note 3. However, for the purpose of complying with the first or third requirement, A may not rely on heads (2)–(4) in the text if the vehicle concerned is (Equality Act 2010 Sch 2 para 3(3)):

    (1)   a hire-vehicle designed and constructed for the carriage of passengers, comprising more than eight seats in addition to the driver's seat and having a maximum mass not exceeding five tonnes;

    (2)   a hire-vehicle designed and constructed for the carriage of goods and having a maximum mass not exceeding 3.5 tonnes;

    (3)   a vehicle licensed under the Local Government (Miscellaneous Provisions) Act 1976 s 48 (see ROAD TRAFFIC vol 90 (2011) PARA 1194) or the Private Hire Vehicles (London) Act 1998 s 7 (see LONDON GOVERNMENT vol 71 (2013) PARA 234) (or under a provision of a local Act corresponding to either of those provisions);

    (4)   a public service vehicle (within the meaning given by the Public Passenger Vehicles Act 1981 s 1: see ROAD TRAFFIC vol 90 (2011) PARA 896);

    (5)   vehicle built or adapted to carry passengers on a railway or tramway (within the meaning, in each case, of the Transport and Works Act 1992: see RAILWAYS AND TRAMWAYS vol 86 (2017) PARA 310);

    (6)   a taxi;

    (7)   a vehicle deployed to transport the driver and passengers of a vehicle that has broken down or is involved in an accident; or

    (8)   a vehicle deployed on a system using a mode of guided transport (within the meaning of the Transport and Works Act 1992: see RAILWAYS AND TRAMWAYS vol 86 (2017) PARA 310).

    For these purposes, a 'hire-vehicle' is a vehicle hired (by way of a trade) under a hiring agreement to which the Road Traffic Offenders Act 1988 s 66 (see ROAD TRAFFIC vol 90 (2011) PARA 869) applies (Equality Act 2010 Sch 2 para 4(1), (2)); and a 'taxi', in England and Wales, is a vehicle:

    (a)   licensed under the Town Police Clauses Act 1847 s 37 (see ROAD TRAFFIC vol 90 (2011) PARA 1181) (Equality Act 2010 Sch 2 para 4(3)(a));

    (b)   licensed under the Metropolitan Public Carriage Act 1869 s 6 (see LONDON GOVERNMENT vol 71 (2013) PARA 233) (Equality Act 2010 Sch 2 para 4(3)(b)); or

    (c)   drawn by one or more persons or animals (Sch 2 para 4(3)(c)).

In the case of a vehicle within heads (1)–(8) above, a relevant device is not an auxiliary aid for the purposes of the third requirement (see PARAS **237, 239**): Sch 2 para 3(8). A 'relevant device' is a device or structure, or equipment, the installation, operation or maintenance of which would necessitate making a permanent alteration to, or which would have a permanent effect on, the internal or external fabric of the vehicle: Sch 2 para 3(9).

In so far as the second requirement (see PARAS **237, 239**) requires A to adopt a reasonable alternative method of providing the service to disabled persons, A may not, for the purpose of complying with the requirement, rely on heads (2)–(4) in the text if the vehicle is a vehicle deployed to transport the driver and passengers of a vehicle that has broken down or is involved in an accident: Sch 2 para 3(4).

5　Equality Act 2010 Sch 2 para 3(2)(c). See notes 3–4.
6　Equality Act 2010 Sch 2 para 3(2)(d). See notes 3–4.

(iii)　Reasonable Adjustments to be made in respect of Leasehold and Commonhold Premises

241.　Duty of controller of let premises to make reasonable adjustments for disabled persons.
Where a person ('A') is a controller of let premises[1], he must comply with the first and third requirements pertaining to reasonable adjustments as set out in the Equality Act 2010[2] as follows[3].

The first requirement is a requirement, where a provision, criterion or practice[4] of A's puts a disabled person[5] at a substantial disadvantage[6] in relation to:
(1)　the enjoyment of the premises[7]; and
(2)　the use of a benefit or facility, entitlement to which arises as a result of the letting[8],
in comparison with persons who are not disabled, to take such steps as it is reasonable[9] to have to take to avoid the disadvantage[10].

The third requirement is a requirement, where a disabled person[11] would, but for the provision of an auxiliary aid[12], be put at a substantial disadvantage in relation to:
(a)　the enjoyment of the premises; and
(b)　the use of a benefit or facility, entitlement to which arises as a result of the letting[13],
in comparison with persons who are not disabled, to take such steps as it is reasonable to have to take to provide the auxiliary aid[14].

1　Equality Act 2010 s 38(8), Sch 4 para 2(1). As to the meaning of 'controller of let premises' see PARA **109** note 2. As to the meaning of 'premises' see PARA **106** note 1.
2　As to the first, second and third requirements as set out in the Equality Act 2010 see PARA **237**.
3　Equality Act 2010 Sch 4 para 2(2). Sch 4 para 2(2) applies only if A receives a request from or on behalf of the tenant or a person entitled to occupy the premises to take steps to avoid the disadvantage or provide the auxiliary aid: Sch 4 para 2(6).
4　As to the meaning of 'provision, criterion or practice' see PARA **237** note 4. For these purposes, the reference to a provision, criterion or practice of A's includes a reference to a term of the letting: Sch 4 para 2(3). The 'terms of letting' include the terms of an agreement relating to it: Sch 4 para 2(10).
5　For these purposes, the reference in the Equality Act 2010 s 20(3) (see text and note 10) or s 20(5) (see text and note 14) to a disabled person is a reference to a disabled person who is a tenant of the premises; or is otherwise entitled to occupy them: Sch 4 para 2(4). Where the relevant disabled person comes within Sch 4 para 2(4)(b) (head (2) in the text), Sch 4 para 4(4)(b) (see PARA **243**) or Sch 4 para 5(4)(c) (not yet in force: see PARA **244**), A must not, because of costs incurred in connection with taking steps to comply with a requirement imposed for the purposes of Sch 4 paras 2, 4 (see PARA **243**) or Sch 4 para 5 (see PARA **244**), subject to a detriment a tenant of the premises or the unit-holder: Sch 4 para 8(1), (2).
　As to the meaning of 'disabled person' see PARA **47**.

6 As to the meaning of 'substantial disadvantage' see PARA 237 note 6. If a term of the letting that prohibits the tenant from making alterations puts the disabled person at the disadvantage referred to in the first requirement, A is required to change the term only so far as is necessary to enable the tenant to make alterations to the let premises so as to avoid the disadvantage: Sch 4 para 2(7).

7 'Enjoyment' of premises means that the tenant should be able to live in his home in the normal manner: see *Beedles v Guinness Northern Counties Ltd* [2011] EWCA Civ 442, [2011] HLR 511; *Dee Thomas-Ashley v Drum Housing Association* [2010] EWCA Civ 265, [2010] 2 P & CR 309.

8 These are referred to as 'relevant matters': see the Equality Act 2010 Sch 4 para 2(5).

9 It is never reasonable for A to have to take a step which would involve the removal or alteration of a physical feature: Equality Act 2010 Sch 4 para 2(8). For these purposes, physical features do not include furniture, furnishings, materials, equipment or other chattels in or on the premises; and none of the following is an alteration of a physical feature (Sch 4 para 2(9)):
    (1)   the replacement or provision of a sign or notice;
    (2)   the replacement of a tap or door handle;
    (3)   the replacement, provision or adaptation of a door bell or door entry system;
    (4)   changes to the colour of a wall, door or any other surface.

10 Equality Act 2010 s 20(3), Sch 4 para 2.

11 See note 5.

12 As to the meaning of 'auxiliary aid' see PARA 237 note 11 For the purposes of the Equality Act 2010 Sch 4 paras 2–4, the following are to be treated as 'auxiliary aids or services' (see the Equality Act 2010 (Disability) Regulations 2010, SI 2010/2128, reg 8(1)):
    (1)   the removal, replacement or provision of any furniture, furnishings, materials, equipment and other chattels;
    (2)   the replacement or provision of any signs or notices;
    (3)   the replacement of any taps or door handles;
    (4)   the replacement, provision or adaptation of any door bell, or any door entry system;
    (5)   changes to the colour of any surface (such as, for example, a wall or door).
Head (1) above does not include the provision of any item which would be a fixture when installed: reg 8(2). It is reasonable to regard a request for a matter falling within heads (1)–(5) above as a request for a controller of premises to take steps in order to provide an auxiliary aid or service: see reg 8(3). For these purposes 'controller of premises' means (Equality Act 2010 (Disability) Regulations 2010, SI 2010/2128, reg 8(4)):
    (a)   in relation to the Equality Act 2010 Sch 4 para 2, the controller of let premises;
    (b)   in relation to Sch 4 para 3 (see PARA 242), the controller of premises that are to let; and
    (c)   in relation to Sch 4 para 4 (see PARA 243), the commonhold association.

13 See note 7.

14 Equality Act 2010 s 20(5), Sch 4 para 2.

242. Duty of controller of premises to let to make reasonable adjustments for disabled persons.

Where a person ('A') is a controller of premises to let[1], A must comply with the first and third requirements pertaining to reasonable adjustments as set out in the Equality Act 2010 as follows[2].

The first requirement is a requirement, where a provision, criterion or practice[3] of A's puts a disabled person[4] at a substantial disadvantage[5] in relation to becoming a tenant of the premises[6] in comparison with persons who are not disabled, to take such steps as it is reasonable[7] to have to take to avoid the disadvantage[8]. The third requirement is a requirement, where a disabled person[9] would, but for the provision of an auxiliary aid[10], be put at a substantial disadvantage in relation to becoming a tenant of the premises in comparison with persons who are not disabled, to take such steps as it is reasonable to have to take to provide the auxiliary aid[11].

1 Equality Act 2010 s 38(8), Sch 4 para 3(1). As to the meaning of 'controller of premises to let' see PARA 109 note 2. As to the meaning of 'premises' see PARA 106 note 1.

2 Equality Act 2010 Sch 4 para 3(2). Schedule 4 para 3(2) applies only if A receives a request by or on behalf of a disabled person within Sch 4 para 3(3) (see note 4) for A to take steps to avoid the disadvantage or provide the auxiliary aid: Sch 4 para 3(5).

    As to the first, second and third requirements see PARA 237.

3   As to the meaning of 'provision, criterion or practice' see PARA 237 note 4.
4   For these purposes, the reference in the Equality Act 2010 s 20(3) (see the text and note 8) or s 20(5) (see the text and note 11) to a disabled person is a reference to a disabled person who is considering taking a letting of the premises: Sch 4 para 3(3). As to the meaning of 'disabled person' see PARA 47.
5   As to the meaning of 'substantial disadvantage' see PARA 237 note 6.
6   See the Equality Act 2010 Sch 4 para 3(4).
7   Nothing in the Equality Act 2010 Sch 4 para 3 requires A to take a step which would involve the removal or alteration of a physical feature: Sch 4 para 3(6). As to the meaning of 'physical feature' see PARA 237 note 9 (applied by Sch 4 para 3(7)).
8   Equality Act 2010 s 20(3), Sch 4 para 3. See also PARA 237.
9   See note 4.
10 As to the meaning of 'auxiliary aid' see PARAS 237 note 11, 241 note 12
11 Equality Act 2010 s 20(5), Sch 4 para 3. See also PARA 237.

243.   Duty of commonhold associations to make reasonable adjustments for disabled persons.

Where a person ('A') is a commonhold association[1], A must comply with the first and third requirements pertaining to reasonable adjustments as set out in the Equality Act 2010 as follows[2].

The first requirement is a requirement, where a provision, criterion or practice[3] of A's puts a disabled person[4] at a substantial disadvantage[5] in relation to the enjoyment of the unit[6] or the use of a benefit or facility, entitlement to which arises as a result of a term of the commonhold community statement or any other applicable term[7] in comparison with persons who are not disabled, to take such steps as it is reasonable[8] to have to take to avoid the disadvantage[9]. The third requirement is a requirement, where a disabled person[10] would, but for the provision of an auxiliary aid[11], be put at a substantial disadvantage in relation to the enjoyment of the unit or the use of a benefit or facility, entitlement to which arises as a result of a term of the commonhold community statement or any other applicable term[12] in comparison with persons who are not disabled, to take such steps as it is reasonable to have to take to provide the auxiliary aid[13].

1   Equality Act 2010 s 38(8), Sch 4 para 4(1). The reference to a 'commonhold association' is a reference to the association in its capacity as the person who manages a commonhold unit: Sch 4 para 4(1). As to the meanings of 'commonhold association' and 'commonhold unit' see PARA 109 note 4.
2   Equality Act 2010 Sch 4 para 4(2). Schedule 4 para 4(2) applies only if A receives a request from or on behalf of the unit-holder or a person entitled to occupy the unit to take steps to avoid the disadvantage or provide the auxiliary aid: Sch 4 para 4(6).
    As to the first, second and third requirements see PARA 237.
3   For these purposes, the reference in the Equality Act 2010 s 20(3) to a provision, criterion or practice of A's includes a reference to a term of the commonhold community statement; or any other term applicable by virtue of the transfer of the unit to the unit-holder: Sch 4 para 4(3). See also generally PARA 237 note 4.
4   For these purposes, the reference in the Equality Act 2010 s 20(3) (see the text and note 9) or s 20(5) (see the text and note 13) to a disabled person is a reference to a disabled person who is the unit-holder; or is otherwise entitled to occupy the unit: Sch 4 para 4(4). As to the meaning of 'disabled person' see PARA 47
5   As to the meaning of 'substantial disadvantage' see PARA 237 note 6. If a term within the Equality Act 2010 Sch 4 para 4(3) (see note 3) that prohibits the unit-holder from making alterations puts the disabled person at the disadvantage referred to in the first requirement, A is required to change the term only so far as is necessary to enable the unit-holder to make alterations to the unit so as to avoid the disadvantage: Sch 4 para 4(7).
6   As to the 'enjoyment' of premises see PARA 241 note 7.
7   Equality Act 2010 Sch 4 para 4(5). The text refers to a term within the Equality Act 2010 Sch 4 para 4(3) (see note 3).

8   It is never reasonable for A to have to take a step which would involve the removal or alteration of a physical feature: Equality Act 2010 Sch 4 para 4(8). As to the meaning of 'physical feature' see PARA 237 note 9 (applied by Sch 4 para 4(8)).

9   Equality Act 2010 s 20(3), Sch 4 para 4. See also PARA 237.

10 See note 4.

11 As to the meaning of 'auxiliary aid' see PARAS 237 note 11, 241 note 12

12 See note 6.

13 Equality Act 2010 s 20(5), Sch 4 para 4. See also PARA 237.

244. Duty of responsible persons in relation to common parts to make reasonable adjustments for disabled persons.

As from a day to be appointed the following provisions have effect[1].

Where a person ('A') is a responsible person in relation to common parts[2], A must comply with the second requirement pertaining to reasonable adjustments as set out in the Equality Act 2010[3]. The second requirement is a requirement, where a physical feature[4] puts a disabled person[5] at a substantial disadvantage[6] in relation to the use of common parts[7] in comparison with persons who are not disabled, to take such steps as it is reasonable[8] to have to take to avoid the disadvantage[9]. If A decides that it is reasonable to take a particular step for these purposes[10], A and the disabled person must agree in writing the rights and responsibilities of each of them in relation to the step[11].

1   At the date at which this volume states the law no day had been appointed for the Equality Act 2010 Sch 4 paras 5, 6, 7 to be brought into force.

2   Equality Act 2010 s 38(8), Sch 4 para 5(1) (not yet in force). As to the meanings of 'responsible person in relation to common parts' and 'common parts' see PARA 109 note 5.

3   Equality Act 2010 Sch 4 para 5(2) (not yet in force). As to the meaning of 'the first, second and third requirements' see PARAS 237, 241. Schedule 4 para 5(2) applies only if A receives a request by or on behalf of a disabled person within Sch 4 para 5(4) (see note 5) for A to take steps to avoid the disadvantage; and the steps requested are likely to avoid or reduce the disadvantage: Sch 4 para 5(6) (not yet in force). See note 5.

4   For these purposes, the reference to a physical feature is a reference to a physical feature of the common parts: Sch 4 para 5(3) (not yet in force).

5   For these purposes, the reference to a disabled person is a reference to a disabled person who:
    (1)   is a tenant of the premises;
    (2)   is a unit-holder;
    (3)   is otherwise entitled to occupy the premises,
    and uses or intends to use the premises as the person's only or main home: Sch 4 para 5(4) (not yet in force). As to the meaning of 'disabled person' see PARA 47.

6   As to a 'substantial disadvantage' see PARA 237 note 6.

7   Equality Act 2010 Sch 4 para 5(5) (not yet in force).

8   In deciding whether it is reasonable to take a step for the purposes of the Equality Act 2010 Sch 4 para 5, A must consult all persons A thinks would be affected by the step: Sch 4 para 6(1) (not yet in force). The consultation must be carried out within a reasonable period of the request being made: Sch 4 para 6(2) (not yet in force). A is not required to have regard to a view expressed against taking a step in so far as A reasonably believes that the view is expressed because of the disabled person's disability: Sch 4 para 6(3) (not yet in force). Nothing in Sch 4 para 6 affects anything a commonhold association is required to do pursuant to the Commonhold and Leasehold Reform Act 2002 Pt 1 (ss 1–70) (see REAL PROPERTY AND REGISTRATION vol 87 (2017) PARA 1103 et seq): Equality Act 2010 Sch 4 para 6(4) (not yet in force). As to the meaning of 'disability' see PARA 47.

9   Equality Act 2010 s 20(4), Sch 4 para 5 (not yet in force).

10 Ie for the purposes of the Equality Act 2010 Sch 4 para 5 (see the text and note 8).

11 Equality Act 2010 Sch 4 para 7(1) (not yet in force). Such an agreement must, in particular, make provision as to the responsibilities of the parties in relation to:
    (1)   the costs of any work to be undertaken (Sch 4 para 7(2)(a) (not yet in force));
    (2)   other costs arising from the work (Sch 4 para 7(2)(b) (not yet in force));
    (3)   the restoration of the common parts to their former condition if the relevant disabled person stops living in the premises (Sch 4 para 7(2)(c) (not yet in force)).

It is always reasonable before the agreement is made for A to insist that the agreement should require the disabled person to pay the costs referred to in heads (1) and (2) above; and the costs of the restoration referred to in head (3) above: Sch 4 para 7(3) (not yet in force). If an agreement under Sch 4 para 7 is made, A's obligations under the agreement become part of A's interest in the common parts and pass on subsequent disposals accordingly: Sch 4 para 7(4) (not yet in force). Regulations may require a party to an agreement under Sch 4 para 7 to provide, in prescribed circumstances, prescribed information about the agreement to persons of a prescribed description: Sch 4 para 7(5) (not yet in force). The regulations may require the information to be provided in a prescribed form: Sch 4 para 7(6) (not yet in force). Regulations may make provision as to circumstances in which an agreement under Sch 4 para 7 is to cease to have effect, in so far as the agreement does not itself make provision for termination: Sch 4 para 7(7) (not yet in force). At the date at which this volume states the law, no such regulations had been made.

(iv) Reasonable Adjustments to be made in the Workplace

245. Reasonable adjustments to be made by employers generally.

Employers[1] are under a duty to make reasonable adjustments for disabled persons[2]. In this respect employers must comply with the first, second and third requirements as follows[3].

The first requirement is a requirement, where a provision, criterion or practice applied by or on behalf of the employer puts a disabled person who is, or has notified the employer that he may be, an applicant for employment, at a substantial disadvantage in relation to deciding to whom to offer employment, or puts a disabled person who is an applicant for employment with the employer, or who is an employee of the employer, at a substantial disadvantage in relation to employment by the employer, in comparison with persons who are not disabled, to take such steps as it is reasonable to have to take to avoid the disadvantage[4].

The second requirement is a requirement, where a physical feature of premises occupied by the employer puts a disabled person who is an applicant for employment by the employer, or an employee of the employer, at a substantial disadvantage in relation to employment by the employer, in comparison with persons who are not disabled, to take such steps as it is reasonable to have to take to avoid the disadvantage[5].

The third requirement is a requirement, where a disabled person who is, or has notified the employer that he may be, an applicant for employment, would but for the provision of an auxiliary aid be put at a substantial disadvantage in relation to deciding to whom to offer employment, or where a disabled person who is an applicant for employment by the employer, or who is an employee of the employer, would but for the provision of an auxiliary aid be put at a substantial disadvantage in relation to employment by the employer, in comparison with persons who are not disabled, to take such steps as it is reasonable to have to take to provide the auxiliary aid[6].

An employer is not subject to a duty to make reasonable adjustments if he does not know, and could not reasonably be expected to know:

(1)   in the case of an applicant for employment or potential applicant for employment, that an interested disabled person is or may be an applicant for the work in question[7]; or

(2)   that an interested disabled person has a disability and is likely to be placed at the disadvantage referred to in the first, second or third requirement[8].

---

1   As to the meaning of 'employer' see PARA 116. If two or more persons are subject to a duty to make reasonable adjustments in relation to the same disabled person, each of them must comply with the duty so far as it is reasonable for each of them to do so: Equality Act 2010 Sch 8 para 2(5).

2 See the Equality Act 2010 s 39(5). As to the meaning of 'disabled person' see PARA 47. The definition of 'interested disabled person' differs according to context. The persons in respect of whom the adjustments are required to be made under these provisions are referred to as 'interested disabled persons': Sch 8 para 4. As to the duty to make reasonable adjustments generally, and in connection with failure to comply with the duty to make adjustments, see PARAS 76, 237–238.

3 Equality Act 2010 Sch 8 paras 1, 2(1).

4 Equality Act 2010 s 20(3), Sch 8 paras 2(2)(a), (c), (3), 5(1). In connection with what amounts to a 'provision, criterion or practice' under the Equality Act 2010 see *Finnigan v Chief Constable of Northumbria Police* [2013] EWCA Civ 1191, (2013) 134 BMLR 1, [2014] 1 WLR 445. As to examples under previous legislation see *Nottinghamshire County Council v Meikle* [2004] EWCA Civ 859, [2004] IRLR 703, CA; *Archibald v Fife Council* [2004] UKHL 32, [2004] 4 All ER 303, [2004] IRLR 651; *Smith v Churchills Stairlifts Ltd* [2005] EWCA Civ 1220, [2006] IRLR 42, [2005] All ER (D) 318 (Oct); *Tarbuck v Sainsbury's Supermarkets Ltd* [2006] IRLR 664, EAT; *Royal Liverpool Children's NHS Trust v Dunsby* [2006] IRLR 351, EAT; *O'Hanlon v Revenue and Customs Comrs* [2007] EWCA Civ 283, [2007] IRLR 404, [2007] All ER (D) 516 (Mar); (cases decided under the Disability Discrimination Act 1995 (repealed)).

5 Equality Act 2010 s 20(4), Sch 8 paras 2(2)(b), (c), (4), 5(1).

6 Equality Act 2010 s 20(5), Sch 8 paras 2(2)(c), (3), 5(1).

7 Equality Act 2010 Sch 8 paras 4, 20(1)(a), (2).

8 Equality Act 2010 Sch 8 paras 4, 20(1)(b) (amended by SI 2011/1060).

246. Reasonable adjustments to be made by employers of disabled contract workers.

Employers[1] are under a duty to make reasonable adjustments for disabled contract workers[2]. In this respect employers must comply with the first, second and third requirements on each occasion that a disabled contract worker is supplied to a principal to do contract work, as follows[3].

The first requirement is a requirement, where a provision, criterion or practice applied by or on behalf of all or most of the principals to whom a disabled contract worker is or might be supplied, is likely to put a disabled contract worker who is, or has notified the employer that he may be, an applicant for employment, at a substantial disadvantage that is the same or similar in the case of each of the principals to whom the worker is or might be supplied, in relation to deciding to whom to offer employment, or is likely put a disabled contract worker who is an applicant for employment with the employer, or who is an employee of the employer, at such a disadvantage in relation to employment by the employer, in comparison with persons who are not disabled, to take such steps to avoid the disadvantage as it would be reasonable for the employer to have to take if the provision, criterion or practice were applied by or on behalf of the employer[4].

The second requirement is a requirement, where a physical feature of premises occupied by each of the principals to whom the worker is or might be supplied is likely to put a disabled contract worker who is an applicant for employment by the employer, or an employee of the employer, at a substantial disadvantage that is the same or similar in the case of each of those principals in relation to employment by the employer, in comparison with persons who are not disabled, to take such steps as it would be reasonable for the employer to have to take to avoid the disadvantage if the premises were occupied by him[5].

The third requirement is a requirement, where a disabled contract worker who is, or has notified the employer that he may be, an applicant for employment, would but for the provision of an auxiliary aid be likely to be put at a substantial disadvantage that is the same or similar in the case of each of the principals to whom the worker is or might be supplied, in relation to deciding to whom to offer employment, or where a disabled person who is an applicant for employment by the employer, or who is an employee of the employer, would but for the provision of an auxiliary aid be likely to be put at a substantial disadvantage that is the same or similar in the case of each of the principals to whom the worker is or might be supplied in relation to employment by the employer, in comparison with persons who are not disabled, to take such steps as it would be reasonable for the employer to have to take to provide the auxiliary aid if he were the person to whom the worker was supplied[6].

An employer is not subject to a duty to make reasonable adjustments if he does not know, and could not reasonably be expected to know:

(1)   in the case of an applicant for employment or potential applicant for employment, that an interested disabled person is or may be an applicant for the work in question[7]; or

(2)   that an interested disabled person has a disability and is likely to be placed at the disadvantage referred to in the first, second or third requirement[8].

1   As to the meaning of 'employer' see PARA 116. If two or more persons are subject to a duty to make reasonable adjustments in relation to the same disabled person, each of them must comply with the duty so far as it is reasonable for each of them to do so: Equality Act 2010 Sch 8 para 2(5).
2   See the Equality Act 2010 s 39(5); and PARAS 245, 155. The definition of 'interested disabled person' differs according to context. The persons in respect of whom the adjustments are required to be made under these provisions are referred to as 'interested disabled persons': Sch 8 para 4. As to the duty to make reasonable adjustments generally, and in connection with failure to comply with the duty to make adjustments, see PARAS 76, 237–238.
3   Equality Act 2010 Sch 8 paras 1, 2(1), 5(2).
4   Equality Act 2010 s 20(3), Sch 8 paras 2(2)(a), (c), (3), 5(1), (3).
5   Equality Act 2010 s 20(4), Sch 8 paras 2(2)(b), (c), (4), 5(1), (4).
6   Equality Act 2010 s 20(5), Sch 8 paras 2(2)(c), (3), 5(1), (5).
7   Equality Act 2010 Sch 8 para 20(1)(a), (2).
8   Equality Act 2010 Sch 8 para 20(1)(b) (amended by SI 2011/1060).

247. Reasonable adjustments to be made by principals in contract work.

Principals in contract work (as well as the employers of contract workers)[1] are under a duty to make reasonable adjustments for disabled persons[2]. In this respect principals must comply with the first, second and third requirements as follows[3].

The first requirement is a requirement, where a provision, criterion or practice applied by or on behalf of the principal puts a contract worker who is, or has notified the principal that he may be, an applicant to do the work, at a substantial disadvantage in relation to contract work that the principal may make available, or puts a contract worker who is supplied to do the work at a substantial disadvantage in relation to contract work that the principal makes available, in comparison with persons who are not disabled, to take such steps as it is reasonable to have to take to avoid the disadvantage[4].

The second requirement is a requirement, where a physical feature of premises occupied by the principal puts a disabled contract worker who is supplied to do the work at a substantial disadvantage in relation to contract work that the principal makes available, in comparison with persons who are not disabled, to take such steps as it is reasonable to have to take to avoid the disadvantage[5].

The third requirement is a requirement, where a disabled contract worker who is, or has notified the principal that he may be, an applicant to do contract work, would but for the provision of an auxiliary aid be put at a substantial disadvantage in relation to contract work that the employer may make available, or where a disabled contract worker who is supplied to do the work would but for the provision of an auxiliary aid be put at a substantial disadvantage in relation to contract work that the principal makes available, in comparison with persons who are not disabled, to take such steps as it is reasonable to have to take to provide the auxiliary aid[6].

A principal is not required to do anything that a disabled person's employer is required[7] to do[8].

1   As to the meaning of 'principal' see PARA 119 note 1; as to the meanings of 'contract worker' and 'contract work' see PARA 119 note 4; as to the meaning of 'employer' see PARA 116. If two or more persons are subject to a duty to make reasonable adjustments in relation to the same disabled person, each of them must comply with the duty so far as it is reasonable for each of them to do so: Equality Act 2010 Sch 8 para 2(5).
2   See the Equality Act 2010 s 41(4); and PARAS 119, 155. The definition of 'interested disabled person' differs according to context. The persons in respect of whom the adjustments are required to be made under these provisions are referred to as 'interested disabled persons': Sch 8 para 4. As to the duty to make reasonable adjustments generally, and in connection with failure to comply with the duty to make adjustments, see PARAS 76, 237–238.
3   Equality Act 2010 Sch 8 paras 1, 2(1).
4   Equality Act 2010 s 20(3), Sch 8 paras 2(2)(a), (c), (3), 6(1).
5   Equality Act 2010 s 20(4), Sch 8 paras 2(2)(b), (c), (4), 6(1).
6   Equality Act 2010 s 20(5), Sch 8 paras 2(2)(c), (3), 6(1).
7   Ie by virtue of the Equality Act 2010 Sch 8 para 5 (see PARA 246).
8   Equality Act 2010 Sch 8 para 6(2).

248.   Reasonable adjustments to be made by partnerships.

A firm or proposed firm[1] is under a duty to make reasonable adjustments for disabled persons[2]. In this respect firms or proposed firms must comply with the first, second and third requirements as follows[3].

The first requirement is a requirement, where a provision, criterion or practice applied by or on behalf of the firm or proposed firm puts a person who is, or has notified the firm or proposed firm that he may be, a candidate for a position as a partner, at a substantial disadvantage in relation to deciding to whom to offer such a position, or puts a candidate for a position as a partner or a partner who holds such a position at a substantial disadvantage in relation to that position, in comparison with persons who are not disabled, to take such steps as it is reasonable to have to take to avoid the disadvantage[4].

The second requirement is a requirement, where a physical feature of premises occupied by the firm or proposed firm puts a candidate for a position as a partner or a partner who holds such a position at a substantial disadvantage in relation to that position, in comparison with persons who are not disabled, to take such steps as it is reasonable to have to take to avoid the disadvantage[5].

The third requirement is a requirement, where a person who is, or has notified the firm or proposed firm that he may be, a candidate for a position as a partner, would but for the provision of an auxiliary aid be put at a substantial disadvantage in relation to deciding to whom to offer such a position, or where a candidate for a position as a partner or a partner who holds such a position would but for the provision of an auxiliary aid be put at a substantial disadvantage in relation to such position, in comparison with persons who are not disabled, to take such steps as it is reasonable to have to take to provide the auxiliary aid[6].

A firm or proposed firm is not subject to a duty to make reasonable adjustments if it does not know, and could not reasonably be expected to know:

(1)   in the case of a candidate for a position as a partner or a potential candidate for a position as a partner, that an interested disabled person is or may be a candidate for the position in question[7]; or

(2)   that an interested disabled person has a disability and is likely to be placed at the disadvantage referred to in the first, second or third requirement[8].

1   As to the meaning of 'firm' see PARA 122 note 1; as to the meaning of 'proposed firm' see PARA 122 note 2. If two or more persons are subject to a duty to make reasonable adjustments in relation to the same disabled person, each of them must comply with the duty so far as it is reasonable for each of them to do so: Equality Act 2010 Sch 8 para 2(5).
2   See the Equality Act 2010 s 44(7); and paras 122, 155. The definition of 'interested disabled person' differs according to context. The persons in respect of whom the adjustments are required to be made under these provisions are referred to as 'interested disabled persons': Sch 8 para 4. As to the duty to make reasonable adjustments generally, and in connection with failure to comply with the duty to make adjustments, see paras 76, 237–238. Where a firm or proposed firm is required by these provisions to take a step in relation to an interested disabled person the cost of taking the step is to be treated as an expense of the firm or proposed firm and the extent to which the disabled person should (if he is or becomes a partner) bear the cost is not to exceed such amount as is reasonable (having regard in particular to his entitlement to share in the firm or proposed firm's profits): Equality Act 2010 Sch 8 para 7(2).
3   Equality Act 2010 Sch 8 paras 1, 2(1).
4   Equality Act 2010 s 20(3), Sch 8 paras 2(2)(a), (c), (3), 7(1).
5   Equality Act 2010 s 20(4), Sch 8 paras 2(2)(b), (c), (4), 7(1).
6   Equality Act 2010 s 20(5), Sch 8 paras 2(2)(c), (3), 7(1).
7   Equality Act 2010 Sch 8 para 20(1)(a), (2).
8   Equality Act 2010 Sch 8 para 20(1)(b) (amended by SI 2011/1060).

249. Reasonable adjustments to be made by limited liability partnerships.

A limited liability partnership ('LLP') or proposed LLP[1] is under a duty to make reasonable adjustments for disabled persons[2]. In this respect LLPs or proposed LLPs must comply with the first, second and third requirements as follows[3].

The first requirement is a requirement, where a provision, criterion or practice applied by or on behalf of the LLP or proposed LLP puts a person who is, or has notified the LLP or proposed LLP that he may be, a candidate for a position as a member, at a substantial disadvantage in relation to deciding to whom to offer such a position, or puts a candidate for a position as a member or a member who holds such a position at a substantial disadvantage in relation to that position, in comparison with persons who are not disabled, to take such steps as it is reasonable to have to take to avoid the disadvantage[4].

The second requirement is a requirement, where a physical feature of premises occupied by the LLP or proposed LLP puts a candidate for a position as a member or a member who holds such a position at a substantial disadvantage in relation to that position, in comparison with persons who are not disabled, to take such steps as it is reasonable to have to take to avoid the disadvantage[5].

The third requirement is a requirement, where a person who is, or has notified the LLP or proposed LLP that he may be, a candidate for a position as a member, would but for the provision of an auxiliary aid be put at a substantial disadvantage in relation to deciding to whom to offer such a position, or where a candidate for a position as a member or a member who holds such a position would but for the provision of an auxiliary aid be put at a substantial disadvantage in relation to such position, in comparison with persons who are not disabled, to take such steps as it is reasonable to have to take to provide the auxiliary aid[6].

An LLP or proposed LLP is not subject to a duty to make reasonable adjustments if it does not know, and could not reasonably be expected to know:

(1)   in the case of a candidate for a position as a member or a potential candidate for a position as a member, that an interested disabled person is or may be a candidate for the position in question[7]; or

(2)   that an interested disabled person has a disability and is likely to be placed at the disadvantage referred to in the first, second or third requirement[8].

1 As to the meaning of 'limited liability partnership' see PARA 123 note 1. If two or more persons are subject to a duty to make reasonable adjustments in relation to the same disabled person, each of them must comply with the duty so far as it is reasonable for each of them to do so: Equality Act 2010 Sch 8 para 2(5).
2 See the Equality Act 2010 s 45(7); and PARAS 123, 155. The definition of 'interested disabled person' differs according to context. The persons in respect of whom the adjustments are required to be made under these provisions are referred to as 'interested disabled persons': Sch 8 para 4. As to the duty to make reasonable adjustments generally, and in connection with failure to comply with the duty to make adjustments, see PARAS 76, 237–238. Where an LLP or proposed LLP is required by these provisions to take a step in relation to an interested disabled person the cost of taking the step is to be treated as an expense of the LLP or proposed LLP and the extent to which the disabled person should (if he is or becomes a member) bear the cost is not to exceed such amount as is reasonable (having regard in particular to his entitlement to share in the LLP or proposed LLP's profits): Equality Act 2010 Sch 8 para 8(2).
3 Equality Act 2010 Sch 8 paras 1, 2(1).
4 Equality Act 2010 s 20(3), Sch 8 paras 2(2)(a), (c), (3), 8(1).
5 Equality Act 2010 s 20(4), Sch 8 paras 2(2)(b), (c), (4), 8(1).
6 Equality Act 2010 s 20(5), Sch 8 paras 2(2)(c), (3), 8(1).
7 Equality Act 2010 Sch 8 para 20(1)(a), (2).
8 Equality Act 2010 Sch 8 para 20(1)(b) (amended by SI 2011/1060).

250. Barristers and their clerks.

A barrister[1] is under a duty to make reasonable adjustments for disabled persons[2]. In this respect barristers and barrister's clerks must comply with the first, second and third requirements as follows[3].

The first requirement is a requirement, where a provision, criterion or practice applied by or on behalf of the barrister or barrister's clerk puts a person who is, or has notified the barrister or barrister's clerk that he may be, an applicant for a pupillage or tenancy, at a substantial disadvantage in relation to deciding to whom to offer a pupillage or tenancy, or puts an applicant for a pupillage or tenancy or a pupil or tenant at a substantial disadvantage in relation to the pupillage or tenancy, in comparison with persons who are not disabled, to take such steps as it is reasonable to have to take to avoid the disadvantage[4].

The second requirement is a requirement, where a physical feature of premises occupied by the barrister or barrister's clerk puts an applicant for a pupillage or tenancy or a pupil or tenant at a substantial disadvantage in relation to a pupillage or tenancy, in comparison with persons who are not disabled, to take such steps as it is reasonable to have to take to avoid the disadvantage[5].

The third requirement is a requirement, where a person who is, or has notified the barrister or barrister's clerk that he may be, an applicant for a pupillage or tenancy, would but for the provision of an auxiliary aid be put at a substantial disadvantage in relation to deciding to whom to offer a pupillage or tenancy, or where an applicant for a pupillage or tenancy or a pupil or tenant would but for the provision of an auxiliary aid be put at a substantial disadvantage in relation to a pupillage or tenancy, in comparison with persons who are not disabled, to take such steps as it is reasonable to have to take to provide the auxiliary aid[6].

A barrister or barrister's clerk is not subject to a duty to make reasonable adjustments if he does not know, and could not reasonably be expected to know:

(1)   in the case of an applicant for a pupillage or tenancy or a potential applicant for a pupillage or tenancy, that an interested disabled person is or may be an applicant for the position in question[7]; or

(2)   that an interested disabled person has a disability and is likely to be
        placed at the disadvantage referred to in the first, second or third
        requirement[8].

1   As to the meaning of 'barrister' see PARA 124 note 1. If two or more persons are subject to a duty
    to make reasonable adjustments in relation to the same disabled person, each of them must comply
    with the duty so far as it is reasonable for each of them to do so: Equality Act 2010 Sch 8 para 2(5).
2   See the Equality Act 2010 s 47(7); and PARAS 124, 155. The persons in respect of whom the
    adjustments are required to be made under these provisions are referred to as 'interested disabled
    persons': Sch 8 para 4. As to the duty to make reasonable adjustments generally, and in connection
    with failure to comply with the duty to make adjustments, see PARAS 76, 237–238.
3   Equality Act 2010 Sch 8 paras 1, 2(1).
4   Equality Act 2010 s 20(3), Sch 8 paras 2(2)(a), (c), (3), 9(1).
5   Equality Act 2010 s 20(4), Sch 8 paras 2(2)(b), (c), (4), 9(1).
6   Equality Act 2010 s 20(5), Sch 8 paras 2(2)(c), (3), 9(1).
7   Equality Act 2010 Sch 8 para 20(1)(a), (2).
8   Equality Act 2010 Sch 8 para 20(1)(b) (amended by SI 2011/1060).

251. Persons making appointments to personal or public offices.
A person who has the power to make an appointment to a personal or public
office[1] is under a duty to make reasonable adjustments for disabled persons[2]. In
this respect such persons must comply with the first, second and third
requirements as follows[3].

The first requirement is a requirement, where a provision, criterion or practice
applied by or on behalf of such a person puts a person who is, or has notified the
person that he may be, seeking an appointment, or a person who is being
considered for an appointment, at a substantial disadvantage in relation to
deciding to whom to offer the appointment, or puts a person who is seeking, or
being considered for, appointment to the office at a substantial disadvantage in
relation to appointment to the office, in comparison with persons who are not
disabled, to take such steps as it is reasonable to have to take to avoid the
disadvantage[4].

The second requirement is a requirement, where a physical feature of premises
under the control of the person and at or from which the functions of the office
concerned are performed puts a person who is seeking, or being considered for,
appointment to an office at a substantial disadvantage in relation to appointment
to the office, in comparison with persons who are not disabled, to take such steps
as it is reasonable to have to take to avoid the disadvantage[5].

The third requirement is a requirement, where a person who is, or has notified
the person that he may be, seeking an appointment, or a person who is being
considered for an appointment, would but for the provision of an auxiliary aid be
put at a substantial disadvantage in relation to deciding to whom to offer the
appointment, or where a person who is seeking, or being considered for,
appointment to an office would but for the provision of an auxiliary aid be put at
a substantial disadvantage in relation to appointment to the office, in comparison
with persons who are not disabled, to take such steps as it is reasonable to have
to take to provide the auxiliary aid[6].

A person making an appointment to a personal or public office is not subject
to a duty to make reasonable adjustments if he does not know, and could not
reasonably be expected to know:

(1)   in the case of a person who is seeking appointment to the office or a
        person who potentially is seeking appointment to the office, that an
        interested disabled person is or may be such a person[7]; or

(2) that an interested disabled person has a disability and is likely to be placed at the disadvantage referred to in the first, second or third requirement[8].

1 As to the meaning of 'personal or public office' see PARAS **125, 126**. If two or more persons are subject to a duty to make reasonable adjustments in relation to the same disabled person, each of them must comply with the duty so far as it is reasonable for each of them to do so: Equality Act 2010 Sch 8 para 2(5).

2 See the Equality Act 2010 ss 49(9)(a), 50(11)(b); and PARAS **125–126, 155**. The persons in respect of whom the adjustments are required to be made under these provisions are referred to as 'interested disabled persons': Sch 8 para 4. As to the duty to make reasonable adjustments generally, and in connection with failure to comply with the duty to make adjustments, see PARAS **76, 237–238**.

3 Equality Act 2010 Sch 8 paras 1, 2(1).
4 Equality Act 2010 s 20(3), Sch 8 paras 2(2)(a), (c), (3), 11.
5 Equality Act 2010 s 20(4), Sch 8 paras 2(2)(b), (c), (4), 11, 14.
6 Equality Act 2010 s 20(5), Sch 8 paras 2(2)(c), (3), 11.
7 Equality Act 2010 Sch 8 para 20(1)(a), (2).
8 Equality Act 2010 Sch 8 para 20(1)(b) (amended by SI 2011/1060).

252. Persons having managerial responsibilities in relation to persons appointed to personal or public offices.

A person who has managerial responsibilities in relation to a person appointed to a personal or public office[1] is under a duty to make reasonable adjustments for disabled persons[2]. In this respect such persons must comply with the first, second and third requirements as follows[3].

The first requirement is a requirement, where a provision, criterion or practice applied by or on behalf of a relevant person puts a person appointed to the office at a substantial disadvantage in relation to the appointment, in comparison with persons who are not disabled, to take such steps as it is reasonable to have to take to avoid the disadvantage[4].

The second requirement is a requirement, where a physical feature of premises under the control of the relevant person and at or from which the functions of the office concerned are performed puts a person appointed to the office at a substantial disadvantage in relation to appointment to the office, in comparison with persons who are not disabled, to take such steps as it is reasonable to have to take to avoid the disadvantage[5].

The third requirement is a requirement, where a person appointed to the office would but for the provision of an auxiliary aid be put at a substantial disadvantage in relation to the appointment, in comparison with persons who are not disabled, to take such steps as it is reasonable to have to take to provide the auxiliary aid[6].

1 Ie a 'relevant person' in relation to an office: see the Equality Act 2010 s 52(1), (6); and PARA **125** note 7. As to the meaning of 'personal or public office' see PARAS **125, 126**. If two or more persons are subject to a duty to make reasonable adjustments in relation to the same disabled person, each of them must comply with the duty so far as it is reasonable for each of them to do so: Equality Act 2010 Sch 8 para 2(5).

2 See the Equality Act 2010 ss 49(9)(b), 50(11)(a); and PARAS **125–126, 155**. The persons in respect of whom the adjustments are required to be made under these provisions are referred to as 'interested disabled persons': Sch 8 para 4. As to the duty to make reasonable adjustments generally, and in connection with failure to comply with the duty to make adjustments, see PARAS **76, 237–238**.

3 Equality Act 2010 Sch 8 paras 1, 2(1).
4 Equality Act 2010 s 20(3), Sch 8 paras 2(2)(a), (c), (3), 12.
5 Equality Act 2010 s 20(4), Sch 8 paras 2(2)(b), (c), (4), 12, 14.
6 Equality Act 2010 s 20(5), Sch 8 paras 2(2)(c), (3), 12.

253. Persons making recommendations or giving approval in connection with appointments to public offices.

A person who has the power to make a recommendation for, or give approval to, an appointment to a public office[1] is under a duty to make reasonable adjustments for disabled persons[2]. In this respect such persons must comply with the first, second and third requirements as follows[3].

The first requirement is a requirement, where a provision, criterion or practice applied by or on behalf of such a person puts a person who is, or has notified the person that he may be, seeking recommendation or approval for appointment to the office, or a person who is being considered for recommendation or approval for appointment to the office, at a substantial disadvantage in relation to deciding who to recommend or approve for appointment to the office, or puts a person who is seeking, or being considered for, appointment to the office at a substantial disadvantage in relation to appointment to the office, in comparison with persons who are not disabled, to take such steps as it is reasonable to have to take to avoid the disadvantage[4].

The second requirement is a requirement, where a physical feature of premises under the control of the person and at or from which the functions of the office concerned are performed puts a person who is seeking, or being considered for, appointment to the office at a substantial disadvantage in relation to appointment to the office, in comparison with persons who are not disabled, to take such steps as it is reasonable to have to take to avoid the disadvantage[5].

The third requirement is a requirement, where a person who is, or has notified the person that he may be, seeking recommendation or approval for appointment to the office, or a person who is being considered for recommendation or approval for appointment to the office, would but for the provision of an auxiliary aid be put at a substantial disadvantage in relation to deciding who to recommend or approve for the appointment, or where a person who is seeking, or being considered for, appointment to the office would but for the provision of an auxiliary aid be put at a substantial disadvantage in relation to the appointment, in comparison with persons who are not disabled, to take such steps as it is reasonable to have to take to provide the auxiliary aid[6].

A person making recommendations or giving approval in connection with appointments to public offices is not subject to a duty to make reasonable adjustments if he does not know, and could not reasonably be expected to know:

(1)   in the case of a person who is seeking recommendation or approval for appointment to the office, or a person who potentially is seeking recommendation or approval for appointment to the office, that an interested disabled person is or may be such a person[7]; or

(2)   that an interested disabled person has a disability and is likely to be placed at the disadvantage referred to in the first, second or third requirement[8].

1   As to the meaning of 'public office' see PARA 127. If two or more persons are subject to a duty to make reasonable adjustments in relation to the same disabled person, each of them must comply with the duty so far as it is reasonable for each of them to do so: Equality Act 2010 Sch 8 para 2(5).

2   See the Equality Act 2010 s 51(4); and PARAS 127, 155. The persons in respect of whom the adjustments are required to be made under these provisions are referred to as 'interested disabled persons': Sch 8 para 4. As to the duty to make reasonable adjustments generally, and in connection with failure to comply with the duty to make adjustments, see PARAS 76, 237–238.

3   Equality Act 2010 Sch 8 paras 1, 2(1).

4   Equality Act 2010 s 20(3), Sch 8 paras 2(2)(a), (2)(c), (3), 13.

5   Equality Act 2010 s 20(4), Sch 8 paras 2(2)(b), (2)(c), (4), 13, 14.

6   Equality Act 2010 s 20(5), Sch 8 paras 2(2)(c), (3), 13.

7 Equality Act 2010 Sch 8 para 20(1)(a), (2).
8 Equality Act 2010 Sch 8 para 20(1)(b) (amended by SI 2011/1060).

254. Qualifications bodies.

A qualifications body[1] is under a duty to make reasonable adjustments for disabled persons[2]. In this respect such qualifications bodies must comply with the first, second and third requirements as follows[3].

The first requirement is a requirement, where a provision, criterion or practice applied by or on behalf of the qualifications body puts a person who is, or has notified the body that he may be, an applicant for conferment of a relevant qualification, at a substantial disadvantage in relation to deciding upon whom to confer the qualification, or puts an applicant for conferment of a relevant qualification, or a person who holds the qualification, at a substantial disadvantage in relation to conferment by the body of the qualification, in comparison with persons who are not disabled, to take such steps as it is reasonable to have to take to avoid the disadvantage[4].

The second requirement is a requirement, where a physical feature of premises occupied by the qualifications body puts an applicant for conferment of a relevant qualification, or a person who holds the qualification, at a substantial disadvantage in relation to conferment by the body of the qualification, in comparison with persons who are not disabled, to take such steps as it is reasonable to have to take to avoid the disadvantage[5].

The third requirement is a requirement, where a person who is, or has notified the qualifications body that he may be, an applicant for conferment of a relevant qualification, would but for the provision of an auxiliary aid be put at a substantial disadvantage in relation to deciding upon whom to confer the qualification, or where an applicant for conferment of a relevant qualification, or a person who holds the qualification, would but for the provision of an auxiliary aid be put at a substantial disadvantage in relation to conferment by the body of the qualification, in comparison with persons who are not disabled, to take such steps as it is reasonable to have to take to provide the auxiliary aid[6].

A qualifications body is not subject to a duty to make reasonable adjustments if it does not know, and could not reasonably be expected to know:

(1)   in the case of an applicant for conferment of a relevant qualification or a potential applicant for such conferment, that an interested disabled person is or may be such an applicant[7]; or

(2)   that an interested disabled person has a disability and is likely to be placed at the disadvantage referred to in the first, second or third requirement[8].

1 As to the meaning of 'qualifications body' see PARA 129 note 1. If two or more persons are subject to a duty to make reasonable adjustments in relation to the same disabled person, each of them must comply with the duty so far as it is reasonable for each of them to do so: Equality Act 2010 Sch 8 para 2(5).
2 See the Equality Act 2010 s 53(6); and PARAS 129, 155. The persons in respect of whom the adjustments are required to be made under these provisions are referred to as 'interested disabled persons': Sch 8 para 4. As to the duty to make reasonable adjustments generally, and in connection with failure to comply with the duty to make adjustments, see PARAS 76, 237–238.
3 Equality Act 2010 Sch 8 paras 1, 2(1).
4 Equality Act 2010 s 20(3), Sch 8 paras 2(2)(a), (c), (3), 15(1). As to the meaning of 'relevant qualification' see PARA 129 note 1. A provision, criterion or practice does not include the application of a competence standard: Sch 8 para 15(2). As to the meaning of 'competence standard' see PARA 129 note 13.
5 Equality Act 2010 s 20(4), Sch 8 paras 2(2)(b), (c), (4), 15(1).
6 Equality Act 2010 s 20(5), Sch 8 paras 2(2)(c), (3), 15(1).

7   Equality Act 2010 Sch 8 para 20(1)(a), (2).
8   Equality Act 2010 Sch 8 para 20(1)(b) (amended by SI 2011/1060).

255. Employment service-providers who provide vocational training.

Where an employment service-provider provides an employment service which is vocational training[1], the provider is under a duty to make reasonable adjustments for disabled persons[2]. In this respect such employment service-providers must comply with the first, second and third requirements as follows[3].

The first requirement is a requirement, where a provision, criterion or practice applied by or on behalf of the employment service-provider puts a person who is, or has notified the provider that he may be, an applicant for the provision of the service, at a substantial disadvantage in relation to deciding to whom to offer to provide the service, or puts a person who applies to the employment service-provider for the provision of the service, or a person to whom the employment service-provider provides the service, at a substantial disadvantage in relation to provision of the service by the provider, in comparison with persons who are not disabled, to take such steps as it is reasonable to have to take to avoid the disadvantage[4].

The second requirement is a requirement, where a physical feature of premises occupied by the employment service-provider puts a person who applies to the employment service-provider for the provision of the service, or a person to whom the employment service-provider provides the service, at a substantial disadvantage in relation to the provision of the service by the provider, in comparison with persons who are not disabled, to take such steps as it is reasonable to have to take to avoid the disadvantage[5].

The third requirement is a requirement, where a person who is, or has notified the employment service-provider that he may be, an applicant for the provision of the service, would but for the provision of an auxiliary aid be put at a substantial disadvantage in relation to deciding to whom to offer to provide the service, or where a person who applies to the employment service-provider for the provision of the service, or a person to whom the employment service-provider provides the service, would but for the provision of an auxiliary aid be put at a substantial disadvantage in relation to the provision of the service by the provider, in comparison with persons who are not disabled, to take such steps as it is reasonable to have to take to provide the auxiliary aid[6].

An employment service-provider is not, in so far as the employment service he provides is vocational training, subject to a duty to make reasonable adjustments if he does not know, and could not reasonably be expected to know:

(1)   in the case of an applicant for the provision of an employment service or a potential applicant for the provision of such a service, that an interested disabled person is or may be such an applicant[7]; or

(2)   that an interested disabled person has a disability and is likely to be placed at the disadvantage referred to in the first, second or third requirement[8].

1   As to the meaning of 'employment service-provider' see PARA 130. As to the meaning of 'vocational training' see the Equality Act 2010 s 56(6)(b); and PARA 130 note 1. If two or more persons are subject to a duty to make reasonable adjustments in relation to the same disabled person, each of them must comply with the duty so far as it is reasonable for each of them to do so: Sch 8 para 2(5).
2   See the Equality Act 2010 s 55(6); and PARAS 130, 155. The persons in respect of whom the adjustments are required to be made under these provisions are referred to as 'interested disabled

persons': Sch 8 para 4. As to the duty to make reasonable adjustments generally, and in connection with failure to comply with the duty to make adjustments, see PARAS 76, 237–238.

3 Equality Act 2010 Sch 8 paras 1, 2(1).
4 Equality Act 2010 s 20(3), Sch 8 paras 2(2)(a), (c), (3), 16.
5 Equality Act 2010 s 20(4), Sch 8 paras 2(2)(b), (c), (4), 16.
6 Equality Act 2010 s 20(5), Sch 8 paras 2(2)(c), (3), 16.
7 Equality Act 2010 Sch 8 para 20(1)(a), (2), (3).
8 Equality Act 2010 Sch 8 para 20(1)(b) (amended by SI 2011/1060).

256. Employment service-providers who do not provide vocational training.

Where an employment service-provider provides an employment service which is not vocational training[1], the provider is under a duty to make reasonable adjustments for disabled persons[2]. In this respect such employment service-providers must comply with the first, second and third requirements as follows[3].

The first requirement is a requirement, where a provision, criterion or practice applied by or on behalf of the employment service-provider puts a person who is, or has notified the provider that he may be, an applicant for the provision of the service, at a substantial disadvantage in relation to the employment service which the employment service-provider provides, or puts a person who applies to the employment service-provider for the provision of the service, or a person to whom the employment service-provider provides the service, at a substantial disadvantage in relation to the employment service which the employment service-provider provides, in comparison with persons who are not disabled, to take such steps as it is reasonable to have to take to avoid the disadvantage[4].

The second requirement is a requirement, where a physical feature of premises occupied by the employment service-provider puts a person who applies to the employment service-provider for the provision of the service, or a person to whom the employment service-provider provides the service, at a substantial disadvantage in relation to the employment service which the employment service-provider provides, in comparison with persons who are not disabled, to take such steps as it is reasonable to have to take to avoid the disadvantage[5].

The third requirement is a requirement, where a person who is, or has notified the employment service-provider that he may be, an applicant for the provision of the service, would but for the provision of an auxiliary aid be put at a substantial disadvantage in relation to the employment service which the employment service-provider provides, or where a person who applies to the employment service-provider for the provision of the service, or a person to whom the employment service-provider provides the service, would but for the provision of an auxiliary aid be put at a substantial disadvantage in relation to the employment service which the employment service-provider provides, in comparison with persons who are not disabled, to take such steps as it is reasonable to have to take to provide the auxiliary aid[6].

1 As to the meaning of 'employment service-provider' see PARA 130. As to the meaning of 'vocational training' see the Equality Act 2010 s 56(6)(b); and PARA 130 note 1. If two or more persons are subject to a duty to make reasonable adjustments in relation to the same disabled person, each of them must comply with the duty so far as it is reasonable for each of them to do so: Sch 8 paras 2(5), 3(1), (4).
2 See the Equality Act 2010 s 55(6); and PARAS 130, 155. The persons in respect of whom the adjustments are required to be made under these provisions are referred to as 'interested disabled persons': Sch 8 para 4. As to the duty to make reasonable adjustments generally, and in connection with failure to comply with the duty to make adjustments, see PARAS 76, 237–238.
3 Equality Act 2010 Sch 8 paras 1, 2(1).
4 Equality Act 2010 s 20(3), Sch 8 paras 2(2)(a), (c), (3), 3(1)–(3), 16.

5 Equality Act 2010 s 20(4), Sch 8 paras 2(2)(b), (c), (4) , 3(1)–(3), 16.
6 Equality Act 2010 s 20(5), Sch 8 paras 2(2)(c), (3) , 3(1)–(3), 16.

257. Reasonable adjustments to be made by trade organisations.

A trade organisation[1] is under a duty to make reasonable adjustments for disabled persons[2]. In this respect trade organisations must comply with the first, second and third requirements as follows[3].

The first requirement is a requirement, where a provision, criterion or practice applied by or on behalf of the organisation puts a person who is, or has notified the organisation that he may be, an applicant for membership of the organisation, at a substantial disadvantage in relation to deciding to whom to offer such membership, or puts an applicant for membership, or a member, at a substantial disadvantage in relation to membership of the organisation, in comparison with persons who are not disabled, to take such steps as it is reasonable to have to take to avoid the disadvantage[4].

The second requirement is a requirement, where a physical feature of premises occupied by the organisation puts an applicant for membership, or a member, at a substantial disadvantage in relation to membership of the organisation, in comparison with persons who are not disabled, to take such steps as it is reasonable to have to take to avoid the disadvantage[5].

The third requirement is a requirement, where a person who is, or has notified the organisation that he may be, an applicant for membership of the organisation, would but for the provision of an auxiliary aid be put at a substantial disadvantage in relation to deciding to whom to offer such membership, or where an applicant for membership, or a member, of the organisation would but for the provision of an auxiliary aid be put at a substantial disadvantage in relation to such membership, in comparison with persons who are not disabled, to take such steps as it is reasonable to have to take to provide the auxiliary aid[6].

A trade organisation is not subject to a duty to make reasonable adjustments if it does not know, and could not reasonably be expected to know:

(1) in the case of an applicant for membership or a potential applicant for membership, that an interested disabled person is or may be such an applicant[7]; or

(2) that an interested disabled person has a disability and is likely to be placed at the disadvantage referred to in the first, second or third requirement[8].

1 As to the meaning of 'trade organisation' see PARA 131 note 1. If two or more persons are subject to a duty to make reasonable adjustments in relation to the same disabled person, each of them must comply with the duty so far as it is reasonable for each of them to do so: Equality Act 2010 Sch 8 para 2(5).
2 See the Equality Act 2010 s 57(6); and PARAS 131, 155. The persons in respect of whom the adjustments are required to be made under these provisions are referred to as 'interested disabled persons': Sch 8 para 4. As to the duty to make reasonable adjustments generally, and in connection with failure to comply with the duty to make adjustments, see PARAS 76, 237–238.
3 Equality Act 2010 Sch 8 paras 1, 2(1).
4 Equality Act 2010 s 20(3), Sch 8 paras 2(2)(a), (c), (3), 17.
5 Equality Act 2010 s 20(4), Sch 8 paras 2(2)(b), (c), (4), 17.
6 Equality Act 2010 s 20(5), Sch 8 paras 2(2)(c), (3), 17.
7 Equality Act 2010 Sch 8 para 20(1)(a), (2).
8 Equality Act 2010 Sch 8 para 20(1)(b) (amended by SI 2011/1060).

258. Reasonable adjustments to be made by local authorities.

A local authority[1] is under a duty to make reasonable adjustments for disabled persons[2]. In this respect local authorities must comply with the first, second and third requirements as follows[3].

The first requirement is a requirement, where a provision, criterion or practice applied by or on behalf of the local authority puts a member of the authority who is carrying out official business at a substantial disadvantage in relation to the carrying-out of that business, in comparison with persons who are not disabled, to take such steps as it is reasonable to have to take to avoid the disadvantage[4].

The second requirement is a requirement, where a physical feature of premises occupied by the organisation puts a member of the authority who is carrying out official business at a substantial disadvantage in relation to the carrying-out of that business, in comparison with persons who are not disabled, to take such steps as it is reasonable to have to take to avoid the disadvantage[5].

The third requirement is a requirement, where a member of the authority who is carrying out official business would but for the provision of an auxiliary aid be put at a substantial disadvantage in relation to the carrying-out of that business, in comparison with persons who are not disabled, to take such steps as it is reasonable to have to take to provide the auxiliary aid[6].

1 As to the meaning of 'local authority' see PARA 132 note 1. If two or more persons are subject to a duty to make reasonable adjustments in relation to the same disabled person, each of them must comply with the duty so far as it is reasonable for each of them to do so: Equality Act 2010 Sch 8 para 2(5).
2 See the Equality Act 2010 s 58(6); and PARAS 132, 155. The persons in respect of whom the adjustments are required to be made under these provisions are referred to as 'interested disabled persons': Sch 8 para 4. As to the duty to make reasonable adjustments generally, and in connection with failure to comply with the duty to make adjustments, see PARAS 76, 237–238.
3 Equality Act 2010 Sch 8 paras 1, 2(1).
4 Equality Act 2010 s 20(3), Sch 8 paras 2(2)(a), (c), (3), 18(1). Regulations may, for these purposes, make provision as to circumstances in which a provision, criterion or practice is, or is not, to be taken to put a disabled person at the disadvantage referred to in the first requirement: Sch 8 para 18(2)(a). At the date at which this volume states the law no such regulations had been made.
5 Equality Act 2010 s 20(4), Sch 8 paras 2(2)(c), (4), 18(1). Regulations may, for these purposes, make provision as to circumstances in which a physical feature is, or is not, to be taken to put a disabled person at the disadvantage referred to in the second requirement: Sch 8 para 18(2)(b). At the date at which this volume states the law no such regulations had been made.
6 Equality Act 2010 s 20(5), Sch 8 paras 2(2)(c), (3), 18(1). Regulations may, for these purposes, make provision as to circumstances in which it is, or in which it is not, reasonable for a local authority to be required to take steps of a prescribed description (Sch 8 para 18(2)(c)) and as to steps which it is always, or which it is never, reasonable for a local authority to take (Sch 8 para 18(2)(d)). At the date at which this volume states the law no such regulations had been made.

259. Reasonable adjustments to be made in connection with occupational pension schemes.

A responsible person in relation to an occupational pension scheme[1] is under a duty to make reasonable adjustments for disabled persons[2]. In this respect local authorities must comply with the first, second and third requirements as follows[3].

The first requirement is a requirement, where a provision, criterion or practice applied by or on behalf of the responsible person puts a person who is or may be a member of the scheme at a substantial disadvantage in relation to the carrying-out of the responsible person's functions in relation to the scheme, in comparison with persons who are not disabled, to take such steps as it is reasonable to have to take to avoid the disadvantage[4].

The second requirement is a requirement, where a physical feature of premises occupied by the responsible person puts a person who is or may be a member of the scheme at a substantial disadvantage in relation to the carrying-out of the responsible person's functions in relation to the scheme, in comparison with persons who are not disabled, to take such steps as it is reasonable to have to take to avoid the disadvantage[5].

The third requirement is a requirement, where a person who is or may be a member of the scheme would but for the provision of an auxiliary aid be put at a substantial disadvantage in relation to the carrying-out of the responsible person's functions in relation to the scheme, in comparison with persons who are not disabled, to take such steps as it is reasonable to have to take to provide the auxiliary aid[6].

1   As to the meaning of 'responsible person' see PARA 134 note 4; as to the meaning of 'occupational pension scheme' see PARA 134 note 1. If two or more persons are subject to a duty to make reasonable adjustments in relation to the same disabled person, each of them must comply with the duty so far as it is reasonable for each of them to do so: Equality Act 2010 Sch 8 para 2(5).
2   See the Equality Act 2010 s 61(11); and PARAS 134, 155. The persons in respect of whom the adjustments are required to be made under these provisions are referred to as 'interested disabled persons': Sch 8 para 4. As to the duty to make reasonable adjustments generally, and in connection with failure to comply with the duty to make adjustments, see PARAS 76, 237–238.
3   Equality Act 2010 Sch 8 paras 1, 2(1).
4   Equality Act 2010 s 20(3), Sch 8 paras 2(2)(a), (c), (3), 19.
5   Equality Act 2010 s 20(4), Sch 8 paras 2(2)(b), (c), (4), 19.
6   Equality Act 2010 s 20(5), Sch 8 paras 2(2)(c), (3), 19.

(v) Reasonable Adjustments to be made by Bodies concerned with Education or Training

260. Reasonable adjustments to be made by schools.
The responsible body of a school[1] is under a duty to make reasonable adjustments for disabled persons[2]. In this respect the school must comply with the first and third requirements as follows[3].

The first requirement is a requirement, where a provision, criterion or practice applied by or on behalf of the school puts a disabled person at a substantial disadvantage in relation to deciding who is to be offered admission as a pupil[4], or puts a disabled pupil at a substantial disadvantage in the provision of education or access to a benefit, facility or service[5], in comparison with persons who are not disabled, to take such steps as it is reasonable to have to take to avoid the disadvantage[6].

The third requirement is a requirement, where a disabled person would, but for the provision of an auxiliary aid, be put at a substantial disadvantage in relation to deciding who is to be offered admission as a pupil, or where a disabled pupil would, but for the provision of such aid, be put at a substantial disadvantage in relation to the provision of education or access to a benefit, facility or service, in comparison with persons who are not disabled, to take such steps as it is reasonable to have to take to provide the auxiliary aid[7].

1   As to the schools to which these provisions apply, and as to the 'responsible bodies' of such schools, see PARA 173 note 1.
2   See the Equality Act 2010 s 85(6); and PARA 194. As to the meaning of 'disabled person' see PARA 47. As to the duty to make reasonable adjustments generally, and as to the failure to comply with that duty see PARAS 76, 237–238.
3   Equality Act 2010 s 98, Sch 13 paras 1, 2(1), (2). In deciding whether it is reasonable for a person to have to take a step for the purpose of complying with the first, second or third requirements, that person must have regard to relevant provisions of a code of practice issued under s 14 (see PARA 67): Sch 13 para 7. If a person has made a 'confidentiality request' of which A is aware, then in

deciding whether it is reasonable for A to have to take a step in relation to that person so as to comply with the first, second or third requirement, A must have regard to the extent to which taking the step is consistent with the request: Sch 13 para 8(1), (2). In a case within Sch 13 para 8(2), a 'confidentiality request' is a request that the nature or existence of a disabled person's disability be treated as confidential and which satisfies either of the following conditions:

(1)   that the request is made by the person's parent (Sch 13 para 8(3), (4)); or

(2)   that it is made by the person and A reasonably believes that the person has sufficient understanding of the nature and effect of the request (Sch 13 para 8(5)).

4   Equality Act 2010 Sch 13 para 2(3)(a), (b)(i), (4)(a).

5   Equality Act 2010 Sch 13 para 2(3)(b)(ii), (4)(b). As to providing or affording access to a benefit, facility or service see PARA 117 note 7.

6   Equality Act 2010 s 20(3), Sch 13 para 2(3).

7   Equality Act 2010 s 20(5), Sch 13 para 2(3).

261. Reasonable adjustments to be made by further and higher education institutions.

The responsible body of an applicable further or higher education institution[1] is under a duty to make reasonable adjustments for disabled persons[2]. In this respect the institution must comply with the first, second and third requirements as follows[3].

The first requirement is a requirement, where a provision, criterion or practice applied by or on behalf of the institution[4] puts a disabled person at a substantial disadvantage in relation to deciding who is to be offered admission as a student[5], puts a disabled student at a substantial disadvantage in the provision of education or access to a benefit, facility or service[6], or puts an interested disabled person[7] at a substantial disadvantage in deciding on whom a qualification is conferred or in relation to a qualification that the institution confers[8], in comparison with persons who are not disabled, to take such steps as it is reasonable to have to take to avoid the disadvantage[9].

The second requirement is a requirement, where a physical feature of premises occupied by the institution puts a disabled person at a substantial disadvantage in relation to deciding who is to be offered admission as a student, puts a disabled student at a substantial disadvantage in the provision of education or access to a benefit, facility or service, or puts an interested disabled person at a substantial disadvantage in deciding on whom a qualification is conferred or in relation to a qualification that the institution confers, in comparison with persons who are not disabled, to take such steps as it is reasonable to have to take to avoid the disadvantage[10].

The third requirement is a requirement, where a disabled person would, but for the provision of an auxiliary aid, be put at a substantial disadvantage in relation to deciding who is to be offered admission as a student, or where a disabled student would, but for the provision of such aid, be put at a substantial disadvantage in the provision of education or access to a benefit, facility or service, or where an interested disabled person would, but for the provision of such aid, be put at a substantial disadvantage in deciding on whom a qualification is conferred or in relation to a qualification that the institution confers, in comparison with persons who are not disabled, to take such steps as it is reasonable to have to take to provide the auxiliary aid[11].

1   As to the institutions to which these provisions apply, and as to the 'responsible bodies' of such institutions, see PARA 182 note 1.

2   See the Equality Act 2010 s 91(9); and PARA 194. As to the meaning of 'disabled person' see PARA 47. As to the duty to make reasonable adjustments generally, and as to the failure to comply with that duty see PARAS 76, 237–238.

3   Equality Act 2010 Sch 13 paras 1, 3(1), (2). As to deciding whether it is reasonable for a person
    to have to take a step for the purpose of complying with the first, second or third requirements see
    further Sch 13 paras 7, 8; and PARA 260 note 3.
4   A provision, criterion or practice does not include the application of a competence standard (ie an
    academic, medical or other standard applied for the purpose of determining whether or not a
    person has a particular level of competence or ability): Equality Act 2010 Sch 13 para 4(2), (3).
5   Equality Act 2010 Sch 13 para 3(3)(c)(i), (4)(a).
6   Equality Act 2010 Sch 13 para 3(3)(c)(ii), (4)(b), (c). As to providing or affording access to a
    benefit, facility or service see PARA 117 note 7.
7   An 'interested' disabled person is a disabled person who is a person who is, or has notified the
    institution that the person may be, an applicant for the conferment of the qualification (in the
    context of deciding upon whom to confer a qualification and is either an applicant for the
    conferment by the institution of the qualification or a person on whom the institution confers the
    qualification) in the context of a qualification that A confers: Equality Act 2010 Sch 13 para 4(1).
    As to references to conferring a qualification see PARA 184 note 4.
8   Equality Act 2010 Sch 13 para 3(3)(c)(iii), (4)(d), (e).
9   Equality Act 2010 s 20(3), Sch 13 para 3(3)(a).
10 Equality Act 2010 s 20(4), Sch 13 para 3(3)(b), (3)(c), (4).
11 Equality Act 2010 s 20(5), Sch 13 para 3(3)(c), (4).

262. Reasonable adjustments to be made in connection with the provision of further or higher education courses.

The responsible body in relation to an applicable course of further or higher education[1] is under a duty to make reasonable adjustments for disabled persons[2]. In this respect the responsible body must comply with the first, second and third requirements (although if the responsible body is the governing body of a maintained school[3] it is not required to comply with the second requirement) as follows[4].

The first requirement is a requirement, where a provision, criterion or practice applied by or on behalf of the responsible body puts a disabled person at a substantial disadvantage in relation to arrangements for enrolling persons on a course of further or higher education secured by the responsible body[5], or puts a disabled person who is enrolled on a course at a substantial disadvantage in the relation to services provided by the responsible body for persons enrolled on the course[6], in comparison with persons who are not disabled, to take such steps as it is reasonable to have to take to avoid the disadvantage[7].

The second requirement is a requirement, where a physical feature of premises occupied by the responsible body puts a disabled person at a substantial disadvantage in relation to arrangements for enrolling persons on a course of further or higher education secured by the responsible body, or puts a disabled person who is enrolled on a course at a substantial disadvantage in the relation to services provided by the responsible body for persons enrolled on the course, in comparison with persons who are not disabled, to take such steps as it is reasonable to have to take to avoid the disadvantage[8].

The third requirement is a requirement, where a disabled person would, but for the provision of an auxiliary aid, be put at a substantial disadvantage in relation to arrangements for enrolling persons on a course of further or higher education secured by the responsible body, or where a disabled person who is enrolled on a course would, but for the provision of such aid, be put at a substantial disadvantage in the relation to services provided by the responsible body for persons enrolled on the course, in comparison with persons who are not disabled, to take such steps as it is reasonable to have to take to provide the auxiliary aid[9].

1   As to the courses to which these provisions apply, and as to the 'responsible bodies' in connection
    with such courses, see PARA 188 note 1.

2   See the Equality Act 2010 s 92(6); and PARA 194. As to the meaning of 'disabled person' see PARA
    47. As to the duty to make reasonable adjustments generally, and as to the failure to comply with
    that duty see PARAS 76, 237–238.
3   See PARA 188 note 1.
4   Equality Act 2010 Sch 13 para 5(1), (2). As to deciding whether it is reasonable for a person to
    have to take a step for the purpose of complying with the first, second or third requirements see
    further Sch 13 paras 7, 8; and PARA 260 note 3.
5   Equality Act 2010 Sch 13 para 5(3)(c)(i), (4)(a).
6   Equality Act 2010 Sch 13 para 5(3)(c)(ii), (4)(b). As to providing or affording access to a benefit,
    facility or service see PARA 117 note 7.
7   Equality Act 2010 s 20(3), Sch 13 para 5(3)(a). As to the meanings of 'enrolment' and 'services'
    see PARA 188 notes 3, 7.
8   Equality Act 2010 s 20(4), Sch 13 para 5(3)(b), (3)(c), (4).
9   Equality Act 2010 s 20(5), Sch 13 para 5(3)(c), (4).

263. Reasonable adjustments to be made in connection with the provision of recreational or training facilities.

A body responsible for the provision of recreational and training facilities[1] is under a duty to make reasonable adjustments for disabled persons[2]. In this respect the responsible body must comply with the first, second and third requirements as follows[3].

The first requirement is a requirement, where a provision, criterion or practice applied by or on behalf of the responsible body puts a disabled person at a substantial disadvantage in relation to the responsible body's arrangements for providing the recreational or training facilities[4], in comparison with persons who are not disabled, to take such steps as it is reasonable to have to take to avoid the disadvantage[5].

The second requirement is a requirement, where a physical feature of premises occupied by the responsible body puts a disabled person at a substantial disadvantage in relation to the responsible body's arrangements for providing the recreational or training facilities, in comparison with persons who are not disabled, to take such steps as it is reasonable to have to take to avoid the disadvantage[6].

The third requirement is a requirement, where a disabled person would, but for the provision of an auxiliary aid, be put at a substantial disadvantage in relation to the responsible body's arrangements for providing the recreational or training facilities, in comparison with persons who are not disabled, to take such steps as it is reasonable to have to take to provide such aid[7].

1   As to the recreational and training facilities to which these provisions apply, and as to the
    'responsible bodies' in connection with such facilities, see PARA 190 note 1.
2   See the Equality Act 2010 s 93(6); and PARA 194. As to the meaning of 'disabled person' see PARA
    47. As to the duty to make reasonable adjustments generally, and as to the failure to comply with
    that duty see PARAS 76, 237–238.
3   Equality Act 2010 Sch 13 para 6(1), (2). As to deciding whether it is reasonable for a person to
    have to take a step for the purpose of complying with the first, second or third requirements see
    further Sch 13 paras 7, 8; and PARA 260 note 3.
4   Equality Act 2010 Sch 13 para 6(3)(c), (4).
5   Equality Act 2010 s 20(3), Sch 13 para 6(3)(a).
6   Equality Act 2010 s 20(4), Sch 13 para 6(3)(b), (3)(c), (4).
7   Equality Act 2010 s 20(5), Sch 13 para 6(3)(c), (4).

264. Reasonable adjustments to be made by qualifications bodies.

Qualifications bodies[1] are under a duty to make reasonable adjustments for disabled persons[2]. In this respect the institution must comply with the first, second and third requirements as follows[3].

The first requirement is a requirement, where a provision, criterion or practice relating to qualifications applied by or on behalf of the institution[4] puts a disabled person at a substantial disadvantage in relation to deciding who is to be offered admission as a student[5], puts a disabled student at a substantial disadvantage in the provision of education or access to a benefit, facility or service[6], or puts an interested disabled person[7] at a substantial disadvantage in deciding on whom a qualification is conferred or in relation to a qualification that the institution confers[8], in comparison with persons who are not disabled, to take such steps as it is reasonable to have to take to avoid the disadvantage[9].

The second requirement is a requirement, where (so far as relating to qualifications) a physical feature of premises occupied by the institution puts a disabled person at a substantial disadvantage in relation to deciding who is to be offered admission as a student, puts a disabled student at a substantial disadvantage in the provision of education or access to a benefit, facility or service, or puts an interested disabled person at a substantial disadvantage in deciding on whom a qualification is conferred or in relation to a qualification that the institution confers, in comparison with persons who are not disabled, to take such steps as it is reasonable to have to take to avoid the disadvantage[10].

The third requirement is a requirement, where (so far as relating to qualifications) a disabled person would, but for the provision of an auxiliary aid, be put at a substantial disadvantage in relation to deciding who is to be offered admission as a student, or where a disabled student would, but for the provision of such aid, be put at a substantial disadvantage in the provision of education or access to a benefit, facility or service, or where an interested disabled person would, but for the provision of such aid, be put at a substantial disadvantage in deciding on whom a qualification is conferred or in relation to a qualification that the institution confers, in comparison with persons who are not disabled, to take such steps as it is reasonable to have to take to provide the auxiliary aid[11].

This duty does not, however, apply to the body in so far as the appropriate regulator[12] specifies provisions, criteria or practices[13] in relation to which the body is not subject to a duty to make reasonable adjustments[14] or is subject to a duty to make reasonable adjustments, but in relation to which such adjustments as the regulator specifies should not be made[15].

1 As to the meaning of 'qualifications body' see PARA **192** note 1.
2 See the Equality Act 2010 s 96(6); and PARA **194**. As to the meaning of 'disabled person' see PARA **47**. As to the duty to make reasonable adjustments generally, and as to the failure to comply with that duty see PARAS **76**, 237–238.
3 Equality Act 2010 Sch 13 paras 3(1), (2), 9(1), (2). As to deciding whether it is reasonable for a person to have to take a step for the purpose of complying with the first, second or third requirements see further Sch 13 paras 7, 8; and PARA **260** note 3.
4 A provision, criterion or practice does not include the application of a competence standard (ie an academic, medical or other standard applied for the purpose of determining whether or not a person has a particular level of competence or ability): Equality Act 2010 Sch 13 para 4(2), (3).
5 Equality Act 2010 Sch 13 para 3(3)(c)(i), (4)(a).
6 Equality Act 2010 Sch 13 para 3(3)(c)(ii), (4)(b), (c). As to providing or affording access to a benefit, facility or service see PARA **117** note 7.
7 An 'interested' disabled person is a disabled person who is a person who is, or has notified the institution that the person may be, an applicant for the conferment of the qualification (in the context of deciding upon whom to confer a qualification and is either an applicant for the conferment by the institution of the qualification or a person on whom the institution confers the qualification (in the context of a qualification that A confers: Equality Act 2010 Sch 13 para 4(1). As to references to conferring a qualification see PARA **184** note 4.
8 Equality Act 2010 Sch 13 para 3(3)(c)(iii), (4)(d), (e).
9 Equality Act 2010 s 20(3), Sch 13 para 3(3)(a).

10 Equality Act 2010 s 20(4), Sch 13 para 3(3)(b), (c), (4).
11 Equality Act 2010 s 20(5), Sch 13 para 3(3)(c), (4).
12 The 'appropriate regulator' is a person prescribed by a Minister of the Crown (in relation to a qualifications body that confers relevant qualifications in England) or the Welsh Ministers (in relation to a qualifications body that confers relevant qualifications in Wales): Equality Act 2010 ss 96(10)(a), (b), 97(7). As to the meaning of 'relevant qualification', and as to the conferment of qualifications, see PARA 192 note 1: for these purposes a relevant qualification is conferred in a part of Great Britain if there are, or may reasonably be expected to be, persons seeking to obtain the relevant qualification who are or will be assessed for those purposes wholly or mainly in that part: ss 96(11), 97(7). As to the meanings of 'England', 'Wales' and 'Great Britain' see PARA 85 note 1; as to the persons so prescribed see the Equality Act 2010 (General Qualifications Bodies) (Appropriate Regulator and Relevant Qualifications) Regulations 2010, SI 2010/2245, regs 3, 4, Sch 1 (amended by SI 2017/705); and the Equality Act 2010 (General Qualifications Bodies Regulator and Relevant Qualifications) (Wales) Regulations 2010, SI 2010/2217.
13 The appropriate regulator must not specify any matter for the purposes of the Equality Act 2010 s 96(7) unless it has consulted such persons as it thinks appropriate (s 96(9)(a)), and must publish matters so specified (including the date from which they are to have effect) in such manner as is prescribed (s 96(9)(b)). In England, an appropriate regulator must publish any matter specified under s 96(7) on the regulator's website: see the Equality Act 2010 (General Qualifications Bodies) (Appropriate Regulator and Relevant Qualifications) Regulations 2010, SI 2010/2245, reg 2.
14 Equality Act 2010 s 96(7)(a). For the purposes of s 96(7) the appropriate regulator must have regard to the need to minimise the extent to which disabled persons are disadvantaged in attaining the relevant qualification because of their disabilities, the need to secure that the relevant qualification gives a reliable indication of the knowledge, skills and understanding of a person upon whom it is conferred, and the need to maintain public confidence in the relevant qualification: ss 96(8), 97(7).
15 Equality Act 2010 s 96(7)(b). See note 14.

(vi) Reasonable Adjustments to be made by Associations

265. Reasonable adjustments to be made by associations.

Associations[1] are under a duty to make reasonable adjustments for disabled persons who:

(1)　are, or are seeking to become or might wish to become, members;
(2)　are associates; or
(3)　are, or are likely to become, guests[2].

In this respect the association must comply with the first, second and third requirements as follows[3].

The first requirement is a requirement, where a provision, criterion or practice of the association puts a disabled person at a substantial disadvantage in relation to:

(a)　access to a benefit, facility or service;
(b)　members' or associates' retaining their rights as such or avoiding having them varied;
(c)　being admitted to membership or invited as a guest[4],

in comparison with persons who are not disabled, to take such steps as it is reasonable to have to take to avoid the disadvantage[5].

The second requirement is a requirement, where a physical feature[6] puts a disabled person at a substantial disadvantage in relation to:

(i)　access to a benefit, facility or service;
(ii)　being admitted to membership or invited as a guest[7],

in comparison with persons who are not disabled, to take such steps as it is reasonable to have to take to avoid the disadvantage, or to adopt a reasonable alternative method of affording access to the benefit, facility or service or of admitting persons to membership or inviting persons as guests[8].

The third requirement is a requirement, where a disabled person would, but for the provision of an auxiliary aid, be put at a substantial disadvantage in relation to:

(A)   access to a benefit, facility or service;

(B)   members' or associates' retaining their rights as such or avoiding having them varied;

(C)   being admitted to membership or invited as a guest[9],

in comparison with persons who are not disabled, to take such steps as it is reasonable to have to take to provide the auxiliary aid[10].

However, these provisions do not require the association to take a step which would fundamentally alter the nature of the benefit, facility or service concerned, or the nature of the association[11]. Nor do they require a member or associate in whose house meetings of the association take place to make adjustments to a physical feature of the house[12].

1   As to the meaning of 'association' see PARA **198**.
2   See the Equality Act 2010 ss 103(1), 107(8), Sch 15 paras 1, 2(2); the Equality Act 2010 Code of Practice — Services, Public Functions and Associations Statutory Code of Practice (2011) paras 12.43–12.45; and PARA **203**. As to discrimination by associations generally see PARAS **198–210**. As to the duty to make reasonable adjustments generally, and as to the failure to comply with that duty see PARAS **76, 237–238**.
3   Equality Act 2010 Sch 15 para 2(1).
4   Equality Act 2010 Sch 15 para 2(4).
5   Equality Act 2010 s 20(3).
6   In relation to the second requirement, a physical feature includes a physical feature brought by or on behalf of the association, in the course of or for the purpose of providing a benefit, facility or service, on to premises other than those that the association occupies (as well as including a physical feature in or on premises that the association occupies): Equality Act 2010 Sch 15 para 2(6).
7   Equality Act 2010 Sch 15 para 2(5).
8   Equality Act 2010 s 20(4), Sch 15 para 2(3). It is not reasonable for an association to have to remove or alter a physical feature where the feature concerned:
     (1)   was provided in or in connection with a building for the purpose of assisting people to have access to the building or to use facilities provided in the building (Equality Act 2010 (Disability) Regulations 2010, SI 2010/2128, reg 9(1)); and
     (2)   satisfies the relevant design standard (Equality Act 2010 (Disability) Regulations 2010, SI 2010/2128, reg 9(2)).
     Whether a physical feature satisfies the relevant design standard is determined in accordance with the Equality Act 2010 (Disability) Regulations 2010, SI 2010/2128, Schedule: see reg 9(3).
9   Equality Act 2010 Sch 15 para 2(4).
10   Equality Act 2010 s 20(5).
11   Equality Act 2010 Sch 15 para 2(7).
12   Equality Act 2010 Sch 15 para 2(8).

(vii) Requirement to Obtain Consent to Make Reasonable Adjustments

266. Generally applicable provisions regarding consent.
In addition to the provisions which set out the reasonable adjustments that particular categories of bodies must make for the benefit of disabled persons[1], the Equality Act 2010 also sets out provisions which apply to all such bodies[2]. These provisions relate primarily to the issues surrounding obtaining the consent of other persons with respect to making reasonable adjustments to premises[3].

1   As to the duty to make reasonable adjustments generally, and as to the failure to comply with that duty see PARAS **76, 237–238**. As to the reasonable adjustments that must be made in the provision of services and the exercise of public functions see the Equality Act 2010 Sch 2; and PARAS **239–240**. As to the reasonable adjustments that must be made in respect of leasehold and commonhold premises see Sch 4; and PARAS **241–244**. As to the reasonable adjustments that must be made in the workplace

see Sch 8; and PARAS 245–259. As to the reasonable adjustments to be made by bodies concerned with education or training see Sch 13; and PARAS 260–264. As to the reasonable adjustments to be made by associations see Sch 15; and PARA 265.

2 See the Equality Act 2010 s 189, Sch 21 para 1; and PARA 267 et seq.

3 See PARA 267 et seq.

267. Binding obligations to obtain consent.

If:

(1) a binding obligation[1] requires a person ('A') A to obtain the consent of another person to an alteration of premises which A occupies[2];

(2) where A is a controller of let premises, a binding obligation requires A to obtain the consent of another person to a variation of a term of the tenancy[3]; or

(3) where A is a responsible person in relation to common parts, a binding obligation requires A to obtain the consent of another person to an alteration of the common parts[4],

then, for the purpose of discharging a duty to make reasonable adjustments[5] it is always reasonable for A to have to take steps to obtain the consent[6], but it is never reasonable for A to have to make the alteration before the consent is obtained[7].

1 For these purposes, a binding obligation is a legally binding obligation in relation to premises, however arising; but the reference to a binding obligation in head (1) or (3) in the text does not include a reference to an obligation imposed by a tenancy: Equality Act 2010 Sch 21 para 2(3).

2 Equality Act 2010 Sch 21 para 2(1)(a).

3 Equality Act 2010 Sch 21 para 2(1)(b).

4 Equality Act 2010 Sch 21 para 2(1)(c).

5 As to the duty to make reasonable adjustments generally, and as to the failure to comply with that duty see PARAS 76, 237–238.

6 Equality Act 2010 Sch 21 para 2(2)(a). The steps referred to in the text do not include applying to a court or tribunal: Sch 21 para 2(4).

7 Equality Act 2010 Sch 21 para 2(2)(b).

268. Landlord's consent.

If:

(1) a person ('A') occupies premises under a tenancy, and he is proposing to make an alteration to the premises so as to comply with a duty to make reasonable adjustments[1], and he would not otherwise be entitled to make the alteration[2]; or

(2) if A is a responsible person in relation to common parts, and he is proposing to make an alteration to the common parts so as to comply with a duty to make reasonable adjustments, and is the tenant of property which includes the common parts, and he would not otherwise be entitled to make the alteration[3],

then the tenancy has effect as if it provided:

(a) for A to be entitled to make the alteration with the written consent of the landlord[4];

(b) for A to have to make a written application for that consent[5];

(c) for the landlord not to withhold the consent unreasonably[6]; and

(d) for the landlord to be able to give the consent subject to reasonable conditions[7].

If a question arises as to whether A has made the alteration (and, accordingly, complied with a duty to make reasonable adjustments), any constraint attributable to the tenancy must be ignored unless A has applied to the landlord in writing for consent to the alteration[8].

Regulations may make provision modifying or supplementing these provisions[9] where A's tenancy is a sub-tenancy[10].

1　As to the duty to make reasonable adjustments generally, and as to the failure to comply with that duty see PARAS 76, 237–238.
2　Equality Act 2010 Sch 21 para 3(1)(a)–(c). A must be treated as not entitled to make the alteration if the tenancy imposes conditions which are to apply if A makes an alteration, or entitles the landlord to attach conditions to a consent to the alteration: Sch 21 para 3(5).
3　Equality Act 2010 Sch 21 para 3(2)(a)–(d). See note 2.
4　Equality Act 2010 Sch 21 para 3(3)(a).
5　Equality Act 2010 Sch 21 para 3(3)(b).
6　Equality Act 2010 Sch 21 para 3(3)(c). As to whether a landlord has withheld consent unreasonably see PARA 269.
7　Equality Act 2010 Sch 21 para 3(3)(d).
8　Equality Act 2010 Sch 21 para 3(4).
9　Ie provision supplementing or modifying the Equality Act 2010 Sch 21 paras 1–6 or provision made under Sch 21 para 6.
10　See the Equality Act 2010 Sch 21 para 6(3), (4). In exercise of this power, the Equality Act 2010 (Disability) Regulations 2010, SI 2010/2128, have been made which modify the Equality Act 2010 Sch 21 in relation to any case where the occupier occupies premises under a sub-tenancy: see the Equality Act 2010 (Disability) Regulations 2010, SI 2010/2128, reg 14. In these circumstances it is provided that except to the extent to which it expressly so provides, any superior lease in respect of the premises has effect in relation to the landlord and tenant who are parties to that superior lease as if it provided:
　　(1)　for the tenant to be entitled to give his consent to the alteration with the written consent of the landlord (Equality Act 2010 Sch 21 para 3(3A)(a) (Sch 21 para 3(3A) added as a modification by SI 2010/2128);
　　(2)　for the tenant to have to make a written application to the landlord for consent if he wishes to give his consent to the alteration (Equality Act 2010 Sch 21 para 3(3A)(b) (as so added);
　　(3)　if such an application is made, for the landlord not to withhold his consent unreasonably (Sch 21 para 3(3A)(c) (as so added); and
　　(4)　for the landlord to be entitled to make his consent subject to reasonable conditions (Sch 21 para 3(3A)(d) (as so added).

269. Whether landlord has reasonably or unreasonably withheld consent to reasonable adjustments.

Regulations may make provision as to the circumstances in which a landlord is taken[1] to have either withheld consent, or withheld consent reasonably or withheld consent unreasonably[2] to a proposed alteration to comply with the duty to make reasonable adjustments[3]. Regulations may make provision as to the circumstances in which a condition subject to which a landlord gives consent is taken to be reasonable, or to be unreasonable[4].

In exercise of these powers, regulations have been made which provide as follows. The landlord ('L') is to be taken to have withheld consent for alterations to premises where, within the period of 42 days beginning with the date on which L receives the application for consent, L either:

(1)　fails to reply consenting to or refusing the alteration; or
(2)　replies consenting to the alteration subject to obtaining the consent of another person required under a superior leave or pursuant to a binding obligation, but fails to seek that consent[5].

However, L is not to be taken to have withheld consent where the applicant fails to submit with the application such plans and specifications as it is reasonable for L to require before consenting to the alteration[6]; and within the period of 21 days beginning with the date on which he receives the application, L replies requesting the applicant to submit such plans and specifications[7]. Where such plans and specifications are submitted to L in response to such a request[8], L is taken to have withheld consent to the alteration where, within the period of 42 days beginning with the date on which he receives those plans and specifications L either:

(a)   fails to reply consenting or refusing the alteration; or

(b)   replies consenting to the alteration subject to obtaining the consent of another person required under a superior lease or pursuant to a binding obligation, but fails to seek that consent[9].

L, who having sought the consent of the other person referred to in heads (2) and (b) above, receives that consent, is taken to have withheld consent to the alteration where, within the period of 14 days beginning with the day on which he receives the consent, L fails to inform the applicant in writing that it has been received[10].

L is to be treated as not having sought another's consent unless he:

(i)   has applied in writing to that person indicating that the occupier has applied for consent to the alteration of the premises in order to comply with a second requirement duty; and L has given his consent conditionally upon obtaining the other person's consent; and

(ii)   submits to that other person any plans and specifications which have been submitted to L[11].

L is to be taken to have acted unreasonably in withholding consent for alterations to the premises where the lease provides that L must give his consent to an alteration of the kind in question and L has withheld his consent to that alteration[12].

L is to be taken to have acted reasonably in withholding consent for alterations to premises where there is a binding obligation requiring the consent of any person to the alteration, L has taken steps to obtain that consent, and that consent has not been given, or has been given subject to a condition making it reasonable for L to withhold consent[13]. L is also to be taken to have acted reasonably in withholding consent for alterations to premises where L does not know, and could not reasonably be expected to know, that the alteration is one which the occupier proposes to make to comply with a second requirement duty[14].

Particular circumstances are prescribed in which a condition, subject to which L has given consent to alterations to premises, is to be taken to be reasonable[15]. These are where the condition is to the effect that:

(A)   the occupier must obtain any necessary planning permission and any other consent or permission required by or under any enactment[16];

(B)   the work must be carried out in accordance with any plans or specifications approved by the L[17];

(C)   L must be permitted a reasonable opportunity to inspect the work (whether before or after it is completed)[18];

(D)   the consent of another person required under a superior lease or a binding agreement must be obtained[19];

(E)   the occupier must repay to the L the costs reasonably incurred in connection with the giving of the consent[20].

1   Ie for the purposes of the Equality Act 2010 Sch 21 (see PARA 266 et seq).
2   Equality Act 2010 Sch 21 para 6(1).
3   As to the duty to make reasonable adjustments generally, and as to the failure to comply with that duty see PARAS 76, 237–238.
4   Equality Act 2010 Sch 21 para 6(2).
5   Equality Act 2010 (Disability) Regulations 2010, SI 2010/2128, reg 10(1), (2). 'To reply' means to reply in writing: reg 10(7)(b). L who, but for the requirements as to time, complies with the requirements of reg 10(2), (4) or (5) is taken to have withheld consent until such time as he so complies: reg 10(6).
6   Equality Act 2010 (Disability) Regulations 2010, SI 2010/2128, reg 10(3)(a).
7   Equality Act 2010 (Disability) Regulations 2010, SI 2010/2128, reg 10(3)(b).

8   Ie a request made in accordance with the Equality Act 2010 (Disability) Regulations 2010, SI 2010/2128, reg 10(3)(b) (see the text and note 7).
9   Equality Act 2010 (Disability) Regulations 2010, SI 2010/2128, reg 10(4). See note 5.
10 Equality Act 2010 (Disability) Regulations 2010, SI 2010/2128, reg 10(5). See note 5.
11 Equality Act 2010 (Disability) Regulations 2010, SI 2010/2128, reg 10(7)(a).
12 Equality Act 2010 (Disability) Regulations 2010, SI 2010/2128, reg 11(1), (2).
13 Equality Act 2010 (Disability) Regulations 2010, SI 2010/2128, reg 12(1), (2)(a).
14 Equality Act 2010 (Disability) Regulations 2010, SI 2010/2128, reg 12(1), (2)(b). As to the second requirement see PARA 237.
15 Equality Act 2010 (Disability) Regulations 2010, SI 2010/2128, reg 13(1).
16 Equality Act 2010 (Disability) Regulations 2010, SI 2010/2128, reg 13(2)(a).
17 Equality Act 2010 (Disability) Regulations 2010, SI 2010/2128, reg 13(2)(b).
18 Equality Act 2010 (Disability) Regulations 2010, SI 2010/2128, reg 13(2)(c).
19 Equality Act 2010 (Disability) Regulations 2010, SI 2010/2128, reg 13(2)(d).
20 Equality Act 2010 (Disability) Regulations 2010, SI 2010/2128, reg 13(2)(e).

270. County Court to determine whether refusal or condition is reasonable.
In certain cases[1] if a person ('A') has applied in writing to the landlord for consent to the alteration[2], and the landlord has refused to give consent or has given consent subject to a condition[3], then A (or a disabled person with an interest in the alteration being made) may refer the matter to the County Court[4].

The County Court must then determine whether the refusal or condition is unreasonable[5], and if it finds that the refusal or condition is unreasonable, it may make such declaration as it thinks appropriate[6]. The County Court may also make an order authorising A to make the alteration specified in the order (and requiring A to comply with such conditions as are so specified)[7].

1   Ie in a case within the Equality Act 2010 Pt 3 (ss 28–31) (services and public functions: see PARAS 84–104), Pt 4 (ss 32–38) (premises: see PARAS 105–115), Pt 6 (ss 84–99) (education: see PARAS 173–197) or Pt 7 (ss 100–107) (associations: see PARAS 198–210).
2   Ie to an alteration which is proposed to be made in order to comply with the duty to make reasonable adjustments. As to the duty to make reasonable adjustments generally, and as to the failure to comply with that duty see PARAS 76, 237–238.
3   Equality Act 2010 Sch 21 para 4(1).
4   Equality Act 2010 Sch 21 para 4(2) (amended by the Crime and Courts Act 2013 Sch 9 para 52). Regulations may make provision modifying or supplementing these provisions where A's tenancy is a sub-tenancy: see the Equality Act 2010 Sch 21 para 6. In exercise of this power, the Equality Act 2010 (Disability) Regulations 2010, SI 2010/2128, have been made which modify the Equality Act 2010 Sch 21 in relation to any case where the occupier occupies premises under a sub-tenancy: see the Equality Act 2010 (Disability) Regulations 2010, SI 2010/2128, reg 14. In relation to any case where the occupier occupies premises under a sub-tenancy, the Equality Act 2010 Sch 21 para 4 has effect as if as follows. Where the tenant of any superior lease in relation to the premises has applied in writing to his landlord for consent to the alteration and that consent has been refused, or the landlord has made his consent subject to one or more conditions, then the occupier, tenant or a disabled person who has an interest in the alteration being made may refer the matter to the County Court: Sch 21 para 4(2A) (added as a modification by SI 2010/2128; amended by virtue of the Crime and Courts Act 2013 Sch 9 para 11).
5   Equality Act 2010 Sch 21 para 4(3).
6   Equality Act 2010 Sch 21 para 4(4)(a).
7   Equality Act 2010 Sch 21 para 4(4)(b).

271. Joining landlord as party to proceedings.
A party to proceedings (that is proceedings relating to a contravention of the duty under the Equality Act 2010 to make reasonable adjustments[1]) may request the employment tribunal or the County Court[2] to direct that the landlord is joined as a party to the proceedings[3]. The court or tribunal must grant the request if it is made before the hearing of the complaint or claim begins[4]. It may refuse the request if it is made after the hearing begins[5], and it must refuse the request if it is made after the claim has been determined[6].

If the landlord is joined as a party to the proceedings, the court or tribunal may determine whether:

(1) the landlord has refused to consent to the alteration;

(2) the landlord has consented subject to a condition;

(3) the refusal or condition was unreasonable[7].

If the court or tribunal finds that the refusal or condition was unreasonable, it may make such declaration as it thinks appropriate[8]. It may also make an order authorising a person ('A') to make the alteration specified in the order (and requiring A to comply with such conditions as are so specified)[9], and it may order the landlord to pay compensation to the claimant[10].

1   Ie a contravention of the Equality Act 2010 by virtue of s 20 (see PARA 237). As to the duty to make reasonable adjustments generally, and as to the failure to comply with that duty see PARAS 76, 237–238.

2   The Equality Act 2010 Sch 21 para 5 uses the term 'judicial authority' to refer to the employment tribunal, the County Court or (in relation to Scotland) sheriff.

3   Equality Act 2010 Sch 21 para 5(1), (2) (amended by virtue of the Crime and Courts Act 2013 Sch 9 para 11).

4   Equality Act 2010 Sch 21 para 5(3)(a). Regulations may make provision modifying or supplementing these provisions where A's tenancy is a sub-tenancy: see Sch 21 para 6. In exercise of this power, the Equality Act 2010 (Disability) Regulations 2010, SI 2010/2128, have been made which modify the Equality Act 2010 Sch 21 in relation to any case where the occupier occupies premises under a sub-tenancy: see the Equality Act 2010 (Disability) Regulations 2010, SI 2010/2128, reg 14. In relation to any case where the occupier occupies premises under a sub-tenancy, the Equality Act 2010 Sch 21 para 5(3)(a) has effect as follows. The court or tribunal must grant the request if it is made before the hearing of the complaint or claim begins, unless it considers that another landlord should be joined as a party to the proceedings: see Sch 21 para 5(3) (modified by SI 2010/2128).

5   Equality Act 2010 Sch 21 para 5(3)(b).

6   Equality Act 2010 Sch 21 para 5(3)(c).

7   Equality Act 2010 Sch 21 para 5(4).

8   Equality Act 2010 Sch 21 para 5(5)(a).

9   Equality Act 2010 Sch 21 para 5(5)(b).

10 Equality Act 2010 Sch 21 para 5(5)(c). An employment tribunal may act in reliance on Sch 21 para 5(5)(c) instead of, or in addition to, acting in reliance on s 124(2) (see PARA 359); but if it orders the landlord to pay compensation it must not do so in reliance on s 124(2): Sch 21 para 5(6). If the County Court orders the landlord to pay compensation, it may not order A to do so: Sch 21 para 5(7) (amended by the Crime and Courts Act 2013 Sch 9 para 52).

(4) IMPROVEMENTS TO DWELLING HOUSES

272. Improvements to let dwelling houses.

The following provisions apply in relation to a lease[1] of a dwelling house if:

(1) the tenancy is not a protected tenancy, a statutory tenancy or a secure tenancy[2]; and

(2) the tenant or another person occupying or intending to occupy the premises is a disabled person[3]; and

(3) the disabled person occupies or intends to occupy the premises as that person's only or main home[4]; and

(4) the tenant is entitled, with the consent of the landlord, to make improvements to the premises[5]; and

(5) the tenant applies to the landlord for consent to make a relevant improvement[6].

'Improvement' means an alteration in or addition to the premises[7], and an improvement to premises is a relevant improvement if, having regard to the disabled person's disability, it is likely to facilitate that person's enjoyment of the premises[8].

Where the tenant applies in writing for the landlord's consent and he refuses to give it, the landlord must give the tenant a written statement of the reason why the consent was withheld[9]. If the landlord neither gives nor refuses to give consent within a reasonable time, consent must be taken to have been unreasonably withheld[10]. If the landlord gives consent subject to a condition which is unreasonable, the consent must be taken to have been unreasonably withheld[11]. If the landlord's consent is unreasonably withheld, it must be taken to have been given[12]. On any question as to whether consent was unreasonably withheld, or whether a condition imposed was unreasonable, it is for the landlord to show that it was not[13].

If the tenant fails to comply with a reasonable condition imposed by the landlord on the making of a relevant improvement, the failure is to be treated as a breach by the tenant of an obligation of the tenancy[14].

1   For these purposes, 'lease' includes a sub-lease or other tenancy: Equality Act 2010 s 190(9).
2   Equality Act 2010 s 190(1)(a). As to protected tenancies and statutory tenancies see the Rent Act 1977 ss 1, 2; and LANDLORD AND TENANT vol 63 (2016) PARA 653 et seq. As to secure tenancies see the Housing Act 1985 s 79; and LANDLORD AND TENANT vol 63 (2016) PARA 1037.
3   Equality Act 2010 s 190(1)(b). As to the meaning of 'disabled person' see PARA 47.
4   Equality Act 2010 s 190(1)(c).
5   Equality Act 2010 s 190(1)(d).
6   Equality Act 2010 s 190(1)(e).
7   Equality Act 2010 s 190(9). An improvement includes:
    (1)   an addition to or alteration in the landlord's fittings and fixtures;
    (2)   an addition or alteration connected with the provision of services to the premises;
    (3)   the erection of a wireless or television aerial;
    (4)   carrying out external decoration.
8   Equality Act 2010 s 190(7). As to the 'enjoyment' of premises see PARA **241** note 7. Section 190(2)–(7) applies only in so far as provision of a like nature is not made by the lease: s 190(8).
9   Equality Act 2010 s 190(2)(a). See note 8.
10 Equality Act 2010 s 190(2)(b). See note 8.
11 Equality Act 2010 s 190(3). See note 8.
12 Equality Act 2010 s 190(4). See note 8.
13 Equality Act 2010 s 190(5). See note 8.
14 Equality Act 2010 s 190(6). See note 8.

(5) EXCEPTIONS IN RELATION TO ACCESSIBILITY ISSUES FOR DISABLED PERSONS

273. No contravention of the Equality Act 2010 where act done under statutory authority.

A person does not contravene the provisions of the Equality Act 2010 relating to disabled persons and transport[1], so far as relating to the protected characteristic of disability[2], if he does anything he must do pursuant to a requirement of an enactment[3]. Nor does a person contravene those provisions so far as relating to the protected characteristics of disability if he does anything he must do pursuant to a relevant requirement or condition imposed by virtue of an enactment[4].

1   Ie the Equality Act 2010 Pt 12 (ss 160–188): see PARAS **211–236**. As to exceptions from the Equality Act 2010 generally, and as to further exceptions in specific circumstances, see PARAS **320–338**.
2   As to disability as a protected characteristic see PARAS **47–55**.

3 Equality Act 2010 Sch 22 para 1(1). As to the meaning of 'enactment' see PARAS 91 note 10, 92 note 8.
4 Equality Act 2010 Sch 22 para 1(1). As to the meaning of 'a relevant requirement or condition' see PARA 92 note 9.

11. DISCRIMINATORY CONTRACTS AND OTHER AGREEMENTS

274. Unenforceable terms in contracts, collective agreements and undertakings.

A term of a contract is unenforceable against a person in so far as it constitutes, promotes or provides for treatment of that person or another person that is of a description prohibited by the Equality Act 2010[1], and a relevant non-contractual term[2] is unenforceable against a person in so far as it constitutes, promotes or provides for treatment of that or another person that is of a description prohibited by the Act in so far as the Act relates to disability[3]. The County Court may, on an application by a person who has an interest in a contract or other agreement which includes a term that is unenforceable by virtue of these provisions, make an order for the term to be removed or modified[4].

A term of a collective agreement[5] is void, and a rule of an undertaking[6] is unenforceable against a person, in so far as it constitutes, promotes or provides for treatment of a description prohibited by the Equality Act 2010[7]. A qualifying person[8] may make a complaint to an employment tribunal that a term is void, or that a rule is unenforceable, as a result of these provisions[9], and if the tribunal finds that the complaint is well-founded it must make an order declaring that the term is void or the rule is unenforceable[10].

1   Equality Act 2010 s 142(1). Treatment is of a prohibited description if it is prohibited by the Equality Act 2010: ss 142(1), 145(1), (2). A reference to treatment of a description prohibited by the Equality Act 2010 does not include treatment in so far as it is treatment that would contravene Pt 1 (ss 1–3) (public sector duty regarding socio-economic inequalities: see PARAS 302–304), or Pt 11 Ch 1 (ss 149–157) (public sector equality duty: see PARAS 276–301): s 148(1), (2). A reference in s 142(1) or s 142(2) (see the text and notes 2–3) to treatment of a description prohibited by the Equality Act 2010 does not include a reference to the inclusion of a term in a contract referred to in s 70(2)(a) (see PARA 143) or s 76(2) (see PARA 117) or a reference to the failure to include a term in a contract as referred to in s 70(2)(b) (see PARA 143): s 142(4). Section 142(4) does not affect the application of s 148(2) to s 142: s 142(5).
2   A relevant non-contractual term is a term which is a term of an agreement that is not a contract and relates to the provision of an employment service within the Equality Act 2010 s 56(2)(a)–(e) (see PARA 130) or to the provision under a group insurance arrangement of facilities by way of insurance: s 142(3). 'Group insurance arrangement' means an arrangement between an employer and another person for the provision by that other person of facilities by way of insurance to the employer's employees (or a class of those employees): s 148(3).
3   Equality Act 2010 s 142(2).
4   Equality Act 2010 s 143(1) (amended by Crime and Courts Act 2013 Sch 9 para 52). An order under the Equality Act 2010 s 143 must not be made unless every person who would be affected by it has been given notice of the application (except where notice is dispensed with in accordance with rules of court) and has been afforded an opportunity to make representations to the County Court: s 143(2). An order under s 143 may include provision in respect of a period before the making of the order: s 143(3).
5   As to the meaning of 'collective agreement' see the Trade Union and Labour Relations (Consolidation) Act 1992 s 178; and EMPLOYMENT vol 41A (2014) PARA 1093 (definition applied by the Equality Act 2010 s 148(4)).
6   A rule of an undertaking is:
    (1)   a rule made by a trade organisation or a qualifications body for application to its members or prospective members, persons on whom it has conferred a relevant qualification or persons seeking conferment by it of a relevant qualification (Equality Act 2010 s 148(5), (6)); or
    (2)   a rule made by an employer for application to employees, persons who apply for employment or persons the employer considers for employment (s 148(5), (7)).
    As to the meaning of 'trade organisation' see s 57(7); and PARA 131 note 1; as to the meanings of 'qualifications body' and 'relevant qualification' see s 54(1)–(3); and PARA 129 note 1 (definitions applied by s 148(8)).

7   Equality Act 2010 s 145(1), (2).
8   In the case of a complaint about a term of a collective agreement:
    (1)   where the term is one made by or on behalf of an employer, a qualifying person is a
           person who is, or is seeking to be, an employee of the employer (Equality Act 2010 s
           146(5));
    (2)   where the term is one made by or on behalf of an organisation of employers, a qualifying
           person is a person who is, or is seeking to be, an employee of an employer who is a
           member of that organisation (s 146(5)); and
    (3)   where the term is one made by or on behalf of an association of organisations of
           employers, a qualifying person is a person who is, or is seeking to be, an employee of an
           employer who is a member of an organisation in that association (s 146(5)).
    In the case of a complaint about a rule of an undertaking:
    (a)   where the rule is one made by or on behalf of an employer, a qualifying person is a
           person who is, or is seeking to be, an employee of the employer (s 146(6));
    (b)   where the rule is one made by or on behalf of a trade organisation or qualifications body,
           a qualifying person is a person who is a person who is, or is seeking to be, a member of
           the organisation or body, a person upon whom the body has conferred a relevant
           qualification, or a person seeking conferment by the body of a relevant qualification (s
           146(6)).
9   Equality Act 2010 s 146(1). A qualifying person may make a complaint under these provisions
    only if the term or rule may in the future have effect in relation to him and, where the complaint
    alleges that the term or rule provides for treatment of a description prohibited by the Equality Act
    2010, the qualifying person may in the future be subjected to treatment that would (if he were
    subjected to it in present circumstances) be of that description: s 146(2).
10 Equality Act 2010 s 146(3). An order under s 146 may include provision in respect of a period
    before the making of the order: s 146(4).

275. Contracting out.

A term of a contract is unenforceable by a person in whose favour it would
operate in so far as it purports to exclude or limit an equality provision (that is a
provision of the Equality Act 2010, or one made under it)[1], and a relevant
non-contractual term[2] is unenforceable by a person in whose favour it would
operate in so far as it purports to exclude or limit an equality provision, in so far
as the provision relates to disability[3]. These provisions do not apply to a contract[4]
which settles[5] a discrimination claim in the civil courts[6] or to a contract which
settles a complaint to an employment tribunal[7] if the contract is made with the
assistance of a conciliation officer or is a qualifying settlement agreement[8].

1   Equality Act 2010 s 144(1).
2   As to the meaning of 'relevant non-contractual term' see the Equality Act 2010 s 142(2); and PARA
    274 note 2 (definition applied by s 144(2)).
3   Equality Act 2010 s 144(2).
4   A contract within the Equality Act 2010 s 144(4) (see the text and notes 7–8) includes a contract
    which settles a complaint relating to a breach of an equality clause or rule or of a
    non-discrimination rule (s 144(5)) and includes an agreement by the parties to a dispute to submit
    the dispute to arbitration if the dispute is covered by a scheme having effect by virtue of an order
    under the Trade Union and Labour Relations (Consolidation) Act 1992 s 212A (see EMPLOYMENT
    vol 41 (2014) PARA 824) and the agreement is to submit the dispute to arbitration in accordance
    with the scheme: Equality Act 2010 s 144(6).
5   Ie a claim within the Equality Act 2010 s 114 (see PARA 351).
6   Equality Act 2010 144(3).
7   Ie a claim within the Equality Act 2010 s 120 (see PARA 357).
8   Equality Act 2010 s 144(4) (amended by the Enterprise and Regulatory Reform Act 2013 s 23(5)).
    A 'qualifying settlement agreement' is a contract in relation to which each of the following
    conditions is met (Equality Act 2010 s 147(1), (2) (amended by the Enterprise and Regulatory
    Reform Act 2013 s 23(6))):
    (1)   the contract is in writing (s 147(3)(a));
    (2)   the contract relates to the particular complaint (s 147(3)(b));

(3)   the complainant has, before entering into the contract, received advice from an independent adviser about its terms and effect (including, in particular, its effect on the complainant's ability to pursue the complaint before an employment tribunal) (s 147(3)(c));

(4)   on the date of the giving of the advice, there is in force a contract of insurance, or an indemnity provided for members of a profession or professional body, covering the risk of a claim by the complainant in respect of loss arising from the advice (s 147(3)(d));

(5)   the contract identifies the adviser (s 147(3)(e)); and

(6)   the contract states that the conditions in heads (3) and (4) are met (s 147(3)(f)).

For this purpose each of the following is an independent adviser:

(a)   a qualified lawyer (s 147(4)(a));

(b)   an officer, official, employee or member of an independent trade union certified in writing by the trade union as competent to give advice and as authorised to do so on its behalf (s 147(4)(b));

(c)   a worker at an advice centre (whether as an employee or a volunteer) certified in writing by the centre as competent to give advice and as authorised to do so on its behalf (s 147(4)(c)); and

(d)   a person of a description specified in the Equality Act 2010 (Qualifying Settlement Agreement Specified Person) Order 2010, SI 2010/2192 (Equality Act 2010 s 147(4)(d)).

For the purposes of s 147(4)(a) a 'qualified lawyer', in relation to England and Wales, is a person who, for the purposes of the Legal Services Act 2007, is an authorised person in relation to an activity which constitutes the exercise of a right of audience or the conduct of litigation (see LEGAL PROFESSIONS vol 65 (2015) PARA 356): Equality Act 2010 s 147(6)(a). As to the meaning of 'independent trade union' see the Trade Union and Labour Relations (Consolidation) Act 1992 s 5; and EMPLOYMENT vol 41 (2014) PARA 904 (definition applied by the Equality Act 2010 s 147(7)).

Despite this, none of the following is an independent adviser to the complainant in relation to a qualifying settlement agreement:

(i)   a person (other than the complainant) who is a party to the contract or the complaint (s 147(5)(a) (amended by the Enterprise and Regulatory Reform Act 2013 s 23(6); and SI 2012/334));

(ii)   a person who is connected to such a person (Equality Act 2010 s 147(5)(b));

(iii)   a person who is employed by a person within head (i) or (ii) above (s 147(5)(c));

(iv)   a person who is acting for a person within head (i) or (ii) above in relation to the contract or the complaint (s 147(5)(d));

(v)   a person within s 147(4)(b) or s 147(4)(c) (ie head (b) or (c) above), if the trade union or advice centre is a person within head (i) or (ii) above (s 147(5)(e));

(vi)   a person within s 147(4)(c) (ie head (c) above) to whom the complainant makes a payment for the advice (s 147(5)(f)).

Two persons are 'connected' for the purposes of s 147(5) if one is a company of which the other (directly or indirectly) has control or both are companies of which a third person (directly or indirectly) has control: s 147(8). Two persons are also connected for these purposes in so far as a connection between them gives rise to a conflict of interest in relation to the contract or the complaint: s 147(9).

12. ADVANCEMENT OF EQUALITY

(1) THE PUBLIC SECTOR EQUALITY DUTY

(i) Public Authorities and Protected Characteristics

276. The protected characteristics for the purposes of public sector equality duty.

For the purposes of the public sector equality duty[1] the relevant protected characteristics are:

(1)   age[2];
(2)   disability[3];
(3)   gender reassignment[4];
(4)   pregnancy and maternity[5];
(5)   race[6];
(6)   religion or belief[7];
(7)   sex[8]; and
(8)   sexual orientation[9].

1   Ie for the purposes of the Equality Act 2010 s 149 (see PARAS 278–284).
2   Equality Act 2010 s 149(7). As to age as a protected characteristic see PARA 46.
3   Equality Act 2010 s 149(7). As to disability as a protected characteristic see PARAS 47–55.
4   Equality Act 2010 s 149(7). As to gender reassignment as a protected characteristic see PARAS 56, 61.
5   Equality Act 2010 s 149(7). As to pregnancy and maternity as a protected characteristic see PARAS 62, 73–74.
6   Equality Act 2010 s 149(7). As to race as a protected characteristic see PARA 58.
7   Equality Act 2010 s 149(7). As to religion or belief as a protected characteristic see PARA 59.
8   Equality Act 2010 s 149(7). As to sex as a protected characteristic see PARA 60.
9   Equality Act 2010 s 149(7). As to sexual orientation as a protected characteristic see PARA 63.

277. The public authorities on which the public sector equality duty is imposed.

The authorities on which the public sector equality duty[1] is imposed are:

(1)   Ministers of the Crown, government departments and officers of the Welsh government and the National Assembly for Wales[2];
(2)   the Armed Forces[3];
(3)   the British Broadcasting Corporation[4], Channel 4[5] and S4C[6];
(4)   the Equality and Human Rights Commission[7];
(5)   the Information Commissioner[8];
(6)   the Children and Family Court Advisory and Support Service[9];
(7)   the Judicial Appointments Commission[10];
(8)   the Legal Services Board[11];
(9)   specified bodies concerned with the administration of criminal justice[12];
(10) the Homes and Communities Agency[13];
(11) Natural England[14];
(12) specified bodies concerned with health, social care and social security[15];
(13) specified bodies concerned with industry, business and finance[16];
(14) specified local government and local administration bodies[17];
(15) other specified educational bodies[18];
(16) Parliamentary and devolved bodies[19];
(17) specified police bodies[20];

(18) specified regulatory bodies[21];

(19) specified transport bodies[22]; and

(20) other specified Welsh public bodies[23] and cross-border Welsh authorities[24].

Authorities may be added to or removed from this list by order[25], and additional duties may by regulations be imposed on a public authority for the purpose of enabling the better performance by the authority of the public sector equality duty[26].

1 Ie the duty imposed by the Equality Act 2010 s 149 (see PARAS 278–284).

2 Ie a Minister of the Crown; a government department (other than the Security Service; the Secret Intelligence Service or the Government Communications Headquarters); the Welsh Ministers; the First Minister for Wales; the Counsel General to the Welsh Government; and a subsidiary of the Welsh Ministers (within the meaning given by the Government of Wales Act 2006 s 134(4)): Equality Act 2010 s 150(1), (2), Sch 19 Pts 1, 2 (amended by virtue of the Wales Act 2014 s 4(4)). As to the Security Service, the Secret Intelligence Service and the Government Communications Headquarters see CONSTITUTIONAL AND ADMINISTRATIVE LAW vol 20 (2014) PARA 243 et seq. As to the Welsh Ministers, the First Minister for Wales and the Counsel General to the Welsh Government and a subsidiary of the Welsh Ministers see the Government of Wales Act 2006 Pt 2 (ss 45–92); and CONSTITUTIONAL AND ADMINISTRATIVE LAW vol 20 (2014) PARA 373 et seq. Where the Welsh Ministers, the First Minister for Wales and the Counsel General to the Welsh Government are required by the Equality Act 2010 (Statutory Duties) (Wales) Regulations 2011, SI 2011/1064 (see PARAS 289–298) to prepare a SEP (see PARA 294), publish a report or do any other thing, they may comply with the duty by acting jointly: reg 19 (amended by virtue of the Wales Act 2014 s 4(4)).

3 Ie any of the armed forces other than any part of the armed forces which is, in accordance with a requirement of the Secretary of State, assisting the Government Communications Headquarters: Equality Act 2010 Sch 19 Pt 1.

4 Ie the British Broadcasting Corporation ('BBC'), except in respect of functions relating to the provision of a content service (within the meaning given by the Communications Act 2003 s 32(7): see TELECOMMUNICATIONS vol 97 (2015) PARA 53); and the reference to the BBC includes a reference to a body corporate which is a wholly owned subsidiary of the BBC, is not operated with a view to generating a profit and undertakes activities primarily in order to promote the BBC's public purposes: Equality Act 2010 Sch 19 Pt 1 (amended by SI 2011/1060).

5 Ie the Channel Four Television Corporation (see BROADCASTING vol 4 (2011) PARA 627 et seq), except in respect of functions relating to the provision of a content service, and the function of carrying on the activities referred to in the Communications Act 2003 s 199 (see BROADCASTING vol 4 (2011) PARA 639): Equality Act 2010 Sch 19 Pt 1 (amended by SI 2011/1060).

6 Ie the Welsh Authority (as defined by the Broadcasting Act 1990 s 56(1): see BROADCASTING vol 4 (2011) PARA 645), except in respect of functions relating to the provision of a content service: Equality Act 2010 Sch 19 Pt 1 (amended by SI 2011/1060).

7 Equality Act 2010 Sch 19 Pt 1 (amended by SI 2011/1060). As to the Commission see PARAS 28–44.

8 Equality Act 2010 Sch 19 Pt 1 (amended by SI 2011/1060). As to the Information Commissioner see CONFIDENCE AND INFORMATIONAL PRIVACY vol 19 (2011) PARA 109 et seq.

9 Equality Act 2010 Sch 19 Pt 1 (amended by SI 2011/1060). As to the Children and Family Court Advisory and Support Service see CHILDREN AND YOUNG PERSONS vol 9 (2017) PARA 225 et seq.

10 Equality Act 2010 Sch 19 Pt 1 (amended by SI 2011/1060). As to the Judicial Appointments Commission see COURTS AND TRIBUNALS vol 24 (2010) PARA 935.

11 Equality Act 2010 Sch 19 Pt 1 (amended by SI 2011/1060). As to the Legal Services Board see LEGAL PROFESSIONS vol 65 (2015) PARA 203.

12 Ie Her Majesty's Chief Inspector of Constabulary (see POLICE AND INVESTIGATORY POWERS vol 84 (2013) PARA 152); Her Majesty's Chief Inspector of the Crown Prosecution Service (see CRIMINAL PROCEDURE vol 27 (2015) PARA 26); Her Majesty's Chief Inspector of Prisons (see PRISONS AND PRISONERS vol 85 (2012) PARA 409); Her Majesty's Chief Inspector of Probation for England and Wales (see SENTENCING vol 92 (2015) PARA 682); the Parole Board for England and Wales (see SENTENCING vol 92 (2015) PARA 699); a recall adjudicator (as defined in the Criminal Justice Act 2003 s 239A: see SENTENCING vol 92 (2015) PARA 705); a probation trust established by an order made under the Offender Management Act 2007 s 5(1) (see SENTENCING vol 92 (2015) PARA 670); and the Youth Justice Board for England and Wales (see CHILDREN AND YOUNG PERSONS vol 10

(2017) PARA 1286 et seq): Equality Act 2010 Sch 19 Pt 1 (amended by the Criminal Justice and Courts Act 2015 Sch 3 para 17; and SI 2011/1060).

13 Equality Act 2010 Sch 19 Pt 1 (amended by SI 2011/1060). As to the Homes and Communities Agency see PLANNING vol 83 (2010) PARA 1454 et seq.

14 Equality Act 2010 Sch 19 Pt 1 (amended by SI 2011/1060). As to Natural England see OPEN SPACES AND COUNTRYSIDE vol 78 (2010) PARA 523.

15 Ie the National Health Service Commissioning Board (see HEALTH SERVICES vol 54 (2017) PARAS 32, 133 et seq); a clinical commissioning group established under the National Health Service Act 2006 s 14D (see HEALTH SERVICES vol 54 (2017) PARAS 35, 151 et seq); the Care Quality Commission (see HEALTH SERVICES vol 54A (2017) PARA 648 et seq; SOCIAL SERVICES vol 95 (2017) PARA 336 et seq); Health Education England (see HEALTH SERVICES vol 54 (2017) PARAS 196–198); the Health Research Authority (see HEALTH SERVICES vol 54 (2017) PARAS 199–202); Social Care Wales (see SOCIAL SERVICES vol 95 (2017) PARA 412 et seq); the Health Service Commissioner for England in respect of the Commissioner's functions set out in the Health Service Commissioners Act 1993 Sch 1 para 11 (see HEALTH SERVICES vol 54A (2017) PARA 682) and the Commissioner's public procurement functions (as defined in the Equality Act 2010 s 155(3): see PARA 297); Monitor (see HEALTH SERVICES vol 54 (2017) PARAS 194–195); an NHS foundation trust within the meaning given by the National Health Service Act 2006 s 30 (see HEALTH SERVICES vol 54 (2017) PARA 244 et seq); an NHS trust established under the National Health Service Act 2006 s 25 (see HEALTH SERVICES vol 54 (2017) PARA 234 et seq); an NHS trust established in Wales under the National Health Service (Wales) Act 2006 s 18 (see HEALTH SERVICES vol 54 (2017) PARAS 97, 98); a Local Health Board established under s 11 (see HEALTH SERVICES vol 54 (2017) PARAS 97, 98); a Community Health Council in Wales (see HEALTH SERVICES vol 54 (2017) PARAS 97, 98); the Board of Community Health Councils in Wales (see HEALTH SERVICES vol 54 (2017) PARAS 97, 98); a Special Health Authority established under the National Health Service Act 2006 s 28 (see HEALTH SERVICES vol 54 (2017) PARA 180 et seq) other than NHS Blood and Transplant (see HEALTH SERVICES vol 54 (2017) PARA 189) and the NHS Business Services Authority (see HEALTH SERVICES vol 54 (2017) PARA 190); the National Institute for Health and Care Excellence (see SOCIAL SERVICES vol 95 (2017) PARA 371); and the Health and Social Care Information Centre (see SOCIAL SERVICES vol 95 (2017) PARA 372): Equality Act 2010 Sch 19 Pt 1 (amended by the Health and Social Care Act 2012 Sch 5 para 182, Sch 13 para 19, Sch 17 para 14, Sch 19 para 13; the Care Act 2014 Sch 5 para 35, Sch 7 para 27; and SI 2011/1060); Equality Act 2010 Sch 19 Pt 2 (amended by SI 2011/1063; and SI 2017/353). As from a day to be appointed, the reference to an NHS trust in the Equality Act 2010 Sch 19 Pt 1 is repealed by the Health and Social Care Act 2012 Sch 14 para 116. At the date at which this volume states the law no such day had been appointed.

16 Ie the Advisory, Conciliation and Arbitration Service (see EMPLOYMENT vol 41A (2014) PARA 1213 et seq); the Bank of England (including the Bank in its capacity as the Prudential Regulation Authority) in respect of its public functions (see FINANCIAL INSTITUTIONS vol 48 (2015) PARA 97 et seq; FINANCIAL SERVICES REGULATION vol 50 (2016) PARA 20); the Civil Aviation Authority (see AVIATION vol 2 (2017) PARA 752 et seq); the Board of the Pension Protection Fund (see PERSONAL AND OCCUPATIONAL PENSIONS vol 80 (2013) PARA 554 et seq); the Coal Authority (see MINES, MINERALS AND QUARRIES vol 76 (2013) PARA 51 et seq); the Construction Industry Training Board; the Engineering Construction Industry Training Board; the Nuclear Decommissioning Authority (see ENERGY AND CLIMATE CHANGE vol 44 (2011) PARA 818 et seq); the Oil and Gas Authority ((see ENERGY AND CLIMATE CHANGE vol 44 (2011) PARA 1034); the Comptroller and Auditor General (see CONSTITUTIONAL AND ADMINISTRATIVE LAW vol 20 (2014) PARAS 494–496); the Financial Conduct Authority (see FINANCIAL SERVICES REGULATION vol 50 (2016) PARA 6 et seq); the National Audit Office (see CONSTITUTIONAL AND ADMINISTRATIVE LAW vol 20 (2014) PARA 492 et seq); the Office of Communications (see TELECOMMUNICATIONS vol 97 (2015) PARA 2 et seq); the Office of Tax Simplification (see CONSTITUTIONAL AND ADMINISTRATIVE LAW vol 20 (2014) PARA 265A); and the Payment Systems Regulator established under the Financial Services (Banking Reform) Act 2013 s 40 (see FINANCIAL INSTITUTIONS vol 48 (2015) PARA 79): Equality Act 2010 Sch 19 Pt 1 (amended by the Budget Responsibility and National Audit Act 2011 Sch 5 para 34; the Financial Services Act 2012 Sch 18 para 131; the Enterprise and Regulatory Reform Act 2013 Sch 4 para 26; the Financial Services (Banking Reform) Act 2013 Sch 4 para 16; the Finance Act 2016 Sch 25 para 15; SI 2011/1060; SI 2017/80; and SI 2017/353).

17 Ie a county council, district council or parish council in England (see LOCAL GOVERNMENT vol 69 (2009) PARA 24 et seq); a county council or county borough council in Wales (see LOCAL GOVERNMENT vol 69 (2009) PARA 37 et seq); a parish meeting constituted under the Local Government Act 1972 s 13 (see LOCAL GOVERNMENT vol 69 (2009) PARA 34); charter trustees

constituted under s 246 for an area in England (see LOCAL GOVERNMENT vol 69 (2009) PARA 108 et seq); the Greater London Authority (see LONDON GOVERNMENT vol 71 (2013) PARA 67 et seq); a London borough council (see LONDON GOVERNMENT vol 71 (2013) PARAS 20–22); the Common Council of the City of London in its capacity as a local authority or port health authority (see LONDON GOVERNMENT vol 71 (2013) PARA 34 et seq); the Sub-Treasurer of the Inner Temple or the Under-Treasurer of the Middle Temple, in that person's capacity as a local authority (see LOCAL GOVERNMENT vol 69 (2009) PARA 5); the London Fire and Emergency Planning Authority (see LONDON GOVERNMENT vol 71 (2013) PARA 315); Transport for London (see LONDON GOVERNMENT vol 71 (2013) PARA 163 et seq); a Mayoral development corporation (see LONDON GOVERNMENT vol 71 (2013) PARA 323); the Council of the Isles of Scilly (see LOCAL GOVERNMENT vol 69 (2009) PARA 36); the Broads Authority established by the Norfolk and Suffolk Broads Act 1988 s 1; a fire and rescue authority constituted by a scheme under the Fire and Rescue Services Act 2004 s 2 or a scheme to which s 4 applies, for an area in England or Wales; a fire and rescue authority created by an order under s 4A (see FIRE AND RESCUE SERVICES vol 51 (2013) PARAS 18, 20); an internal drainage board which is continued in being by virtue of the Land Drainage Act 1991 s 1 for an area in England (see WATER AND WATERWAYS vol 101 (2009) PARAS 569–572); a National Park authority established by an order under the Environment Act 1995 s 63 for an area in England or Wales (see OPEN SPACES AND COUNTRYSIDE vol 78 (2010) PARA 526); a Passenger Transport Executive for an integrated transport area in England (within the meaning of the Transport Act 1968 Pt 2 (ss 9–23A)) (see ROAD TRAFFIC vol 89 (2011) PARA 47 et seq); a port health authority constituted by an order under the Public Health (Control of Disease) Act 1984 s 2 for an area in England (see ENVIRONMENTAL QUALITY AND PUBLIC HEALTH vol 45 (2010) PARA 102); a waste disposal authority established by virtue of an order under the Local Government Act 1985 s 10(1) (see LOCAL GOVERNMENT vol 69 (2009) PARA 17); a joint authority established under Pt 4 (ss 23–42) for an area in England (see LOCAL GOVERNMENT vol 69 (2009) PARA 47) (including, by virtue of the Local Transport Act 2008 s 77(9), an Integrated Transport Authority established under Pt 5 (ss 77–102D) (see ROAD TRAFFIC vol 89 (2011) PARAS 48–49); a sub-national transport body established under the Local Transport Act 2008 s 102E (see ROAD TRAFFIC vol 89 (2011) PARA 48B); a body corporate established pursuant to an order under the Local Government Act 1985 s 67 (see LOCAL GOVERNMENT vol 69 (2009) PARA 17); a joint committee constituted in accordance with the Local Government Act 1972 s 102(1)(b) for an area in England (see LOCAL GOVERNMENT vol 69 (2009) PARA 371); a joint board which is continued in being by virtue of s 263(1) for an area in England (see LOCAL GOVERNMENT vol 69 (2009) PARA 10); a Local Commissioner in England as defined by the Local Government Act 1974 s 23(3) (see LOCAL GOVERNMENT vol 69 (2009) PARA 839), in respect of the Commissioner's functions under ss 29(6A), 34G(6) (see LOCAL GOVERNMENT vol 69 (2009) PARA 859) and the Apprenticeships, Skills, Children and Learning Act 2009 s 210(5) (repealed), and the Commissioner's public procurement functions (as defined in the Equality Act 2010 s 155(3) (see PARA 297); a combined authority established by an order made under the Local Democracy, Economic Development and Construction Act 2009 s 103(1) (see TRADE AND INDUSTRY vol 97 (2015) PARA 1092); an economic prosperity board established by an order made under s 88(1) (see TRADE AND INDUSTRY vol 97 (2015) PARA 1086); and an urban development corporation established by an order made under the Local Government, Planning and Land Act 1980 s 135 (see PLANNING vol 83 (2010) PARA 1581): Sch 19 Pt 1 (amended by the Localism Act 2011 Sch 22 para 62; the Local Audit and Accountability Act 2014 Sch 12 para 114; the Cities and Local Government Devolution Act 2016 Sch 5 para 31; the Policing and Crime Act 2017 Sch 1 para 85; SI 2011/1060; and SI 2017/353); Equality Act 2010 Sch 19 Pt 2 (amended by SI 2011/1063). As from a day to be appointed, the reference to the London Fire and Emergency Planning Authority is repealed and replaced with a reference to the London Fire Commissioner: see the Policing and Crime Act 2017 Sch 2 para 116. At the date at which this volume states the law no such day had been appointed. As to the meaning of 'relevant Welsh authority' for the purposes of the Equality Act 2010 Sch 19 Pt 2 see s 157(1), (2). As from a day to be appointed, s 157(2) is prospectively substituted by the Wales Act 2017 Sch 6 para 84(1), (2). At the date at which this volume states the law no such day had been appointed.

18 Ie the governing body of an educational establishment maintained by an English or Welsh local authority (within the meaning of the Education and Inspections Act 2006 s 162) (see EDUCATION vol 35 (2015) PARA 26); the governing body of an institution in England or Wales within the further education sector (within the meaning of the Further and Higher Education Act 1992 s 91(3)) (see EDUCATION vol 35 (2015) PARA 555); the governing body of an institution in England or Wales within the higher education sector (within the meaning of s 91(5)) (see EDUCATION vol 35 (2015) PARA 619); the Higher Education Funding Councils for England and Wales (see EDUCATION

vol 35 (2015) PARA 691); the Education Workforce Council (see EDUCATION vol 36 (2015) PARA 1075); Her Majesty's Chief Inspector of Education and Training in Wales (see EDUCATION vol 36 (2015) PARA 1148); Qualifications Wales (see EDUCATION vol 36 (2015) PARA 855); a local authority with respect to the pupil referral units it establishes and maintains by virtue of the Education Act 1996 s 19 (see EDUCATION vol 35 (2015) PARA 427); and the proprietor of a City Technology College, a City College for Technology of the Arts, or an academy (see EDUCATION vol 35 (2015) PARA 346): Equality Act 2010 Sch 19 Pt 1 (amended by SI 2011/1060; and SI 2017/353); Equality Act 2010 Sch 19 Pt 2 (amended by the Qualifications Wales Act 2015 Sch 1 para 40; SI 2011/1060; and by virtue of the Education (Wales) Act 2014 s 2(1)).

19 Ie the National Assembly for Wales Commission (see CONSTITUTIONAL AND ADMINISTRATIVE LAW vol 20 (2014) PARA 366); the Parliamentary Commissioner for Administration, in respect of the Commissioner's functions set out in the Parliamentary Commissioner Act 1967 s 3(1), (1A) (see CONSTITUTIONAL AND ADMINISTRATIVE LAW vol 20 (2014) PARA 633) and the Commissioner's public procurement functions (as defined in the Equality Act 2010 s 155(3)) (see PARA 297): Sch 19 Pt 1 (amended by SI 2011/1060).

20 Ie the British Transport Police Force (see POLICE AND INVESTIGATORY POWERS vol 84 (2013) PARA 30); a chief constable of a police force maintained under the Police Act 1996 s 2 (see POLICE AND INVESTIGATORY POWERS vol 84 (2013) PARA 52); the Chief Inspector of the UK Border Agency (see IMMIGRATION AND ASYLUM vol 57 (2012) PARA 200); the Civil Nuclear Police Authority (see ENERGY AND CLIMATE CHANGE vol 44 (2011) PARA 916 et seq); the College of Policing (see POLICE AND INVESTIGATORY POWERS vol 84 (2013) PARA 180); the Commissioner of Police for the City of London (see POLICE AND INVESTIGATORY POWERS vol 84 (2013) PARA 122); the Metropolitan Police Commissioner (see POLICE AND INVESTIGATORY POWERS vol 84 (2013) PARA 117); the Common Council of the City of London in its capacity as a police authority (see POLICE AND INVESTIGATORY POWERS vol 84 (2013) PARA 55); the Independent Police Complaints Commission (see POLICE AND INVESTIGATORY POWERS vol 84 (2013) PARA 287 et seq); a police and crime commissioner established under the Police Reform and Social Responsibility Act 2011 s 1 (see POLICE AND INVESTIGATORY POWERS vol 84 (2013) PARA 56 et seq); the Mayor's Office for Policing and Crime established under s 3 (see LONDON GOVERNMENT vol 71 (2013) PARA 303); a Port Police Force established under an order made under the Harbours Act 1964 s 14 (see PORTS AND HARBOURS vol 85 (2012) PARAS 27–29); the Port Police Force established under the Port of London Act 1968 Pt 10 (ss 154–160); a Port Police Force established under the Harbours, Docks and Piers Clauses Act 1847 s 79 (see PORTS AND HARBOURS vol 85 (2012) PARA 160): Equality Act 2010 Sch 19 Pt 1 (amended by the Police Reform and Social Responsibility Act 2011 Sch 16 paras 380, 383; the Crime and Courts Act 2013 Sch 8 para 183; the Anti-social Behaviour, Crime and Policing Act 2014 Sch 11 para 96; and SI 2011/1060). As from a day to be appointed, the reference to the Independent Police Complaints Commission is repealed and references to the Director General of the Independent Office for Police Conduct and the Independent Office for Police Conduct are added by the Policing and Crime Act 2017 Sch 9 para 72. At the date at which this volume states the law no such day had been appointed.

21 Ie the Association of Chartered Certified Accountants, in respect of its public functions; the Disclosure and Barring Service (see SOCIAL SERVICES vol 95 (2017) PARA 265), the Gambling Commission (see LEISURE AND ENTERTAINMENT vol 68 (2016) PARA 731), the Gangmasters and Labour Abuse Authority (see AGRICULTURAL PRODUCTION AND MARKETING vol 1A (2017) PARA 320); the General Optical Council, in respect of its public functions (see MEDICAL PROFESSIONS vol 74 (2011) PARA 319 et seq), the General Osteopathic Council, in respect of its public functions (see MEDICAL PROFESSIONS vol 74 (2011) PARA 526), the General Pharmaceutical Council, in respect of its public functions (see MEDICAL PROFESSIONS vol 74 (2011) PARA 785), the Health and Care Professions Council, in respect of its public functions (see MEDICAL PROFESSIONS vol 74 (2011) PARA 916), the Independent Monitor appointed under the Police Act 1997 s 119B (see SENTENCING vol 92 (2015) PARA 655); the Pensions Regulator (see PERSONAL AND OCCUPATIONAL PENSIONS vol 80 (2013) PARA 479 et seq); the Security Industry Authority (see TRADE AND INDUSTRY vol 97 (2015) PARA 980 et seq); the Chartered Institute of Patent Attorneys, in respect of its public functions; the Council for Licensed Conveyancers, in respect of its public functions (see LEGAL PROFESSIONS vol 66 (2015) PARA 937 et seq); the General Chiropractic Council, in respect of its public functions (see MEDICAL PROFESSIONS vol 74 (2011) PARA 604); the General Council of the Bar, in respect of its public functions (see LEGAL PROFESSIONS vol 66 (2015) PARA 814 et seq); the General Dental Council, in respect of its public functions (see MEDICAL PROFESSIONS vol 74 (2011) PARA 407 et seq); the General Medical Council, in respect of its public functions (see MEDICAL

PROFESSIONS vol 74 (2011) PARA 179 et seq); the Health and Safety Executive (see HEALTH AND SAFETY AT WORK vol 52 (2014) PARA 326 et seq); the Office for Nuclear Regulation (see ENERGY AND CLIMATE CHANGE vol 44 (2011) PARA 815A); the Insolvency Practitioners Association, in respect of its public functions; the Institute of Chartered Accountants in England and Wales, in respect of its public functions; the Institute of Legal Executives, in respect of its public functions (see LEGAL PROFESSIONS vol 66 (2015) PARA 1044 et seq); the Institute of Trade Mark Attorneys, in respect of its public functions (see TRADE MARKS AND TRADE NAMES vol 97A (2014) PARA 38); the Law Society of England and Wales, in respect of its public functions (see LEGAL PROFESSIONS vol 65 (2015) PARA 439 et seq); the Nursing and Midwifery Council, in respect of its public functions (see MEDICAL PROFESSIONS vol 74 (2011) PARA 692 et seq); and the Office of the Immigration Services Commissioner (see IMMIGRATION AND ASYLUM vol 57 (2012) PARA 204): Equality Act 2010 Sch 19 Pt 1 (amended by the Energy Act 2013 Sch 12 para 102; SI 2011/1060; and SI 2017/353).

22 Ie High Speed Two (HS2) Ltd (see RAILWAYS AND TRAMWAYS vol 86 (2017) PARA 335); Highways England Company Ltd (see HIGHWAYS, STREETS AND BRIDGES vol 55 (2012) PARA 54A); and Network Rail Limited (see RAILWAYS AND TRAMWAYS vol 86 (2017) PARAS 83, 101): Equality Act 2010 Sch 19 Pt 1 (amended by SI 2017/353).

23 Ie the Auditor General for Wales (see LOCAL GOVERNMENT vol 69 (2009) PARA 796); the Public Services Ombudsman for Wales (see the Public Services Ombudsman (Wales) Act 2005; and CONSTITUTIONAL AND ADMINISTRATIVE LAW vol 20 (2014) PARA 640); the Arts Council for Wales(see NATIONAL CULTURAL HERITAGE vol 77 (2016) PARA 958); the National Museums and Galleries of Wales (see NATIONAL CULTURAL HERITAGE vol 77 (2016) PARA 922 et seq); the National Library of Wales (see NATIONAL CULTURAL HERITAGE vol 77 (2016) PARA 902 et seq); the Sports Council for Wales (see NATIONAL CULTURAL HERITAGE vol 77 (2016) PARA 961); the Welsh Language Commissioner (see the Welsh Language (Wales) Measure 2011; and CONSTITUTIONAL AND ADMINISTRATIVE LAW vol 20 (2014) PARA 408); the Commissioner for Older People in Wales (see PARAS 305–317); and the Children's Commissioner for Wales (see CHILDREN AND YOUNG PERSONS vol 9 (2017) PARA 188 et seq); the Wales Audit Office (see CONSTITUTIONAL AND ADMINISTRATIVE LAW vol 20 (2014) PARA 403): Equality Act 2010 Sch 19 Pt 2 (amended by the Public Audit (Wales) Act 2013 Sch 4 para 92; SI 2011/1063; SI 2012/990; and SI 2013/755).

24 Ie the Environment Agency(see ENVIRONMENTAL QUALITY AND PUBLIC HEALTH vol 45 (2010) PARA 68 et seq); the Natural Resources Body for Wales (see ENVIRONMENTAL QUALITY AND PUBLIC HEALTH vol 45 (2010) PARA 59); NHS Blood and Transplant (see HEALTH SERVICES vol 54 (2017) PARA 189); the NHS Business Services Authority (see HEALTH SERVICES vol 54 (2017) PARA 190); and the Student Loans Company Ltd: Equality Act 2010 Sch 19 Pt 4 (added by SI 2011/1060; and amended by SI 2013/755). As to the meaning of 'cross-border Welsh authority' for these purposes see the Equality Act 2010 s 157(1), (3).

25 See the Equality Act 2010 ss 151, 152, 154, 155; and the Equality Act 2010 (Specific Duties and Public Authorities) Regulations 2017, SI 2017/353.

26 See PARAS 285–298.

(ii) General Duties imposed on Public Authorities

278. The public sector equality duty.

A public authority[1] must, in the exercise of its functions[2], have due regard[3] to the need to:

    (1)   eliminate discrimination, harassment[4], victimisation[5] and any other prohibited conduct[6];

    (2)   advance equality of opportunity between persons who share a relevant protected characteristic[7] and persons who do not share it[8];

    (3)   foster good relations between persons who share a relevant protected characteristic and persons who do not share it[9].

The duty (known as the 'public sector equality duty') arises whenever a decision is taken which may have an impact on matters covered by the duty[10]: the object of these provisions is that the potential equality impact of a given decision should always be taken into account[11]. A failure in respect of a performance of a duty imposed by or under these provisions does not confer a cause of action at private law[12]. There are a number of exceptions to this duty relating to the provision of education and other children's services[13], the operation of immigration and nationality functions[14], and the operation of judicial functions[15].

Additional specific duties, pursuant to complying with the public sector equality duty, are also imposed on the applicable authorities[16].

1 As to the public authorities to which these duties apply see the Equality Act 2010 Sch 19; and PARA 277. A public authority specified in Sch 19 is subject to the duty imposed by s 149(1) (see the text and notes 2–9) in relation to the exercise of all of its functions unless it is referred to in Sch 19 only in respect of certain specified functions, in which case it is subject to the duty under s 149(1) only in respect of the exercise of those functions: s 150(3), (4).

2 The 'functions' to which these provisions apply include decisions made in individual cases: these provisions are not restricted to functions involving the formulation of policy: see *Pieretti v Enfield London Borough Council* [2010] EWCA Civ 1104 at [26], [2011] 2 All ER 642, [2010] LGR 944 per Wilson LJ (decided under the Disability Discrimination Act 1995 s 49A (repealed)). Regard must be had in advance of taking the decision in question (*R (on the application of Elias) v Secretary of State for Defence* [2006] EWCA Civ 1293 at [274], [2006] 1 WLR 3213, [2006] IRLR 934 per Arden LJ; *R (on the application of Bailey) v Brent London Borough Council* [2011] EWCA Civ 1586 at [75], [2012] LGR 530 per Pill LJ)), and the obligation is one that continues throughout the process (*R (on the application of Brown) v Secretary of State for Work and Pensions* [2008] EWHC 3158 (Admin) at [95], [2009] PTSR 1506 per Aiken LJ). The public sector equality duty is limited to the functions which the public authority has exercised, not those which it could exercise if it chose to do so: *R (on the application of BAPIO Action Ltd) v Royal College of General Practitioners* [2014] All ER (D) 131 (Apr). The public sector equality duty does not generally apply to the passing of resolutions by a local authority following a debate: *R (on the application of Jewish Rights Watch, t/a Jewish Human Rights Watch) v Leicester City Council; R (on the application of Jewish Rights Watch, t/a Jewish Human Rights Watch) v Gwynedd Council; R (on the application of Jewish Rights Watch, t/a Jewish Human Rights Watch) v City and County of Swansea* [2016] EWHC 1512 (Admin), [2016] All ER (D) 164 (Jun).

3 Ie regard that is appropriate in all the circumstances: see *R (on the application of Baker) v Secretary of State for Communities and Local Government* [2008] EWCA Civ 141, [2008] LGR 239, [2008] 2 P & CR 119 (decided under the Race Relations Act 1976 s 71 (repealed)). The nature of the regard to be had is dependent on the level of observable impact: see *R (on the application of Hajrula) v London Councils* [2011] EWHC 448 (Admin) at [58]–[59], [2011] All ER (D) 119 (Apr). Regard must be had to all limbs of the duty and active steps must be taken to achieve compliance: see *R (on the application of E) v Governing Body of Jews Free School* [2008] EWHC 1535 (Admin) at [206], [2008] ELR 445 per Munby J (revsd on other grounds [2009] EWCA Civ 626, [2009] 4 All ER 375, [2009] ELR 407; [2009] UKSC 15, [2010] 2 AC 728, [2010] 1 All ER 319) (decided under the Race Relations Act 1976 ss 1, 3 (repealed)). Compliance with the duty does not demand a particular outcome or result: *R (on the application of Baker) v Secretary of State for Communities and Local Government*.

4 As to the meaning of 'harassment' see the Equality Act 2010 s 26; and PARA 79.

5 As to the meaning of 'victimisation' see the Equality Act 2010 ss 27, 86; and PARA 81.

6 Equality Act 2010 s 149(1)(a). 'Prohibited conduct' for these purposes is conduct that is prohibited by or under the Equality Act 2010: s 149(1)(a). A reference to conduct that is prohibited by or under the Equality Act 2010 includes a reference to a breach of an equality clause or rule (see PARA 117 note 4) and a breach of a non-discrimination rule (see PARA 134 notes 4–10): s 149(8). Compliance with the duties in s 149 may involve treating some persons more favourably than others; but that is not to be taken as permitting conduct that would otherwise be prohibited conduct: s 149(6).

7 As to the relevant protected characteristics for these purposes see PARA 276.

8 Equality Act 2010 s 149(1)(b). As to having due regard to advancing equality of opportunity between persons who share a relevant protected characteristic and persons who do not share it see further s 149(3), (4); and PARA 280.

9 Equality Act 2010 s 149(1)(c). See also *R (on the application of LH) v Shropshire Council* [2014] EWCA Civ 404, [2014] All ER (D) 06 (May). As to fostering good relations between persons who share a relevant protected characteristic and persons who do not share it see further s 149(5); and PARA 281.

10 See *R (on the application of Watkins-Singh) v Governing Body of Aberdare Girls' High School* [2008] EWHC 1865 (Admin) at [97], [2008] All ER (D) 376 (Jul), [2008] ELR 561, per Silber J (decided under the Race Relations Act 1976 s 71 (repealed)).

11 See *R (on the application of E) v Governing Body of Jews Free School* [2008] EWHC 1535 (Admin) at [206], [2008] ELR 445 per Munby J (revsd on other grounds [2009] EWCA Civ 626, [2009] 4 All ER 375, [2009] ELR 407; [2009] UKSC 15, [2010] 2 AC 728, [2010] 1 All ER 319) (decided under the Race Relations Act 1976 ss 1, 3 (repealed)). See also *R (on the application of Harris) v Haringey London Borough Council (Equality and Human Rights Commission intervening)* [2010] EWCA Civ 703, [2010] LGR 713 (decided under the Race Relations Act 1976 s 71 (repealed)); *Bracking v Secretary of State for Work and Pensions* [2013] EWCA Civ 1345, [2013] All ER (D) 75 (Nov); *R (on the application of Aspinall) (formerly including Bracking) v Secretary of State for Work and Pensions (Equality and Human Rights Commission intervening)* [2014] EWHC 4134 (Admin), [2014] All ER (D) 90 (Dec).

12 Equality Act 2010 s 156.

13 See PARA 282.

14 See PARA 283.

15 See PARA 284.

16 See the Equality Act 2010 (Specific Duties and Public Authorities) Regulations 2017, SI 2017/353; the Equality Act 2010 (Statutory Duties) (Wales) Regulations 2011, SI 2011/1064; and PARAS 285–288 (England), 289–298 (Wales). Failure to comply with the specific duties will not make a breach of the public sector equality duty inevitable: see *R (on the application of Brown) v Secretary of State for Work and Pensions* [2008] EWHC 3158 (Admin) at [176], [2009] PTSR 1506 per Aiken LJ (decided under the Disability Discrimination Act 1995 (repealed)).

279.　Duty of non-public authorities exercising public functions.

A person who is not a public authority but who exercises public functions[1] must, in the exercise of those functions, have due regard to the need to:

(1)　eliminate discrimination, harassment[2], victimisation[3] and any other prohibited conduct[4];

(2)　advance equality of opportunity between persons who share a relevant protected characteristic[5] and persons who do not share it[6];

(3)　foster good relations between persons who share a relevant protected characteristic and persons who do not share it[7].

A failure in respect of a performance of a duty imposed by or under these provisions does not confer a cause of action at private law[8]. There are a number of exceptions to this duty relating to the provision of education and other children's services[9], the operation of immigration and nationality functions[10], and the operation of judicial functions[11].

1 A 'public function' is a function that is a function of a public nature for the purposes of the Human Rights Act 1998: Equality Act 2010 s 150(5). As to functions of a public nature for those purposes see RIGHTS AND FREEDOMS vol 88A (2013) PARA 26. These provisions (ie s 149(2): see the text and notes 2–7) do not apply to the House of Commons (Sch 18 para 4(1)(a), (2)(a)), the House of Lords (Sch 18 para 4(1)(a), (2)(b)), the National Assembly for Wales (Sch 18 para 4(1)(a), (2)(d)), the General Synod of the Church of England (Sch 18 para 4(1)(a), (2)(e)), the Security Service (Sch 18 para 4(1)(a), (2)(f)), the Secret Intelligence Service (Sch 18 para 4(1)(a), (2)(g)), the Government Communications Headquarters (Sch 18 para 4(1)(a), (2)(h)) or a part of the armed forces which is, in accordance with a requirement of the Secretary of State, assisting the Government Communications Headquarters (Sch 18 para 4(1)(a), (2)(i)), or to the exercise of a function in connection with proceedings in the House of Commons or the House of Lords or a function in connection with proceedings in the National Assembly for Wales (other than a function of the Assembly Commission) (Sch 18 para 4(1)(b), (3)(a), (c)). As to the House of Commons see PARLIAMENT vol 78 (2010) PARAS 892–989; as to the House of Lords see PARLIAMENT vol 78 (2010) PARAS 828–891; as to the National Assembly for Wales see CONSTITUTIONAL AND ADMINISTRATIVE LAW vol 20 (2014) PARA 351 et seq; as to the General Synod of the Church of England see ECCLESIASTICAL LAW vol 34 (2011) PARA 100 et seq; as to the Security Service, the Secret Intelligence Service and the Government Communications Headquarters see CONSTITUTIONAL AND ADMINISTRATIVE LAW vol 20 (2014) PARA 243 et seq. As to the meaning of 'the Assembly Commission' see the Government of Wales Act 2006 s 27; and CONSTITUTIONAL AND ADMINISTRATIVE LAW vol 20 (2014) PARA 366 (definition applied by the Equality Act 2010 s 157(1), (4)).

　　A Minister of the Crown may by order amend the Equality Act 2010 Sch 18 so as to add, vary or omit an exception to s 149 (Sch 18 para 5(1)), although any provision so made may not amend

Sch 18 so as to omit an exception in Sch 18 para 3 (see PARA 284), so as to omit an exception in Sch 18 para 4(1) so far as applying for the purposes of Sch 18 para 4(2)(a)–(e) or (3) (see above), or so as to reduce the extent to which such an exception applies (Sch 18 para 5(2)). Any amending orders so made will be recorded to the applicable provision.

2   As to the meaning of 'harassment' see the Equality Act 2010 s 26; and PARA 79.
3   As to the meaning of 'victimisation' see the Equality Act 2010 ss 27, 86; and PARA 81.
4   Equality Act 2010 s 149(1)(a), (2). As to 'prohibited conduct' for these purposes, and compliance with these duties, see PARA 278 note 6.
5   As to the relevant protected characteristics for these purposes see PARA 276.
6   Equality Act 2010 s 149(1)(b), (2). As to having due regard to advancing equality of opportunity between persons who share a relevant protected characteristic and persons who do not share it see further s 149(3), (4); and PARA 280.
7   Equality Act 2010 s 149(1)(c), (2). As to fostering good relations between persons who share a relevant protected characteristic and persons who do not share it see further s 149(5); and PARA 281.
8   Equality Act 2010 s 156.
9   See PARA 282.
10 See PARA 283.
11 See PARA 284.

280. Advancing equality of opportunity.

Having due regard to the need to advance equality of opportunity between persons who share a relevant protected characteristic[1] and persons who do not share it[2] involves having due regard, in particular, to the need to:

(1)   remove or minimise disadvantages suffered by persons who share a relevant protected characteristic that are connected to that characteristic[3];

(2)   take steps to meet the needs of persons who share a relevant protected characteristic that are different from the needs of persons who do not share it[4]; and

(3)   encourage persons who share a relevant protected characteristic to participate in public life or in any other activity in which participation by such persons is disproportionately low[5].

1   As to the relevant protected characteristics for these purposes see PARA 276.
2   Ie in the context of the Equality Act 2010 s 149(1) (see PARAS 278, 279).
3   Equality Act 2010 s 149(3)(a).
4   Equality Act 2010 s 149(3)(b). The steps involved in meeting the needs of disabled persons that are different from the needs of persons who are not disabled include, in particular, steps to take account of disabled persons' disabilities: s 149(4).
5   Equality Act 2010 s 149(3)(c).

281. Fostering good relations.

Having due regard to the need to foster good relations between persons who share a relevant protected characteristic[1] and persons who do not share it[2] involves having due regard, in particular, to the need to tackle prejudice[3] and promote understanding[4].

1   As to the relevant protected characteristics for these purposes see PARA 276.
2   Ie in the context of the Equality Act 2010 s 149(1) (see PARAS 278–279).
3   Equality Act 2010 s 149(5)(a).
4   Equality Act 2010 s 149(5)(b).

282. Exception relating to the provision of education and other children's services.

The public sector equality duty[1], so far as relating to age[2], does not apply to the exercise of a function relating to:

(1)   the provision of education to pupils in schools[3];
(2)   the provision of benefits, facilities or services to pupils in schools[4];
(3)   the provision[5] of accommodation, benefits, facilities or services in community homes[6]; or
(4)   the provision[7] of accommodation, benefits, facilities or services pursuant to arrangements by the Secretary of State relating to the accommodation of children[8].

1   Ie the duty imposed by the Equality Act 2010 s 149 on public authorities and authorities exercising functions of a public nature (see PARAS 278, 279).
2   As to age as a protected characteristic see PARA 46. As to the protected characteristics for the purposes of the public sector equality duty see PARA 276.
3   Equality Act 2010 Sch 18 para 1(1)(a). As to the meanings of 'pupil' and 'school' see the Education Act 1996 ss 3(1), 4; and EDUCATION vol 35 (2015) PARAS 20, 91 (definitions applied by the Equality Act 2010 s 89(3)(a), (5)(a), Sch 18 para 1(2)).
4   Equality Act 2010 Sch 18 para 1(1)(b).
5   Ie pursuant to the Children Act 1989 s 53(1) (see CHILDREN AND YOUNG PERSONS vol 10 (2017) PARA 1008).
6   Equality Act 2010 Sch 18 para 1(1)(c).
7   Ie pursuant to the Children Act 1989 s 82(5) (see CHILDREN AND YOUNG PERSONS vol 9 (2017) PARA 173).
8   Equality Act 2010 Sch 18 para 1(1)(d). As to the Secretary of State see PARA 4.

283. Exception relating to immigration and nationality functions.

In relation to the exercise of immigration and nationality functions[1], the public sector equality duty[2] has effect as if the duty to advance equality of opportunity between persons who share a relevant protected characteristic[3] and persons who do not share it[4] does not apply to the protected characteristics of age[5], race[6] or religion or belief[7].

1   'Immigration and nationality functions' means functions exercisable by virtue of the Immigration Acts (excluding the Immigration Act 1971 ss 28A–28K in so far as they relate to criminal offences), the British Nationality Act 1981, the British Nationality (Falkland Islands) Act 1983, the British Nationality (Hong Kong) Act 1990, the Hong Kong (War Wives and Widows) Act 1996, the British Nationality (Hong Kong) Act 1997, the Special Immigration Appeals Commission Act 1997, or a provision made under the European Communities Act 1972 s 2(2), or of EU law, which relates to the subject matter of any such enactment: Equality Act 2010 Sch 18 para 2(2) (amended by SI 2010/2279). As to the meaning of 'enactment' see PARA 91 note 10.
2   Ie the duty imposed by the Equality Act 2010 s 149 on public authorities and authorities exercising functions of a public nature (see PARAS 278, 279).
3   As to the protected characteristics for the purposes of the public sector equality duty see PARA 276.
4   Ie the duty imposed by the Equality Act 2010 s 149(1)(b) (see PARAS 278–279).
5   As to age as a protected characteristic see PARA 46.
6   As to race as a protected characteristic see PARA 58. For this purpose 'race' means race so far as relating to nationality or ethnic or national origins: Equality Act 2010 Sch 18 para 2(1).
7   Equality Act 2010 Sch 18 para 2(1). As to religion or belief as a protected characteristic see PARA 59.

284. Exception relating to judicial functions.

The public sector equality duty[1] does not apply to the exercise of a judicial function[2] or a function exercised on behalf of, or on the instructions of, a person exercising a judicial function[3].

1   Ie the duty imposed by the Equality Act 2010 s 149 on public authorities and authorities exercising functions of a public nature (see PARAS 278, 279).
2   References to a judicial function include a reference to a judicial function conferred on a person other than a court or tribunal: Equality Act 2010 Sch 18 para 3(2).
3   Equality Act 2010 Sch 18 para 3(1).

(iii) Specific Duties imposed on Public Authorities

A.   ENGLAND AND WALES

285. Duty to publish information concerning compliance with the public sector equality duty.

Certain public authorities[1] are required to publish information to demonstrate their compliance with the public sector equality duty[2]. The information a public authority publishes in compliance with this requirement must include, in particular, information relating to persons who share a relevant protected characteristic[3] who are its employees[4] and other persons affected by its policies and practices[5]. Publication is annual[6], and must be in such a manner that the information is accessible to the public[7].

1   As to the authorities to which these requirements apply see PARA **288**.
2   Equality Act 2010 (Specific Duties and Public Authorities) Regulations 2017, SI 2017/353, reg 4(1). The 'public sector equality duty' is the duty imposed by the Equality Act 2010 s 149(1) (see PARAS **278–279**). The Equality Act 2010 (Specific Duties and Public Authorities) Regulations 2017, SI 2017/353, are made pursuant to the Equality Act 2010 s 153(1), under which a Minister of the Crown may by regulations impose duties on a public authority specified in Sch 19 Pt 1 (see PARA **277**) for the purpose of enabling the better performance by the authority of the duty imposed by s 149(1). Before making such regulations the Minister must consult the Equality and Human Rights Commission: s 153(4). As to supplementary provisions in connection with the exercise of this power see s 155. As to the Commission see PARAS **28–44**.
3   As to the relevant protected characteristics see PARA **276**.
4   Equality Act 2010 (Specific Duties and Public Authorities) Regulations 2017, SI 2017/353, reg 4(3)(a). Regulation 4(3)(a) does not apply to a public authority with fewer than 150 employees: reg 4(4).
5   Equality Act 2010 (Specific Duties and Public Authorities) Regulations 2017, SI 2017/353, reg 4(3)(b).
6   The public authorities required to publish information pursuant to these provisions must publish that information not later than 30th March 2018; and subsequently at intervals of not greater than one year beginning with the date of last publication: Equality Act 2010 (Specific Duties and Public Authorities) Regulations 2017, SI 2017/353, reg 4(2).
7   Equality Act 2010 (Specific Duties and Public Authorities) Regulations 2017, SI 2017/353, reg 6(1). A public authority may comply with a duty to publish information imposed by reg 4 by publishing the information within another published document: see reg 6(2).

286. Duty to comply with gender pay gap reporting requirements.

Specified public authorities[1] must publish the following gender pay gap information[2]:

(1)   the difference between the mean hourly rate of pay of male full-pay relevant employees[3] and that of female full-pay relevant employees; and the difference between the median hourly rate of pay of male full-pay relevant employees and that of female full-pay relevant employees[4];

(2)   the difference between the mean bonus pay paid to male relevant employees and that paid to female relevant employees; and the difference between the median bonus pay paid to male relevant employees and that paid to female relevant employees[5];

(3)   the proportions of male and female relevant employees who were paid bonus pay[6]; and

(4)   the proportions of male and female full-pay relevant employees in the lower, lower middle, upper middle and upper quartile pay bands[7].

The relevant public authority must publish the information required within the period of 12 months beginning with the snapshot date[8]. In compiling such information, a relevant public authority is not required to include data relating to a relevant employee if the employee is employed under a contract personally to do work and the public authority does not have, and it is not reasonably practicable for the public authority to obtain, the data[9].

1   As to the authorities to which these requirements apply see PARA 288.

2   The information is to be published for 2017 and each subsequent year: see the Equality Act 2010 (Specific Duties and Public Authorities) Regulations 2017, SI 2017/353, reg 3, Sch 1 para 2(1). The requirement in Sch 1 para 2(1) to publish information is a requirement that that information be published on the public authority's website in a manner that is accessible to all its employees and to the public and for a period of at least three years beginning with the date of publication: see Sch 1 para 14(1). A relevant public authority must also publish the information on a website designated for that purpose by the Secretary of State: see Sch 1 para 14(2). As to other publication options where the relevant public authority comprises one of the armed forces see Sch 1 para 14(3), (4).

3   'Full-pay relevant employee' means a relevant employee who is not, during the relevant pay period, being paid at a reduced rate or nil as a result of the employee being on leave: see the Equality Act 2010 (Specific Duties and Public Authorities) Regulations 2017, SI 2017/353, Sch 1 para 1(1). 'Relevant employee' means a person who is employed by, (or in the case of Crown employment, under or for the purposes of) the relevant public authority on the snapshot date (ie 31 March in the year to which the information required by Sch 1 para 2 relates): Sch 1 para 1(1). 'Relevant pay period' means the pay period within which the snapshot date falls; and 'leave' includes annual leave; maternity, paternity, adoption, parental or shared parental leave; sick leave; and special leave: Sch 1 paras 1(1), 5(2). For these purposes, 'employment' means employment under a contract of employment, a contract of apprenticeship or a contract personally to do work, and Crown employment (within the meaning of the Employment Rights Act 1996 s 191(3): see EMPLOYMENT vol 39 (2014) PARA 163) (Equality Act 2010 (Specific Duties and Public Authorities) Regulations 2017, SI 2017/353, reg 2(1)); and the Employment Rights Act 1996 s 191(4) (see EMPLOYMENT vol 39 (2014) PARA 163) applies for these purposes as it applies for the purposes set out in that provision: Equality Act 2010 (Specific Duties and Public Authorities) Regulations 2017, SI 2017/353, reg 2(2).

4   See the Equality Act 2010 (Specific Duties and Public Authorities) Regulations 2017, SI 2017/353, Sch 1 para 2(1)(a), (1)(b). As to determination of the difference between the mean hourly rate of pay of male full-pay relevant employees and that of female full-pay relevant employees see Sch 1 paras 3, 5–8. As to determination of the difference between the median hourly rate of pay of male full-pay relevant employees and that of female full-pay relevant employees see Sch 1 paras 3, 5–7, 9. 'Hourly rate of pay' is defined in Sch 1 para 6.

5   See the Equality Act 2010 (Specific Duties and Public Authorities) Regulations 2017, SI 2017/353, Sch 1 para 2(1)(c), (1)(d). As to determination of the difference between the mean bonus pay paid to male relevant employees and that paid to female relevant employees see Sch 1 para 10. As to determination of the difference between the median bonus pay paid to male relevant employees and that paid to female relevant employees see Sch 1 para 11. 'Bonus pay' is defined in Sch 1 para 4.

6   See the Equality Act 2010 (Specific Duties and Public Authorities) Regulations 2017, SI 2017/353, Sch 1 para 2(1)(e). As to determination of the proportions of male and female relevant employees who were paid bonus pay see Sch 1 para 12.

7   See the Equality Act 2010 (Specific Duties and Public Authorities) Regulations 2017, SI 2017/353, Sch 1 para 2(1)(f). As to determination of the proportions of male and female full-pay relevant employees in the lower, lower middle, upper middle and upper quartile pay bands see Sch 1 para 13.

8   See the Equality Act 2010 (Specific Duties and Public Authorities) Regulations 2017, SI 2017/353, Sch 1 para 2(2). As to the 'snapshot date' see note 3.

9   See the Equality Act 2010 (Specific Duties and Public Authorities) Regulations 2017, SI 2017/353, Sch 1 para 2(3).

287. Publication of equality objectives.

Specified public authorities[1] must prepare and publish one or more objectives it thinks it should achieve in order to:

(1)   eliminate discrimination, harassment[2], victimisation[3] and any other prohibited conduct[4];

(2)   advance equality of opportunity between persons who share a relevant protected characteristic[5] and persons who do not share it[6];

(3)   foster good relations between persons who share a relevant protected characteristic and persons who do not share it[7].

An objective so published must be specific and measurable[8]. Publication is annual[9], and must be in such a manner that the information is accessible to the public[10].

1 As to the authorities to which these requirements apply see PARA 288.
2 As to the meaning of 'harassment' see the Equality Act 2010 s 26; and PARA 79.
3 As to the meaning of 'victimisation' see the Equality Act 2010 ss 27, 86; and PARA 81.
4 Equality Act 2010 s 149(1)(a); Equality Act 2010 (Specific Duties and Public Authorities) Regulations 2017, SI 2017/353, reg 5(1). As to 'prohibited conduct' for these purposes see PARA 278 note 6. As to the making of these regulations see PARA 285 note 2.
5 As to the relevant protected characteristics for these purposes see PARA 276.
6 Equality Act 2010 s 149(1)(b); Equality Act 2010 (Specific Duties and Public Authorities) Regulations 2017, SI 2017/353, reg 5(1). As to having due regard to advancing equality of opportunity between persons who share a relevant protected characteristic and persons who do not share it see further s 149(3), (4); and PARA 280.
7 Equality Act 2010 s 149(1)(c); Equality Act 2010 (Specific Duties and Public Authorities) Regulations 2017, SI 2017/353, reg 5(1). As to fostering good relations between persons who share a relevant protected characteristic and persons who do not share it see further s 149(5); and PARA 281.
8 Equality Act 2010 (Specific Duties and Public Authorities) Regulations 2017, SI 2017/353, reg 5(3).
9 The objectives must be published not later than 30th March 2018 (save where transitional provisions apply); and subsequently at intervals of not greater than four years beginning with the date of last publication: see the Equality Act 2010 (Specific Duties and Public Authorities) Regulations 2017, SI 2017/353, reg 5(2). As to where transitional provisions apply see reg 9.
10 Equality Act 2010 (Specific Duties and Public Authorities) Regulations 2017, SI 2017/353, reg 6(1). A public authority may comply with a duty to publish information imposed by reg 5 by publishing the information within another published document: see reg 6(2).

288. Authorities subject to the specific duties.
The public authorities required to publish information demonstrating their compliance with the public sector equality duty[1] and to publish equality objectives[2] are:
(1)   any of the armed forces other than any part of the armed forces which is, in accordance with a requirement of the Secretary of State, assisting the Government Communications Headquarters[3];
(2)   the British Broadcasting Corporation[4], Channel 4[5] and S4C[6];
(3)   the Equality and Human Rights Commission[7];
(4)   the Information Commissioner[8];
(5)   the Children and Family Court Advisory and Support Service[9];
(6)   the Judicial Appointments Commission[10];
(7)   the Legal Services Board[11];
(8)   specified bodies concerned with the administration of criminal justice[12];
(9)   certain further and higher education bodies[13];
(10)   the Environment Agency[14];
(11)   the Homes and Communities Agency[15];
(12)   Natural England[16];
(13)   specified bodies concerned with health, social care and social security[17];
(14)   specified bodies concerned with industry, business and finance[18];
(15)   specified local government bodies[19];
(16)   Ministers of the Crown and government departments[20];
(17)   the National Assembly for Wales Commission[21];
(18)   the Scottish Parliamentary Corporate Body[22];
(19)   specified police bodies[23];

(20)   specified regulatory bodies[24]; and
(21)   specified transport bodies[25].

1 Ie pursuant to the Equality Act 2010 (Specific Duties and Public Authorities) Regulations 2017, SI 2017/353, reg 4 (see PARA 285).

2 Ie pursuant to the Equality Act 2010 (Specific Duties and Public Authorities) Regulations 2017, SI 2017/353, reg 5 (see PARA 287).

3 Equality Act 2010 (Specific Duties and Public Authorities) Regulations 2017, SI 2017/353, Sch 2. As to the Government Communications Headquarters see CONSTITUTIONAL AND ADMINISTRATIVE LAW vol 20 (2014) PARA 245.

4 Ie the British Broadcasting Corporation ('BBC'), except in respect of functions relating to the provision of a content service (within the meaning given by the Communications Act 2003 s 32(7): see TELECOMMUNICATIONS vol 97 (2015) PARA 53); the reference to the BBC includes a reference to a body corporate which is a wholly owned subsidiary of the BBC, is not operated with a view to generating a profit, and undertakes activities primarily in order to promote the BBC's public purposes: Equality Act 2010 (Specific Duties and Public Authorities) Regulations 2017, SI 2017/353, Sch 2.

5 Ie the Channel Four Television Corporation (see BROADCASTING vol 4 (2011) PARA 627 et seq), except in respect of functions relating to the provision of a content service (within the meaning given by the Communications Act 2003 s 32(7)), and the function of carrying on the activities referred to in s 199 (see BROADCASTING vol 4 (2011) PARA 639)): Equality Act 2010 (Specific Duties and Public Authorities) Regulations 2017, SI 2017/353, Sch 2.

6 Ie the Welsh Authority (as defined by the Broadcasting Act 1990 s 56(1): see BROADCASTING vol 4 (2011) PARA 645), except in respect of functions relating to the provision of a content service (within the meaning given by the Communications Act 2003 s 32(7)): Equality Act 2010 (Specific Duties and Public Authorities) Regulations 2017, SI 2017/353, Sch 2.

7 Equality Act 2010 (Specific Duties and Public Authorities) Regulations 2017, SI 2017/353, Sch 2. As to the Commission see PARAS 28–44.

8 Equality Act 2010 (Specific Duties and Public Authorities) Regulations 2017, SI 2017/353, Sch 2. As to the Information Commissioner see CONFIDENCE AND INFORMATIONAL PRIVACY vol 19 (2011) PARA 109.

9 Equality Act 2010 (Specific Duties and Public Authorities) Regulations 2017, SI 2017/353, Sch 2. As to the Children and Family Court Advisory and Support Service see CHILDREN AND YOUNG PERSONS vol 9 (2017) PARA 225 et seq.

10 Equality Act 2010 (Specific Duties and Public Authorities) Regulations 2017, SI 2017/353, Sch 2. As to the Judicial Appointments Commission see COURTS AND TRIBUNALS vol 24 (2010) PARA 935.

11 Equality Act 2010 (Specific Duties and Public Authorities) Regulations 2017, SI 2017/353, Sch 2. As to the Legal Services Board see LEGAL PROFESSIONS vol 65 (2015) PARA 203.

12 Ie the Criminal Cases Review Commission (see CRIMINAL PROCEDURE vol 28 (2015) PARA 790 et seq); Her Majesty's Chief Inspector of Constabulary (see POLICE AND INVESTIGATORY POWERS vol 84 (2013) PARA 152); Her Majesty's Chief Inspector of the Crown Prosecution Service (see CRIMINAL PROCEDURE vol 27 (2015) PARA 26); Her Majesty's Chief Inspector of Prisons (see PRISONS AND PRISONERS vol 85 (2012) PARA 409); Her Majesty's Chief Inspector of Probation for England and Wales (see SENTENCING vol 92 (2015) PARA 682); the Parole Board for England and Wales (see SENTENCING vol 92 (2015) PARA 699); a probation trust established by an order made under the Offender Management Act 2007 s 5(1) (see SENTENCING vol 92 (2015) PARA 670); and the Youth Justice Board for England and Wales (see CHILDREN AND YOUNG PERSONS vol 10 (2017) PARA 1286 et seq): Equality Act 2010 (Specific Duties and Public Authorities) Regulations 2017, SI 2017/353, Sch 2.

13 Ie the governing body of an educational establishment maintained by an English local authority (within the meaning of the Education and Inspections Act 2006 s 162) (see EDUCATION vol 35 (2015) PARA 26); the governing body of an institution in England within the further education sector (within the meaning of the Further and Higher Education Act 1992 91(3)) (see EDUCATION vol 35 (2015) PARA 555); the governing body of an institution in England within the higher education sector (within the meaning of s 91(5)) (see EDUCATION vol 35 (2015) PARA 619); the Higher Education Funding Council for England (see EDUCATION vol 35 (2015) PARA 691); a local authority in England with respect to the pupil referral units it establishes and maintains by virtue of the Education Act 1996 s 19 (see EDUCATION vol 35 (2015) PARA 427); and the proprietor of a City Technology College, City College for Technology of the Arts, or an academy (see EDUCATION

vol 35 (2015) PARA 364); and the Student Loans Company Limited: Equality Act 2010 (Specific Duties and Public Authorities) Regulations 2017, SI 2017/353, Sch 2.

14 Equality Act 2010 (Specific Duties and Public Authorities) Regulations 2017, SI 2017/353, Sch 2. As to the Environment Agency see ENVIRONMENTAL QUALITY AND PUBLIC HEALTH vol 45 (2010) PARA 68 et seq.

15 Equality Act 2010 (Specific Duties and Public Authorities) Regulations 2017, SI 2017/353, Sch 2. As to the Homes and Communities Agency see HOUSING vol 56 (2017) PARA 2.

16 Equality Act 2010 (Specific Duties and Public Authorities) Regulations 2017, SI 2017/353, Sch 2. As to Natural England see OPEN SPACES AND COUNTRYSIDE vol 78 (2010) PARA 523.

17 Ie the Care Quality Commission (see HEALTH SERVICES vol 54A (2017) PARA 648 et seq); a clinical commissioning group established under the National Health Service Act 2006 s 14D (see HEALTH SERVICES vol 54 (2017) PARAS 35, 151 et seq); Health Education England (see HEALTH SERVICES vol 54 (2017) PARAS 196–198); the Health Research Authority (see HEALTH SERVICES vol 54 (2017) PARAS 199–202); the Health and Social Care Information Centre (see SOCIAL SERVICES vol 95 (2017) PARA 372); Monitor (see HEALTH SERVICES vol 54 (2017) PARAS 194–195); an NHS foundation trust within the meaning given by the National Health Service Act 2006 s 30 (see HEALTH SERVICES vol 54 (2017) PARA 244); an NHS trust established in England under s 25 (see HEALTH SERVICES vol 54 (2017) PARA 235); the National Health Service Commissioning Board (see HEALTH SERVICES vol 54 (2017) PARAS 32, 133 et seq); the National Institute for Health and Care Excellence (see SOCIAL SERVICES vol 95 (2017) PARA 371); a Special Health Authority established under s 28 (see HEALTH SERVICES vol 54 (2017) PARA 180): Equality Act 2010 (Specific Duties and Public Authorities) Regulations 2017, SI 2017/353, Sch 2. Monitor and the NHS Trust Development Authority (see HEALTH SERVICES vol 54 (2017) PARA 192) may jointly comply with the obligations imposed by the Equality Act 2010 (Specific Duties and Public Authorities) Regulations 2017, SI 2017/353 (see PARAS 285–287) as if they were a single public authority: reg 7.

18 Ie the Advisory, Conciliation and Arbitration Service (see EMPLOYMENT vol 41A (2014) PARA 1213 et seq); the Bank of England in respect of its public functions (see FINANCIAL INSTITUTIONS vol 48 (2015) PARA 97 et seq); the Board of the Pension Protection Fund (see PERSONAL AND OCCUPATIONAL PENSIONS vol 80 (2013) PARA 554 et seq); the Civil Aviation Authority (see AVIATION vol 2 (2017) PARA 752 et seq); the Coal Authority (see MINES, MINERALS AND QUARRIES vol 76 (2013) PARA 51 et seq); the Construction Industry Training Board; the Engineering Construction Industry Training Board; the Financial Conduct Authority (see FINANCIAL SERVICES REGULATION vol 50 (2016) PARA 6 et seq); the National Audit Office (see CONSTITUTIONAL AND ADMINISTRATIVE LAW vol 20 (2014) PARA 492); the Nuclear Decommissioning Authority (see ENERGY AND CLIMATE CHANGE vol 44 (2011) PARA 818 et seq); the Office for Budget Responsibility (see CONSTITUTIONAL AND ADMINISTRATIVE LAW vol 20 (2014) PARA 475); the Office of Communications (see TELECOMMUNICATIONS vol 97 (2015) PARA 2 et seq); the Oil and Gas Authority ((see ENERGY AND CLIMATE CHANGE vol 44 (2011) PARA 1034); and the Prudential Regulation Authority (see FINANCIAL SERVICES REGULATION vol 50 (2016) PARA 20 et seq): Equality Act 2010 (Specific Duties and Public Authorities) Regulations 2017, SI 2017/353, Sch 2.

19 Ie a body corporate established pursuant to an order under the Local Government Act 1985 s 67 (see LOCAL GOVERNMENT vol 69 (2009) PARA 17); a combined authority established by an order made under the Local Democracy, Economic Development and Construction Act 2009 s 103(1) (see TRADE AND INDUSTRY vol 97 (2015) PARA 1092); the Common Council of the City of London in its capacity as a local authority or port health authority (see LONDON GOVERNMENT vol 71 (2013) PARA 34 et seq); the Council of the Isles of Scilly (see LOCAL GOVERNMENT vol 69 (2009) PARA 36); a county council or district council in England (see LOCAL GOVERNMENT vol 69 (2009) PARA 24 et seq); an economic prosperity board established by an order made under the Local Democracy, Economic Development and Construction Act 2009 s 88(1) (see TRADE AND INDUSTRY vol 97 (2015) PARA 1086); a fire and rescue authority constituted by a scheme under the Fire and Rescue Services Act 2004 s 2 or a scheme to which s 4 applies, for an area in England (see FIRE AND RESCUE SERVICES vol 51 (2013) PARAS 18, 20); the Greater London Authority (see LONDON GOVERNMENT vol 71 (2013) PARA 67 et seq); a joint committee constituted in accordance with the Local Government Act 1972 s 102(1)(b) for an area in England (see LOCAL GOVERNMENT vol 69 (2009) PARA 371); a London borough council (see LONDON GOVERNMENT vol 71 (2013) PARAS 20–22); the London Fire and Emergency Planning Authority (see LONDON GOVERNMENT vol 71 (2013) PARA 315); a National Park authority established by an order under the Environment Act 1995 s 63 for an area in England (see OPEN SPACES AND COUNTRYSIDE vol 78 (2010) PARA 526); a Passenger Transport

Executive for an integrated transport area in England (within the meaning of the Transport Act 1968 Pt 2 (ss 9–23A)) (see ROAD TRAFFIC vol 89 (2011) PARA 47 et seq); and Transport for London (see LONDON GOVERNMENT vol 71 (2013) PARA 163 et seq): Equality Act 2010 (Specific Duties and Public Authorities) Regulations 2017, SI 2017/353, Sch 2.

20 Ie a government department other than the Security Service, the Secret Intelligence Service or the Government Communications Headquarters; and a Minister of the Crown: Equality Act 2010 (Specific Duties and Public Authorities) Regulations 2017, SI 2017/353, Sch 2. As to the Security Service, the Secret Intelligence Service and the Government Communications Headquarters see CONSTITUTIONAL AND ADMINISTRATIVE LAW vol 20 (2014) PARA 243 et seq.

21 Equality Act 2010 (Specific Duties and Public Authorities) Regulations 2017, SI 2017/353, Sch 2. As to the Commission see CONSTITUTIONAL AND ADMINISTRATIVE LAW vol 20 (2014) PARA 366.

22 Equality Act 2010 (Specific Duties and Public Authorities) Regulations 2017, SI 2017/353, Sch 2.

23 Ie the British Transport Police Force (see POLICE AND INVESTIGATORY POWERS vol 84 (2013) PARA 30); a chief constable of a police force maintained under the Police Act 1996 s 2 (see POLICE AND INVESTIGATORY POWERS vol 84 (2013) PARA 52); the Chief Inspector of the UK Border Agency (see IMMIGRATION AND ASYLUM vol 57 (2012) PARA 200); the Civil Nuclear Police Authority (see ENERGY AND CLIMATE CHANGE vol 44 (2011) PARA 916 et seq); the Commissioner of Police for the City of London (see POLICE AND INVESTIGATORY POWERS vol 84 (2013) PARA 122); the Metropolitan Police Commissioner (see POLICE AND INVESTIGATORY POWERS vol 84 (2013) PARA 117); the Common Council of the City of London in its capacity as a police authority (see POLICE AND INVESTIGATORY POWERS vol 84 (2013) PARA 55); the Independent Police Complaints Commission (see POLICE AND INVESTIGATORY POWERS vol 84 (2013) PARA 287 et seq); the Mayor's Office for Policing and Crime established under the Police Reform and Social Responsibility Act 2011 s 3 (see LONDON GOVERNMENT vol 71 (2013) PARA 303); and a police and crime commissioner established under the Police Reform and Social Responsibility Act 2011 s 1 (see POLICE AND INVESTIGATORY POWERS vol 84 (2013) PARA 56 et seq): Equality Act 2010 (Specific Duties and Public Authorities) Regulations 2017, SI 2017/353, Sch 2.

24 Ie the Disclosure and Barring Service (see SOCIAL SERVICES vol 95 (2017) PARA 265), the Gambling Commission (see LEISURE AND ENTERTAINMENT vol 68 (2016) PARA 731), the Gangmasters and Labour Abuse Authority (see AGRICULTURAL PRODUCTION AND MARKETING vol 1A (2017) PARA 320); the General Council of the Bar, in respect of its public functions (see LEGAL PROFESSIONS vol 66 (2015) PARA 814 et seq); the Health and Safety Executive (see HEALTH AND SAFETY AT WORK vol 52 (2014) PARA 326 et seq); the Law Society of England and Wales, in respect of its public functions (see LEGAL PROFESSIONS vol 65 (2015) PARA 439 et seq); the Office for Nuclear Regulation (see ENERGY AND CLIMATE CHANGE vol 44 (2011) PARA 815A); the Pensions Regulator (see PERSONAL AND OCCUPATIONAL PENSIONS vol 80 (2013) PARA 479 et seq); and the Security Industry Authority (see TRADE AND INDUSTRY vol 97 (2015) PARA 980 et seq): Equality Act 2010 (Specific Duties and Public Authorities) Regulations 2017, SI 2017/353, Sch 2.

25 Ie High Speed Two (HS2) Ltd (see RAILWAYS AND TRAMWAYS vol 86 (2017) PARA 335); Highways England Company Ltd (see HIGHWAYS, STREETS AND BRIDGES vol 55 (2012) PARA 54A); and Network Rail Limited (see RAILWAYS AND TRAMWAYS vol 86 (2017) PARAS 83, 101): Equality Act 2010 Sch 19 Pt 1 (amended by SI 2017/353).

B.   WALES

289. Equality objectives.

An authority[1] in Wales must:

(1)   publish objectives that are designed to enable it to better perform the public sector equality duty ('equality objectives')[2];

(2)   publish a statement setting out the steps that it has taken or intends to take in order to fulfil each objective and how long the authority expects it will take in order to fulfil each objective[3]; and

(3)   make such arrangements as it considers appropriate for monitoring the progress that it makes and the effectiveness of the steps that it takes in order to fulfil its equality objectives[4].

An authority must, when considering what its equality objectives should be, have due regard to the need to have equality objectives that address the causes of differences in pay between persons who do and do not have protected characteristics[5]. When considering what its equality objectives should be and when designing any equality objective (or any revision to such an objective) the authority must comply with the engagement provisions[6] and have due regard to relevant information[7] that it holds[8]. Publication is as the authority considers appropriate[9], and objectives are subject to periodic review and revision[10]. If an authority does not publish an equality objective in respect of one or more of the protected characteristics[11], or if it has[12] identified a gender pay difference[13] but has not published an equality objective to address the causes of that difference[14], it must publish reasons for its decision not to do so[15].

1   Ie an authority specified in the Equality Act 2010 Sch 19 Pt 2; 'authorities' is construed accordingly: Equality Act 2010 (Statutory Duties) (Wales) Regulations 2011, SI 2011/1064, reg 2. The Equality Act 2010 (Statutory Duties) (Wales) Regulations 2011, SI 2011/1064, are made pursuant to the Equality Act 2010 s 153(2), under which the Welsh Ministers may by regulations impose duties on a public authority specified in Sch 19 Pt 2 (see PARA 277) for the purpose of enabling the better performance by the authority of the duty imposed by s 149(1) (see PARAS 278–279). Before making such regulations the Ministers must consult the Equality and Human Rights Commission: s 153(4). As to supplementary provisions in connection with the exercise of this power see s 155. As to the Commission see PARAS 28–44.
2   Equality Act 2010 (Statutory Duties) (Wales) Regulations 2011, SI 2011/1064, reg 3(1). The 'public sector equality duty' is the duty imposed by the Equality Act 2010 s 149(1) (see PARAS 278–279).
3   Equality Act 2010 (Statutory Duties) (Wales) Regulations 2011, SI 2011/1064, reg 3(2)(a).
4   Equality Act 2010 (Statutory Duties) (Wales) Regulations 2011, SI 2011/1064, reg 3(2)(b). An authority must keep under review, and may at any time revise or remake, the arrangements it has made to comply with reg 3(2)(b): reg 13(1), (2), (3)(i).
5   An authority must, when considering what its equality objectives should be, have due regard to the need to have equality objectives that address the causes of any differences between the pay of any person or persons employed by the authority (P) who (as the case may be) has a protected characteristic or share a protected characteristic, and those who do not where either the first or second condition is met: Equality Act 2010 (Statutory Duties) (Wales) Regulations 2011, SI 2011/1064, reg 11(1)(a), (b). The first condition is that the difference is for a reason that is related to the fact that P has or share that protected characteristic (as the case may be); the second condition is that it appears to the authority to be reasonably likely that the difference is for a reason that is related to the fact that P has or share that protected characteristic (as the case may be): reg 11(1). 'Employment', 'employees' and 'persons employed' are to be construed in accordance with the Equality Act 2010 s 83 (see PARA 116): Equality Act 2010 (Statutory Duties) (Wales) Regulations 2011, SI 2011/1064, reg 2. As to the protected characteristics see PARA 276.
6   As to the engagement provisions see PARA 298.
7   'Relevant information' means information that relates to compliance (or otherwise) by the authority with the public sector equality duty: Equality Act 2010 (Statutory Duties) (Wales) Regulations 2011, SI 2011/1064, reg 2. As to information about compliance with the public sector equality duty see PARA 290.
8   Equality Act 2010 (Statutory Duties) (Wales) Regulations 2011, SI 2011/1064, reg 4(1).
9   Equality Act 2010 (Statutory Duties) (Wales) Regulations 2011, SI 2011/1064, reg 4(2)(b). The authority must first have complied with the requirement to publish equality objectives by 2 April 2012: reg 4(2)(a). The authority must take all reasonable steps to ensure that the published objectives are accessible by persons who share one or more protected characteristics: reg 6.
10 An authority must review each of its equality objectives not later than the end of the period of four years beginning with the date that the objective was first published and subsequently at intervals not later than the end of the period of four years beginning with the date of the last review of the objective: Equality Act 2010 (Statutory Duties) (Wales) Regulations 2011, SI 2011/1064, reg 4(3). An authority may carry out a review of any of its equality objectives at any other time (reg 4(4)), and may revise or remake an equality objective at any time (reg 4(5)). If an authority does any of the things referred to in reg 4(5) it must either amend the statement published by it under reg 3(2) or publish a new statement (reg 4(7)), and if an authority does any of the things referred to in reg 4(5) in respect of a gender pay equality objective it must either amend the action plan published by it under reg 12(1) (see PARA 293) or publish a new action plan (reg 12(2)). If an authority

revises an objective without remaking it then the authority must, as soon as possible after making the revision, publish the revision or the objective as revised (as it considers appropriate): reg 4(6). See note 9.

11 Equality Act 2010 (Statutory Duties) (Wales) Regulations 2011, SI 2011/1064, reg 3(3). The requirement under reg 3(3) applies even if an authority publishes an equality objective for the purpose referred to in reg 11(1) (see the text and note 5) (and for that reason such an objective is to be ignored for the purpose of reg 3(3): reg 3(4).

12 Ie in accordance with the Equality Act 2010 (Statutory Duties) (Wales) Regulations 2011, SI 2011/1064, reg 11(1) (see the text and note 5).

13 'Gender pay difference' means any difference between the pay of a woman and a man, or women and men, who are employed by an authority and where either the first or second condition is met: Equality Act 2010 (Statutory Duties) (Wales) Regulations 2011, SI 2011/1064, reg 2. The first condition is that the difference is for a reason that is related to the protected characteristic of sex; and the second condition is that it appears to the authority to be reasonably likely that the difference is for a reason that is related to the protected characteristic of sex: reg 2. As to the protected characteristic of sex see PARA 60. In connection with gender pay differences see further PARA 293 (pay and action plans).

14 Equality Act 2010 (Statutory Duties) (Wales) Regulations 2011, SI 2011/1064, reg 11(3).

15 Equality Act 2010 (Statutory Duties) (Wales) Regulations 2011, SI 2011/1064, regs 3(4), 11(3).

290. Information about compliance with public sector equality duty.

Provision is made in connection with the identification and publication of information relating to compliance (or otherwise) by the authority[1] with the public sector equality duty[2] ('relevant information')[3]. An authority in Wales must make such arrangements as it considers appropriate to ensure that, from time to time, it identifies relevant information that it holds[4], identifies and collects relevant information that it does not hold[5] and publishes relevant information that it holds and which it considers appropriate to publish[6]. These arrangements must also contain arrangements for identifying and collecting information about any differences between the pay of persons who have or share protected characteristics and those who do not[7] and the causes of any such differences[8].

An authority must keep under review, and may at any time revise or remake, the arrangements it has made to comply with these provisions[9].

1 As to the meaning of 'authority' see PARA 289 note 1.

2 The 'public sector equality duty' is the duty imposed by the Equality Act 2010 s 149(1) (see PARAS 278–279).

3 Equality Act 2010 (Statutory Duties) (Wales) Regulations 2011, SI 2011/1064, reg 2. As to the making of these regulations see PARA 289 note 1. An authority is not required to publish information if to do so would constitute a breach of confidence actionable by any person or of the Data Protection Act 1998 (see CONFIDENCE AND INFORMATIONAL PRIVACY vol 19 (2011) PARA 95 et seq), or the authority would be entitled to refuse to produce the information in or for the purposes of proceedings in a court or tribunal in England and Wales: Equality Act 2010 (Statutory Duties) (Wales) Regulations 2011, SI 2011/1064, reg 20. The authority must take all reasonable steps to ensure that the published information is accessible by persons who share one or more protected characteristics: reg 6. As to the protected characteristics see PARA 276.

4 Equality Act 2010 (Statutory Duties) (Wales) Regulations 2011, SI 2011/1064, reg 7(1)(a). For these purposes an authority holds relevant information if:

   (1)   it is held by the authority, otherwise than on behalf of another person (reg 7(2)(a));
   (2)   it is held by another person on behalf of the authority (reg 7(2)(b)); or
   (3)   it is held by the authority on behalf of another person and that person has consented to the authority using the information for the purpose of compliance by the authority with the public sector equality duty and the duties under the Equality Act 2010 (Statutory Duties) (Wales) Regulations 2011, SI 2011/1064 (reg 7(2)(c)(i)), or use of the information by the authority for the purpose of compliance by it with those duties is not contrary to law and is reasonable, having regard to all the circumstances including, in particular, the nature of the information and the circumstances in which it was obtained by the authority (reg 7(2)(c)(ii), (3)).

The identification of relevant information includes identifying such information by means of carrying out an assessment of whether there are:

(a) things done by the authority that contribute to the authority complying (or otherwise) with the public sector equality duty (reg 7(4)(a)); and

(b) things that it could do that would be likely to contribute to compliance by the authority with that duty (reg 7(4)(b)).

When carrying out such an assessment the authority must comply with the engagement provisions and have due regard to relevant information that it holds: reg 7(5). As to the engagement provisions see PARA 298. The arrangements referred to in reg 7(1) had to ensure that, not later than 2 April 2012, the authority carried out an assessment referred to in reg 7(4) and published relevant information that it held and which it considered appropriate to publish: reg 7(6).

5 Equality Act 2010 (Statutory Duties) (Wales) Regulations 2011, SI 2011/1064, reg 7(1)(b).
6 Equality Act 2010 (Statutory Duties) (Wales) Regulations 2011, SI 2011/1064, reg 7(1)(c).
7 Ie persons referred to in the Equality Act 2010 (Statutory Duties) (Wales) Regulations 2011, SI 2011/1064, reg 11(1) (see PARA 289).
8 Equality Act 2010 (Statutory Duties) (Wales) Regulations 2011, SI 2011/1064, reg 11(2).
9 Equality Act 2010 (Statutory Duties) (Wales) Regulations 2011, SI 2011/1064, reg 13(1), (2), (3)(ii). The provisions referred to in the text are those contained in reg 7(1) (see the text and notes 4–6).

291. Impact and monitoring of policies and practices.

An authority[1] in Wales must make such arrangements as it considers appropriate for:

(1) assessing the likely impact of its proposed policies and practices on its ability to comply with the public sector equality duty[2];

(2) assessing the impact of any policy or practice that the authority has decided to review, or revision that the authority proposes to make to a policy or practice, on its ability to comply with that duty[3];

(3) monitoring the impact of its policies and practices on its ability to comply with that duty[4]; and

(4) publishing reports in respect of any assessment that:
   (a) is referred to in head (1) or (2) above; and
   (b) shows that the impact or likely impact (as the case may be) on the authority's ability to comply with that duty is substantial[5].

An authority must keep under review, and may at any time revise or remake, the arrangements it has made to comply with these provisions[6].

1 As to the meaning of 'authority' see PARA 289 note 1.
2 Equality Act 2010 (Statutory Duties) (Wales) Regulations 2011, SI 2011/1064, reg 8(1)(a). The 'public sector equality duty' is the duty imposed by the Equality Act 2010 s 149(1) (see PARAS 278–279). When carrying out an assessment referred to in the Equality Act 2010 (Statutory Duties) (Wales) Regulations 2011, SI 2011/1064, reg 8(1)(a) or reg 8(1)(b) (see heads (1) and (2) in the text), the authority must comply with the engagement provisions and have due regard to relevant information that it holds: 8(3). As to relevant information see PARA 290. As to the engagement provisions see PARA 298. As to the making of these regulations see PARA 289 note 1.
3 Equality Act 2010 (Statutory Duties) (Wales) Regulations 2011, SI 2011/1064, reg 8(1)(b). See note 2.
4 Equality Act 2010 (Statutory Duties) (Wales) Regulations 2011, SI 2011/1064, reg 8(1)(c).
5 Equality Act 2010 (Statutory Duties) (Wales) Regulations 2011, SI 2011/1064, reg 8(1)(d). Reports under reg 8(1)(d) must set out, in particular:
   (1) the purpose of the proposed policy or practice, the policy or practice, or the proposed revision to a policy or practice, that has been assessed (reg 8(2)(a));
   (2) a summary of the steps that the authority has taken to carry out the assessment (reg 8(2)(b));
   (3) a summary of the information that the authority has taken into account in the assessment (reg 8(2)(c));
   (4) the results of the assessment (reg 8(2)(d)); and
   (5) any decisions taken by the authority in relation to those results (reg 8(2)(e)).
An authority is not required to publish information if to do so would constitute a breach of confidence actionable by any person or of the Data Protection Act 1998 (see CONFIDENCE AND INFORMATIONAL PRIVACY vol 19 (2011) PARA 95 et seq), or the authority would be entitled to refuse

to produce the information in or for the purposes of proceedings in a court or tribunal in England and Wales: Equality Act 2010 (Statutory Duties) (Wales) Regulations 2011, SI 2011/1064, reg 20. The authority must take all reasonable steps to ensure that published reports are accessible by persons who share one or more protected characteristics: reg 6. As to the protected characteristics see PARA 276.

6   Equality Act 2010 (Statutory Duties) (Wales) Regulations 2011, SI 2011/1064, reg 13(1), (2), (3)(iii).

292. Training and collection of employment information.

An authority[1] in Wales must, in each year, collect the following information[2]:

(1)   the number of persons employed[3] by the authority at the relevant date in that year[4];

(2)   the number of persons employed by the authority at that date broken down by job[5];

(3)   the number of persons employed by the authority at that date broken down by grade (where an authority operates a grade system in respect of its employees)[6];

(4)   the number of persons employed by the authority at that date broken down by pay[7];

(5)   the number of persons employed by the authority at that date broken down by contract type (including, but not limited to permanent and fixed-term contracts)[8];

(6)   the number of persons employed by the authority at that date broken down by working pattern (including, but not limited to full-time, part-time and other flexible working arrangements)[9];

(7)   the number, during the reporting period[10] ending with the relevant date in that year, of persons who have applied for employment with the authority (excluding persons already employed by the authority)[11];

(8)   the number, during the reporting period ending with the relevant date in that year, of the authority's employees who have changed position within the authority including the number who applied to change position and the number who were successful (or otherwise) in their application[12];

(9)   the number, during the reporting period ending with the relevant date in that year, of the authority's employees who have applied for training, the number who were successful (or otherwise) in their application[13], and the number who completed the training[14];

(10)   the number, during the reporting period ending with the relevant date in that year, of the authority's employees who were or are involved in grievance procedures by reason of either being the person who made an accusation against another or being the person against whom an accusation was made[15];

(11)   the number, during the reporting period ending with the relevant date in that year, of the authority's employees who were or are the subject of disciplinary proceedings[16]; and

(12)   the number, during the reporting period ending with the relevant date in that year, of the authority's employees who left the employment of the authority[17].

The authority must publish the information it has collected in accordance with these provisions[18].

An authority must also make such arrangements as it considers appropriate for promoting amongst its employees knowledge and understanding of the public sector equality duty and the statutory Welsh duties[19] and for using its performance assessment procedures (if any) to identify and address the training needs of its employees in relation to those duties[20].

1   As to the meaning of 'authority' see PARA 289 note 1.
2   Nothing in the Equality Act 2010 (Statutory Duties) (Wales) Regulations 2011, SI 2011/1064, reg 9 (see the text and notes 3–18) is to be relied upon by an authority so as to require any person to whom reg 9 applies to provide information to the authority: reg 9(5). This applies to any employee of the authority and any person who applies for employment with the authority: reg 9(6). As to the meanings of 'employment', 'employees' and 'persons employed' see PARA 289 note 5. As to the making of these regulations see PARA 289 note 1.
3   In the Equality Act 2010 (Statutory Duties) (Wales) Regulations 2011, SI 2011/1064, reg 9(1) (other than reg 9(1)(b)) any reference to the number of persons or employees includes, in respect of each protected characteristic, the numbers who share the protected characteristic: reg 9(2). As to the protected characteristics see PARA 276.
4   Equality Act 2010 (Statutory Duties) (Wales) Regulations 2011, SI 2011/1064, reg 9(1)(a). See note 3. The 'relevant date' is 31 March: reg 2.
5   Equality Act 2010 (Statutory Duties) (Wales) Regulations 2011, SI 2011/1064, reg 9(1)(b)(i). In the Equality Act 2010 (Statutory Duties) (Wales) Regulations 2011, SI 2011/1064, reg 9(1)(b), the reference to the number of persons employed includes, in respect of the protected characteristic of sex, the number who are women and the number who are men: reg 9(3).
6   Equality Act 2010 (Statutory Duties) (Wales) Regulations 2011, SI 2011/1064, reg 9(1)(b)(ii). See note 5.
7   Equality Act 2010 (Statutory Duties) (Wales) Regulations 2011, SI 2011/1064, reg 9(1)(b)(iii). See note 5.
8   Equality Act 2010 (Statutory Duties) (Wales) Regulations 2011, SI 2011/1064, reg 9(1)(b)(iv). See note 5.
9   Equality Act 2010 (Statutory Duties) (Wales) Regulations 2011, SI 2011/1064, reg 9(1)(b)(v). See note 5.
10 'Reporting period' means the period 1 April to 31 March: Equality Act 2010 (Statutory Duties) (Wales) Regulations 2011, SI 2011/1064, reg 2.
11 Equality Act 2010 (Statutory Duties) (Wales) Regulations 2011, SI 2011/1064, reg 9(1)(c)(i). See note 3.
12 Equality Act 2010 (Statutory Duties) (Wales) Regulations 2011, SI 2011/1064, reg 9(1)(c)(ii). See note 3.
13 Equality Act 2010 (Statutory Duties) (Wales) Regulations 2011, SI 2011/1064, reg 9(1)(c)(iii). See note 3.
14 Equality Act 2010 (Statutory Duties) (Wales) Regulations 2011, SI 2011/1064, reg 9(1)(c)(iv). See note 3.
15 Equality Act 2010 (Statutory Duties) (Wales) Regulations 2011, SI 2011/1064, reg 9(1)(c)(v). See note 3.
16 Equality Act 2010 (Statutory Duties) (Wales) Regulations 2011, SI 2011/1064, reg 9(1)(c)(vi). See note 3.
17 Equality Act 2010 (Statutory Duties) (Wales) Regulations 2011, SI 2011/1064, reg 9(1)(c)(vii). See note 3.
18 Equality Act 2010 (Statutory Duties) (Wales) Regulations 2011, SI 2011/1064, reg 9(4). An authority is not required to publish information if to do so would constitute a breach of confidence actionable by any person or of the Data Protection Act 1998 (see CONFIDENCE AND INFORMATIONAL PRIVACY vol 19 (2011) PARA 95 et seq), or the authority would be entitled to refuse to produce the information in or for the purposes of proceedings in a court or tribunal in England and Wales: Equality Act 2010 (Statutory Duties) (Wales) Regulations 2011, SI 2011/1064, reg 20. The authority must take all reasonable steps to ensure that published information is accessible by persons who share one or more protected characteristics: reg 6.
19 Ie the duties in the Equality Act 2010 (Statutory Duties) (Wales) Regulations 2011, SI 2011/1064.
20 Equality Act 2010 (Statutory Duties) (Wales) Regulations 2011, SI 2011/1064, reg 10. An authority must keep under review, and may at any time revise or remake, the arrangements it has made to comply with reg 10: reg 13(1), (2), (3)(iv).

293. Pay and action plans.
An authority[1] in Wales must publish an action plan[2] setting out:

(1) any policy of the authority that relates to the need to address the causes of any gender pay difference[3];
(2) any gender pay equality objective[4] published by it[5];
(3) any revision to a gender pay equality objective or any revised gender pay equality objective it is required[6] to publish[7];
(4) information it is required to publish[8] in respect of any gender pay equality objective[9];
(5) any reasons for failing to publish an equality objective addressing the causes of a gender pay difference that it is required[10] to publish[11].

Where an authority revises or remakes a gender pay equality objective it must either amend the action plan published by it under these provisions or publish a new action plan[12].

1 As to the meaning of 'authority' see PARA 289 note 1.
2 The authority must take all reasonable steps to ensure that the published plan is accessible by persons who share one or more protected characteristics: Equality Act 2010 (Statutory Duties) (Wales) Regulations 2011, SI 2011/1064, reg 6. As to the protected characteristics see PARA 276. As to the making of these regulations see PARA 289 note 1.
3 Equality Act 2010 (Statutory Duties) (Wales) Regulations 2011, SI 2011/1064, reg 12(1)(a). As to the meaning of 'gender pay difference' see PARA 289 note 13.
4 'Gender pay equality objective' means an equality objective that relates to the need to address the causes of any gender pay difference and which the authority has published: Equality Act 2010 (Statutory Duties) (Wales) Regulations 2011, SI 2011/1064, reg 2. As to an authority's equality objectives generally see PARA 289.
5 Equality Act 2010 (Statutory Duties) (Wales) Regulations 2011, SI 2011/1064, reg 12(1)(b).
6 Ie in accordance with the Equality Act 2010 (Statutory Duties) (Wales) Regulations 2011, SI 2011/1064, reg 4(6) (see PARA 289 note 10).
7 Equality Act 2010 (Statutory Duties) (Wales) Regulations 2011, SI 2011/1064, reg 12(1)(c).
8 Ie in accordance with the Equality Act 2010 (Statutory Duties) (Wales) Regulations 2011, SI 2011/1064, reg 3(2)(a) (see PARA 289 note 3).
9 Equality Act 2010 (Statutory Duties) (Wales) Regulations 2011, SI 2011/1064, reg 12(1)(d).
10 Ie in accordance with the Equality Act 2010 (Statutory Duties) (Wales) Regulations 2011, SI 2011/1064, reg 11(3) (see PARA 289 note 14).
11 Equality Act 2010 (Statutory Duties) (Wales) Regulations 2011, SI 2011/1064, reg 12(1)(e).
12 See Equality Act 2010 (Statutory Duties) (Wales) Regulations 2011, SI 2011/1064, reg 12(2); and PARA 289 note 10.

294. Strategic equality plans.

An authority[1] in Wales must make a Strategic Equality Plan ('SEP') containing a statement setting out:

(1) a description of the authority[2];
(2) the authority's equality objectives[3];
(3) in respect of each of those objectives, the steps that the authority has taken or intends to take in order to fulfil the objective and how long the authority expects it will take in order to fulfil the objective[4];
(4) the arrangements that it has made or intends to make[5] for the purpose of monitoring the progress it makes and the effectiveness of the steps it takes in order to fulfil its equality objectives[6];
(5) the arrangements that it has made or intends to make[7] for the purposes of identifying, collecting and publishing relevant information[8];
(6) the arrangements that it has made or intends to make[9] for the purpose of assessing and monitoring the impact of its policies and practices on its compliance with the public sector equality duty[10];

(7) the arrangements that it has made or intends to make[11] for the purpose of promoting an understanding of the public sector equality duty amongst its employees[12];

(8) its pay and action plan[13]; and

(9) such other matters that are relevant to compliance with the public sector equality duty as the authority considers appropriate[14].

In making, remaking or revising[15] a SEP the authority must comply with the engagement provisions[16] and have due regard to relevant information[17] that it holds[18]. The authority must keep under review its SEP and any revisions made to the SEP[19]. An authority must publish its SEP as soon as possible after the SEP is made or remade[20]: if an authority revises its SEP without remaking it then the authority must, as soon as possible after making the revisions, publish the revisions or the SEP as revised (as it considers appropriate)[21].

1 As to the meaning of 'authority' see PARA 289 note 1.
2 Equality Act 2010 (Statutory Duties) (Wales) Regulations 2011, SI 2011/1064, reg 14(1), (2)(a). As to the making of these regulations see PARA 289 note 1.
3 Equality Act 2010 (Statutory Duties) (Wales) Regulations 2011, SI 2011/1064, reg 14(2)(b). As to an authority's equality objectives generally see PARA 289.
4 Equality Act 2010 (Statutory Duties) (Wales) Regulations 2011, SI 2011/1064, reg 14(2)(c).
5 Ie the arrangements that the authority has made or intends to make to comply with the Equality Act 2010 (Statutory Duties) (Wales) Regulations 2011, SI 2011/1064, reg 3(2)(b) (see PARA 289).
6 Equality Act 2010 (Statutory Duties) (Wales) Regulations 2011, SI 2011/1064, reg 14(2)(d)(i).
7 Ie the arrangements that the authority has made or intends to make to comply with the Equality Act 2010 (Statutory Duties) (Wales) Regulations 2011, SI 2011/1064, reg 7(1) (see PARA 290).
8 Equality Act 2010 (Statutory Duties) (Wales) Regulations 2011, SI 2011/1064, reg 14(2)(d)(ii).
9 Ie the arrangements that the authority has made or intends to make to comply with the Equality Act 2010 (Statutory Duties) (Wales) Regulations 2011, SI 2011/1064, reg 8(1) (see PARA 291).
10 Equality Act 2010 (Statutory Duties) (Wales) Regulations 2011, SI 2011/1064, reg 14(2)(d)(iii). The 'public sector equality duty' is the duty imposed by the Equality Act 2010 s 149(1) (see PARAS 278–279).
11 Ie the arrangements that the authority has made or intends to make to comply with the Equality Act 2010 (Statutory Duties) (Wales) Regulations 2011, SI 2011/1064, reg 10 (see PARA 292).
12 Equality Act 2010 (Statutory Duties) (Wales) Regulations 2011, SI 2011/1064, reg 14(2)(d)(iv).
13 Ie the plan referred to in the Equality Act 2010 (Statutory Duties) (Wales) Regulations 2011, SI 2011/1064, reg 12 (see PARA 293): reg 14(2)(e).
14 Equality Act 2010 (Statutory Duties) (Wales) Regulations 2011, SI 2011/1064, reg 14(3).
15 The authority may revise or remake its SEP at any time: Equality Act 2010 (Statutory Duties) (Wales) Regulations 2011, SI 2011/1064, reg 14(4).
16 As to the engagement provisions see PARA 298.
17 As to the meaning of 'relevant information' see PARA 289 note 7.
18 Equality Act 2010 (Statutory Duties) (Wales) Regulations 2011, SI 2011/1064, reg 15(1).
19 Equality Act 2010 (Statutory Duties) (Wales) Regulations 2011, SI 2011/1064, reg 15(5). In complying with this duty the authority must have due regard to relevant information that it holds and any other information that the authority considers would be likely to assist it in the review: reg 15(6).
20 Equality Act 2010 (Statutory Duties) (Wales) Regulations 2011, SI 2011/1064, reg 15(2). An authority may comply with the duty to publish its SEP (and any revisions to the SEP) by setting out the SEP as part of another published document or within a number of other published documents: reg 15(4). The authority must take all reasonable steps to ensure that the published SEP is accessible by persons who share one or more protected characteristics: reg 6. As to the protected characteristics see PARA 276.
   Authorities were required to have made their first SEP's not later than 2 April 2012: reg 14(1).
21 Equality Act 2010 (Statutory Duties) (Wales) Regulations 2011, SI 2011/1064, reg 15(3).

295. Authorities' reports on compliance with public sector equality duty.

An authority[1] in Wales must, in respect of each reporting period[2], publish a report setting out:

(1)   the steps that the authority has taken to identify and collect relevant information[3];
(2)   in respect of relevant information that it holds, how the authority has used that information for the purpose of complying with the public sector equality duty[4] and the statutory Welsh duties[5];
(3)   the authority's reasons for not collecting any relevant information that it has identified but does not hold[6];
(4)   the progress that the authority has made in order to fulfil each of its equality objectives[7];
(5)   a statement by the authority of the effectiveness of its arrangements for identifying and collecting relevant information and the steps it has taken in order to fulfil each of its equality objectives[8]; and
(6)   the information that the authority is required to publish[9] pursuant to the collection of employment information unless the authority has already published that information[10].

The authority may, if it considers it appropriate to do so, include in a report any other matter that is relevant to compliance by the authority with the public sector equality duty and the statutory Welsh duties[11]. The report must be published not later than the relevant date[12] in the year following the year in which the applicable reporting period ends[13].

1   As to the meaning of 'authority' see PARA 289 note 1.
2   As to the meaning of 'reporting period' see PARA 292 note 10.
3   Equality Act 2010 (Statutory Duties) (Wales) Regulations 2011, SI 2011/1064, reg 16(1), (2)(a). As to the meaning of 'relevant information' see PARA 289 note 7. As to the making of these regulations see PARA 289 note 1.
4   The 'public sector equality duty' is the duty imposed by the Equality Act 2010 s 149(1) (see PARAS 278–279).
5   Equality Act 2010 (Statutory Duties) (Wales) Regulations 2011, SI 2011/1064, reg 16(2)(b). The 'statutory Welsh duties' are the duties in the Equality Act 2010 (Statutory Duties) (Wales) Regulations 2011, SI 2011/1064.
6   Equality Act 2010 (Statutory Duties) (Wales) Regulations 2011, SI 2011/1064, reg 16(2)(c).
7   Equality Act 2010 (Statutory Duties) (Wales) Regulations 2011, SI 2011/1064, reg 16(2)(d). As to an authority's equality objectives generally see PARA 289.
8   Equality Act 2010 (Statutory Duties) (Wales) Regulations 2011, SI 2011/1064, reg 16(2)(e).
9   Ie pursuant to the Equality Act 2010 (Statutory Duties) (Wales) Regulations 2011, SI 2011/1064, reg 9(4) (see PARA 292).
10   Equality Act 2010 (Statutory Duties) (Wales) Regulations 2011, SI 2011/1064, reg 16(2)(f).
11   Equality Act 2010 (Statutory Duties) (Wales) Regulations 2011, SI 2011/1064, reg 16(3).
12   As to the meaning of 'relevant date' see PARA 292 note 4.
13   Equality Act 2010 (Statutory Duties) (Wales) Regulations 2011, SI 2011/1064, reg 16(1). The authority may comply with the duty to publish a report under reg 16(1) by setting out its report (including any matter referred to in reg 16(3): see the text and note 11) as part of another published document or within a number of other published documents: reg 16(4). An authority is not required to publish information if to do so would constitute a breach of confidence actionable by any person or of the Data Protection Act 1998 (see CONFIDENCE AND INFORMATIONAL PRIVACY vol 19 (2011) PARA 95 et seq), or the authority would be entitled to refuse to produce the information in or for the purposes of proceedings in a court or tribunal in England and Wales: Equality Act 2010 (Statutory Duties) (Wales) Regulations 2011, SI 2011/1064, reg 20. The authority must take all reasonable steps to ensure that the published report is accessible by persons who share one or more protected characteristics: reg 6. As to the protected characteristics see PARA 276.

296. Reports by Welsh Ministers on authorities' compliance with public sector equality duty.
The Welsh Ministers[1] must publish reports setting out an overview of the progress made by authorities[2] in Wales towards compliance by those authorities with the public sector equality duty[3]. Such reports must be published not later

than 31 December 2014[4], not later than 31 December 2016[5], and subsequently at intervals not later than the end of each successive period of four years beginning with the date that the last report was[6] published[7], and must[8] cover the period since the date that the last report[9] was published[10].

The Welsh Ministers were also required to publish a report setting out an overview of the progress made by authorities towards compliance by them with the public sector equality duty so far as it related to persons who share the protected characteristic of disability[11].

Reports under these provisions are also required to set out the Welsh Ministers' proposals for the coordination of action by authorities so as to bring about further progress towards compliance by those authorities with the public sector equality duty[12].

1 As to the Welsh Ministers see the Government of Wales Act 2006 Pt 2 (ss 45–92); and CONSTITUTIONAL AND ADMINISTRATIVE LAW vol 20 (2014) PARA 373 et seq.
2 As to the meaning of 'authority' see PARA 289 note 1.
3 Equality Act 2010 (Statutory Duties) (Wales) Regulations 2011, SI 2011/1064, reg 17(1). As to the making of these regulations see PARA 289 note 1. The 'public sector equality duty' is the duty imposed by the Equality Act 2010 s 149(1) (see PARAS 278–279). The authority must take all reasonable steps to ensure that the published report is accessible by persons who share one or more protected characteristics: Equality Act 2010 (Statutory Duties) (Wales) Regulations 2011, SI 2011/1064, reg 6. As to the protected characteristics see PARA 276.
4 Equality Act 2010 (Statutory Duties) (Wales) Regulations 2011, SI 2011/1064, reg 17(2)(a)(i).
5 Equality Act 2010 (Statutory Duties) (Wales) Regulations 2011, SI 2011/1064, reg 17(2)(b)(i).
6 Ie in accordance with the Equality Act 2010 (Statutory Duties) (Wales) Regulations 2011, SI 2011/1064, reg 17(2)(a)(i) (see the text and note 4) or reg 17(2)(b)(i) (see the text and note 5), as the case may be.
7 Equality Act 2010 (Statutory Duties) (Wales) Regulations 2011, SI 2011/1064, reg 17(2)(a)(ii), (b)(ii).
8 Ie other than in the case of the first reports required to be published in accordance with the Equality Act 2010 (Statutory Duties) (Wales) Regulations 2011, SI 2011/1064, reg 17(2)(a)(i) (see the text and note 4), 17(2)(b)(i) (see the text and note 5).
9 Ie under the Equality Act 2010 (Statutory Duties) (Wales) Regulations 2011, SI 2011/1064, reg 17(2)(b) (see the text and notes 5–7).
10 Equality Act 2010 (Statutory Duties) (Wales) Regulations 2011, SI 2011/1064, reg 17(3).
11 Equality Act 2010 (Statutory Duties) (Wales) Regulations 2011, SI 2011/1064, reg 17(4)(a). As to the protected characteristic of disability see PARAS 47–55. This report was required to be published not later than 31 December 2011 and was required additionally to contain information relating to the period 2 December 2008 to 5 April 2011 that the Welsh Ministers would have been required to include in a report under the Disability Discrimination (Public Authorities) (Statutory Duties) Regulations 2005, SI 2005/2966, reg 5 (revoked), by virtue of reg 5(2)(a), if those regulations were in force: Equality Act 2010 (Statutory Duties) (Wales) Regulations 2011, SI 2011/1064, reg 17(4)(b).
12 Equality Act 2010 (Statutory Duties) (Wales) Regulations 2011, SI 2011/1064, reg 17(5).

297. Public procurement and the public sector equality duty.
Where an authority[1] in Wales that is a contracting authority[2] proposes to award a public contract[3] or conclude a framework agreement[4] that is regulated by the Public Sector Directive[5] on the basis of an offer which is the most economically advantageous, it must have due regard to whether the award criteria should include considerations relevant to its performance of the public sector equality duty[6]. Where an authority in Wales that is a contracting authority proposes to stipulate conditions relating to the performance of such an agreement it must have due regard to whether the conditions should include considerations relevant to its performance of the public sector equality duty[7].

1 As to the meaning of 'authority' see PARA 289 note 1.

2 'Contracting authorities' means the state, regional or local authorities, bodies governed by public law or associations formed by one or more such authorities or one or more such bodies governed by public law: see European Parliament and Council Regulation (EU) 2014/24 (OJ L94, 28.3.2014, p 65) on public procurement and repealing Directive 2014/18/EC, as amended from time to time ('the Public Sector Directive'), art 2.1(1) (definition applied by the Equality Act 2010 s 155(3) (amended by SI 2016/275); and the Equality Act 2010 (Statutory Duties) (Wales) Regulations 2011, SI 2011/1064, reg 18(3)). 'Bodies governed by public law' is defined in European Parliament and Council Regulation (EU) 2014/24 (OJ L94, 28.3.2014, p 65) art 2.1(4).

3 'Public contracts' means contracts for pecuniary interest concluded in writing between one or more economic operators and one or more contracting authorities and having as their object the execution of works, the supply of products or the provision of services: European Parliament and Council Regulation (EU) 2014/24 (OJ L94, 28.3.2014, p 65) art 2.1(5) (definition applied by the Equality Act 2010 s 155(3) (as amended: see note 2); and the Equality Act 2010 (Statutory Duties) (Wales) Regulations 2011, SI 2011/1064, reg 18(3)). 'Economic operator' is defined in European Parliament and Council Regulation (EU) 2014/24 (OJ L94, 28.3.2014, p 65) art 2.1(10).

4 A 'framework agreement' means an agreement between one or more contracting authorities and one or more economic operators, the purpose of which is to establish the terms governing contracts to be awarded during a given period, in particular with regard to price and, where appropriate, the quantity envisaged: European Parliament and Council Regulation (EU) 2014/24 (OJ L94, 28.3.2014, p 65) art 33.1 (definition applied by the Equality Act 2010 s 155(3) (as amended: see note 2); and the Equality Act 2010 (Statutory Duties) (Wales) Regulations 2011, SI 2011/1064, reg 18(3)).

5 Ie European Parliament and Council Regulation (EU) 2014/24 (OJ L94, 28.3.2014, p 65) (amended by Commission Delegated Regulation (EU) 2015/2170 (OJ L307, 25.11.2015, p 5)) and implemented by the Public Contracts Regulations 2015, SI 2015/102: see notes 2–4; and CONSTITUTIONAL AND ADMINISTRATIVE LAW vol 20 (2014) PARA 528A.

6 Equality Act 2010 (Statutory Duties) (Wales) Regulations 2011, SI 2011/1064, reg 18(1), (3). The 'public sector equality duty' is the duty imposed by the Equality Act 2010 s 149(1) (see PARAS 278–279).

7 Equality Act 2010 (Statutory Duties) (Wales) Regulations 2011, SI 2011/1064, reg 18(2).

298. The engagement provisions.

Where an authority is required[1] to comply with the 'engagement provisions' in carrying out any activity, compliance with those provisions means that in carrying out that activity the authority:

(1) must involve such persons as the authority considers represent the interests of persons who share one or more of the protected characteristics[2] and have an interest in the way that the authority carries out its functions[3];

(2) may involve such other persons as the authority considers appropriate[4]; and

(3) may consult such persons as the authority considers appropriate[5].

1 Ie by any provision of the Equality Act 2010 (Statutory Duties) (Wales) Regulations 2011, SI 2011/1064.

2 As to the protected characteristics see PARA 276.

3 Equality Act 2010 (Statutory Duties) (Wales) Regulations 2011, SI 2011/1064, reg 5(1), (2)(a).

4 Equality Act 2010 (Statutory Duties) (Wales) Regulations 2011, SI 2011/1064, reg 5(2)(b). In reaching a decision under reg 5(2)(b) or (c) the authority must have regard to the need to involve or consult (as the case may be), so far as is reasonably practicable to do so, persons who share one or more of the protected characteristics and have an interest in the way that the authority carries out its functions: reg 5(3).

5 Equality Act 2010 (Statutory Duties) (Wales) Regulations 2011, SI 2011/1064, reg 5(2)(c). See note 4.

(iv) Positive Action

299. Positive action.

If a person reasonably thinks that:

(1)   persons who share a protected characteristic[1] suffer a disadvantage connected to the characteristic[2];

(2)   persons who share a protected characteristic have needs that are different from the needs of persons who do not share it[3]; or

(3)   participation in an activity by persons who share a protected characteristic is disproportionately low[4],

he is not prohibited[5] from taking any action[6] which is a proportionate means of achieving the aim of:

(a)   enabling or encouraging persons who share the protected characteristic to overcome or minimise that disadvantage[7];

(b)   meeting those needs[8]; or

(c)   enabling or encouraging persons who share the protected characteristic to participate in that activity[9].

These provisions[10] do not allow for the taking of action which involves treating a person (A) more favourably in connection with recruitment[11] or promotion than another person (B) because A has the protected characteristic but B does not[12]. However, such action may be taken in a specific employment context if a person (P) reasonably thinks that persons who share a protected characteristic suffer a disadvantage connected to the characteristic or participation in an activity by persons who share a protected characteristic is disproportionately low[13], provided that A is properly qualified[14] and the process is non-discriminatory[15] and proportionate[16].

These provisions do not apply to such positive action as is permitted in connection with the selection of party political candidates[17].

1   As to the protected characteristics see PARA 45.
2   Equality Act 2010 s 158(1)(a).
3   Equality Act 2010 s 158(1)(b).
4   Equality Act 2010 s 158(1)(c).
5   Ie prohibited by the Equality Act 2010. These provisions (ie ss 158, 159) do not enable anything to be done that is prohibited by or under an enactment other than the Equality Act 2010: ss 158(6), 159(6).
6   Regulations may specify action, or descriptions of action, to which the Equality Act 2010 s 158(2) (see the text and notes 7–9) does not apply: s 158(3). At the date at which this volume states the law no such regulations had been made.
7   Equality Act 2010 s 158(2)(a).
8   Equality Act 2010 s 158(2)(b).
9   Equality Act 2010 s 158(2)(c).
10 Ie the Equality Act 2010 s 158 (see the text and notes 1–9).
11 'Recruitment' means a process for deciding whether to offer employment to a person, make contract work available to a contract worker, offer a person a position as a partner in a firm or proposed firm, offer a person a position as a member of an LLP or proposed LLP, offer a person a pupillage or tenancy in barristers' chambers, offer a person an appointment to a personal office, offer a person an appointment to a public office, recommend a person for such an appointment or approve a person's appointment to a public office, or offer a person a service for finding employment: Equality Act 2010 s 159(5).
12 Equality Act 2010 ss 158(4)(a), 159(3).
13 See the Equality Act 2010 s 159(1), (2), which provides that in those circumstances Pt 5 (ss 39–83) (work: see PARAS 116–172) does not prohibit the taking of action within s 159(3) (see the text and notes 10–12) with the aim of enabling or encouraging persons who share the protected characteristic to overcome or minimise the identified disadvantage or participate in the specified activity.
14 Ie A is as qualified as B to be recruited or promoted: Equality Act 2010 s 159(4)(a).
15 Ie P does not have a policy of treating persons who share the protected characteristic more favourably in connection with recruitment or promotion than persons who do not share it: Equality Act 2010 s 159(4)(b).
16 Ie taking the action in question is a proportionate means of achieving the aim referred to in the Equality Act 2010 s 159(2) (see note 13): s 159(4)(c).

17 The Equality Act 2010 s 158 (see the text and notes 1–12) does not apply to anything which is permitted by virtue of s 104 (selection of candidates: see PARA 209): s 158(4)(b). If s 104(7) is repealed by virtue of s 105 (time-limited provision), s 158 will not apply to anything that would have been so permitted but for the repeal: s 158(5).

(v) Compliance

300. Powers of Equality and Human Rights Commission with respect to the public sector equality duty.

The Equality and Human Rights Commission[1] may assess the extent to which or the manner in which a person has complied with the public sector equality duty[2]. Provision is made in connection with the conduct of assessments[3].

Where the Commission has carried out such an assessment and thinks that a person has failed to comply with the general public sector equality duty[4], it may give the person a notice relating to the results of the assessment requiring him to comply with the duty[5] and to give the Commission[6] written information of steps taken or proposed for the purpose of complying with the duty[7]. Such a notice may also be given in respect of specific duties imposed pursuant to the public sector equality duty[8] whether or not such an assessment has been carried out[9]. A person who receives a notice under these provisions must comply with it[10] (although there are also circumstances in which the recipient may disregard or request the cancellation of the notice[11]), and if the Commission thinks that a person to whom a notice has been given has failed to comply with a requirement of the notice, the Commission may apply to the court[12] for an order requiring the person to comply[13].

1 As to the Commission see PARAS 28–44.
2 Equality Act 2006 s 31(1) (ss 31(1), 32(1) substituted, s 32(4), (9), (11) amended, by the Equality Act 2010 Sch 26 paras 73, 74 (amended by SI 2010/2279)). The public sector equality duty is a duty under or by virtue of the Equality Act 2010 s 149 (see PARAS 278–284), s 153 (imposition of specific duties: see PARAS 285 (England), 289 (Wales)), or s 154 (see PARA 277). This power is without prejudice to the generality of the Equality Act 2006 s 16 (power of Commission to conduct inquiries: see PARA 339) and s 20 (power of Commission to conduct investigations: see PARA 347): s 31(3).
3 See the Equality Act 2006 Sch 2; and PARAS 340–344.
4 Ie has failed to comply with the Equality Act 2006 s 149 (see PARAS 278–284).
5 Equality Act 2006 s 32(1), (2)(a), (4) (s 32(1) as substituted: see note 2). A notice under s 32 may require a person to give the Commission information required by the Commission for the purposes of assessing compliance with the duty; in which case the notice must specify the period within which the information is to be given (which must begin with the date on which the notice is received and shall not exceed three months) (s 32(3)(a)) and the manner and form in which the information is to be given (s 32(3)(b)).
6 Ie within the period of 28 days beginning with the date on which the person receives the notice: Equality Act 2006 s 32(2)(b).
7 Equality Act 2006 s 32(2)(b). A notice under s 32 does not oblige a person to give information that he is prohibited from disclosing by virtue of an enactment or that he could not be compelled to give in proceedings before the High Court: s 32(6).
8 Ie under the Equality Act 2010 s 153 or s 154 (see PARAS 277, 285, 289).
9 Equality Act 2006 s 32(2).
10 Equality Act 2006 s 32(5).
11 See the Equality Act 2006 s 32(7), Sch 2 paras 11, 14; and PARA 342.
12 For these purposes, 'court' means the High Court (where the notice related to a duty under the Equality Act 2010 s 149) or the County Court (where the notice related to a duty by virtue of s 153 or 154): Equality Act 2006 s 32(9) (as amended (see note 2); further amended by the Crime and Courts Act 2013 Sch 9 para 52(1)(b), (2)).
13 Equality Act 2006 s 32(8). A notice under s 32 must specify a time before which the Commission may not make an application under s 32(8) in respect of the notice: s 32(10). Legal proceedings in

relation to a duty by virtue of the Equality Act 2010 s 153 or s 154 may be brought by the Commission in accordance with the Equality Act 2006 s 32(8) and may not be brought in any other way: s 32(11) (as amended: see note 2).

301. Agreements not to issue compliance notices.

The Equality and Human Rights Commission[1] may enter into an agreement with a person under which:

(1)   the person undertakes not to commit a breach of the public sector equality duty[2] and to take, or refrain from taking, other specified action[3]; and

(2)   the Commission undertakes not to issue a compliance notice[4] in respect of any breach of the kind so specified[5].

The Commission may enter into such an agreement only if it thinks that the person has committed such a breach[6].

1 As to the Commission see PARAS **28–44**.
2 Equality Act 2006 ss 23(1)(a)(i), (5), 34(2) (s 34(2) amended by the Equality Act 2010 Sch 26 para 76(1)–(3) (amended by SI 2010/2279)). The public sector equality duty is a duty under or by virtue of the Equality Act 2010 s 149, s 153 or s 154: see PARAS **276–298**. By virtue of the Equality Act 2006 ss 23(5), 34(2) (as so amended) these provisions also apply to the provisions relating to disabled persons and transport under the Equality Act 2010 Pt 12 (ss 160–188) (see PARAS **211, 213, 215–236**) and the provisions relating to improvements to let dwelling houses (ie s 190: see PARA **272**).
3 Equality Act 2006 s 23(1)(a)(ii). Specified action which may include the preparation of a plan for the purpose of avoiding an unlawful act: Equality Act 2006 s 23(1)(a)(ii).
4 Ie undertakes not to proceed against the person under the Equality Act 2006 s 32 (see PARA **300**).
5 Equality Act 2006 s 23(1)(b).
6 Equality Act 2006 s 23(2). A person will not be taken to admit to a breach by reason only of entering into an agreement under these provisions: s 23(3).

(2) REDUCTION OF SOCIO–ECONOMIC INEQUALITIES

302. Authorities subject to the public sector duty regarding socio-economic inequalities.

As from a day to be appointed the authorities in relation to which the public sector duty regarding socio-economic inequalities[1] applies are:

(1)   a Minister of the Crown[2];

(2)   a government department other than the Security Service, the Secret Intelligence Service or the Government Communications Headquarters[3];

(3)   a county council or district council in England[4];

(4)   the Greater London Authority[5];

(5)   a London borough council[6];

(6)   the Common Council of the City of London in its capacity as a local authority[7];

(7)   the Council of the Isles of Scilly[8]; and

(8)   a police and crime commissioner established for an area in England[9].

As from a day to be appointed the duty may be imposed on additional authorities, or imposed for different purposes, and authorities may be removed from the scope of the duty, by regulations[10].

1 Ie the duty imposed by the Equality Act 2010 s 1 (not yet in force) (see PARA **303**).
2 Equality Act 2010 s 1(3)(a) (not yet in force: see PARA **303** note 1).

3   Equality Act 2010 s 1(3)(b) (not yet in force: see PARA 303 note 1). As to the Security Service, the Secret Intelligence Service and the Government Communications Headquarters see CONSTITUTIONAL AND ADMINISTRATIVE LAW vol 20 (2014) PARA 243 et seq.

4   Equality Act 2010 s 1(3)(c) (not yet in force: see PARA 303 note 1). As to county councils and district councils in England see LOCAL GOVERNMENT vol 69 (2009) PARA 24 et seq.

5   Equality Act 2010 s 1(3)(d) (not yet in force: see PARA 303 note 1). As to the Greater London Authority see LONDON GOVERNMENT vol 71 (2013) PARA 67 et seq.

6   Equality Act 2010 s 1(3)(e) (not yet in force: see PARA 303 note 1). As to the London borough councils see LONDON GOVERNMENT vol 71 (2013) PARAS 20–22.

7   Equality Act 2010 s 1(3)(f) (not yet in force: see PARA 303 note 1). As to the Common Council of the City of London see LONDON GOVERNMENT vol 71 (2013) PARA 34 et seq.

8   Equality Act 2010 s 1(3)(g) (not yet in force: see PARA 303 note 1). As to the Council of the Isles of Scilly see LOCAL GOVERNMENT vol 69 (2009) PARA 36.

9   Equality Act 2010 s 1(3)(k) (not yet in force (see PARA 303 note 1); amended by the Police Reform and Social Responsibility Act 2011 Sch 16 paras 380, 381). As to police and crime commissioners see POLICE AND INVESTIGATORY POWERS vol 84 (2013) PARA 85 et seq.

10   A Minister of the Crown may by regulations amend the Equality Act 2010 s 1 (see the text and notes 1–9; and PARA 303) so as to add a public authority (ie an authority that has functions of a public nature) to the authorities that are subject to the duty under s 1(1), remove an authority from those that are subject to the duty, make the duty apply, in the case of a particular authority, only in relation to certain functions that it has, or, in the case of an authority to which the application of the duty is already restricted to certain functions, remove or alter the restriction (s 2(1), (2) (not yet in force: see PARA 303 note 1)): provision so made may not impose a duty on an authority in relation to any devolved Scottish functions (ie functions exercisable in or as regards Scotland and not relating to reserved matters (within the meaning of the Scotland Act 1998)) (Equality Act 2010 s 2(3), (11)(a) (s 2(3) not yet in force (see PARA 303 note 1); s 2(11) amended by the Scotland Act 2016 s 38(1), (5), (8))) or devolved Welsh functions (ie functions relating to matters in respect of which functions are exercisable by the Welsh Ministers, the First Minister for Wales or the Counsel General to the Welsh Government, or to matters within the legislative competence of the National Assembly for Wales) (Equality Act 2010 s 2(3), (11)(b) (not yet in force (see PARA 303 note 1); s 2(11) as so amended; s 2(11)(b) amended by virtue of the Wales Act 2014 s 4(4)(a))). As from a day to be appointed, the Equality Act 2010 s 2(11)(b) is repealed by the Wales Act 2017 Sch 6 para 83(1), (3). At the date at which this volume states the law no such day had been appointed. The Welsh Ministers may by regulations amend the Equality Act 2010 s 1 so as to add a relevant authority to the authorities that are subject to the duty under s 1(1), remove a relevant authority from those that are subject to the duty, make the duty apply, in the case of a particular relevant authority, only in relation to certain functions that it has, or, in the case of a relevant authority to which the application of the duty is already restricted to certain functions, remove or alter the restriction (s 2(4) (not yet in force: see PARA 303 note 1)): for this purpose 'relevant authority' means an authority whose functions are exercisable only in or as regards Wales, are wholly or mainly devolved Welsh functions, and correspond or are similar to those of an authority for the time being specified in s 1(3) (see the text and notes 2–9) or referred to in s 1(4) (repealed) (s 2(6) (not yet in force: see PARA 303 note 1). As from a day to be appointed, for the purpose of the power conferred by s 2(4), 'relevant authority' means a devolved Welsh authority (within the meaning given by the Government of Wales Act 2006 s 157A (see LOCAL GOVERNMENT)) whose functions correspond or are similar to those of an authority for the time being specified in the Equality Act 2010 s 1(3) (see the text and notes 1–9) or referred to in s 1(4) (repealed): see s 2(6) (not yet in force (see PARA 303 note 1); prospectively amended by the Wales Act 2017 Sch 6 para 83(1), (2)). At the date at which this volume states the law no such day had been appointed. Before making such regulations the Welsh Ministers must consult a Minister of the Crown: Equality Act 2010 s 2(7) (not yet in force (see PARA 303 note 1); amended by the Scotland Act 2016 s 38(1), (5), (6)). Regulations under the Equality Act 2010 s 2 may make any amendments of s 1 that appear to the Minister or Ministers to be necessary or expedient in consequence of provision made under s 2(1) or (as the case may be) s 2(4) (s 2(8) (not yet in force: see PARA 303 note 1)); provision made by the Welsh Ministers in reliance on s 2(8) may, in particular, amend s 1 so as to confer on the Ministers a power to issue guidance (s 2(9)(a) (not yet in force (see PARA 303 note 1); amended by the Scotland Act 2016 s 38(1), (5), (6))), require a relevant authority to take into account any guidance issued under a power conferred by virtue of the Equality Act 2010 s 2(9)(a) (s 2(9)(b) (not yet in force: see PARA 303 note 1)), or disapply s 1(2) in consequence of the imposition of a requirement by virtue of s 2(9)(b) (s 2(9)(c) (not yet in force: see PARA 303 note 1)). Before issuing

guidance under a power conferred by virtue of s 2(9)(a) the Welsh Ministers must take into account any guidance issued by a Minister of the Crown under s 1 and consult a Minister of the Crown: s 2(10) (not yet in force (see PARA 303 note 1); amended by the Scotland Act 2016 s 38(1), (5), (7)). At the date at which this volume states the law no regulations had been made under the Equality Act 2010 s 2. As from a day to be appointed, the provisions of s 2(9), (10) are repealed by the Wales Act 2017 s 45(1), (3). At the date at which this volume states the law, no such day had been appointed. As to the Welsh Ministers, the First Minister for Wales and the Counsel General to the Welsh Government, and their functions, see the Government of Wales Act 2006 Pt 2 (ss 45–92); and CONSTITUTIONAL AND ADMINISTRATIVE LAW vol 20 (2014) PARA 373 et seq. As to the matters which are within the legislative competence of the National Assembly for Wales see ss 108, 109, Sch 7; and STATUTES AND LEGISLATIVE PROCESS vol 96 (2012) PARAS 993–1008.

303. Duty on authorities to have regard to desirability of reducing disadvantage of socio-economic inequality.

As from a day to be appointed[1] applicable authorities[2] are required, when making decisions of a strategic nature about how to exercise their functions, to have due regard to the desirability of exercising them in a way that is designed to reduce the inequalities of outcome which result from socio-economic disadvantage[3]. This does not include any inequalities experienced by a person as a result of being a person subject to immigration control[4].

A failure in respect of a performance of this duty does not confer a cause of action at private law[5].

1 At the date at which this volume states the law the provisions of the Equality Act 2010 ss 1–3 have not been brought into force. See PARA 302; and the text and notes 2–5.
2 As to the authorities to which the public sector duty regarding socio-economic inequalities applies see PARA 302.
3 Equality Act 2010 s 1(1) (not yet in force: see note 1). In deciding how to fulfil a duty to which it is subject under s 1(1), an authority must take into account any guidance issued in accordance with s 1(2A): s 1(2) (not yet in force; amended by the Scotland Act 2016 s 38(1)–(3)). The guidance to be taken into account is: in the case of a duty imposed on an authority in relation to devolved Scottish functions, guidance issued by the Scottish Ministers; in the case of a duty imposed on an authority in relation to devolved Welsh functions, guidance issued by the Welsh Ministers; and, in any other case, guidance issued by a Minister of the Crown: Equality Act 2010 s 1(2A) (added by the Scotland Act 2016 s 38(1), (2), (4); not yet in force). As to the meaning of 'devolved Scottish functions' and 'devolved Welsh functions' see PARA 302 note 10. As to the Welsh Ministers see PARA 4.
4 Equality Act 2010 s 1(6) (not yet in force: see note 1). The reference to 'a person subject to immigration control' is a reference to a person who is so subject within the meaning given the Immigration and Asylum Act 1999 s 115(9) (see IMMIGRATION AND ASYLUM vol 57 (2012) PARA 335).
5 Equality Act 2010 s 3 (not yet in force: see note 1).

304. Agreements not to issue compliance notices.

The Equality and Human Rights Commission[1] may enter into an agreement with a person under which:

(1)   the person undertakes not to commit a breach of the public sector duty regarding socio-economic inequalities[2] and to take, or refrain from taking, other specified action[3]; and

(2)   the Commission undertakes not to issue a compliance notice[4] in respect of any breach of the kind so specified[5].

The Commission may enter into such an agreement only if it thinks that the person has committed such a breach[6].

1 As to the Commission see PARAS 28–44.
2 Equality Act 2006 ss 23(1)(a)(i), (5), 34(2) (s 34(2) amended by the Equality Act 2010 Sch 26 para 76(1)–(3) (amended by SI 2010/2279)). The public sector duty regarding socio-economic inequalities is a duty under or by virtue of the Equality Act 2010 s 1: see PARAS 302–303. By virtue

of the Equality Act 2006 ss 23(5), 34(2) (as so amended) these provisions also apply to the provisions relating to disabled persons and transport under the Equality Act 2010 Pt 12 (ss 160–188) (see PARAS **211, 213, 215–236**) and the provisions relating to improvements to let dwelling houses (ie s 190: see PARA **272**).

3   Equality Act 2006 s 23(1)(a)(ii). Specified action which may include the preparation of a plan for the purpose of avoiding an unlawful act: s 23(1)(a)(ii).
4   Ie undertakes not to proceed against the person under the Equality Act 2006 s 32 (see PARA **300**).
5   Equality Act 2006 s 23(1)(b).
6   Equality Act 2006 s 23(2). A person will not be taken to admit to a breach by reason only of entering into an agreement under these provisions: s 23(3).

(3) THE COMMISSIONER FOR OLDER PEOPLE IN WALES

305. The office and general functions of the Commissioner for Older People in Wales.
The office of Commissioner for Older People in Wales[1] was established in 2006[2]. The general functions of the Commissioner are to:

(1)   promote awareness of the interests of older people in Wales[3] and of the need to safeguard those interests[4];

(2)   promote the provision of opportunities for, and the elimination of discrimination against, older people in Wales[5];

(3)   encourage best practice in the treatment of older people in Wales[6];

(4)   keep under review the adequacy and effectiveness of law affecting the interests of older people in Wales[7].

These powers are exercisable only in relation to fields in which functions are exercisable by the Welsh Ministers, the First Minister for Wales or the Counsel General to the Welsh Government[8]. The Commissioner may consider, and make representations to the Welsh Ministers, the First Minister for Wales or the Counsel General to the Welsh Government about, any matter relating to the interests of older people in Wales[9].

Provision is made by the Commissioner for Older People (Wales) Act 2006 concerning such matters as the appointment and remuneration of the Commissioner, his power to appoint staff, and other administrative and financial matters pertaining to the office[10].

The Act does not authorise or require the Commissioner to discharge a function in relation to a matter to the extent that the matter is the subject of legal proceedings before, or has been determined by, a court or tribunal[11]. Nor does the Act authorise or require the Commissioner to discharge a prescribed function which by virtue of an enactment is also dischargeable by a prescribed person[12].

1   Or, in Welsh, Comisiynydd Pobl Hyn Cymru: see the Commissioner for Older People (Wales) Act 2006 s 1.
2   Ie on 14 October 2006: see the Commissioner for Older People (Wales) Act 2006 ss 1(1), 23, 30; the Commissioner for Older People (Wales) Act 2006 (Commencement) Order 2006, SI 2006/2699, arts 1, 2.
3   'Older person' means a person aged 60 or over (Commissioner for Older People (Wales) Act 2006 s 24(1), (2)); and 'older person in Wales' means an older person:
    (1)   who is ordinarily resident in Wales (s 24(3)(a));
    (2)   to or in respect of whom regulated services in Wales are provided (s 24(3)(b)); or
    (3)   to or in respect of whom relevant services (as to the meaning of which see PARA **307** note 2) are provided by or on behalf of, or under arrangements with, a person mentioned in Sch 3 (s 24(3)(c)).
    'Regulated services in Wales' means services which are provided in Wales by or in a regulated establishment or agency (ie an establishment or agency where the person carrying it on or managing it is required to be registered in respect of it under the Care Standards Act 2000 Pt 2 (ss

11–42): Commissioner for Older People (Wales) Act 2006 s 26(1), (2), (3). The services provided by or in a regulated establishment or agency are to be treated as provided by the person who carries it on: s 26(4).

In considering what constitutes the interests of older people in Wales, the Commissioner must have regard to the United Nations Principles for Older Persons adopted by the General Assembly of the United Nations on 16 December 1991: see the Commissioner for Older People (Wales) Act 2006 s 25.

4 Commissioner for Older People (Wales) Act 2006 s 2(1)(a).
5 Commissioner for Older People (Wales) Act 2006 s 2(1)(b).
6 Commissioner for Older People (Wales) Act 2006 s 2(1)(c).
7 Commissioner for Older People (Wales) Act 2006 s 2(1)(d).
8 Commissioner for Older People (Wales) Act 2006 s 2(2) (amended by SI 2007/1388; and by virtue of the Wales Act 2014 s 4(4)(a)). As to Welsh devolution see further STATUTES AND LEGISLATIVE PROCESS vol 96 (2012) PARAS 986–1029, 1033–1044. As to the Welsh Ministers see PARA 4.
9 Commissioner for Older People (Wales) Act 2006 s 2(3) (amended by SI 2007/1388).
10 See the Commissioner for Older People (Wales) Act 2006 s 1(2), Sch 1 (amended by SI 2007/1388). The Commissioner is a corporation sole and is not to be regarded as the servant or agent of the Crown or as enjoying any status, immunity or privilege of the Crown: see the Commissioner for Older People (Wales) Act 2006 Sch 1 para 1. Regulations may make provision as to the appointment and term of office of the Commissioner: see Sch 1 para 2; and the Commissioner for Older People in Wales (Appointment) Regulations 2007, SI 2007/396. As to the provision made as regards remuneration and payments see the Commissioner for Older People (Wales) Act 2006 Sch 1 paras 3, 7 (amended by SI 2007/1338). The Commissioner must appoint a deputy Commissioner who may discharge the functions of the Commissioner when the Commissioner is for any reason unable to act: see the Commissioner for Older People (Wales) Act 2006 Sch 1 para 4. The Commissioner has power to appoint such other staff as he thinks necessary for assisting him in the discharge of his functions: see Sch 1 paras 4, 5. He must make reports to the Welsh Ministers relating to the discharge of his functions: see s 15, Sch 1 para 8 (s 15 amended by SI 2007/1388; and the Welsh Language (Wales) Measure 2011 s 21, Sch 3 paras 7, 8); and the Commissioner for Older People in Wales Regulations 2007, SI 2007/398, regs 14–17 (amended by SI 2008/1512).

Provision is made regarding the financial matters of office: see the Commissioner for Older People (Wales) Act 2006 Sch 1 para 9 (estimates of income and expenses), Sch 1 paras 10, 11, 12 (amended by SI 2007/1388) (keeping of accounts, and audit), Commissioner for Older People (Wales) Act 2006 Sch 1 para 22; Commissioner for Older People in Wales Regulations 2007, SI 2007/398, reg 18 (financial year). The Auditor General for Wales may carry out examinations into the economy, efficiency and effectiveness with which the Commissioner has used his resources in discharging his functions (although this does not entitle the Auditor General for Wales to question the merits of the policy objectives of the Commissioner): see Sch 1 paras 13, 14. A document purporting to be duly executed under the seal of the Commissioner or to be signed by him or on his behalf is to be received in evidence and, unless the contrary is proved, taken to be so executed or signed: Sch 1 para 15. Subject to any directions given by the Welsh Ministers, the Commissioner may do anything (including acquire or dispose of any property or rights) which is calculated to facilitate, or is conducive or incidental to, the discharge of his functions: see Sch 1 para 19 (amended by SI 2007/1388). As from a day to be appointed, the Commissioner for Older People (Wales) Act 2006 Sch 1 para 14 is repealed by the Wales Act 2017 Sch 6 para 65. At the date at which this volume states the law, no such day had been appointed.

The Commissioner for Older People (Wales) Act 2006 also makes consequential amendments to other legislation: see s 22, Sch 1 paras 6, 16–18, 20, 21, Sch 4 (amended by the Social Services and Well-being (Wales) Act 2014 Sch 3 paras 32, 34).
11 Commissioner for Older People (Wales) Act 2006 s 21(1).
12 Commissioner for Older People (Wales) Act 2006 s 21(2).

306. Review of the discharge of functions of various bodies.

For the purpose of safeguarding and promoting the interests of older people in Wales[1], the Commissioner for Older People in Wales[2] may review the effect on them of:

(1)   the discharge or proposed discharge of a function of the Welsh Ministers, the First Minister for Wales or the Counsel General to the Welsh Government, including the making or proposed making of subordinate legislation[3];

(2)   a failure by the Welsh Ministers, the First Minister for Wales or the Counsel General to the Welsh Government to discharge a function[4];

(3)   the discharge or proposed discharge in relation to Wales of a relevant function[5] of a person specified in the Commissioner for Older People (Wales) Act 2006[6];

(4)   a failure by such a person to discharge a relevant function in relation to Wales[7].

1   As to the meaning of 'older person in Wales' see PARA 305 note 3.

2   As to the office of the Commissioner see PARA 305.

3   Commissioner for Older People (Wales) Act 2006 s 3(1)(a), (4) (s 3(1) amended by SI 2007/1388; and by virtue of the Wales Act 2014 s 4(4)(a)). As to Welsh devolution see further CONSTITUTIONAL AND ADMINISTRATIVE LAW vol 20 (2014) PARA 75 et seq. 'Subordinate legislation' has the same meaning as in the Interpretation Act 1978: see the Commissioner for Older People (Wales) Act 2006 s 3(3); and STATUTES AND LEGISLATIVE PROCESS vol 96 (2012) PARA 1030.

4   Commissioner for Older People (Wales) Act 2006 s 3(1)(b) (as amended: see note 3).

5   A 'relevant function' is:
     (1)   in the case of a person who is a family health service provider in Wales (see below), a function dischargeable in relation to the provision of any of the family health services which the person has entered into a contract, undertaken, or made arrangements, to provide (Commissioner for Older People (Wales) Act 2006 s 3(2)(a));
     (2)   in the case of a person who is an independent provider in Wales (see below), a function dischargeable in relation to the provision of any of the independently provided services which the person has made arrangements to provide (s 3(2)(b));
     (3)   in the case of any other person mentioned in Sch 2, any function of the person (s 3(2)(c)).
'Family health service provider in Wales' means (see the Commissioner for Older People (Wales) Act 2006 s 27(1) (definition amended by the National Health Service (Consequential Provisions) Act 2006 s 2, Sch 1 paras 305, 306)):
     (a)   a person who provides services under a contract entered into by that person with a Local Health Board under the National Health Service (Wales) Act 2006 s 42 or s 57;
     (b)   a person who has undertaken to provide in Wales general ophthalmic services under the National Health Service (Wales) Act 2006 Pt 6, or pharmaceutical services under Pt 7 Ch 1;
     (c)   an individual who provides in Wales primary medical services or primary dental services in accordance with arrangements made under s 50 or s 64 (except as an employee of, or otherwise on behalf of, a Welsh health service body or an independent provider in Wales).
'Welsh health service body' means (see the Commissioner for Older People (Wales) Act 2006 s 27(1) (definition amended by SI 2007/1388)):
     (i)   the Welsh Ministers, to the extent that they discharge functions in relation to the National Health Service;
     (ii)   a Local Health Board;
     (iii)   an NHS trust managing a hospital or other establishment or facility in Wales;
     (iv)   a Special Health Authority discharging functions in relation to Wales.
'Independent provider in Wales' means a person who provides services of any kind in Wales under arrangements with a Welsh health service body or a family health service provider in Wales, and is not a Welsh health service body or a family health service provider in Wales: Commissioner for Older People (Wales) Act 2006 s 27(1). This definition and the definition of 'family health service provider in Wales' may be amended by the Welsh Ministers: see s 27(2), (3) (amended by SI 2007/1388). As to the Welsh Ministers see PARA 4.
    As to the health service in Wales see further HEALTH SERVICES vol 54 (2017) PARA 97.

6   Commissioner for Older People (Wales) Act 2006 s 3(1)(c). The persons are specified in Sch 2 (amended by the Qualifications Wales Act 2015 Sch 1 para 39; the Regulation and Inspection of Social Care (Wales) Act 2016 Sch 3 paras 51, 52; SI 2012/990; and SI 2013/755) as follows:
     (1)   a county council, county borough council or community council in Wales (see LOCAL GOVERNMENT vol 69 (2009) PARA 37 et seq);
     (2)   a joint board (see LOCAL GOVERNMENT vol 69 (2009) PARA 10) the constituent authorities of which are all county or county borough councils in Wales;
     (3)   a fire and rescue authority in Wales constituted by a scheme under the Fire and Rescue Services Act 2004 s 2 or a scheme to which s 4 applies (see FIRE AND RESCUE SERVICES vol 51 (2013) PARAS 18, 20);

(4)   Social Care Wales (see SOCIAL SERVICES vol 95 (2017) PARA 412 et seq);

(5)   a Local Health Board (see HEALTH SERVICES vol 54 (2017) PARAS 97, 98);

(6)   an NHS trust (see HEALTH SERVICES vol 54 (2017) PARA 97, 98) managing a hospital or other establishment or facility in Wales;

(7)   a Special Health Authority (see HEALTH SERVICES vol 54 (2017) PARAS 97, 98) discharging functions in relation to Wales;

(8)   the Wales Centre for Health (see HEALTH SERVICES vol 54 (2017) PARAS 97, 98);

(9)   a family health service provider in Wales (see note 5);

(10)   an independent provider in Wales (see note 5);

(11)   Health Professions Wales (or Proffesiynau Iechyd Cymru) (see MEDICAL PROFESSIONS vol 74 (2011) PARAS 916, 938);

(12)   the National Leadership and Innovations Agency for Healthcare;

(13)   the National Council for Education and Training for Wales (whose functions are now exercised by the Welsh Government's Department for Children, Education, Lifelong Learning and Skills);

(14)   the Office of Her Majesty's Chief Inspector of Education and Training in Wales (or Prif Arolygydd Ei Mawrhydi dros Addysg a Hyfforddiant yng Nghymru) (see EDUCATION vol 36 (2015) PARA 1148);

(15)   the Higher Education Funding Council for Wales (see EDUCATION vol 35 (2015) PARA 691 et seq);

(16)   a further education corporation (see EDUCATION vol 35 (2015) PARA 559 et seq) discharging functions in relation to Wales;

(17)   a higher education corporation (see EDUCATION vol 35 (2015) PARA 619 et seq) discharging functions in relation to Wales;

(18)   an institution in Wales falling within the Further and Higher Education Act 1992 s 91(5)(a) (see EDUCATION vol 35 (2015) PARA 619);

(19)   the governing body of a maintained school (see EDUCATION vol 35 (2015) PARA 99) in Wales at which further education is provided;

(20)   Qualifications Wales (see EDUCATION vol 36 (2015) PARA 855);

(21)   the Arts Council of Wales (see NATIONAL CULTURAL HERITAGE vol 77 (2016) PARA 958);

(22)   the Sports Council for Wales (see NATIONAL CULTURAL HERITAGE vol 77 (2016) PARA 961);

(23)   the Wales Tourist Board (see TRADE AND INDUSTRY vol 97 (2015) PARA 1028);

(24)   the National Library of Wales (see NATIONAL CULTURAL HERITAGE vol 77 (2016) PARA 902 et seq);

(25)   the National Museums and Galleries of Wales (see NATIONAL CULTURAL HERITAGE vol 77 (2016) PARA 889);

(26)   the Royal Commission on the Ancient and Historical Monuments of Wales (see NATIONAL CULTURAL HERITAGE vol 77 (2016) PARA 811);

(27)   a National Park authority for a National Park in Wales (see OPEN SPACES AND COUNTRYSIDE vol 78 (2010) PARA 526 et seq);

(28)   the Natural Resources Body for Wales (see OPEN SPACES AND COUNTRYSIDE vol 78 (2010) PARA 523 et seq);

(29)   the Environment Agency (see ENVIRONMENTAL QUALITY AND PUBLIC HEALTH vol 45 (2010) PARA 68 et seq);

(30)   the Forestry Commissioners (see FORESTRY vol 52 (2014) PARA 37 et seq);

(31)   the Welsh Development Agency (dissolved) (see TRADE AND INDUSTRY vol 97 (2015) PARA 1051 et seq);

(32)   Comisiynydd y Gymraeg (The Welsh Language Commissioner) (see CONSTITUTIONAL AND ADMINISTRATIVE LAW vol 20 (2014) PARA 408); and

(33)   an agricultural wages committee (see AGRICULTURAL PRODUCTION AND MARKETING vol 1A (2017) PARAS 296, 298) for an area wholly in, or consisting of, Wales.

The Welsh Ministers have power to amend this list in the Commissioner for Older People (Wales) Act 2006 Sch 2 by adding or omitting a person, or by changing the description of a person: see s 4 (amended by SI 2007/1388).

7   Commissioner for Older People (Wales) Act 2006 s 3(1)(d).

307. Commissioner's power to review the effectiveness of arrangements.

The Commissioner for Older People in Wales[1] may review advocacy arrangements, complaints arrangements and whistle-blowing arrangements (and the operation of any such arrangements) for the purpose of ascertaining whether, and to what extent, they are effective in safeguarding and promoting the interests of relevant older people in Wales[2]. The Commissioner may also assess the effect on relevant older people in Wales of a person's failure to make any such arrangements[3].

'Advocacy arrangements' are arrangements made by a person for making persons available to represent the views and wishes of relevant older people in Wales, and for making persons available to provide relevant older people in Wales with advice and support of a prescribed kind[4]. 'Complaints arrangements' are arrangements made[5] for dealing with complaints or representations which are made by or on behalf of a relevant older person in Wales, and in respect of relevant services[6] provided to relevant older people in Wales by or on behalf of the person who has made the arrangements[7]. 'Whistle-blowing arrangements' are arrangements made[8] for ensuring that proper action is taken in response to a disclosure of potentially adverse information[9].

Information is potentially adverse if it may tend to show that, in the course of, or in connection with, the provision of relevant services:

(1)   a criminal offence has been committed;

(2)   a person has failed to comply with a legal obligation to which he is subject;

(3)   the health or safety of a person has been endangered;

(4)   the dignity of a person has been violated;

(5)   information tending to show a matter falling within any of heads (1) to (4) has been deliberately concealed[10].

Regulations may confer power on the Commissioner to require prescribed persons to provide any information which the Commissioner thinks it necessary or expedient to have for the purposes of his functions in relation to reviewing arrangements[11], and for the purposes of determining whether a recommendation made in a report following the discharge of his functions in relation to reviewing arrangements has been complied with[12]. In exercise of this power, regulations have been made which enable the Commissioner to require certain specified persons[13] to provide him with information, recorded in any form, which the Commissioner considers necessary or expedient to have for the purposes of:

(a)   reviewing arrangements in relation to advocacy, complaints or whistle-blowing[14];

(b)   assessing the effect of the failure of any person to make such arrangements[15]; and

(c)   determining whether a recommendation made in a report following a review of such arrangements has been complied with[16].

1   As to the office of the Commissioner see PARA 305.
2   Commissioner for Older People (Wales) Act 2006 s 5(1), (2). As to the meaning of 'older person in Wales' see PARA 305 note 3. 'Relevant older people in Wales' are (see s 6(1), (2), Sch 3):
    (1)   older people to or in respect of whom regulated services in Wales (see PARA 305 note 3) are provided; or
    (2)   older people to or in respect of whom relevant services (see below) are provided by or on behalf of, or under arrangements with any of the following persons:
        (a)   a county council or county borough council in Wales (see LOCAL GOVERNMENT vol 69 (2009) PARA 37 et seq);
        (b)   a Local Health Board (see HEALTH SERVICES vol 54 (2017) PARAS 97, 98);

(c)   an NHS trust (see HEALTH SERVICES vol 54 (2017) PARAS 97, 98) managing a hospital or other establishment or facility in Wales;

(d)   a Special Health Authority (see HEALTH SERVICES vol 54 (2017) PARAS 97, 98) discharging functions in relation to Wales;

(e)   a family health service provider in Wales (see PARA 306 note 5);

(f)   the National Council for Education and Training for Wales (whose functions are now exercised by the Welsh Government's Department for Children, Education, Lifelong Learning and Skills);

(g)   an independent provider in Wales (see PARA 306 note 5);

(h)   a further education corporation (see EDUCATION vol 35 (2015) PARA 559 et seq) discharging functions in relation to Wales;

(i)   a higher education corporation (see EDUCATION vol 35 (2015) PARA 619 et seq) discharging functions in relation to Wales;

(j)   an institution in Wales falling within the Further and Higher Education Act 1992 s 91(5)(a) (see EDUCATION vol 35 (2015) PARA 619);

(k)   the governing body of a maintained school (see EDUCATION vol 35 (2015) PARA 99) in Wales at which further education is provided.

The Welsh Ministers may by order amend the Commissioner for Older People (Wales) Act 2006 Sch 3 by adding or omitting a person, or by changing the description of a person: see s 7 (amended by SI 2007/1388). As to the power of the Welsh Ministers to make orders and regulations by statutory instrument see the Commissioner for Older People (Wales) Act 2006 s 28 (amended by SI 2007/1388; and by virtue of the Wales Act 2014 s 4(4)(a)). As to the Welsh Ministers generally see PARA 4.

A 'relevant service' is:

(i)   in the case of the Welsh Ministers, the First Minister for Wales or the Counsel General to the Welsh Government (see CONSTITUTIONAL AND ADMINISTRATIVE LAW vol 20 (2014) PARA 373 et seq), any service which they provide (Commissioner for Older People (Wales) Act 2006 s 6(4)(a) (substituted by SI 2007/1388; and amended by virtue of the Wales Act 2014 s 4(4)(a));

(ii)   in the case of a person providing regulated services in Wales, any of those services (Commissioner for Older People (Wales) Act 2006 s 6(4)(b));

(iii)   in the case of a person who is a family health service provider in Wales, any of the family health services which the person provides (s 6(4)(c));

(iv)   in the case of a person who is an independent provider in Wales, any of the independently provided services which the person provides (s 6(4)(d));

(v)   in the case of any other person mentioned in Sch 3 (see heads (a)–(k) above), any service the person provides (s 6(4)(e));

(vi)   in the case of a person providing services in Wales on behalf of, or under arrangements with, a person mentioned in Sch 3 (see heads (a)–(k) above), any service which the person provides in Wales on behalf of, or under arrangements with, a person mentioned in Sch 3 (see heads (a)–(k) above), and which would, if provided by the person mentioned in Sch 3 (see heads (a)–(k) above) be a relevant service falling within heads (iii)–(v) (s 6(4)(f)).

3   Commissioner for Older People (Wales) Act 2006 s 5(3).

4   Commissioner for Older People (Wales) Act 2006 s 5(4). The kind of advice and support to relevant older people in Wales which is prescribed for these purposes is the provision of advice and support which is intended to enable and assist them to express their views and wishes orally or using any other means of communication, and the provision of advice (including information) about their rights and welfare: see the Commissioner for Older People in Wales Regulations 2007, SI 2007/398, reg 3.

5   Ie arrangements made by:

(1)   the Welsh Ministers;

(2)   the First Minister for Wales;

(3)   the Counsel General to the Welsh Government;

(4)   a person providing regulated services in Wales;

(5)   a person mentioned in the Commissioner for Older People (Wales) Act 2006 Sch 3 (see note 2 heads (a)–(k));

(6)   a person providing services in Wales on behalf of, or under arrangements with, a person mentioned in Sch 3 (see note 2 heads (a)–(k)).

6   As to the relevant services see note 2.

7   Commissioner for Older People (Wales) Act 2006 s 5(5), s 6(3) (amended by SI 2007/1388; and by virtue of the Wales Act 2014 s 4(4)(a)).

8   See note 5.
9   Commissioner for Older People (Wales) Act 2006 s 5(6).
10   Commissioner for Older People (Wales) Act 2006 s 5(7).
11   Ie his functions under the Commissioner for Older People (Wales) Act 2006 s 5 (see the text and notes 1–10).
12   Commissioner for Older People (Wales) Act 2006 s 6(5).
13   The prescribed persons are listed in the Commissioner for Older People in Wales Regulations 2007, SI 2007/398, reg 4(2) (amended by SI 2008/1512; and by virtue of the Wales Act 2014 s 4(4)(a)) as follows:
     (1)   in relation to the provision of regulated services in Wales, the providers or former providers of such services, employees or former employees of such providers or former providers, persons who work or worked for such providers or former providers in a voluntary capacity, and members and employees of the Welsh Government and former members and employees of the 1998 Assembly and the Welsh Government;
     (2)   members (including elected members), directors, executives, officers and employees of a relevant person, former members, directors, executives, officers and employees of a relevant person and persons who work or worked for a relevant person in a voluntary capacity;
     (3)   the receiver or manager of the property, the liquidator or provisional liquidator or the trustee in bankruptcy, as the case may be, of a person who is or has been a relevant person or who provides or provided services described in head (1).
   For the purposes of heads (2) and (3) above, 'relevant person' means the 1998 Assembly, the Welsh Government, any person mentioned in the Commissioner for Older People (Wales) Act 2006 Sch 3 providing services to or in respect of an older person in Wales or a person providing such services on behalf of or under arrangements with that person: Commissioner for Older People in Wales Regulations 2007, SI 2007/398, reg 4(3) (amended by SI 2008/1512; and by virtue of the Wales Act 2014 s 4(4)(a)).
14   Commissioner for Older People in Wales Regulations 2007, SI 2007/398, reg 4(1)(a).
15   Commissioner for Older People in Wales Regulations 2007, SI 2007/398, reg 4(1)(b).
16   Commissioner for Older People in Wales Regulations 2007, SI 2007/398, reg 4(1)(c). If such information is held by means of a computer or in any other form, the Commissioner may require any person having charge of, or otherwise concerned with the operation of, the computer or other device holding that information to make the information available, or produce the information, in a visible and legible form: reg 19.

308. Provision of assistance to older persons making complaints etc.

Regulations under the Commissioner for Older People (Wales) Act 2006 may confer power on the Commissioner for Older People in Wales[1] to give assistance[2] to a person who is or has been an older person in Wales[3]:

(1)   in making a complaint or representation to or in respect of the Welsh Ministers, the First Minister for Wales or the Counsel General to the Welsh Government[4];

(2)   in making a complaint or representation to or in respect of a person providing regulated services in Wales[5], in respect of the provision of those services[6];

(3)   in making a complaint or representation to or in respect of a certain specified person[7], in relation to anything done or omitted to be done by that person the effect of which is subject to review[8];

(4)   in making a complaint or representation to or in respect of a person providing services on behalf of or under arrangements with a certain specified person[9], in respect of the provision of a relevant service[10];

(5)   in any procedure, proceedings or prospective proceedings of a prescribed description[11].

In exercise of this power, regulations have been made regarding the provision of assistance to older persons in making complaints and representations[12]. In deciding whether to provide assistance the Commissioner may take account of the financial and other assistance available to the older person in Wales in relation to the proceedings, complaint or representation concerned including assistance under the Access to Justice Act 1999[13].

1   As to the office of the Commissioner see PARA 305.
2   Assistance includes financial assistance, and arranging for a person to provide representation or give advice or assistance: Commissioner for Older People (Wales) Act 2006 s 8(4). The regulations may provide for assistance to be given on conditions including (in the case of financial assistance) conditions requiring repayment in prescribed circumstances: s 8(5). Where the Commissioner decides to provide financial assistance to an older person in Wales, the assistance may be provided subject to either or both of the following conditions:
    (1)   that the Commissioner may recover the reasonable cost of providing the assistance from any sums paid by other parties for this purpose in the proceedings concerned (and for this purpose, it is immaterial whether the sums paid by other parties are payable by virtue of a decision of a court or tribunal, an agreement reached to avoid proceedings or to bring them to an end, or otherwise) (Commissioner for Older People in Wales Regulations 2007, SI 2007/398, reg 6(1), (2)(a), (3));
    (2)   that the assistance provided does not duplicate assistance which has been or may be provided under any enactment (reg 6(2)(b)).
    As to the power of the Welsh Ministers to make orders and regulations by statutory instrument see the Commissioner for Older People (Wales) Act 2006 s 28 (amended by SI 2007/1388). As to the Welsh Ministers generally see PARA 4.
3   As to the meaning of 'older person in Wales' see PARA 305 note 3. See also the Commissioner for Older People (Wales) Act 2006 s 8(2).
4   Commissioner for Older People (Wales) Act 2006 s 8(1)(a) (amended by SI 2007/1388; and by virtue of the Wales Act 2014 s 4(4)(a)). As to the regulations made see the Commissioner for Older People in Wales Regulations 2007, SI 2007/398, reg 5(1)(a). As to Welsh devolution see further CONSTITUTIONAL AND ADMINISTRATIVE LAW vol 20 (2014) PARA 75 et seq.
5   As to the meaning of 'regulated services in Wales' see PARA 305 note 3.
6   Commissioner for Older People (Wales) Act 2006 s 8(1)(b). As to the regulations made see the Commissioner for Older People in Wales Regulations 2007, SI 2007/398, reg 5(1)(a).
7   Ie a person mentioned in the Commissioner for Older People (Wales) Act 2006 Sch 3 (see heads (a)–(k) in PARA 307 note 2).
8   Commissioner for Older People (Wales) Act 2006 s 8(1)(c). As to the regulations made see the Commissioner for Older People in Wales Regulations 2007, SI 2007/398, reg 5(1)(a). As to review under the Commissioner for Older People (Wales) Act 2006 s 3 see PARA 306.
9   See note 7.
10 Commissioner for Older People (Wales) Act 2006 s 8(1)(d). As to the regulations made see the Commissioner for Older People in Wales Regulations 2007, SI 2007/398, reg 5(1)(a). For these purposes, 'relevant service' means a service which is a relevant service for the purposes of the Commissioner for Older People (Wales) Act 2006 s 5 by virtue of s 6(4)(f) (see PARA 307 note 2): s 8(6).
11 Commissioner for Older People (Wales) Act 2006 s 8(1)(e). A description of procedure or proceedings may be so prescribed only if it relates to anything the effect of which is subject to review under s 3; the provision of regulated services in Wales; or the provision of a relevant service on behalf of, or under arrangements with, a person mentioned in Sch 3 (see heads (a)–(k) in PARA 307 note 2): s 8(3). In exercise of this power, regulations have been made which prescribe the following proceedings for the purposes of s 8(1)(e):
    (1)   proceedings which concern the provision to or in respect of an older person in Wales of regulated services in Wales (Commissioner for Older People in Wales Regulations 2007, SI 2007/398, reg 5(2)(a));
    (2)   proceedings which concern the provision of services to or in respect of an older person in Wales by any person mentioned in the Commissioner for Older People (Wales) Act 2006 Sch 3 (see heads (a)–(k) in PARA 307 note 2) or any person providing services on behalf of or under arrangements with that person (Commissioner for Older People in Wales Regulations 2007, SI 2007/398, reg 5(2)(b)); or
    (3)   proceedings which concern the effect on an older person in Wales of the exercise or proposed exercise of any function of the 1998 Assembly, the Welsh Ministers, the First Minister or the Counsel General or a person mentioned in the Commissioner for Older People (Wales) Act 2006 Sch 2 (see PARA 306 note 6) (Commissioner for Older People in Wales Regulations 2007, SI 2007/398, reg 5(2)(c) (amended by SI 2008/1512)).

The Commissioner may provide assistance to an older person in Wales in relation to such proceedings listed in heads (1)–(3) above where, in the reasonable opinion of the Commissioner, the proceedings relate to matters which have a more general application or relevance to the interests of older people in Wales than in the particular proceedings concerned: Commissioner for Older People in Wales Regulations 2007, SI 2007/398, reg 5(1)(b).

12 See the Commissioner for Older People in Wales Regulations 2007, SI 2007/398, regs 5, 6; and notes 2–11.

13 Commissioner for Older People in Wales Regulations 2007, SI 2007/398, reg 5(3). Regulation 5 does not affect the law and practice as to who may represent a person in relation to any proceedings: reg 5(4).

309. Examination of particular cases.

Regulations may make provision for the examination by the Commissioner for Older People in Wales[1] of the cases of particular persons who are or have been older people in Wales[2], in connection with the Commissioner's functions under the Commissioner for Older People (Wales) Act 2006[3]. Such regulations may include provision about the types of cases which may be examined, the circumstances in which an examination may be made and the procedure for conducting an examination, including provision about the representation of parties[4]. They may also make provision requiring persons to provide the Commissioner with information, or requiring persons who hold or are accountable for information to provide the Commissioner with explanations or other assistance for:

(1)   the purposes of an examination;

(2)   the purposes of determining whether a recommendation made in a report following an examination has been complied with[5].

The regulations may make provision for the payment by the Commissioner of sums in respect of expenses or allowances to persons who attend or provide information, explanations or other assistance for either of the purposes mentioned above[6].

In exercise of this power, regulations have been made which authorise the Commissioner to examine the cases of particular persons who are or who have been older people in Wales:

(a)   to or in respect of whom regulated services in Wales[7] are being or have been provided;

(b)   to or in respect of whom services are being or have been provided by any of the persons specified in the Commissioner for Older People (Wales) Act 2006[8] or persons providing such services on behalf of or under arrangements with any of those persons; or

(c)   who are ordinarily resident in Wales and who are being or have been affected by the exercise or proposed exercise of any function of the 1998 Assembly, the Welsh Ministers, the First Minister or the Counsel General or a person specified in the Commissioner for Older People (Wales) Act 2006[9],

where the cases relate to issues concerning the provision of such services or the effect on the older person of the exercise of such functions[10].

However, the Commissioner may only examine the case of a particular person who is or has been an older person in Wales where:

(i)   a representation is made to the Commissioner by the person concerned (or if the person concerned is unable for any reason to make such a representation, where a representation is made to the Commissioner on behalf of the person concerned by a person who appears to the Commissioner to be an appropriate person to act on behalf of the person concerned);

(ii)   the Commissioner considers that the representation raises a question of principle which has a more general application or relevance to the interests of older people in Wales than in the particular case concerned; and

(iii)   the Commissioner has taken into account whether the issues involved in the case have been or are being formally considered in any way by other persons and if they have not or are not whether, in the Commissioner's opinion, they are more suitable for consideration by other persons[11].

The Commissioner must follow procedural rules concerning the conduct of the examination[12]. In conducting an examination he may require certain persons[13] to provide information which appears to him to be necessary for the purposes of the examination, and determining whether a recommendation made in a report following an examination of a case has been complied with[14]. The Commissioner may, if it is considered necessary for the purposes of an examination, require certain persons[15] to attend in person to provide information, explanation or assistance[16]. However, he may only require attendance in person if reasonable written notice of the proposed date of attendance and the information, explanation or assistance required by the Commissioner has been given to that person[17]. In connection with attendance in person, the Commissioner may issue witness summonses and administer oaths or affirmations and may permit a person to be represented[18].

Where the Commissioner decides not to conduct an examination he must prepare a statement of reasons for that decision and send copies of it to the person who made the representation in relation to the case and such other persons as the Commissioner considers appropriate[19].

1   As to the office of the Commissioner see PARA 305.
2   As to the meaning of 'older person in Wales' see PARA 305 note 3.
3   Commissioner for Older People (Wales) Act 2006 s 10(1), (3). The reference in the text to the Commissioner's functions under the Act does not include his powers under ss 2(3), 9 (see PARAS 305, 310), to the extent that they are exercised in relation to a field in which neither the Welsh Minsters, the First Minister for Wales nor the Counsel General to the Welsh Government have functions: s 10(2) (amended by SI 2007/1388; and by virtue of the Wales Act 2014 s 4(4)(a)). As to the general functions of the Commissioner see PARA 305. As to the power of the Welsh Ministers to make orders and regulations by statutory instrument see the Commissioner for Older People (Wales) Act 2006 s 28 (amended by SI 2007/1388). As to the Welsh Ministers generally see PARA 4.
4   Commissioner for Older People (Wales) Act 2006 s 10(4).
5   Commissioner for Older People (Wales) Act 2006 s 10(5), (6). For the purposes mentioned in heads (1) and (2) in the text, the Commissioner has the same powers as the High Court in respect of the attendance and examination of witnesses (including the administration of oaths and affirmations and the examination of witnesses abroad), and the provision of information: s 10(7). However, no person is to be compelled to give any evidence or provide any information which he could not be compelled to give or provide in civil proceedings before the High Court: s 10(8).
6   Commissioner for Older People (Wales) Act 2006 s 10(9).
7   As to the meaning of 'regulated services in Wales' see PARA 305 note 3.
8   Ie any of the persons mentioned in the Commissioner for Older People (Wales) Act 2006 Sch 3 (see heads (a)–(k) in PARA 307 note 2).
9   Ie a person specified in the Commissioner for Older People (Wales) Act 2006 Sch 2 (see PARA 306 note 6).
10 Commissioner for Older People in Wales Regulations 2007, SI 2007/398, regs 7, 8 (amended by SI 2008/1512).
11 Commissioner for Older People in Wales Regulations 2007, SI 2007/398, reg 9.
12 Where the Commissioner decides to conduct an examination he must:
    (1)   produce terms of reference of the examination (Commissioner for Older People in Wales Regulations 2007, SI 2007/398, reg 10(1)(a));

(2)   send the terms of reference to the person who made a representation in relation to the case in accordance with head (i) in the text (reg 10(1)(b));

(3)   send written notice of the proposed examination and copies of the terms of reference to the person in respect of whose provision of services or the exercise of whose functions is to be examined (reg 10(1)(c));

(4)   afford to the person being examined, and if he or she so desires, his or her representative, an opportunity to make representations in writing or in person in relation to the matters being examined (reg 10(1)(d)).

13 Ie:

(1)   in relation to the provision of regulated services in Wales, the providers or former providers of such services, employees or former employees of such providers or former providers and persons who work or worked for such providers or former providers in a voluntary capacity and members and employees of the Welsh Government and former members and employees of the 1998 Assembly and the Welsh Government (Commissioner for Older People in Wales Regulations 2007, SI 2007/398, reg 11(3)(a) (amended by SI 2008/1512); and by virtue of the Wales Act 2014 s 4(4)(a));

(2)   members (including elected members), directors, executives, officers and employees of a relevant person, former members, directors, executives, officers and employees of a relevant person (see below) and persons who work or worked for a relevant person in a voluntary capacity (Commissioner for Older People in Wales Regulations 2007, SI 2007/398, reg 11(3)(b));

(3)   the receiver or manager of the property, the liquidator or provisional liquidator or the trustee in bankruptcy, as the case may be, of a person who is or has been a relevant person (see below) or who provides or provided services described in head (1) (reg 11(3)(c)).

For the purposes of heads (2) and (3), 'relevant person' means the 1998 Assembly, the Welsh Government, any person mentioned in the Commissioner for Older People (Wales) Act 2006 Sch 2 (see PARA 306 note 6), any other person exercising a function of the Welsh Ministers, the First Minister or the Counsel General or of any person mentioned in Sch 2, or any person providing services to or in respect of older people in Wales on behalf of or under arrangements with any person mentioned in Sch 3 (see heads (a)–(k) in PARA 307 note 2): Commissioner for Older People in Wales Regulations 2007, SI 2007/398, reg 11(4) (definition amended by SI 2008/1512; and by virtue of the Wales Act 2014 s 4(4)(a)).

14 Commissioner for Older People in Wales Regulations 2007, SI 2007/398, reg 11(1). If such information is held by means of a computer or in any other form, the Commissioner may require any person having charge of, or otherwise concerned with the operation of, the computer or other device holding that information to make the information available, or produce the information, in a visible and legible form: reg 19. In conducting an examination the Commissioner may require a person to provide the Commissioner with an explanation of, or assistance in relation to any matters which are the subject of the examination, or any information provided under reg 11(1): see reg 11(2). Expenses may be paid where a person provides information to the Commissioner pursuant to reg 11(1): see reg 20.

15 Ie the persons who are required to provide information under the Commissioner for Older People in Wales Regulations 2007, SI 2007/398, reg 11(1) (see the text and note 14); or to provide an explanation or assistance under reg 11(2) (see note 14): reg 12(2).

16 Commissioner for Older People in Wales Regulations 2007, SI 2007/398, reg 12(1). Expenses may be paid where a person attends before the Commissioner pursuant to reg 12: see reg 20.

17 Commissioner for Older People in Wales Regulations 2007, SI 2007/398, reg 12(3).

18 Commissioner for Older People in Wales Regulations 2007, SI 2007/398, reg 12(4). See also the Commissioner for Older People (Wales) Act 2006 s 10(7), (8); and note 5.

19 Commissioner for Older People in Wales Regulations 2007, SI 2007/398, reg 10(2).

310.   Research, assistance, education and guidance.

The Commissioner for Older People in Wales[1] may, in connection with any of his functions:

(1)   undertake or commission research;

(2)   give assistance (including financial assistance[2]) to another to undertake or commission research;

(3)   carry out or commission the carrying out of educational activities;

(4)   give assistance to another to carry out or commission the carrying out of educational activities[3].

He may also issue guidance on best practice in connection with any matter relating to the interests of older people in Wales[4]. Such guidance may be issued to the Welsh Ministers, the First Minister for Wales or the Counsel General to the Welsh Government, persons specified in the Commissioner for Older People (Wales) Act 2006[5], and persons providing regulated services in Wales[6]. Such persons must have regard to the guidance in discharging their functions[7]. In discharging his statutory functions in respect of such persons, the Commissioner may have regard to the extent to which the person has complied with any applicable guidance issued under these provisions[8].

1   As to the office of the Commissioner see PARA 305.
2   Commissioner for Older People (Wales) Act 2006 s 9(2). See also PARA 33.
3   Commissioner for Older People (Wales) Act 2006 s 9(1).
4   Commissioner for Older People (Wales) Act 2006 s 12(1). As to the meaning of 'older person in Wales' see PARA 305 note 3. Before issuing guidance the Commissioner must consult such persons as he thinks appropriate: s 12(3).
5   Ie the persons specified in the Commissioner for Older People (Wales) Act 2006 Sch 2 (see PARA 306 note 6). As to the Welsh Ministers see PARA 4.
6   Commissioner for Older People (Wales) Act 2006 s 12(2) (amended by SI 2007/1388; and by virtue of the Wales Act 2014 s 4(4)(a)). As to the meaning of 'regulated services in Wales' see PARA 305 note 3.
7   See the Commissioner for Older People (Wales) Act 2006 s 12(4).
8   See the Commissioner for Older People (Wales) Act 2006 s 12(5). As to the functions of the Commissioner see PARA 305 et seq.

311. Obstruction of the Commissioner or his staff etc dealt with as contempt of court.

If the Commissioner for Older People in Wales[1] is satisfied that a person:
(1)   without lawful excuse, has obstructed him or a member of his staff in the discharge of any of his functions[2] under regulations concerning the examination of cases[3];
(2)   without lawful excuse, has failed to comply with certain requirements[4] to provide information[5]; or
(3)   has done an act or made an omission in relation to an examination[6] which, if the examination were proceedings in the High Court, would constitute contempt of court[7],

he may issue a certificate to that effect to the High Court[8]. The High Court may then inquire into the matter and, if it is satisfied that a condition mentioned in heads (1) to (3) above is met in relation to the person, it may deal with him in any manner in which it could have dealt with him if he had committed contempt in relation to the High Court[9].

1   As to the office of the Commissioner see PARA 305.
2   Ie any of his functions under regulations made under the Commissioner for Older People (Wales) Act 2006 s 10 (see PARA 309).
3   Commissioner for Older People (Wales) Act 2006 s 11(2)(a).
4   Ie a requirement to provide information which was imposed in the exercise of a power conferred by regulations made under the Commissioner for Older People (Wales) Act 2006 s 6(5) (review of arrangements: see PARA 307) or s 10(5) (examination of cases: see PARA 309).
5   Commissioner for Older People (Wales) Act 2006 s 11(2)(b).
6   Ie an examination under regulations made under the Commissioner for Older People (Wales) Act 2006 s 10 (see PARA 309).
7   Commissioner for Older People (Wales) Act 2006 s 11(2)(c).
8   Commissioner for Older People (Wales) Act 2006 s 11(1).

9   Commissioner for Older People (Wales) Act 2006 s 11(3). As to contempt of court see further
CONTEMPT OF COURT vol 22 (2012) PARA 1 et seq.

312. Power to enter premises and interview older people.

In order to exercise his function of safeguarding and promoting the interests of older people in Wales[1] by reviewing the discharge of functions[2] and reviewing the effectiveness of advocacy, complaints and whistle-blowing complaints[3], the Commissioner for Older People in Wales[4] (or a person authorised by him) may at any reasonable time enter any premises (other than a private dwelling) for the purpose of interviewing an older person accommodated or cared for there[5], and may at any reasonable time interview the older person, if they consent[6]. Such an interview must be conducted, if the older person requires another person to be present, in that other person's presence[7]. Otherwise, it must conducted in the presence of others only to the extent that the older person and the Commissioner have consented to their being present[8].

Regulations may be made, conferring a similar power on the Commissioner (or a person authorised by him) for any purpose connected with the Commissioner's other functions[9].

1   As to the meaning of 'older person in Wales' see PARA 305 note 3.
2   Ie under the Commissioner for Older People (Wales) Act 2006 s 3 (see PARA 306).
3   Ie under the Commissioner for Older People (Wales) Act 2006 s 5 (see PARA 307).
4   As to the office of the Commissioner see PARA 305.
5   Commissioner for Older People (Wales) Act 2006 s 13(1)(a), (3).
6   Commissioner for Older People (Wales) Act 2006 s 13(1)(b), (3).
7   Commissioner for Older People (Wales) Act 2006 s 13(2)(a).
8   Commissioner for Older People (Wales) Act 2006 s 13(2)(b).
9   See the Commissioner for Older People (Wales) Act 2006 s 14(1), (3), (4). However, this does not apply to the Commissioner's powers under ss 2(3), 9, to the extent that they are exercised in a field in which neither the Welsh Minsters, the First Minister for Wales nor the Counsel General to the Welsh Government have functions; and nor does it apply to the Commissioner's powers under s 13: s 14(2) (amended by SI 2007/1388; and by virtue of the Wales Act 2014 s 4(4)(a)). As to the Welsh Ministers see PARA 4.

313. Communication between the Commissioner and older people in Wales.

The Commissioner for Older People in Wales[1] must take reasonable steps to ensure that older people in Wales[2] are made aware of the existence and functions of the Commissioner's office[3], its location and the ways in which they may communicate with the Commissioner and his staff[4]. He must take reasonable steps to ensure that older people are encouraged to communicate with him and his staff[5], and that the views of older people are sought concerning how the Commissioner should exercise his functions, as well as to the content of the Commissioner's annual work programme[6]. Reasonable steps must also be taken by the Commissioner and his staff to make themselves available to such older people in the older persons' locality[7].

In exercising these functions, the Commissioner must have regard to what he reasonably considers to be the needs and circumstances of such older people[8].

1   As to the office of the Commissioner see PARA 305.
2   As to the meaning of 'older person in Wales' see PARA 305 note 3.
3   Commissioner for Older People in Wales Regulations 2007, SI 2007/398, reg 13(1)(a).
4   See the Commissioner for Older People in Wales Regulations 2007, SI 2007/398, reg 13(1)(b).
5   Commissioner for Older People in Wales Regulations 2007, SI 2007/398, reg 13(1)(c).
6   Commissioner for Older People in Wales Regulations 2007, SI 2007/398, reg 13(1)(d).
7   Commissioner for Older People in Wales Regulations 2007, SI 2007/398, reg 13(1)(e).
8   Commissioner for Older People in Wales Regulations 2007, SI 2007/398, reg 13(2).

314. Commissioner's collaboration with other ombudsmen.

Where it appears to the Commissioner for Older People in Wales[1] that he is entitled to examine a particular case[2] and it is one which could also be the subject of an investigation by the Public Services Ombudsman for Wales[3], then if the Commissioner considers it appropriate, he must inform the Ombudsman about the case, and consult him in relation to it[4]. The Commissioner and the Ombudsman may then co-operate with each other in relation to the case, conduct a joint examination of the case, and prepare and publish a joint report in relation to the examination[5]. There is power for the application of this provision to be extended by the Welsh Ministers[6].

Where it appears to the Commissioner that a case which he is examining[7], or considering whether to examine, relates to or raises a matter which could be the subject of an investigation by another ombudsman (the 'connected matter'), then if the Commissioner considers it appropriate, he may (as respects the Welsh Language Commissioner) or must (as respects another ombudsman) inform the other ombudsman[8] about the connected matter[9]. Where the Commissioner considers that the case also relates to or raises a matter which he is entitled to examine himself[10], he may (as respects the Welsh Language Commissioner) or must (as respects another ombudsman) also, if he considers it appropriate, inform the other ombudsman about the Commissioner's proposals for the investigation of the case, and consult the other ombudsman about those proposals[11]. Where the Commissioner and the other ombudsman consider that they are entitled to investigate, respectively, the older people matter and the connected matter they may co-operate with each other in the separate investigation of each of those matters, act together in the investigation of those matters, and prepare and publish a joint report containing their respective conclusions in relation to the matters they have each investigated[12].

Where the Commissioner considers that the case is not one which relates to or raises a matter that he is entitled to examine himself, and that it is appropriate to do so, he may (as respects the Welsh Language Commissioner) or must (as respects another ombudsman) inform the person whose case it is, or another person interested in it that he thinks fit, about how to secure the referral of the connected matter to the other ombudsman[13].

1 As to the office of the Commissioner see PARA 305.
2 Ie under regulations made under the Commissioner for Older People (Wales) Act 2006 s 10 (see PARA 309). As to the power of the Welsh Ministers to make orders and regulations by statutory instrument see the Commissioner for Older People (Wales) Act 2006 s 28 (amended by SI 2007/1388). As to the Welsh Ministers generally see PARA 4.
3 As to the Public Services Ombudsman for Wales see LOCAL GOVERNMENT vol 69 (2009) PARA 843 et seq.
4 Commissioner for Older People (Wales) Act 2006 s 16(1), (2).
5 Commissioner for Older People (Wales) Act 2006 s 16(3).
6 The Welsh Ministers may by order provide that the Commissioner for Older People (Wales) Act 2006 s 16 is also to apply where it appears to the Commissioner that a case could be the subject of an investigation by a person who is specified in the order as if references in s 16 to the Public Services Ombudsman for Wales were references to that person: s 16(4) (amended by SI 2007/1388). Before making such an order, the Welsh Ministers must consult the Commissioner and any other persons they think appropriate: Commissioner for Older People (Wales) Act 2006 s 16(5) (amended by SI 2007/1388). At the date at which this volume states the law, no such order had been made.
7 Ie in accordance with regulations made under the Commissioner for Older People (Wales) Act 2006 s 10 (see PARA 309).
8 'Other ombudsman' means the Public Services Ombudsman for Wales, the Children's Commissioner for Wales or the Welsh Language Commissioner: Commissioner for Older People

(Wales) Act 2006 s 17(6) (amended by the Welsh Language (Wales) Measure 2011 Sch 3 paras 7, 9(d)). For these purposes, 'investigation' includes examination and inquiry: s 17(7). As to the Children's Commissioner for Wales see CHILDREN AND YOUNG PERSONS vol 9 (2017) PARAS 204–211; and as to the Welsh Language Commissioner see CONSTITUTIONAL AND ADMINISTRATIVE LAW vol 20 (2014) PARA 408. The Welsh Ministers may by order amend the Commissioner for Older People (Wales) Act 2006 s 17(6) by adding or omitting a person, or by changing the description of a person, but before making such an order they must consult the Commissioner and any other persons they think appropriate: s 17(8), (9) (amended by SI 2007/1388). In exercise of this power, the Welsh Language Commissioner was added by the Welsh Language (Wales) Measure 2011 Sch 3 paras 7, 9.

9   Commissioner for Older People (Wales) Act 2006 s 17(1), (2) (amended by the Welsh Language (Wales) Measure 2011 s 21, Sch 3 paras 7, 9(a)).
10 Such a matter is referred to in the legislation as the 'older people matter'.
11 Commissioner for Older People (Wales) Act 2006 s 17(3) (amended by the Welsh Language (Wales) Measure 2011 Sch 3 paras 7, 9(b)).
12 Commissioner for Older People (Wales) Act 2006 s 17(4).
13 Commissioner for Older People (Wales) Act 2006 s 17(5) (amended by the Welsh Language (Wales) Measure 2011 s 21, Sch 3 paras 7, 9(c)).

315. Disclosure of information obtained by the Commissioner.

The Commissioner for Older People in Wales[1] may disclose certain information[2] obtained by him in the exercise of his functions in certain specified circumstances[3]. Such information must not be disclosed except where its disclosure is authorised as follows[4].

The Commissioner may disclose such information only:

(1)   for the purpose of the discharge of any of his functions[5];

(2)   if he is satisfied that the disclosure is to a permitted person[6] and is:

    (a)   appropriate for the purpose of the discharge by the permitted person of any of his functions; and

    (b)   in the public interest[7];

(3)   for the purpose of proceedings for an offence of perjury alleged to have been committed in the course of an examination by the Commissioner[8];

(4)   for the purpose of an inquiry with a view to the taking of such proceedings[9];

(5)   for the purpose of proceedings under the Commissioner for Older People (Wales) Act 2006 for contempt[10];

(6)   if the information is to the effect that a person is likely to constitute a threat to the health or safety of one or more persons and the disclosure is to a person to whom the Commissioner thinks it should be disclosed in the public interest[11];

(7)   if the disclosure is to the Information Commissioner, and the information is information which appears to the Commissioner to relate to:

    (a)   a matter in respect of which the Information Commissioner could exercise certain statutory powers of enforcement[12]; or

    (b)   the commission of certain offences[13];

(8)   if the information was obtained by the Commissioner more than 70 years before the date of the disclosure and the disclosure is to a person to whom the Commissioner thinks it should be disclosed in the public interest[14].

1 As to the office of the Commissioner see PARA 305.
2 This only applies to the following information (Commissioner for Older People (Wales) Act 2006 s 18(1) (amended by the Social Services and Well-being (Wales) Act 2014 Sch 3 para 33)):
    (1)   information obtained by the Commissioner in the discharge of any of his functions;

(2)　information obtained by the Commissioner from the Public Services Ombudsman for Wales by virtue of the Public Services Ombudsman (Wales) Act 2005 s 34V (working jointly with the Commissioner for Older People in Wales: see SOCIAL SERVICES vol 95 (2017) PARA 358);

(3)　information obtained by the Commissioner from another ombudsman by virtue of any provision in an enactment relating to that ombudsman which corresponds to any provision of the Commissioner for Older People (Wales) Act 2006 s 17 (see PARA 314);

(4)　information obtained by the Commissioner from the Information Commissioner by virtue of the Freedom of Information Act 2000 s 76 (disclosure between Information Commissioner and ombudsmen: see CONSTITUTIONAL AND ADMINISTRATIVE LAW vol 20 (2014) PARA 461).

3　See the Commissioner for Older People (Wales) Act 2006 s 18; and the text and notes 4–14.

4　Commissioner for Older People (Wales) Act 2006 s 18(2).

5　Commissioner for Older People (Wales) Act 2006 s 18(3)(a).

6　'Permitted person' means: the Welsh Ministers (see CONSTITUTIONAL AND ADMINISTRATIVE LAW vol 20 (2014) PARA 375); the First Minister for Wales (see CONSTITUTIONAL AND ADMINISTRATIVE LAW vol 20 (2014) PARA 374); the Counsel General to the Welsh Government (see CONSTITUTIONAL AND ADMINISTRATIVE LAW vol 20 (2014) PARA 376); the Public Services Ombudsman for Wales (see LOCAL GOVERNMENT vol 69 (2009) PARA 843 et seq); the Children's Commissioner for Wales (see CHILDREN AND YOUNG PERSONS vol 9 (2017) PARAS 204–211); the Children's Commissioner (see CHILDREN AND YOUNG PERSONS vol 9 (2017) PARAS 200–203; the Commissioner for Children and Young People for Northern Ireland; a housing ombudsman appointed in accordance with a scheme approved under the Housing Act 1996 s 51 (see HOUSING vol 56 (2017) PARAS 130–140); a council for a county or county borough in Wales (see LOCAL GOVERNMENT vol 69 (2009) PARA 37 et seq); a council for a county or district in England (see LOCAL GOVERNMENT vol 69 (2009) PARA 24 et seq); a council for a London borough (see LONDON GOVERNMENT vol 71 (2013) PARAS 20–22); a chief of police of a police force for a police area (see POLICE AND INVESTIGATORY POWERS vol 84 (2013) PARA 123 et seq); and the chief constable of the British Transport Police Force (see POLICE AND INVESTIGATORY POWERS vol 84 (2013) PARA 30): Commissioner for Older People (Wales) Act 2006 s 18(9) (amended by SI 2007/1388; and by virtue of the Wales Act 2014 s 4(4)(a)). The Welsh Ministers may by order amend the definition of 'permitted person' by adding or omitting a person or by changing a description of a person: Commissioner for Older People (Wales) Act 2006 s 18(10) (amended by SI 2007/1388). As to the power of the Welsh Ministers to make orders and regulations by statutory instrument see the Commissioner for Older People (Wales) Act 2006 s 28 (amended by SI 2007/1388). As to the Welsh Ministers generally see PARA 4.

7　Commissioner for Older People (Wales) Act 2006 s 18(3)(b), (4). In determining for these purposes whether disclosure of information is in the public interest, the Commissioner must take into account the interests of any person to whom the information relates, and such other persons he thinks appropriate: s 18(5).

8　Commissioner for Older People (Wales) Act 2006 s 18(3)(c). The reference in the text to an examination is to one by the Commissioner under regulations made under s 10 (see PARA 309).

9　Commissioner for Older People (Wales) Act 2006 s 18(3)(d). The reference in the text to proceedings is to those mentioned in s 18(3)(c) (see head (3) in the text).

10　Commissioner for Older People (Wales) Act 2006 s 18(3)(e). The reference in the text to proceedings is to those under s 11 (see PARA 311).

11　Commissioner for Older People (Wales) Act 2006 s 18(3)(f). See note 7.

12　Ie a matter in respect of which the Information Commissioner could exercise a power conferred by the Data Protection Act 1998 Pt 5 (ss 40–50), the Freedom of Information Act 2000 s 48, Pt 4 (ss 50–56) (see CONFIDENCE AND INFORMATIONAL PRIVACY vol 19 (2011) PARAS 7, 152 et seq): Commissioner for Older People (Wales) Act 2006 s 18(7).

13　Commissioner for Older People (Wales) Act 2006 s 18(3)(g), (6). The reference in the text to offences is to those under any provision of the Data Protection Act 1998 (other than Sch 9 para 12 (obstruction of execution of a warrant)); or the Freedom of Information Act 2000 s 77 (offence of altering etc records with intent to prevent disclosure): Commissioner for Older People (Wales) Act 2006 s 18(8).

14　Commissioner for Older People (Wales) Act 2006 s 18(3)(h). See note 7.

316. Protection against defamation.

For the purposes of the law of defamation, certain matters enjoy either absolute or qualified privilege[1]. The following are absolutely privileged:

(1)   the publication of a matter by the Commissioner for Older People in Wales[2] in a report on the discharge of his functions[3];
(2)   the publication in communications between the Commissioner and the Public Services Ombudsman for Wales or another ombudsman of a matter which the Commissioner is permitted to disclose to that ombudsman in order to discharge his functions[4];
(3)   the publication in communications from the Commissioner to:
       (a)   the person whose case is being examined;
       (b)   a person whose conduct is the subject of the examination;
       (c)   a person with whom the Commissioner is communicating for the purpose of obtaining information about the case; and
       (d)   a person acting on behalf of a person falling within heads (a) to (c),
(4)   of a matter in connection with an examination by the Commissioner into a particular case[5].

However, the publication in communications from a person falling within heads (a) to (d)[6], to the Commissioner of a matter in connection with an examination by the Commissioner into a particular case[7] has qualified, rather than absolute, privilege[8].

1   As to the law of defamation see generally DEFAMATION vol 32 (2012) PARA 501 et seq. As to absolute privilege see DEFAMATION vol 32 (2012) PARA 594 et seq. As to qualified privilege see DEFAMATION vol 32 (2012) PARA 609 et seq.
2   As to the office of the Commissioner see PARA 305.
3   Commissioner for Older People (Wales) Act 2006 s 19(1)(a). The reference in the text to a report is to one made under regulations made under s 15 or Sch 1 para 8 (see the Commissioner for Older People in Wales Regulations 2007, SI 2007/398, regs 14–17; and PARA 305). As to the power of the Welsh Ministers to make orders and regulations by statutory instrument see the Commissioner for Older People (Wales) Act 2006 s 28 (amended by SI 2007/1388). As to the Welsh Ministers generally see PARA 4.
4   Commissioner for Older People (Wales) Act 2006 s 19(1)(b). As to the meaning of 'other ombudsman' see PARA 314 note 8; definition applied by s 19(4). The reference in the text to matters which the Commissioner is permitted to disclose to another ombudsman is to those matters which he is permitted to disclose by virtue of s 18(3)(a) (see PARA 315).
5   Commissioner for Older People (Wales) Act 2006 s 19(1)(c), (3). The reference in the text to examination by the Commissioner into a case is to examination into a case under regulations made under s 10 (see PARA 309).
6   Ie a person mentioned in the Commissioner for Older People (Wales) Act 2006 s 19(3) (see the text and note 5).
7   Ie into a case under regulations made under the Commissioner for Older People (Wales) Act 2006 s 10 (see PARA 309).
8   Commissioner for Older People (Wales) Act 2006 s 19(2). See also note 1.

317. Complaints procedure in respect of the Commissioner.

The Commissioner for Older People in Wales[1] must establish a procedure for the investigation of complaints made in respect of his actions or omissions relating to the discharge of his functions[2]. This procedure must cover:
(1)   how a complaint may be made;
(2)   the person to whom a complaint may be made;
(3)   the period within which consideration of a complaint must begin and should be concluded; and
(4)   action that the Commissioner must consider taking in response to a complaint[3].

The Commissioner may amend the procedure from time to time[4].

1   As to the office of the Commissioner see PARA 305.

2   Commissioner for Older People (Wales) Act 2006 s 20(1). Before establishing the procedure the
    Commissioner must consult the Welsh Ministers and obtain their approval: see s 20(4), (5)
    (amended by SI 2007/1833). At the date at which this volume states the law, the complaints
    procedure was available on the website for the Commissioner (see www.olderpeoplewales.com).
    As to the Welsh Ministers see PARA 4.
3   Commissioner for Older People (Wales) Act 2006 s 20(2).
4   Commissioner for Older People (Wales) Act 2006 s 20(3). Before amending the procedure the
    Commissioner must consult the Welsh Ministers and obtain their approval: see s 20(4), (5) (as
    amended: see note 2).

(4) DISABLED PERSONS' RIGHT TO CONTROL PROVISION OF SERVICES

318. Greater choice for disabled persons in relation to relevant services.
The purpose of Part 2 of the Welfare Reform Act 2009[1] is to enable disabled
people aged 18 or over to exercise greater choice in relation to, and greater control
over, the way in which relevant services are provided to or for them, in cases
where the provision of the relevant services is a function of a relevant authority[2].
The term 'relevant services' means services which are provided to or for the
benefit of a disabled person (whether or not in connection with his disability), and
which relate to one or more of the following matters[3]:

(1)   the provision of further education for the disabled person[4];
(2)   facilitating the undertaking by the disabled person of further education
       or higher education[5];
(3)   the provision of training for the disabled person[6];
(4)   securing employment for the disabled person[7];
(5)   facilitating the disabled person's continued employment[8];
(6)   enabling the disabled person to live independently or more
       independently in their home[9];
(7)   the provision of residential accommodation for the disabled person[10];
(8)   enabling the disabled person to overcome barriers to participation in
       society[11];

Relevant services also include the provision by or on behalf of a relevant authority
to or for the benefit of a disabled person of grants or loans relating to one or more
of the matters mentioned in heads (1) to (8) above[12]. Certain services are, however,
specifically excluded[13], and provision as to direct payments relating to such
services are made by other legislation[14].

1   Ie the Welfare Reform Act 2009 Pt 2 (ss 38–50).
2   Welfare Reform Act 2009 s 38. 'Relevant authority' means:
    (1)   a Minister of the Crown (which includes the Scottish Ministers and the Welsh Ministers)
           or government department (s 40(1)(a), (5));
    (2)   the Scottish Ministers (s 40(1)(b));
    (3)   the Welsh Ministers (s 40(1)(c));
    (4)   a local authority (ie a local authority within the meaning of the Local Government Act
           1972 (see LOCAL GOVERNMENT vol 69 (2009) PARA 23), the Greater London Authority
           (see LONDON GOVERNMENT vol 71 (2013) PARA 67 et seq), the Common Council of the
           City of London (see LONDON GOVERNMENT vol 71 (2013) PARA 34 et seq) in its capacity
           as a local authority, or the Council of the Isles of Scilly (see LOCAL GOVERNMENT vol 69
           (2009) PARA 36)) (s 40(1)(d), (4));
    (5)   a person or body whose functions are exercised on behalf of the Crown (s 40(1)(e));
    (6)   any other body which meets conditions A and B as follows:
           (a)   condition A being that the body is established by virtue of Her Majesty's
                  prerogative or by an enactment or is established in any other way by a Minister
                  of the Crown acting as such or by a government department; and

      (b)   condition B being that the body's revenues derive wholly or mainly from public funds (s 40(1)(f), (2), (3)).

3 Welfare Reform Act 2009 s 39(1).

4 Welfare Reform Act 2009 s 39(2)(a), (8). As to further education see EDUCATION vol 35 (2015) PARA 555 et seq.

5 Welfare Reform Act 2009 s 39(2)(b), (8). As to higher education see EDUCATION vol 35 (2015) PARA 619 et seq.

6 Welfare Reform Act 2009 s 39(2)(c).

7 Welfare Reform Act 2009 s 39(2)(d). 'Employment' includes self-employment: s 50.

8 Welfare Reform Act 2009 s 39(2)(e).

9 Welfare Reform Act 2009 s 39(2)(f).

10 Welfare Reform Act 2009 s 39(2)(g).

11 Welfare Reform Act 2009 s 39(2)(h).

12 Welfare Reform Act 2009 s 39(3).

13 In relation to England and Wales, the following are excluded services:
      (1)   community care services (see, in relation to England, the Care Act 2014 Pt 1 (ss 1–80) or the Mental Health Act 1983 s 117; in relation to Wales, the Social Services and Well-being (Wales) Act 2014 Pt 4 (ss 32–58) or the Mental Health Act 1983 s 117; and MENTAL HEALTH AND CAPACITY vol 75 (2013) PARA 945; SOCIAL SERVICES vol 95 (2017) PARA 8 et seq) Welfare Reform Act 2009 ss 39(6)(a), 50 (amended by SI 2015/157; SI 2015/914; and SI 2016/413);
      (2)   services provided under the Children Act 1989 s 17 (provision of services for children in need, their families and others: see CHILDREN AND YOUNG PERSONS vol 10 (2017) PARA 789) or the Social Services and Well-being (Wales) Act 2014 ss 37–39 (meeting care and support needs of children: see SOCIAL SERVICES vol 95 (2017) PARAS 30–32): Welfare Reform Act 2009 s 39(6)(b) (amended by SI 2016/413).
    There is power to repeal the provision in the Welfare Reform Act 2009 s 39(6) which excludes community care services: see s 48.

14 Welfare Reform Act 2009 s 39(4). This is subject to s 44(4) (which relates to pilot schemes: see PARA 319) and to s 48 (which gives power to repeal the exclusion of community care services): see s 39(5).

319. Power to make regulations enabling exercise of greater choice and control as respects services.

The appropriate authority[1] may by regulations[2] make any provision that would in its opinion serve the purpose of Part 2 of the Welfare Reform Act 2009[3] (which is to enable disabled people aged 18 or over to exercise greater choice in relation to, and greater control over, the way in which relevant services are provided to or for them, in cases where the provision of the relevant services is a function of a relevant authority)[4].

Such regulations may, in particular, make provision for and in connection with requiring a relevant authority to take the following steps in relation to a disabled person ('P') for whom it is obliged, or has decided, to provide, or arrange the provision of, relevant services:

(1)   to inform P of the right to control conferred by virtue of the regulations, of the value of the relevant services to which P is entitled and of the choices available to P by virtue of the regulations[5];

(2)   to work with P to determine the outcomes to be achieved by the provision of the relevant services[6];

(3)   to work with P to prepare a support plan setting out how those outcomes will be achieved[7];

(4)   to work with P to review and revise the support plan in prescribed circumstances[8];

(5)   if P so requests, to make payments to P in respect of P securing the provision of an equivalent service[9];

(6)   to the extent that P chooses to receive relevant services provided or arranged by the relevant authority, to provide, or arrange for them to be provided, in accordance with P's support plan as far as it is reasonably practicable to do so[10].

The regulations may specify who is or is not to be treated as a disabled person for any purpose of the regulations[11], and may also make provision:

(a)   about the circumstances in which a relevant authority is to be taken to have decided to provide a relevant service to a person[12];

(b)   as to matters to which a relevant authority must, or may, have regard when making a decision for the purposes of a provision of the regulations[13]; and

(c)   as to steps which a relevant authority must, or may, take before, or after, it makes a decision for the purposes of the regulations[14].

They may also enable or require the disclosure of information by one relevant authority to another for prescribed purposes[15].

The regulations may vary the conditions attached to any power of a relevant authority to provide financial assistance to disabled people, and they may vary the conditions attached to any power of a relevant authority to provide financial assistance to another relevant authority in connection with the provision of relevant services to disabled people by the other authority[16]. They may also require a relevant authority exercising any function under the regulations to have regard to any guidance given from time to time by the appropriate authority[17].

Regulations may make provision enabling any request or consent required for the purposes of the regulations to be made or given on behalf of a disabled person who lacks mental capacity by a person of a prescribed description[18].

Provision is made for pilot schemes to be introduced where the regulations have effect for a limited period only[19] with a view to ascertaining the extent to which their provisions contribute to achieving their purpose[20], the extent of any beneficial effects on the lives of the disabled people affected, and the extent of any financial burden imposed on the relevant authorities to which the regulations relate[21]. A pilot scheme may provide that it applies only in specified areas[22], or to certain specified classes of person[23].

1   The Secretary of State is the appropriate authority (Welfare Reform Act 2009 s 45(1), (2)), except that:

(1)   in relation to provision that would be within the legislative competence of the Scottish Parliament if it were included in an Act of that Parliament, the Scottish Ministers are the appropriate authority (s 45(2)(a));

(2)   in relation to provision that would be within the legislative competence of the National Assembly for Wales if it were included in a Measure of the Assembly (or, if regulations are made after the Assembly Act provisions come into force, an Act of the Assembly), the Welsh Ministers are the appropriate authority (s 45(2)(b));

(3)   in relation to provision that does not fall within head (2) and relates to relevant services in Wales with respect to which functions are exercisable by a Minister of the Crown, and by the Welsh Ministers, the First Minister for Wales (the 'First Minister') or the Counsel General to the Welsh Government (the 'Counsel General'), then the Secretary of State or the Welsh Ministers are the appropriate authority (s 45(2)(c), (5) (s 45 amended by virtue of the Wales Act 2014 s 4(4)(a)); and

(4)   in relation to provision that does not fall within head (2) or (3) and relates to relevant services in Wales with respect to which functions are exercisable by the Welsh Ministers, the First Minister or the Counsel General, the Welsh Ministers are the appropriate authority (Welfare Reform Act 2009 s 45(2)(D)).

Any power of the Secretary of State to make regulations under s 41 is exercisable only with the consent of the Treasury, and does not include power to make provision removing or modifying any function of the Welsh Ministers, the First Minister or the Counsel General, or make provision conferring or imposing any function on the Welsh Ministers, the First Minister or the Counsel

General: s 45(3). As to the Secretary of State and the Welsh Ministers see PARA 4. As to the Treasury see CONSTITUTIONAL AND ADMINISTRATIVE LAW vol 20 (2014) PARAS 262–265.

Any power of the Welsh Ministers to make regulations under s 41 by virtue of head (3) or (4) above does not include power to make provision removing or modifying any function of a Minister of the Crown (including the Treasury), or conferring or imposing any function on a Minister of the Crown: s 45(4), (5).

2 Such regulations are to be made by statutory instrument (see the Welfare Reform Act 2009 s 41(1), and before laying before Parliament or the National Assembly for Wales a draft of the statutory instrument, the appropriate authority must publish draft regulations in such manner as it thinks fit, and invite representations to be made to it about the draft, during a specified period of not less than 12 weeks, by persons appearing to it to be affected by the proposals (see ss 47, 49).

At the date at which this volume states the law, only pilot regulations have been made: see the Disabled Peoples' Right to Control (Pilot Scheme) (England) Regulations 2010, SI 2010/2862 (no longer in force); and note 21.

3 See the Welfare Reform Act 2009 s 41(1), 46. The text refers to the Welfare Reform Act 2009 Pt 2 (ss 38–50).

4 See the Welfare Reform Act 2009 s 38; and PARA 318. As to the meaning of 'relevant services' see PARA 318. As to the meaning of 'relevant authority' see PARA 318 note 2.

5 Welfare Reform Act 2009 s 41(2)(a).

6 Welfare Reform Act 2009 s 41(2)(b).

7 Welfare Reform Act 2009 s 41(2)(c).

8 Welfare Reform Act 2009 s 41(2)(d).

9 Welfare Reform Act 2009 s 41(2)(e). Regulations under s 41 making provision by virtue of s 41(2)(e) are referred to as 'direct payments regulations'. Provision may be made concerning direct payments (ie payments made by a relevant authority under the regulations) including the circumstances in which they are required, and any conditions to be complied with, and manner in which they are to be paid: see s 42.

10 Welfare Reform Act 2009 s 41(2)(f).

11 Welfare Reform Act 2009 s 41(3)(a).

12 Welfare Reform Act 2009 s 41(3)(b).

13 Welfare Reform Act 2009 s 41(3)(c).

14 See the Welfare Reform Act 2009 s 41(3)(d).

15 Welfare Reform Act 2009 s 41(4).

16 Welfare Reform Act 2009 s 41(5)(a), (b).

17 Welfare Reform Act 2009 s 41(6).

18 See the Welfare Reform Act 2009 s 43(1), (2). The reference in the text to a person who lacks capacity is to one who lacks capacity within the meaning of the Mental Capacity Act 2005, in relation to the decision concerned (see MENTAL HEALTH AND CAPACITY vol 75 (2013) PARAS 597–719).

19 Ie a period not exceeding 36 months: see the Welfare Reform Act 2009 s 44(1).

20 Ie for the purpose of the Welfare Reform Act 2009 Pt 2 (see the text and notes 1–4).

21 See the Welfare Reform Act 2009 s 44(2), (3). The Disabled Peoples' Right to Control (Pilot Scheme) (England) Regulations 2010, SI 2010/2862, which were made under these provisions ceased to have effect by virtue of reg 1(4) (amended by SI 2012/3048).

22 The Disabled Peoples' Right to Control (Pilot Scheme) (England) Regulations 2010, SI 2010/2862, operated in the following pilot areas: the London borough of Barnet, the metropolitan district of Barnsley, the metropolitan district of Bury, the non-metropolitan district of Epsom and Ewell, the county of Essex, the non-metropolitan district of Leicester, the metropolitan district of Manchester, the London borough of Newham, the non-metropolitan district of Reigate and Banstead, the metropolitan district of Sheffield, the metropolitan district of Stockport, and the metropolitan district of Trafford: reg 3 (amended by SI 2012/3048) (no longer in force).

23 See the Welfare Reform Act 2009 s 44(5). As to provision regarding the cessation of pilot schemes, replacement pilot schemes and reports on the operation of the scheme see s 44(6)–(8).

13. EXCEPTIONS FROM THE EQUALITY ACT 2010

(1) SCOPE OF EXCEPTIONS

320. Exceptions to the provisions of the Equality Act 2010.
There are a number of exceptions to the general provisions of the Equality Act 2010 in the areas of:

(1)   national security[1];

(2)   acts carried out pursuant to statutory requirements[2];

(3)   acts carried out pursuant to pre-existing statutory provisions for the protection of women[3];

(4)   religion[4];

(5)   charities[5];

(6)   supported employment for the disabled[6];

(7)   nationality or residence[7];

(8)   sport[8]; and

(9)   the provision of communal accommodation[9].

There are also a number of exceptions which are specific to the 'arenas' of discrimination enumerated by the Equality Act 2010, namely services and public functions[10], premises[11], work[12], education[13] and associations[14].

1   See PARA 321.
2   See PARA 322.
3   See PARA 323.
4   See PARA 324.
5   See PARA 325.
6   See PARA 326.
7   See PARA 327.
8   See PARA 328.
9   See PARA 329.
10 See PARAS 91–104.
11 See PARAS 110–115.
12 See PARAS 156–172.
13 See PARAS 195–197.
14 See PARAS 204–208.

(2) GENERAL EXCEPTIONS FROM THE EQUALITY ACT 2010

321. Exception for national security.
A person does not contravene the Equality Act 2010[1] only by doing, for the purpose of safeguarding national security, anything it is proportionate to do for that purpose[2].

1   As to the introduction of the Equality Act 2010 see PARA 1.
2   Equality Act 2010 s 192.

322. Exceptions for acts carried out pursuant to statutory requirements.
Acts carried out pursuant to a requirement of an enactment or pursuant to a relevant requirement or condition imposed by virtue of an enactment will not necessarily contravene the provisions of the Equality Act 2010 prohibiting discrimination in the arenas of services[1], premises[2], work[3], education[4],

associations[5], and disabled persons and transport[6], so far as relating to the protected characteristics of age[7], disability[8], religion or belief[9], sex[10], and sexual orientation[11].

1   Ie the Equality Act 2010 Pt 3 (ss 28–31) (see PARAS 84–104).
2   Ie the Equality Act 2010 Pt 4 (ss 32–38) (see PARAS 105–115).
3   Ie the Equality Act 2010 Pt 5 (ss 39–83) (see PARAS 116–172).
4   Ie the Equality Act 2010 Pt 6 (ss 84–99) (see PARAS 173–197).
5   Ie the Equality Act 2010 Pt 7 (ss 100–107) (see PARAS 198–210).
6   Ie the Equality Act 2010 Pt 12 (ss 160–188) (see PARAS 211–236).
7   As to age as a protected characteristic see PARA 46.
8   As to disability as a protected characteristic see PARAS 47–55.
9   As to religion or belief as a protected characteristic see PARA 59.
10   As to sex as a protected characteristic see PARA 60.
11   See the Equality Act 2010 Sch 22 para 1(1), (2); and PARA 92 (exceptions relating to the provision of services), PARA 110 (exceptions relating to premises), PARA 156 (exceptions relating to work), PARA 195 (exceptions relating to education), PARA 207 (exceptions relating to associations), PARA 273 (exceptions relating to disabled persons and transport). As to sexual orientation as a protected characteristic see PARA 63. As to the meaning of 'enactment' see PARA 92 note 8.

323. Exceptions for acts carried out pursuant to pre-existing statutory provisions for the protection of women.

The provisions of the Equality Act 2010 relating to discrimination in the workplace[1] and in education[2] are not contravened, so far as relating to the protected characteristics of pregnancy and maternity[3], and sex[4], by certain acts done in compliance with pre-existing statutory provisions for the protection of women[5].

1   Ie the Equality Act 2010 Pt 5 (ss 39–83) (see PARAS 116–172).
2   Ie the Equality Act 2010 Pt 6 (ss 84–99) (see PARAS 173–197).
3   As to pregnancy and maternity as a protected characteristic see PARAS 62, 73–74.
4   As to sex as a protected characteristic see PARA 60.
5   See the Equality Act 2010 Sch 22 para 2; and PARAS 158 (exceptions relating to work), 197 (exceptions relating to education).

324. Exceptions relating to religion.

The provisions of the Equality Act 2010 prohibiting discrimination in the workplace[1] and the provisions of that Act generally[2], are not contravened by acts done pursuant to statutory provisions concerning employment in schools of a religious character[3]. Religious organisations do not contravene the provisions of the Equality Act 2010 relating to services[4], premises[5], or associations[6], if they do specified acts connected with their religion which discriminate on grounds of religion or belief[7] or sexual orientation[8].

It is not a contravention of the Equality Act 2010 for a charity[9] to require members[10], or persons wishing to become members, to make a statement which asserts or implies membership or acceptance of a religion or belief[11].

1   Ie the Equality Act 2010 Pt 5 (ss 39–83) (see PARAS 116–172).
2   As to the application of the Equality Act 2010 see PARAS 1–4.
3   See the Equality Act 2010 Sch 22 paras 3, 4; and PARA 162.
4   Ie the Equality Act 2010 Pt 3 (ss 28–31) (see PARAS 84–104).
5   Ie the Equality Act 2010 Pt 4 (ss 32–38) (see PARAS 105–115).
6   Ie the Equality Act 2010 Pt 7 (ss 100–107) (see PARAS 198–210).
7   As to religion or belief as a protected characteristic see PARA 59.
8   See the Equality Act 2010 Sch 23 para 2; and PARAS 97 (exceptions relating to the provision of services), 112 (exceptions relating to premises), 208 (exceptions relating to associations).

9   As to the meaning of 'charity', and as to exceptions relating to charities generally, see PARA 325.
    These provisions (ie the Equality Act 2010 s 193(5)) apply only if the charity, or an organisation
    of which it is part, first imposed such a requirement before 18 May 2005 and the charity or
    organisation has not ceased since that date to impose such a requirement: s 193(6).
10 For this purpose 'membership' is membership of any description; a reference to a 'member' is to
    be construed accordingly: Equality Act 2010 s 194(6).
11 Equality Act 2010 s 193(5). For this purpose restricting the access by members to a benefit, facility
    or service to those who make such a statement is to be treated as imposing such a requirement: s
    193(5).

325.   Exceptions relating to charities.

A person does not contravene the Equality Act 2010[1] (other than in so far as
applying to race so far as relating to colour[2], or in certain employment-related
contexts[3]) only by restricting the provision of benefits to persons who share a
protected characteristic[4] if the person acts in pursuance of a charitable instrument[5]
and the provision of the benefits is:

(1)   a proportionate means of achieving a legitimate aim[6]; or
(2)   for the purpose of preventing or compensating for a disadvantage linked
        to the protected characteristic[7].

It is not a contravention of the Equality Act 2010 for a charity to require
members, or persons wishing to become members, to make a statement which
asserts or implies membership or acceptance of a religion or belief[8]. It is not a
contravention of the provisions of the Equality Act 2010 relating to services[9] for
a person, in relation to an activity which is carried on for the purpose of
promoting or supporting a charity, to restrict participation in the activity to
persons of one sex[10].

The Charity Commission for England and Wales[11] does not contravene the
Equality Act 2010 only by exercising a function in relation to a charity in a
manner which the regulator thinks is expedient in the interests of the charity,
having regard to the charitable instrument[12].

1   As to the introduction of the Equality Act 2010 see PARA 1.
2   Equality Act 2010 s 194(1), (2). As to race as a protected characteristic see PARA 58.
3   The Equality Act 2010 s 193(1) (see the text and notes 1–2, 4–7) does not apply (except so far as
    relating to disability) to a contravention of ss 39–41 (protection of employees: see PARAS 117–119)
    or (so far as relating to the provision of vocational training) s 55 (service providers in employment:
    see PARA 130): s 193(9), (10). As to disability as a protected characteristic see PARAS 47–55.
4   As to the protected characteristics generally see PARA 45 et seq.
5   Equality Act 2010 s 193(1)(a). 'Charitable instrument' means an instrument establishing or
    governing a charity (including an instrument made or having effect before the 1 October 2010 (ie
    the date on which ss 193, 194 were brought into force by the Equality Act 2010 (Commencement
    No 4, Savings, Consequential, Transitional, Transitory and Incidental Provisions and Revocation)
    Order 2010, SI 2010/2317)): Equality Act 2010 s 194(4). As to the meaning of 'charity' see the
    Charities Act 2011 s 1(1); and CHARITIES vol 8 (2015) PARA 1 (definition applied by the Equality
    Act 2010 s 194(3) (amended by the Charities Act 2011 Sch 7 para 144)). As to the construction
    of charitable instruments enabling the provision of benefits to persons of a class defined by
    reference to colour see the Equality Act 2010 s 193(4); and PARA 58.
6   Equality Act 2010 s 193(1)(b), (2)(a). See *Catholic Care (Diocese of Leeds) v Charity Commission
    for England and Wales* [2012] UKUT 395 (TCC), [2013] 2 All ER 1114, [2013] 1 WLR 2105.
7   Equality Act 2010 s 193(2)(b).
8   See the Equality Act 2010 s 193(5), (6); and PARA 324.
9   Ie the Equality Act 2010 s 29 (see PARAS 85–88).
10 Equality Act 2010 s 193(7).
11 As to the Charity Commission for England and Wales see CHARITIES vol 8 (2015) PARA 543 et seq.
12 Equality Act 2010 ss 193(8), 194(5)(a).

326. Exceptions relating to supported employment for the disabled.

It is not a contravention of the Equality Act 2010[1] for:

(1)   a person who provides supported employment[2] to treat persons who have the same disability or a disability of a prescribed description more favourably than those who do not have that disability or a disability of such a description in providing such employment[3]; or

(2)   a Minister of the Crown to agree to arrangements for the provision of supported employment which will, or may, have that effect[4].

1   As to the introduction of the Equality Act 2010 see PARA 1.
2   'Supported employment' means facilities provided, or in respect of which payments are made, under the Disabled Persons (Employment) Act 1944 s 15 (see EMPLOYMENT vol 40 (2014) PARA 610): Equality Act 2010 s 194(7).
3   Equality Act 2010 s 193(3)(a). At the date at which this volume states the law no description of disability had been prescribed for these purposes.
4   Equality Act 2010 s 193(3)(b).

327. Exceptions relating to nationality or residence.

A person does not contravene the provisions of the Equality Act 2010 relating to services[1], premises[2], work[3] or education[4], if he does an act which is authorised by statute or by the executive which discriminates on grounds of nationality[5] or residence[6]. Nor does a person contravene the Equality Act 2010 by making or continuing in force rules restricting to persons of particular birth, nationality, descent or residence, employment with the Crown or with certain public bodies[7].

A person who:

(1)   selects one or more persons to represent a country, place or area or a related association, in a sport or game or other activity of a competitive nature[8]; or

(2)   does anything in pursuance of the rules of a competition so far as relating to eligibility to compete in a sport or game or other such activity[9],

does not contravene the Equality Act 2010[10] only because of the nationality or place of birth of another or because of the length of time the other has been resident in a particular area or place[11].

A person (A) does not contravene the Equality Act 2010, so far as relating to nationality, only by providing a non-resident (B)[12] with training[13], if A thinks that B does not intend to exercise in Great Britain[14] skills B obtains as a result[15].

1   Ie the Equality Act 2010 Pt 3 (ss 28–31): see PARAS **84–104**.
2   Ie the Equality Act 2010 Pt 4 (ss 32–38): see PARAS **105–115**.
3   Ie the Equality Act 2010 Pt 5 (ss 39–83): see PARAS **116–172**.
4   Ie the Equality Act 2010 Pt 6 (ss 84–99): see PARAS **173–197**.
5   Nationality is a component of the protected characteristic of race: see PARA 58.
6   See the Equality Act 2010 Sch 23 para 1; and PARAS **95** (exceptions relating to the provision of services), 111 (exceptions relating to premises), 157 (exceptions relating to work), 196 (exceptions relating to education).
7   See the Equality Act 2010 Sch 22 para 5; and PARA **159**.
8   Equality Act 2010 s 195(6)(a).
9   Equality Act 2010 s 195(6)(b).
10 Ie the Equality Act 2010 (see PARAS **1–4**).
11 Equality Act 2010 s 195(5). As to exceptions relating to sport generally see PARA **328**.
12 A 'non-resident' is a person who is not ordinarily resident in an EEA state (or, in the case of training provided by the armed forces or Secretary of State for purposes relating to defence, Great Britain): Equality Act 2010 Sch 23 para 4(2), (5)(a). As to the Secretary of State see PARA 4.
13 The reference to providing B with training is:

(1)   if A employs B in relevant employment, a reference to doing anything in or in connection with the employment (Equality Act 2010 Sch 23 para 4(3)(a));

(2)   if A as a principal allows B to do relevant contract work, a reference to doing anything in or in connection with allowing B to do the work (Sch 23 para 4(3)(b)); or

(3)   in a case within head (1) or (2) above or any other case, a reference to affording B access to facilities for education or training or ancillary benefits (Sch 23 para 4(3)(c)).

Employment or contract work is relevant if its sole or main purpose is the provision of training in skills (or, in the case of training provided by the armed forces or Secretary of State for purposes relating to defence, if it is for purposes including the provision of training in skills): Sch 23 para 4(4), (5)(b). As to the meanings of 'contract work' and 'principal' see s 41; and PARA 119 (definitions applied by Sch 23 para 4(6)).

14 As to the meaning of 'Great Britain' see PARA 85 note 1.
15 Equality Act 2010 Sch 23 para 4(1).

328. Exceptions relating to sport.

A 'gender-affected activity' is a sport, game or other activity of a competitive nature in circumstances in which the physical strength, stamina or physique of average persons of one sex would put them at a disadvantage compared to average persons of the other sex as competitors in events involving the activity[1]. A person does not contravene the Equality Act 2010[2], so far as relating to the protected characteristic of sex[3], only by doing anything in relation to the participation of another as a competitor in a gender-affected activity[4].

An 'age-banded activity' is a sport, game or other activity of a competitive nature in circumstances in which the physical or mental strength, agility, stamina, physique, mobility, maturity or manual dexterity of average persons of a particular age group would put them at a disadvantage compared to average persons of another age group as competitors in events involving the activity[5]. A person does not contravene the Equality Act 2010, so far as relating to age discrimination[6], only by doing anything in relation to the participation of another as a competitor in an age-banded activity if it is necessary to do so to secure in relation to the activity fair competition or the safety of competitors[7], to comply with the rules of a national or international competition[8], or to increase participation in that activity[9].

There are also exceptions relating to the selection of competitors for national and regional teams[10], and exceptions relating to transsexual persons and sport, in the context of the provision of services[11] and the disposal and management of premises[12].

1   Equality Act 2010 s 195(3). In considering whether a sport, game or other activity is gender-affected in relation to children, it is appropriate to take account of the age and stage of development of children who are likely to be competitors: s 195(4). For a general discussion of the provisions of s 195 see *Chief Inspector of Education, Children's Services and Skills v Interim Executive Board of Al-Hijrah School (Secretary of State for Education intervening)* [2017] EWCA Civ 1426, [2017] All ER (D) 79 (Oct).

2   As to the introduction of the Equality Act 2010 see PARA 1.

3   As to sex as a protected characteristic see PARA 60.

4   Equality Act 2010 s 195(1).

5   Equality Act 2010 s 195(8) (s 195(7), (8) added by SI 2012/2466). The Equality Act 2010 (Age Exceptions) Order 2012, SI 2012/2466, was made under the Equality Act 2010 s 197: see PARA 96 note 2.

6   As to age as a protected characteristic see PARA 46.

7   Equality Act 2010 s 195(7)(a) (as added: see note 5).

8   Equality Act 2010 s 195(7)(b) (as added: see note 5).

9   Equality Act 2010 s 195(7)(c) (as added: see note 5).

10 See the Equality Act 2010 s 195(5), (6); and PARA 327.

11 Ie the Equality Act 2010 s 29 (see s 195(2); and PARA 104).

12 Ie the Equality Act 2010 ss 33, 34, or s 35 (see s 195(2); and PARA 115).

329. Exceptions relating to the provision of communal accommodation.
A person does not contravene the Equality Act 2010[1], so far as relating to sex discrimination[2] or gender reassignment discrimination[3], only because of anything done in relation to the admission of persons to communal accommodation[4] or the provision of a benefit, facility or service linked to the accommodation[5]. 'Communal accommodation' is residential accommodation which includes dormitories or other shared sleeping accommodation which for reasons of privacy should be used only by persons of the same sex[6], and may include:

(1)   shared sleeping accommodation for men and for women[7];
(2)   ordinary sleeping accommodation[8];
(3)   residential accommodation all or part of which should be used only by persons of the same sex because of the nature of the sanitary facilities serving the accommodation[9].

These provisions do not apply for the purposes of the provisions of the Equality Act 2010 prohibiting discrimination in the workplace[10] unless such arrangements as are reasonably practicable are made to compensate for the refusal[11] of use of the accommodation[12] or the refusal[13] of provision of the benefit, facility or service[14].

1   As to the introduction of the Equality Act 2010 see PARA 1.
2   As to sex as a protected characteristic see PARA 60.
3   As to gender reassignment as a protected characteristic see PARAS 56, 61.
4   Equality Act 2010 Sch 23 para 3(1)(a). Schedule 23 para 3(1)(a) does not apply unless the accommodation is managed in a way which is as fair as possible to both men and women (Sch 23 para 3(2)), and in applying Sch 23 para 3(1)(a) account must be taken of whether and how far it is reasonable to expect that the accommodation should be altered or extended or that further accommodation should be provided and the frequency of the demand or need for use of the accommodation by persons of one sex as compared with those of the other (Sch 23 para 3(3)). In applying Sch 23 para 3(1)(a) in relation to gender reassignment, account must also be taken of whether and how far the conduct in question is a proportionate means of achieving a legitimate aim: Sch 23 para 3(4).
5   Equality Act 2010 Sch 23 para 3(1)(b). A benefit, facility or service is linked to communal accommodation if it cannot properly and effectively be provided except for those using the accommodation and a person could be refused use of the accommodation in reliance on Sch 23 para 3(1)(a) : Sch 23 para 3(7).
6   Equality Act 2010 Sch 23 para 3(5).
7   Equality Act 2010 Sch 23 para 3(6)(a).
8   Equality Act 2010 Sch 23 para 3(6)(b).
9   Equality Act 2010 Sch 23 para 3(6)(c).
10 Ie the Equality Act 2010 Pt 5 (ss 39–83) (see PARAS 116–172).
11 Ie in a case where the Equality Act 2010 Sch 23 para 3(1)(a) applies (see the text and notes 1–4).
12 Equality Act 2010 Sch 23 para 3(8)(a).
13 Ie in a case where the Equality Act 2010 Sch 23 para 3(1)(b) applies (see the text and notes 1–5).
14 Equality Act 2010 Sch 23 para 3(8)(b).

(3) EXCEPTIONS RELATING TO PARTICULAR ARENAS OF DISCRIMINATION

330. Exceptions to the provisions on services and public functions.
There are exceptions to the provisions of the Equality Act 2010 prohibiting discrimination in the context of services and public functions[1] relating to:

(1)   specified constitutional and armed forces matters[2];
(2)   things done pursuant to the requirements of an enactment[3];
(3)   education[4];
(4)   health care[5];

(5)   nationality, residence and immigration[6];
(6)   religion, belief and charity[7];
(7)   insurance and other financial matters[8];
(8)   marriage[9];
(9)   the provision of different services for different genders[10];
(10)   the provision of certain age-based services[11];
(11)   broadcasting[12];
(12)   transport[13]; and
(13)   transsexual persons and sport[14].

1 Ie the Equality Act 2010 Pt 3 (ss 28–31) (see PARAS **84–104**). As to exceptions from the Equality Act 2010 generally, and as to further exceptions in specific circumstances, see PARAS **321–329**.
2 See PARA **91**.
3 See PARA **92**.
4 See PARA **93**.
5 See PARA **94**.
6 See PARAS **95–96**.
7 See PARA **97**.
8 See PARA **98**.
9 See PARA **99**.
10 See PARA **100**.
11 See PARA **101**.
12 See PARA **102**.
13 See PARA **103**.
14 See PARA **104**.

331. Exceptions to the provisions on premises.
There are exceptions to the provisions of the Equality Act 2010 prohibiting discrimination in the disposal and management of premises[1] relating to:
(1)   things done pursuant to the requirements of an enactment[2];
(2)   nationality or residence[3];
(3)   religion or belief[4];
(4)   owner occupiers[5];
(5)   small premises[6]; and
(6)   transsexual persons and sport[7].

1 Ie the Equality Act 2010 Pt 4 (ss 32–38) (see PARAS **105–115**). As to exceptions from the Equality Act 2010 generally, and as to further exceptions in specific circumstances, see PARAS **321–329**.
2 See PARA **110**.
3 See PARA **111**.
4 See PARA **112**.
5 See PARA **113**.
6 See PARA **114**.
7 See PARA **115**.

332. Exceptions to the provisions on work.
There are exceptions to the provisions of the Equality Act 2010 prohibiting discrimination in the workplace[1] relating to:
(1)   things done pursuant to the requirements of an enactment[2];
(2)   nationality or residence[3];
(3)   provision made for the protection of women[4];
(4)   Crown employment and public office[5];
(5)   occupational requirements[6];
(6)   age and duration of service[7]; and

(7)   benefits, public services and insurance contracts[8].

1   Ie the Equality Act 2010 Pt 5 (ss 39–83) (see PARAS 116–172). As to exceptions from the Equality Act 2010 generally, and as to further exceptions in specific circumstances, see PARAS 321–329.
2   See PARA 156.
3   See PARA 157.
4   See PARA 158.
5   See PARA 159.
6   See PARAS 160–163.
7   See PARAS 164–169.
8   See PARAS 170–172.

333. Exceptions to the provisions on education.
There are exceptions to the provisions of the Equality Act 2010 prohibiting discrimination in education[1] relating to:
(1)   things done pursuant to the requirements of an enactment[2];
(2)   nationality or residence[3]; and
(3)   provision made for the protection of women[4].

1   Ie the Equality Act 2010 Pt 6 (ss 84–99) (see PARAS 173–197). As to exceptions from the Equality Act 2010 generally, and as to further exceptions in specific circumstances, see PARAS 321–329.
2   See PARA 195.
3   See PARA 196.
4   See PARA 197.

334. Exceptions to the provisions on associations.
There are exceptions to the provisions of the Equality Act 2010 prohibiting discrimination by associations[1] relating to:
(1)   things done pursuant to the requirements of an enactment[2];
(2)   the restriction of membership to persons who share a protected characteristic[3];
(3)   membership concessions for persons of a particular age group[4];
(4)   membership restrictions to pregnant women on grounds of health and safety[5]; and
(5)   religion or belief[6].

1   Ie the Equality Act 2010 Pt 7 (ss 100–107) (see PARAS 198–210). As to exceptions from the Equality Act 2010 generally, and as to further exceptions in specific circumstances, see PARAS 321–329.
2   See PARA 207.
3   See PARA 204.
4   See PARA 205.
5   See PARA 206.
6   See PARA 208.

(4) EXCEPTIONS RELATING TO THE PROVISION OF INFORMATION SOCIETY SERVICES

335. Application of legislation to providers of information society services.
An 'information society service' is any service normally provided for remuneration[1], at a distance, by means of electronic equipment for the processing (including digital compression) and storage of data, and at the individual request of a recipient of a service[2]. Where a person concerned with the provision of an information society service (an 'information society service provider') is

established[3] in Great Britain, the Equality Act 2010 applies to anything done by the person in an EEA state (other than the United Kingdom) in providing the service as it would apply if the act in question were done by the person in Great Britain[4]; and where an information society service provider is established in an EEA state (other than the United Kingdom), the Act does not apply to anything done by the person in providing the service[5].

1   The requirement that services normally be provided for remuneration has caused problems in a number of cases. In *Metropolitan International Schools Ltd (t/a Skillstrain and/or Train2game) v Designtechnica Corpn (t/a Digital Trends)* [2009] EWHC 1765 (QB), [2010] 3 All ER 548, [2010] IP & T 1065, the court had, inter alia, to consider whether the search engine Google should be classed as an information society service provider. Although the matter was not felt to be free from doubt, it was held that the fact that any users can access its services free of charge, and that Google earned income indirectly from advertisers, was sufficient to bring it within the scope of the definition.

2   See the Equality Act 2010 Sch 25 para 7(2), (3) (amended by virtue of the Interpretation Act 1978 s 20A); Parliament and Council Directive (EC) 2000/31 (OJ L178, 17.7.2000, p 1) on certain legal aspects of information society services, in particular electronic commerce, in the internal market ('the Electronic Commerce Directive') recital 17, art 2(a) (which refers to Parliament and Council Directive (EC) 98/34 (OJ L204, 21.7.1998, p 37) laying down a procedure for the provision of information in the field of technical standards and regulations, art 1(2) (replaced by European Parliament and Council Directive (EU) 2015/1535 (OJ L241, 17.9.2015, p 1) laying down a procedure for the provision of information in the field of technical regulations and of rules on Information Society services, art 1(1)(b)) 'Recipient' means a person who (whether for professional purposes or not) uses an information society service, in particular for seeking information or making it accessible: Equality Act 2010 Sch 25 para 7(4). As to the Electronic Commerce Directive see INFORMATION TECHNOLOGY LAW vol 57 (2012) PARAS 587–598.

3   An information society service-provider is 'established' in a country or territory if the service-provider effectively pursues an economic activity using a fixed establishment in that country or territory for an indefinite period and is a national of an EEA state or a body mentioned in the Treaty on the Functioning of the European Union (Rome, 25 March 1957; TS 1 (1973); Cmnd 5179) art 54: Equality Act 2010 Sch 25 para 7(5) (amended by SI 2012/1809). The Treaty (commonly abbreviated to 'TFEU') was formerly known as the Treaty Establishing the European Community; it has been renamed and its provisions renumbered by the Treaty of Lisbon Amending the Treaty on European Union and the Treaty Establishing the European Community (Lisbon, 13 December 2007, ECS 13 (2007); Cm 7294). The presence or use in a particular place of equipment or other technical means of providing an information society service is not itself sufficient to constitute the establishment of a service-provider: Equality Act 2010 Sch 25 para 7(6). Where it cannot be decided from which of a number of establishments an information society service is provided, the service is to be regarded as provided from the establishment at the centre of the information society service provider's activities relating to that service: Equality Act 2010 Sch 25 para 7(7).

4   Equality Act 2010 Sch 25 para 1. As to the meanings of 'Great Britain' and 'United Kingdom' see PARA 85 note 1.

5   Equality Act 2010 Sch 25 para 2.

336.   Information society service providers acting as mere conduits.

An information society service provider[1] does not contravene the Equality Act 2010[2] only by providing so much of an information society service as consists in the provision of access to a communication network[3] or the transmission in a communication network of information provided by the recipient of the service[4], provided that the service provider does not:

(1)   initiate the transmission[5];
(2)   select the recipient of the transmission[6]; or
(3)   select or modify the information contained in the transmission[7].

1   As to the meanings of 'information society service' and 'information society service provider' see PARA 335.

2   Ie pursuant to the provisions of the Equality Act 2010 Sch 25 paras 1, 2 (see PARA 335).

3   Equality Act 2010 Sch 25 para 3(1)(a). For these purposes the provision of access to a communication network, and the transmission of information in a communication network, includes the automatic, intermediate and transient storage of the information transmitted so far as the storage is solely for the purpose of carrying out the transmission in the network (Sch 25 para 3(3)), although Sch 25 para 3(3) does not apply if the information is stored for longer than is reasonably necessary for the transmission (Sch 25 para 3(4)).
4   Equality Act 2010 Sch 25 para 3(1)(b). As to the transmission of information in a communication network see note 3.
5   Equality Act 2010 Sch 25 para 3(2)(a).
6   Equality Act 2010 Sch 25 para 3(2)(b).
7   Equality Act 2010 Sch 25 para 3(2)(c).

337. Information society service providers caching information.

Where an information society service[1] consists in the transmission in a communication network of information provided by a recipient of the service[2] the information society service provider[3] does not contravene the Equality Act 2010[4] only by doing anything in connection with the automatic, intermediate and temporary storage of information so provided if:

(1)   the storage of the information is solely for the purpose of making more efficient the onward transmission of the information to other recipients of the service at their request[5]; and

(2)   the service-provider does not modify the information[6], complies with such conditions as are attached to having access to the information[7], and (where applicable[8]) expeditiously removes the information or disables access to it[9].

1   As to the meaning of 'information society service' see PARA 335.
2   Equality Act 2010 Sch 25 para 4(1). As to the 'recipient' of a service see PARA 335 note 2.
3   As to the meaning of 'information society service provider' see PARA 335.
4   Ie pursuant to the provisions of the Equality Act 2010 Sch 25 paras 1, 2 (see PARA 335).
5   Equality Act 2010 Sch 25 para 4(2)(a).
6   Equality Act 2010 Sch 25 para 4(2)(b), (3)(a).
7   Equality Act 2010 Sch 25 para 4(3)(b).
8   Ie if the service-provider obtains actual knowledge that the information at the initial source of the transmission has been removed from the network, access to it has been disabled, or a court or administrative authority has required the removal from the network of, or the disablement of access to, the information: Equality Act 2010 Sch 25 para 4(4).
9   Equality Act 2010 Sch 25 para 4(3)(c).

338. Information society service providers hosting information.

An information society service provider[1] does not contravene the Equality Act 2010[2] only by doing anything in providing so much of an information society service as consists in the storage of information provided by a recipient of the service[3], if:

(1)   the service provider had no actual knowledge when the information was provided that its provision amounted to a contravention of the Act[4]; or

(2)   on obtaining actual knowledge that the provision of the information amounted to a contravention of the Act, the service provider expeditiously removed the information or disabled access to it[5].

1   As to the meanings of 'information society service' and 'information society service provider' see PARA 335.
2   Ie pursuant to the provisions of the Equality Act 2010 Sch 25 paras 1, 2 (see PARA 335).
3   As to the 'recipient' of a service see PARA 335 note 2. These provisions do not apply if the recipient of the service is acting under the authority of the control of the service provider: Equality Act 2010 Sch 25 para 5(2).

4   Equality Act 2010 Sch 25 para 5(1)(a).
5   Equality Act 2010 Sch 25 para 5(1)(b).

14. ENFORCEMENT AND PROCEDURE

(1) INQUIRIES AND INVESTIGATIONS BY THE EQUALITY AND HUMAN RIGHTS COMMISSION

(i) Inquiries by the Equality and Human Rights Commission

339. Commission's power to conduct inquiries.
The Equality and Human Rights Commission[1] may conduct an inquiry[2] into a matter relating to any of its duties concerning equality and diversity[3] and human rights[4].

If, in the course of an inquiry, the Commission begins to suspect that a person may have committed an unlawful[5] act:

(1)   in continuing the inquiry the Commission must, so far as possible, avoid further consideration of whether or not the person has committed an unlawful act[6];

(2)   the Commission may commence an investigation[7] into that question[8];

(3)   the Commission may use information or evidence acquired in the course of the inquiry for the purpose of the investigation[9]; and

(4)   the Commission must so far as possible ensure[10] that any aspects of the inquiry which concern the person investigated, or may require his involvement, are not pursued while the investigation is in progress[11].

The report of an inquiry may not state[12] that a specified or identifiable person has committed an unlawful act[13], and must not otherwise refer to the activities of a specified or identifiable person unless the Commission thinks that the reference will not harm the person, or that it is necessary in order for the report adequately to reflect the results of the inquiry[14]. However, an inquiry is not prevented from considering or reporting a matter relating to human rights[15].

Before settling a report of an inquiry which records findings which in the Commission's opinion are of an adverse nature and relate[16] to a specified or identifiable person the Commission must send a draft of the report to the person, specify a period of at least 28 days during which he may make written representations about the draft, and consider any representations made[17].

1   As to the establishment of the Commission see PARA 28.
2   At the date at which this volume states the law, the Commission's published Compliance and enforcement policy can be found on the Commission's website.
3   Ie under the Equality Act 2006 s 8 (see PARA 32).
4   Equality Act 2006 s 16(1) (amended by the Enterprise and Regulatory Reform Act 2013 s 64(8)). As to the Commission's duties concerning human rights see the Equality Act 2006 s 9; and PARA 33. As to the conduct of inquiries see further s 16(6), Sch 2; and PARA 340 et seq.
5   As to the meaning of 'unlawful' see PARA 32 note 8.
6   Equality Act 2006 s 16(2)(a).
7   Ie under the Equality Act 2006 s 20 (see PARA 347).
8   Equality Act 2006 s 16(2)(b).
9   Equality Act 2006 s 16(2)(c).
10   This may be by aborting or suspending the inquiry or otherwise: see the Equality Act 2006 s 16(2)(d).
11   Equality Act 2006 s 16(2)(d).
12   Ie whether expressly or by necessary implication: see the Equality Act 2006 s 16(3)(a).
13   Equality Act 2006 s 16(3)(a).
14   Equality Act 2006 s 16(3)(b).

15 The Equality Act 2006 s 16(2), (3) does not prevent an inquiry from considering or reporting a matter relating to human rights (whether or not a necessary implication arises in relation to the Equality Act 2010: Equality Act 2006 s 16(4) (amended by the Equality Act 2010 s 211(1), Sch 26 paras 61, 66; SI 2010/2279).
16 Ie whether expressly or by necessary implication: see the Equality Act 2006 s 16(5).
17 Equality Act 2006 s 16(5)(a), (b), (c).

340. Terms of reference for inquiries, investigations and assessments.
Before conducting an inquiry[1] the Equality and Human Rights Commission[2] must:

(1)   publish the terms of reference of the inquiry in a manner that it thinks is likely to bring the inquiry to the attention of persons whom it concerns or who are likely to be interested in it; and

(2)   in particular, give notice of the terms of reference to any persons specified in them[3].

Before conducting an investigation[4] the Commission must:

(a)   prepare terms of reference specifying the person to be investigated and the nature of the unlawful act which the Commission suspects;

(b)   give the person to be investigated notice of the proposed terms of reference;

(c)   give the person to be investigated an opportunity to make representations about the proposed terms of reference;

(d)   consider any representations made; and

(e)   publish the terms of reference once settled[5].

Before conducting an assessment of a person's compliance with a duty[6] the Commission must:

(i)   prepare terms of reference,

(ii)   give the person notice of the proposed terms of reference,

(iii)   give the person an opportunity to make representations about the proposed terms of reference,

(iv)   consider any representations made, and

(v)   publish the terms of reference once settled[7].

These requirements apply in relation to revised terms of reference as they apply in relation to original terms of reference[8].

1   Ie an inquiry under the Equality Act 2006 s 16 (see PARA 339).
2   As to the establishment of the Commission see PARA 28.
3   Equality Act 2006 Sch 2 paras 1, 2.
4   Ie an investigation under the Equality Act 2006 s 20 (see PARA 347).
5   Equality Act 2006 Sch 2 paras 1, 3.
6   Ie an assessment under the Equality Act 2006 s 31 (see PARA 300).
7   Equality Act 2006 Sch 2 paras 1, 4.
8   Equality Act 2006 Sch 2 para 5.

341. Opportunity for persons to make representations.
The Equality and Human Rights Commission[1] must make arrangements for giving persons an opportunity to make representations in relation to inquiries, investigations and assessments[2]. In particular, in the course of an investigation, inquiry or assessment the Commission must give any person specified in the terms of reference an opportunity to make representations[3].

The Commission is under a duty to consider such representations[4]. However, where it thinks it appropriate, the Commission may refuse to consider representations made neither by nor on behalf of a person specified in the terms of reference, or refuse to consider representations made on behalf of a person specified in the terms of reference by a person who is not a relevant lawyer[5]. If the Commission refuses to consider representations[6] it must give the person who makes them written notice of its decision and the reasons for it[7].

1 As to the establishment of the Commission see PARA 28.
2 Equality Act 2006 Sch 2 para 6(1). Such arrangements may, but need not, include arrangements for oral representations: Sch 2 para 7. As to inquiries under s 16 see PARA 339. As to investigations under s 20 see PARA 347. As to assessments under s 31 see PARA 300.
3 Equality Act 2006 Sch 2 para 6(2).
4 Equality Act 2006 Sch 2 para 8(1).
5 Equality Act 2006 Sch 2 para 8(2) (amended by the Legal Services Act 2007 s 208(1), Sch 21 para 152(a)). 'Relevant lawyer' means (1) an advocate or solicitor in Scotland; or (2) a person who, for the purposes of the Legal Services Act 2007, is an authorised person in relation to an activity which constitutes the exercise of a right of audience or the conduct of litigation (within the meaning of that Act): Equality Act 2006 Sch 2 para 8(2A) (added by the Legal Services Act 2007 s 208(1), Sch 21 para 152(b)).
6 Ie in reliance on the Equality Act 2006 Sch 2 para 8(2) (see the text and note 5).
7 Equality Act 2006 Sch 2 para 8(3).

342. Requirement to provide evidence to the Commission.

In the course of an inquiry, investigation or assessment[1] the Equality and Human Rights Commission may give a notice to any person[2] requiring him to:

(1)	provide information in his possession;
(2)	produce documents in his possession; or
(3)	give oral evidence[3].

Such a notice may include provision about the form of information, documents or evidence, or timing[4]. It may not require a person to provide information that he is prohibited from disclosing by virtue of an enactment[5]; nor may it require a person to do anything that he could not be compelled to do in proceedings before the High Court[6]. The notice may not require a person to attend at a place unless the Commission undertakes to pay the expenses of his journey[7].

The recipient of a notice may apply to the County Court to have the notice cancelled on the grounds that the requirement imposed by the notice is unnecessary having regard to the purpose of the inquiry, investigation or assessment to which the notice relates, or is otherwise unreasonable[8].

Where the Commission thinks that a person has failed without reasonable excuse to comply with a notice, or is likely to fail without reasonable excuse to comply with such a notice[9], then it may apply to the County Court for an order requiring a person to take such steps as may be specified in the order to comply with the notice[10].

A person commits an offence if without reasonable excuse he:

(a)	fails to comply with a notice or an order to comply with a notice;
(b)	falsifies anything provided or produced in accordance with a notice or an order to comply with a notice; or
(c)	makes a false statement in giving oral evidence in accordance with a notice[11].

However, where a person is given a notice he must disregard it, and notify[12] the Commission that he is disregarding it, in so far as he thinks it would require him to:

(i)	to disclose sensitive information[13];
(ii)	to disclose information which might lead to the identification of an employee or agent of an intelligence service (other than one whose identity is already known to the Commission)[14];

(iii)   to disclose information which might provide details of processes used in recruiting, selecting or training employees or agents of an intelligence service[15];

(iv)   to disclose information which might provide details of, or cannot practicably be separated from, information falling within any of heads (i) to (iii)[16]; or

(v)   to make a disclosure of information relating to an intelligence service which would prejudice the interests of national security[17].

Where the Commission receives information or documents from or relating to an intelligence service in response to a notice[18], the Commission must store and use the information or documents in accordance with any arrangements specified by the Secretary of State[19].

The recipient of a notice may apply to the High Court to have the notice cancelled on the grounds that the requirement imposed by the notice is undesirable for reasons of national security, other than for the reason that it would require a disclosure of a kind to which heads (i) to (v) apply[20].

1   Ie an inquiry under the Equality Act 2006 s 16 (see PARA 339), an investigation under s 20 (see PARA 347) or an assessment under s 31 (see PARA 300).
2   Equality Act 2006 Sch 2 para 9. As to the establishment of the Commission see PARA 28.
3   Equality Act 2006 Sch 2 para 10(1).
4   Equality Act 2006 Sch 2 para 10(2).
5   Equality Act 2006 Sch 2 para 10(3)(a).
6   Equality Act 2006 Sch 2 para 10(3)(b).
7   Equality Act 2006 Sch 2 para 10(3)(c).
8   Equality Act 2006 Sch 2 para 11 (Sch 2 paras 11, 12(2) amended by the Crime and Courts Act 2013 Sch 9 para 52).
9   Equality Act 2006 Sch 2 para 12(1).
10 Equality Act 2006 Sch 2 para 12(2) (as amended: see note 8).
11 Equality Act 2006 Sch 2 para 13(1). A person who is guilty of an offence under Sch 2 para 13 is liable on summary conviction to a fine not exceeding level 5 on the standard scale: Sch 2 para 13(2). As to the powers of magistrates' courts to issue fines on summary conviction see SENTENCING vol 92 (2015) PARA 176.
12 The Equality Act 2006 Sch 2 para 14(3) provides that where, in response to a notice, a person notifies the Commission that he is disregarding it, then:
    (1)   Schedule 2 paras 12, 13 do not apply in relation to that part of the notice under Sch 2 para 9 to which the notice under Sch 2 para 14(1) relates;
    (2)   the Commission may apply to the tribunal established by the Regulation of Investigatory Powers Act 2000 s 65 (see POLICE AND INVESTIGATORY POWERS vol 84A (2013) PARA 649) for an order requiring the person to take such steps as may be specified in the order to comply with the notice;
    (3)   the following provisions of the Regulation of Investigatory Powers Act 2000 apply in relation to proceedings under the Equality Act 2006 Sch 2 para 14 as they apply (with any necessary modifications) in relation to proceedings under the Regulation of Investigatory Powers Act 2000: s 67(7), (8), (10)–(12) (determination), s 68 (procedure), s 69 (rules) (see POLICE AND INVESTIGATORY POWERS vol 84A (2013) PARAS 651–653); and
    (4)   the tribunal must determine proceedings by considering the opinion of the person who gave the notice under the Equality Act 2006 Sch 2 para 14(1) in accordance with the principles that would be applied by a court on an application for judicial review of the giving of the notice.
13 See the Equality Act 2006 Sch 2 para 14(1)(a) (amended by the Justice and Security Act 2013 Sch 2 para 6). The following information is sensitive information (see the Justice and Security Act 2013 Sch 1 para 5; and CONSTITUTIONAL AND ADMINISTRATIVE LAW vol 20 (2014) PARA 247):
    (1)   information which might lead to the identification of, or provide details of, sources of information, other assistance or operational methods available to the Security Service, the Secret Intelligence Service, GCHQ or any part of a government department, or any part of Her Majesty's forces, which is engaged in intelligence or security activities;
    (2)   information about particular operations which have been, are being or are proposed to be undertaken in pursuance of any of the functions of those bodies; and

(3)   information provided by, or by an agency of, the Government of a country or territory outside the United Kingdom where that Government does not consent to the disclosure of the information.

'Intelligence service' means the Security Service, the Secret Intelligence Service, and the Government Communications Headquarters: Equality Act 2006 Sch 2 para 14(2). As to the Security Service, the Secret Intelligence Service and the Government Communications Headquarters see CONSTITUTIONAL AND ADMINISTRATIVE LAW vol 20 (2014) PARA 243 et seq.

14 Equality Act 2006 Sch 2 para 14(1)(b).
15 Equality Act 2006 Sch 2 para 14(1)(c).
16 Equality Act 2006 Sch 2 para 14(1)(d).
17 Equality Act 2006 Sch 2 para 14(1)(e).
18 Ie a notice under the Equality Act 2006 Sch 2 para 9 (see the text and notes 1–2).
19 Equality Act 2006 Sch 2 para 14(4). As to the Secretary of State see PARA 4.
20 Equality Act 2006 Sch 2 para 14(5).

343. Reports and recommendations by the Commission.

The Equality and Human Rights Commission[1] must publish a report of its findings on an inquiry, investigation or assessment[2].

In relation to an investigation, before settling a report recording a finding that a person has committed an unlawful act[3] or has failed to comply with a requirement or undertaking, the Commission must send a draft of the report to the person, specify a period of at least 28 days during which he may make written representations about the draft, and must consider any representations made[4].

The Commission may make recommendations as part of a report of an inquiry, investigation or assessment, or in respect of a matter arising in the course of an inquiry, investigation or assessment[5]. A recommendation may be addressed to any class of person[6].

A court or tribunal may have regard to a finding of the report of an inquiry, investigation or assessment, but must not treat it as conclusive[7]. A person to whom a recommendation in the report of an inquiry, investigation or assessment is addressed must have regard to it[8].

1 As to the establishment of the Commission see PARA 28.
2 Equality Act 2006 Sch 2 para 15. As to inquiries under s 16 see PARA 339. As to investigations under s 20 see PARA 347. As to assessments under s 31 see PARA 300.
3 As to the meaning of 'unlawful' see PARA 32 note 8.
4 Equality Act 2006 s 20(4).
5 Equality Act 2006 Sch 2 para 16(1).
6 Equality Act 2006 Sch 2 para 16(2).
7 Equality Act 2006 Sch 2 para 17.
8 Equality Act 2006 Sch 2 para 18.

344. Matters excluded from consideration by the Commission.

An inquiry, investigation or assessment[1] by the Equality and Human Rights Commission[2] may not question (whether expressly or by necessary implication) the findings of a court or tribunal[3].

An inquiry may not consider whether an intelligence service[4] has acted (or is acting) in a way which is incompatible with a person's human rights, nor consider other matters concerning human rights in relation to an intelligence service[5].

1 As to inquiries under s 16 see PARA 339. As to investigations under s 20 see PARA 347. As to assessments under s 31 see PARA 300.
2 As to the establishment of the Commission see PARA 28.
3 Equality Act 2006 Sch 2 para 19.
4 As to the meaning of 'intelligence service' see PARA 39 note 18.
5 Equality Act 2006 Sch 2 para 20.

(ii) Investigations by the Equality and Human Rights Commission

345. Unlawful acts to which the investigative provisions apply.
The Equality and Human Rights Commission[1] has power to investigate[2] the commission of acts which are unlawful under the Equality Act 2010[3] and, where applicable, to order the preparation of action plans for the purpose of addressing the unlawfulness[4]. For these purposes[5], an act[6] is 'unlawful' if it is contrary to any of the provisions of the Act[7]; but an act will not be 'unlawful' by reason only of the fact that it contravenes the public sector duty regarding socio-economic inequalities[8], the public sector equality duty[9], the provisions relating to disabled persons and transport[10] or the provisions relating to improvements to let dwelling houses[11]. In most cases[12], for the purposes of the provisions relating to the Commission's investigative and enforcement powers[13], it is immaterial whether the Commission knows or suspects that a person has been or may be affected by the unlawful act or application[14].

1 As to the Commission see PARAS **28–44**.
2 At the date at which this volume states the law, the Commission's published Compliance and enforcement policy can be found on the Commission's website.
3 As to the Equality Act 2010 see PARAS **1–4**; as to the Commission's investigatory powers see further PARAS **346–350**.
4 As to the preparation of action plans see further PARA **349**. The Commission may agree with persons not to proceed with an investigation, or not to issue an unlawful act notice, in return for an undertaking not to commit an unlawful act or to refrain from other specified activities: see the Equality Act 2006 s 23; and PARA **350**.
5 Ie for the purposes of the Equality Act 2006 Pt 1 (ss 1–42).
6 'Act' includes deliberate omission: Equality Act 2006 s 35.
7 Equality Act 2006 s 34(1) (s 34(1), (2) amended, by the Equality Act 2010 Sch 26 para 76(1)–(3) (amended by SI 2010/2279)). For the purposes of the Commission's investigative and enforcement powers (ie the Equality Act 2006 ss 20–24: see PARAS **346–350**), an unlawful act includes making arrangements to act in a particular way which would, if applied to an individual, amount to a contravention mentioned in s 24A(1)(a) (see note 11): s 24A(3) (s 24A added by the Equality Act 2010 Sch 26 para 68).
8 Ie a duty under or by virtue of the Equality Act 2010 s 1 (see PARAS **302–303**).
9 Ie a duty under or by virtue of the Equality Act 2010 s 149, s 153 or s 154 (see PARAS **276–301**).
10 Ie a duty under or by virtue of the Equality Act 2010 Pt 12 (ss 160–188) (see PARAS **211, 213, 215–236**).
11 Equality Act 2006 s 34(2) (as amended: see note 6). As to the provisions relating to improvements to let dwelling houses (ie the Equality Act 2010 s 190) see PARA **272**.
12 Ie in relation to:
   (1)   an act which is unlawful because, by virtue of any of the Equality Act 2010 ss 13–18 (discrimination other than indirect discrimination: see PARAS **67–74**), it amounts to a contravention of any of Pt 3 (ss 28–31) (services and public functions: see PARAS **84–104**), Pt 4 (ss 32–38) (premises: see PARAS **105–115**), Pt 5 (ss 39–83) (work: see PARA **116–172**), Pt 6 (ss 84–99) (education: see PARAS **173–197**) or Pt 7 (ss 100–107) (associations: see PARAS **198–210**) (Equality Act 2006 s 24A(1)(a) (as added: see note 7));
   (2)   an act which is unlawful because it amounts to a contravention of the Equality Act 2010 s 60(1) (enquiries about disability and health in a recruitment context: see PARA **133**) or to a contravention of s 111 or s 112 (instructing, causing, inducing or aiding contraventions: see PARAS **82, 83, 351**) that relates to a contravention of s 60(1)) (Equality Act 2006 s 24A(1)(b) (as so added));
   (3)   an act which is unlawful because it amounts to a contravention of the Equality Act 2010 s 106 (information about diversity in range of election candidates etc: see PARA **210**) (Equality Act 2006 s 24A(1)(c) (as so added));
   (4)   an act which is unlawful because, by virtue of the Equality Act 2010 s 108(1) (relationships that have ended: see PARAS **70, 80**) it amounts to a contravention of any of Pts 3, 4, 5, 6 or Pt 7 (Equality Act 2006 s 24A(1)(d) (as so added)); or

(5)   the application of a provision, criterion or practice which, by virtue of the Equality Act
2010 s 19 (indirect discrimination: see PARA 75) amounts to a contravention of that Act
(Equality Act 2006 s 24A(1)(e) (as so added)).

13 Ie for the purposes of the Equality Act 2006 ss 20–24 (see PARAS 346–350).
14 Equality Act 2006 s 24A(2) (as added: see note 7).

346. Injunctions.

If the Equality and Human Rights Commission[1] thinks that a person is likely
to commit an unlawful act[2] it may apply to the County Court for an injunction
restraining the person from committing the act[3].

1   As to the Commission see PARAS 28–44.
2   As to the acts which are unlawful for these purposes see PARA 345.
3   Equality Act 2006 s 24(1)(a) (amended by the Crime and Courts Act 2013 Sch 9 para 52(1)(b),
(2)). See, for example, *Equality and Human Rights Commission v Griffin* [2010] EqLR 42. An
injunction under these provisions may not impose on a person concerned with the provision of an
information society service consisting of access to a communication network or the transmission
in a communication network of information provided by the recipient of the service (ie a service
of a description given in the Equality Act 2010 Sch 25 para 3(1): see PARA 336), the transmission
in a communication network of information provided by a recipient of the service (ie a service of
a description given in Sch 25 para 4(1): see PARA 337), or so much of an information society
service as consists in the storage of information provided by a recipient of the service (ie a service
of a description given in Sch 25 para 5(1): see PARA 338), a liability the imposition of which would
contravene Parliament and Council Directive (EC) 2000/31 (OJ L178, 17.7.2000, p 1) on certain
legal aspects of information society services, in particular electronic commerce, in the internal
market ('the Electronic Commerce Directive'), arts 12, 13 or art 14 or a general obligation of the
description given in art 15: Equality Act 2010 Sch 25 paras 6, 7(3). As to the Directive see
INFORMATION TECHNOLOGY LAW vol 57 (2012) PARAS 587–598.

347. Investigations and unlawful act notices.

The Equality and Human Rights Commission[1] may investigate whether or not
a person has committed an unlawful act[2], but only if it suspects that the person
concerned may have committed the act[3]. Provision is made in connection with the
conduct of investigations[4]. If a person is or has been the subject of such an
investigation[5] and the Commission is satisfied that he has committed an unlawful
act[6], the Commission may give that person an 'unlawful act notice'[7] specifying the
unlawful act[8] and the provision of the Equality Act 2010 by virtue of which the
act is unlawful[9]. A notice may require the person to whom it is given to prepare
an action plan for the purpose of avoiding repetition or continuation of the
unlawful act[10] and recommend action to be taken by the person for that purpose[11]:
the Commission may also investigate a failure to comply with any such
requirement[12].

The Commission may agree not to investigate a person or issue an unlawful act
notice where that person undertakes not to commit the unlawful act and to take
or refrain from taking specified action[13], and may investigate whether a person has
complied with such an undertaking[14].

1   As to the Commission see PARAS 28–44.
2   Equality Act 2006 s 20(1)(a). As to the acts which are unlawful for these purposes see PARA 345.
3   Equality Act 2006 s 20(2). A suspicion for the purposes of s 20(2) may (but need not) be based on
the results of, or a matter arising during the course of, an inquiry under s 16 (see PARA 339): s
20(3).
4   See the Equality Act 2006 s 20(5), Sch 2; and PARAS 340–344.
5   Equality Act 2006 s 21(1)(a).
6   Equality Act 2006 s 21(1)(b).
7   Equality Act 2006 s 21(1). A notice must inform the recipient of the effect of s 21(5)–(7) (appeals:
see PARA 348), s 20(1)(b) (see the text and note 12) and s 24(1) (injunctions: see PARA 346): s
21(3).

8   Equality Act 2006 s 21(2)(a).
9   Equality Act 2006 s 21(2)(b) (amended by the Equality Act 2010 Sch 21 para 67 (amended by SI 2010/2279)). There is a right of appeal against an unlawful act notice: see the Equality Act 2006 s 21(5)–(7); and PARA 348.
10 Equality Act 2006 s 21(4)(a). In connection with action plans see further PARA 349.
11 Equality Act 2006 s 21(4)(b). In connection with agreements to take action see further PARAS 349–350.
12 Equality Act 2006 s 20(1)(b).
13 See the Equality Act 2010 s 23; and PARA 350.
14 Equality Act 2006 s 20(1)(c).

348. Appeals against unlawful act notices.

A person who is given an unlawful act notice[1] may, within the period of six weeks beginning with the day on which the notice is given, appeal against the notice on the grounds:

(1)   that he has not committed the unlawful act specified in the notice[2]; or
(2)   that a requirement for the preparation of an action plan[3] is unreasonable[4].

The appeal is to the court or tribunal to which a claim in respect of the alleged unlawful act[5] could be made, that is to say, the County Court or the employment tribunal[6]. On the appeal the court or tribunal may affirm, annul or vary a notice or requirement, and may make an order for costs or expenses[7].

1   As to the giving of unlawful act notices see PARA 347.
2   Equality Act 2006 s 21(5)(a).
3   Ie a requirement imposed under the Equality Act 2006 s 21(4)(a) (see PARA 347). In connection with action plans see further PARA 349.
4   Equality Act 2006 s 21(5)(b).
5   As to the acts which are unlawful for these purposes see PARA 345.
6   See the Equality Act 2006 s 21(7) (amended by the Crime and Courts Act 2013 Sch 9 para 52(1)(b), (2)). As to the County Court see COURTS AND TRIBUNALS vol 24 (2010) PARAS 758–802. As to the constitution and jurisdiction of employment tribunals generally see EMPLOYMENT vol 41A (2014) PARA 1399 et seq; as to proceedings before employment tribunals see EMPLOYMENT vol 41A (2014) PARA 1453 et seq.
7   See the Equality Act 2006 s 21(6).

349. Action plans.

Where a person has been given an unlawful act notice[1] which requires him[2] to prepare an action plan, the notice must specify a time by which the person must give the Equality and Human Rights Commission[3] a first draft plan[4], which the Commission may approve or require to be revised[5]. The Commission may apply to the County Court for an order requiring a person to give the Commission a first draft plan by a time specified in the order[6], for an order requiring a person who has given the Commission a revised draft plan to prepare and give to the Commission a further revised draft plan[7], or for an order requiring a person, over a five year period[8], to act in accordance with the action plan or take specified action for a similar purpose[9]. Failure to comply with any such order is an offence[10].

An action plan may be varied by agreement between the Commission and the person who prepared it[11].

1   Ie a notice under the Equality Act 2006 s 21 (see PARA 347).
2   Ie under the Equality Act 2006 21(4)(a) (see PARA 347).
3   As to the Commission see PARAS 28–44.
4   Equality Act 2006 s 22(1), (2).
5   After receiving a first draft plan from a person the Commission must either approve it (Equality Act 2006 s 22(3)(a)) or give the person a notice which states that the draft is not adequate, requires the

person to give the Commission a revised draft by a specified time, and may make recommendations about the content of the revised draft (s 22(3)(b)). The provisions of s 22(3) apply in relation to a revised draft plan as they apply in relation to a first draft plan: s 22(4). As to the consideration by the Commission of the adequacy of a draft action plan see s 22(8), Sch 2 paras 10–14 (but omitting references to oral evidence); and PARA 342.

6   Equality Act 2006 s 22(6)(a) (amended by the Crime and Courts Act 2013 Sch 9 para 52(1)(b), (2)).
7   Equality Act 2006 s 22(6)(b). In these circumstances an order must require the revised draft plan to be given by a time specified in the order (s 22(6)(b)(i)) and in accordance with any directions about the plan's content specified in the order (s 22(6)(b)(ii)).
8   Ie during the period of five years beginning with the date on which an action plan prepared by a person comes into force: Equality Act 2006 s 22(6)(c). An action plan comes into force:
    (1)   if the period of six weeks beginning with the date on which a first draft or revised draft is given to the Commission expires without the Commission giving a notice under s 22(3)(b) (see note 5) or applying for an order under s 22(6)(b) (see note 7) (s 22(5)(a)); or
    (2)   upon a court's declining to make an order under s 22(6)(b) in relation to a revised draft of the plan (s 22(5)(b)).
9   Equality Act 2006 s 22(6)(c).
10 A person commits an offence if without reasonable excuse he fails to comply with an order under the Equality Act 2006 s 22(6); and a person guilty of such an offence is liable on summary conviction to a fine not exceeding level 5 on the standard scale: s 22(9). As to the powers of magistrates' courts to issue fines on summary conviction see SENTENCING vol 92 (2015) PARA 176.
11 Equality Act 2006 s 22(7).

350.   Agreements not to investigate or issue unlawful act notice in return for restraint of unlawful acts.

The Equality and Human Rights Commission[1] may enter into an agreement with a person under which:

(1)   the person undertakes not to commit an unlawful act of a specified kind[2] and to take, or refrain from taking, other specified action[3]; and

(2)   the Commission undertakes not to investigate the person or issue an unlawful act notice[4] or in respect of any unlawful act of the kind so specified[5].

The Commission may enter into such an agreement only if it thinks that the person has committed an unlawful act[6], and an agreement may be entered into whether or not the person is or has been[7] the subject of an investigation[8]. The Commission may investigate whether a person has complied with an undertaking under these provisions[9], and if it thinks that a party to an agreement under these provisions has failed to comply, or is likely not to comply, with an undertaking under the agreement, may apply to the County Court for an order requiring the person to comply with his undertaking and to take such other action as the court may specify[10].

1   As to the Commission see PARAS 28–44.
2   Equality Act 2006 s 23(1)(a)(i). As to the acts which are unlawful for these purposes see PARA 345.
3   Equality Act 2006 s 23(1)(a)(ii). Specified action which may include the preparation of a plan for the purpose of avoiding an unlawful act: 23(1)(a)(ii).
4   Ie undertakes not to proceed against the person under the Equality Act 2006 s 20 or s 21 (see PARA 347).
5   Equality Act 2006 s 23(1)(b).
6   Equality Act 2006 s 23(2). A person will not be taken to admit to the commission of an unlawful act by reason only of entering into an agreement under these provisions: s 23(3).
7   Ie under the Equality Act 2006 s 20 (see PARA 347).
8   Equality Act 2006 s 23(4)(a). An agreement under s 23 may include incidental or supplemental provision (which may include provision for termination in specified circumstances) and may be varied or terminated by agreement of the parties: s 23(4)(b), (c).
9   See the Equality Act 2010 s 20(1)(c); and PARA 347.

10 Equality Act 2006 s 24(2), (3) (amended by the Crime and Courts Act 2013 Sch 9 para 52(1)(b), (2)).

(2) JURISDICTION TO DETERMINE CLAIMS UNDER THE EQUALITY ACT 2010

(i) Contraventions relating to Services, Public Functions, Premises, Education and Associations

A.   GENERAL JURISDICTION OF THE COUNTY COURT

351. Jurisdiction of the County Court.

The County Court has jurisdiction[1] to determine a claim relating to a contravention[2] of:

(1)   the provisions[3] relating to services and public functions[4] (apart from certain immigration cases)[5];

(2)   the provisions[6] relating to premises[7];

(3)   the provisions[8] relating to education[9] (apart from certain cases involving disabled pupils)[10]; and

(4)   the provisions[11] relating to associations[12] (apart from cases relating to diversity in political candidates)[13].

The County Court also has jurisdiction to determine claims relating to ancillary prohibited conduct relating to those provisions[14]. Provision is made in connection with the time within which proceedings on a claim must be brought[15] and for the remedies that the court may order[16].

1   In proceedings in England and Wales on a claim within the Equality Act 2010 s 114(1) (see the text and notes 2–13), the power under the County Courts Act 1984 s 63(1) (appointment of assessors: see CIVIL PROCEDURE vol 12 (2015) PARA 921) must be exercised unless the judge is satisfied that there are good reasons for not doing so: Equality Act 2010 s 114(7). As to the appointment of assessors see *Cary v Metropolitan Police Comr* [2014] EWCA Civ 987, [2014] EqLR 707, [2015] ICR 71 (an assessor should be a person of skill and experience in the matter to which the proceedings relate; but does not need to have special skills relating to the particular protected characteristic at issue). As to the role of assessors see further *Ahmed v Governing Body of University of Oxford* [2002] EWCA Civ 1907, [2003] 1 All ER 915, [2003] 1 WLR 995; *Appiah v Governing Body of Bishop Douglass Roman Catholic High School Governors* [2007] EWCA Civ 10, [2007] IRLR 264, [2007] ICR 897 (both decided under the Race Relations Act 1975 (repealed)). As to the exercise of this jurisdiction see PARAS 352–356. As to procedural provisions in connection with the burden of proof and the applicability of previous findings in proceedings see PARA 365.

2   The reference to a contravention of the Equality Act 2010 includes a reference to a breach of an equality clause or rule: s 113(5). For the purposes of Pt 9 (ss 113–141):

(1)   a contravention of s 108 (discrimination or harassment in relationships that have ended: see PARAS 70, 80, 237) relates to the Part of the Equality Act 2010 that would have been contravened if the relationship had not ended (s 108(6));

(2)   a contravention of s 111 (instructing, causing or inducing contraventions: see PARA 82) is to be treated as relating:

(a)   in a case within s 111(5)(a) (see PARA 82), to the Part of the Equality Act 2010 which, because of the relationship between A and B, A is in a position to contravene in relation to B (s 111(9)(a)); or

(b)   in a case within s 111(5)(b) (see PARA 82), to the Part of the Equality Act 2010 which, because of the relationship between B and C, B is in a position to contravene in relation to C (s 111(9)(b)); and

(3)   a contravention of s 112 (aiding contraventions: see PARA 83) is to be treated as relating to the provision of the Act to which the basic contravention relates (s 112(5)).

Part 9 applies to a contravention of s 110 (liability of employees or agents: see PARA 120) by an employee or agent as if it were a contravention by a principal or employer: s 110(6). Part 9 Ch 2 (ss 114–119) and Pt 9 Ch 3 (ss 120–126) do not apply to proceedings relating to an equality clause or rule except in so far as Pt 9 Ch 4 (ss 127–135) provides for that: s 113(6). As to the meanings of 'equality clause' and 'equality rule' see PARA 117 note 4. As to jurisdiction over contraventions of the Equality Act 2010 generally see PARA 6. Where a claim or complaint is transferred in accordance with s 140 (concurrent litigation: see PARA) a reference to a claim within s 114(1) includes a reference to a claim transferred to a court under s 140: s 140(4)(a).

3   Ie the Equality Act 2010 Pt 3 (ss 28–31): see PARAS 84–104.
4   Equality Act 2010 s 114(1)(a) (amended by the Crime and Courts Act 2013 Sch 9 para 52).
5   The Equality Act 2010 s 114(1)(a) does not apply to a claim within s 115 (immigration cases: see PARA 352): s 114(2).
6   Ie the Equality Act 2010 Pt 4 (ss 32–38): see PARAS 105–115.
7   Equality Act 2010 s 114(1)(b).
8   Ie the Equality Act 2010 Pt 6 (ss 84–99): see PARAS 173–197.
9   Equality Act 2010 s 114(1)(c).
10 The Equality Act 2010 s 114(1)(c) does not apply to a claim within s 116 (matters involving disabled pupils), which will instead be heard by the First-tier Tribunal or the Special Educational Needs Tribunal for Wales (see PARA 356): s 114(3).
11 Ie the Equality Act 2010 Pt 7 (ss 100–107) (see PARAS 198–210).
12 Equality Act 2010 s 114(1)(d).
13 The Equality Act 2010 s 114(1)(d) does not apply to a contravention of s 106 (information about diversity in range of candidates: see PARA 210): s 114(4).
14 Ie the Equality Act 2010 s 108 (relationships that have ended: see PARA 70), s 111 (instructing, causing or inducing contraventions: see PARA 82) or s 112 (aiding contraventions: see PARA 83) that relates to Pt 3, Pt 4, Pt 6 or Pt 7: s 114(1)(e) (as amended: see note 4).
15 See PARA 353.
16 See PARA 355.

352. No County Court jurisdiction in certain immigration cases.

The County Court does not have jurisdiction to determine a claim relating to a contravention of the provisions on services and public functions[1] if the claim relates to the act of an immigration authority[2] in taking:

(1)   a decision under the Immigration Acts[3] relating to the entitlement of a person to enter or remain in the United Kingdom[4];

(2)   a decision on an appeal under the immigration provisions relating to such a decision[5],

and:

(a)   the question whether the act is a contravention of the provisions on services and public functions has been or could be raised on an appeal which is pending[6], or could be brought, under the immigration provisions[7]; or

(b)   it has been decided on an appeal under those provisions that the act is not a contravention of the provisions on services and public functions[8].

The decision in question is not subject to challenge in proceedings on a claim relating to a contravention of the provisions on services and public functions[9] or affected by the decision of the court in such proceedings[10].

1   Ie jurisdiction under the Equality Act 2010 s 114 (see PARA 351) relating to a contravention of Pt 3 (ss 28–31) (see PARAS 84–104). As to the meaning of 'contravention' for these purposes see PARA 6 note 12. As to jurisdiction over contraventions of the Equality Act 2010 generally see PARA 6. As to procedural provisions in connection with the burden of proof and the applicability of previous findings in proceedings see PARA 365.
2   Each of the following is an immigration authority for these purposes: the Secretary of State; an immigration officer; and a person responsible for the grant or refusal of entry clearance (within the meaning of the Immigration Act 1971 s 33(1): see IMMIGRATION AND ASYLUM vol 57 (2012) PARA 28): Equality Act 2010 s 115(4). As to the Secretary of State see PARA 4.

3   As to the Immigration Acts see IMMIGRATION AND ASYLUM.
4   Equality Act 2010 ss 114(2), 115(6)(a). The decision referred to in the text is a 'relevant decision' for the purposes of s 115. As to the meaning of 'United Kingdom' see PARA 85 note 1.
5   Equality Act 2010 ss 114(2), 115(6)(b). The decision referred to in the text is a 'relevant decision' for the purposes of s 115.
6   An appeal is pending if it is pending for the purposes of the Nationality, Immigration and Asylum Act 2002 s 104 (see IMMIGRATION AND ASYLUM vol 57 (2012) PARA 402) or (as the case may be) for the purposes of s 104 as it is applied by the Special Immigration Appeals Commission Act 1997 s 2(2)(j) (see IMMIGRATION AND ASYLUM vol 57 (2012) PARA 436): Equality Act 2010 s 115(7).
7   Equality Act 2010 s 115(1)(a). For these purposes, a power to grant permission to appeal out of time must be ignored: s 115(3). For the purposes of proceedings on a claim within s 114(1)(a) (see PARA 351) a decision in proceedings on a claim mentioned in s 115(1) that an act is a contravention of Pt 3 is binding (s 114(5)(a)) and it does not matter whether the act occurs outside the United Kingdom (s 114(5)(b)) The 'immigration provisions' are the Special Immigration Appeals Commission Act 1997 (see IMMIGRATION AND ASYLUM vol 57 (2012) PARAS 430–456) or the Nationality, Immigration and Asylum Act 2002 Pt 5 (ss 81–115) (see IMMIGRATION AND ASYLUM vol 57 (2012) PARA 391 et seq): Equality Act 2010 s 115(5). The provisions of s 115 apply in relation to reviews under the Special Immigration Appeals Commission Act 1997 ss 2D, 2E (see IMMIGRATION AND ASYLUM vol 57 (2012) PARAS 400, 434A) as they apply in relation to appeals under the immigration provisions: Equality Act 2010 s 115(8) (added by the Justice and Security Act 2013 Sch 2 para 12; and amended by the Immigration Act 2014 Sch 9 para 59).
8   Equality Act 2010 s 115(1)(b).
9   Ie a claim within the Equality Act 2010 s 114(1)(a) (see PARA 351).
10 Equality Act 2010 s 115(2).

353. Time limits for bringing claims.

Proceedings on a claim before the County Court[1] may not in general be brought after the end of the period of six months starting with the date of the act to which the claim relates[2] or such other period as the County Court thinks just and equitable[3], although special provision is made in connection with complaints under the student complaints scheme[4], certain cross-border disputes referred for mediation[5], certain disputes subject to alternative dispute resolution ('ADR')[6] and certain immigration matters[7].

1   Ie proceedings on a claim within the Equality Act 2010 s 114 (see PARA 351).
2   Equality Act 2010 s 118(1)(a) (amended by SI 2011/1133; and SI 2015/1392). For the purposes of s 118, conduct extending over a period is to be treated as done at the end of the period and failure to do something is to be treated as occurring when the person in question decided on it: Equality Act 2010 s 118(6). In the absence of evidence to the contrary, a person is to be taken to decide on failure to do something when he does an act inconsistent with doing it or if he does no inconsistent act, on the expiry of the period in which that person might reasonably have been expected to do it: s 118(7).
3   Equality Act 2010 s 118(1)(b). See note 2.
4   See the Equality Act 2010 s 118(2), (3) (s 118(2) amended by the Enterprise and Regulatory Reform Act 2013, s 64(12), (13)(a)).The 'student complaints scheme' means a scheme for the review of qualifying complaints (within the meaning of the Higher Education Act 2004 s 12: see EDUCATION vol 36 (2015) PARA 1090) that is provided by the designated operator (within the meaning of s 13(5)(b): see EDUCATION vol 36 (2015) PARA 1091): Equality Act 2010 s 118(8). Where the claim relates to the act of a qualifying institution and a complaint relating to the act is referred under the student complaints scheme before the end of the period of 6 months starting with the date of the act (s 118(3)), s 118(1)(a) (see the text and notes 1–2) has effect as if for 6 months there was substituted 9 months (s 118(2) (as so amended)). As to the meaning of 'qualifying institution' see the Higher Education Act 2004 s 11; and EDUCATION vol 36 (2015) PARA 1090) (definition applied by the Equality Act 2010 s 118(8)). As from a day to be appointed, s 118(8) (definition of 'qualifying institution') is amended by the Higher Education and Research Act 2017 s 89(6). At the date at which this volume states the law no such day had been appointed.
5   Where a time limit is set by the Equality Act 2010 s 118(1)(a) (see the text and notes 1–2), s 118(2) (see note 4) or s 129(3) (see PARA 361) in relation to the whole or part of a dispute to which Parliament and Council Directive (EC) 2008/52 (OJ L136, 24.5.2008, p 3) on certain aspects of mediation in civil and commercial matters ('the Mediation Directive') art 8.1 applies (a 'relevant dispute'), a mediation in relation to the relevant dispute starts before the time limit expires, and,

if not extended by these provisions, the time limit would expire before the mediation ends or less than eight weeks after it ends, the time limit expires instead at the end of 8 weeks after the mediation ends: Equality Act 2010 s 140A(1)(a), (d), (2), (3) (s 140A added by SI 2011/1133). As to the meanings of 'mediation' and 'mediator' see the Mediation Directive art 3(a), (b) (definitions applied by the Equality Act 2010 s 140A(1)(b), (c) (as so added)). In the case of any relevant dispute, references in s 140A to a mediation are references to the mediation so far as it relates to that dispute, and references to a party are to be read accordingly: s 140A(12) (as so added). If such a time limit has been extended by s 140A, these provisions apply to the extended time limit as they apply to that time limit: s 140A(4) (as so added). Where more than one time limit applies in relation to a relevant dispute, the extension by s 140A(3) of one of those time limits does not affect the others: s 140A(8) (as so added). Where a court or tribunal has power under s 118(1)(b) to extend a period of limitation, the power is exercisable in relation to the period of limitation as extended by s 140A: s 140A(13) (as so added).

For the purposes of s 140A, a mediation starts on the date of the agreement to mediate that is entered into by the parties and the mediator (s 140A(9) (as so added)) ends on the date of the first of these to occur:

(1)   the parties reach an agreement in resolution of the relevant dispute (s 140A(10)(a) (as so added));

(2)   a party completes the notification of the other parties that it has withdrawn from the mediation (s 140A(10)(b) (as so added));

(3)   a party to whom a qualifying request (ie a request by a party that another (A) confirm to all parties that A is continuing with the mediation) is made fails to give a response reaching the other parties within 14 days of the request (s 140A(10)(c), (11) (as so added));

(4)   the parties, after being notified that the mediator's appointment has ended (by death, resignation or otherwise), fail to agree within 14 days to seek to appoint a replacement mediator (s 140A(10)(d) (as so added)); or

(5)   the mediation otherwise comes to an end pursuant to the terms of the agreement to mediate(s 140A(10)(e) (as so added)).

The limits set out in s 118 are subject to these provisions: s 118(1) (as amended: see note 2).

6   Where a time limit is set by the Equality Act 2010 s 118(1)(a) (see the text and notes 1–2), s 118(2) (see note 4) in relation to the whole or part of a dispute to which Parliament and Council Directive (EU) 2013/11 (OJ L165 18.6.2013, p 63) on alternative dispute resolution for consumer disputes and amending Regulation (EC) 2006/2004 and Directive (EC) 2009/22 (Directive on Consumer ADR) art 12(1) applies (a 'relevant dispute'), a non-binding ADR procedure in relation to the relevant dispute starts before the time limit expires, and if not extended by these provisions, the time limit would expire before the non-binding ADR procedure ends or less than eight weeks after it ends, then, for the purposes of initiating judicial proceedings, the time limit expires instead at the end of eight weeks after the non-binding ADR procedure ends: Equality Act 2010 s 140AA(1)(a), (f), (2), (3) (s 140AA added by SI 2015/1392). 'Non-binding ADR procedure' means an ADR procedure the outcome of which is not binding on the parties: Equality Act 2010 s 140AA(1)(e). As to the meaning of 'ADR procedure' see the ADR Directive art 4(1)(g) (definition applied by the Equality Act 2010 s 140AA(1)(d) (as so added)). In the case of any relevant dispute, references in s 140AA to a non-binding ADR procedure are references to the non-binding ADR procedure so far as it relates to that dispute, and references to a party are to be read accordingly: s 140AA(9). If such a time limit has been extended by s 140AA, these provisions apply to the extended time limit as they apply to that time limit: s 140AA(4) (as so added). Where more than one time limit applies in relation to a relevant dispute, the extension by s 140AA(3) of one of those time limits does not affect the others: s 140AA(5) (as so added). Where a court or tribunal has power under s 118(1)(b) to extend a period of limitation, the power is exercisable in relation to the period of limitation as extended by s 140AA: s 140AA(10) (as so added).

For the purposes of s 140AA, a non-binding ADR procedure starts in relation to a relevant dispute on the date when the dispute is first sent or otherwise communicated to the ADR entity in accordance with the entity's rules regarding the submission of complaints: s 140AA(6) (as so added). As to the meaning of 'ADR entity' see the ADR Directive art 4(1)(h) (definition applied by the Equality Act 2010 s 140AA(1)(b) (as so added)). For the purposes of s 140AA, the non-binding ADR procedure ends on the date of the first of these to occur:

(1)   the parties reach an agreement in resolution of the relevant dispute (s 140AA(7)(a) (as so added));

(2)   a party completes the notification of the other parties that it has withdrawn from the non-binding ADR procedure (s 140AA(7)(b) (as so added));

(3)   a party to whom a qualifying request (ie a request by a party that another (A) confirm to all parties that A is continuing with the non-binding ADR procedure) is made fails to give a response reaching the other parties within 14 days of the request (s 140AA(7)(c), (8) (as so added));

(4)   that the ADR entity notifies the party that submitted the relevant dispute to the ADR entity that, in accordance with its policy, the ADR entity refuses to deal with the relevant dispute (s 140AA(7)(d) (as so added));

(5)   after the parties are notified that the ADR entity can no longer act in relation to the relevant dispute (for whatever reason), the parties fail to agree within 14 days to submit the dispute to an alternative ADR entity (s 140AA(7)(e) (as so added));

(6)   the non-binding ADR procedure otherwise comes to an end pursuant to the rules of the ADR entity (s 140AA(7)(f) (as so added)).

The limits set out in s 118 are subject to these provisions: s 118(1) (as amended: see note 2).

7   If it has been decided under the immigration provisions that the act of an immigration authority in taking a relevant decision is a contravention of the Equality Act 2010 Pt 3 (ss 28–31), proceedings on the claim may not be brought after the end of the period of 6 months starting with the day after the expiry of the period during which, as a result of s 114(2) (no County Court jurisdiction in certain immigration cases: see PARA 352), proceedings could not be brought in reliance on s 114(1)(a) (see PARA 351) or such other period as the County Court thinks just and equitable: s 118(1), (5). As to the meaning of 'immigration authority', 'immigration provisions' and 'relevant decision' see s 115; and PARA 352 notes 2, 4, 5, 7 (definitions applied by s 118(8)).

354. Exclusion from proceedings where there are national security considerations.

Rules of court may, in relation to proceedings on a claim within the jurisdiction of the County Court[1] confer power on the court, where the court thinks it expedient to do so in the interests of national security:

(1)   to exclude from all or part of the proceedings the claimant or pursuer, a representative of the claimant or pursuer, or an assessor[2]; and

(2)   to permit a claimant, pursuer or representative who has been excluded to make a statement to the court before the commencement of the proceedings, or part of the proceedings, to which the exclusion relates[3].

The rules may also confer power to take steps to keep secret all or part of the reasons for the court's decision[4].

At the date at which this volume states the law no such rules had been made.

1   Ie claims within the Equality Act 2010 s 114 (see PARA 351).
2   Equality Act 2010 s 117(1), (2). The Attorney General may appoint a person to represent the interests of a claimant or pursuer in, or in any part of, proceedings to which an exclusion by virtue of this provision relates: s 117(5). A person may be appointed under s 117(5) only if he is a person who, for the purposes of the Legal Services Act 2007, is an authorised person in relation to an activity which constitutes the exercise of a right of audience or the conduct of litigation (see LEGAL PROFESSIONS vol 65 (2015) PARA 356): Equality Act 2010 s 117(6)(a). A person so appointed is not responsible to the person whose interests he is appointed to represent: s 117(7).
3   Equality Act 2010 s 117(3).
4   Equality Act 2010 s 117(4).

355. Remedies.

If the County Court finds that there has been a contravention of an applicable provision[1] it has power to grant any remedy which could be granted by the High Court in proceedings in tort or on a claim for judicial review[2], although the power to award damages is restricted in cases of unintended indirect discrimination[3]. An award of damages may include compensation for injured feelings (whether or not it includes compensation on any other basis)[4]. The County Court must not grant a remedy other than an award of damages or the making of a declaration unless satisfied that no criminal matter[5] would be prejudiced by doing so[6]. The County Court must not grant an interim injunction unless satisfied that no criminal matter would be prejudiced by doing so[7], and must grant an application to stay proceedings under the applicable provisions on grounds of prejudice to a criminal matter unless satisfied the matter will not be prejudiced[8].

1   Ie a provision referred to in the Equality Act 2010 s 114(1) (see PARA 351).
2   Equality Act 2010 s 119(1), (2) (s 119(1) amended by the Crime and Courts Act 2013 Sch 9 para 52).
3   If the County Court finds that a contravention of a provision referred to in the Equality Act 2010 s 114(1) is established by virtue of s 19 (see PARA 75) but is satisfied that the provision, criterion or practice was not applied with the intention of discriminating against the claimant or pursuer, the court must not make an award of damages unless it first considers whether to make any other disposal: s 119(5), (6).
4   Equality Act 2010 s 119(4). As to the calculation of any damages in compensation for injury to feelings see *Pereira de Souza v Vinci Construction (UK) Ltd* [2017] EWCA Civ 979, [2017] IRLR 844; and *Vento v Chief Constable of West Yorkshire (No 2)* [2002] EWCA Civ 1871, [2003] IRLR 102, [2003] ICR 318.
5   'Criminal matter' means an investigation into the commission of an alleged offence, a decision whether to commence criminal proceedings, or criminal proceedings: Equality Act 2010 s 141(9).
6   Equality Act 2010 s 119(7).
7   Equality Act 2010 s 114(6)(a).
8   Equality Act 2010 s 114(6)(b).

B.   JURISDICTION OF TRIBUNALS IN MATTERS RELATING TO DISABLED PUPILS

356.   Jurisdiction of Tribunals.

A claim that a responsible body[1] has contravened the provisions relating to discrimination in schools[2] because of a person's disability may be made to the First-tier Tribunal in England or the Special Educational Needs Tribunal in Wales[3]. There are exceptions to this in connection with admissions decisions[4] and certain exclusions decisions[5] in circumstances where appeal arrangements[6] have been made: in those circumstances, a claim that a responsible body[7] has, because of a person's disability, contravened the provisions relating to discrimination in schools must be made under the appeal arrangements[8], and the body hearing the claim has the powers it has in relation to an appeal under the appeal arrangements[9].

Tribunal claims (not brought under appeal arrangements) may be made by the person's parent[10] or, in Wales (except in the case of appeals relating to admissions arrangements or exclusions[11]), by the person himself[12]. Proceedings on a claim may not be brought after the end of the period of six months starting with the date when the conduct complained of occurred[13], although the Tribunal may consider a claim which is out of time[14]. If the Tribunal finds that the contravention has occurred it may make such order as it thinks fit[15]. Procedural provision is made in connection with the bringing of claims[16] and, so far as relating to Wales, in connection with the appointment of persons to resolve disputes on behalf of the disabled child in question[17] and the provision of independent advocacy services[18].

The County Court does not have jurisdiction to determine a claim to which these provisions apply[19].

1   As to the meaning of 'responsible body' see the Equality Act 2010 s 85(9); and PARA 173 note 1 (definition applied by Sch 17 para 1).
2   Ie the Equality Act 2010 Pt 6 Ch 1 (ss 84–89) (see PARA 173 et seq).
3   Equality Act 2010 s 116(3), Sch 17, paras 1–3 (Sch 17 para 3 amended by the Children and Families Act 2014 s 60). As to the meanings of 'England' and 'Wales' see PARA 85 note 1. As to the meaning of 'contravention' for these purposes see PARA 6 note 12. As to jurisdiction over contraventions of the Equality Act 2010 generally see PARA 6. As to the First-tier Tribunal see COURTS AND TRIBUNALS vol 24 (2010) PARA 874 et seq; as to the Special Educational Needs

Tribunal in Wales see EDUCATION vol 36 (2015) PARAS 1034–1037. As to procedural provisions inconnection with the burden of proof and the applicability of previous findings in proceedings see PARA 365.

A party to any proceedings under Pt 6 Ch 1 before the Welsh Tribunal may appeal to the Upper Tribunal on any point of law arising from a decision made by the Welsh Tribunal in those proceedings: see the Disability Discrimination Act 1995 s 28JA(1) (s 28JA added by SI 2008/2833; repealed by the Equality Act 2010 Sch 27 (amended by SI 2010/2279); saved for these purposes by the Equality Act 2010 (Commencement No 4, Savings, Consequential, Transitional, Transitory and Incidental Provisions and Revocation) Order 2010, SI 2010/2317, art 6). Such an appeal may be brought only if, on an application made by the party concerned, the Welsh Tribunal or the Upper Tribunal has given its permission for the appeal to be brought: Disability Discrimination Act 1995 s 28JA(2) (as so added and saved). The Tribunals, Courts and Enforcement Act 2007 s 12 (proceedings on appeal to Upper Tribunal: see COURTS AND TRIBUNALS vol 24 (2010) PARA 928) applies in relation to appeals to the Upper Tribunal under the Disability Discrimination Act 1995 s 28JA as it applies in relation to appeals to it under the Tribunals, Courts and Enforcement Act 2007 s 11, but as if references to the First-tier Tribunal were references to the Welsh Tribunal: Disability Discrimination Act 1995 s 28JA(3) (as so added and saved).

4   An admissions decision is a decision of a kind mentioned in the School Standards and Framework Act 1998 s 94(1) or (2) (see EDUCATION vol 35 (2015) PARA 251) or a decision as to the admission of a person to an academy school or an alternative provision academy taken by the responsible body or on its behalf: Equality Act 2010 Sch 17 para 13(5) (Sch 17 paras 13(4), (5), 14(1), (5) amended, Sch 17 para 14(4) substituted, by the Education Act 2011 Sch 1 paras 11–13, Sch 15 para 2).

5   Ie decisions of a kind mentioned in the Education Act 2002 s 52(3) (see EDUCATION vol 35 (2015) PARA 517) in relation to a school in Wales: Equality Act 2010 Sch 17 para 14(1), (5) (as amended: see note 4).

6   In the case of admissions decisions, 'appeal arrangements' are arrangements under the School Standards and Framework Act 1998 s 94 (see EDUCATION vol 35 (2015) PARA 251) or academy arrangements (as defined in the Academies Act 2010 s 1: see EDUCATION vol 35 (2015) PARA 346) between the responsible body for an academy and the Secretary of State, enabling an appeal to be made by the person's parent against the decision: Equality Act 2010 Sch 17 para 13(4) (as amended: see note 4). In the case of exclusions decisions to which these provisions apply, 'appeal arrangements' are arrangements under the Education Act 2002 s 52(3) enabling an appeal to be made against an exclusion decision: Equality Act 2010 Sch 17 para 14(4) (as so substituted). As to the Secretary of State see PARA 4.

7   In the context of the bringing of claims under appeal arrangements relating to exclusions decisions in Wales 'responsible body', in relation to a maintained school, includes the discipline committee of the governing body if that committee is required to be established as a result of regulations made under the Education Act 2002 s 19 (see EDUCATION vol 35 (2015) PARA 195); and 'maintained school' has the meaning given in the School Standards and Framework Act 1998 s 20(7) (see EDUCATION vol 35 (2015) PARA 106): Equality Act 2010 Sch 17 para 14(6), (7).

8   Equality Act 2010 Sch 17 paras 13(1), (2), 14(1), (2) (Sch 17 para 14(1) as amended: see note 4).

9   Equality Act 2010 Sch 17 paras 13(3), 14(3).

10 Equality Act 2010 Sch 17 para 3 (as amended: see note 3).

11 Ie claims to which the Equality Act 2010 Sch 17 para 13 or Sch 17 para 14 applies: Sch 17 para 3A(2) (Sch 17 paras 3A, 4(2A), 6(3)(ca), 6A–6E added, Sch 17 para 6(2)(a) amended, by the Education (Wales) Measure 2009 ss 9–16 (substituted by SI 2011/1651)).

12 Equality Act 2010 Sch 17 para 3A(1) (as added: see note 11). The relevant person's right to claim is exercisable concurrently with the right of the relevant person's parent under Sch 17 para 3: Sch 17 para 3A(3) (as so added). The exercise of rights under Sch 17 para 3A is subject to provision made by regulations under Sch 17 paras 6, 6A (as to which see the text and notes 16–18): Sch 17 para 3A(4) (as so added).

13 Equality Act 2010 Sch 17 para 4(1). In Wales, this period may be extended by three months where the dispute has been referred for conciliation: see Sch 17 para 4(2A) (Sch 17 para 4(2A) as added (see note 11); amended by the Enterprise and Regulatory Reform Act 2013 s 64(14)). If the contravention is attributable to a term in a contract, the conduct is to be treated as extending throughout the duration of the contract: Equality Act 2010 Sch 17 para 4(5)(a). Conduct extending over a period is to be treated as occurring at the end of the period: Sch 17 para 4(5)(b). Failure to do something is to be treated as occurring when the person in question decided on it: Sch 17 para 4(5)(c). In the absence of evidence to the contrary, a person (P) is to be taken to decide on failure to do something when P acts inconsistently with doing it or if P does not act inconsistently, on the expiry of the period in which P might reasonably have been expected to do it: Sch 17 para 4(6).

14 Equality Act 2010 Sch 17 para 4(3). Schedule 17 para 4(3) does not apply if the Tribunal has previously decided under that provision not to consider a claim: Sch 17 para 4(4).
15 Equality Act 2010 Sch 17 para 5(1), (2). The power under Sch 17 para 5(2) may, in particular, be exercised with a view to obviating or reducing the adverse effect on the person of any matter to which the claim relates and does not include power to order the payment of compensation: Sch 17 para 5(3).
16 See the Equality Act 2010 Sch 17 paras 6, 6C, 6E (Sch 17 para 6 as amended and Sch 17 paras 6C, 6E as added: see note 11) and the Special Educational Needs Tribunal for Wales Regulations 2012, SI 2012/322 (proceedings on a claim to the Special Educational Needs Tribunal in Wales).
17 See the Equality Act 2010 Sch 17 para 6A (as added: see note 11). A local authority in Wales must arrange for the provision of advice and information about matters relating to disability discrimination in schools: see Sch 17 paras 6B, 6E (as so added).
18 See the Equality Act 2010 Sch 17 para 6D, 6E (as added: see note 11).
19 See the Equality Act 2010 ss 114(3), 116(1)(a), (b), (2), which provide that the powers of the County Court to determine a claim relating to a contravention of Pt 6 (education) (see PARA 6) do not apply to a claim which may be made to the First-tier Tribunal or the Special Educational Needs Tribunal for Wales under Sch 17 or to a claim which may be made in accordance with appeal arrangements within the meaning of Sch 17 paras 13, 14 (see the text and notes 4–9).

(ii) Contraventions relating to Work

357. Jurisdiction of employment tribunals.

An employment tribunal has jurisdiction to determine:

(1) a complaint relating to a contravention of the provisions relating to work[1] and a complaint relating to ancillary prohibited conduct relating to those provisions[2] (subject to certain restrictions relating to armed forces cases[3]);

(2) an application by a responsible person[4] for a declaration as to the rights of that person and a worker[5] in relation to a dispute about the effect of a non-discrimination rule in an occupational pension scheme[6];

(3) an application by the trustees or managers of an occupational pension scheme for a declaration as to their rights and those of a member in relation to a dispute about the effect of a non-discrimination rule[7]; and

(4) a question that relates to a non-discrimination rule and is referred[8] to the tribunal[9].

Provision is made in connection with the time within which proceedings on a complaint or application must be brought[10], and for the remedies that the tribunal may order[11].

1 Equality Act 2010 s 120(1)(a). The provisions relating to work are Pt 5 (ss 39–83) (see PARAS 116–172), although the provisions of s 120 do not apply to s 60(1) (enquiries about disability and health: see PARA 133): s 120(8). Section 120(1)(a) does not apply to a contravention of s 53 (discrimination by qualifications bodies: see PARA 129) in so far as the act complained of may, by virtue of an enactment, be subject to an appeal or proceedings in the nature of an appeal: s 120(7). As to the necessary requirements for such an appeal see *Michalak v General Medical Council* [2017] UKSC 71. The availability of judicial review does not preclude an employment tribunal from hearing a complaint against a medical qualifications body under the Equality Act 2010 s 120 where no statutory appeal to the High Court or internal review or appeal is provided for: *Michalak v General Medical Council* [2016] EWCA Civ 172, [2017] 2 All ER 534, [2016] All ER (D) 206 (Mar); affd [2017] UKSC 71. As to the meaning of 'contravention' see PARA 351 note 2. As to the meaning of 'enactment' see PARA 91 note 10. As to the exercise of this jurisdiction see PARAS 360–364). As to the constitution and jurisdiction of employment tribunals generally see EMPLOYMENT vol 41A (2014) PARA 1399 et seq; as to proceedings before employment tribunals see EMPLOYMENT vol 41A (2014) PARA 1453 et seq. This power is subject to s 121: see note 3. As to procedural provisions in connection with the burden of proof and the applicability of previous findings in proceedings see PARA 365.

Where a claim or complaint is transferred in accordance with s 140 (concurrent litigation: see PARA6) a reference to a complaint within s 120(1) includes a reference to a complaint transferred to an employment tribunal under s 140: s 140(4)(b).

2 Equality Act 2010 s 120(1)(b). The reference to ancillary prohibited conduct in the text is a reference to a contravention of the Equality Act 2010 s 108 (relationships that have ended), s 111 (instructing, causing or inducing contraventions) or s 112 (aiding contraventions) that relates to Pt 5 (see PARAS 70, 80, 82–83, 237, 351).

3 The Equality Act 2010 s 120(1) (see the text and notes 1–2) does not apply to a complaint relating to an act done when the complainant was serving as a member of the armed forces unless the complainant has made a service complaint (ie a complaint under the Armed Forces Act 2006 s 340A(1) or s 340A(2): see ARMED FORCES vol 3 (2011) PARA 756B) about the matter (Equality Act 2010 ss 121(1)(a), 141(8) (definition substituted by the Armed Forces (Service Complaints and Financial Assistance) Act 2015 Schedule para 15) and the complaint has not been withdrawn (Equality Act 2010 s 121(1)(b)). Where the complaint is dealt with by a person or panel appointed by the Defence Council by virtue of the Armed Forces Act 2006 s 340C(1)(a) (see ARMED FORCES vol 3 (2011) PARA 756B), it is to be treated for the purposes of the Equality Act 2010 s 121(1)(b) as withdrawn if the period allowed in accordance with service complaints regulations for bringing an appeal against the person's or panel's decision expires, and either the complainant does not apply to the Service Complaints Ombudsman for a review by virtue of the Armed Forces Act 2006 s 340D(6) (review of decision that appeal brought out of time cannot proceed); or the complainant does apply for such a review and the Ombudsman decides that an appeal against the person's or panel's decision cannot be proceeded with: Equality Act 2010 s 121(2) (s 121(2) substituted, s 121(3), (4) repealed by the Armed Forces (Service Complaints and Financial Assistance) Act 2015 Schedule para 13(2), (3)). The making of a complaint to an employment tribunal in reliance on the Equality Act 2010 s 120(1) does not affect the continuation of the procedures set out in service complaint regulations: s 121(5) (amended by the Armed Forces (Service Complaints and Financial Assistance) Act 2015 Schedule para 13(4)). 'Service complaints regulations' means regulations made under the Armed Forces Act 2006 s 340B(1) (see): Equality Act 2010 s 121(6) (added by the Armed Forces (Service Complaints and Financial Assistance) Act 2015 Schedule paras 12, 13(1), (5)). As to the Service Complaints Ombudsman see ARMED FORCES vol 3 (2011) PARA 756B.

   The service complaint which must be brought before there can be an application to a tribunal must be a valid service complaint, so if that complaint is brought out of time there cannot be a complaint to a tribunal: see *Molaudi v Ministry of Defence* (2011) UKEAT/0463/10, [2011] ICR D19, [2011] All ER (D) 72 (May) (decided under the Race Relations Act 1976 (repealed)).

4 As to the meaning of 'responsible person' see the Equality Act 2010 s 61(4); and PARA 134 note 4 (definition applied by s 120(2)).

5 A reference to a 'worker' is a reference to the person to the terms of whose work the proceedings in question relate: Equality Act 2010 s 141(3). A reference to the terms of a person's work is to be construed in accordance with Pt 5 Ch 3 (ss 64–80) (equality of terms: see PARAS 136–153): s 141(4).

6 See the Equality Act 2010 s 120(2). As to the non-discrimination rule see PARA 134: in proceedings before an employment tribunal on a complaint relating to a breach of a non-discrimination rule, the employer is to be treated as a party and is accordingly entitled to appear and be heard: s 120(5). Nothing in s 120 affects such jurisdiction as the High Court or the County Court has in relation to a non-discrimination rule: s 120(6) (amended by the Crime and Courts Act 2013 Sch 9 para 52). If it appears to a court in which proceedings are pending that a claim or counter-claim relating to a non-discrimination rule could more conveniently be determined by an employment tribunal, the court may strike out the claim or counter-claim: Equality Act 2010 s 122(1). If in proceedings before a court a question arises about a non-discrimination rule, the court may (whether or not on an application by a party to the proceedings) refer the question, or direct that it be referred by a party to the proceedings, to an employment tribunal for determination, and stay the proceedings in the meantime: s 122(2).

7 Equality Act 2010 s 120(3). A reference to a member of an occupational pension scheme includes a reference to a prospective member: s 141(5).

8 Ie by virtue of the Equality Act 2010 s 122 (see note 6).

9 Equality Act 2010 s 120(4).

10 See PARA 358.

11 See PARA 359.

358. Time limits for bringing proceedings.

Proceedings on a complaint to an employment tribunal[1] may not in general be brought after the end of the period of three months starting with the date of the act to which the complaint relates[2] or such other period as the tribunal thinks just and equitable[3], although special provision is made in connection with applicable armed forces cases[4], certain cross-border disputes referred to mediation[5] and in order to facilitate conciliation before institution of proceedings[6].

1   Ie proceedings on a complaint within the Equality Act 2010 s 120 (see PARA 357).
2   Equality Act 2010 s 123(1)(a) (amended by the Enterprise and Regulatory Reform Act 2013 Sch 2 para 43; and SI 2011/1133). For these purposes, conduct extending over a period is to be treated as done at the end of the period and failure to do something is to be treated as occurring when the person in question decided on it: Equality Act 2010 s 123(3). See *Hendricks v Metropolitan Police Comr* [2002] EWCA Civ 1686, [2003] 1 All ER 654, [2003] IRLR 96, where Mummery LJ said at [52]: 'the question is whether [there] is an 'act extending over a period' as distinct from a succession of unconnected or isolated specific acts, for which time would be given to run from the date when each specific act was committed'. See also *Aziz v FDA* [2010] EWCA Civ 304, (2010) 154 Sol Jo (no 14) 29. In the absence of evidence to the contrary, a person is to be taken to decide on failure to do something when he does an act inconsistent with doing it or, if he does no inconsistent act, on the expiry of the period in which he might reasonably have been expected to do it: s 123(4). In connection with time limits under these provisions see *Okoro v Taylor Woodrow Construction Ltd* [2012] EWCA Civ 1590, [2013] ICR 580, [2012] All ER (D) 23 (Dec) (decided under the Race Relations Act 1976 (repealed)); *Charles v Tesco Stores Ltd* [2012] EWCA Civ 1663, [2013] EqLR 260, [2012] All ER (D) 141 (Dec) (decided under the Race Relations Act 1976 (repealed)).
3   Equality Act 2010 s 123(1)(b). The 'just and equitable' provision gives the tribunal a wider discretion than under the equivalent power in general employment law (where the test is 'reasonably practicable'): see eg *Hutchison v Westward Television Ltd* [1977] IRLR 69, EAT (decided under the Sex Discrimination Act 1975 (repealed)); *Gloucester Working Men's Club and Institute v James* [1986] ICR 603, EAT; *British Coal Corpn v Keeble* [1997] IRLR 336 (decided under the Sex Discrimination Act 1975 (repealed)); *Biggs v Somerset County Council* [1996] IRLR 203.
4   Proceedings may not be brought in reliance on the Equality Act 2010 s 121(1) (see PARA 357) after the end of the period of 6 months starting with the date of the act to which the proceedings relate or such other period as the employment tribunal thinks just and equitable: s 123(2).
5   Where a time limit is set by the Equality Act 2010 s 123(1)(a) (see the text and note 2) in relation to the whole or part of a dispute to which Parliament and Council Directive (EC) 2008/52 (OJ L136, 24.5.2008, p 3) on certain aspects of mediation in civil and commercial matters ('the Mediation Directive') art 8.1 applies (a 'relevant dispute'), a mediation in relation to the relevant dispute starts before the time limit expires, and, if not extended by these provisions, the time limit would expire before the mediation ends or less than four weeks after it ends, the time limit expires instead at the end of four weeks after the mediation ends: Equality Act 2010 s 140A(1)(a), (d), (5), (6) (s 140A added by SI 2011/1133). If such a time limit has been so extended, these provisions apply to the extended time limit as they apply to the original time limit: Equality Act 2010 s 140A(7) (as so added). Where more than one time limit applies in relation to a relevant dispute, the extension by these provisions of one of those time limits does not affect the others: s 140A(8) (as so added). Where a court or tribunal has power under s 123(1)(b) (see the text and note 3) to extend a period of limitation, the power is exercisable in relation to the period of limitation as extended by s 140A: s 140A(13) (as so added). As to the meanings of 'mediation' and 'mediator' for these purposes, and as to the calculation of the dates on which mediations start and end, see s 140A(1)(b), (c), (9)–(11); and PARA 353 note 5.
    The limits set out in s 123 are subject to the provisions contained in s 140A: s 123(1) (as amended: see note 2).
6   Except in relation to a dispute that is (or so much of a dispute as is) a relevant dispute for the purposes of the Equality Act 2010 s 140A, where a time limit is set by s 123(1)(a), in working out when the time limit set by s 123(1)(a) expires the period beginning with the day after Day A and ending with Day B is not to be counted: s 140B(1), (3) (s 140B added by the Enterprise and Regulatory Reform Act 2013 Sch 2 para 45). Day A is the day on which the complainant or applicant concerned complies with the requirement in the Employment Tribunals Act 1996 s 18A(1) (see EMPLOYMENT vol 39 (2014) PARA 152) in relation to the matter in respect of which the proceedings are brought, and Day B is the day on which the complainant or applicant concerned receives or, if earlier, is treated as receiving (by virtue of regulations made under s 18A(11)) the certificate issued under s 18A(4): Equality Act 2010 s 140B(2). If the time limit set by s 123(1)(a) would expire during the period beginning with Day A and ending one month after Day B, the time

limit expires instead at the end of that period: s 140B(4). The power conferred on the employment tribunal by s 123(1)(b) to extend the time limit set by s 123(1)(a) is exercisable in relation to that time limit as extended by s 140B: s 140B(5).

The limits set out in s 123 are subject to the provisions contained in s 140B: s 123(1) (as amended: see note 2).

359. Remedies.

If an employment tribunal finds that there has been a contravention of an applicable provision[1] it may make a declaration as to the rights of the complainant and the respondent in relation to the matters to which the proceedings relate[2], order the respondent to pay compensation to the complainant[3], or make an appropriate recommendation[4], although the power to award compensation is restricted in cases of unintended indirect discrimination[5]. Additional remedies are available to the tribunal in relation to contraventions involving occupational pension schemes[6].

1 Ie a contravention of a provision referred to in the Equality Act 2010 s 120(1) (see PARA 357).
2 Equality Act 2010 s 124(1), (2)(a).
3 Equality Act 2010 s 124(2)(b). The amount of compensation which may be awarded under s 124(2)(b) corresponds to the amount which could be awarded by the County Court under s 119 (see PARA 355): s 124(6) (amended by the Crime and Courts Act 2013 Sch 9 para 52). See also note 5; and in connection with contraventions involving the membership of occupational pension schemes, see note 6. This will include compensation for injury to feelings, assessed in accordance with *Pereira de Souza v Vinci Construction (UK) Ltd* [2017] EWCA Civ 979, [2017] IRLR 844; and *Vento v Chief Constable of West Yorkshire (No 2)* [2002] EWCA Civ 1871, [2003] IRLR 102, [2003] ICR 318.
  Regulations may make provision for enabling an employment tribunal to include interest on an amount awarded by it in proceedings under the Equality Act 2010 and specifying the manner in which, and the periods and rate by reference to which, the interest is to be determined: s 139(1). Regulations may modify the operation of an order made under the Employment Tribunals Act 1996 s 14 (power to make provision as to interest on awards: see EMPLOYMENT vol 41A (2014) PARA 1481) in so far as it relates to an award in proceedings under the Equality Act 2010: s 139(2). As to the applicable regulations see the Employment Tribunals (Interest on Awards in Discrimination Cases) Regulations 1996, SI 1996/2803 (amended by the Employment Rights (Dispute Resolution) Act 1998 s 1(2); and by SI 2013/1669) (made under the Race Relations Act 1976 s 56(5), (6) (repealed) and the Disability Discrimination Act 1995 s 17A(6), (7) (repealed); continued in force by the Equality Act 2010 (Commencement No 4, Savings, Consequential, Transitional, Transitory and Incidental Provisions and Revocation) Order 2010, SI 2010/2317, art 21(1), Sch 7).
4 Equality Act 2010 s 124(2)(c). An appropriate recommendation is a recommendation that within a specified period the respondent takes specified steps for the purpose of obviating or reducing the adverse effect of any matter to which the proceedings relate: s 124(3) (s 124(3), (7) amended by, s 125 repealed by, the Deregulation Act 2015 s 2(1), (2)(a), (b)). If a respondent fails, without reasonable excuse, to comply with an appropriate recommendation, the tribunal may, if an order was made under the Equality Act 2010 s 124(2)(b) (see the text and note 3), increase the amount of compensation to be paid (s 124(7)(a) (as so amended)); if no such order was made, make one (s 124(7)(b)).
5 If the tribunal finds that a contravention is established by virtue of the Equality Act 2010 s 19 (see PARA 75) but is satisfied that the provision, criterion or practice was not applied with the intention of discriminating against the complainant, the tribunal must not order the respondent to pay compensation to the complainant pursuant to s 124(2)(b) (see the text and note 3) unless it first considers whether to act under s 124(2)(a) (see the text and note 2) or s 124(2)(c) (see the text and note 4): s 124(4), (5).
6 If an employment tribunal finds that there has been a contravention of a provision referred to in the Equality Act 2010 s 120(1) in relation to the terms on which persons become members of an occupational pension scheme (s 126(1)(a)) or the terms on which members of an occupational pension scheme are treated (s 126(1)(b)), then in addition to anything which may be done by the tribunal under s 124 (see the text and notes 1–6), the tribunal may also by order declare that the complainant has a right to be admitted to the scheme (if the complaint relates to the terms on which persons become members of a scheme) (s 126(2)(a)) or that the complainant has a right to membership of the scheme without discrimination (if the complaint relates to the terms on which members of the scheme are treated) (s 126(2)(b)). An order under s 126(2) may make provision as

to the terms on which or the capacity in which the claimant is to enjoy the admission or membership (s 126(4)(a)) and may have effect in relation to a period before the order is made (s 126(4)(b)). However, the tribunal may not make an order for the payment of compensation under s 124(2)(b) (see the text and note 3) unless the compensation is for injured feelings or the order is made by virtue of s 124(7) (see note 4): s 126(1), (3). As to the meaning of 'occupational pension scheme' see PARA **134** note 1.

(iii) Contraventions relating to Equality Clauses and Rules

360. Jurisdiction of employment tribunals.

An employment tribunal has jurisdiction to determine:

(1)   a complaint relating to a breach of an equality clause or rule[1];

(2)   an application by a responsible person[2] for a declaration as to the rights of that person and a worker[3] in relation to a dispute about the effect of an equality clause or rule[4];

(3)   an application by the trustees or managers of an occupational pension scheme[5] for a declaration as to their rights and those of a member in relation to a dispute about the effect of an equality rule[6]; and

(4)   a question that relates to an equality clause or rule and is referred[7] to the tribunal[8].

The tribunal's jurisdiction in these matters is subject to certain restrictions relating to armed forces cases[9]. Provision is made in connection with the time within which proceedings on a complaint or application must be brought[10], and for the remedies that the tribunal may order[11]. Provision is also made for determining, where necessary in proceedings under these provisions, whether work is of equal value[12].

1   Equality Act 2010 s 127(1). This includes jurisdiction to determine a complaint arising out of a breach of an equality clause or rule; and a reference in Pt 9 Ch 4 (ss 127–135) (see the text and notes 2–12; and PARAS **361–364**) to a complaint relating to such a breach is to be read accordingly: s 127(2). As to the meanings of 'equality clause' and 'equality rule' see PARA **117** note 4. As to the constitution and jurisdiction of employment tribunals generally see EMPLOYMENT vol 41A (2014) PARA 1399 et seq; as to proceedings before employment tribunals see EMPLOYMENT vol 41A (2014) PARA 1453 et seq. Nothing in s 127 affects such jurisdiction as the High Court or the County Court has in relation to an equality clause or rule: s 127(9) (amended by Crime and Courts Act 2013 Sch 9 para 52). As to procedural provisions in connection with the burden of proof and the applicability of previous findings in proceedings, and the collection of information see PARA **365**.
        In proceedings before an employment tribunal on a complaint relating to a breach of an equality rule, the employer is to be treated as a party and is accordingly entitled to appear and be heard: Equality Act 2010 s 127(8).
2   As to the meaning of 'responsible person' see the Equality Act 2010 s 80(4); and PARA **142** note 2 (definition applied by s 141(2)).
3   As to the meaning of 'worker' see PARA **357** note 5; and for the purposes of proceedings relating to an equality rule (see PARAS **140, 141**) or a non-discrimination rule (see PARA **134**), a reference to a worker includes a reference to a member of the occupational pension scheme in question: Equality Act 2010 s 141(3). A reference to a member of an occupational pension scheme includes a reference to a prospective member: s 141(5).
4   Equality Act 2010 s 127(3).
5   As to the meaning of 'occupational pension scheme' see PARA **134** note 1.
6   Equality Act 2010 s 127(4).
7   Ie by virtue of the Equality Act 2010 s 128(2), which provides that if in proceedings before a court a question arises about an equality clause or rule, the court may (whether or not on an application by a party to the proceedings), refer the question, or direct that it be referred by a party to the proceedings, to an employment tribunal for determination, and stay the proceedings in the meantime. In this regard see further PARA **362**. If it appears to a court in which proceedings are

pending that a claim or counter-claim relating to an equality clause or rule could more conveniently be determined by an employment tribunal, the court may strike out the claim or counter-claim: s 128(1).

8 Equality Act 2010 s 127(5).
9 Equality Act 2010 s 127(1). These provisions of s 127 do not apply to a complaint relating to an act done when the complainant was serving as a member of the armed forces unless the complainant has made a service complaint about the matter and the complaint has not been withdrawn: s 127(6). As to the meaning of 'service complaint' see PARA 357 note 3. The provisions of s 121(2)–(6) (see PARA 357 note 3) apply for the purposes of s 127(6) as they apply for the purposes of s 121(1): s 127(7) (amended by the Armed Forces (Service Complaints and Financial Assistance) Act 2015 Schedule para 14).
10 See PARA 361.
11 See PARA 364.
12 See the Equality Act 2010 s 131; and PARA 362.

361. Time limits for bringing proceedings.

Proceedings on a complaint or application relating to a breach of an equality clause or rule[1] may not in general be brought in an employment tribunal after the end of a specified period (the 'qualifying period')[2] which varies depending on whether the case in question is a stable work case[3], a concealment case[4], an incapacity case[5] or a standard case[6], although special provision is made in connection with certain cross-border disputes referred for mediation and in order to facilitate conciliation before institution of proceedings[7].

1 Ie a complaint relating to a breach of an equality clause or rule and an application for a declaration referred to in the Equality Act 2010 s 127(3), (4) (see PARA 360). As to the meanings of 'equality clause' and 'equality rule' see PARA 117 note 4.
2 Equality Act 2010 s 129(1), (2).
3 A stable work case is a case where the proceedings relate to a period during which there was a stable working relationship between the worker and the responsible person (including any time after the terms of work had expired): Equality Act 2010 s 130(1), (3). If the complaint or application relates to terms of work other than terms of service in the armed forces, the qualifying period in a stable work case (providing it is not also a concealment or incapacity case (see notes 4, 5) or both) is the period of 6 months beginning with the day on which the stable working relationship ended: s 129(3), (4). See *Slack v Cumbria County Council* [2009] EWCA Civ 293, [2009] IRLR 463, [2009] All ER (D) 54 (Apr) (decided under the Equal Pay Act 1970 (repealed)); *Fox v North Cumbria University Hospitals NHS* [2010] EWCA Civ 729, [2010] IRLR 804, [2010] All ER (D) 267 (Jun) (decided under the Equal Pay Act 1970 (repealed)). As to the meaning of 'worker' see PARAS 357 note 5, 360 note 3. As to the meaning of 'responsible person' see PARA 360 note 2. As to a reference to the terms of a person's work see PARA 357 note 5.
4 A concealment case in proceedings relating to an equality clause is a case where the responsible person deliberately concealed a qualifying fact from the worker and the worker did not discover (or could not with reasonable diligence have discovered) the qualifying fact until after the relevant day (Equality Act 2010 s 130(1), (4)); and a concealment case in proceedings relating to an equality rule is a case where the employer or the trustees or managers of the occupational pension scheme in question deliberately concealed a qualifying fact from the member and the member did not discover (or could not with reasonable diligence have discovered) the qualifying fact until after the relevant day (s 130(1), (5)). A qualifying fact for the purposes of s 130(4) or s 130(5) is a fact which is relevant to the complaint and without knowledge of which the worker or member could not reasonably have been expected to bring the proceedings: s 130(6). The relevant day for the purposes of s 129 is the last day of the employment or appointment or the day on which the stable working relationship between the worker and the responsible person ended: s 130(10). The qualifying period in a concealment case which is not also an incapacity case (see note 5) is the period of 6 months (or, if the complaint or application relates to terms of service in the armed forces, 9 months), beginning with the day on which the worker discovered (or could with reasonable diligence have discovered) the qualifying fact: s 129(3), (4). The qualifying period in a case which is a concealment case and an incapacity case is the period of 6 months (or, if the complaint or application relates to terms of service in the armed forces, 9 months) beginning with

the later of the days on which the period would begin if the case were merely a concealment or incapacity case: Equality Act 2010 s 129(3), (4). As to the meaning of 'occupational pension scheme' see PARA **134** note 1.

5   An incapacity case in proceedings relating to an equality clause is a case where the worker had an incapacity during the period of 6 months (or, if the complaint or application relates to terms of service in the armed forces, 9 months), beginning with the later of the relevant day (or the last day of the period of service during which the complaint arose) or the day on which the worker discovered (or could with reasonable diligence have discovered) the qualifying fact deliberately concealed from the worker by the responsible person (Equality Act 2010 s 130(1), (7), (8)); and an incapacity case in proceedings relating to an equality rule is a case where the member of the occupational pension scheme in question had an incapacity during the period of 6 months beginning with the later of the relevant day or the day on which the member discovered (or could with reasonable diligence have discovered) the qualifying fact deliberately concealed from the member by the employer or the trustees or managers of the scheme (s 130(1), (9)). A person has an incapacity if he has not attained the age of 18 or lacks capacity (within the meaning of the Mental Capacity Act 2005: see MENTAL HEALTH AND CAPACITY vol 75 (2013) PARA 603): Equality Act 2010 s 141(6). The qualifying period in an incapacity case which is not also a concealment case (see note 4) is the period of 6 months (or, if the complaint or application relates to terms of service in the armed forces, 9 months), beginning with the day on which the worker ceased to have the incapacity: s 129(3), (4). As to the qualifying period in a case which is a concealment case and an incapacity case see note 4.

6   A standard case is a case which is not a stable work case (see note 3), a concealment case (see note 4), an incapacity case (see note 5) or a concealment case and an incapacity case: Equality Act 2010 s 130(1), (2). The qualifying period in a standard case is the period of 6 months beginning with the last day of the employment or appointment (or, if the complaint relates to terms of service in the armed forces, the period of 9 months beginning with the last day of the period of service during which the complaint arose): s 129(3), (4).

7   The limits set out in the Equality Act 2010 s 129 are subject to the provisions relating to mediation in cross-border disputes contained in s 140A (see PARA **353** note 6), and the provisions relating to conciliation before institution of proceedings contained in s 140B (see PARA **358**) (s 129(3) (amended by the Enterprise and Regulatory Reform Act 2013 Sch 2 para 44; and SI 2011/1133)), except where the complaint relates to terms of service in the armed forces, in which case the limits set out in the Equality Act 2010 s 129 are subject to the provisions relating to conciliation before institution of proceedings contained in s 140B (see PARA **358**) only (s 129(4) (amended by the Enterprise and Regulatory Reform Act 2013 Sch 2 para 44)).

362.   Assessment of whether work is of equal value.

Where, in proceedings before an employment tribunal relating to a breach of an equality clause or rule[1], a question arises as to whether one person's work is of equal value to another's, the tribunal may, before determining the question, require a member of the panel of independent experts[2] to prepare a report on the question[3]. If the tribunal requires the preparation of such a report (and does not withdraw the requirement[4]), it must not determine the question unless it has received the report[5].

Where a question arises in proceedings as to whether the work of one person (A) is of equal value to the work of another (B), and A's work and B's work have been given different values by a job evaluation study[6], the tribunal must determine that A's work is not of equal value to B's work unless it has reasonable grounds for suspecting that the evaluation contained in the study was based on a system that discriminates because of sex[7] or is otherwise unreliable[8].

1   Ie proceedings before an employment tribunal on a complaint relating to a breach of an equality clause or rule or a question referred to the tribunal by virtue of the Equality Act 2010 s 128(2) (see PARA **360** note 7): s 131(1).

2   A reference to a member of the panel of independent experts is a reference to a person who is for the time being designated as such by the Advisory, Conciliation and Arbitration Service (ACAS) for these purposes and who is neither a member of the Council of ACAS nor one of its officers or members of staff: Equality Act 2010 s 131(8). As to ACAS see EMPLOYMENT vol 41A (2014) PARA 1213 et seq.

3   Equality Act 2010 s 131(2).

4 The tribunal may withdraw a requirement under the Equality Act 2010 s 131(2): s 131(3). If the tribunal withdraws such a requirement it may request the panel member to provide it with specified documentation and make such other requests to that member as are connected with the withdrawal of the requirement: s 131(3).

5 Equality Act 2010 s 131(4).

6 Equality Act 2010 s 131(5). As to the meaning of 'job evaluation study' see s 80(5); and PARA 137 note 7 (definition applied by s 131(9)).

7 Equality Act 2010 s 131(6)(a). For these purposes, a system discriminates because of sex if a difference (or coincidence) between values that the system sets on different demands is not justifiable regardless of the sex of the person on whom the demands are made: s 131(7). See *Armstrong (HBJ Claimants) v Glasgow City Council* [2017] CSIH 56, [2017] IRLR 993, Court of Session, Inner House.

8 Equality Act 2010 s 131(6)(b). See *HBJ Claimants v Glasgow City Council Court of Session (Inner House, Second Division)* [2017] CSIH 56, [2017] IRLR 993.

363. Special procedure on equal value claims.

Where there are proceedings before an employment tribunal involving an equal value claim[1] the procedural rules for employment tribunals[2] apply with specified modifications[3]. These modified procedural rules require the tribunal to conduct the following hearings:

(1)   a stage 1 equal value hearing[4];

(2)   a stage 2 equal value hearing[5];

(3)   a final hearing[6].

There may be more than one stage 1 or stage 2 equal value hearing in any case[7].

Where the tribunal has decided to require an independent expert to prepare a report on the question whether the claimant's work is of equal value to that of the comparator[8], it may at any stage of the proceedings, on its own initiative or on the application of a party, order the independent expert to assist the tribunal in establishing the facts on which the independent expert may rely in preparing the report[9].

1 Ie a claim relating to a breach of a sex equality clause or rule within the meaning of the Equality Act 2010 in a case involving work within s 65(1)(c) (see PARA 137). As to sex equality clauses see PARA 139; and as to sex equality rules see PARA 140. As to an assessment by a member of the panel of independent experts as to whether work is of equal value see PARA 362.

2 Ie as set out in the Employment Tribunals (Constitution and Rules of Procedure) Regulations 2013, SI 2013/1237, reg 13(1), Sch 1 (see EMPLOYMENT vol 41A (2014) PARA 1486 et seq).

3 See the Employment Tribunals (Constitution and Rules of Procedure) Regulations 2013, SI 2013/1237, reg 13(2)(b), Sch 3; and EMPLOYMENT vol 41A (2014) PARA 1491. As to the general power to manage proceedings see Sch 3 r 2; and EMPLOYMENT vol 41A (2014) PARA 1491.

4 As to the conduct of a stage 1 equal value claim and the standard orders to be made see the Employment Tribunals (Constitution and Rules of Procedure) Regulations 2013, SI 2013/1237, Sch 3 rr 3, 4, 9; and EMPLOYMENT vol 41A (2014) PARA 1492.

5 As to the conduct of a stage 2 equal value claim and the standard orders to be made see the Employment Tribunals (Constitution and Rules of Procedure) Regulations 2013, SI 2013/1237, Sch 3 rr 6, 7; and EMPLOYMENT vol 41A (2014) PARA 1493.

6 As to the conduct of the final hearing see the Employment Tribunals (Constitution and Rules of Procedure) Regulations 2013, SI 2013/1237, Sch 3 r 8; and EMPLOYMENT vol 41A (2014) PARA 1494.

7 See the Employment Tribunals (Constitution and Rules of Procedure) Regulations 2013, SI 2013/1237, Sch 3 r 12(2); and EMPLOYMENT vol 41A (2014) PARAS 1492–1493.

8 See the Employment Tribunals (Constitution and Rules of Procedure) Regulations 2013, SI 2013/1237, Sch 3 r 1(2). 'Comparator' means the person of the opposite sex to the claimant in relation to whom the claimant alleges that his or her work is of equal value: see Sch 3 r 1(2). As to duties and powers of the independent expert, use of the report and questions which may be put to experts see Sch 3 rr 9–11; and EMPLOYMENT vol 41A (2014) PARAS 1491, 1492. See also PARA 362.

9   See the Employment Tribunals (Constitution and Rules of Procedure) Regulations 2013, SI 2013/1237, Sch 3 r 5; and EMPLOYMENT vol 41A (2014) PARA 1492.

364. Remedies.

If in proceedings before an employment tribunal or a court on a complaint or claim relating to a breach of an equality clause[1], other than a breach with respect to membership of or rights under an occupational pension scheme[2], the court or tribunal finds that there has been a breach of the equality clause, it may make a declaration as to the rights of the parties in relation to the matters to which the proceedings relate[3] or order an award by way of arrears of pay or damages in relation to the complainant or claimant[4].

If a court or tribunal finds that there has been a breach of an equality rule[5] or a breach of an equality clause with respect to membership of, or rights under, an occupational pension scheme:

(1)   it may make a declaration as to the rights of the parties in relation to the matters to which the proceedings relate[6];

(2)   it must not order arrears of benefits or damages or any other amount to be paid to the complainant[7],

and if the breach relates to a term on which persons become members of the scheme, the court or tribunal may declare that the complainant is entitled to be admitted to the scheme with effect from a specified date[8]. If the breach relates to a term on which members of the scheme are treated, the court or tribunal may declare that the complainant is, in respect of a specified period, entitled to secure the rights that would have accrued if the breach had not occurred[9].

If a court or tribunal finds, on a complaint by a pensioner member[10] of an occupational pension scheme relating to a breach of an equality clause or rule with respect to a term on which the member is treated, that there has been such a breach, it may:

(a)   make a declaration as to the rights of the complainant and the respondent in relation to the matters to which the proceedings relate[11];

(b)   order an award by way of arrears of benefits or damages or of any other amount in relation to the complainant[12].

1   As to such proceedings see PARAS 357–360. As to the meaning of 'equality clause' see PARA 117 note 4.
2   Equality Act 2010 ss 132(1), 135(1), (12). As to the meaning of 'occupational pension scheme' see PARA 134 note 1.
3   Equality Act 2010 s 132(2)(a).
4   Equality Act 2010 ss 132(2)(b), 135(1), (12). The court or tribunal may not order a payment under s 132(2)(b) in respect of a time before the arrears day: s 132(3). In relation to a standard case, the arrears day is the day falling 6 years before the day on which the proceedings were instituted; and in relation to a concealment case or an incapacity case (or a case which is both), the arrears day is the day on which the breach first occurred: s 132(4). A standard case is a case which is not a concealment case, an incapacity case or a concealment case and an incapacity case: s 135(2). A concealment case in relation to an equality clause is a case where the responsible person deliberately concealed a qualifying fact (as defined by s 130: see PARA 361 note 4) from the worker (s 135(3)(a)) and the worker commenced the proceedings (or, in relation to terms of service, made a service complaint) before the end of the period of 6 years beginning with the day on which the worker discovered (or could with reasonable diligence have discovered) the qualifying fact (s 135(3)(b), (10)); and an incapacity case is a case where the worker or member had an incapacity when the breach first occurred (s 135(5)(a)) and commenced the proceedings (or, in relation to terms of service, made a service complaint) before the end of the period of 6 years beginning with the day on which the worker or member ceased to have the incapacity (s 135(5)(b), (10)). As to the meaning of 'worker' see PARAS 357 note 5, 360 note 3. As to the meaning of 'responsible person' see PARA 360 note 2. As to the meaning of 'incapacity' see PARA 361 note 5. As to the meaning of 'service complaint' see PARA 357 note 3.

Regulations may make provision for enabling an employment tribunal to include interest on an amount awarded by it in proceedings under the Equality Act 2010 and specifying the manner in which, and the periods and rate by reference to which, the interest is to be determined: s 139(1). Regulations may modify the operation of an order made under the Employment Tribunals Act 1996 s 14 (power to make provision as to interest on awards: see EMPLOYMENT vol 41A (2014) PARA 1481) in so far as it relates to an award in proceedings under the Equality Act 2010: s 139(2). As to regulations made see the Employment Tribunals (Interest on Awards in Discrimination Cases) Regulations 1996, SI 1996/2803 (amended by SI 1998/1658; SI 2003/1660; SI 2003/1661; SI 2006/1031; SI 2013/1669).

5   As to the meaning of 'equality rule' see PARA 117 note 4.
6   Equality Act 2010 s 133(1), (2)(a).
7   Equality Act 2010 s 133(2)(b). Section 133(2)(b) does not apply if the proceedings are proceedings to which s 134 (see the text and notes 10–12) applies: s 133(3).
8   Equality Act 2010 s 133(4). A date specified for the purposes of s 133(4) must not be before 8 April 1976: s 133(5). 8 April 1976 is the date on which the European Court of Justice gave its judgment in Case C-43/75 *Defrenne v Sabena* [1981] 1 All ER 122, [1976] ECR 455, ECJ (in which the Court, in holding that the principle of equal pay was directly effective, held that what was then the Treaty on European Union art 119 (see now the Treaty on the Functioning of the European Union (Rome, 25 March 1957; TS 1 (1973); Cmnd 5179) art 157) should not be applied to periods of service before the judgment).
9   Equality Act 2010 s 133(6). A period specified for the purposes of s 133(6) must not be before 17 May 1990: s 133(7). If the court or tribunal makes a declaration under s 133(6) the employer must provide such resources to the scheme as are necessary to secure for the complainant (without contribution or further contribution by the complainant or other members) the rights referred to in s 133(6): s 133(8). 17 May 1990 is the date on which the European Court of Justice gave its judgment in Case C-262/88 *Barber v Guardian Royal Exchange Assurance Group* [1991] 1 QB 344, [1990] 2 All ER 660, ECJ (which established that occupational pensions were 'pay' for the purposes of what was then the Treaty on European Union art 119 (see now the Treaty on the Functioning of the European Union art 157)).
10 A reference to a pensioner member of a scheme includes a reference to a person who is entitled to the present payment of pension or other benefits derived through a member: Equality Act 2010 s 135(1), (11).
11 Equality Act 2010 s 134(1), (2)(a).
12 Equality Act 2010 s 134(2)(b). The court or tribunal must not order an award under s 134(2)(b) in respect of a time before the arrears day: s 134(3). In relation to a standard case, the arrears day is the day falling 6 years before the day on which the proceedings were commenced; and in relation to a concealment case or an incapacity case (or a case which is both), the arrears day is the day on which the breach first occurred: s 134(5). A concealment case in relation to an equality rule is a case where the employer or the trustees or managers of the occupational pension scheme in question deliberately concealed a qualifying fact (as defined by s 130: see PARA 361 note 4) from the member, and the member commenced the proceedings before the end of the period of 6 years beginning with the day on which the member discovered (or could with reasonable diligence have discovered) the qualifying fact: s 135(1), (4).
    If the court or tribunal orders an award under s 134(2)(b), the employer must provide such resources to the scheme as are necessary to secure for the complainant (without contribution or further contribution by the complainant or other members) the amount of the award: s 134(4).

(3) PROCEDURAL MATTERS: BURDEN OF PROOF

365. Burden of proof.

If, in any proceedings relating to a contravention[1] of the Equality Act 2010[2], there are facts from which the court or applicable tribunal[3] could decide, in the absence of any other explanation, that a person (A) contravened the provision concerned, the court or applicable tribunal must hold that the contravention occurred[4], although this does not apply if A shows that A did not contravene the provision[5]. These provisions do not apply to proceedings for an offence[6]. As the application of these provisions[7] is to take effect at the conclusion of proceedings, it will not normally be possible therefore to apply to strike out a claim[8].

A finding in relevant proceedings[9] in respect of an act which has become final[10] is to be treated as conclusive in proceedings under the Equality Act 2010[11].

1 As to the meaning of 'contravention' see PARA 351 note 2. The reference to a contravention of the Equality Act 2010 includes a reference to a breach of an equality clause or rule: s 136(4). As to the meanings of 'equality clause' and 'equality rule' see PARA 117 note 4.

2 As to the Equality Act 2010 see PARAS 1–4.

3 In these provisions a reference to the court includes a reference to an employment tribunal (see EMPLOYMENT vol 41A (2014) PARA 1399 et seq), the Special Immigration Appeals Commission (see IMMIGRATION AND ASYLUM vol 57 (2012) PARAS 430–456), the First-tier Tribunal (see COURTS AND TRIBUNALS vol 24 (2010) PARA 874 et seq) and the Special Educational Needs Tribunal for Wales (see EDUCATION vol 36 (2015) PARAS 1034–1037): Equality Act 2010 s 136(6)(a)–(e).

4 Equality Act 2010 s 136(1), (2). See *Hewage v Grampian Health Board* [2012] UKSC 37, [2012] 4 All ER 447, [2012] IRLR 870; and for guidance see *Wong v Igen Ltd* [2005] EWCA Civ 142 at [76], [2005] 3 All ER 812, [2005] ICR 931 per Peter Gibson LJ. Where a claim or complaint is transferred in accordance with the Equality Act 2010 s 140 (concurrent litigation: see PARA 6) a court or tribunal may not make a decision that is inconsistent with an earlier decision in proceedings arising out of the conduct: s 140(5).

5 Equality Act 2010 s 136(3). See *Efobi v Royal Mail Group Ltd* (2017) UKEAT/0203/16/DA, [2017] All ER (D) 96 (Sep). In *Efobi v Royal Mail Group Ltd*, Laing J said at [78]–[79]: 'It may therefore be misleading to refer to a shifting of the burden of proof as this implies, contrary to the language of [the Equality Act 2010] s 136(2), that Parliament has required a claimant to prove something. It does not appear to me that it has done . . . I acknowledge that this is not the way in which s 136 is interpreted in the Explanatory Notes . . . Explanatory Notes may be an admissible aid to the construction of a statute in order to establish contextual factors, but in so far as they reveal the government's views about the scope of statutory language, they cannot be treated as reflecting the will of Parliament, which is to be deduced from the language of the statute in question (*Westminster City Council v National Asylum Support Service* [2002] UKHL 38 at [5]–[6], [2002] 1 WLR 2956 per Lord Steyn).

In earlier cases, it has been held that the burden of proof is not reversed merely on accusation: a prima facie case is required: see eg *University of Huddersfield v Wolff* [2004] IRLR 534, EAT (decided under the Sex Discrimination Act 1975 (repealed)); *Sinclair Roche and Temperley v Heard* [2004] IRLR 763, [2004] All ER (D) 432 (Jul), EAT; *Maksymiuk v Bar Roma Partnership* [2012] EqLR 917, [2012] All ER (D) 377 (Jul), EAT.

6 Equality Act 2010 s 136(5).

7 Ie the Equality Act 2010 s 136 (see the text and notes 1–6).

8 See *Efobi v Royal Mail Group Ltd* (2017) UKEAT/0203/16/DA at [78], [2017] All ER (D) 96 (Sep) per Laing J.

9 'Relevant proceedings' are proceedings before a court or employment tribunal under any of the Race Relations Act 1968 s 19 or s 20, the Equal Pay Act 1970, the Sex Discrimination Act 1975, the Race Relations Act 1976, the Sex Discrimination Act 1986 s 6(4A), the Disability Discrimination Act 1995, the Equality Act 2006 Pt 2 (ss 44–80), the Employment Equality (Religion and Belief) Regulations 2003, SI 2003/1660, the Employment Equality (Sexual Orientation) Regulations 2003, SI 2003/1661, the Employment Equality (Age) Regulations 2006, SI 2006/1031, and the Equality Act (Sexual Orientation) Regulations 2007, SI 2007/1263 (all repealed or revoked): Equality Act 2010 s 137(2).

10 A finding becomes final when an appeal against the finding is dismissed, withdrawn or abandoned or when the time for appealing expires without an appeal having been brought: Equality Act 2010 s 137(3).

11 Equality Act 2010 s 137(1).

INDEX

Discrimination

References are to paragraph numbers; superior figures refer to notes

References are to paragraph numbers; superior figures refer to notes

References are to paragraph numbers; superior figures refer to notes

References are to paragraph numbers; superior figures refer to notes

References are to paragraph numbers; superior figures refer to notes